75.00

D0142829

No Longer Property of
Fr. Leonard Alvey Library
Brescia University

Routledge Revivals

Routledge Revivals

Women, Health, and Medicine in America

GARLAND REFERENCE LIBRARY OF
THE SOCIAL SCIENCES (VOL. 483)

© 1990 Rima D. Apple
All Rights Reserved

Library of Congress Cataloging-in-Publication Data

Women, health, and medicine in America: a historical handbook /
edited by Rima D. Apple.
    p. cm. —(Garland reference library of social science: v.
483)
    Includes bibliographical references.
    ISBN 0-8240-8447-0
    1. Women—United States—Health and hygiene—
History. 2. Women healers—United States—History. 3. Women
in medicine—United States—History. I. Apple, Rima D. (Rima
Dombrow), 1944- . II. Series.
RA564.85.W664   1990
610'.82—dc20   90-2719

610.82
W872

Cover and Book Design by
Renata Gomes

Printed in the United States of America

WOMEN, HEALTH, AND MEDICINE IN AMERICA

A *Historical Handbook*

EDITED BY RIMA D. APPLE

GARLAND PUBLISHING, INC.
NEW YORK & LONDON 1990

BRESCIA COLLEGE LIBRARY
OWENSBORO, KENTUCKY

85111

BRESCIA COLLEGE LIBRARY
OWENSBORO, KENTUCKY

IN LOVING MEMORY OF MY MOTHER,
VIOLET GOLDBERG DOMBROW

TABLE OF CONTENTS

• • • ————————— • • •

ACKNOWLEDGMENTS

• • • —————— • • •

This book owes its form and substance to the contributions of many people. I am especially grateful to those who agreed to serve on the editorial board: Janet Golden, Judith Walzer Leavitt, Susan Reverby, and Martha Verbrugge. They have consistently supported me through the entire project. I was encouraged when I approached each with the idea for this book. They gave cogent counsel, sometimes on short notice: suggesting topics to be included, recommending authors and referees, carefully reading and reviewing many chapters.

The authors responded to my requests for manuscripts and revisions with enthusiasm, creativity, and understanding. I appreciate the time and energy they expended in the production of the following pages and their commitment to the project. Moreover, each chapter was carefully considered by members of the advisory board familiar with the topic at hand. I know that the authors join me in thanking these previously anonymous reviewers for their generous and constructive suggestions. I am happy now to acknowledge their names: Susan Bell, Charlotte Borst, Joan Brumberg, Allan Brandt, Gretchen Condran, Norman Gevitz, Laurie Glass, Gerald Grob, Allison Heisch, Elizabeth Keeney, Susan Lederer, Diana Long, Constance McGovern, Gloria Moldow, Laura Mumford, John Parascandola, Martin Pernick, Virginia Quiroga, Ronald Numbers, David Rosner, Todd Savitt, Barbara Sicherman, Susan Smith, Mariamne Whatley, James Whorton, and Diane Worzala.

Marie Ellen Larcada and Kennie Lyman, of Garland Publishing, have maintained confidence in the project since its inception. Phone conversations with them could revive a flagging spirit. I appreciate the help of Christopher Hoolihan of the Edward G. Miner Library, University of Rochester Medical Center, and Christine Schelshorn and Myrna

Williamson of the Iconographic Collections, State Historical Society of Wisconsin, in locating some of the photographs reproduced in the pictorial essay. I am grateful to Elizabeth Berg Diez for her indexing expertise.

Special words of thanks are reserved for Diane Mary Chase Worzala and Michael W. Apple. They continue to provide intellectual rigor and reassurance, in the appropriate doses, when needed.

The professional lives of us all have intersected with this book. These intersections, and the book in turn, affected and were affected by events beyond our scholarly concerns. Since I began this project, we have encountered birth and death, wedding and divorce, sickness and health. Thus this professional project has been, undeniably, a social creation, a blend of voices whose ranges and tones reflect personal scholarship and life experiences. The completed composition exhibits the rewards of such collaboration.

Rima D. Apple

INTRODUCTION

◆ ◆ ◆ ———————— ◆ ◆ ◆

Rima D. Apple

Women are, and always have been, givers of health care as well as its recipients. We are, and have been, the objects of medical study, even while we challenge the hypotheses and conclusions of the medical sciences. Furthermore, women are not, and never were, alone with their ills or without assistance in caring for the health of their families and neighbors. Women aided women, sometimes through a clearly articulated vision of sisterhood or feminist impulse; in other instances simple neighborliness or need directed their actions. Men too offered assistance, though sometimes they went beyond offering help to insist that women unquestioningly follow their direction. Advice and support came from myriad professional and nonprofessional sources: friends, educators, health reformers, and health practitioners. Also women's needs have shaped health systems and health-care institutions. Women's health care and especially the conditions under which women birth have ramifications far beyond the health and well-being of the individual mother and child; they frequently serve as a gauge for society's conscience and faith in the future.

Yet, despite our significance, women, with the exception of "great ladies" such as Elizabeth Blackwell, have been largely absent from standard histories of medicine and health until quite recently. Today, due to the efforts of a growing number of historians and social scientists, our history is no longer a blank page. Slowly we have mapped outlines sketching the complex and interrelated elements that have formed and are forming the health experiences of women in America. Some of the earliest studies, which appeared in the 1940s and 1950s, told the stories of "great women" in the health-care field and of "great men" who worked in areas of women's health. Publications like *The First Woman Doctor: The Story of*

Elizabeth Blackwell[1] and "Fifty Years of Medical Progress: Medicine as a Science: Obstetrics,"[2] profiled pioneering women and major medical contributions. Since the 1970s, however, the flowering of historical research has produced a richer, more nuanced picture.[3]

In the 1970s much of this new history was highly polemical, a reflection of the influence of the women's health movement and more general women's movement which revealed past and present injustices.[4] These discussions often saw women as victims of the medical profession and as oppressed by contemporary medical theory that claimed women could not escape their physiology and its inevitable physical problems. Documenting the ways in which medicine defined and attempted to control women's lives, authors such as Barbara Ehrenreich and Deirdre English and Ann Douglas Wood stimulated further research into a host of issues involving the role of medical professionals in the lives of women. Scholars began to delineate the complex and dynamic relationships between women (as patients and practitioners) and medicine (both practice and theory). Rather than positing the oppression, repression, and suppression of women, this literature moved women from the periphery to the center. Women's historical voices could now be heard. Researchers such as Regina Morantz-Sanchez and Charles Rosenberg and Carroll Smith-Rosenberg asked new questions about the role of gender in society, intertwining the methodologies and approaches of social and medical history with a feminist vision.[5] True, the discipline of women's

---

[1] Rachel Baker, *The First Woman Doctor: The Story of Elizabeth Blackwell* (New York: Julian Messner, 1944).

[2] Fred C. Irving, "Fifty Years of Medical Progress: Medicine as a Science: Obstetrics," *New England Journal of Medicine* 244 (1951): 91–100.

[3] The work of Judith Walzer Leavitt, for example, "Ten Years of Historical Research on Women and Health," in *A Decade of Research in Women's Studies: A Colloquium Series,* 1987 (Madison: University of Wisconsin, Women's Studies Research Center, n.d.) pp. 1–19 has been most useful in stimulating my understanding of the historical development of the field. See also Ellen Lewin and Virginia Olesen, eds., *Women, Health and Healing: Toward a New Perspective* (New York: Tavistock, 1985), esp. their introduction, pp. 1–24.

[4] See for example Barbara Ehrenreich and Deirdre English, *Witches, Midwives, and Nurses: A History of Women Healers* (Old Westbury, NY: Feminist Press, 1973); Ehrenreich and English, *Complaints and Disorders: The Sexual Politics of Sickness* (Old Westbury, NY: Feminist Press, 1973); Ann Douglas Wood, "'The Fashionable Disease': Women's Complaints and Their Treatment in Nineteenth-century America," *Journal of Interdisciplinary History* 4 (1973): 25–52.

[5] Regina Markell Morantz, "The Perils of Feminist History," *Journal of Interdisciplinary History* 4 (1973): 649–60; Carroll Smith-Rosenberg and Charles Rosenberg, "The Female Animal: Medical and Biological Views of Woman and Her Role in Nineteenth-century America," *Journal of American History* 60 (1973): 332–56.

health history also continued to celebrate the role of women in the health-care system, but not uncritically and not necessarily from the vantage point of male institutions. Scholars explored the importance of women-oriented and feminist enterprises such as the New England Hospital for Women.[6]

Scholars of women's health history also paid increasing attention to the role of women's agency. Women were not, are not, passive recipients of medical advice and therapeutics; we were not, are not, defined by male-constructed medical theories. We are active participants who at times resist, at times embrace, and at times create the conditions in which we find ourselves. Recognition of women's personal power immeasurably enriched history in general and the history of health in particular.[7]

Much of the research published in the 1970s and early 1980s focused on nineteenth-century women. At this time a dominant theme, addressed either directly or indirectly by scholars through a variety of different lenses, was the health state of women. Interest in the subject was stirred in part by the recognition that most earlier studies relied extensively on prescriptive and medical literature. Historians sought to move beyond the rhetoric of the nineteenth century to understand something about the way women experienced life. Were American women of the previous century sickly? Though there has been no single study analyzing this question, several parts of the puzzle have been discussed and some patterns are emerging.

When we talk about health status today, we frequently begin with statistical evidence. Nineteenth-century health statistics are fragmentary, imprecise, and subject to widely varying interpretations. We do know that incidences of previously endemic diseases and frequently occurring conditions such as tuberculosis, diphtheria, and scarlet fever were in decline. Birth rates were falling. Some analyses suggest that women's life expectancy was on the rise throughout the century. We do not have enough numerical evidence, however, to draw any firm conclusions.[8]

---

[6] Mary Roth Walsh, "*Doctors Wanted: No Women Need Apply*": Sexual Barriers in the Medical Profession, *1835–1975* (New Haven: Yale University Press, 1977).

[7] See for example Linda Gordon's skillful blending of social and economic analysis with women's experiences in *Woman's Body, Woman's Right: A Social History of Birth Control in America* (New York: Grossman, 1976).

[8] For an analysis on nineteenth-century mortality statistics, see Martha H. Verbrugge, *Able-bodied Womanhood: Personal Health and Social Change in Nineteenth-century Boston* (New York: Oxford University Press, 1988), esp. pp. 102–4.

Moreover, health status is more a question of morbidity than mortality, and those data are virtually nonexistent. In any case, complete statistical studies would not tell the whole story. The question of the health status of American women involves more than numbers.

Indirect evidence from observers suggests that nineteenth-century women were not as healthy as their predecessors. Contemporary physicians, commentators, and women themselves wrote as if women (the term assumed white, middle-class women) were sickly, particularly when compared with women of previous generations. To understand these perceptions we must rely on impressionistic evidence. Fictional accounts, such as the oft-cited example of Charlotte Perkins Gilman's *The Yellow Wallpaper*,[9] provide us with a critical portrayal of women's mental health in an earlier era. Biographical studies—Alice James, sister of William and Henry, is a frequently mentioned case—also demonstrate the social and familial factors influencing health and beliefs about health.[10] In published contemporary studies, medical tracts and private case records, physicians described patients they were treating, claiming linkage between the conditions they saw, female physiology, social roles, and life styles.[11] This type of analysis also appeared in the works of nonmedical writers and health reformers who, for example, recognized female "invalidness" and blamed it on "unnatural" eating habits. Some recognized hazards specific to wage-earning women such as the debilitating effects and dangerous situations faced in the sweatshop or factory. For other commentators the dictates of fashion created ill-health: how could a woman breathe properly or take in sufficient nourishment when encased in a steel corset and dragged down with pounds of heavy skirts?[12] Culpability rested with the woman or with society depending upon the analysis of the commentator. Some claimed that women must be aware of their physical limitations and consequently those who ignored the special needs of their bodies were irresponsible. Others indicted the demands society placed on women.

Ultimately, there will probably be no answer to the question of whether nineteenth-century women were sickly. Expectations of health,

---

9   Charlotte Perkins Gilman, *The Yellow Wallpaper* (New York: Feminist Press, 1973).
10 See for example Jean Strouse, *Alice James: A Biography* (Boston: Houghton Mifflin, 1980).
11 Prime examples are Edward Clarke, *Sex in Education* (Boston: J. R. Osgood, 1873) and Dio Lewis, "The Health of American Women," *North American Review* 135 (1882): 503–10.
12 Mrs. R[achel] B[rooks] Gleason, "Women's Dress," *Water-Cure Journal* 11 (1851).

environmental conditions, the effects of poverty, and other factors we
are only slowly beginning to recognize contribute to health and to our
perceptions of health. We cannot peel away layers of beliefs and interpretations to disclose some underlying "reality." At this time, what we
can say is that commentators considered "female invalidism" among
white middle-class women common. And, what is most significant, such
women themselves frequently concurred. As Catharine Beecher concluded in her inquiry into the status of American women's health,
published in 1855,

> . . . the *standard of health* among American women is so low that few
> have a correct idea of *what a healthy woman is.* I have again and again
> been told by ladies that they were "perfectly healthy," who yet, on
> close inquiry, would allow that they were subject to frequent attacks of
> neuralgia, or to periodic nervous headaches, or to local ailments, to
> which they had become so accustomed, that they were counted as
> "nothing at all." A woman who has tolerable health finds herself so
> much above the great mass of her friends in this respect, that she feels
> herself a prodigy of good health.[13]

Such comments about women's conditions have been supplemented
with more direct evidence, as we unearth further data from women
themselves, describing and analyzing their own situations. Historians and
archivists continue to discover and reclaim women's private writings,
and we are learning more and more about the daily lives of women
across the country. These diaries and correspondence collections allow
us to get closer to women's own perceptions about their lives and their
health. We learn how women reacted to specific diseases or conditions
such as influenza and prolapsed uterus, and how they coped with more
general conditions such as the fatigue of childbearing and the demands of
fashion.[14] There are problems with such evidence. It is highly individualistic, and the historian must be careful generalizing from the life experience of one or a few actors. Furthermore, it is usually quite class- and
race-specific. Many of these data are from the writings of white, middle-
class and upper-class literate women. We are only gradually uncovering

---

[13] Catharine Beecher, *Letters to the People on Health and Happiness* (New York: Harper &
Bros., 1855), reprinted in Nancy F. Cott, ed., *Root of Bitterness: Documents in the Social
History of American Women* (New York: E. P. Dutton, 1972), p. 264.

[14] Two recent examples are Elizabeth Hampsten, *Read This Only to Yourself: The Private
Writings of Mid-western Women, 1880–1920* (Bloomington: Indiana University Press,
1982) and Sylvia D. Hoffert, *Private Matter: American Attitudes toward Childbearing and
Infant Nurture in the Urban North, 1800–1860* (Urbana: University of Illinois Press,
1989).

direct evidence about the lives of working-class women, women of color, and immigrant women.[15]

Since the 1970s scholars have explored the factors that shaped women's health and health care; they have looked back to earlier eras and on into the twentieth century. Much of this research has focused on women's activities as health practitioners[16] and on women's active involvement in the maintenance of their own health.[17] Unfortunately, this scholarship is scattered in a host of monographs and journal literature.[18] A reader interested in the variety of historical issues involving women's health and health care has no single source to turn to for an overview of our current historical knowledge. This book is intended to fill that important need. Scholars from history and the social sciences have surveyed the field, bringing together pertinent research addressing various aspects of women's health history. They have provided a synthesis of essential works, monographs, and articles, highlighting the contributions of each to the question under study. Where a field does not have a well-developed secondary literature, the authors have identified publications that present notable background material and discuss research to

[15] Interesting examples include Nancy Schrom Dye, "Modern Obstetrics and Working Class Women: The New York Midwifery Dispensary, 1890–1920," *Journal of Social History* 20 (1987): 549–64 and Sydney Stahl Weinberg, *The World of Our Mothers: The Lives of Jewish Immigrant Women* (Chapel Hill: University of North Carolina Press, 1988).

[16] This literature is cited throughout this volume and in the bibliographic appendix. A few examples of this diversity of recent research include: Janet Golden, "Trouble in the Nursery: Physicians, Families, and Wet Nurses at the End of the Nineteenth Century," in *"To Toil the Livelong Day": America's Women at Work, 1780–1980*, ed. by Carol Groneman and Mary Beth Norton (Ithaca: Cornell University Press, 1987), pp. 125–37; Gloria Moldow, *Women Doctors in Gilded-Age Washington: Race, Gender, and Professionalization* (Urbana: University of Illinois Press, 1987); Regina Markell Morantz-Sanchez, *Sympathy and Science: Women Physicians in American Medicine* (New York: Oxford University Press, 1985); and Susan M. Reverby, *Ordered to Care: The Dilemma of American Nursing, 1850–1945* (Cambridge, MA: Cambridge University Press, 1987).

[17] Some recent work in this area include: Verbrugge, *Able-bodied Womanhood*; Rima D. Apple, *Mothers and Medicine: A Social History of Infant Feeding, 1890–1950* (Madison: University of Wisconsin Press, 1987); Joan Jacobs Brumberg, *Fasting Girls: The Emergence of Anorexia Nervosa as a Modern Disease* (Cambridge: Harvard University Press, 1988); Judith Walzer Leavitt, *Brought to Bed: Child-bearing in America, 1750–1950* (New York: Oxford University Press, 1986). See the following chapters and the bibliographic appendix for more references.

[18] An exception is Judith Walzer Leavitt, ed., *Women and Health in America: Historical Readings* (Madison: University of Wisconsin Press, 1984), which collects previously published articles.

be pursued. Moreover, each chapter points to questions needing further investigation.

The following chapters view women as actors and reactors, as healers and patients, as well as objects of medical theory and research and sociological analysis. Two themes appear consistently throughout the book. The first involves medicalization, that is, the increasing encroachment of professional medicine into areas previously considered outside the purview of medical practice. For example, childbirth, once "natural," came to be defined as "pathological."[19] The second major theme involves an enlargement of our conceptions of health and medicine. Many authors clearly and carefully document the ideological, social, cultural, economic, technological, as well as scientific factors that inform our health beliefs and medical values.

The book begins with a section on definitions of health and disease which provide crucial background for interpreting women's health concerns. Adele Clarke investigates how social scientists have employed the concept of female life cycle in their analyses. She suggests that despite the possible pitfall of biological determinism, life-cycle analysis can be a useful lens for viewing women's health history. Lois Verbrugge offers a study of sex-specific morbidity and mortality differentials, discussing hypotheses that have been posed to explain the apparent contradiction between women's higher rates of morbidity and lower rates of mortality when compared with men in the twentieth century. Nancy Sahli analyzes the history of definitions of sexuality and socially appropriate sexual behavior. She shows how medically informed attitudes gained increasing currency in the twentieth century and relates sexuality to wider social and political issues. The critical changes in childbirth practices—the shift from woman-centered to medically managed, the move from home to hospital—are examined by Janet Bogdan. She discusses how time, place, and class influenced women's birthing experiences. Edward Beardsley deals with the impact of race on the health and health care of black women, demonstrating the influence of racial beliefs both on the view of African Americans and on the availability of health services.

In the section on orthodox health care, Nancy Tomes analyzes the role of gender in constructing views of mental health and in the presentation of treatment, in institutions and outside of institutions. She also

---

[19] Another, less studied case is that of menopause. See for instance, Susan E. Bell, "Changing Ideas: The Medicalization of Menopause," *Social Science and Medicine* 24 (1987): 535–42.

discusses sex differentials in self-reporting, diagnosis, and treatment of
mental illness and the social and cultural components involved in the
manifestations of illness. Two medical specialties that take women's
health as their arena, gynecological surgery and obstetrics, are studied by
Judith Roy and Charlotte Borst, respectively. Their investigations highlight the roles played by professionalization and gender relations in the
development of new medical specialties. In a chapter on reproductive
health, Suzanne Poirier is concerned with the medical, social, cultural
and technological forces that shaped beliefs about women's reproductive
powers and rights. These include eugenics, contraception, abortion, and
reproductive technologies. Joan Lynaugh studies the move from home
care to institutionalized health care over the past two hundred years,
including the social and cultural factors that influenced the development
of institutions ranging from out-patient dispensaries to large hospital
complexes. She also describes the roles of women as caregivers in these
institutions.

Health care has never been the exclusive domain of orthodox, or in
the nineteenth century, allopathic, medicine. The next section presents
some of the alternatives developed by and utilized by women over the
past two centuries. Medical sects of homeopathy, eclecticism, and hydropathy, which have attracted much historical attention in the last
several decades, are examined by Naomi Rogers. These groups appealed
to women both as patients and as practitioners. In other instances,
women turned away from professional medical assistance (either orthodox or sectarian) and instead preferred health practices informed by self-
help manuals and instructions handed down from mother to daughter
and friend to friend. Additional health-care advice came from patent-
medicine manufacturers. Using gender as a tool of analysis, Susan Cayleff considers the literature that seeks to explain these choices. In a study
of religion and medicine, Jonathan Butler and Rennie Schoepflin present
women who founded significant and distinctive American religious denominations and whose medical teachings widely influenced health beliefs and practices in this country.

The social and political dynamics of women's health are addressed
in the next section of the book. Martha Verbrugge documents how
health educators and physical educators act as "socializers," teaching
socially acceptable definitions of gender identity while stretching those
definitions. One group of women reformers used just such a socially
acceptable definition of womanhood, woman as childbearer, to push for
legislation to protect women workers and to promote maternal and child
health benefits, a phenomenon discussed by Molly Ladd-Taylor. An-

thony Bale studies a previously overlooked topic: women's toxic experiences. He surveys situations in which women faced health- and life-threatening conditions as a result of their employment and corporate greed; he identifies women in the forefront of fights to clean up the workplace and the environment and to fight negligent pharmaceutical companies.

Several of the earlier chapters discuss the roles women played in health care; the final section of the book focuses specifically on women as health-care providers. Judy Litoff provides an overview of our current knowledge about the rise and demise of the midwife in America. Ellen Baer argues that only recently has the historical and contemporary importance of nursing as women's work and nursing in the health-care system gained recognition. Regina Morantz-Sanchez analyzes current historiography that provides an increasingly complex picture of women as physicians in the United States. Gregory Higby with Teresa Gallagher surveys a newly emerging area of history, the story of women in the pharmacy profession.

Edward Morman, with the assistance of Jill Gates Smith and Margaret Jerrido, compiled a comprehensive topical bibliography of recent scholarship in the history of women, health, and medicine. The bibliography will provide guidance to the reader who wishes to pursue various topics raised in this book. This bibliographical material is crucial because this book is an inclusive, but not conclusive, investigation of women's health history. Many aspects are just now gaining historiographic recognition; others have yet to attract focused attention.

One of the goals of this book has been to stimulate further research. We know little about the health issues of immigrant and minority women (with the exception of some studies on black women) and we know even less about minority women in the health professions.[20] Class is another influential, understudied factor in health and disease. In addition, there are only scattered studies of the health of women wage-earners. In the last few decades we have explored women as physicians, midwives, nurses, and now pharmacists; but there is a host of other health-care careers that have not been studied in depth. Comparisons between twentieth-century female-dominated occupations, such as medical technology, and male-dominated ones, such as dentistry, could

---

[20] Some recent additions to the literature include Moldow, *Women Doctors in Gilded-Age Washington*; Darlene Clark Hine, *Black Women in White: Racial Conflict and Cooperation in the Nursing Profession, 1890–1950* (Bloomington: Indiana University Press, 1989).

provide valuable insights into the role of gender in our society. Women's activity as medical consumers deserves much more study. How, for example, did the development of the sanitary napkin influence women's lives? How did the move from home medical care to highly institutionalized medical care alter women's role as domestic healers and their mothering (parenting) practices? Infertility research is a topic hotly debated in the media today; a topic without an analytic history. The role of government funding and policy in facilitating and limiting women's access to health care, in areas such as abortion and Medicaid, demands critical historical analysis. The reader can undoubtedly multiply this list manyfold.

The history of women's health is a vibrant, growing area of research which has considerable resonances for today's health concerns. In the past two decades, we have produced an outline map, and are sketching in the contours and details. In so doing we have gained a much greater appreciation for the complexities involved in the relationships between physical status and economic, social, and environmental factors contributing to our perceptions of health and disease, as well as the roles played by theory, medical practice, and institution-building in the creation of healthful conditions and the identification and treatment of sickliness. To continue the geographical analogy, these chapters demonstrate how far we have come in drawing our historical map. This is not to say that there is nothing left but to fill in details. Whole areas are as yet unexplored, and even previously examined areas need new research. Moreover, as in cartography, a new, as-yet undeveloped perspective may alter our view. We are familiar with global maps in which north is at the top and south the bottom. What a different sense of the world we get from a map in which the two are reversed; we see the relationships between continents and countries in a new light.[21] The use of gender as a tool, the recognition of women's agency, both have enhanced our vision. The ways in which future research may reorient our perspective are unknown, but this interim map of historical scholarship already documents the power and significance of gender analysis in understanding society and transforming history.

---

[21] On the changing perceptions with new projections, see John Noble Wilford, "The Impossible Quest for the Perfect Map," *New York Times*, October 25, 1988.

DEFINITIONS
OF HEALTH
AND DISEASE

· · · —————— · · ·

♦ ♦ ♦ ──────── ♦ ♦ ♦

WOMEN'S HEALTH: LIFE-CYCLE ISSUES

Adele E. Clarke

The area of life-cycle perspectives on women's health is fraught with tensions and contradictions both within feminist scholarly communities and without, and both within and across disciplinary boundaries.[1] In fact, any attempt to address women's cyclicity immediately places scholars in a domain which has been controversial for hundreds of years. The topic is highly charged culturally, medically, scientifically, and politically. An understanding of the varied disciplinary and interdisciplinary usages of and debates about life-cycle perspectives is thus especially important for the interdisciplinary field of women's studies. This essay begins with a brief overview of the scholarly development of life-cycle perspectives within which women's lives and cycles have been situated. It next addresses life-cycle overviews in the history of women's health and the literatures on adolescence, menstruation, menopause, reproductive sciences, and aging. While life-cycle perspectives remain problematic, they can be adapted for use in historical research, and some suggestions are offered in conclusion.

LIFE-CYCLE PERSPECTIVES

Religious, philosophical, and medical approaches to understanding human existence have been based in life-cycle, birth-to-death, perspec-

---

[1] Support for this work was provided by the NIMH Postdoctoral Program in Organizations and Mental Health, Department of Sociology, Stanford University. I am most grateful for helpful comments on an earlier version from Diana Long, Karen Offen, and Rima Apple.

tives for thousands of years.[2] In modern scholarship shortly after the turn of the century, anthropologists refined such perspectives into analytic tools for understanding the social organization of culture, frameworks within which cultures could be comparatively examined. (Margaret Mead's *Coming of Age in Samoa* is a classic example.[3])

In framing the multi-disciplinary field of human development after World War II, Erik Erikson and others further developed the life-cycle perspective as a distinctive theoretical approach also known as the life span or life course.[4] Beginning in the 1960s, psychologists, biologists, anthropologists, sociologists, historical demographers, family historians, and historians of women have all worked in this tradition. Two models have predominated. The first is a biologically oriented "normative crisis model" which assumes that individuals must pass through the often stressful stages of development in the proper sequence or risk impaired development (paralleling theories of embryonic development). The second model centers on a socially based "timing-of-events" conception in which an "average expectable life cycle" becomes the yardstick for assessing life events (or their absence) in terms of normative expectations for a given age.[5]

Historians of women drawing upon life-cycle perspectives have generally focused on documentary history, family history, women's history, and historical demographic issues.[6] Most have adopted the "timing-of-events" model, using the chronological approach of the life cycle to situate women's experiences within historical chronologies. That is, for historians of women the life cycle has often been more of an organizing device than a theoretical perspective.

---

[2] See, for example, Erwin H. Ackerknecht, *A Short History of Medicine* (Baltimore: Johns Hopkins University Press, 1968).

[3] This was originally published in 1928; see Margaret Mead, *Coming of Age in Samoa*, third ed. (New York: William Morrow, 1961).

[4] For example, see Erik Erikson, *Childhood and Society* (New York: Norton, 1950); and his *Identity: Youth and Crisis* (New York: Norton, 1968). The field certainly has earlier roots, especially in psychology. See W. R. Looft, ed., *Developmental Psychology: A Book of Readings* (New York: Holt, Rinehart and Winston, 1972).

[5] Alice S. Rossi, "Life-Span Theories and Women's Lives," *Signs* 6 (1980): 4–32, esp. pp. 9–17.

[6] See, for example, Gerda Lerner, ed., *The Female Experience: An American Documentary* (Indianapolis: The Bobbs-Merrill Co., 1977); Tamara K. Hareven, ed., *Transitions: The Family and the Life Course in Historical Perspective* (New York: Academic Press, 1978).

Life-cycle historians, sociologists, and others did not raise the fundamental issues of gender differences in developmental and life-cycle experiences until the recent wave of feminist scholarship began in the 1960s. Some feminist scholars then sought to reformulate life-cycle perspectives to take gender into account and to address issues of particular concern to women. While, as Alice S. Rossi notes, "A major focus of life-course research is the search for social patterns in the timing, duration, spacing and order of life events,"[7] gender issues are salient as social patterns for males and females vary considerably both in terms of developmental stages and age expectations.[8] Working within the interdisciplinary life-cycles theoretical tradition, subsequent efforts have attempted to integrate biological, anthropological, and sociological perspectives on gender.[9]

In the 1970s, in sharp dialogue with these works, other feminist scholars mounted serious critiques of such developmental perspectives, emphasizing both problems of method and of the assumptions underlying life-cycle approaches.[10] Particular criticisms have been directed at biosocial models.[11] This decade-old debate recently resumed in 1982 in response to Carol Gilligan's book, *In A Different Voice*, which reinter-

---

[7] Rossi, "Life-Span Theories," p. 7.

[8] See Alice S. Rossi, "Equality Between the Sexes: An Immodest Proposal," *Daedalus* 93 (Spring, 1964): 607–52; Alice S. Rossi, ed., *Gender and the Life Course* (New York: Aldine Pubs., 1984); Rossi, "Life-Span Theories"; Matilda White Riley and Ann Foner, eds., *Aging and Society* (New York: Russell Sage, 1968).

[9] See Alice S. Rossi, "A Biosocial Perspective on Parenting," *Daedalus* 106 (1977): 1–31. For more recent work, see Kathleen A. McClusky and Hayne W. Reese, eds., *Life-Span Developmental Psychology: Historical and Generational Effects* (Orlando, FL: Academic Press, 1984); and Jane Lancaster et al., eds., *Parenting Across the Lifespan: Biosocial Dimensions* (New York: Aldine De Gruyter, 1987).

[10] See, for example, Phyllis Chesler, "Patient and Patriarch: Women in the Psychotherapeutic Relationship," in *Woman in Sexist Society*, ed. Vivian Gornick and Barbara K. Moran (New York: Basic Books, 1971), pp. 362–92; and Naomi Weisstein, "Psychology Constructs the Female, or the Fantasy Life of the Male Psychologist," in *Woman in Sexist Society*, ed. Gornick and Moran, pp. 207–24. Both Chesler and Weisstein specifically critique the work of Erikson, as did many other early feminist works. An excellent overview is provided by Carolyn Wood Sherif, "Bias in Psychology," in *The Prism of Sex: Essays in the Sociology of Knowledge*, ed. Julia A. Sherman and Evelyn Tornton Beck (Madison: University of Wisconsin Press, 1979), pp. 93–133; Margaret Cerullo, Judith Stacey and Wini Breines, "Alice Rossi's Sociobiology and Anti-feminist Backlash," *Berkeley Journal of Sociology* 22 (1977): 167–78; Nancy Chodorow, "Considerations on a Biosocial Perspective on Parenting," *Berkeley Journal of Sociology* 22 (1977): 179–97.

[11] See Harriet Engel Gross, et al., "Considering A Biosocial Perspective on Parenting," *Signs* 4 (1979): 695–717.

prets Lawrence Kohlberg's model and stages of moral development through a focus on women rather than men.[12]

The life-cycle perspective is tidy, neat, and orderly. It trundles us along a familiar path from birth to death—a path we presumably all follow. It is this very familiarity that can breed not contempt but tacit, unreflective acceptance of a highly narrowed view. That narrowed view is the assumption of the existence of widespread social norms—that "most people" or "most women" will experience X in Y way at Z time in their lives. In sharp contrast, the recent wave of feminist scholarship has emphasized seeking to understand the *diversity* of women's experiences and in women's own terms.[13]

There has also been recognition that, in the process of constructing fields of inquiry, emphasizing one thing necessarily means deemphasizing another.[14] The normative emphases in life-cycle research thereby require the deemphasis of the diversity and full range of variation of women's experiences. Because the focus is on the normative, "negative cases" and/or categories of people who do not fit the model are ignored. For example, a key criticism of life-cycle approaches has been that they tend to ignore important differences of race, class, and ethnicity.[15] More-

---

[12] Carol Gilligan, *In A Different Voice: Psychological Theory and Women's Development* (Cambridge: Harvard University Press, 1982). For critiques, see Linda Kerber, et al., "On *In A Different Voice*: An Interdisciplinary Forum," *Signs* 11 (Winter, 1966): 304–33; see also Maxine Baca Zinn, et al., "The Costs of Exclusionary Practices in Women's Studies," *Signs* 11 (Winter, 1986): 290–303.

[13] See, for example, Sandra Harding, "Struggling for Self Definition" [Review of Mary Field Belensky et al., *Women's Ways of Knowing: The Development of Self, Voice and Mind* (New York: Basic Books, 1986)], *Women's Review of Books* 4 (March 1987): 6–7. Another very sophisticated epistemological statement on these issues is Dorothy Smith, "A Sociology for Women," in *The Prism of Sex*, ed. Sherman and Beck, pp. 135–87, also reprinted in Dorothy E. Smith, *The Everyday World as Problematic: A Feminist Sociology* (Boston: Northeastern University, 1987), pp. 49–103. A lovely, important and reflexive essay on research processes—including a reassessment of her own earlier work in these terms—is offered by Carroll Smith-Rosenberg, "Hearing Women's Words: A Feminist Reconstruction of History," in her *Disorderly Conduct: Visions of Gender in Victorian America* (New York: Oxford University Press, 1985), pp. 11–52.

[14] See, for example, Susan Leigh Star, "Introduction: The Sociology of Science and Technology," *Social Problems* 35 (June, 1988): 197–205.

[15] See, for example, Gross, et al., "Considering"; Kerber, et al., "On *In A Different Voice*"; and Baca Zinn, et al., "The Costs or Exclusionary Practices"; Irving Kenneth Zola, "Oh Where, Oh Where Has Ethnicity Gone?" in *Ethnicity and Aging: Theory Research and Policy*, ed. Donald E. Gelfand and Alfred J. Kutzik (New York: Springer, 1979), pp. 66–80, esp. p. 67. For a bibliography on minority women's health covering both historical and contemporary issues, see Sheryl Ruzek et al., eds., *Minority Women, Health and Healing in the U.S.: Selected Bibliography and Resources*, 1986. Available from the Women, Health and Healing Program, Department of Social and Behavioral Sciences, University of California, San Francisco, CA 94143-0612.

over, life-cycle approaches deemphasize the incredible variety of subcultures and social worlds in which human lives are lived and which render them meaningful. Such differences as geographic region, urban versus rural, religious and political influences, and sexual preference, among others, are rendered invisible.

Further, there are serious questions about whether norms are descriptive of actual behavior or prescriptions for behavior or, ultimately, whether norms exist in meaningful ways. One alternative view is that, while there are situated expectations or local social conventions of which participants are aware, participants constantly negotiate their actual behavior in any given situation.[16] Norms can thus be perceived in terms of what Carl Degler called "what ought to be" compared to "what was," a fundamental distinction in women's history.[17]

Ultimately, what comes closest to being "normative" (though it is itself highly varied) is biological development and patterns of change with aging from birth to death. Because of this, life-cycle perspectives in women's health history (but also in many other areas) have centered on biological events and processes. In fact, Pat Jalland and John Hooper's documentary history of women's health begins with an extensive section on "The Epochs/Ages of Female Life" and "The Biological Destiny of Women."[18] Here we see how medical men and women constructed female life-cycle stages as biologically determined. Not surprisingly, the criticism of biological reductionism has been routinely leveled at life-cycle research.[19]

---

[16] See also the critique of functional analyses by Martha Verbrugge, "Women and Medicine in Nineteenth Century America," *Signs* 1 (1976): 957–72, esp. pp. 966–7.

[17] See Carl Degler, "What Ought To Be and What Was: Women's Sexuality in the Nineteenth Century," *American Historical Review* 79 (1974): 1467–90, reprinted in *Women and Health in America: Historical Readings*, ed. Judith Walzer Leavitt (Madison: University of Wisconsin, 1984), pp. 40–56.

[18] Pat Jalland and John Hooper, eds., *Women From Birth to Death: The Female Life Cycle in Britain, 1830–1914* (Atlantic Highlands, NJ: Humanities Press International, 1986).

[19] The most extensive feminist critique by a variety of authors is the response to Rossi by Gross et al., "Considering." Critiques of life-cycle perspectives' biological bases have also come from feminist critics of science who have questioned not only the structures of science but also its contents. See, for example, Ruth Bleier, *Science and Gender: A Critique of Biology and Its Theories on Women* (New York: Pergamon, 1984); Evelyn Fox Keller, *Reflections on Gender and Science* (New Haven: Yale University Press, 1985); Sandra Harding and Jean F. O'Barr, eds., *Sex and Scientific Inquiry* (Chicago: University of Chicago Press, 1987); Ruth Hubbard, Mary Sue Henifin, and Barbara Fried, eds., *Biological Woman: The Convenient Myth* (New York: Schenkman, 1982); Anne Fausto-Sterling, *Myths of Gender: Biological Theories About Women and Men* (New York: Basic Books, 1985); and Marion Lowe and Ruth Hubbard, eds., *Woman's Nature: Rationalizations of Inequality* (New York: Pergamon, 1983).

An additional problem derives from the invariable emphasis in female life-cycle perspectives on both the normative and the pathological aspects of reproduction. Male life-cycle perspectives often pay little or no attention to reproductive issues. This is especially true in terms of male reproductive physiology which has been understudied in both biology and medicine, including clinical pathology.[20] Such unequal treatment of male and female reproduction in life-cycle perspectives thus further distorts our understanding of people's lives.

In sum, the history of research based in life-cycle perspectives is one of disciplinary variety and long-standing political and scholarly debate. In fact, because of its focus on the biological aspects of women's lives, the life-cycles literature is the site of important debates about the political value of the traditional work of women in carrying on the generations.[21]

Importantly, these debates are not merely scholarly but of broad political consequence in terms of women's health. It is life-cycle events and processes, especially those involving reproductive cycles, that are typically the historically and personally significant "moments" when medicine enters women's lives, for women's biological cycles have been profoundly medicalized. Medicalization is the process through which more and more aspects of human living and bodily function have come to be defined as medical "problems" or as requiring the ministrations of medicine in some way. It has increased as the profession of medicine has expanded over the nineteenth and twentieth centuries, especially but not only in the Western world.[22]

In Catherine Kohler Riessman's words, "The medical model is used from birth to death in the social construction of reality."[23] The medicali-

---

[20] Naomi Pfeffer has called attention to the fact that until recently there was no equivalent medical specialty to gynecology focused on the male reproductive system. See Naomi Pfeffer, "The Hidden Pathology of the Male Reproductive System," in *The Sexual Politics of Reproduction*, ed. Hilary Homans (Brookfield, VT: Gower, 1985), pp. 30–44.

[21] I am indebted to Diana Long for clarification of this point.

[22] For excellent general discussions of medicalization with historical analyses, see Peter Conrad and Joseph W. Schneider, *Deviance and Medicalization: From Badness to Sickness* (St. Louis: C. V. Mosby, 1980); Peter Conrad and Joseph W. Schneider, "Looking at Levels of Medicalization: A Comment on Strong's Critique of the Thesis of Medical Imperialism," *Social Science and Medicine* 14A (1980): 75–79; Robert Crawford, "A Cultural Account of 'Health': Control, Release and the Social Body," in *Issues in the Political Economy of Health Care*, ed. John McKinlay (New York: Tavistock, 1984), pp. 60–103; Robert Crawford, "Healthism and the Medicalization of Everyday Life," *International Journal of Health Services* 10 (1980): 365–89; and John Ehrenreich, ed., *The Cultural Crisis of Modern Medicine* (New York: Monthly Review Press, 1978).

[23] Catherine Kohler Riessman, "Women and Medicalization: A New Perspective," *Social Policy* 14 (1983): 3–18, esp. p. 3.

zation thesis rests on the argument that what we consider illness, even what we consider health, and certainly what we consider medicine is socially, culturally, and historically defined. Concepts such as health, illness, and medicine are constructed and implemented by people who have sufficient power both to define "reality" for others and to act on that reality. The tremendous variations in human social arrangements concerning health, illness, and disease demonstrated in anthropological and other cross-cultural studies serve as documentation of the degree to which illness, health, and medicine are culturally specific.[24] At heart, this perspective assumes that "the way things are," the status quo at any given place and time, both could have been different and can yet be different—that social arrangements have changed and are changing.[25]

It is therefore not surprising that analyses of medicalization and the social construction of health and illness focus intently on power relations and on the power of medicine as an institution of social control.[26] The central question is *cui bono*—who benefits? This question has consistently been at the heart of feminist analyses of women's experiences of health and illness.[27] Especially but not only because of women's greater role in human reproduction, women's health issues have consistently been more vulnerable than men's to medicalization processes.[28]

---

[24] See, for example, Patricia Whelehan, ed., *The Anthropology of Women's Health* (South Hadley, MA: Bergin and Garvey, 1987).

[25] In addition to the medicalization literature cited above, see Eliot G. Mischler, "The Social Construction of Illness," in *Social Contexts of Health, Illness and Patient Care*, ed. E. G. Mischler et al., (Cambridge, MA: Cambridge University Press, 1981), p. 141–68; and Peter Wright and Andrew Treacher, eds., *The Problem of Medical Knowledge: Examining the Social Construction of Medicine* (Edinburgh: Edinburgh University Press, 1982).

[26] For the classic statement of this view, see Irving Kenneth Zola, "Medicine as an Institution of Social Control," *Sociological Review* 20 (1972): 487–504, reprinted in Ehrenreich, *The Cultural Crisis*, pp. 80–100. For some negative views of the medicalization thesis see, for example, Roy Porter and Andrew Wear, eds., *Problems and Methods in the History of Medicine* (London: Croom Helm, 1987), esp. pp. 1–9; P. M. Strong, "Sociological Imperialism and the Profession of Medicine: A Critical Examination of the Thesis of Medical Imperialism," *Social Science and Medicine* 13a (1979): 12–23.

[27] See, for example, Barbara Ehrenreich and Deirdre English, *Complaints and Disorders: The Sexual Politics of Sickness* (Old Westbury, NY: Feminist Press, 1973); and Sheryl B. Ruzek, *The Women's Health Movement: Feminist Alternatives to Medical Control* (New York: Praeger, 1979).

[28] Medicalization has included an array of industrialization processes as well. See Adele E. Clarke, "The Industrialization of Human Reproduction, 1890–1990," Plenary address, Conference of University of California Women's Programs, Davis, 1988.

The most impressive analysis of the medicalization of women's health to date is Riessman's, for she takes us beyond the inadequate but often terminal analysis that "men are the problem," a view that characterized much early feminist work in the field. She renders complex processes in their full complexity, noting:

> . . . feminists have not always emphasized the ways in which women have simultaneously gained and lost with the medicalization of their life's problems. Nor have scholars always noted the fact that women actively participated in the construction of the new medical definitions, nor discussed the reasons that led to their participation . . . To cast [women] in the passive role is to perpetuate the very kinds of assumptions about women that feminists have been trying to challenge.[29]

Because of the frequent emphasis on biological processes, life-cycle perspectives can similarly cast women as passively progressing through prescribed eras and experiences. Life-cycle perspectives are thus particularly vulnerable to unwittingly incorporating the medicalized model through the very structuring of the life cycle around biological—and progressively biomedical—events. Such assumptions can prevent us from discovering how women have conceived and handled these phenomena on their own terms—the heart of the feminist task, both historically and contemporarily.

With these caveats, we can now turn to the life-cycles literature in women's health history.

LIFE CYCLE OVERVIEWS

Several documentary histories of women have taken an explicit life-cycle perspective. In seeking to move beyond male-oriented conceptual frameworks, Gerda Lerner's pioneering effort, *The Female Experience*, focuses on the experiences of ordinary women, proceeding from personal and family domains framed by the life cycle to institutional domains outside the domestic sphere.[30] Jalland and Hooper's volume, *Women from Birth to Death*, focuses on Great Britain, while Erna Olafson Hellerstein, Leslie Parker Hume, and Karen M. Offen's *Victorian Women*

---

[29] Riessman, "Women and Medicalization," p. 3. Here Reissman provides analyses of the medicalization of childbirth, abortion, contraception, premenstrual syndrome, physical appearance/"getting thin," and mental health issues.

[30] Lerner, *The Female Experience*.

includes documents from England, France, and the United States be-cause, "For all their differences, the three countries formed . . . a trans-atlantic culture that tells us more about Victorian attitudes and institu-tions than we could learn from a single nation."[31] British and European medical and scientific research and theories are also important to under-stand because American physicians and other life scientists relied heavily upon them until well after the turn of the century. Sources like Gerald L. Geison's *Physiology in the American Context, 1850–1940* provide a good overview.[32]

Like many other works using life-cycle perspectives, the documen-tary accounts draw on these perspectives in order to frame female life experiences from birth to death and to distinguish them from those typical of boys and men. That such differences in experience are lifelong and often life-pervasive has been a central feminist argument. The books described above all offer excellent overview essays and section introduc-tions which, while they do not focus exclusively on health, do serve to situate such concerns in their wider social contexts. (Specific women's health concerns over the life cycle addressed in these volumes are discussed topically below.)

Yet because they focus predominantly on white women, these vol-umes do not reflect the diversity of American women's life-cycle expe-riences. While available documentary accounts of racial and ethnic minority women's lives such as Dorothy Sterling's *We Are Your Sisters: Black Women in the Nineteenth Century* offer few materials directly on health, they do provide excellent contextual materials.[33] In addition, there are a number of works which broadly frame racial and ethnic

---

[31] Jalland and Hooper, *Women from Birth to Death*; and Erna Olafson Hellerstein, Leslie Parker Hume, and Karen M. Offen, eds., *Victorian Women: A Documentary Account of Women's Lives in Nineteenth Century England, France and the United States* (Stanford: Stanford University Press, 1981), p. i. These volumes are excellent resources for teaching women's health history, enriching the curriculum by adding women's voices on their own terms.

[32] See, for example, Gerald L. Geison, ed., *Physiology in the American Context, 1850–1940* (Bethesda, MD: American Physiological Society, 1987).

[33] See Dorothy Sterling, ed., *We Are Your Sisters: Black Women in the Nineteenth Century* (New York: Norton, 1984); Gerda Lerner, ed., *Black Women in White America: A Documentary History* (New York: Pantheon Books, 1971); and Bert J. Loewenberg and Ruth Bogin, eds., *Black Women in Nineteenth Century American Life* (University Park, PA: Pennsylvania State University Press, 1976).

women's lives and raise issues of class diversity more explicitly.[34] While these works tend to focus on family and household arrangements, all enrich a life-cycle perspective on women's health, for the life cycle is, after all, socially embedded.

Life-cycle perspectives have been used routinely to construct special and limited spheres for women.[35] Nineteenth-century physicians and scientists employed a number of medical and biological justificatory arguments in attempts to confine middle- and upper-class women to newly-bounded domestic childbearing and rearing domains and to prevent them from entering expanding economic and civic worlds outside the home.[36] These nineteenth-century arguments were based on a "new" presumption of biological difference between the sexes which Thomas

---

[34] These include Jacqueline Jones, "My Mother Was Much of a Woman: Black Women, Work and Family Under Slavery," *Feminist Studies* 8 (1982): 235–70; Eugene D. Genovese, "Life in the Big House," in his *Roll, Jordan, Roll: The World the Slaves Made* (New York: Pantheon/Random House, 1974), excerpted and reprinted in *A Heritage of Her Own: Toward a New Social History of American Women*, ed. Nancy F. Cott and Elizabeth H. Pleck (New York: Simon and Schuster, 1979), pp. 290–7; Laurence A. Glasco, "The Life Cycles and Household Structure of American Ethnic Groups: Irish, Germans and Native Born Whites in Buffalo, New York, 1855," *Journal of Urban History* 1 (1975): 339–64, reprinted in *A Heritage*, ed. Cott and Pleck, pp. 268–89; Ann Gordon and Mari Jo Buhle, "Sex and Class in Colonial and Nineteenth Century America," in *Liberating Women's History*, ed. Berenice A. Carroll (Urbana: University of Illinois Press, 1978), pp. 278–300; Herbert G. Guttman, "Marital and Sexual Norms Among Slave Women," in his *The Black Family in Slavery and Freedom, 1750–1925* (New York: Pantheon/Random House, 1976), also excerpted and reprinted in *A Heritage*, ed. Cott and Pleck, pp. 298–310; Charles Rosenberg, "Sexuality, Class and Role in Nineteenth Century America," *American Quarterly* 25 (1973): 131–54, reprinted in his *No Other Gods: On Science and American Social Thought* (Baltimore: Johns Hopkins University, 1976), pp. 71–88; Sydney Weinberg, *The World of Our Mothers: Lives of Jewish Immigrant Women* (Chapel Hill: University of North Carolina, 1988); Elizabeth Ewen, *Immigrant Women in the Land of Dollars: Life and Culture on the Lower East Side, 1890–1925* (New York: Monthly Review Press, 1985); Kathy Peiss, *Cheap Amusements: Working Women and Leisure in Turn of the Century New York* (Philadelphia: Temple University Press, 1986); and Judith E. Smith *Family Connections: A History of Italian and Jewish Immigrant Lives in Providence Rhode Island, 1900–1940* (Albany: State University of New York Press, 1985). For a corrective view of the daily life of middle-class white British women, see Patricia Branca, "Image and Reality: The Myth of the Idle Victorian Woman," in *Clio's Consciousness Raised: New Perspectives on the History of Women*, ed. Mary S. Hartman and Lois Banner (New York: Harper and Row, 1974), pp. 179–91.

[35] The classic work on separate spheres remains Barbara Welter, "The Cult of True Womanhood, 1820–1860," *American Quarterly* 18 (1966): 151–74.

[36] Carroll Smith-Rosenberg and Charles Rosenberg, "The Female Animal: Medical and Biological Views of Woman and Her Role in Nineteenth Century America," *Journal of American History* 60 (1973): 332–56, reprinted in *Women and Health*, ed. Leavitt, pp. 12–27, also reprinted in Rosenberg, *No Other Gods*, pp. 54–70.

Laqueur asserts did not occur until the late eighteenth century.[37] Prior to this time, a hierarchical model of biology predominated with white, Northern European men, of course, atop the whole chain of being. Women had been seen as inferior to but not fundamentally different from men. Female reproductive organs were construed as underdeveloped parallels to those of males. This hierarchical biological model was displaced in the late eighteenth century by a model of complementary biological difference upon which different proper spheres of activity were subsequently predicated.

Londa Schiebinger asserts that even skeletal structure was presumed to be similar until the eighteenth century, although the male skeleton was the "human" model.[38] As the presumption of fundamental difference took root, female skeletons were studied and distinguished from those of males in significant ways: they had wider pelvises, smaller ribcages, and smaller skulls. Considerable scientific effort was then devoted to documenting women's smaller skulls and therefore smaller brain capacity.[39] Women's reproductive capacities were seen to be skeletally dominant. Some scientists even argued that women's evolutionary development must have been arrested in order for them to be so different.[40]

---

[37] Thomas Laqueur, "Orgasm, Generation and the Politics of Reproductive Biology," in *The Making of the Modern Body: Sexuality and Society in the Nineteenth Century*, ed. Catherine Gallagher and Thomas Laqueur (Berkeley: University of California, 1987), pp. 1–41.

[38] Londa Schiebinger, "Skeletons in the Closet: The First Illustrations of the Female Skeleton in Eighteenth Century Anatomy," in *The Making of the Modern Body*, ed. Gallagher and Laqueur, pp. 42–82.

[39] See, for example, Elizabeth Fee, "Nineteenth Century Crainiology: The Study of the Female Skull," *Bulletin of the History of Medicine* 53 (1979): 415–33; Stephen J. Gould, *The Mismeasure of Man* (New York: Norton, 1981), esp. pp. 103–112; John S. Haller and Robin M. Haller, *The Physician and Sexuality in Victorian America* (Urbana: University of Illinois, 1974), pp. 47–61; and Joan Burstyn, *Victorian Education and the Ideal of Womanhood* (New Brunswick, NJ: Rutgers University Press, 1984).

[40] See, for example, Barbara Ehrenreich and Deirdre English, *For Her Own Good: 150 Years of the Experts' Advice to Women* (New York: Anchor Doubleday, 1979), pp. 104–8. However, problems for women with evolutionary theory continue today; see, for example, Adrienne L. Zihlman, "Gathering Stories for Hunting Human Nature: Review Essay," *Feminist Studies* 11 (1985): 365–77; Mina Davis Caulfield, "Sexuality in Human Evolution: What is 'Natural' in Sex?" *Feminist Studies* 11 (1985): 343–63; Donna Haraway, "Primatology is Politics by Other Means," in *Feminist Approaches to Science*, ed. Ruth Bleier (New York: Pergamon, 1986), pp. 77–118; Evelyn Fox Keller, "Reproduction and the Central Project of Evolutionary Theory," *Biology and Philosophy* 2 (1987): 73–86; Jane B. Lancaster, "Evolutionary Perspectives on Sex Differences in the Higher Primates," in *Gender and the Life Course*, ed. Rossi, pp. 3–27; Helen Longino and Ruth Doell, "Body, Bias and Behavior: A Comparative Analysis of Reasoning in Two Areas of Biological Science," *Signs* 9 (1983): 206–27; and Elizabeth Lloyd, *All About Eve: Evolutionary Explanations of Women's Sexuality* (Princeton: Princeton University Press, forthcoming).

Subsequent medical and biological arguments of fundamental sex differences moved from anatomical into more physiological domains. In studying the history of nineteenth-century research on reproductive phenomena, John Farley found that for many biologists, sexual reproduction was the means of reproduction employed by those species in which a distinctive reproductive individual, the female, had been formed.[41] These biologists then argued that reproductive capacity therefore determined the place of females in the division of labor.

Biological and medical arguments for this division of labor typically centered on the tyranny of women's reproductive organs and functions—at times the uterus, at times the ovaries, at times menstruation, at times childbearing, at times childrearing, at times menopause—over women's consciousness and women's lives. Such arguments "formed an ideological system rigid in its support of tradition, yet infinitely flexible in the particular mechanisms which could be made to explain and legitimate woman's role."[42] What Carroll Smith-Rosenberg called "the cycle of femininity" from puberty to menopause was debilitating, if not disabling, and made women unfit for wider social roles.[43] Men's reproductive systems exercised no parallel control over them according to these formulations.

Several early works in the recent wave of feminist scholarship took these life-cycle issues in varied directions. Drawing upon the "normative crisis model" of the life cycle, Smith-Rosenberg studied Victorian medical attitudes toward the "puberty-to-menopause" phase of women's lives as expressed in physicians' professional and popular writings. She examined how physicians' individual psychological needs "to express deeply ambivalent feelings about sexuality," their broader social needs to defend "woman's traditional social place," and their needs as medical professionals all were met through asserting an ideology of the "cycle of femininity." In this early work, women's needs, the meanings women themselves gave to such phenomena, and the social and economic forces

---

[41] John Farley, "The Sexless Age," in his *Gametes and Spores: Ideas About Sexual Reproduction, 1750–1914* (Baltimore: Johns Hopkins University, 1982), pp. 110–28.

[42] Smith-Rosenberg and Rosenberg, "The Female Animal," in *Women and Health*, ed. Leavitt, p. 13.

[43] Carroll Smith-Rosenberg, "The Cycle of Femininity: Puberty to Menopause in Nineteenth Century America," *Feminist Studies* 1 (Winter/Spring 1973): 58–72, reprinted in *Clio's Consciousness Raised*, ed. Hartman and Banner, pp. 23–37, and in *Disorderly Conduct*, ed. Smith-Rosenberg, pp. 182–96.

shaping the larger worlds within which they occurred were largely ignored, omissions Smith-Rosenberg's later work acknowledges.[44]

In contrast, Barbara Ehrenreich and Dierdre English analyzed the same biomedical arguments as part of "the rise of the experts" in a system of medical and scientific social and economic control.[45] They argued that the medical construction of "femininity as a disease" was necessary to create and sustain the gender-based structure of sexual-economic relations and the sexual division of labor, and to ensure the rise of the medical profession as the impacts of industrialization reverberated more widely. They specifically examined working-class and minority women's exclusion from the middle-class role of invalid and middle-class women's forms of resistance to that role.

In a different vein, a more recent work drawing upon life-cycle approaches by Nancy M. Theriot attempts to view the major changes of the nineteenth century through women's own eyes as they acted and reacted in making their lives.[46] Theriot advances an ambitious theory of female intergenerational identity formation, integrating historical, sociological, and psychological perspectives. She contrasts the generation of middle-class women born in the early to middle nineteenth century with that of their daughters. Her focus is on how those daughters used their own material experiences to modify and reshape their mothers' visions of womanhood, motherhood, and the life course to fit their own new circumstances and needs as the century progressed. Their changed circumstances included improved control over health and birth pain through medical intervention. Their responses to such changes included a new approach to mothering based on active socialization of children rather than passive modeling of goodness. Professional motherhood replaced suffering motherhood.

---

[44] Smith-Rosenberg, "Hearing Women's Words," pp. 25–9. Problems with both the functional and psychological analyses offered by Smith-Rosenberg and Rosenberg have been detailed by Verbrugge. See Verbrugge, "Women and Medicine," pp. 966–7.

[45] See Ehrenreich and English, *Complaints and Disorders*; Barbara Ehrenreich and Dierdre English, *Witches, Midwives and Nurses: A History of Women Healers* (Old Westbury, NY: Feminist Press, 1973); and the more fully developed argument in Ehrenreich and English, *For Her Own Good*. Their work is intentionally more popular, echoing consciousness-raising stylistics which often feel alien in scholarly worlds. However, their early formulations of "The Sexual Politics of Sickness" and of the shift to second- or third-class status of women's roles as healers were major founding documents of the contemporary women's health movement both within and outside the academy.

[46] Nancy M. Theriot, *The Biosocial Construction of Femininity: Mothers and Daughters in Nineteenth Century America* (Westport, CT: Greenwood Press, 1988).

The broader frameworks of these authors provide an orientation to the more focused studies centered on particular life-cycle stages to which we next turn.

CHILDHOOD, ADOLESCENCE AND PUBERTY

Aside from studies of chlorosis, little work in the history of health and medicine has been done on female childhood and adolescence. Documentary data on childhood are strong, but little is focused on health issues.[47] In terms of childhood diseases, Edward Shorter's work specifies childhood rickets as a "scourge of adult women" because of the consequent life-long pelvic deformities which affected childbearing.[48]

There has been no historical work on puberty before the nineteenth century aside from documentary data. During the nineteenth century, both physicians and laypersons understood puberty to be a time of "physiological crisis." In her study of physicians' clinical and scientific work, Smith-Rosenberg found dominant the idea that "The ovaries begin their dictatorship of woman's life at puberty," a perilous journey into womanhood that resembled *Pilgrim's Progress*.[49] The standard view was that the way in which a girl negotiated these dangers would shape not only her childbearing years but also her menopause. Therefore adolescent girls were to focus intently on the healthy development of their reproductive organs and the regulation of their menses. A strict regimen was recommended along with extensive maternal surveillance to assure compliance. According to physicians, the first menstruation could be "a primal feminine scene" fraught with dangers if mothers were

---

[47] Cott offers an excerpt from William Alcott's *The Young Woman's Books of Health*; see Nancy F. Cott, ed., *Root of Bitterness: Documents of the Social History of American Women* (New York: E. P. Dutton, 1972), pp. 277–84. Lerner offers materials on varied experiences of childhood; see Lerner, *The Female Experience*, pp. 3–40. Hellerstein, Hume and Offen provide some materials on puberty and educational issues; see their *Victorian Women*, pp. 8–116. Jalland and Hooper's materials center on menstruation, education, chlorosis, hysteria and "corset-mania"; see their *Women From Birth to Death*, pp. 53–116. Sterling's materials center on the experience of Black female slave children, giving sorely needed breadth to the life-cycle perspective; see Stirling, *We Are Your Sisters*, pp. 1–13. See also Jo B. Paoletti, "Clothing and Gender in America: Children's Fashions, 1890–1920," *Signs* 13 (1987): 136–43.

[48] Edward Shorter, *A History of Women's Bodies* (New York: Basic Books, 1982), pp. 22–28; and Edward Shorter, "Women's Diseases Before 1900," *New Directions in Psycho History* [In Honor of Erik Erikson], ed. M. Albin, R. J. Devlin and G. Heeger (Lexington, KY: D. C. Heath, 1980), pp. 183–208. However, this work is of dubious scholarly reliability due to extensive speculation beyond the data.

[49] Smith-Rosenberg, "Puberty to Menopause," in her *Disorderly Conduct*, p. 184.

not there to help.[50] As in other areas of historical research, there are often confusing contradictions between what Carl Degler has termed "what ought to be and what was."[51]

It is within this "puberty as crisis" framework that the ongoing debate in the history of medicine about the etiology of chlorosis and its very conceptualization as a disease entity must be examined. As a disease, chlorosis was found almost exclusively among young girls, either premenstrually or in early menstrual years, and was known for some time as "the virgin's disease." The symptoms associated with chlorosis at various times included general debility and listlessness, amenorrhea, emaciation, pica (eating non-food substances such as clay), melancholia and depression, facial pallor (with or without the green tinge which led to its name of "the green sickness"), nausea, and vomiting.[52] After appearing in the medical literature for centuries and after being described as epidemic during the nineteenth century, chlorosis essentially disappeared as a disease entity early in this century. The current debate centers on what chlorosis was, what it was thought to be and why, for the study of chlorosis involves the analysis of the social construction of illness and disease.

The first historical study, by Robert Hudson, is in the classic tradition of the history of diseases.[53] Hudson chronicles the nosology of chlorosis and asserts that it was ultimately designated as a form of iron-deficiency anemia in 1936. He also discusses other diseases likely to have been misdiagnosed as chlorosis at different times due to lack of medical knowledge, and reviews the variety of specific iron treatments applied. He speculatively relates its common name of "the green sickness" to corseting practices. (Although chlorosis was also seen to occur in men, such men were often feminized in medical writings.)

Carl Figlio analyzes chlorosis as an explicitly female illness, involving both gender and class patterns of domination.[54] He finds different modes

---

50 Smith-Rosenberg has retrospectively noted that she did not adequately distinguish between the prescriptive and the descriptive in this paper. See Smith-Rosenberg, "Hearing Women's Words," pp. 25–9.
51 Degler's analysis focused on female sexuality but seems apt here as well. See Degler, "What Ought to Be and What Was."
52 I. S. L. Loudon, "Chlorosis, anaemia and anorexia nervosa," British Medical Journal 281 (December 1980): 1669–75.
53 Robert Hudson, "The Biography of Disease: Lessons from Chlorosis," Bulletin of the History of Medicine 51 (1977): 448–63.
54 Carl Figlio, "Chlorosis and Chronic Disease in Nineteenth Century Britain: The Social Constitution of Somatic Illness in a Capitalist Society," International Journal of Health Services 8 (1978): 589–617, reprinted in Women and Health: The Politics of Sex in Medicine, ed. Elizabeth Fee (New York: Baywood Press, 1983), pp. 213–41.

85111   610.82   Brescia College Library
                W872   Owensboro, Kentucky

of medical thinking related to different classes of female chlorotic patients. Physicians blamed middle- and upper-class female "troubles"—including chlorosis—on lives of indolence, artificiality, and inactivity characteristic of being "better off." For treatment, they recommended a "wholesome" if childlike outdoor regimen. While physicians also saw and diagnosed chlorosis in working-class girls, they tended to ignore it (as they ignored many occupational and class-related health issues) or to attribute it to urban rather than rural living, a "choice" the working-class girl had made herself. For Figlio, the "ideological work of medicine supported class stratification by establishing social distance between the classes . . ." even in disease etiology.[55]

Like Hudson, I. S. L. Loudon follows the classic approaches of the history of disease. He argues that chlorosis was not simply a form of anemia (although this was a secondary feature), but was a functional disorder closely related to anorexia nervosa. Its routine association with a "capricious or depraved appetite," including nausea, vomiting, bulimia, and pica, supports his point. Anorexia was framed as a diagnostic category in the late nineteenth century, shortly after laboratory methods permitted the diagnosis of anemia. Thus by the twentieth century, chlorosis as a diagnostic category may have been replaced in medical practice by these and other categories, and "Anorexia nervosa may not be a 'modern' disorder in historical terms."[56]

A. Clair Siddall asks why the incidence of chlorosis was "epidemic" in the nineteenth century and why it disappeared so precipitously at the turn of this century.[57] He suggests that some proportion of its incidence may have been iatrogenic (medically caused), since the timing of the rise of chlorosis in the nineteenth century overlapped with physicians' becoming the primary providers of obstetrical and gynecological care. Physicians' common use of blood-letting as treatment for a wide variety of female ailments at the time would have contributed to anemia, and Siddall asserts that the decline in blood-letting occurred at generally the same time as the decline in chlorosis.

---

[55] Figlio, "Chlorosis," p. 236.

[56] Loudon, "Chlorosis, Anaemia, and Anorexia Nervosa," p. 1675. Loudon views his own conclusions as highly compatible with those of Figlio. Beeson also briefly reviews chlorosis, noting some theories that tight corseting was causal. See Paul B. Beeson, "Some Diseases that Have Disappeared," *The American Journal of Medicine* 68 (June, 1980): 806–11.

[57] A. Clair Siddall, "Chlorosis—Etiology Reconsidered," *Bulletin of the History of Medicine* 56 (1982): 254–60.

Joan Jacobs Brumberg finds that previous studies "do not provide adequate cultural explanations for why it was that chlorosis was so prevalent among a single age and sex group."[58] In classic feminist fashion, Brumberg takes the patients seriously, but she also attempts to broaden the life-cycle view to situate chlorosis in the context of its "life and times" in order to examine the complex interplay of adolescent physiology, medicine, and social and family life at the turn of the century. She found that, in contrast with their British counterparts, American physicians tended to view all girls as at least potentially chlorotic regardless of class, and in ways which fed into the overarching "femininity-as-disease" and "puberty-as-crisis" theses. Chlorotic girls were thereby constructed as younger versions of the sickly, feminine women sentimentalized by the Victorians.

More recently, Theriot agrees with Loudon that anorexia was a significant proportion of chlorosis and that psychological factors were central to its etiology.[59] As part of her larger project, she analyzes the nineteenth-century epidemic of "green sickness" as reflecting daughters' ambivalence, conflict, and covert rebellion against the long-suffering model of the female role personified by their mothers' generation. Chlorosis avoided direct confrontation with mothers and, if physicians' regimens were followed, involved increased maternal caretaking. Girls could thereby delay becoming the women they did not want to be. Theriot thus extends Brumberg's analysis of the chlorosis epidemic. Both agree that by the twentieth century, "mothers and daughters had moved beyond invalidism and chlorosis"[60] to new models of womanhood.

These were not necessarily healthy models, as Brumberg's recent work on the emergence of anorexia nervosa in the late nineteenth century attests.[61] "Wasting was in style," and "picky eating" was very common among young girls, especially meat avoidance which likely contributed to that segment of chlorosis which was iron-deficiency

---

[58] Joan Jacobs Brumberg, "Chloritic Girls, 1870–1920: A Historical Perspective on Female Adolescence," *Child Development* 53 (1982): 1468–77, reprinted in *Women and Health*, ed. Leavitt, pp. 186–95, esp. p. 186. Works in the history of adolescence more broadly are well cited by both Figlio and Brumberg.

[59] Theriot, *The Biosocial Construction of Femininity*, pp. 119–32.

[60] Brumberg, "Chloritic Girls," p. 193.

[61] See Joan Jacobs Brumberg, *Fasting Girls: The Emergence of Anorexia Nervosa as a Modern Disease* (Cambridge: Harvard University Press, 1988). For a more thorough discussion of Brumberg's work, see "Historical Perspectives on Women and Mental Illness" by Nancy Tomes in this volume.

anemia.[62] Brumberg further asserts that it is probable that in the late nineteenth and early twentieth centuries the earlier stages of anorexia were often misdiagnosed as chlorosis. A thorough explanation of the issues surrounding chlorosis would draw on aspects of the work of all these authors. As Rosenberg has stated, "A disease is no absolute physical entity but a complex intellectual construction, an amalgam of biological state and social definition."[63]

MENSTRUATION

Considerably more historical research has been done on menstruation than on puberty, although documentary materials, especially by women, remain slim and derive mainly from nineteenth-century sources. Jalland and Hooper's documents are largely medical, although they do provide a brief account of a shift in advice books at the turn of this century from an emphasis on pain and horror to a notion of menstruation as part of "good health."[64] Studies of puberty and menstruation in the seventeenth and eighteenth centuries are obviously sorely needed to determine how different nineteenth-century views were from those of earlier periods.

Menarche, too, is understudied, with the clear exception of the declining age at which it has occurred over the past two hundred years or so. This decline is largely attributed to socioeconomic improvements which led to earlier overall physical growth in weight and bone mass, both of which correlate with earlier menarche.[65] At heart, the lower age at menarche reflects improvements in both nutrition and public health, since the decline in age tends to occur first among the upper classes.

Victorian prescriptive medical views on menarche were rigid and reeked of a "blame-the-victim" mentality. As Barbara Charlesworth Gelpi notes:

---

[62] Brumberg, *Fasting Girls*, p. 171, 176.
[63] Charles E. Rosenberg, *The Cholera Years* (Chicago: University of Chicago Press, 1962), p. 5, n. 8.
[64] Jalland and Hooper, *Women From Birth to Death*, pp. 53–76.
[65] See, for example, Peter Laslett, "Age at Menarche in Europe Since the Eighteenth Century," *Journal of Interdisciplinary History* II (1971): 221–36, reprinted in *Marriage and Fertility: Studies in Interdisciplinary History*, ed. Robert I. Rotberg and Theodore K. Rabb (Princeton: Princeton University Press, 1980), pp. 285–300; and Sir John Dewhurst, "The Menarche," in *Female Puberty and Its Abnormalities*, ed. Sir John Dewhurst (New York: Churchill Livingstone, 1984), pp. 25–47. For a basic review, see Ingrid Swenson and Beverly Havens, "Menarch and Menstruation: A Review of the Literature," *Journal of Community Health Nursing* 4 (1987): 199–210.

The flow was to begin neither too early (a sign of excessive sexuality, probably masturbation, and a diet larded with the red meats and spices that were inappropriate for a young girl) nor too late (a sign of an overstimulated mind drawing energy from the reproductive organs). The "right" time was between fourteen and eighteen, and fifteen or sixteen the ideal.[66]

Similarly rigid views were advanced by physicians on menstruation. Drawing together the dribs and drabs published on menstruation in the nineteenth century, Elaine and English Showalter's pioneering study found that the central issues for Victorians were its debilitating effects on women (which did not end at puberty) as well as the taboos and distaste surrounding it, a distaste which extended to pornographers.[67]

Almost all the recent histories of women, and especially those attending to menstruation, discuss the intense debate in the nineteenth century over whether women's reproductive capacities were endangered by education, especially higher education.[68] Criticism of women's education was predicated on a "zero-sum energy" theory which asserted that if a girl's energies were used in mental efforts such as education, they would be somehow "drawn away" from her reproductive organs which would then suffer deformities of development at their most crucial stage with life-long negative consequences. Working-class girls were not seen as endangered because they supposedly did not go to work until after their menses were established and did not enervate themselves by "brain work."[69]

Showalter and Showalter argue that the nature of the debate itself was ideological rather than scientific. They quote M. Carey Thomas, the first President of Bryn Mawr College, on the faculty's genuine anxieties

---

[66] Barbara Charlesworth Gelpi, "Introduction to Part I," in *Victorian Women*, ed. Hellerstein, Hume and Offen, p. 19.

[67] See Elaine Showalter and English Showalter, "Victorian Women and Menstruation," *Victorian Studies* 24 (1970), reprinted in *Suffer and Be Still: Women in the Victorian Age*, ed. Martha Vicinus (Urbana: University of Illinois, 1972), pp. 36–44.

[68] Documentary materials are found in Hellerstein, Hume and Offen, *Victorian Women*, pp. 68–94; and Jalland and Hooper, *Women from Birth to Death*, pp. 77–86. An excellent overview of the debate and documentary history from *Popular Science Monthly* c1870–1890 is provided by Louise Michelle Newman, ed., *Men's Ideas/Women's Realities: Popular Science, 1870–1915* (New York: Pergamon Press, 1985), pp. 54–104. Historical works which address the debate to some limited degree include Smith-Rosenberg, "Puberty to Menopause"; Sheila Rothman, *Woman's Proper Place: A History of Changing Ideals and Practices, 1870 to the Present* (New York: Basic Books, 1978), pp. 13–61; and Mabel Collins Donnelly, *The American Victorian Woman: The Myth and the Reality* (Westport, CT: Greenwood Press, 1986), pp. 35–41.

[69] See, for example, Hellerstein, Hume, and Offen, *Victorian Women*, p. 20.

that physicians might be correct that girls could not stand the strain of college education. During the 1870s, Thomas made her mother read a treatise on the subject and "was much cheered by her remark that, as neither she nor any of the women she knew, had ever seen girls or women of the kind described in Dr. Clarke's book, we might as well act as if they did not exist."[70] (Women's responses were then and have continued to be empirical in nature and have become more systematically so over the twentieth century, as discussed below.)

Carroll Smith-Rosenberg and Charles Rosenberg focus on a functional analysis of normative prescriptions for the female role in nineteenth-century medical and other literatures.[71] Physicians argued that the uterus and brain were connected through the then-regnant nervous system, rendering women vulnerable to reproductive diseases through "reflex irritation" of the brain.[72] Many physicians asserted a decline in American women's health attributable to such brain irritation via education, and expressed concern about consequences for future generations. Women physicians and others responded with calls for women's physical education to complement their mental education, and argued that "Looks, not books, are the murderers of American women."[73] That is, women themselves much more commonly blamed the fashions of corseting and the tremendous weight of long skirts and petticoats for their menstrual ills.[74]

Ehrenreich and English view the "zero-sum energy" theory as "a miniature economic system, with the various parts—like classes or interest groups—competing for a limited supply of resources." While men

---

[70] Showalter and Showalter, "Victorian Women," in *Suffer and Be Still*, ed. Vicinus, p. 42.

[71] Smith-Rosenberg and Rosenberg, "The Female Animal," in *Women and Health*, ed. Leavitt, esp. pp. 15–17.

[72] Hormonal theories of chemical regulation of bodily function were not strongly advanced until the 1890s and were not widely accepted before the turn of the century. Prior to that time, the nervous system was believed to predominate in such regulation. See, for example, Merriley Borell, "Organotherapy, British Physiology and Discovery of the Internal Secretions," *Journal of the History of Biology* 9 (1976): 235–68.

[73] Sarah Stevenson, as quoted by Smith-Rosenberg and Rosenberg, "The Female Animal," in *Women and Health*, ed. Leavitt, p. 17. See also Martha Verbrugge, "Knowledge and Power: Health and Physical Education for Women in America" in this volume; and Paul Atkinson, "Fitness, Feminism and Schooling," in *The Nineteenth Century Woman: Her Cultural and Physical World*, ed. Sara Delamont and Lorna Duffin (New York: Barnes and Noble, 1978), pp. 92–133.

[74] See, for example, Haller and Haller, *The Physician and Sexuality*, esp. pp. 141–186; and Fred E. H. Schroeder, "Feminine Hygiene, Fashion and the Emancipation of American Women," *American Studies* 17 (1976): 101–110.

were encouraged to "back the brain," women were "urged to throw their weight behind the uterus" to sustain the appropriate division of social and economic labor. Ehrenreich and English argue that the goal of this ideology was to keep women from competing directly with men as workers for a piece of the limited economic pie.[75]

Women obviously resisted the "zero-sum" ideology, and feminists and their allies responded to its advocates head-on, especially fighting the theory that menstrual debility was worsened by education. Vern Bullough and Martha Voight offer the strongest review to date of women's and their male allies' empirical responses.[76] They situate the debate within the chaos of medical knowledge and theories, concluding that it was physicians' "emotional attachments" or "political prejudices" rather than their science which led to medical theories of menstrual debility. R. O. Valdiserri provides an account of Dr. Mary Putnam Jacobi's pioneering work on the question of rest during menstruation, mention of which is oddly missing from the Bullough and Voight essay.[77]

Two recent studies counter the middle-class bias of most of this literature by focusing on employed women and menstrual issues. Karen Offen examines the sexual politics and menstrual consequences of the use of dual-treadle sewing machines, finding that nineteenth-century French physicians differentially identified problems with their use according to whether those physicians did or did not support women's employment in general.[78] One medical opponent saw the machines as causing extensive vaginal discharge, extreme genital arousal (including observed orgasms at ateliers), and menstrual problems, including hemorrhages induced by arousal. A physician who supported women's right to work and who took an occupational health perspective found through a survey that the negative effects of treadle machines were minimal as long as women were not overworked. Debility was not necessarily menstrually induced. He also successfully prescribed using the treadle machine for women suffering from dysmenorrhea!

---

[75] Ehrenreich and English, *For Her Own Good*, p. 114.
[76] See Vern Bullough and Martha Voight, "Women, Menstruation and Nineteenth Century Medicine," *Bulletin of the History of Medicine* 47 (1973): 66–82, reprinted in *Women and Health*, ed. Leavitt, pp. 28–38.
[77] See R. O. Valdiserri, "Menstruation and Medical Theory: An Historical Overview," *Journal of the American Medical Women's Association* 38 (1983): 66–70.
[78] Karen Offen, "Powered by a Woman's Foot: A Documentary Introduction to the Sexual Politics of the Sewing Machine in Nineteenth Century France," *Women's Studies International Forum* 11 (1988): 93–101.

Sioban Harlow has analyzed American research on menstruation and work published from c1875 to 1975.[79] Early workplace studies of American women also centered on their menstrual debility (rather than occupational health risks and poor working conditions), and were often accompanied by questions about whether women ought to be employed at all. Subsequent research has not supported hypotheses that normal menstruation impairs a woman's capacity to work, or that dysmenorrhea causes inefficiency or absenteeism. Both Harlow and Randi Daimon Koeske offer new theoretical frameworks for reconceptualizing research on menstruation.[80]

Assessing the literature on menstruation, it seems clear that more systematic analyses of women's empirical responses to menstrual debility theories are needed, including materials at least up to World War II and in relation to work, education, and other aspects of women's lives. Moreover, these need to be linked with shifts at the turn of the century to conceptions of menstruation as a normal and healthy process, part of a shift to new models of womanhood and motherhood.[81] For example, Jalland and Hooper refer to a *Lancet* article of 1926, declaring that Victorian attitudes toward menstruation had disappeared forever because of scientific advances and because women's capacities to work despite menstruation had been demonstrated during World War I.[82] But no historical studies have adequately addressed changes in women's own perspectives or in medical views of menstruation in the late nineteenth and early twentieth centuries.

Most contemporary studies of menstruation also utilize historical perspectives. Two popular feminist books in this tradition, aimed at understanding and lifting "the curse," have helpful bibliographies and

---

[79] Sioban Harlow, "Function and Disfunction: An Historical Critique of the Literature on Menstruation and Work," *Health Care for Women International* 7 (1986): 39–50, reprinted in *Culture, Society and Menstruation*, ed. Virginia Olesen and Nancy Fugate Woods (Washington, D.C.: Hemisphere, 1986), pp. 39–50. A more far-ranging review of the literature can be found in Sioban Harlow, "The Association Between Weight, Exercise, and Stress and Variation in Menstrual Bleeding Patterns" (Ph.D. diss., Johns Hopkins University, 1988).

[80] Randi Daimon Koeske, "Lifting the Curse of Menstruation: Toward a Feminist Perspective on the Menstrual Cycle," *Women and Health* 8 (1983): 1–16, reprinted in *Lifting the Curse of Menstruation: A Feminist Appraisal of the Influence of Menstruation on Women's Lives*, ed. Sharon Golub (New York: Haworth Press, 1983), pp. 1–16.

[81] See, for example, Linda Gordon, *Woman's Body, Woman's Right: A Social History of Birth Control in America* (New York: Penguin Books, 1976); Rothman, *Woman's Proper Place*; Theriot, *The Biosocial Construction*; and Ehrenreich and English, *For Her Own Good*.

[82] Jalland and Hooper, *Women From Birth to Death*, p. 56.

provocative insights.[83] Janet Sayers provides a feminist theoretical account of the social construction of menstruation, drawing on historical
data.[84] Sophie Laws argues that "Women's experience is so thoroughly
suppressed that the true picture of what the range of effects of the cycle
are cannot be available to us."[85] A recent historically-framed anthropological study of American women's relations with their bodies by Emily
Martin begins to address this very point by using women's own voices
generating their own categories of experience.[86] The "rule of silence"[87]
which surrounded menstruation is losing its force.

Laws also analyzes the rise of premenstrual tension as a medical
construction which has historically segmented part of women's continuous experience of cyclic change as a means of enhancing medical social
control.[88] Amanda Rittenhouse extends this analysis of PMS through a
content analysis of medical, popular and feminist literatures: From 1931
to 1980, medical and popular views were virtually identical; from 1981
to 1985, these became distinguishable with the popular literature sus-
taining stereotypes about women while the medical literature eschews
them and a new but largely reactive feminist literature emerged; since
1985, the feminist literature has offered its own analyses of the causes
and consequences of PMS.[89]

There is an intriguing if preliminary literature on the history of
means of managing menstrual flow. American women traditionally used
rags or napkins, sometimes specially made and reserved for this purpose,
and routinely soaked and boiled.[90] The development of commerical

---

[83] Paula Weideger, *Menstruation and Menopause: The Physiology and Psychology, the Myth and the Reality* (New York: Alfred A. Knopf, 1976); and Janice Delaney, Mary Jane Lupton and Emily Toth, *The Curse: A Cultural History of Menstruation*, rev. ed. (Urbana: University of Illinois Press, 1988).

[84] Janet Sayers, *Biological Politics: Feminist and Anti-Feminist Perspectives* (New York: Methuen, 1982), pp. 107–24.

[85] Sophie Laws, "The Sexual Politics of Pre-Menstrual Tension," *Women's Studies International Forum* 6 (1983): 19–31, esp. p. 20. See also Esther Rome, "Premenstrual Syndrome (PMS) Examined Through a Feminist Lens," *Health Care for Women International* 7 (1986): 145–52.

[86] Emily Martin, *The Woman in the Body: A Cultural Analysis of Reproduction* (Boston: Beacon Press, 1987).

[87] Smith-Rosenberg, "Puberty to Menopause."

[88] Laws, "The Sexual Politics."

[89] See Amanda Rittenhouse, "The Emergence of Premenstrual Syndrome: The Social History of a Women's Health 'Problem'," (Ph.D. diss., University of California, San Francisco, 1989).

[90] Showalter and Showalter, "Victorian Women," in *Suffer and Be Still*, ed. Vicinus, p. 41.

hygiene products signaled the entry of industry into this reproductive process.[91] Documentary materials illuminate the transition from rags and diapers to disposable "sanitary towels" in Victorian Britain. Displayed at meetings of the Obstetrical Society of London, they could also be purchased with a "towel cremator."[92] In the U.S., sanitary pads along with rubber belts were mail-order items available from Montgomery Ward catalogs in 1895 and from Sears, Roebuck in 1897.[93] Disposable sanitary napkins, placed on the market by Johnson and Johnson in 1896 as "Lister's Towels," were shortly withdrawn due to lack of sales, likely due to lack of advertising of such "unmentionables."[94] During World War I, French nurses discovered that the cellulose material used for bandaging wounds absorbed menstrual flow better than cloth diapers.[95] Using war-surplus cellulose wadding, Kotex napkins were produced by Kimberly-Clark in 1921; they were widely advertised in the 1920s using images of nurses and became a $19-million business by 1929.[96] No major innovations in this technology occurred until adhesive-backed pads eliminated the need for sanitary belts after 1970.[97]

Disposable commercial tampons, invented in 1933 by the Tampax Company, immediately generated considerble controversy "as an engine of contraception, masturbation or defloration." They had gradually gained acceptance by a significant minority of women when toxic shock syndrome was identified in 1978 and confirmed to be associated with tampon use in 1985. This new controversy has embroiled manufacturers, the Food and Drug Administration, and women's health advocates

---

[91] Clarke, "Industrialization."
[92] Jalland and Hooper, *Women From Birth to Death*, pp. 56, 73-4.
[93] Whether these were continually available thereafter is unclear. See Schroeder, "Feminine Hygiene," pp. 106-109. Schroeder attempts to link disposable sanitary pads with the shortening and lightening of skirts, dubiously assuming that the commercial products of the day were vast improvements on rags of various sorts.
[94] See Vern L. Bullough, "Female Physiology, Technology and Women's Liberation," in *Dynamos and Virgins Revisited: Women and Technological Change in History*, ed. Martha Moore Trescott (Metuchen, NJ: Scarecrow Press, 1979), pp. 233-51, esp. pp. 245-6; and Delaney, Lupton, and Toth, *The Curse*, pp. 138-50. Bullough drew on patent data while Delaney, Lupton, and Toth obtained company and product histories.
[95] Delaney, Lupton, and Toth, *The Curse*, p. 139.
[96] Bullough, "Female Physiology," p. 246. See also Vern L. Bullough, "Archives: Merchandising the Sanitary Napkin: Lillian Gilbreth's 1927 Survey," *Signs* 10 (1985): 615-27.
[97] Delaney, Lupton, and Toth, *The Curse*, p. 139.

in continued negotiations about product safety, inserting warnings in packages, and labeling absorbency levels.[98]

Only two other technologies for managing menstrual flow have been developed to date, and neither is widely used. In 1969, the Tassaway, a diaphragm-like disposable plastic cup worn in the vagina, was introduced.[99] The menstrual extraction method was developed in the recent women's health movement.[100] As Judith Walzer Leavitt has noted, ambitious histories of the development of the full array of feminine hygiene products and technologies are sorely needed.[101] Such studies would link well with growing interest in relations between medical and other sciences and industry. The commercial development of menstrual products has been aptly characterized as the transition "From Rags to Riches" since today there are approximately fifty brand-name napkins and tampons, and annual sales are approximately $500 million.[102]

MENOPAUSE

A fully developed life-course perspective on women's health would turn next to studies of the health and illnesses of adult women. In this volume, these are addressed by Lois Verbrugge, and so we now turn to studies of menopause. Two facts should be noted: not until after 1900 did American women's life expectancy exceed fifty years, and in 1900 only 4.1% of the U.S. population was over 65.[103] Thus before the twentieth century, many women died before experiencing menopause.

It is ironic, then, that the documentary data on menopause are more extensive than those on menstruation, although again much of it is

---

[98] Delaney, Lupton, and Toth, *The Curse*, p. 139, 144–5. See also Virginia L. Olesen, "Analyzing Emergent Issues in Women's Health: The Case of the Toxic Shock Syndrome," in *Culture, Society and Menstruation*, ed. Olesen and Woods, pp. 51–62. For a chronological approach see S. D. Helgerson, "Toxic Shock Syndrome: Tampons, Toxins and Time—The Evolution of Understanding an Illness," *Women and Health* 6 (1981): 93–104.

[99] Delaney, Lupton, and Toth, *The Curse*, p. 140.

[100] Lorraine Rothman, "The Development of Menstrual Extraction in the Women's Health Movement," in *The Menstrual Cycle: Vol. I—A Synthesis of Interdisciplinary Research*, ed. Alice J. Dan, Effie A. Graham and Carol P. Beecher (New York: Springer, 1980), pp. 312–17.

[101] Leavitt, *Women and Health*, p. ii. See also Nancy Reame, "Menstrual Health Products, Practices and Problems," *Women and Health* 8 (1983): 37–52, reprinted in *Lifting the Curse*, ed. Golub, pp. 37–52.

[102] Delaney, Lupton, and Toth, *The Curse*, p. 138.

[103] Hellerstein, Hume, and Offen, *Victorian Women*, pp. 452–3.

medical, as the "rule of silence" which surrounded menstruation held across the cycle of femininity.[104] These documentary materials illustrate the bleak if not grotesque picture painted by medical writers of the end of women's reproductive years, although some did acknowledge that postmenopausal life could be delightful.[105]

In one of the few historical studies emphasizing menopause, Smith-Rosenberg asserts that, like puberty, it was seen as a physiological crisis the resolution of which would shape a woman's remaining life.[106] The portrait of menopause itself was grim, with a host of possible ailments and diseases lurking. However, a lovely "Indian summer" or "golden age" of life was a possible outcome if the travails of menopause were survived. Medical men found the most significant cause of menopausal disease to be violations of the feminine role and/or engaging in sexual intercourse during or after menopause. A renewed commitment to asexual domesticity was their routine prescription.

Smith-Rosenberg also sought to understand how women themselves viewed menopause and found utter ambivalence. On the one hand, there would be freedom from menstruation, pregnancy, and childrearing, a "release from a world of troubles." On the other hand, rough waters needed to be negotiated to reach the other side.[107] It seems that many of the illnesses and diseases older women suffered from, such as cancer, were linked by physicians—and perhaps by women themselves—to menopause.[108] This confounding of menopause with pathological diseases and/or with chronic diseases of old age has apparently continued up to the present,[109] and future research needs to address this more directly.

Historical change in public information about menopause is the focus of another study. Linda S. Mitteness's content analysis of articles in the popular media in the U.S. from 1900 to 1976 reveals that the ambivalence described by Smith-Rosenberg was characteristic up to

---

[104] Smith-Rosenberg, "Puberty to Menopause."
[105] Jalland and Hooper, *Women From Birth to Death*, pp. 281-4, 287-99; and Hellerstein, Hume and Offen, *Victorian Women*, pp. 462-7.
[106] Smith-Rosenberg, "Puberty to Menopause."
[107] Smith-Rosenberg also offers a variety of psychological explanations for the varied perspectives put forth. See "Puberty to Menopause," in her *Disorderly Conduct*, pp. 191-4.
[108] See also Shorter's discussion of uterine cancer in his *A History*, pp. 245-6.
[109] See, for example, Ann M. Voda, Myra Dinnerstein, and Sheryl R. O'Donnell, eds., *Changing Perspectives on Menopause* (Austin: University of Texas, 1982).

1950.[110] Menopause was then considered a natural physiological event not requiring medical intervention. However, after 1950, negative statements focused on loss of youth and loss of sexuality grew more common and, after 1960, increased substantially. There is likely some connection between these characterizations and the fact that before 1960, estrogen replacement therapy was only recommended for severe menopausal symptoms, while more recently it has been recommended for an increasing array of symptoms, mild as well as severe.

While historical research on menopause is scanty, a considerable amount of work has been done on estrogen replacement therapies (ERT). Susan Bell pioneered in this area, examining the intellectual roots of the medicalization of menopause in the 1930s and 1940s and its definition as a hormonal "deficiency disease."[111] Bell found that medical specialists developed three basic models of menopause—biological, psychological, and environmental—each of which contributed to its medicalization. Both the then-emergent paradigm of reproductive endocrinology and the availability, in 1938, of a new drug (diethylsylbestrol or DES) usable in treatment of menopausal women justified and permitted implementation of that medicalization. The view that developed in the 1930s of menopause as a deficiency disease exists virtually unchanged in the medical literature today. Bell's discussion of medical specialists' ambivalence about science and its clinical applicability in the 1930s and 1940s is especially helpful in understanding how nonmonolithic medicine was.

Also within a medicalization framework, Frances B. McCrea examines the "second wave" of attempted medical designation of menopause as a deficiency disease, which occurred during the 1960s and 1970s.[112] At this historical juncture, feminists responded with an alternative view, arguing that the problem as not menopause but its medicalization. Patricia A. Kaufert and Sonja M. McKinlay focus on the debate about ERT within the American medical world between 1970 and 1973. They trace both the research community's case against estrogen and clinicians' strategies for rehabilitating ERT despite research demonstrating asso-

---

[110] Linda A. Mitteness, "Historical Changes in Public Information About the Menopause," *Urban Anthropology* 12 (1983): 161–79.

[111] Susan Bell, "The Synthetic Compound Diethylsilbesterol (DES) 1938–1941: The Social Construction of a Medical Treatment" (Ph.D. diss., Brandeis University, 1980); and Susan Bell, "Changing Ideas: The Medicalization of Menopause," *Social Science and Medicine* 24 (1987): 535–42. DES is discussed more fully below.

[112] Frances B. McCrea, "The Politics of Menopause: The 'Discovery' of a Deficiency Disease," *Social Problems* 31 (1983): 111–23.

ciated risks.[113] They draw here on an extensive critical review of the clinical and medical research literatures on menopause.[114] Recently, Kaufert and Gilbert have generated a set of criteria by which to assess whether a particular phenomenon has been medicalized.[115] After reviewing the literature on the medicalization of menopause and studying Canadian women's experiences of menopause, they conclude that the biomedical model is neither fully developed nor fully applied by physicians to menopause. That is, there is a wide range of practice regarding menopause by physicians, as Margaret Lock found.[116] Moreover, women's experiences are wide-ranging in terms of the presence, absence, and kinds of medical intervention. A host of ethical issues are, however, raised by physician/patient interactions leading to the prescription of ERT, as Virginia Olesen has ably pointed out.[117]

A comparative perspective is brought to bear in a paper by Frances B. McCrea and Gerald E. Markle which contrasts the history of the development and application of ERT in the United States and the United Kingdom.[118] Here they illuminate conflicts situated within different health systems among physicians, feminists and consumers, regulatory bodies, and the pharmaceutical industry. These negotiations have led to radically different use patterns. In the U.S., with its fee-for-service system in which patients or their insurers pay for drug purchases directly, ERT is extensively advertised and prescribed. In the U.K., where medical care including prescriptions is state-funded, ERT is much less frequently prescribed.

---

[113] Patricia A. Kaufert and Sonja M. McKinlay, "Estrogen Replacement Therapy: The Production of Medical Knowledge and the Emergence of Policy," in Women, Health and Healing: Toward a New Perspective, ed. Ellen Lewin and Virginia Olesen (New York: Methuen/Tavistock, 1985), pp. 113–38.

[114] Sonja M. McKinlay and John B. McKinlay, "Selected Studies of the Menopause: An Annotated Bibliography," Journal of Biosocial Science 5 (1973): 533–55.

[115] Patricia A. Kaufert and Penny Gilbert, "Women, Menopause and Medicalization," Culture, Medicine and Psychiatry 10 (1986): 7–22.

[116] See Margaret Lock, "Models and Practice in Medicine: Menopause as Syndrome or Life Transition?" in Physicians of Western Medicine, ed. R. A. Hahn and A. D. Gaines (Boston: D. Riedel, 1985), pp. 115–140.

[117] Virginia Olesen, "Sociological Observations on Ethical Issues Implicated in Estrogen Replacement Therapy at Menopause," in Changing Perspectives on Menopause, ed. Voda, Dinnerstein, and O'Donnell, pp. 346–60.

[118] Frances B. McCrea and Gerald E. Markle, "The Estrogen Replacement Controversy in the USA and UK: Different Answers to the Same Question?" Social Studies of Science 14 (1984): 1–26.

As in the area of menstruation, a variety of contemporary studies of menopause have included but not centered on historical aspects.[119] Pauline Bart and Marilyn Grossman's work demonstrates the continuity of nineteenth-century medical conceptions.[120] Maryvonne Gognalons-Nicolet brings an explicit life-cycle perspective to bear on menopause, arguing that studies must situate it historically and socially.[121] And an intriguing essay by Kaufert examines *both* medical and feminist views of menopause as cultural myths.[122]

REPRODUCTIVE SCIENCE AND ENDOCRINOLOGY

Over the past decade or so, many feminist scholars have come to understand that both medicine and science are socially constructed and that these constructions have quite consistently, though not invariably, disadvantaged women. This recognition has led to the flurry of feminist science studies noted earlier, many of which challenge the content of science as biased.[123] As the studies of ERT and DES demonstrate, there is also an emergent trend toward research that integrates the histories of medicine, science, and women's health issues.[124] One such area gradually receiving more scholarly attention is the history of reproductive science and endocrinology. Because life-cycle studies in the history of

[119] See Weideger, *Menstruation and Menopause*, pp. 195–218; and Delaney, Lupton and Toth, *The Curse*, pp. 213–40.

[120] See Pauline Bart and Marilyn Grossman, "Menopause," in *The Woman Patient: Medical and Psychological Interfaces*, ed. Malka T. Notman and Carol Nadelson (New York: Plenum Press, 1978), pp. 337–54; and Marilyn Grossman and Pauline Bart, "Taking the Men Out of Menopause," in *Biological Woman*, ed. Hubbard, Henifin and Fried, pp. 185–206.

[121] See Maryvonne Gognalons-Nicolet, "The Crossroads of Menopause: A Chance and a Risk for the Aging Process of Women," in *Older Women: Issues and Prospects*, ed. and trans. Elizabeth W. Markson (Lexington, MA: Lexington Books/D.C. Heath, 1983), pp. 37–48.

[122] Patricia Kaufert, "Myth and the Menopause," *Sociology of Health and Illness* 4 (1982): 141–65.

[123] See note 13. Three basic works with strong bibliographies are Harding and O'Barr, *Sex and Scientific Inquiry*; Hubbard, Henifin and Fried, *Biological Woman*; and Sue V. Rosser, *Teaching Science and Health from a Feminist Perspective* (New York: Pergamon, 1986).

[124] Susan Bell and Susan Reverby are currently working on a book that will demonstrate the importance of such integrated analytic perspectives.

women's health are essentially reproductive-cycle studies, a brief review of this area is appropriate here.[125]

A modern physiological reproductive science did not emerge until c1910, when the first English-language volume on the topic was published.[126] There were, of course, a variety of largely morphological and anatomical researchers preceding this. John Farley's outstanding volume covers these developments up to c1914, carefully situating the early study of reproductive phenomena in its usual scientific contexts of hereditary and evolutionary questions.[127] A key factor in the emergence of modern reproductive science was the "discovery" of hormones as "chemical messengers" which regulate bodily function. Merriley Borell and Diana Long Hall pioneered in this area. Borell's work addresses the rise of British general and reproductive endocrinology,[128] while Long Hall's work has focused largely on the rise of the endocrinological paradigm and the ensuing sexual politics of sex differences.[129] Nelly Oudshoorn's recent work focuses on endocrinology and the conceptualization of sex, c1920 to 1940 and on the making of sex hormones.[130] And my own work addresses the rise of American reproductive science

---

[125] Histories of the various reproductive technologies are not included here. The major secondary works are cited and the primary literature is available through their citations. Historical works by both reproductive scientists themselves and by historians and others are listed.

[126] F. H. A. Marshall, *The Physiology of Reproduction* (London: Longmans, Green and Co., 1910).

[127] See Farley, *Gametes and Spores.*

[128] See Merriley Borell, "Biologists and the Promotion of Birth Control Research, 1918–1938," *Journal of the History of Biology* 20 (1987): 57–87; Merriley Borell, "Organotherapy and the Emergence Reproductive Endocrinology," *Journal of the History of Biology* 18 (1986): 1–30; and Borell, "Organotherapy." The best general reference on the history of endocrinology is Victor Cornelius Medvei, *A History of Endocrinology* (Lancaster, PA: MTP Press, 1982).

[129] See Diana Long Hall, "Biology, Sex Hormones and Sexism in the 1920s," *Philosophical Forum* 5 (1974): 81–96, reprinted in *Women and Philosophy: Toward a Theory of Liberation*, ed. C. C. Gould and M. W. Wartovsky (New York: G. P. Putnam's, 1976), pp. 81–96; Diana Long Hall, "The Social Implications of the Scientific Study of Sex," *The Scholar and the Feminist* 4 (New York: The Women's Center of Barnard College), pp. 11–21; and Diana E. Long, "Physiological Identity of American Sex Researchers Between the Two World Wars," in *Physiology in the American Context, 1850–1940*, ed. Gerald L. Geison (Bethesda, MD: American Physiological Society, 1987), pp. 263–78.

[130] Nelly Oudshoorn, "Endocrinologists and the Conceptualization of Sex, 1920–1940," *Journal of the History of Biology*, forthcoming; and Nelly Oudshoorn, "On the Making of Sex Hormones: Research Materials and the Production of Knowledge," *Social Studies of Science*, forthcoming.

in biology, medicine, and agriculture c1910 to 1940.[131] The focus is on the centrality of endocrinology, patterns of research support, and changing relations with birth-control advocates.

Reproductive scientists themselves have made important contributions here. George W. Corner and Alan S. Parkes offer both autobiographical and historical information on the growth of reproductive endocrinology,[132] and Carl Hartman provides a helpful overview of the research.[133] Roy O. Greep and his associates also provide an historical overview, along with remarkable and invaluable historical charts of research within given problem areas in reproductive science.[134] Sophie D. Aberle and George Corner have written an informative institutional history of the major funding source of reproductive science from 1922 to 1947, which also outlines research done under its auspices.[135]

There is very little history qua history of the study of menstruation in reproductive science.[136] John Dewhurst provides a brief overview of

---

[131] See Adele E. Clarke, "Research Materials and Reproductive Science in the United States, 1910-1940" in *Physiology*, ed. Geison, pp. 323-50; Adele E. Clarke, "Embryology and the Development of American Reproductive Science, 1910-1945," in *The American Expansion of Biology*, ed. Keith Benson, Ronald Rainger, and Jane Maienschein (New Brunswick, NJ: Rutgers University Press, forthcoming); Adele E. Clarke, "A Social Worlds Research Adventure: The Case of Reproductive Science," in *Theories of Science in Society*, ed. Thomas Gieryn and Susan Cozzens (Bloomington: Indiana University Press, forthcoming); and Adele E. Clarke, "Emergence of the Reproductive Research Enterprise: A Sociology of Biological, Medical and Agricultural Science in the United States, 1910-1940" (Ph.D. diss., University of California, San Francisco, 1985).

[132] George W. Corner, *Seven Ages of a Medical Scientist*; also see his *The Hormones in Human Reproduction* (Princeton: Princeton University, 1942, 1947; New York: Atheneum, 1963); Alan S. Parkes, "The Rise of Reproductive Endocrinology, 1926-1940: The Dale Lecture for 1965," *Journal of Endocrinology* 34 (1966): xx-xxxii.

[133] Carl Hartman, *Science and the Safe Period: A Compendium of Human Reproduction* (Baltimore: Williams and Wilkins, 1962).

[134] Roy O. Greep, M. A. Koblinsky and F. S. Jaffe, *Reproduction and Human Welfare: A Challenge to Research* (Boston: MIT for the Ford Foundation, 1976); and Roy O. Greep and Marjorie A. Koblinsky, eds., *Frontiers in Reproduction and Fertility Control: A Review of the Reproductive Sciences and Contraceptive Development* (Boston: MIT for the Ford Foundation, 1977).

[135] Sophie D. Aberle and George W. Corner, *Twenty-Five Years of Sex Research: History of the National Research Council Committee for Research in Problems of Sex, 1922-1947* (Philadelphia: W. B. Saunders, 1953).

[136] Two overview articles by feminist scholars are inadequately historical. See Alice J. Dan, "Historical Perspective on Menstrual Cycle Research," in *The Menstrual Cycle, Vol. I*, ed. Dan, Graham and Beecher, pp. 1-7; and Barbara Sommer, "Menstrual Cycle Research: Yesterday, Today and Tomorrow," *The Menstrual Cycle Vol. II: Research and Implications for Women's Health*, ed. Pauline Komnenich et al., (New York: Springer, 1981), pp. 193-99.

menarche.[137] Research on the menstrual cycle has been historically summarized by Guy E. Abraham, Rudolf F. Vollman, and Carl G. Hartman,[138] while R. A. H. Kinch provides some work on dysmenorrhea.[139]

Even less historical study of menopause has been done in basic or clinical reproductive science, with the exception of a strong critical review of the historical clinical and scientific literatures.[140] Madeleine Goodman's contemporary review article raises important conceptual points,[141] and Wulf H. Utian offers a short review.[142]

A considerable number of historical studies have focused on the discovery and applications of DES. First synthesized in 1938, this nonsteroidal compound with the properties of natural estrogen was only finally acknowledged to be carcinogenic in 1971, despite consistent evidence reported in the interim. Susan E. Bell provides a superb analysis of the development of DES as an FDA-approved medical technology between 1938 and 1941.[143] She demonstrates how the issues of safety, efficacy, and efficiency were negotiated among the four participating communities or sets of actors from medicine, science, the pharmaceuti-

---

[137] Dewhurst, "The Menarche."
[138] Guy E. Abraham, "The Normal Menstrual Cycle," in *Endocrine Causes of Menstrual Disorders*, ed. James R. Givens (Chicago: Year Book Medical Publishers, 1977), pp. 15–44; Rudolf F. Vollman, *The Menstrual Cycle: Major Problems in Obstetrics and Gynecology Vol. 7* (Philadelphia: W. B. Saunders, Co., 1977); Hartman, *Science and the Safe Period*. Research on menstruation was not undertaken until the 1920s, and a solid animal-based understanding of the cycle was not clear until the 1930s at which time clinical research expanded dramatically. See, for example, the four major reviews of the scientific literature on menstruation done in the 1930s, in which most of the citations are to work done in the 1920s and 1930s: George W. Corner, "The Nature of the Menstruation Cycle," *Medicine* 12 (1933): 61–82; Carl G. Hartman, *Time of Ovulation in Women* (Baltimore: Williams and Wilkins, 1936); George W. Bartelmez, "Menstruation," *Physiological Reviews* 17 (1937): 28–72; Hugo Ehrenfest, "Menstruation and Its Disorders," *American Journal of Obstetrics and Gynecology* 34 (1937): 530–729 and 1051–76. Corner's autobiography provides a good narrative summary of the early work; see Corner, *Seven Ages of a Medical Scientist*. These works provide good saturation of the field up to World War II.
[139] R. A. H. Kinch, "Dysmenorrhea: A Historical Perspective," in *Premenstrual Syndrome and Dysmenorrhea*, ed. R. A. H. Kinch (Baltimore-Munich: Urban and Schwarzenberg, 1985), pp. 79–85.
[140] See McKinlay and McKinlay, "Selected Studies of the Menopause."
[141] Madeleine Goodman, "Toward a Biology of Menopause," *Signs* 5 (1980): 739–54.
[142] Wulf H. Utian, "The Background: Historical Aspects," in *Menopause in Modern Perspective: A Guide to Clinical Practice*, ed. Wulf H. Utian (New York: Appleton-Century-Crofts, 1980), pp. 1–10.
[143] Susan E. Bell, "A New Model of Medical Technology Development: A Case Study of DES," in *Research in the Sociology of Health Care, Vol. 4*, ed. Julius Roth and Sheryl Ruzek (Greenwich, CT: JAI Press, 1986), pp. 1–32. See also Bell, "The Synthetic Compound Diethylsilbesterol (DES) 1938–1941."

cal industry, and the state in its regulatory capacity. Moving beyond linear or phase models,[144] Bell provides the most sophisticated framework to date with which to capture the complex social and historical processes of medical innovation.

Within a larger study of medical disasters, Dutton examines DES vis-à-vis the elusive goal of drug safety.[145] DES had an array of both clinical and agricultural applications, and the development of each use is traced up to the present, focusing on the warning signs that emerged in each arena and the ways in which they were discounted or dismissed. The transformation of DES from wonder drug to cause of the first known human occurence of transplacental carcinogenesis, from livestock-fattener to suspected cause of premature sexual development in children under ten who ate the meat, is a story of "reluctant regulation" by both the Food and Drug Administration and the U.S. Department of Agriculture, according to Dutton.

Roberta J. Apfel and Susan M. Fisher, relying upon Bell's work, begin with a historical overview of the development of DES and its biological activity.[146] The volume goes on to analyze the psychological ramifications of DES use among pregnant women and their daughters and sons, and the consequences of the DES disaster for physician/patient relationships. In sharp contrast to Dutton, they conclude that scandals such as that surrounding DES are "intrinsic to the very structure of modern medicine."[147] Moreover, they believe that such disasters are unavoidable if medical science is to advance. Their work has been cogently criticized by Richard Gillam and Barton Bernstein on these grounds.[148]

---

[144] See, for example, John B. McKinlay, "From 'Promising Report' to 'Standard Procedure': Seven Stages in the Career of a Medical Innovation," *Milbank Memorial Fund Quarterly: Health and Society* 59 (1981): 374–411.

[145] Dutton draws deeply on Bell's historical work and the chapter is an excellent synthesis on the topic. Diana B. Dutton, "DES and the elusive goal of drug safety," *Worse than the Disease: Pitfalls of Medical Progress* (Cambridge, MA: Cambridge University Press, 1988), pp. 31–90.

[146] Chapters 1 and 2 are the most worthwhile, although not all references cited are actually provided. See Roberta J. Apfel and Susan M. Fisher, *To Do No Harm: DES and the Dilemmas of Modern Medicine* (New Haven: Yale University Press, 1984).

[147] Apfel and Fisher, *To Do No Harm*, p. 8.

[148] See Richard Gillam and Barton Bernstein, "Doing Harm: The DES Tragedy and Modern American Medicine," *The Public Historian* 9 (1987): 57–82. See also, Barbara Seaman and Gideon Seaman, *Women and the Crisis in Sex Hormones* (New York: Bantam, 1977); Susan G. Hadden, "DES and the Assessment of Risk," in *Controversy: Politics of Technical Decisions*, ed. Dorothy Nelkin (Beverly Hills: Sage, 1979); Cynthia L. Orenberg, *DES: The Complete Story* (New York: St. Martin's Press, 1981); and Robert Meyers, *DES: The Bitter Pill* (New York: Seaview/Putnam, 1983).

OLDER WOMEN'S HEALTH, AGING, AND DYING

Very few historical studies have been done on older women's health, aging, and dying. This demonstrates the fragmented and partial nature of the use of life-cycle perspectives in women's health history, as aging issues are obviously crucial to the life cycle. There are, however, some remarkable documentary materials available, many with strong introductory essays.[149]

In the literature on aging itself, Tamara K. Hareven explicitly situates aging within the life course in important ways.[150] There have also been some historical and comparative studies, and even some attention to cultural and sub-cultural variations in the situations and experiences of the aged. Modernization and industrialization theories are central concerns and the focus is largely on work, family issues, and the relative status of the aged.[151] Alfred J. Kutzik provides a solid historical perspective on American social provision for the aged from the colonial era to 1940, with special emphasis on race and ethnic variations.[152] Though it does not particularly attend to gender, this work renders the situations of the elderly poor quite vividly.

When aging and health are addressed in the literature on aging, research generally centers on contemporary health care economics and family issues. Here old age and illness are equated, and too often gender issues are ignored. The exception is recent work on women as "hidden" caregivers for the elderly, with some recognition that the elderly are usually frail women and are typically cared for by their daughters,

---

149 See Lerner, *The Female Experience*, pp. 148–200; Marilyn Yalom, "Introduction to Part IV." In Hellerstein, Hume and Offen, *Victorian Women*, pp. 452–510; and Jalland and Hooper, *Women From Birth to Death*, pp. 281–318.

150 Tamara K. Hareven, "The Life Course and Aging in Historical Perspective," in *Aging and Life Course Transitions: An Interdisciplinary Perspective*, ed. Tamara K. Hareven and Kathleen J. Adams (New York: The Guilford Press, 1982), pp. 1–26.

151 See, for example, Tamara K. Hareven, *Family Time and Industrial Time: The Relationship Between the Family and Work in A New England Industrial Community* (Cambridge, MA: Cambridge University Press, 1982); Tamara K. Hareven, "Modernization and Family History: Perspectives on Social Change," *Signs* 2 (1976): 190–206; and Jill S. Quadagno, *Aging in Early Industrial Society: Work, Family and Social Policy in Nineteenth Century England* (New York: Academic, 1982).

152 Alfred J. Kutzik, "American Social Provision for the Aged: An Historical Perspective," in *Ethnicity and Aging: Theory Research and Policy*, ed. Donald E. Gelfand and Alfred J. Kutzik (New York: Springer, 1979), pp. 32–65.

daughters-in-law, and poorly paid female nursing home aides.[153] Historical and interdisciplinary studies could valuably pursue some of these rich themes.

SUGGESTIONS FOR FURTHER RESEARCH

Throughout this essay, many avenues for further research have been specified. The question addressed here is how life-cycle perspectives can be brought to bear on women's health history while avoiding their obvious pitfalls. I believe there are two different approaches which can both be valuably utilized.

The first is simply to use the life-cycle framework as a chronological organizing device, as many studies have done, shorn of *both* its classic modeling dimensions of developmental crisis *and* normative age expectations. Moreover, rather than attempt to trundle across the entire life cycle in a single book or article, particular stages should be the sole focus of individual studies. That is, the complexities we can easily perceive when thinking *across* the life cycle must be matched by the complexity of concerns addressed *within* particular life-cycle stages.

Within a given stage or phase, researchers can then seek out the full range of variation of female experiences of that phase during a particular historical era or across several eras, including women's conceptions of the very categories of their experience. Emphasis would be on the diversity of women's experiences of a particular life-cycle stage. Such diversities should certainly include but not be limited to race, class, ethnicity, sexual preference, urban or rural setting, and geographic region. Alternatively, research could focus on a single stage or a few stages as experienced within a particular identifiable social group.[154] Ulti-

---

[153] See, for example, Helen Evers, "The Frail Elderly Woman: Emergent Questions in Aging and Women's Health," in *Women, Health and Healing*, ed. Lewin and Olesen, pp. 86–112; Janet Finch and Dulcie Groves, "By Women, For Women: Caring for the Frail Elderly," *Women's Studies International Forum* 5 (1982): 427–38; Janet Finch and Dulcie Groves, eds., *A Labour of Love* (London: Routledge and Kegan Paul, 1983); R. Stone, G. Cafferata, and J. Sangl, "Caregivers of the Frail Elderly: A National Profile," *The Gerontologist* 27 (1987): 616–26. For policy concerns with historical perspectives, see Jane Sprague Zones, Carroll L. Estes and Elizabeth A. Binney, "Gender, Public Policy and the Oldest Old," *Ageing and Society* 7 (1987): 275–302; and Dean Rodeheaver, "When Old Age Became a Social Problem, Women Were Left Behind," *The Gerontologist* 27 (1987): 741–6.

[154] This is the approach taken in Jane Lewis, ed., *Labor and Love: Women's Experience of Home and Family, 1850–1940* (London: Basil Blackwell, 1986).

mately, this approach would yield comparative portraits of different stages across time and across socially meaningful groups.[155]

A second approach involves taking up the serious feminist challenge to reframe historical eras of relevance to women's experiences and to discover women's own categories of experience within them. Many historians have noted that women's history disputes the conventional periodizations of history.[156] In this approach, the questions that must be asked of life-cycle eras or phases are, "Whose categories are they and do they represent women's conceptualizations?" The core problem here remains the danger of lapsing into normative perspectives that exclude the diversity which has existed and continues to exist. Both feminist periodizations and new categories of female experience are vulnerable to being construed as normative unless the full range of variation is carefully addressed. To pursue this second alternative, interdisciplinary research could be extremely fruitful. For example, feminist scholars from an array of disciplines have been wrestling intensely with the problems of discovering women's own conceptual categories of experience around menstruation, menopause and their bodies more generally.[157]

[155] Bell's recent work offers important conceptual assistance here, providing an interactive yet sequential model, which focuses on the multiplicity of factors coming into play at a given stage and their interrelations over time. While in this article her model is applied to the development of medical technologies, it offers a suberb critique of linear models and provides a much broader analytic framework for our consideration. See Bell, "A New Model of Medical Technology Development."

[156] See, for example, Joan Kelly, Women, History and Theory: The Essays of Joan Kelly (Chicago: University of Chicago Press, 1984).

[157] See for example, Yewoubdar Beyene, "Cultural Significance and Physiological Manifestations of Menopause," Culture, Medicine and Psychiatry 10 (1986): 47–71; Yewoubdar Beyene, From Menarche to Menopause: Reproductive Lives of Peasant Women in Two Cultures (Albany: State University of New York Press, 1989); Dona Lee Davis, "Cultural Significance and Physiological Manifestations of Menopause: A Biocultural Analysis," Culture, Medicine and Psychiatry 10 (1986): 73–87; Margaret Lock, "Introduction: Anthropological Approaches to Menopause: Questioning Received Wisdom," Culture, Medicine and Psychiatry 10 (1986): 1–6; Margaret Lock, "Ambiguities of Aging: Japanese Experience and Perceptions of Menopause," Culture, Medicine and Psychiatry 10 (1986): 23–48; Margarita Artschwager Kay, "Meanings of Menstruation to Mexican American Women," The Menstrual Cycle Vol. 2, ed. Komnenich et al., pp. 114–23; Whelehan, The Anthropology of Women's Health; Martin, The Woman in the Body. See also works cited earlier as drawing on historical perspectives, Smith, "A Sociology for Women"; and Smith, The Everyday World; and Shulamit Reinharz, Social Science Methods, Feminist Voices: Readings and Interpretations (New York: Pergamon Press, 1987).

Both alternatives would improve the utility of life-cycle perspectives for understanding women's health experiences historically. For as Harriet Engel Gross has aptly stated, we need both to stop genuflecting to biology and stop ignoring the body as we seek to understand women's lives.[158]

---

[158] Gross, "Considering." p. 697.

2

PATHWAYS OF HEALTH
AND DEATH

Lois M. Verbrugge

INTRODUCTION

In contemporary health statistics, the largest differentials in rates of illness, disability, and death are related to age. Typically, rates rise across adult ages, and especially steeply at older ages (65+). Sex ranks second: Women's experience of daily symptoms, their prevalence rates for many chronic conditions, their experience of short and long-term disability due to health problems, and their use of professional health services exceed men's within each age group. Nevertheless, women's rates of mortality are strikingly lower than men's.

What causes these sex differentials has much to do with prior personal and social histories. The health status of any individual and any society at a given time is the consequence of past exposures and therapies as well as current ones. Whether we are able to understand the precise causes of sex differentials, or only able to see their distilled outcome in rates and other health-status measures, depends on scientific sophistication and energy.

Advances in the collection and processing of health information over the past century mean we now see levels and differentials that were only intuited or scantly recorded before. We now regularly report the health status of women and men with good accuracy and precision. Still, what we know descriptively about sex differentials is sparse compared to social needs and future scientific capabilities. How health information is

Preparation of this article was facilitated by a Special Emphasis Research Career Award (K01 AG00394) from the National Institute on Aging. This article is a gift to William J. Bogard, for the beckoning pathways sprung to bloom.

interpreted has also changed greatly. Viewed as the "weaker sex" only a century ago, women are now considered the sturdier sex by most biologists and health scientists, with regard to longevity potential and intrinsic vulnerability to fatal pathologies.[1] Interpretations of sex differentials will continue to change, hopefully in ever more veridical directions. In short, our knowledge about population health is always bounded empirically and culturally—ideally less so as time goes on. As scientists, we strive to recognize those limitations and then proceed to tell the truth as accurately and fairly as possible.

CONTENTS

This article begins with contemporary statistics to highlight differences in health and death experiences of women and men. I concentrate on enduring rather than evanescent differences. Explanations for the differences are stated and evaluated. Then trends in health and mortality during the twentieth century and trends in sex differences are presented. Health and mortality prospects for women and men in the twenty-first century and forecasts of their position relative to each other are discussed. I note the shift from a young to an aged population and the rising importance of older women as a social force and as a concern for medicine and rehabilitation. Finally, the failure of statistics to see the dynamics of health—the health pathways that individuals take over their lifetimes—is considered.

Some basic features of the article should be mentioned:

(1) I discuss adults (ages 18+) rather than the whole age span since chronic morbidity and death are infrequent in childhood and youth. Although sex differences do exist in pre-adult years (poorer health for boys up to adolescence, and higher mortality for them at all pre-adult ages), they are relatively small compared to adult ages.[2]

(2) The rates summarized and discussed are age-specific ones (for age groups) unless otherwise noted. In health statistics, age groups are com-

---

[1] For example, see Ashley Montagu, *The Natural Superiority of Women* (New York: Collier Books, 1978); David T. Purtilo and John L. Sullivan, "Immunological Bases for Superior Survival of Females," *American Journal of Diseases of Childhood* 133 (1979): 1251–53; Estelle R. Ramey and Peter Ramwell, "The Relationship of the Sex Hormone/Prostaglandin Interaction to Female and Male Longevity," in *The Changing Risk of Disease in Women: An Epidemiologic Approach*, ed. E. B. Gold (Lexington, MA: D. C. Heath and Co., 1984), pp. 25–36.

[2] John H. Dingle, George F. Badger, and William S. Jordan, *Illness in the Home* (Cleveland, OH: Case Western Reserve University Press, 1964); Mary Grace Kovar, "Health Status of U.S. Children and Use of Medical Care," *Public Health Reports* 97 (1982): 3–15; Lois M. Verbrugge, "Sex Differentials in Health," *Public Health Reports* 97 (1982): 17–37.

)NTEMPORARY HEALTH PROFILES

Health surveys repeatedly show that women have higher rates of
:ss and disability than men. This excess appears in every adult age
ιp, being most pronounced for acute conditions and short-term
bility in reproductive ages (18–44), and for chronic conditions and
)ciated disability in mid- or late life. Despite their lower levels of
lbeing throughout life, women tend to live longer than men. Two
stions rise immediately: Why is there apparently a contradiction
ween sex differentials in health and mortality? And why do sex
erences exist at all in health and mortality?

We begin this section with a summary of contemporary health and
rtality levels for both sexes, and the general size of sex differentials.[6,7]

---

eviews and ample data on sex differentials in health are in Esther Hing, Mary Grace
ovar, and Dorothy P. Rice, "Sex Differences in Health and Use of Medical Care:
Jnited States, 1979." Vital and Health Statistics, series 3, no. 24. DHHS publ. no.
PHS) 83-1408. (Hyattsville, MD: National Center for Health Statistics, 1983); Con-
:ance A. Nathanson, "Sex, Illness, and Medical Care: A Review of Data, Theory, and
1ethod," Social Science and Medicine 11 (1977): 13–25; "Sex Roles as Variables in the
terpretation of Morbidity Data: A Methodological Critique," International Journal of
pidemiology 7 (1978): 253–62; Constance A. Nathanson and Gerda Lorenz, "Women
nd Health: The Social Dimensions of Biomedical Data," in Women in the Middle Years,
d. J. Z. Giele (New York: Wiley, 1982), pp. 37–87; Lois M. Verbrugge, "Sex Differen-
ials in Morbidity and Mortality in the United States," Social Biology 23 (1976): 275–96;
'Females and Illness: Recent Trends in Sex Differences in the United States," Journal of
łealth and Social Behavior 17 (1976): 387–403; "Sex Differentials in Health," Public
łealth Reports 97 (1982): 417–37; "Women and Men: Mortality and Health of Older
'eople," in Aging in Society: Selected Reviews of Recent Research, eds. M. W. Riley, B. B.
łess, and K. Bond (Hillsdale, NJ: Lawrence Erlbaum Assoc., 1983), pp. 139–74; "A
Iealth Profile of Older Women with Comparisons to Older Men," Research on Aging 6
1984): 291–322; "Gender and Health: An Update on Hypotheses and Evidence,"
ournal of Health and Social Behavior 26 (1985): 156–82; "From Sneezes to Adieux:
itages of Health for American Men and Women," in Health in Aging: Sociological Issues
ınd Policy Directions, eds. R. A. Ward and S. B. Tobin (New York: Springer, 1987),
)p. 17–57; "Gender, Aging, and Health," in Aging and Health: Perspectives on Gender,
Race, Ethnicity, and Class, ed. K. S. Markides (Newbury Park, CA: Sage, 1989), pp. 23–
′8; Lois M. Verbrugge and Deborah L. Wingard, "Sex Differentials in Health and
Mortality," Women and Health 12 (1987): 103–45; Ingrid Waldron, "An Analysis of
Causes of Sex Differences in Mortality and Morbidity," in The Fundamental Connection
Between Nature and Nurture, eds. W. R. Gove and G. R. Carpenter (Lexington, MA:
D. C. Heath and Co., 1982), pp. 69–115; "Sex Differences in Illness Incidence, Progno-
sis and Mortality: Issues and Evidence," Social Science and Medicine 17 (1983): 1107–
!3; Deborah L. Wingard, "The Sex Differential in Morbidity, Mortality, and Lifestyle,"
in Annual Review of Public Health, vol. 5, eds. L. Breslow, J. E. Fielding, and L. B. Lave
(Palo Alto, CA: Annual Reviews, 1984): pp. 433–58.
Reviews and data on sex differentials in mortality, with emphasis on the United States,
are in Eileen M. Crimmins, "The Changing Patterns of American Mortality Decline,
1940–77, and Its Implications for the Future," Population and Development Review 7

monly split into young (18–44), middle-aged (45–64),
persons. The total adult population's health is a funct
specific rates and age distribution (percents of people in
When studying trends, demographers prefer age-standa
plying age-specific rates of various years to a fixed age d
allowing only rates to change and pretending age distrib

(3) We will focus on physical health. Physical a
dominant propellers of disability and mortality, though
and cognitive deficits do increase in their causal impo
Besides this, national health surveys have long separat
mental health, studying one but not both. (A key data
article is the National Health Interview Survey, which vi
mental disorders.) In short, issues of pertinence and
examine physical health alone.[3]

(4) Health statistics provide aggregate estimates c
people. These are needed for health-services planning an
whole nation. The statistics can legitimately be used to sta
for individuals or average profiles for subgroups. These a
to convey stereotypes. Thus, sex differentials discussee
tendencies of men and women to differ, but do not im
different health experiences for men versus women.

(5) The only way to demonstrate that women ar
compare them to men, and vice versa. Studying just w
thinner empirical and less steady theoretical results. Th
stance is a standard one in sociology. Readers will find t
says as much about men as women.

A few terms need definition: (1) I shall use the 1
broadly to encompass both morbidity and disability.[4] Mor
symptoms, diseases, and impairments. Disability refers to
of morbidity for physical and social functioning. (2) The
used in a demographic manner, simply to indicate the two
compared.[5]

---

[3] See "Historical Perspectives on Women and Mental Illness" by Nanc
volume.

[4] This article will not review sex differences in health-services use and
and therapeutic health behaviors. Many of the reviews cited herein hav
references on the topic.

[5] By contrast, in sociology the terms "sex" and "gender" are used to sup
refers to features due solely to biology, and gender to features caused
biological, social, and cultural factors.

The contradiction is then untangled. Lastly, reasons why sex differences in health and mortality exist are considered.

Morbidity

Acute conditions are transient. (In national health statistics, they can last no more than three months). Women's incidence rates of acute conditions overall are 20–30% greater than men's (TABLE 1). A female excess appears in all main categories: infective/parasitic diseases, respiratory conditions, digestive system conditions, injuries (at ages 45+, but not 18–44), and the residual "all other acute conditions." The last category contains reproductive conditions, ear diseases, headache, genital tract and urinary disorders, and skin/musculoskeletal conditions. Even when reproductive conditions are excluded, a sizable sex difference still persists for this last category.

Chronic conditions are long-term health problems; they can be diseases or structural/sensory impairments. They are essentially permanent in a person's life, though their symptoms and progression can sometimes be controlled by drugs, lifestyle changes, and other therapeutic regimens. The key distinction for our discussion is between fatal (life-threatening) and nonfatal conditions. Prevalence rates for nonfatal chronic conditions are typically higher for women (TABLE 2). Women's disadvantage is especially large for some musculoskeletal problems, most digestive disorders, thyroid diseases, anemias, migraine headache,

---

(1981): 229–54; "Life Expectancy and the Older Population," *Research on Aging* 6 (1984): 490–514; Lois A. Fingerhut, "Changes in Mortality Among the Elderly, United States, 1940–78," *Vital and Health Statistics*, series 3, nos. 22 and 22a. DHHS publ. no. (PHS) 82-1406, 84-1406a. (Hyattsville, MD: National Center for Health Statistics, 1982, 1984); A. Joan Klebba, Jeffrey D. Maurer, and Evelyn J. Glass, "Mortality Trends: Age, Color, and Sex, United States, 1950–69." *Vital and Health Statistics*, series 20, no. 15. DHEW publ. no. (HRA) 74-1852. (Rockville, MD: National Center for Health Statistics, 1973); Metropolitan Life Insurance Co., "New High for Expectation of Life," *Statistical Bulletin* 68, no. 3 (1987): 8–14; "Women's Longevity Advantage Declines," *Statistical Bulletin* 69, no. 1 (1988): 18–23. Readers are encouraged to scan across years of the *Statistical Bulletin*, since it frequently presents data on health and mortality of U.S. women and men. Constance A. Nathanson, "Sex Differences in Mortality," in *Annual Review of Sociology*, vol. 10, eds. R. H. Turner and J. F. Short (Palo Alto, CA: Annual Reviews, 1984), pp. 191–213; S. Jay Olshansky and A. Brian Ault, "The Fourth Stage of the Epidemiologic Transition: The Age of Delayed Degenerative Diseases," *Milbank Memorial Fund Quarterly/Health and Society* 64 (1986): 355–91; Ira Rosenwaike, *The Extreme Aged in America* (Westport, CT: Greenwood Press, 1985); Lois M. Verbrugge, "Sex Differentials in Morbidity and Mortality in the United States"; Verbrugge, "Recent Trends in Sex Mortality Differentials in the United States," *Women and Health* 5 (1980): 17–37; Verbrugge and Wingard, "Sex Differentials in Health and Mortality"; Ingrid Waldron, "Why Do Women Live Longer Than Men?", *Social Science and Medicine* 10 (1976): 349–62.

TABLE 1. INCIDENCE OF ACUTE CONDITIONS, BY AGE-SEX, U.S., 1985.

(No. of conditions per 100 persons per year)

Age:	18–44			45+		
	Men	Women	F/M[a]	Men	Women	F/M
All acute conditions	140.7	193.0	1.37	95.7	117.1	1.22
Infective and parasitic conditions	12.8	21.6	1.69	5.4	5.9	1.09
Respiratory conditions	69.5	96.4	1.39	49.8	59.0	1.18
Upper resp. cond.	27.3	41.2	1.51	21.3	25.7	1.21
Influenza	37.0	49.7	1.34	24.8	29.1	1.17
Other resp. cond.	5.1	5.6	1.10	3.8	4.2	1.11
Digestive system conditions	4.8	8.0	1.67	4.5	6.2	1.38
Injuries	38.2	23.7	0.62	15.4	19.5	1.27
All other acute conditions	15.4	43.3	2.81	20.6	26.4	1.28
(Excl. reproductive conds.)[b]	15.4	33.7	2.19	20.6	26.2	1.27

SOURCE: National Health Interview Survey, 1985. Derived from Table 2 in *Vital and Health Statistics*, series 10, no. 160. DHHS publ. no. (PHS) 86-1588. Hyattsville, MD: National Center for Health Statistics. 1986.

[a] Sex ratio: Female incidence rate divided by male incidence rate.
[b] Excluding all sex-specific conditions (reproductive and genital tract) for women, their rates are 29.4 and 25.4, and ratios 1.91 and 1.23.

46

urinary conditions, and varicose veins. A special comment is needed about arthritis, since it is the leading chronic problem for women in mid- and late life, and the first or second rank one for men those ages. Women's prevalence rates for this often painful and limiting condition exceed men's by about 50%. Men have higher rates for relatively few nonfatal conditions, mostly some sensory and skeletal impairments (see bottom of Table 2). Altogether these data offer striking evidence of women's greater burden from nonfatal diseases, the conditions that bother but do not kill. The situation completely reverses for fatal chronic conditions (TABLE 3). Here, men consistently have excess rates.

Incidence and prevalence rates tell us simply about the presence of conditions, but not the suffering they cause for people. Health-diary studies in which respondents record symptoms and health actions daily for several weeks or months show how health problems penetrate everyday life. Not surprisingly, daily symptoms are more frequent for women than men at all ages (TABLE 4).

The incidence, prevalence, and symptom rates all point toward greater frequency of illness for women day by day, year by year. More time is spent feeling unwell. But women's illness burden also adds up in another way: Higher risks of experiencing most illness conditions, with the exceptions noted, imply that women end up with more chronic problems (this is called comorbidity) at any age. Thus, their health problems are more extensive both over time and at any given time.

In the midst of these differences, there is nevertheless a striking similarity. Even though rates differ so much, women and men tend to suffer from fundamentally the same health problems. And this similarity increases with age. The evidence: (1) Men's and women's lists of leading acute ailments are very similar (TABLE 5). Flu and the common cold dominate the list for both young men and women. The roster of other leading titles is essentially the same (though injuries tend to rank higher for men than women). For ages 45+, when rates of acute conditions fall sharply and pregnancy vanishes from women's lives, the leading titles and ranks become almost identical. (2) Women's and men's lists of leading chronic conditions are also very similar (TABLE 6). Respiratory problems top the list for young adults of both sexes. Fatal conditions are essentially absent for both. In midlife, the lists for both women and men become a more diverse mix of nonfatal problems, precursors to fatal ones (high blood pressure), and just a few fatal conditions (ischemic heart disease for men, diabetes for both women and men). At older ages, fatal circulatory problems become more prominent for both sexes. Still, their lists remain dominated by nonfatal impairments and diseases,

TABLE 2. SEX RATIOS (F/M) FOR SELECTED NONFATAL CHRONIC CONDITIONS, U.S., 1983–1985.[a]

Age:	18–44	45–64	65–74	75+
Arthritis	1.56	1.59	1.43	1.40
Sciatica	2.12	1.85	1.25	1.30*
Bunion	3.33	4.36	3.48*	3.34*
Bursitis	1.31	1.31	1.29	1.37
Dermatitis	1.88	1.59	1.62	1.76
Trouble with corns and calluses	1.57	1.82	1.65	2.63
Def./orth.impairment-back	1.35	1.09	1.31	1.89
Cataracts	0.52*	1.11	2.06	1.56
Diseases of retina	1.14	1.32	1.22*	1.32*
Gallstones	3.38	1.64	2.55*	1.43*
Gastritis and duodenitis	1.33	1.54	1.48	1.89*
Chronic enteritis and colitis	1.72	2.12	2.62*	2.58*
Spastic colon	4.18	4.05	6.24*	2.25*
Diverticula of intestines	3.83*	2.52	2.30	2.27
Frequent constipation	4.41	3.53	2.83	1.56
Thyroid diseases	8.27	6.51	5.16*	3.43*

Condition				
Anemias	12.96	4.78	1.75	2.88*
Migraine headache	2.97	2.75	2.97*	2.45*
Neuralgia and neuritis	1.38	1.79	1.99	1.15*
Bladder infection/disorders	9.83	4.82	2.37	2.06
Heart rhythm disorders	1.82	1.43	1.42	1.65
Varicose veins	4.69	3.33	2.50	2.23
Hay fever without asthma	1.16	1.23	1.23	1.11
Chronic sinusitis	1.35	1.23	1.24	1.19
BUT:				
Gout	0.25*	0.39	0.40	0.69
Intervertebral disc disorders	0.69	0.86	0.72	0.86*
Visual impairments	0.40	0.51	0.77	0.91
Hearing impairments	0.64	0.54	0.68	0.77
Absence of upper/lower extrem.	0.16*	0.21*	0.29	0.22*
Paralysis, complete or partial	0.45	0.75	0.71	1.03
Tinnitus	1.13	0.79	1.01	0.93
Hernia of abdominal cavity	0.65	0.82	1.06	0.98

SOURCE: Calculated from unpublished data for the National Health Interview Survey, 1983–85, provided to the author by the National Center for Health Statistics.

* High relative standard error (over 30%) for one or both rates.

a Based on prevalence rates (conditions per 1,000 persons). See also Table 6, footnote a. Only half the titles with excess female rates are shown here (contact author for ratios for further titles).

49

TABLE 3. SEX RATIOS (F/M) FOR SELECTED FATAL CHRONIC CONDITIONS, U.S., 1983–1985.

Age:	18–44	45–64	65–74	75+
Ischemic heart disease	0.79	0.49	0.60	0.82
Other selected heart diseases	1.40	0.97	0.86	1.03
Cerebrovascular disease	1.05	0.68	0.55	0.78
Atherosclerosis	0.60*	0.46	0.77	0.99
Malignant neop. of lung/bronchus	0.33*	0.71*	1.00*	0.36*
Emphysema	0.80*	0.41	0.34	0.16
Ulcer of stomach/duodenum	1.05	0.97	0.69	1.44
Liver disease incl. cirrhosis	0.55	0.77	0.40*	0.47*
BUT:				
Diabetes[a]	1.25	1.11	1.16	0.98
High blood pressure[b]	0.86	1.08	1.30	1.61
Chronic bronchitis[c]	1.89	1.96	1.59	1.13
Asthma[c]	1.54	1.41	0.92	0.82

SOURCE: Calculated from unpublished data for the National Health Interview Survey, 1983–85, provided to the author by the National Center for Health Statistics.
*High relative standard error (over 30%) for one or both rates.

[a] Death rates from diabetes are also similar for men and women.
[b] A risk factor for fatal circulatory diseases. Women's higher prevalence rates are thought to reflect earlier diagnosis and control, compared to men.
[c] Fatal in severe forms; most cases are bothersome but have low fatality risk.

especially women's. For both sexes, skeletal impairments diminish in importance with age, and sensory ones rise.

In sum, women and men are distinguished more by their frequency of morbidity than by the conditions they typically suffer. I shall continue to emphasize women's excess rates for nonfatal conditions and men's for fatal conditions, but these tendencies lie within a context of basic similarity in the problems experienced by both groups.

Disability

Acute and chronic problems often induce people to restrict their activities. The impact of acute conditions generally goes no farther than reducing daily activities for a while or staying in bed. But chronic conditions pose long-term threats for physical and social functioning; for example, making walking a painful and difficult enterprise, or forcing people to quit th' 'r jobs.[8]

Statistics split disability into short-term versus long-term impact. Short-term disability is due to both acute and chronic problems. Women consistently have higher rates: They restrict their activities for health problems about 25% more days each year than men do, and spend about 40% more days in bed per year on average. The differences are largest during women's reproductive years (ages 18–44). But even when reproductive problems are removed, a sizable sex difference in disability remains at these ages.[9]

Long-term disability refers to compromised physical and social activities, due largely to chronic conditions. For physical disability, women have notably higher rates of difficulty for all indicators (mobility, other motions, strength, endurance). Their disadvantage is especially pronounced in tasks requiring strength or involving the lower extremities.[10] For social disability, sex differences are more mixed and also harder to interpret: (1) In working ages (defined as 18–69), men are more likely to report severe limitations in their major role, but women surpass them for

---

[8] General introductions to disability are in Joan C. Cornoni-Huntley et al., "Epidemiology of Disability in the Oldest Old: Methodologic Issues and Preliminary Findings," *Milbank Memorial Fund Quarterly/Health and Society* 63 (1985): 350–76; Lawrence D. Haber, "Disabling Effects of Chronic Disease and Impairment," *Journal of Chronic Diseases* 24 (1971): 469–87; Kenneth G. Manton and Beth J. Soldo, "Dynamics of Health Changes in the Oldest Old: New Perspectives and Evidence," *Milbank Memorial Fund Quarterly/Health and Society* 63 (1985): 206–85; Saad Z. Nagi, "An Epidemiology of Disability Among Adults in the United States," *Milbank Memorial Fund Quarterly/ Health and Society* 54 (1976): 439–67; World Health Organization, *International Classification of Impairments, Disabilities, and Handicaps* (Geneva, 1980). Readers are cautioned that the terms used in disability research vary widely now and do not necessarily match the ones used in this chapter.

[9] Selected data on short-term disability are in Verbrugge, "Gender and Health." Readers who want to see the most recent disability rates should consult *Vital and Health Statistics*, series 10, annual issue on "Current Estimates From the National Health Interview Survey, United States" for a given year.

[10] Data on physical disability by sex are in Daniel J. Foley et al., "Physical Functioning," in *Established Populations for Epidemiologic Studies of the Elderly: Resource Data Book*, ed. J. Cornoni-Huntley et al., NIH publ. no. 86-2443. (Bethesda, MD: National Institute on Aging, 1986), pp. 56–94; Lawrence D. Haber, "Disabling Effects of Chronic Disease and Impairment—II. Functional Capacity Limitations," *Journal of Chronic Diseases* 26 (1973): 127–51 (data are for work-disabled people); Alan M. Jette and Laurence G. Branch, "The Framingham Disability Study: II. Physical Disability Among the Aging," *American Journal of Public Health* 71 (1981): 1211–16; Alan M. Jette and Laurence G. Branch, "Musculoskeletal Impairment Among the Noninstitutionalized Aged," *International Rehabilitation Medicine* 6 (1984): 157–61.

TABLE 4. RATES OF DAILY SYMPTOMS, FOR AGE-SEX GROUPS.

(Based on prospective health diaries. Two community studies.)

Detroit	Men			Women		
	18–44	45–64	65+	18–44	45–64	65+
	(Averages in 6 weeks)					
No. symptomatic days	13.1	11.2	17.9	17.6	18.5	18.1
No. syndromes of symptoms[a]	16.3	13.0	30.9	25.8	28.7	31.0
No. specific symptoms	25.0	17.7	46.7	41.6	44.6	40.6[b]
(N)	157	59	27	213	98	35

Southfield	Men			Women		
	62–74	75+	All 62+	62–74	75+	All 62+
			(Averages in 2 weeks)			
No. specific symptoms	15.0	15.9	15.2	18.2	29.6	22.6
(N)	48	12	60	50	32	82

SOURCE: Health In Detroit Study, 1978; Needs of the Elderly Study III, 1984. The Health In Detroit Study had a probability sample of white adult (ages 18+) residents of the Detroit metropolitan area. They kept daily health records for 6 weeks. Data are standardized to 6 weeks for each person to adjust for dropout. See: Lois M. Verbrugge, "Health diaries," *Medical Care*, 1980, 18: 73–95. The Needs of the Elderly Study had a probability sample of older adult (ages 60+, 1982) residents of the Detroit suburb of Southfield. During NES III, respondents kept health diaries for a total of 6 weeks (in three separate time segments). Data here are from the first 2-week segment; not adjusted for dropout, which occurred for only several cases. See: William Rakowski, Mara Julius, Tom Hickey, Lois M. Verbrugge, and Jeffrey B. Halter, "Daily symptoms and behavioral responses: Results with a health diary for older adults," *Medical Care*, 1988, 26: 278–297.
N - Number of respondents.

[a] A syndrome is a collection of related symptoms, as identified by the diary-keeper.
[b] Older Detroit women have lower symptom rates than men. This anomaly may be due to narrowing sex differences at older ages, or to unstable rates from the small samples of older persons.

TABLE 5. LEADING ACUTE CONDITIONS, FOR AGE-SEX GROUPS, U.S., 1985.

(Conditions per 100 persons per year)[a]

	MEN, 18–44	WOMEN, 18–44
1	Influenza, 37.0	Influenza, 49.7
2	Common cold, 21.4	Common cold, 30.7
3	Sprains/strains, 10.6	Other upper resp. infections, 10.5
4	Contusions/superficial injuries, 8.3	Delivery & other pregnancy/puerp. cond., 9.6
5	Open wounds/lacerations, 8.3	Other infective/parasitic diseases, 9.3
6	Other current injuries[b], 6.7	Viral infections NOS, 9.2
7	Other upper resp. infections[c], 5.9	Sprains/strains, 6.7
8	Other infective/parasitic diseases[d], 5.0	Contusions/superficial inj., 5.8
9	Viral infections NOS, 4.8	Other current injuries, 5.2
10	Fractures/dislocations, 4.4	Open wounds/lacerations, 4.5

54

	MEN, 45+	WOMEN, 45+
1	Influenza, 24.8	Influenza, 29.1
2	Common cold, 17.7	Common cold, 21.1
3	Sprains/strains, 4.4	Other current injuries, 5.7
4	Other current injuries, 4.1	Contusions/superficial inj., 5.1
5	Other upper resp. infections, 3.6	Other upper resp. infections, 4.6
6	Viral infections NOS, 3.5	Acute musculoskeletal conditions, 4.6
7	Acute musculoskeletal conditions, 3.5	Fractures/dislocations, 4.0
8	Contusions/superficial inj., 3.1	Viral infections NOS, 3.7
9	—	—
10	—	—

SOURCE: National Health Interview Survey, 1985. Derived from Tables 2, 7 in *Vital and Health Statistics*, Series 10, No. 160. DHHS Publ. No. (PHS) 86-1588. Hyattsville, MD: National Center for Health Statistics. 1986.
NOS - Unspecified ("not otherwise specified").
— - Rates for all other titles are very low (less than 2 per 100), so not ranked.

[a] Rankings are based on 29 titles; one title (a residual in "all other acute conditions") is excluded from the rankings. For tied rates, ranks were determined by checking population estimates (numerator counts).
[b] Residual; excludes fractures/dislocations, sprains/strains, open wounds/lacerations, contusions/superficial injuries.
[c] Except common cold.
[d] Residual; excludes common childhood diseases, intestinal virus NOS, viral infections NOS.

TABLE 6. LEADING CHRONIC CONDITIONS, FOR AGE-SEX GROUPS, 1983–85, UNITED STATES.

(Conditions per 1,000 persons. Average annual rate.)[a,b]

	MEN, 18–44		WOMEN, 18–44	
1	Chronic sinusitis, 136	N	Chronic sinusitis, 183	N
2	Hay fever without asthma, 104	N	Hay fever without asthma, 120	N
3	High blood pressure, 66	'F'	Def./orth. impairment-back[c], 82	I
4	Hearing impairment, 63	I	Migraine headache, 73	N
5	Def./orth. impairment-back, 61	I	Arthritis, 64	N
6	Def./orth. imp.-lower extrem., 53	I	Diseases of female genital organs[d], 63	N
7	Hemorrhoids, 48	N	Hemorrhoids, 58	N
8	Visual impairment, 43	I	High blood pressure, 57	'F'
9	Arthritis, 41	N	Dermatitis, 54	N
10	Indigestion, 29	N	Chronic bronchitis, 51	'F'
11	Dermatitis, 29	N	Other chronic headache, 42	N
12	Chronic bronchitis, 27	'F'	Asthma, 41	'F'
13	Asthma, 26	'F'	Hearing impairment, 40	I
14	Color blindness, 26	I	Varicose veins, 39	N
15	Migraine headache, 25	N	Def./orth. imp.-lower extrem., 38	I

56

MEN, 45-64

#	Condition	
1	High blood pressure, 254	'F'
2	Arthritis, 214	N
3	Hearing impairment, 196	I
4	Chronic sinusitis, 163	N
5	Ischemic heart disease, 87	F
6	Def./orth. impairment-back, 87	I
7	Hay fever without asthma, 79	N
8	Hemorrhoids, 76	N
9	Def./orth. imp.-lower extrem., 72	I
10	Visual impairment, 62	I
11	Diabetes, 52	F
12	Tinnitus, 51	N
13	Hernia of abdominal cavity, 45	N
14	Bursitis, 41	N
15	Intervertebral disc disorders, 41	I

WOMEN, 45-64

#	Condition	
1	Arthritis, 339	N
2	High blood pressure, 274	'F'
3	Chronic sinusitis, 198	N
4	Hearing impairment, 106	I
5	Hay fever without asthma, 98	N
6	Def./orth. impairment-back, 95	I
7	Varicose veins, 88	N
8	Hemorrhoids, 72	N
9	Chronic bronchitis, 65	'F'
10	Migraine headache, 59	N
11	Diabetes, 57	F
12	Bursitis, 54	N
13	Def./orth. imp.-lower extrem., 53	I
14	Heart rhythm disorders, 48	N
15	Corns and calluses, 47	N

MEN, 65–74

1	Arthritis, 371	N
2	High blood pressure, 349	'F'
3	Hearing impairment, 318	I
4	Ischemic heart disease, 190	F
5	Chronic sinusitis, 147	N
6	Tinnitus, 90	N
7	Diabetes, 90	F
8	Visual impairment, 83	I
9	Other selected heart diseases, 79	F
10	Atherosclerosis, 77	F
11	Def./orth. impairment-back, 77	I
12	Hemorrhoids, 75	N
13	Emphysema, 73	F
14	Hernia of abdominal cavity, 71	N
15	Def./orth. imp.-lower extrem., 64	I

WOMEN, 65–74

1	Arthritis, 528	N
2	High blood pressure, 454	'F'
3	Hearing impairment, 216	I
4	Chronic sinusitis, 182	N
5	Cataracts, 125	N
6	Ischemic heart disease, 114	F
7	Diabetes, 104	F
8	Varicose veins, 100	N
9	Def./orth. impairment-back, 100	I
10	Tinnitus, 91	N
11	Hemorrhoids, 82	N
12	Heart rhythm disorders, 81	N
13	Chronic bronchitis, 80	'F'
14	Def./orth. imp.-lower extrem., 80	I
15	Hernia of abdominal cavity, 75	N

#	MEN, 75+[a][b]		WOMEN, 75+[a][b]	
1	Hearing impairment, 447	I	Arthritis, 566	N
2	Arthritis, 405	N	High blood pressure, 459	'F'
3	High blood pressure, 286	'F'	Hearing impairment, 343	I
4	Cataracts, 178	N	Cataracts, 278	N
5	Ischemic heart disease, 158	F	Chronic sinusitis, 153	N
6	Visual impairment, 144	I	Visual impairment, 132	I
7	Chronic sinusitis, 128	N	Ischemic heart disease, 130	F
8	Atherosclerosis, 111	F	Frequent constipation, 119	N
9	Other selected heart diseases, 104	F	Atherosclerosis, 110	F
10	Cerebrovascular disease, 98	F	Varicose veins, 109	N
11	Diabetes, 93	F	Heart rhythm disorders, 108	N
12	Tinnitus, 79	N	Other selected heart diseases, 107	F
13	Emphysema, 79	F	Def./orth. imp.-back, 101	I
14	Frequent constipation, 76	N	Diabetes, 91	F
15	Diseases of prostate[d], 76	F	Def./orth. imp.-lower extrem., 89	I

SOURCE: Calculated from unpublished data for the National Health Interview Survey, 1983–85, provided to the author by the National Center for Health Statistics.

a The titles originate in six lists of specific conditions, queried to sampled households (one list per household). The lists cover high prevalence conditions and other selected conditions of public health importance, but exclude mental disorders. Rates for 95 titles, encompassing all chronic conditions (except mental) in the International Classification of Diseases, were computed and evaluated for ranks. They are rounded to integers for presentation. All rates shown here have low sampling error (relative standard error 30% or less).

b On the right of each column, conditions are noted with I for impairment, N for nonfatal disease, and F for fatal disease. (N includes conditions potentially fatal but rarely so in the modern era.) 'F' is for high blood pressure, asthma (young adult ages), and chronic bronchitis; see footnotes in TABLE 3.

c Deformity or orthopedic impairment.

d Includes cancer. For women 17–44, malignancies are 3% of all conditions in this title. For men 75+, they are 12%.

mild and moderate limitations.[11] ("Severe" means unable to do one's major role, whether it is paid employment or housekeeping; "moderate" is limited in amount/kind of major activity; "mild" is limited in other secondary activities such as shopping or church attendance.) It is hard to see direct reflections of illness in these rates because the physical demands that men and women face in their main roles probably differ on average. (Women still choose housekeeping more often than men, and even in the very same role there can be differences in physical demand.) Thus, social as well as morbidity aspects penetrate the disability statistics. Still, though the differences are hard to interpret precisely, they are genuine measures of the ultimate social impact of health problems. (2) It is currently conventional to measure social disability for older people by their ability to do basic personal care and household-management activities. Among people living in the community (noninstitutional), women are more likely to have difficulty doing routine personal and household tasks. (Examples of personal tasks are dressing self and getting to/using toilet; examples of household tasks are doing light housework and managing money.) The sex differences tend to increase with age; thus, women's problems are especially obvious among very elderly persons (85+). Some people have so much trouble they must rely on another person to help them get the job done. This is called dependency. Rates of dependency are much lower than rates of difficulty, but the sex differentials look the same. Women are more likely than men to be dependent for household tasks at all ages, and for personal-care tasks at advanced ages (80+; no difference at ages 65–79).[12] (3) Institutional residence is considered a form of disability since it signals inability to function

---

[11] Summary data are in Verbrugge, "Gender and Health," and Verbrugge, "Gender, Aging, and Health." See also Mitchell P. LaPlante, *Data on Disability from the National Health Interview Survey, 1983–85.* (Washington, D.C.: National Institute on Disability and Rehabilitation Research, U.S. Department of Education, 1988); Nagi, "An Epidemiology of Disability."

[12] The concept of basic activities of daily living (personal care) is discussed in Sidney Katz and C. Amechi Akpom, "A Measure of Primary Sociobiological Functions," *International Journal of Health Services* 6 (1976): 493–507; and of instrumental activities of daily living (household management) in M. Powell Lawton and Elaine M. Brody, "Assessment of Older People: Self-Maintaining and Instrumental Activities of Daily Living," *The Gerontologist* 9 (1969): 179–86. Data on difficulty and dependency for these tasks are in Deborah Dawson, Gerry Hendershot, and John Fulton, "Aging in the Eighties: Functional Limitations of Individuals Age 65 Years and Over," *Advance Data*, no. 133. (Hyattsville, MD: National Center for Health Statistics, 1987); Barbara A. Feller, "Americans Needing Help to Function at Home," *Advance Data*, no. 92

adequately in the community for medical or social reasons. Institutional residence is more common for older women than older men. Among residents, women residents typically have higher disability levels for personal care than same-age men residents.[13]

Mortality

An ultimate disadvantage for males surfaces in death. Males' overall mortality rate is currently 70% higher than females' (1985; age-adjusted). The male excess appears at all ages. For example, the sex mortality ratio (M/F) for 1985 is 1.80 for ages 45–54, 1.84 at 55–64, 1.81 at 65–74, 1.63 at 74–85, and 1.28 at 85+.[14] Life expectancy portrays these rates in a compact manner: The average number of years of life for a newborn boy was 71.2 in 1985, compared to 78.2 for a girl.[15] Even at age 85, female life expectancy is higher: 6.4 years versus 5.1.[16] Males have higher mortality from all leading causes of death (diseases of heart, malignant neoplasms, cerebrovascular diseases, acci-

(Hyattsville, MD: National Center for Health Statistics, 1983); Jette and Branch, "Framingham Disability Study"; Candace L. Macken, "A Profile of Functionally Impaired Elderly Persons Living in the Community," *Health Care Financing Review* 7 (1986): 33–49; Ethel Shanas, "Health and Incapacity in Later Life," in *Older People in Three Industrial Societies*, ed. E. Shanas et al. (New York: Atherton Press, 1968).

13 National data come from the National Nursing Home Survey (National Center for Health Statistics) and the decennial population census (U.S. Bureau of the Census). For the first, see Esther Hing, Edward Sekscenski, and Genevieve Strahan, "The National Nursing Home Survey: 1985 Summary for the United States." *Vital and Health Statistics*, series 13, no. 97. DHHS publ. no. (PHS) 89-1758. (Hyattsville, MD: National Center for Health Statistics, 1989); Esther Hing and Beulah K. Cypress, "Use of Health Services by Women 65 Years of Age and Over, United States, 1979." *Vital and Health Statistics*, series 13, no. 59. DHHS publ. no. (PHS) 81-1720. (Hyattsville, MD: National Center for Health Statistics, 1981). Data for the 1985 NNHS are forthcoming in issues of Series 13. For census data, see the special volume published on institutional residents subsequent to each census.

14 Note the decline from middle to advanced ages. The sex-mortality ratio follows a curvilinear pattern across age, with lowest values at the beginning and end of life, and highest values at ages 15–24. Data for 1985 are from *Monthly Vital Statistics Report*, vol. 36, no. 5, Supplement (Hyattsville, MD: National Center for Health Statistics, 1987), and *Vital Statistics of the United States*, 1985, vol. 2, part A (Hyattsville, MD: National Center for Health Statistics). Annual mortality statistics can be found in these two publications (the first for advance data, the second for detailed final data).

15 Life expectancy condenses age-specific mortality rates of a given year. It serves as a forecast of the average number of years remaining for individuals at an index age, x, assuming they experience the current rates. If rates actually change as they age, the forecast will be surpassed (mortality rates fall) or not achieved (mortality rates rise).

16 Life-table data for 1985 are from *Vital Statistics of the United States*, 1985, *Life Tables*, volume 2, section 6. DHHS publ. no. (PHS) 88-1104. (Hyattsville, MD: National Center for Health Statistics, 1988).

dents, chronic obstructive pulmonary diseases, pneumonia/influenza, suicide, chronic liver disease/cirrhosis, atherosclerosis).[17]

Despite the pronounced sex differences in mortality rates, there is fundamental similarity in causes of death. The lists of leading causes, and the ranks of those causes, are very similar for men and women.[18]

Summary

Women's lives are filled with more health problems—higher incidence of acute conditions, higher prevalence of most nonfatal chronic ones, more frequent botheration by health problems. Their higher levels of disability are an understandable consequence. Compared to men, women's symptoms are more likely to be bothersome but not life-threatening, and their limitations are mild or moderate rather than severe until advanced ages. The conjunction of more nonfatal problems and fewer fatal ones means more total years of life—and also more years of sickness and dysfunction. By contrast, men's lives are freer of illness, discomfort, and disability. But when ill health does strike, it is more likely to be via fatal chronic diseases. These abbreviate men's lives. Which sex pays the higher price? There is no single answer. Women's compromised life quality and men's compromised longevity are both high prices.

Nevertheless, behind these profound differences lies a basic similarity that should not be overlooked. Women and men encounter largely the same health problems in their lifetimes. Our comparisons of leading titles (for acute conditions, chronic conditions, causes of death) always show fundamental similarities. What differs for women and men are the *paces* of these health problems, with fatal conditions entering men's lives earlier and nonfatal ones entering women's lives earlier.

A Contradiction is Untangled

The seeming contradiction of "higher female morbidity, but higher male mortality" vanishes in face of the data above. Men have higher age-specific prevalence rates for fatal conditions, and it is these which ultimately drive their earlier mortality. Women have higher rates of transient ailments and of chronic conditions that bother but do not kill, and these largely account for their higher levels of discomfort and restriction during life.

---

[17] These titles are in rank order (1–6,8–10) by total number of deaths in the U.S., 1985. Diabetes (rank 7) is an anomaly; it has virtually equal rates for males and females since the 1970's. For most of the century, female rates were slightly higher.

[18] See tables in Verbrugge, "Gender, Aging, and Health."

Morbidity statistics focus on current problems and recent disability, so they are well-suited to showing women's excess in that regard. If instead morbidity statistics captured longitudinal health experiences of individuals, they would show not only a larger cumulative burden among women but also—and importantly—the earlier onset and possibly faster progression of fatal diseases among men. We can only hypothesize about such longitudinal differences now. Mortality statistics are the only overt signal of men's ultimate disadvantage, offering minimal insight into men's significant health decrements while living.

Reasons for Sex Differences

There are five categories of explanations for sex differences in health and mortality: (1) biological risks; these are intrinsic genetic and hormonal differences between males and females, (2) acquired risks; these are risks of illness and injury encountered in one's work and leisure activities, (3) psychosocial aspects of symptoms and care; called "illness behavior" in medical sociology, (4) health-reporting behavior; this concerns how men and women talk about their health problems to others, and (5) prior health care; or how one's care for health problems affects future health. Biological and acquired risks determine the occurrence of disease, injury, and impairment. Psychosocial factors then come into play—in perception of symptoms, evaluation of their cause and severity, choice and continuation of therapeutic actions, and short and long-term disability. Willingness to discuss health problems becomes pertinent when people are interviewed. Lastly, health care for a prior problem can influence one's current and future health experiences.[19,20]

---

[19] Reasons for sex differences in mortality are discussed in Marshall J. Graney, "An Exploration of Social Factors Influencing the Sex Differential in Mortality," *Sociological Symposium* 28 (1979): 1–26; William R. Hazzard, "The Sex Differential in Longevity," in *Principles of Geriatric Medicine*, eds. R. Andres, E. L. Bierman, and W. R. Hazzard (New York: McGraw Hill, (1984), pp. 72–81; G. Herdan, "Causes of Excess Male Mortality in Man," *Acta Genetica et Statistica Medica* (now called *Human Heredity*) 3 (1952): 351–76; Constance Holden, "Why Do Women Live Longer Than Men?", *Science* (October 9, 1987): 158–60; Alan D. Lopez and Lado T. Ruzicka, eds., *Sex Differentials in Mortality: Trends, Determinants, and Consequences*. Miscellanous series, no. 4. (Canberra, Australia: Department of Demography, Australian National University, 1983) (the book contains Proceedings of a WHO conference on sex differentials in mortality); Francis C. Madigan, "Are Sex Mortality Differentials Biologically Caused?," *Milbank Memorial Fund Quarterly* 35 (1957): 202–23; Nathanson, "Sex Differences in Mortality"; Verbrugge, "Sex Differentials in Morbidity and Mortality in the United States"; Verbrugge and Wingard, "Sex Differentials in Health and Mortality"; Waldron, "Why Do Women Live Longer Than Men?"; Waldron, "An Analysis of Causes

It is widely held by researchers, and increasing scientific evidence suggests, that men are disadvantaged by both biological and acquired risks for the development of fatal diseases and for experience of injuries. What lies behind women's greater tendency to develop nonfatal diseases has not been discussed, and it is a real mystery. The diseases are so diverse, no small array of risk factors (acquired or biological) is plausible. Far less epidemiologic and biomedical research has been devoted to etiology of nonfatal diseases than fatal ones. When the answers finally come, they will illuminate this aspect of sex differences. Similarly, women's higher rates of acute conditons are not yet explained. Symptom perception and predispositions to take care of symptoms are thought to be stronger among women. But the research evidence to date shows only small sex differences, in the direction just stated. Thinking about the matter in a theoretical way: sex differences in symptom-response are more likely when people confront "nonserious" health problems (nonfatal chronic conditions and mild acute ones) than "serious" ones (fatal diseases or severe acute conditions). For the latter, the illness is so overt and threatening, men and women are likely to respond similarly. Even if psychosocial differences prove rather small, their repeated expression does add up toward more health attentiveness, more care, and more accommodation over a lifetime for women. For reporting factors, it is often claimed that women are more willing to talk about their health problems and that they remember health events better. But the research evidence on this issue is scant; the evidence to date shows no sex differences. Finally, women's more attentive care for health problems may lead to earlier diagnosis of serious conditions, earlier and more persistent management for them, and ultimately longer lifetimes, compared to men. If supported by data, this hypothesis will show that

---

of Sex Differences"; Ingrid Waldron, "Sex Differences in Human Mortality: The Role of Genetic Factors," *Social Science and Medicine* 17 (1983): 321-33; "What Do We Know About Causes of Sex Differences in Mortality? A Review of the Literature," *Population Bulletin of the United Nations* 18 (1986): 59-76; "The Contribution of Smoking to Sex Differences in Mortality," *Public Health Reports* 101 (1986): 163-73.

[20] For explanations of sex differences in health, readers are referred especially to David Mechanic, "Sex Illness, Illness Behavior, and the Use of Health Services," *Social Science and Medicine* 12B (1976): 207-14; Constance A. Nathanson, "Illness and the Feminine Role: A Theoretical Review," *Social Science and Medicine* 9 (1975): 57-62; Nathanson, "Sex, Illness, and Medical Care: A Review"; Verbrugge, "Females and Illness: Recent Trends"; Lois M. Verbrugge, "Female Illness Rates and Illness Behavior: Testing Hypotheses About Sex Differences in Health," *Women and Health* 4 (1979): 61-79; Verbrugge, "Gender and Health." The last reference is a comprehensive review of hypotheses and research evidence.

women's higher morbidity actually contributes to lower mortality by prompting more care! The evidence is not yet in.

Summing up, I offer some judgments about the relative importance of the five factors. (1) What lies behind sex differences in diseases, impairment, and injury? Acquired risks rank first; social and recreational activities, stresses, and environmental exposures during life are the prime causes of health problems for each sex, and for differentials between them. Prior health care may rank next, giving a cumulative advantage to women. Biological risks come last. (Where do psychosocial and reporting factors fit in? They become pertinent when the data are obtained from health surveys. I hypothesize that their importance is lower than the other three factors.) (2) For mortality, the three principal reasons stack up in the same manner. Although biology ranks last, it is not negligible. The contribution of hormonal and genetic factors to sex mortality differences is hard to guess (my own is that 10–20% of the contemporary difference is due to biology) and will be very difficult to estimate quantitatively. (3) What lies behind sex differences in disability? Women's higher levels of day-to-day, year-to-year morbidity are the principal factor. (Morbidity, in turn, is the net product of acquired risks, prior health care, and biological factors.) Psychosocial factors rank second; they are pervasive aspects of illness experience and behavior in life, and they operate to boost women's responses to symptoms. Health-reporting factors come in last, maybe increasing women's survey reports of disability a little.[21]

These are hypotheses. The relative importance of the five factors in explaining sex differentials in morbidity, disability, and mortality is not known yet quantitatively. What *has* been accomplished in recent years are careful and comprehensive statements of the factors that must be considered, theoretically and empirically, in finding the answers. The basic scientific task ahead is to locate specific factors that influence health and mortality, and also differ in their presence among males and females. Both aspects are necessary for an explanation; neither suffices alone. High interest in sex differences assures us that coming decades will bring forth many detailed answers, which together will produce broad conclusions about the relative importance of social and biological factors. The most intriguing questions of all—"Are women intrinsically sturdier than men? In what biological ways? How much sturdier?"—will

---

[21] The same ranking of factors can explain women's more frequent use of health services.

not be answered soon. But I believe that scientific imagination and intelligence will eventually produce firm responses.

HEALTH AND MORTALITY TRENDS IN THE TWENTIETH CENTURY

The sex differentials in health and mortality evident in the late twentieth century are not new. This section considers their persistence and course over the past century.

All countries establish a vital registration system (for births, deaths, marriages) long before a national health survey program. Our knowledge of mortality trends is thus much richer than of morbidity trends, so we start with mortality.

Mortality Trends

Mortality data for the entire United States are available since 1933 (for selected states, 1880 to 1932). Demographers typically place confidence in figures starting at the century mark, 1900.

A profound epidemiological transition occurred in the twentieth century: Deaths, initially dominated by external and infectious/parasitic causes, are now due largely to chronic diseases (especially cardiovascular and neoplastic). Short-term perturbations in mortality rates, typically due to wars or epidemics, have largely disappeared. Death rates have fallen substantially in all age groups for both sexes. But the locus of gains has shifted; initially larger for children in this century, they are now (since the late 1960's) concentrated among older people.[22]

Sex differentials in mortality widened in the 20th century, particularly since 1930. In 1900, females had only a slight advantage over males: Their life expectancy at birth was 50.9, compared to 47.9 for males. The ratio of male to female mortality rates was 1.10 (age-adusted). In 1985, the sex difference was far larger: Life expectancies at birth were 78.2 and 71.2, respectively, and the sex mortality ratio was

---

[22] For the epidemiologic transition, see Abdel R. Omran, "The Epidemiologic Transition: A Theory of the Epidemiology of Population Change," *Milbank Memorial Fund Quarterly* 49 (1971): 509–38; "Epidemiologic Transition in the United States," *Population Bulletin* 32, no. 2, 1977 (Washington, D.C.: Population Reference Bureau). For mortality trends, see references at the beginning of the Contemporary Health Profiles section; and Jacob A. Brody, Dwight B. Brock, and T. Franklin Williams, "Trends in the Health of the Elderly Population," in *Annual Review of Public Health*, vol. 8, eds. L. Breslow, J. E. Fielding, and L. B. Lave (Palo Alto, CA: Annual Reviews, 1987), pp. 211–34; Monroe Lerner and Odin W. Anderson, *Health Progress in the United States* (Chicago: The University of Chicago Press, 1963).

1.75.[23] It is important to recognize that widening of the sex differential—that is, increasing the male excess—can come about by (a) mortality rates rising faster for males than for females, (b) rates falling faster for females than males, or (c) rising rates for males but falling ones for females. Thus, one must always turn back to mortality levels for each sex and note their trends in order to explain changes in the differential. Stated very generally, the principal reason for the widening gap in the twentieth century has been smaller mortality improvements overall and in most leading causes for men, than for women. This is (b) above. An additional factor in the decades before 1940, but not important since then, was the decline in reproduction-related mortality for women. This is also (b); being a sex-specific cause, it amounted to zero change for men but marked gain for women.[24] In short, for most of the century, women's advantage became larger and larger.

[23] For sex-mortality ratio, 1900: Metropolitan Life Insurance Co., *Statistical Bulletin*, 1980, 61 no. 2, 1985: *Monthly Vital Statistics Report*, *1987*, 36 no. 5, supplement (Hyattsville, MD: National Center for Health Statistics). For expectation of life, 1900 to 1985: Joseph F. Faber and Alice H. Wade, "Life Tables for the United States: 1900–2050," *Actuarial Study* no. 89. SSA publ. no. 11-11536 (Washington, D.C.: Office of the Actuary, Social Security Administration).

[24] Trends in the sex-mortality differential in the twentieth century are examined in Philip E. Enterline, "Causes of Death Responsible for Recent Increases in Sex Mortality Differentials in the United States," *Milbank Memorial Fund Quarterly* 39 (1961): 312–28; Ellen M. Gee and Jean E. Veevers, "Accelerating Sex Differentials in Mortality: An Analysis of Contributing Factors," *Social Biology* 30 (1983): 75–85; Allan Johnson, "Recent Trends in Sex Mortality Differentials in the United States," *Journal of Human Stress* 3 (1977): 22–32; S. L. N. Rao, "On Long-Term Mortality Trends in the United States, 1850–1968," *Demography* 10 (1973): 405–19; Robert R. Retherford, "Tobacco Smoking and the Sex Mortality Differential," *Demography* 9 (1972): 203–16; Retherford, *The Changing Sex Differential in Mortality* (Westport, CT: Greenwood Press, 1975); Verbrugge, "Recent Trends in Sex Mortality Differentials." Earlier studies on sex-mortality differentials that permit an historical perspective are in Antonio Ciocco, "Sex Differences in Morbidity and Mortality," *Quarterly Review of Biology* 15 (1940): 59–73, 192–210; L. I. Dublin, A. J. Lotka, and M. Spiegelman, *Length of Life* (New York: Ronald Press, 1949); Wilson T. Sowder, "Why is the Sex Difference in Mortality Increasing?," *Public Health Reports* 69 (1954): 860–64; Wilson T. Sowder and James O. Bond, "Problems Associated With the Increasing Ratio of Male Over Female Mortality," *Journal of the American Geriatrics Society* 4 (1956): 956–62; George J. Stolnitz, "A Century of International Mortality Trends: II," *Population Studies* 10 (1956): 17–42; Dorothy G. Wiehl, "Sex Differences in Mortality in the United States," *Milbank Memorial Fund Quarterly* 16 (1938): 145–55. Global (multi-national) analyses of patterns in sex-mortality differentials are in Alan D. Lopez, "The Sex Mortality Differential in Developed Countries," in *Sex Differentials in Mortality*, eds. Lopez and Ruzicka, pp. 53–120; Samuel H. Preston, "Older Male Mortality and Cigarette Smoking: A Demographic Analysis." *Population Monograph* no. 7 (Berkeley: Institute of International Studies, University of California, 1970); "An International Comparison of Excessive Adult Mortality," *Population Studies* 24 (1970): 5–20;

In the late 1970s, the situation began to change.[25] Although both sexes continue to experience mortality improvements, their gains are more comparable than before, and this acts to stabilize the sex differential. Quite certainly, a new era is before us in which the mortality gap will hold steady or even narrow. Some journalists have advanced a short-sighted explanation for this—that women are reaping pernicious consequences from stresses in multiple work and family roles due to their increased labor-force participation in recent years. But the truth is complex and longer-sighted, having more to do with (a) changes made by women decades ago such as increased smoking after World War II, or (b) their reaching limits of possible gain from medical and lifestyle improvements sooner than men.[26,27]

Morbidity and Disability Trends

From the late 1920's to the mid-1950's, a number of population-health surveys were sponsored by the United States government.[28] These

---

Mortality Patterns in National Populations (New York: Academic Press, 1976), chapter 6; Samuel H. Preston and James A. Weed, "Causes of Death Responsible for International and Intertemporal Variation in Sex Mortality Differentials," *World Health Statistics Report* 29 (1976): 144–214.

[25] First noted in Verbrugge, "Recent Trends in Sex Mortality Differentials." Since then, various issues of the *Statistical Bulletin* (Metropolitan Life Insurance Co.) have reported on the new situation.

[26] With regard to the second point: A disadvantaged group typically gains more in the presence of medical and social improvements. Their higher rates drop farther in absolute and often relative terms compared to the advantaged group (in this instance, women).

[27] For discussions of women's roles and health, see Debra Froberg, Dwenda Gjerdingen, and Marilyn Preston, "Multiple Roles and Women's Mental and Physical Health: What Have We Learned?," *Women and Health* 11 (1986): 79–96; Mary Ann Haw, "Women, Work, and Stress: A Review and Agenda for the Future," *Journal of Health and Social Behavior* 23 (1982): 132–44; Glorian Sorensen and Lois M. Verbrugge, "Women, Work, and Health," in *Annual Review of Public Health*, vol. 8, eds. L. Breslow, J. E. Fielding, and L. B. Lave (Palo Alto, CA: Annual Reviews, 1987), pp. 235–51; Lois M. Verbrugge and Jennifer H. Madans, "Social Roles and Health Trends of American Women," *Milbank Memorial Fund Quarterly/Health and Society* 63 (1985): 691–735. All three articles have extensive reference lists.

[28] For descriptions of these surveys, see Selwyn D. Collins, "Sickness Surveys," in *Administrative Medicine*, ed. H. Emerson (New York: Nelson, 1951), pp. 511–35; Commission on Chronic Illness, *Chronic Illness in a Large City: The Baltimore Study*, vol. 4 of *Chronic Illness in the United States* (Cambridge, MA: Harvard University Press, 1957), chapter 1; Mortimer Spiegelman, *Introduction to Demography* (Chicago, IL: The Society of Actuaries, 1955); Kenneth R. Wilcox, *Comparison of Three Methods for the Collection of Morbidity Data by Household Survey*, Ph.D. dissertation (Ann Arbor, MI: Department of Epidemiology, School of Public Health, 1963), Chapter 1. Besides such broad health surveys, well-known community-based studies for special topics are discussed in I. I. Kessler and M. L. Levin, eds., *The Community as an Epidemiologic*

yielded painstakingly-produced tables with rates of illness and restricted activity by age, sex, and condition. Pressure to have an ongoing survey covering the entire population mounted in the 1950's, and Congressional legislation in 1956 authorized it. The National Health Interview Survey (NHIS) was launched in July 1957 and has been collecting health data for the civilian noninstitutional population continuously since then.

The early surveys consistently show higher acute and chronic morbidity and higher disability days for females. The excess is smallest for children (sometimes it is a small male excess) and largest for reproductive ages. Males have higher accident/injury rates.[29] The NHIS has shown similar differentials since its inception, and it has provided clearer distinctions of the morbidity areas that disfavor women (acute conditions, chronic nonfatal ones) versus those which disfavor men (injuries at young adult ages, impairments, chronic fatal diseases). Notions of disability have expanded to include activities of daily living for older people, and these augment the evidence of excess female disability.

What has happened to population health over the century? And have sex differences changed so women report more, or fewer, problems relative to men than decades ago? The questions are impossible to answer easily for the whole century since the early surveys do not match

---

Laboratory (Baltimore: Johns Hopkins University Press, 1970). Other community-based studies have been started since then, especially under the aegis of the National Institute on Aging and the National Institute of Mental Health.

[29] Ciocco, "Sex Differences in Morbidity and Mortality"; Selwyn D. Collins, "Cases and Days of Illness Among Males and Females, with Special Reference to Confinement to Bed," Public Health Reports 55 (1940): 47–94; "A Review and Study of Illness and Medical Care." Public Health Monograph no. 48. PHS publ. no. 544. (Washington, D.C.: Public Health Service, 1957); Selwyn D. Collins, Katharine S. Trantham, and Josephine L. Lehmann, "Sickness Experience in Selected Areas of the United States." Public Health Monograph no. 25. (Washington, D.C.: Public Health Service, 1955); Commission on Chronic Illness, Chronic Illness in a Rural Area: The Hunterdon Study, vol. 3 of Chronic Illness in the United States (Cambridge, MA: Harvard University Press, 1959); Commission on Chronic Illness, Chronic Illness in a Large City (cited above); David E. Hailman, "The Prevalence of Disabling Illness Among Male and Female Workers and Housewives." Public Health Bulletin no. 260. (Washington, D.C.: Public Health Service, 1941); Lerner and Anderson, Health Progress in the United States, Chapter 10; Milbank Memorial Fund, Morbidity Survey in Baltimore, 1938–1943. (New York: Milbank Memorial Fund, 1957), see esp. chapters by Collins, Phillips, and Oliver; Downes; Downes and Keller; Jackson, "Morbidity Among Males, and Females'; Jackson, "Duration of Disabling Acute Illness"; Sally Preas and Ruth Phillips, "The Severity of Illness Among Males and Females," Millbank Memorial Fund Quarterly 20 (1942): 221–44; Edgar Sydenstricker, "The Illness Rate Among Males and Females," Public Health Reports 42, (1927): 1939–57; "Sex Differences in the Incidence of Certain Diseases at Different Ages," Public Health Reports 43 (1928): 1259–76.

up easily with NHIS. But NHIS itself has changed relatively little since 1957, so the period since then can be readily studied for trends.[30]

Since the late 1950's, age-specific prevalence rates have increased for most fatal diseases and also for some prominent nonfatal ones, especially arthritis and other musculoskeletal conditions. Short-term diability rates have increased for middle-aged and older people, largely since 1970. Long-term disability rates have increased sharply among middle-aged women and men, and less obviously for older people. These rises occur at all levels of disability, severe to mild. Overall, the bulk of empirical evidence points toward worsening health among U.S. adults.[31]

A number of reasons can account for this: (a) improved medical and lifestyle management of fatal chronic conditions, so ill people stay alive longer; (b) people's increased awareness of their chronic diseases due to improved diagnostic techniques, more frequent visits to physicians, and more frankness by physicians toward patients; (c) more willingness and ability to adopt the sick role for both short and long periods; and (d) improvements in survey techniques, so fuller reports of illness and disability are elicited.[32] Debate over the importance of these factors, and even

[30] Changes were made in 1967–68 and 1982. See National Center for Health Statistics, Health Interview Survey Procedure, 1957–1974. *Vital and Health Statistics*, series 1, no. 11. DHEW publ. no. (HRA) 75-1311. (Rockville, MD: 1975); The National Health Interview Survey Design, 1973–84, and Procedures, 1975–83. *Vital and Health Statistics*, series 1, no. 18. DHHS publ. no. (PHS) 85-1320. (Hyattsville, MD: 1985).

[31] Trends toward worsening health are also reported for children in Paul W. Newacheck, Peter P. Budetti, and Neal Halfon, "Trends in Activity-Limiting Chronic Conditions Among Children," *American Journal of Public Health* 76 (1986): 178–84; Paul W. Newacheck, Peter P. Budetti, and Peggy McManus, "Trends in Childhood Disability," *American Journal of Public Health* 74 (1984): 232–36.

[32] Comprehensive reviews of research on recent health trends are in Steven H. Chapman, Mitchell P. LaPlante, and Gail R. Wilensky, "Life Expectancy and Health Status of the Aged," *Social Security Bulletin* 49, no. 10 (1986): 24–48; Lois M. Verbrugge, "Recent, Present, and Future Health of American Adults," in *Annual Review of Public Health*, vol. 10, eds. L. Breslow, J. E. Fielding, and L. B. Lave (Palo Alto, CA: Annual Reviews, 1989), pp. 333–61. Reasons for worsening population health are discussed in Jacob A. Brody, "Prospects for an Ageing Population," *Nature* 315 (1985): 463–66; Chapman, LaPlante, and Wilensky, "Life Expectancy and Health Status"; Alain Colvez and Madeleine Blanchet, "Disability Trends in the United States Population 1966–76: Analysis of Reported Causes," *American Journal of Public Health* 71 (1981): 464–71; Jacob J. Feldman, "Work Ability of the Aged Under Conditions of Improving Mortality," *Milbank Memorial Fund Quarterly/Health and Society* 61 (1983): 430–44; Dorothy P. Rice and Mitchell P. LaPlante, "Chronic Illness, Disability, and Increasing Longevity," in *Ethics and Economics of Long-Term Care*, eds. S. Sullivan and M. Ein Lewin (Washington, D.C.: American Enterprise Institute, 1988); Edward L. Schneider and Jacob A. Brody, "Aging, Natural Death, and the Compression of Morbidity: Another View," *New England Journal of Medicine* 309 (1983): 854–56; Lois M. Verbrugge, "Longer Life

the direction of the health trends, is very active. My own judgment, shared by most other observers of the data, is that the rising morbidity and disability rates are intimately tied to falling mortality rates, which began a sharp downward turn in 1968. This is (a) above. Deaths have been delayed by secondary prevention; namely, control of fatal diseases so they advance less rapidly. This leads to lower case-fatality rates. The marginal survivors gain some years of life but are already ill and very vulnerable to acquiring new diseases. The subpopulation of marginal survivors is numerous because the mortality gains have been striking, especially for cardiovascular diseases. Simultaneously, people with less advanced disease have made gains too, and their symptoms and limitations are milder than otherwise (i.e., if the secondary prevention successes had not occurred). This subpopulation is very large, far greater than the number of marginal survivors. In short, prevalence rates have risen but the average severity of conditions has probably become milder.

I also believe that better and earlier diagnosis has increased awareness of existing disease, and that positive incentives for disability have increased. These are genuinely social reasons that also boost illness and disability rates. I do not think that survey techniques are an important factor behind the trends. Methodology changes influence data discontinuously, in the same year as the changes. Yet the observed trends are essentially continuous over time.[33]

The trends noted have occurred for both women and men. Have sex differences changed? Since it is hard enough to ascertain the trends in rates with certainty, review of the data for trends in sex differentials is a delicate endeavor. One study, for the 1957 to 1972 period, shows larger increases in chronic morbidity and severe disability for men than women.[34] As the data series lengthens, it will be able to sustain close scrutiny for changes in sex differentials, and discussion of their compatibility with changes in sex-mortality differentials.

But Worsening Health? Trends in Health and Mortality of Middle-Aged and Older Adults," *Milbank Memorial Fund Quarterly/Health and Society* 62 (1984): 475–519; Verbrugge, "Recent, Present, and Future Health"; Martynas A. Ycas, "Recent Trends in Health Near the Age of Retirement: New Findings from the Health Interview Survey," *Social Security Bulletin* 50, no. 2 (1987): 5–30.

[33] For a contrasting view, see Ronald W. Wilson and Thomas F. Drury, "Interpreting Trends in Illness and Disability: Health Statistics and Health Status," in *Annual Review of Public Health*, vol. 5, eds. L. Breslow, J. E. Fielding, and L. B. Lave (Palo Alto, CA: Annual Reviews, 1984), pp. 83–106.

[34] Verbrugge, "Females and Illness: Recent Trends."

In sum, we cannot trace the course of women's and men's health over the century easily. We must rely on occasional surveys until the mid-1950's and the good stream of NHIS data since then. The surveys to mid-century need more attention from demographically-inclined historians, and the NHIS from 1957 on needs more quantitative analysis to locate trends with certainty.

HEALTH AND MORTALITY FUTURES IN THE TWENTY-FIRST CENTURY

The unprecedented and unanticipated mortality declines since the late 1960's have urged more thinking about potentials of population health and longevity.[35] What is our direction for the next fifty to one hundred years? Will recent mortality improvements be sustained? Will the social burden of illness revealed in health surveys continue to rise? How fast will changes occur? Is it feasible to attain a life expectancy at birth of 100 by 2040, or 2090?

Future scenarios of health and mortality hinge on assumptions about three forms of prevention: (a) tertiary; this is saving people at the brink of death by costly medical measures, (b) secondary; this is controlling fatal diseases by medical and lifestyle interventions so they advance less rapidly, and (c) primary; this is reducing the incidence (clinical onset) of diseases. Strides in tertiary prevention happened in mid-century, and there is increasing public and even clinician resistance to furthering this kind of prevention. Contemporary medicine is distinctive for its emphasis on secondary prevention. Little is known about primary prevention, how to prevent chronic diseases from occurring at all to individuals.

Forecasts now being made are based largely on careful thinking and guesses about the three types of prevention, rather than formal quantitative models about presence of risk factors in the population, morbidity incidence and prevalence, and their implications for mortality. Lacking the foundation of such models, I shall state in narrative fashion a plausible course for coming decades, in my judgment.

The twenty-first century holds not just one health future but several sequenced in time. The near future will continue recent trends in health

---

[35] Kenneth G. Manton, "Changing Concepts of Morbidity and Mortality in the Elderly Population," *Milbank Memorial Fund Quarterly/Health and Society* 60 (1982): 183–244; "Past and Future Life Expectancy Increases at Later Ages: Their Implications for the Linkage of Chronic Morbidity, Disability, and Mortality," *Journal of Gerontology* 41 (1986): 672–81; Verbrugge, "Recent, Present, and Future Health."

and mortality, with secondary prevention the lead actor. Despite rising prevalence rates of chronic disease and disability, measures of severity will show a "shift toward mildness." Diseases, though present, will have less impact on people's lives. Five or six decades ahead, there will be an intermediate period with powerful pushes from both secondary and primary prevention. We may then see a larger percent of older people in vigorous health, as well as a larger percent in very poor health. A century hence, disease onsets may be delayed until near life's end for many people. But complete prevention, meaning that people avoid disease in their lifetimes and ultimately die from "natural aging" processes, is not likely to be common.[36]

Thus, we can anticipate continuing advances in disease control and gradually increasing ones in primary prevention. Population-health statistics, focused on prevalence rates, will "worsen" for the next several decades but then slowly turn around to show improving health. (The shift toward mildness that is occurring now and that will continue may be missed by statistics, since severity is seldom ascertained.) Accompanying these health trends, mortality rates will continue to fall. Some scientists think the advances will be swift and widespread, and that life expectancy at birth in 2040 will far surpass the Social Security Administration projection of 83.4 for females and 75.7 for males.[37] Others think that continuing degradation of outdoor and indoor environments, impact of AIDS, and violent deaths will offset medical/lifestyle gains, and those projections are too optimistic.

Sex differentials in mortality and health are likely to narrow over the next century, exchanging their twentieth-century course for a very different one. The narrowing will come about by greater similarity between men and women in risk factors and psychosocial ones pertinent to health. Is it too much to anticipate that men will adopt more caretaking attitudes toward self and others, and more enthusiasm about regular medical contacts and preventive health behaviors? And that women will become increasingly engaged in remunerative and satisfying jobs, feel

---

[36] This notion is called the "compression of morbidity"; it assumes both complete disease prevention and a fixed upper limit to average life expectation for humans. See James F. Fries, "Aging, Natural Death, and the Compression of Morbidity," *New England Journal of Medicine* 303 (1980): 130–35; "The Compression of Morbidity," *Milbank Memorial Fund Quarterly/Health and Society* 61 (1983): 397–419.

[37] Joseph F. Faber and Alice H. Wade, Life Tables for the United States: 1900–2050. *Actuarial Study*, no. 89. SSA publ. no. 11-11536. (Washington, D.C.: Office of the Actuary, Social Security Administration: 1983).

happier and less stressed, and pursue more strenuous leisure activities?[38] If these occur, the results will be improved physical wellbeing, less disability, lower mortality—and smaller sex differences.

Some popular hypotheses must be felled: It is often claimed that women's mortality rates will *rise* to meet men's as they "behave more like men." This is unreasonable. More plausibly, one might assert that both sexes will continue to experience mortality declines, but women's may be slower than men's in coming decades. Even this is overly simplistic and ignores the extensive benefits women stand to accrue from fuller participation in productive and political roles. There is a general lesson here: Any forecast about future sex differentials must make some explicit assumptions about (a) how women and men change in personal behaviors and exposures, receipt of medical and rehabilitation advances, social attitudes about sickness and disability or even biological stamina; and (b) what the ensuing effects are on rates and the sex difference. Forecasts without assumptions should inspire doubt and be viewed as prophecy rather than science.

AN AGING SOCIETY

At any time, the aggregate burden of illness and disability in a population depends on age-specific rates for each sex and the population distribution by age-sex. Simply put, it is a function of "rates times weights." So far in this article, we have discussed rates in the past, present, and future. Now we consider population dynamics; that is, the weights.

The U.S. population has aged considerably in the twentieth century. In 1900, 4.0% of the total population were ages 65+, and just 0.2% were ages 85+. In 1985, the figures were 12.0 and 1.1, respectively. This general aging is accompanied by two important features, called "aging-within-aging" and "feminization of the elderly." The 65+ group is itself aging, with increasing percents among them being very old (85+). And

---

[38] For viewpoints about forthcoming changes in sex differentials, see Michel A. Ibrahim, "The Changing Health State of Women," *American Journal of Public Health* 70 (1980): 120–21; Charles E. Lewis and Mary Ann Lewis, "The Potential Impact of Sexual Equality on Health," *New England Journal of Medicine* 297 (1977): 863–69; Constance A. Nathanson and Alan D. Lopez, "The Future of Sex Mortality Differentials in Industrialized Countries: A Structural Hypothesis," *Population Research and Policy Review* 6 (1987): 123–36; Lois M. Verbrugge, "Unveiling Higher Morbidity for Men: The Story," in *Social Structures and Human Lives*, vol. 1 of *Social Change and the Life Course*, ed. M. W. Riley (Newbury Park, CA: Sage Pub., 1988), pp. 138–60.

the percent female is increasing in the 65+ group. TABLE 7 shows both of these features, comparing 1900 with 1980.

Aging has been a persistent feature of U.S. population dynamics throughout the century, fueled initially by secular declines in fertility rates and in recent decades by large mortality declines concentrated at older ages.[39] Aging-within-aging has been especially rapid in this recent period of mortality decline. Feminization of the elderly has been ongoing since the 1930's.

The twentieth century will stand out as the era in which the U.S. population aged. All of the above dynamics will continue into the twenty-first century but at a slower pace than before.[40] TABLE 7 shows current projections for 2040 and 2080, adjacent to figures for the twentieth century.

Increasing percents of old people, especially very old ones and women, will change both the volume and composition of population health over the long run. The shifting age distribution alone will push upward rates of illness, disability, and mortality for the whole population. (This is because weights will increase at the ages with highest rates.) Feminizing will augment the importance of chronic conditions that are symptomatic and disabling, but not themselves life-threatening, such as arthritis, osteoporosis, incontinence, varicose veins, and digestive disorders. Social and economic problems—loneliness, poverty, and feelings of helplessness and insecurity—will also ascend, often reflecting blunted opportunities and socialization for women in their earlier years. But if women use their "power of numbers," the views and attitudes expressed by very elderly people will be largely women's, and this can open

---

[39] Eileen M. Crimmins, "The Changing Pattern of American Mortality Decline"; Ira Rosenwaike, "A Demographic Portrait of the Oldest Old," *Milbank Memorial Fund Quarterly* 63 (1985): 187–205; Rosenwaike, *The Extreme Aged in America* (Westport, CT: Greenwood Press, 1985); Jacob S. Siegel and Maria Davidson, "Demographic and Socioeconomic Aspects of Aging in the United States," *Current Population Reports*, series P-23, no. 138. (Washington, D.C.: Bureau of the Census, 1984); Beth J. Soldo, "America's Elderly in the 1980s," *Population Bulletin*, vol. 35, no. 4. (Washington, D.C.: Population Reference Bureau, 1980); Cynthia M. Taeuber, "America in Transition: An Aging Society." *Current Population Reports*, series P-23, no. 138. (Washington, D.C.: Bureau of the Census, 1983); Barbara Boyle Torrey, Kevin Kinsella, and Cynthia M. Taeuber, "An Aging World," *International Population Reports*, series P-95, no. 78. (Washington, D.C.: Bureau of the Census, 1987); Paul E. Zopf, Jr., *America's Older Population* (Houston, TX: Cap and Gown Press, 1986).

[40] When the Baby Boom cohort born between 1946 and 1959 reaches older ages, there will be some added propulsion to aging. But this will occur in a general context of slowed aging.

TABLE 7. AGING OF THE UNITED STATES POPULATION, 1900–2080.[a]

	1900	1980	2040	2080
Aging				
Percent of population ages 65+	4.0	11.3	21.1	22.1
Percent of population ages 85+	0.2	1.0	4.1	5.3
Aging Within Aging				
Among persons 65+, percent ages 85+	4.0	8.8	19.3	23.9
Feminization of the Elderly				
Among persons 65+, percent female	49.5	59.7	58.8	58.4
Among persons 85+, percent female	55.6	69.6	69.7	68.6

SOURCE: For 1900: Cynthia M. Taeuber. America in Transition: An Aging Society. *Current Population Reports*, Series P-23, No. 128. Bureau of the Census, U.S. Department of Commerce. Washington, D.C. 1983; and Forrest E. Linder and Robert D. Grove. *Vital Statistics Rates in the United States, 1900–1940*. Bureau of the Census, U.S. Department of Commerce. Washington, D.C.: Government Printing Office. 1943. For 1980: Taeuber, America in Transition; and Jacob S. Siegel and Maria Davidson. "Demographic and Socioeconomic Aspects of Aging in the United States," *Current Population Reports*, Series P-23, No. 138. Bureau of the Census, U.S. Department of Commerce. Washington, D.C. 1984. For 2040 and 2080: John C. Wilkin. Social Security Area Population Projections, 1983. *Actuarial Study*, No. 88. SSA Publ. No. 11-11535. Office of the Actuary, Social Security Administration, Department of Health and Human Services. 1983.

[a] Projected figures for 2040 and 2080, using Alternative II.

political and social opportunities for those who were very dependent before. All of the changes just stated ensue directly from changes in age-sex composition of the population.

If age-specific rates change as well, as proposed in the prior section, then the needs for symptom relief, special aids, medical and rehabilitation services, home assistance, congregate housing, and nursing beds will rise dramatically for a number of decades, before the power of primary prevention acts to lower those rates.

Thus, the pronounced declines in mortality of the twentieth century, with their special relationship to secondary prevention and older ages, have both welcome and unwelcome consequences. They provide more years of life to individuals on average, but also increase the percent of ill older people. This pattern of events is not unique to the United

States; it is a typical phase that developed societies will pass through at some point.

INDIVIDUAL AND SOCIETAL TRAJECTORIES

Health and mortality statistics tell us a population's state of health at a calendar time. They say little about the dynamics of health actually experienced by individuals over their lives.

For individuals, health has many important dimensions besides simple presence or absence of a problem. First, there are movements "to and fro"—acute condition onsets and recoveries spread throughout a year, flares and remissions of chronic conditions, insidious development of dysfunction and welcome returns of function. Second, there is multiplicity to health problems. Chronic ailments tend to accrete over life, and dysfunctions also show a net increase, even though specific ones may vary from year to year. Lastly, there is synergism. Multiple conditions interact to hasten disability, and multiple disabilities interact to sap stamina and spirit. Health statistics have little to say about these three aspects of individual health. Yet they are perceived clearly by people and are fundamental components of physical wellbeing and life quality.

To visualize the great difference between individual and societal trajectories, consider FIGURE 1. The survival curves shown state proportions of the population who are *not* in each state at a given age; i.e., they have survived the event so far. The curves are based on age-sex specific statistics for a given year. Changes in the shapes and position of these curves occur over time, and watching them tells us about societal trajectories, either empirically witnessed or forecast ahead. For example, in the next several decades, continuing emphasis on secondary prevention will make the morbidity and disability curves move inward (worsening health) and the mortality curve outward (improving mortality).

Where are individuals? The curves are commonly offered as typical trajectories for individuals, showing probabilities of being in given states at each age and asserting a standard sequence of events over life.[41] But an individual's actual course looks quite different. She or he crosses lines of

---

[41] Two central assumptions are made: that each state is absorbing (once entered, never left) and that the states are hierarchical (people in a given state have all the "lesser" ones as well). These assumptions will be relaxed in future research as data and methods on transition rates between states advance.

FIGURE 1. SURVIVAL CURVES
OF MORBIDITY, DISABILITY
AND MORTALITY.

(Percent surviving to given age without the event)

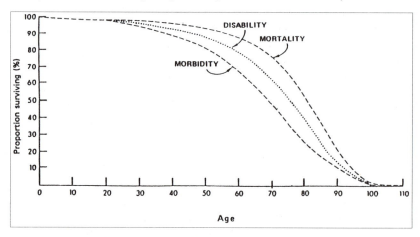

SOURCE: Kenneth G. Manton and Beth J. Soldo, "Dynamics of Health Changes in the
Oldest Old: New Perspectives and Evidence," *Milbank Memorial Fund Quarterly/Health
and Society*, 63(1985):206–85.

morbidities at different ages and moves back and forth across lines of
disabilities. Death is crossed just once.

Even if we have the data to see societal and individual trajectories,
the genuine task of science is to explain them. Here a sense of personal
histories becomes essential. For most people, chronic illnesses and death
come in middle or older ages. Their timing and type are explained by
risks extending over the individual's whole life, not just contemporary
risks. People now 90 were born in the nineteenth century. People who
will be 90 in 2040 are Baby Boomers, and everyone who will be 65+ in
that year is already alive. Health attitudes, lifestyle behaviors, and stress
responses are enduring features for individuals, and they are largely set
in place in the first twenty to twenty-five years of one's life. Thus, states
of health for individuals and society at any time bear immense, quiet
imprints of personal and social history. The lags between risk factors and

their health/mortality outcomes, and the accretion of risks over a lifetime into those outcomes, must always be recognized.

The pathways that women and men take differ somewhat: Women's lives are more filled with sickness and disability, due to greater tendencies to acquire nonfatal chronic problems plus lesser ones to acquire fatal problems. The longer average lifetimes earned by the second feature can be undone by the first. Men die sooner, having suffered fewer years of trouble while alive.

There is no "contradiction" whatsoever in females' higher morbidity rates and males' higher mortality rates, and the label should be abandoned. Those empirical facts emerge from differences in health pathways traced by the sexes; women tend to tarry, while men exit with undue swiftness. Exposures during life are the main reason for this, though biology also plays some part. Finding the causes of fatal diseases and ways to alleviate their progression will keep men with us longer. But it is just as important to find causes and controls for nonfatal diseases, so that women and men can in comfort and vigor tarry together.

3

SEXUALITY AND WOMAN'S SEXUAL NATURE

Nancy Sahli

What is the most appropriate definition of women's sexuality and how should it be interpreted historically? Contemporary historians and researchers on sexual attitudes and behavior have attempted to answer these questions, particularly in the context of broader issues relating to women's gender role, identity, and overall position in society. Noted sex-researcher and educator Mary Steichen Calderone defines sexuality as "the whole person, including his or her thoughts, experiences, learnings, ideas, values, and imaginings, as these have to do with his being male or her being female," thereby making sexuality almost synonymous with all of human life.[1]

Others have attached narrower meanings to the term, focusing on specific sexual ideas, attitudes, and behaviors, such as those related to sexual preference and identity, but excluding such areas as gender role, pregnancy and childbirth, contraception, and sex discrimination. Even these narrower definitions fail to answer the question, "What is sexual behavior?" Is it only that behavior which can lead ultimately to orgasm? Or, as many feminist scholars and theorists would agree, does this definition impose a male-oriented model on women, whose sexual feelings and erotic responses are much more diffuse and less focused on the performance of a particular sequence of actions leading to a specific action or goal?

---

[1] Mary Steichen Calderone and Eric W. Johnson, *The Family Book about Sexuality* (New York: Harper & Row, 1981).

Obviously, there are no easy answers to these questions, and if the definitions of women's sexuality are diverse, so is the literature which relates to it. Beginning in the early nineteenth century, however, when much of the work in this field began to appear, certain trends are clearly visible. An understanding of these trends is essential before the historiography of women's sexuality can be summarized and evaluated.

First, at that time, the dividing line between professional and popular literature was very thin. Little was known about human reproductive and sexual physiology, and would-be scientific writers aiming at an audience of physicians often showed little difference in either their ideas or manner of presentation from authors writing for popular audiences. Hearsay was accepted as fact, and empirical evidence was absent more often than not. Not until well into the twentieth century did organized scientific research into human sexual behavior develop. Masters and Johnson's groundbreaking study of the physiology of human sexual response was published in 1966.[2] It is important to remember, however, that empirical and statistical research can be, and often is, influenced by economic, political, and social factors. Moreover, funding and institutional support for some types of research are available only in certain economic and political climates.

Clitoridectomy, venereal disease, hysteria, and coital frequency were but a few of the topics relating to women's sexuality covered by physicians and other scientific professionals writing in the nineteenth century. These writers set forth a wide range of theories, in some cases based on actual observation, but in others derived from folklore or traditional concepts of "truth." The nineteenth century was a time of great advances in gynecological surgery and the treatment of other disorders of the sexual organs of women. Yet, as G. J. Barker-Benfield has observed, such innovations in treatment were not always motivated by the highest ideals.[3] Isaac Baker Brown, who espoused clitoridectomy as a cure for insanity and other conditions affecting women, had his opponents, but he also had followers in both his native Britain and in the United States.[4]

---

[2] William H. Masters and Virginia E. Johnson, *Human Sexual Response* (Boston: Little, Brown, 1966). This study, which was the culmination of twelve years of research work, was followed by the same authors' *Human Sexual Inadequacy* (Boston: Little, Brown, 1970) and the less successful *Homosexuality in Perspective* (Boston: Little, Brown, 1979).

[3] G. J. Barker-Benfield, *The Horrors of the Half-known Life: Male Attitudes toward Women and Sexuality in Nineteenth-century America* (New York: Harper & Row, 1976).

[4] Isaac Baker Brown's views are articulated in his *On the Curability of Certain Forms of Insanity, Epilepsy, Catalepsy, and Hysteria in Females* (London: Robert Hardwicke, 1866), a work not unfamiliar to American medical practitioners. See also his article "Clitoridectomy," *British Medical Journal* 1 (January 5, 1867): 18.

Physicians commonly took moral stands on issues such as birth control and abortion, and masturbation was seen not only as a disease but as the cause of a wide range of problems ranging from nymphomania to tuberculosis.[5]

Obviously, too, much of the material about women was written by men, whose ideas were in turn tempered by their own subjective, culturally bound preconceptions of what women's normal sexuality ought to be. There was, however, some difference of opinion. A common viewpoint, held by William Acton and others, argued that women were asexual and lacked an active sexuality. Some writers advanced the contrasting argument that women were such intensely sexual creatures that their sexuality could lead them into such dangers as masturbation and nymphomania.[6] Women writers, though in a distinct minority, were not completely free from these dominant strains of thought. Yet, while Elizabeth Blackwell joined with her male colleagues in condemning masturbation, in *The Human Element in Sex* she also called for a recognition of women's sexual nature, and of possible differences between the sexuality of women and men.[7] Despite these general characteristics, the range of medical and scientific opinion on women's sexuality by the late nineteenth and early twentieth centuries was far more diverse than some historians would have us believe. In 1904, for example, C. W. Malchow, a Minneapolis physician, called for a recognition of the periodicity of women's sexual desire and the existence of three erogenous zones: the clitoris, vagina, and breasts—ideas that would be substantiated by laboratory research only much later in the century.[8]

---

[5] See, for example, H. Tristam Engelhardt, Jr., "The Disease of Masturbation: Values and the Concept of Disease," *Bulletin of the History of Medicine* 48, no. 2 (Summer 1974): 234–48; reprinted in *Sickness and Health in America: Readings in the History of Medicine and Public Health*, ed. Judith W. Leavitt and Ronald L. Numbers (Madison: University of Wisconsin Press, 1978), pp. 15–23.

[6] William Acton, *The Functions and Disorders of the Reproductive Organs in Youth, in Adult Age, and in Advanced Life. Considered in their Physiological, Social, and Psychological Relations* (London: John Churchill, 1857).

[7] Elizabeth Blackwell, *The Human Element in Sex: A Medical Enquiry into the Relation of Sexual Physiology to Christian Morality* (London: J. & A. Churchill, 1884). *The Human Element in Sex* emphasizes the importance of chastity as a means of sexual and social self-control.

[8] C. W. Malchow, *The Sexual Life: A Scientific Treatise Designed for Advanced Students and the Professions, Embracing the Natural Sexual Impulse, Normal Sexual Habits and Propagation, Together with Sexual Physiology and Hygiene* (Minneapolis: Burton, 1904). An extremely popular work, *The Sexual Life* ran to at least twenty-seven printings and was still being issued as late as 1931.

Medical and scientific writing is not the only variety of literature on sexuality. Another type, generally called "prescriptive" literature, is written for popular audiences, and is frequently characterized by a variety of viewpoints, as well as lack of attention to scientifically developed evidence. This can be seen in works ranging in chronology from "Aristotle's" *Masterpiece* (1813) to William Josephus Robinson's *Woman: Her Sex and Love Life* (1917).[9] George W. Savory, for example, recommended "the sexual gymnastics of the Egyptian dancing girls" as a means to health, while Alice Stockham advocated reading works by Browning and Emerson prior to coitus.[10] Plagiarism, especially in the nineteenth century, was not uncommon, and some authors, clearly motivated by commercial gain, issued the same work at different times under different titles. Authors or firms they controlled often published their own works, selling them mail-order and using them to advertise products and services ranging from sexual counseling to patent medicine and, of course, other advice books.

Especially in the nineteenth century, prescriptive literature was intended to serve broader purposes of social reform. Some writers, such as Henry C. Wright, called for women's control of sexual relations; others, such as the Fowler brothers, connected sexual behavior to broader philosophical questions, such as the "science" of phrenology.[11] John Humphrey Noyes claimed that male continence not only heightened women's sexual pleasure, but led its practitioners along the road to spiritual perfection.[12] Although throughout the nineteenth century women began in increasing numbers to prescribe for their own sex, most of the literature directed toward women continued to be written by men,

---

[9] The *Masterpiece* was one of several sections in Aristotle [pseud.], *The Works of Aristotle, the Famous Philosopher* (New England [sic]: Printed for the Proprietor, 1813); William Josephus Robinson, *Woman: Her Sex and Love Life* (New York: Critic and Guide, 1917). The *Masterpiece* was perhaps the most widely read popular medical book in America prior to the mid-nineteenth century. Robinson's book also enjoyed a wide readership and was frequently reprinted.

[10] George Washington Savory, *Marriage: Its Science and Ethics* (Chicago: Stockham Publishing Co., 1900); Alice B. Stockham, *Karezza: Ethics of Marriage*, new rev. ed. (Chicago: Stockham Publishing Co., 1903).

[11] Henry C. Wright, *Marriage and Parentage; Or, the Reproductive Element in Man, as a Means to His Elevation and Happiness* (Boston: Bela Marsh, 1955); Lorenzo Niles Fowler, *The Principles of Phrenology and Physiology Applied to Man's Social Relations* (New York: L. N. & O. S. Fowler, 1842); Orson S. Fowler, *Amativeness: Embracing the Evils and Remedies of Excessive and Perverted Sexuality, Including Warning and Advice to the Married and Single*, new rev. ed. (New York: Fowler & Wells, 1889).

[12] John Humphrey Noyes, *Male Continence* (Oneida, NY: Oneida Community, 1872).

often reflecting their own goals of domination and control of women's sexual expression.

By the end of the nineteenth century, several new developments were taking place, which were reflected in medical/scientific as well as prescriptive literature. The free-love movement questioned the rationale for confining sexual relations to conventional marriage, while the social-purity movement sought to impose a uniform chastity on men and women alike. Prostitution came under continual and steady fire, particularly because of its role in fostering the spread of venereal diseases. Sexual variations, or "perversions" (as they were then known), were being widely discussed for the first time by European and American sexologists. Richard von Krafft-Ebing and Havelock Ellis, for example, defined as pathological the ways in which women love other women.[13] Prior to that time, despite occasional reference to Sappho and her followers, writers such as William Rounseville Alger had stressed the spiritual qualities of women's friendships.[14] The new definitions, often based on male models of homosexual behavior, created a stereotyped image of lesbians as man-hating, masculine misfits, outcasts of society whose sexual preference rendered them sick, if not actually dangerous. As Lillian Faderman, Carroll Smith-Rosenberg, and others have demonstrated, close friendships between women were redefined as examples of lesbian sexuality, images that persisted into the post-World War II era.[15]

Also beginning in the late nineteenth century, with the work of such pioneers as Robert Latou Dickinson and Clelia Duel Mosher, researchers started to collect aggregate data documenting women's sexual

---

[13] Richard von Krafft-Ebing, *Psychopathia Sexualis*, trans. Harry E. Wedeck (New York: G. P. Putnam's Sons, 1965); Havelock Ellis, "Sexual Inversion," *Studies in the Psychology of Sex*, vol. 2, pt. 2. (New York: Random House, 1936). Krafft-Ebing's classic taxonomy of sexual variations was originally published in 1886 and served as the source of data for such subsequent theorists as Sigmund Freud. Ellis's study, which first appeared in a German-language translation published in Leipzig in 1896, was the first volume to appear of what would become the *Studies in the Psychology of Sex*.

[14] William Rounseville Alger, *The Friendships of Women* (Boston: Roberts Brothers, 1868).

[15] Lillian Faderman, *Surpassing the Love of Men: Romantic Friendship and Love between Women from the Renaissance to the Present* (New York: William Morrow, 1981); Carroll Smith-Rosenberg, "The Female World of Love and Ritual: Relations between Women in Nineteenth-century America," *Signs* 1, no. 1 (Autumn 1975): 1–29; Carroll Smith-Rosenberg, "The New Woman as Androgyne: Social Disorder and Gender Crisis, 1870–1936," in her *Disorderly Conduct: Visions of Gender in Victorian America* (New York: Alfred A. Knopf, 1985), pp. 245–96. "The Female World" is also reprinted in *Disorderly Conduct*.

attitudes and behavior in the United States.[16] Working as individuals, often with no firm methodology or consistent strategy for data collection, these individuals nevertheless recognized the need for empirical evidence at a time when subjective opinions too often passed for scientific proof. By the 1920s, advances in social-science methodology and the provision of institutional bases for support of survey operations gave a new dimension to sex research. Katharine Bement Davis's *Factors in the Sex Life of Twenty-Two Hundred Women*, although not without its flaws, set new standards for this kind of work and clearly demonstrated the feasibility of gathering information on sexual behavior from the general population.[17]

Concurrent with this rise in scientific attention was a change in the focus of prescriptive literature. An emphasis on sexual technique and women's sexual satisfaction characterized much of the advice literature appearing after World War I, a development made possible to no small degree by increasing liberalization of legal attitudes and restrictions regarding obscenity. Not only had the federal law forbidden the importation of certain types of "sexual" literature (Marie Stopes's *Married Love* was judged to be not obscene only in 1931), but individual states restricted the dissemination both of explicit sex information and of other materials relating to birth control as well.[18] From the 1930s on, popular marriage manuals such as the Dutch import *Ideal Marriage*, by T. H. Van de Velde, which included a detailed discussion of sexual technique, enjoyed a wide readership.[19] It was not until the 1960s, however, that works began to appear—*The Sensuous Woman, The Joy*

---

[16] Robert Latou Dickinson and Lura Beam, *The Single Woman: A Medical Study in Sex Education* (Baltimore: Williams & Wilkins, 1934); Robert Latou Dickinson and Lura Beam, *A Thousand Marriages: A Medical Study of Sex Adjustment* (Baltimore: Williams & Wilkins, 1931); Clelia Duel Mosher, *The Mosher Survey: Sexual Attitudes of 45 Victorian Women*, ed. James MaHood and Kristine Wenburg (New York: Arno Press, 1980). Citations to other surveys may be found in the chapter "Behavior and Attitudes: Surveys and Other Studies," in Nancy Sahli, *Women and Sexuality in America: A Bibliography* (Boston: G. K. Hall, 1984).

[17] Katharine Bement Davis, *Factors in the Sex Life of Twenty-Two Hundred Women* (New York: Harper, 1929).

[18] Marie Charlotte Carmichael Stopes, *Married Love: A New Contribution to the Solution of Sex Difficulties* (New York: Eugenics Publishing Co., 1931). Marie Stopes was one of the early twentieth century's best-known birth-control advocates. *Married Love* attempted to diagnose the causes of unhappy marriages and offered advice on improving the sexual aspects of marriage. It was the subject of an obscenity trial in 1931 (*United States* v. *One Obscene Book Entitled Married Love*, 48 F. 2nd 821 [1931]).

[19] Theodoor Hendrik Van de Velde, *Ideal Marriage, Its Physiology and Technique*, trans. [Frances Worsley] Stella Browne (New York: Random House, 1930).

of Sex, and others—that challenged the premise that marriage was the only suitable basis for sexual relations. Reflecting the similar trend in medical and scientific research of separating reproductive and sexual functions in women, these new manuals achieved an over-the-counter frankness hitherto unknown in literature intended for general audiences.[20]

Other consistent patterns characterized prescriptive literature beginning in the early twentieth century. Women's sexuality was seen typically as being qualitatively different from that of men, but was nevertheless regarded as an active force. Decisions regarding the appropriateness and frequency of sexual relations were, for the most part, deemed to be the responsibility of the individuals involved, although variations on conventional heterosexual behavior elicited varied opinions. Calls for sexual freedom do not, however, equate with a rise in feminist consciousness on the part of the authors, many of whom continued to reflect male-centered attitudes toward women.

In addition to these trends, other patterns in the literature on women's sexuality have evolved during the twentieth century. The feminist movement of the late nineteenth and early twentieth centuries brought in its wake a rash of studies examining questions relating to woman's nature and role. How does woman's nature as a sexual being influence her position in society? How, in turn, has a traditionally male-dominated power structure determined woman's role? How do women perceive their own sexuality, and to what extent do they agree or disagree with an ideology that would define their economic, social, and political roles in terms of their sexuality and destiny as wives and mothers?

In attempting to relate questions of woman's sexuality to broader problems of society and politics, authors have frequently chosen to focus on specific institutions that bridge the gap. Marriage was perhaps the most susceptible of these in the late nineteenth and early twentieth centuries. Free-love advocates such as Victoria Woodhull argued for an end to what they called sexual slavery, while Judge Ben Lindsey and his fellow supporters of companionate marriage sought radical reform of the traditional marriage relationship.[21] More contemporary quasi-political

---

[20] Joan Terry Garrity [J., pseud.], *The Sensuous Woman: The First How-to Book for the Female Who Yearns to Be All Woman* (New York: Lyle Stuart, 1969); Alexander Comfort, ed., *The Joy of Sex: A Cordon Bleu Guide to Lovemaking* (New York: Crown, 1972).

[21] Madeleine Stern, ed., *The Victoria Woodhull Reader* (Weston, MA: M & S Press, 1974) includes the essential writings. For a useful summary of the ideas of companionate marriage see Christina Simmons, "Companionate Marriage and the Lesbian Threat," *Frontiers* 4, no. 3 (Fall 1979): 54–59.

studies appearing in the wake of the resurgence of the women's movement in the 1960s, such as Susan Brownmiller's *Against Our Will: Men, Women and Rape* and Phyllis Chesler's *Women and Madness*, although not without their flaws, examined areas in which ideas about women's sexuality have been used by men and male-dominated institutions as the means for denying women the integrity of their minds and bodies and did much to raise women's consciousness regarding these issues.[22]

The development of psychoanalytic technique in the tradition of Sigmund Freud has been another factor influencing attitudes toward women's sexuality in this century. Although this is by no means the only school of psychological theory to have gained acceptance and influence in the twentieth century, its emphasis on the sexual origins of neuroses, as well as the pervading influence of psychosexual development on psychological functioning, has led it to play a major role in defining how women have been seen as sexual beings in twentieth-century American society.[23] As Juliet Mitchell emphasized in *Psychoanalysis and Feminism*, Freud's followers ond popularizers sometimes distorted his original theories. Yet this observation fails to confront other key problems in the psychoanalytic approach, such as its reliance on specific, often atypical, case analyses as the proof for much more widely reaching theories. There has also been a tendency to regard orthodox Freudian theory as irrefutable, leading to the ostracism of revisionists such as Karen Horney by their more conservative colleagues.[24] The laboratory research of Masters and Johnson played a critical role in initiating the questioning of some classical psychoanalytic tenets, such as the transfer of sexual sensitivity from the clitoris to the vagina. This new scientific data, coupled with an awareness of the role that Freud's own cultural milieu and traditions played in determining his thinking, led to a reevaluation in the 1970s and 1980s of much psychoanalytic and psychiatric theory and writing. Mary Jane Sherfey's *The Nature and Evolution of Female Sexuality*, Jean Strouse's *Women and Analysis*, and Ethel Spector Person's *Signs* article,

---

[22] Susan Brownmiller, *Against Our Will: Men, Women and Rape* (New York: Simon and Schuster, 1975); Phyllis Chesler, *Women and Madness* (Garden City, NY: Doubleday, 1972).

[23] See the chapter "Contributions of Psychoanalysis," in Nancy Sahli, *Women and Sexuality in America*.

[24] See Karen Horney, *Feminine Psychology*, ed. Harold Kelman (New York: W. W. Norton, 1967).

"Sexuality as the Mainstay of Identity," are all reflective of this direction.[25]

By 1929, when Katharine Bement Davis published *Factors in the Sex Life of Twenty-Two Hundred Women*, knowledge of women's sexuality was light-years away from the Victorian days of William Acton and Elizabeth Blackwell. Relaxation of censorship codes following World War I, plus a liberalization of attitudes regarding permissible sexual behavior, not only increased the amount of literature on sex available to the general public, but changed the content of that literature as well.

Although World War II brought a temporary hiatus to much research on sexuality, it had little impact on the work of Alfred C. Kinsey. Begun in the late 1930s, and funded by grants from the National Research Council, an organization that supported some of the major sex research projects of that time, his *Sexual Behavior in the Human Female* was published in 1953.[26] While Kinsey was completing his monumental task, William H. Masters was beginning the groundbreaking studies which he eventually published, along with colleague Virginia E. Johnson, as *Human Sexual Response* and *Human Sexual Inadequacy*.

The 1970s saw the initiation of yet another generation of surveys, such as those undertaken by Shere Hite, in part as a response to the public's increased desire for information about sexual practices, itself an outgrowth of the so-called sexual revolution and the rise of laboratory-based sex research.[27] Many of these surveys were also seen as moneymakers by their developers and publishers, a fact reflected in their methodological problems. Lack of attention to possible differences reflecting race, class, and ethnicity is also apparent. It should be remembered, however, that sex research is still a comparatively new field; refinement and specialization of both research populations and research techniques should be expected to follow in the wake of more general studies.

---

[25] Mary Jane Sherfey, *The Nature and Evolution of Female Sexuality* (New York: Random House, 1972); Jean Strouse, ed., *Women and Analysis: Dialogues on Psychoanalytic Views of Femininity* (New York: Grossman, 1974); and Ethel Spector Person, "Sexuality as the Mainstay of Identity: Psychoanalytic Perspectives," *Signs* 5, no. 4 (Summer 1980): 605–30. While these works express a revisionist viewpoint, they are by no means similar in their hypotheses or conclusions.

[26] Alfred C. Kinsey, et al., *Sexual Behavior in the Human Female* (Philadelphia: W. B. Saunders, 1953).

[27] See, for example, Shere Hite, *The Hite Report: A Nationwide Study on Female Sexuality* (New York: Macmillan, 1976); Carol Tavris and Susan Sadd, *The Redbook Report on Female Sexuality: 100,000 Married Women Disclose the Good News about Sex* (New York: Delacorte Press, 1977); and Linda Wolfe, *The Cosmo Report* (New York: Arbor House, 1981).

Feminist theory also experienced a rebirth after World War II, slowly at first, as a result of works such as Simone de Beauvoir's *The Second Sex*, and then in a landslide after the appearance of Betty Friedan's *The Feminine Mystique*.[28] New social science and laboratory research on women's sexuality, such as that conducted by Masters and Johnson, was incorporated into feminist theory. Other developments at this time which contributed substantially to increasing understanding of women's sexuality were the growth of historical research on human sexuality and women's history, the development of new attitudes toward sexual dysfunction and methods for its treatment, and an ever-increasing openness toward sexual matters in all areas of American life. Thinking and writing about women's sexuality, while still governed more than we would care to admit by stereotypes and social conditioning, has tended to move away from folklore, misinformation, and subjective pontificating toward objectivity, rationality, scientific analysis, and a new recognition of women's real concerns and needs.

How then have historians responded to and interpreted women's sexuality? First, it should come as no surprise that monographic and periodical literature in the history of human sexuality has developed only within the past twenty years. The rise of the new social history and women's history as fields of historical inquiry, the contemporary search for the roots of women's oppression as well as continuity in feminist philosophy, and a heightened awareness and availability of research resources have led to an interest in and an acceptance of the validity of historical research in women's sexuality. As John D'Emilio has observed, work in women's history has uncovered many of the sources used for the study of the history of sexuality, and the interrelationship between women's traditional roles and sexual behavior has led to close ties between the history of women and the history of sexuality.[29]

Because sex itself was so long tabooed and neglected as a subject of legitimate research, however, historians in this field have had to face several barriers which, in turn, have led to creative redefinitions of subject matter and historical periodization. One of the most obvious, of course, is the lack of an established historiographical tradition and methodology other than that used in the writing of more conventional

---

[28] Simone de Beauvoir, *The Second Sex*, trans. and ed. H. M. Parshley (New York: Knopf, 1953); Betty Friedan, *The Feminine Mystique* (New York: W. W. Norton, 1963).
[29] John D'Emilio, "Introduction," *The Maryland Historian* [special issue on the history of gender and sexuality] 18, no. 1 (Spring/Summer 1987): 1–4.

social and intellectual history. As historians of women so rightly point out, traditional bases of periodization simply do not apply to many questions of women's lives and sexuality. Attempts to relate sexual attitudes and behavior to broader issues of economic, political, and social concern have only just begun and are often hampered by the sheer breadth of material relating to the sexual realm. Even defining what is meant by sexuality and whether the same parameters outline men's and women's lives is an unresolved issue.

The nineteenth century, or the "Victorian period," as some would call it, has exerted a special fascination for historians of women's sexuality in America. This is not surprising, for sources for the study of women's sexuality prior to that time are difficult to identify, especially because of a comparative lack of either prescriptive or medical literature on the topic prior to the 1830s and 1840s. (Even then the medical literature tended to focus on obstetrics and gynecology rather than non-reproductive sexual behavior, while prescriptive literature encompassed all aspects of women's behavior.) Nancy Cott is one of the few historians to have examined women's sexuality in the late eighteenth and early nineteenth centuries. In her article "Passionlessness: An Interpretation of Victorian Sexual Ideology, 1790–1850," she argues that a major change in views of women's sexuality took place between the seventeenth and nineteenth centuries as a dominant Anglo-American definition of women as particularly sexual beings was transformed into the view that women's sexual appetites were much smaller than those of men. Linking this change to the rise of evangelical religion, Cott sees passionlessness as a positive force, which replaced sexual determinism with the new view emphasizing woman's moral character as her chief motivating force.[30]

Cott, like many other historians of women's sexuality, relies heavily on prescriptive literature as a resource. Although such dependence is difficult to avoid, it can lead to a false equation of such literature with actual behavior, a point noted by Carl N. Degler in his 1974 article, "What Ought to Be and What Was: Women's Sexuality in the Nineteenth Century."[31] Prescriptive and medical literature taken on its own terms, however, can remain a valuable resource, as shown by Charles E.

---

[30] Nancy F. Cott, "Passionlessness: An Interpretation of Victorian Sexual Ideology, 1790–1850," *Signs* 4, no. 2 (Winter 1978): 219–36.

[31] Carl N. Degler, "What Ought to Be and What Was: Women's Sexuality in the Nineteenth Century," *American Historical Review* 79, no. 5 (December 1974): 1467–90.

Rosenberg in "Sexuality, Class and Role in 19th-century America," an important theoretical article tracing the main currents of nineteenth-century sexual attitudes as reflected in prescriptive literature.[32] Among other common themes, Rosenberg found that although woman's sexuality was consistently linked to her maternal function and masturbation was consistently decried, nineteenth-century America still accorded validity to a variety of sexual behavior options.

A more repressive view of women's sexual options in Victorian America is taken by G. J. Barker-Benfield, whose *The Horrors of the Half-known Life* and other works argue that nineteenth-century American men manipulated female sexuality to serve nationalistic goals of control and dominance.[33] Unfortunately, Barker-Benfield's supporting evidence is taken too much out of context to be convincing without further research and analysis. Similarly lacking in empirical evidence are the two chapters dealing in part with women's sexuality in John S. Haller and Robin M. Haller's *The Physician and Sexuality in Victorian America*.[34] Although the Hallers err in equating recommended with actual behavior, their work does form a useful introduction to nineteenth-century prescriptive literature.

Feminist attitudes and rhetoric about sexuality are explored by Linda Gordon and Ellen Dubois in the article, "Seeking Ecstasy on the Battlefield: Danger and Pleasure in Nineteenth-century Feminist Sexual Thought." Gordon and Dubois identify two patterns in feminist sexual thought. The first reflected the social purity perspective that warned of the dangers of sex, but saw little of its positive potential. The second, espoused by a minority of "sex radicals," championed free love and other forms of liberated heterosexual behavior, but failed to address the sexual options available to most women. Neither "school" dealt with issues of homoeroticism.[35]

Non-feminist historians have also specialized in studying free love and sexual ideology in nineteenth-century utopian communities. Louis J.

---

[32] Charles E. Rosenberg, "Sexuality, Class and Role in 19th-century America," *American Quarterly* 25, no. 2 (May 1973): 131–53.

[33] G. J. Barker-Benfield, *The Horrors of the Half-known Life*; Graham John Barker-Benfield, "The Spermatic Economy: A Nineteenth-century View of Sexuality," *Feminist Studies* 1, no. 1 (1972): 45–74.

[34] See chapters three and four of John S. Haller, Jr., and Robin M. Haller, *The Physician and Sexuality in Victorian America* (Urbana: University of Illinois Press, 1974).

[35] Linda Gordon and Ellen Dubois, "Seeking Ecstasy on the Battlefield: Danger and Pleasure in Nineteenth-century Feminist Sexual Thought," *Feminist Studies* 9, no. 1 (Spring 1983): 7–25.

Kern's *An Ordered Love* examines sex roles and sexuality among the Shakers, Mormons, and the followers of John Humphrey Noyes at Oneida.[36] Kern found that although sexual behavior and roles in these groups varied widely from the conventional practices of the time, they nevertheless were predicated on an ideology of women's inferiority and male dominance. A less satisfactory work on a similar topic is Raymond Lee Muncy's *Sex and Marriage in Utopian Communities: 19th-century America*.[37] Muncy argues that monogamous marriage was the primary institution of traditional society that caused concern among communitarians, chiefly because it placed family welfare above the good of the community as a whole. The study is marred by Muncy's failure to perceive how the innate biases of his sources have influenced his own arguments.

Also dealing with the sexual "fringe" is Hal D. Sears' *The Sex Radicals*, which traces the connections between feminist free-love ideology, which stressed woman's right to control her own body and to be mistress of her own person, and other threads of nineteenth-century radicalism: anarchism, libertarianism, secularism, and spiritualism.[38] Sears's study is rich in sources and detail and is suggestive of many additional lines of research into the history of female sexuality and its ties to feminism and other radical reforms.

The study of women's affectional and sexual relationships with one another has been the focus of considerable research. Perhaps the first work to examine this topic in an historical perspective was Jeannette H. Foster's *Sex Variant Women in Literature*, which examines lesbians in the Western literary tradition, both as authors and as subjects.[39] Originally published in 1956, Foster's work was reprinted in 1975, and has had a significant influence on subsequent literary and historical studies of lesbians, especially as a bibliographic source. Also building on the work of Foster was Jane Rule, whose *Lesbian Images* (1975) was the first work coming out of the contemporary women's movement to explore images of lesbians (defined by Rule as women who love other women) and the

---

[36] Louis J. Kern, *An Ordered Love: Sex Roles and Sexuality in Victorian Utopias—the Shakers, the Mormons, and the Oneida Community* (Chapel Hill: University of North Carolina Press, 1981).

[37] Raymond Lee Muncy, *Sex and Marriage in Utopian Communities: 19th-century America* (Bloomington: Indiana University Press, 1973).

[38] Hal D. Sears, *The Sex Radicals: Free Love in High Victorian America* (Lawrence: Regents Press of Kansas, 1977).

[39] Jeannette H. Foster, *Sex Variant Women in Literature* (Baltimore: Diana Press, 1975).

role of lesbian authors of fiction, biography, and autobiography.[40] Looked at from the perspective of 1989, Rule's chapters on "recent" nonfiction and individual works seem to provide sparse coverage of this topic, a clear indication of how far lesbian authors and literature have come in the intervening years.

Perhaps the most influential and best known of the recent historical writing on lesbian history is Carroll Smith-Rosenberg's now-classic article, "The Female World of Love and Ritual," which paints a rich picture of loving relationships between women in the nineteenth century. While not denying that these relationships may have had a sexual or homoerotic component, Smith-Rosenberg argues that twentieth-century tendencies to dichotomize such behavior into heterosexual and homosexual categories obscure the complexity of the sexual and emotional spectrum in which these women lived. Smith-Rosenberg's work is also significant for its use of personal letters and diaries from thirty-five families as aggregate evidence, thereby demonstrating the possibilities for documenting sexual and emotional attitudes and behavior in the absence of surveys, case studies, and other similar sources often used by contemporary researchers.

Several studies have built on and more fully developed the ideas originally expressed in "The Female World of Love and Ritual." Nancy Sahli's 1979 article, "Smashing: Women's Relationships Before the Fall," shows how the loving relationships described by Smith-Rosenberg became increasingly suspect in the late nineteenth and early twentieth centuries.[41] This was due largely to the pejorative definition of such relationships as sexually and emotionally abnormal by sexologists, psychiatrists, and other scientific and medical researchers and writers at that time. Drawing a similar conclusion is Lillian Faderman's *Surpassing the Love of Men*, which traces patterns of women's erotic relationships with other women from the sixteenth century to the present. Faderman found that the change in attitudes which took place in the late nineteenth century, drastically altering the emotional options available to women, was a result of medical and psychiatric ideas, the pejorative identification of women's love relationships with feminism and independence, and the negative portrayal of female same-sex relationships in literature written by men. Faderman's key point is clear: that expectations for same-sex

[40] Jane Rule, *Lesbian Images* (Garden City, NY: Doubleday, 1975).
[41] Nancy Sahli, "Smashing: Women's Relationships before the Fall," *Chrysalis* no. 8 (1979): 17–27.

relationships are culturally determined, changing over time, and that a male-dominated culture has the power to define what is "normal" and "permissible" where women's relationships are concerned.

The transition from nineteenth to twentieth century definitions and attitudes is also explored by Carroll Smith-Rosenberg in "The New Woman as Androgyne." This article, which demonstrates the connection between social ideology and attitudes toward women's sexuality, also explores the use of language, imagery, and symbolism in their relationship to sexual and political experience. Another study of the early twentieth century, Christina Simmons's "Companionate Marriage and the Lesbian Threat," demonstrates that proponents of the companionate marriage ideology of the 1920s and 1930s used lesbianism as a metaphor for women's autonomy in various forms in an attempt to perpetuate a single role for women, one focused on marriage and the service of men.

Two useful compilations of primary sources for the study of lesbian history in the United States, although not without their problems in dealing with women, are Jonathan Ned Katz's *Gay American History* and *Gay/Lesbian Almanac*, which reprint documentary sources, periodical literature, and other printed matter from the colonial period to the twentieth century.[42] Despite the existence of these two published volumes, additional work needs to be done to identify sources for the study of all aspects of women's sexuality.

In addition to lesbian history, two other topics relating to the study of women's sexuality have led to the development of monographs and other interpretive historical studies: prostitution and twentieth-century sex research. Although work done in the latter field cannot be said to focus solely on women, understanding the field of sex research generally is essential for any scholar attempting to use social science and laboratory studies as sources for historical research. One of the earliest assessments, Sophie D. Aberle and George W. Corner's *Twenty-five Years of Sex Research*, provides information on funding priorities and research networks between 1922 and 1947.[43] The work of Alfred C. Kinsey and

---

[42] Jonathan Ned Katz, *Gay American History: Lesbians and Gay Men in the U.S.A.* (New York: Crowell, 1976), and *Gay/Lesbian Almanac: A New Documentary* (New York: Harper & Row, 1983). A perceptive review of the latter volume by Leila J. Rupp can be found in *Signs* 9, no. 4 (Summer 1984): 712–15.

[43] Sophie D. Aberle and George W. Corner, *Twenty-five Years of Sex Research: History of the National Research Council Committee for Research in Problems of Sex 1922–1947* (Philadelphia: W. B. Saunders, 1953).

the Institute for Sex Research at Indiana University is documented in an as-yet unpublished dissertation by James H. Jones, "The Origins of the Institute for Sex Research: A History."[44] Jones's study includes information on the policies of such key organizations as the Committee for Research in Problems of Sex of the National Research Council, the Bureau of Social Hygiene, the Rockefeller Foundation, and Indiana University. Likewise, Wardell B. Pomeroy's 1972 biography of Kinsey is particularly useful for its description of the climate in which sex researchers tried to do their work and of the opposition to the criticism of *Sexual Behavior in the Human Female* after its publication.[45]

A broader view is taken by historian Paul A. Robinson in *The Modernization of Sex*, a critique of the major writing of Havelock Ellis, Alfred C. Kinsey, William Masters, and Virginia Johnson.[46] Although Robinson compares the work of these various authors to one another, he does not compare their work with that of their contemporaries. Additional research is clearly needed to assess the work of more contemporary researchers such as Shere Hite, in terms of their methodology, the relationship of their findings and techniques to those used by researchers in the past, and the reception of their work and its impact on society. Although significant privacy issues are inevitable, historians now and in the future should have access to the survey data used by these researchers in its original form if it is to be used for any sort of meaningful analysis.

Although prostitution is often characterized as an economic and social condition rather than a sexual one, its use of sex as a commodity brings it under the purview of any investigation of women's sexuality. Prostitution is one of the most thoroughly investigated subjects relating to women's sexuality, largely because of the existence of rich and diverse sources for the study of this topic. Also, studies of prostitution in historical perspective frequently cut across disciplinary lines, involving the study of sexual behavior, public policy, venereal disease, women's economic position and role in society, and many more topics.

Several recent monographic studies demonstrate this interdisciplinary approach. Barbara Meil Hobson's *Uneasy Virtue: The Politics of*

---

[44] James H. Jones, "The Origins of the Institute for Sex Research: A History" (Ph.D. diss., Indiana University, 1972).

[45] Wardell B. Pomeroy, *Dr. Kinsey and the Institute for Sex Research* (New York: Harper & Row, 1972).

[46] Paul A. Robinson, *The Modernization of Sex: Havelock Ellis, Alfred Kinsey, William Masters and Virginia Johnson* (New York: Harper & Row, 1976).

Prostitution and the American Reform Tradition, provides an overview of the subject from the 1820s to the present, with particular focus on nineteenth-century New England.[47] Mark Thomas Connelly's *The Response to Prostitution in the Progressive Era* provides an excellent overview of the subject during this period and examines such topics as women's roles, venereal disease, and the role of "new" immigrants in both the image and actuality of prostitution.[48] Even more useful and evocative is Ruth Rosen's *The Lost Sisterhood: Prostitution in America, 1900–1918*, which complements and expands on Connelly's work and provides a somewhat more feminist perspective.[49]

Studies focusing on particular regions and ethnic groups provide the basis for comparison and contrast. Marion S. Goldman's *Gold Diggers & Silver Miners: Prostitution and Social Life on the Comstock Lode* uses a sociological perspective in its examination of prostitutes and prostitution in nineteenth-century Virginia City, Nevada.[50] Goldman's study makes especially skillful use of local history resources and displays a keen sensitivity to its subjects as individuals that is sometimes absent from works examining prostitution primarily from a public-policy or other regulatory perspective. Anne M. Butler's *Daughters of Joy, Sisters of Misery: Prostitutes in the American West, 1865–90* looks at prostitution from the perspective of the West as a developing region with significant populations of single men—cowboys, soldiers, miners—willing to pay for sexual services and pays particular attention to the economic forces that led women to take up a life of prostitution.[51] Like Goldman, Butler tries to personalize and humanize her subject as much as possible and avoids facile stereotyping.

---

47 Barbara Meil Hobson, *Uneasy Virtue: The Politics of Prostitution and the American Reform Tradition* (New York: Basic Books, 1987). One of the first historians to explore prostitution in relation to public policy was John C. Burnham. See his "Medical Inspection of Prostitutes in America in the Nineteenth Century: The St. Louis Experiment and Its Sequel," *Bulletin of the History of Medicine* 45, no. 3 (May/June 1971): 203–18.

48 Mark Thomas Connelly, *The Response to Prostitution in the Progressive Era* (Chapel Hill: University of North Carolina Press, 1980).

49 Ruth Rosen, *The Lost Sisterhood: Prostitution in America, 1900–1918* (Baltimore: Johns Hopkins University Press, 1982). For insight into the life of one prostitute see Ruth Rosen and Sue Davidson, eds., *The Maimie Papers* (Old Westbury, NY: The Feminist Press, 1977).

50 Marion S. Goldman, *Gold Diggers & Silver Miners: Prostitution and Social Life on the Comstock Lode* (Ann Arbor: University of Michigan Press, 1981).

51 Anne M. Butler, *Daughters of Joy, Sisters of Misery: Prostitutes in the American West, 1865–90* (Urbana and Chicago: University of Illinois Press, 1985).

Other specialized topics as diverse as nineteenth-century Chinese and Japanese prostitutes in America and brothel life in St. Paul, Minnesota, have also been explored by contemporary historians.[52] The existence of similar source materials—court records and newspaper accounts to name two—in different regions of the country makes it possible to develop comparative studies assessing regional and other differences and similarities in an historical perspective.

Although venereal disease is a topic often dealt with in monographs on prostitution, only one work has attempted to present an overview of this topic in an historical perspective. Allan M. Brandt's *No Magic Bullet: A Social History of Venereal Disease in the United States Since 1880* does not focus specifically on women, but it does include sufficient information on the political and social context of venereal disease, its prevention and treatment, to be a useful starting point for further work on this topic.[53]

Likewise, only one serious work of historical scholarship has attempted to develop a synthesis that examines both male and female sexuality in America: John D'Emilio and Estelle Freedman's *Intimate Matters: A History of Sexuality in America*.[54] The existence of only one such work incorporating the findings and perspectives of the historical research and social movements that have occurred during the past twenty years demonstrates the difficulty of developing a synthesis at this stage of historical research and writing in the field of sexuality. It also demonstrates the need for more research studies on specific topics that could then be used as the basis for further development of synthetic works, as well as for refinement of periodization, historiography, and historical-research methodology. The study of women's sexuality, like the study of the history of sexuality as a whole, has thus far been heavily focused on description rather than analysis. Perhaps this is only natural,

---

52 See, for example, Lucie Cheng Hirata, "Free, Indentured, Enslaved: Chinese Prostitutes in Nineteenth-century America," *Signs* 5, no. 1 (Autumn 1979); Yuji Ichioka, "Ameyuke-san: Japanese Prostitutes in Nineteenth Century America," *Amerasia Journal* 4, no. 1 (1977): 1–21; Joan Hori, "Japanese Prostitution in Hawaii During the Immigration Period," *Hawaiian Journal of History* 15 (1981): 113–23; Joel Best, "Careers in Brothel Prostitution: St. Paul, 1865–1883," *Journal of Interdisciplinary History* 12, no. 4 (Spring 1982): 597–619. Especially evocative because of its extensive use of visual resources is Al Rose, *Storyville, New Orleans: Being An Authentic, Illustrated Account of the Notorious Red-Light District* (University: University of Alabama Press, 1974).

53 Allan M. Brandt, *No Magic Bullet: A Social History of Venereal Disease in the United States since 1880* (New York: Oxford University Press, 1985).

54 John D'Emilio and Estelle Freedman, *Intimate Matters: A History of Sexuality in America* (New York: Harper & Row, 1988).

given the newness of the field, for most historical scholarship regardless of the specific field passes through phases of growth and development: description and fact-finding in traditional sources, analysis, synthesis, revisionist analysis, and increasingly specialized description, often leading to the use of new sources and methodologies or new configurations of traditional sources. This can readily be seen in the use of quantitative methodology in the study of political history or in the examination of specific localities or groups in society by the "new" social history.

One characteristic in the historical literature thus far is its emphasis on certain specialized topics or populations—nineteenth-century sex radicals, lesbians, prostitutes—that do not reflect the majority of women in the population. With the exception of one short article on the work on Clelia Duel Mosher, we do not have published historical analyses of the numerous sex-research surveys (Davis, Hite, Kinsey, and others) done since the late nineteenth century.[55] Research needs to be done on the historical differences in women's sexuality and sexual behavior in the United States as influenced by their age, class, ethnic background, demographic or geographic background, and similar factors. We need perceptive analyses of visual imagery, popular-culture media forms, and the relationship of prescriptive literature to real behavior. We need less ghettoization of sexuality as a field of inquiry and more integration of research in this area into other work on women's history and social history.

Historians, as we have seen, have demonstrated that the sources are there with which to explore this field. The study of the history of sexuality and women's sexuality in particular can challenge our most deeply held biases and misconceptions. We may not always "like" what we learn, but the excitement of using the past to reveal truths to which we can relate as individuals in the present will always make this one of the most intellectually stimulating and emotionally satisfying fields of historical inquiry.

---

[55] See the chapter "Behavior and Attitudes: Surveys and Other Studies" in Nancy Sahli, *Women and Sexuality in America*. Two other works that may be useful in defining topics for further research are Barbara Ehrenreich, Elizabeth Hess, and Gloria Jacobs, *Remaking Love: The Feminization of Sex* (Garden City, NY: Anchor Press/Doubleday, 1986), and Meryl Altman, "Everything They Always Wanted You to Know: The Ideology of Popular Sex Literature," in *Pleasure and Danger*, ed. Carole S. Vance (Boston: Routledge & K. Paul, 1984).

4

· · · —————— · · ·

CHILDBIRTH IN AMERICA,
1650 to 1990
Janet Carlisle Bogdan

Until the 1970s, our knowledge of childbirth history was principally an inferred one, derived mainly from the writings of medical historians. Historians of medicine traditionally stressed the progressive history of scientific advance in obstetrics, the field of medicine concerned with childbirth, and dwelled on the life histories of leading practitioners.[1] From this history we learned how doctors interpreted changes in the management of the physiological act of birth—what represented problems to doctors and how doctors succeeded in overcoming these problems. We did not learn what represented problems to the *women* giving birth, however, or how their helpers participated in their births. From traditional medical history we also learned the broad outlines of how women's experience of childbirth changed during America's history from a female affair presided over by midwives, to one defined and dominated by medical men. Medical history, however, told us little about how changes in the management of birthing affected women's experience of birth or about women's reactions to and participation in such changes. Nor did it suggest how birth fit into women's lives or what an actual birth was like. What knowledge we *could* gain about childbirth

---

[1] Irving S. Cutter and Henry R. Viets, *A Short History of Midwifery* (Philadelphia: W. B. Saunders & Co., 1933); Palmer Findley, *The Story of Childbirth* (New York: Doubleday, Doran & Company, 1933); Harvey Graham [Isaac Harvey Flack], *Eternal Eve* (Altrincham: William Heinemann, 1950); Herbert Thoms, *Chapters in American Obstetrics* (Springfield, IL: Charles C. Thomas, 1933).

in more than its physiological aspects came from social historians writing about period customs or about women's lives.[2]

Beginning in the late 1960s, however, scholarship began to emerge that examined pregnancy, childbirth, and the lying-in period as social phenomena and as aspects of women's lives rather than solely or principally as phenomena of medical history.[3] Moreover, study of medical history began to include questions concerning its political and social context.[4] Part of the "new social history" that focused on the whole social, racial, economic, and ethnic spectrum of participants in history-making, childbirth history began to consider all women giving birth, the poor as well as the privileged, the bondswoman as well as the bondholder's wife. Today the investigation continues into the experience of others formerly considered either outside the historical mainstream or lost to real historical investigation: the immigrant, the slave, the social and geographical isolate. This new scholarship, then, has broadened the investigation of both obstetrics and women's lives; we now study childbirth history in a variety of contexts: medical, demographic, cultural, social, economic, professional, and symbolic, to name but a few. We recognize that as a social institution, the particulars of childbirth experience and management reflect the organization of social relationships in the larger society. As that society or those relationships undergo changes, so do its institutions. Childbirth changed as America changed. It is still changing, but continues to reflect the cultural logic. In the essay that follows, I will focus on childbirth itself, on how and why, and to what effect historians are discovering this central event in women's lives changed since the seventeenth century in America.

Women's attitudes toward and behavior during birth are shaped and conditioned by the demands and expectations of family, peers, community, and often religion. What a woman expects from her childbirth experience, what she will do, what she will fear and not fear, how she will

---

[2] Alice Morse Earle, *Customs and Fashions in Old New England* (New York: Charles Scribner's Sons, 1893; Alice Morse Earle, *Colonial Days in Old New York* (New York: Charles Scribner's Sons, 1896); Eleanor Flexner, *Century of Struggle* (1959; reprint New York: Atheneum, 1974); Julia Cherry Spruill, *Women's Work and Life in the Southern Colonies* (1938; reprint New York: W. W. Norton, 1972).

[3] Claire Elizabeth Fox, "Pregnancy, Childbirth and Early Infancy in Anglo-American Culture: 1675–1830," (Ph.D. dissertation, University of Pennsylvania, 1966).

[4] Barbara Ehrenreich and Deirdre English, *Witches, Midwives and Nurses: A History of Women Healers* (Old Westbury, NY: The Feminist Press, 1973); Frances Kobrin, "The American Midwife Controversy: A Crisis of Professionalization," *Bulletin of the History of Medicine* 40 (1966): 350–66.

interpret what is happening to her, and what in fact *will* happen when she gives birth, depend in large measure upon how her society defines what birth should be and where she fits in the various hierarchies and value systems of that society. Contemporary Americans accept childbirth as medically centered. One in a long series of procreation-related events punctuating women's lives, it is primarily defined and understood by medical people. Women are encouraged to check constantly on the normality of their procreative system events—onset of menstruation, birth control, pregnancy, abortion and miscarriage, labor, childbirth, postpartum conditions, and so on. Procreative normality is the central component of Americans' view of female healthiness. We are acutely aware that something might go wrong and typically feel we need medical expertise to assess normality and to accomplish care.

Certainly part of our willingness to view the body's procreative processes as needing medical surveillance is that the major procreative event, childbirth, is a rare one in most women's lives.[5] Childbirth happens only once or twice in our own personal physical experience, and is also infrequent in extended family or even neighborhood or friendship group life. For an event which can have such profound consequences during the remainder of a woman's life, women of any era would choose to avail themselves of whatever opportunities exist to enhance its out-come. No wonder we turn to medical advice, advice we consider scientific aid, in the project of birth. When we think of a childbirth in America, in fact, most would think of a medical scene. Although childbirth in contemporary America actually occurs in an assortment of settings with a variety of attendants, the dominant image of women giving birth is probably of a medical team surrounding a draped body to which are attached the various IV bottles and equipment needed for the team to deliver a healthy baby for the mother: a medical procedure over which a team of experts—doctor(s), nurses, technicians, both men and women—presides. For an increasing percentage of women in America,

---

[5] The total fertility rate in the United States today (i.e., the number of children born to a woman experiencing the average fertility for each year of her reproductive life) is 1.8, down from a twentieth-century high of 3.56 among whites and 4.24 among nonwhites. See Ansley J. Coale and Melvin Zelnick, *New Estimates of Fertility and Population in the United States* (Princeton: Princeton University Press, 1963), p. 35; Population Reference Bureau, *1988 World Population Data Sheet*; "Fertility Tables for Birth Cohorts by Color: United States, 1917–1973," U.S. Department of Health, Education, and Welfare, National Center for Health Statistics, Rockville, MD, April 1976; *Statistical Abstract of the United States*, 103rd Edition, Bureau of the Census, U.S. Department of Commerce, 1983.

in fact, childbirth *is* a surgical event; their infants are brought into the world by cesarean section.[6]

In seventeenth-century America, surgery represented the last desperate hope to salvage a woman's life threatened by a stalled or abnormal delivery. Except in rare cases, those associated with medicine were not even connected to the childbirth event. Most of what we consider the preserve of medicine in the 1980s was part of the seventeenth-century woman's *domestic* responsibilities both among the groups immigrating to the New World and among native peoples. Although variations certainly characterized the ways different groups managed childbirth in the rugged realities of the New World, all shared the tradition that only women attended other women at this pivotal event in their lives. It might be many women, or only a few, and the rituals of the childbirth might vary, but it was the women who knew about birth.

Early generations of American women knew about birth in part because it was everpresent in their everyday lives. Almost every white woman of childbearing age was married and most were having babies. Current estimates suggest, in fact, that fertility in early America was higher than in any European country at the time and, at more than eight births per woman over the course of her childbearing years, higher even than any present day national population.[7]

A first birth for these early American women typically came within a year or so after marriage vows were exchanged. Around age twenty-one,

---

[6] The cesarean birth rate has been rising steadily in the past few decades in America. In 1970, cesareans accounted for 5.5% of all U.S. births; in 1975, for 10.4%; in 1980, for 15%; in 1985, for 22.7%; and in 1987, for 24.4%. "C-Sections: New Guidelines May Reverse Trends," *Syracuse Herald Journal*, October 28, 1988; Milt Freudenheim, "The Effort to Curb Cesarean Rate," *The New York Times*, January 10, 1989; Gina Kolata, "New York Seeks to Reduce Rates of Cesarean Births," *The New York Times*, January 27, 1989.

[7] On rates of marriage in the white population, see Robert V. Wells, *Revolutions in Americans' Lives* (Westport, CT: Greenwood Press, 1982), pp. 41–43, and Mary Beth Norton, *Liberty's Daughters, The Revolutionary Experience of American Women, 1750–1860* (Boston: Little, Brown and Company, 1980), pp. 41–42. Wells points out that the slave status of many black Americans meant they could not legally marry.

For fertility-rate patterns in the United States, see Coale and Zelnick, *New Estimates of Fertility*, p. 35. Kenya presently has one of the highest birth rates in the world at 8 births per woman. John R. Weeks, *Population*, 4th ed. (Belmont, CA: Wadsworth Publishing Co., 1989), pp. 89–90. In *A Little Commonwealth* (New York: Oxford University Press, 1970), p. 68, John Demos found an average of more than eight births per woman among seventeenth-century Plymouth Colony families; Philip Greven also found over eight births per family in his sample of twenty-nine families settling in Andover between 1645 and 1660. See his "Family Structure in Seventeenth-Century Andover, Massachusetts," *William and Mary Quarterly* 3, no. 23 (1966): 237.

then, the cycle of conception, pregnancy, birth, nursing, weaning, and conception began that would occupy most months for the next twenty to twenty-five years of their lives. Although abortions, miscarriages, still-births, and infant deaths (which would foreshorten the nursing period) might interrupt the twenty- to thirty-month cycle, it would soon begin again.[8] Using sources such as men's diaries, court records, and a variety of prescriptive writings, historians such as Laurel Ulrich and Catherine Scholten have been able to comment on the childbirth orientation of much of women's daily activities at least in New England during the first generations of settlement. In a way that may be difficult for a woman of the 1980s to imagine, childbirth—her own, her sister's, her friend's, her neighbor's, even her mother's—was a fact and focus of everyday life, an everpresent influence on what a woman's daily round of cares and activities might be. When and how a woman could travel and where, what she might plant in her spring garden and harvest in the fall, when she sewed and mended, for whom and what, all were affected by her point in the procreative cycle or for what aspect of help she would soon be called upon to provide for a woman neighbor or relative.[9]

Because literacy among women rose in the eighteenth century, from that period on, we have *women's* letters and diaries as well to draw upon in order to understand the meaning and experience of childbirth in their lives. In her recent history of childbirth in America, Judith Leavitt draws upon diaries kept by the Holyoke family women of Salem, Massachusetts, to illustrate the cycle of what she calls "bodily reproductive duties" in the lives of eighteenth- and nineteenth-century women. These day-to-day chronicles of what and for whom women performed the daily duties of eighteenth-and nineteenth-century life attest to both the pervasiveness and centrality of matters of childbirth in women's lives. Mary Vial Holyoke, for example, gave birth to twelve children in the first twenty-three years of her married life, of whom three lived to adulthood. Sarah Everett Hale experienced eleven childbirths and at least that many more pregnancies in her first twenty years of marriage. At her twenty-fifth wedding anniversary in 1841, Hale wrote in her diary that seven of her children still lived while four had been taken, one at age seven. For

---

[8] Laurel Thatcher Ulrich. *Good Wives: Image and Reality in the Lives of Women in Northern New England, 1650–1750* (New York: Alfred A. Knopf, 1982), pp. 135–45.
[9] Ulrich, *Good Wives*, 139–45; Catherine M. Scholten, *Childbearing in American Society: 1650–1850* (New York: New York University Press, 1985), pp. 8–30.

both these women, and countless others like them, most days of married life were lived preparing for or recovering from childbirth.[10]

Since the rituals and beliefs about birth grow out of a culture's experience and tradition, the experience of childbirth would vary from place to place and time to time. A seventeenth-century Puritan woman, married and wealthy, would have a different childbirth experience than a contemporary Fox Indian woman to the west of her, or an indentured servant woman to the south of her, for example. A Fox Indian woman might give birth in a small isolated brush shelter with her mother, mother-in-law, and midwife present and assisting; she might kneel or lay supine on the ground during her labor while she held a strap suspended from the shelter roof on which she pulled whenever her contractions were intense; she might use special potions mixed and given her by the midwife who might assist not only by giving herbal drinks to ease her pain, but also by circling outside the shelter while singing special songs and chanting. This expectant mother might never utter a cry during her entire painful ordeal, a behavior traditionally expected of all Fox Indian parturients; nor would she fear this pain or fear the pain of subsequent childbirths. Also traditional for this new mother would be that she stay in her isolated shelter—that she be separated from her husband after the birth—for thirty or forty days.[11]

A pious seventeenth-century Puritan would also be attended by a midwife and other women. She would most likely enjoy the company and aid of a whole contingent of women, however, rather than just a mother and a mother-in-law. Like her Indian counterpart, she would be separated from the rest of the household, but in a special room or in a space curtained off from the rest of the household, rather than in a temporary hut constructed at some distance from her home. Also like her Indian counterpart, she would be encouraged to bear her pains silently, not so much to assure bravery and forebearance in future generations, but rather to prove that she had prayed sufficiently and had appropriately resigned herself to her God's will in this dangerous trial. To complain too much when the intensity of labor reached its zenith would be a woeful admission of her lack of faith in God's plan.

---

[10] Judith Walzer Leavitt. *Brought to Bed: Childbearing in America, 1750–1950* (New York: Oxford University Press, 1986), pp. 13–19; Scholten, *Childbearing in American Society*, pp. 31–49.

[11] James Axtell, *The Indian Peoples of Eastern America: A Documentary History of the Sexes* (New York: Oxford University Press, 1981), pp. 28–29.

Not all seventeenth-century immigrants to what are now coastal northeastern states were Puritans, of course. Whether the new arrivals were English or, if they lived farther down the eastern New World coast, Dutch or even African; however, their childbirth beliefs and practices were a melange of herbal medicine, folklore, and magic. Specifics of practices might vary from one group to another, but whether it was a midwife circling the birthing hut singing chants to resuscitate a stalled labor in the case of the Fox Indian woman, or a New England matron wearing a loadstone around her neck to assure that her labor did not start too early, she was acting out of traditional folk or perhaps magic beliefs.

Whether aided by magic or herbs, the seventeenth-century immigrant parturient would have the benefit of generations of accumulated wisdom about ways to ease the trials of childbirth. The women attending her might prepare a tea infused from amber, saffron, ground cumin seed, sage, and comfrey, for example, to help the birth along. To further encourage easy passage of the fetus and to ease the mother-to-be's pain, the women might prepare a steaming pot of wild pennyroyal decoction for her to sit over. As the labor and delivery progressed, they might offer other herbal preparations: myrrh to hasten the delivery, mint syrup to quell nausea, fern paste to keep the perineum pliant during the delivery of the head and shoulders, a basil or rue decoction to expel a tardy afterbirth, bayberry tea to control bleeding after the delivery, and perhaps a betony root preparation as a prophylactic against hysterics following the ordeal. Moreover, if the new mother's milk did not flow well within a few days after the birth, the midwife could give her a tea made from the leaves, seeds, and root of the bugloss plant or an anise syrup, or even boiled turnips along with the water they were boiled in. If her breasts became sore, a not-uncommon complaint of new mothers, a paste of oatmeal and sage could be prepared. To complete her recovery from the birth, a new mother might take sassafras tea, a tonic often relied upon for childbirth recovery.[12]

---

[12] Cotton Mather, *The Angel of Bethesda* (*An Essay Upon the Common Maladies of Mankind*), ed. Gordon W. Jones. (Barre, MA: American Antiquarian Society and Barre Publishers, 1972), pp. 246–47; Ann Leighton, *Early American Gardens 'For Meate or Medicine'* (Boston: Houghton Mifflin, 1966), pp. 237, 247, 263, 349, 382, 399.

Katsi Cook, a lay midwife of the Mohawk Nation at Akwesasne, in a lecture on Native American midwifery, mentioned some of the same preparations Mather referred to as part of current Iroquois midwifery practice, e.g., fern paste. February 16, 1981, Syracuse, New York.

EIGHTEENTH-CENTURY CHANGES
IN BIRTH PRACTICES

Traditional beliefs about variations in the physiological aspects of birth, about why childbirth differed from one woman to another, about how a childbirth was best conducted, and about who and under what conditions different members of the community should be present, changed in America as everyday life changed, as religion declined as a central organizing principle of belief and everyday life and as economic realities and relationships changed. Whereas in early America women were the acknowledged experts about and at birth, by the middle of the eighteenth century their expertise began to be questioned. Groundwork for change in attendance customs and the source of best knowledge about childbirth began in sixteenth-century France when women in substantial numbers began to give birth in hospitals under the watchful eyes not only of midwives, but also of doctors. Until this opportunity to regularly observe the process of ordinary birth, doctors had seen only the abnormal, the unusual birth. Anatomical drawings, previously based on a combination of historical notions of organs and on animal or autopsy dissections, were closely tied to the contemporary idea that the uterus was but an inverted penis.[13] When birth was institutionalized, different descriptions of the birth process began to emerge, descriptions based in a spreading Enlightenment ideology championing the ascendancy of nature and natural laws. From the Enlightenment vantage point, birth was a natural process that proceeded by laws of its own. Through close observation, measurement, and recording of the birth process, early French doctors aimed to uncover these natural laws and rationally to describe and explain the heretofore mysterious process of birth.[14]

Eschewing what they redefined as magical and superstitious ideas about the birth process, doctors with access to the normal births of the desperate poor who peopled early hospital beds worked out what they named as scientific descriptions, in pictures and words, of the birth process. Heralding their new understanding as based upon a rational process of observation and likening the body and the birth process to the

---

[13] Thomas Laqueur, "Orgasm, Generation, and the Politics of Reproductive Biology," *Representations* 14 (Spring, 1986): 2.
[14] Richard W. Wertz and Dorothy C. Wertz, *Lying-In: A History of Childbirth in America* (New York: Free Press, 1977), pp. 31–34.

machine the new "scientific midwifery" celebrated, doctors both implicitly and explicitly trivialized and degraded the traditional, experience-based knowledge women and midwives had about birth.[15]

While French doctors were expanding their knowledge and understanding of the birth process through observation, the English were working on *techniques* for putting this new knowledge to work in the service of their occupation as barber-surgeons who were sometimes called by midwives to surgically extract a fetus. Since the British medical tradition did not include hospital-based clinical opportunities to observe and assist or direct birth attendance, these British surgeons created their own opportunities by setting up private clinics at which they would assist poor women during delivery *and* demonstrate their techniques to students who paid them for this opportunity.[16]

It was the British attention to technique and to passing on their newly acquired skills to apprentices that most visibly affected women's birth experiences over the next three hundred years in America. A number of these apprentices migrated across the Atlantic beginning in the mid-eighteenth century, bringing with them not only their claim to education in the new science of midwifery, but also their claim to possess life-saving tools, the forceps, with which they could rescue birthing women from otherwise hopeless situations. Young American men, in their turn, crossed the Atlantic to Britain and France and in their years of medical training there picked up both practical and theoretical experience in midwifery. Returning home with the same implied if not explicit claims as earlier men-midwives, these young American physicians began appearing at the bedsides of middle- and upper-class urban women. At first they attended along with the traditional midwife, but by the early years of the nineteenth century, they were on their way to replacing them. These returning physicians also helped to establish medical schools in America which would serve to certify numbers of other men as birth attendants by virtue of their education.[17] Though women were invited to the earliest midwifery instruction efforts in America, they were not invited for "medical" training as were the men;

---

[15] Walter Radcliffe, *The Secret Instrument* (London: William Heinemann, 1947), pp. 19–29; Wertz and Wertz, *Lying In*, pp. 32–33; William Ray Arney, *Power and the Profession of Obstetrics* (Chicago: University of Chicago Press, 1982), pp. 24–25.

[16] Wertz and Wertz, *Lying In*, pp. 34–37; Jane Bauer Donegan, *Women and Men Midwives: Medicine, Morality, and Misogyny in Early America* (Westport, CT: Greenwood Press, 1978), pp. 59–82.

[17] This story is well told in Donegan, *Women and Men Midwives*, pp. 89–135.

rather they were invited to learn what were suitable behaviors for midwives at an uncomplicated or normal birth and to learn the circumstances under which they should call in a physician.

THE DIFFERENCE MALE ATTENDANCE MADE

What difference did it make to women giving birth in the mid-eighteenth century that men as physicians or men-midwives began to be present at births? How did a male presence affect women's experience of birth, if it did so at all? To some extent, even to consider having a male present and assisting at a childbirth suggests that women's ideas about and experience of birth had already undergone dramatic change. As I noted earlier, from earliest times childbirth was a women's rite, a "mystery" to men in the words of standard contemporary midwives' oaths. Knowing about birth and caring for a birthing woman were thought to be part of women's domestic knowledge and repertoire of domestic skills. Women were consultants, nurturers, consolers, helpers, and confidants throughout the nine months prior to a birth as well as during and after the childbirth event itself. Women had confidence in other women because not only had they experienced birth but they had also attended other women's births. Other women understood what the parturient or expectant mother was experiencing and could provide appropriate encouragement and aid when necessary. To shift from an expectation of this kind of help to that promised by physicians—knowledge of birth gained through education rather than experience, and attendance oriented to altering the course of the birth rather than assisting in the course that birth would naturally take—implies that in women's eyes, childbirth had become an event they might affect rather than one to which they must be resigned. It also suggests that childbirth was at least partially viewed in more than its traditional natural or domestic light. One would not call in a physician or a male to take charge of a domestic duty. When women decided that calling in a physician to attend at birth was appropriate, they had begun to consider birth as possibly a disease, the view that educated physicians advocated.

In altering the childbirth ritual to allow the possibility of a man or men at the birth, women had to be willing to change many of its traditional aspects. They gave up the comfort and security of an all-female ritual, for one thing. They faced constriction of their physical freedom for another. Physicians wanted birthing women placed on their backs or on their sides so they would have better access for internal examination or "touching," and for forceps, should they want to use them. Thus, whereas before women could move around freely during the hours of travail or labor and give birth in the position that felt most comfortable for them—sitting on a birthing stool or a chair, or resting on or between the knees of one of their women attendants, or even simply squatting, perhaps—and *then* be "brought to bed," now they would have to plan to give birth in bed. These were middle- and upper-class urban white women, after all, whose code of behavior called for appropriate attention to bodily modesty. In this circumstance, modesty meant being completely covered.[18] On the one hand, then, women could anticipate additional and perhaps unknown intervention by the new childbirth attendants. On the other hand, they would have to agree to curtail their own movement during the event for propriety's sake and for the comfort of all present.

Women also had to anticipate sharing or giving up the female control which had characterized the childbirth rite through the ages. Not only because physicians were male would they enter the birthing chamber as the ones assumed to be in charge, but also because physicians were entering with the mantle of "science" worn conspicuously, if only symbolically. Leavitt reminds us in her *Brought to Bed*, however, that women's control was only *shared* with the new attendants at birth, not given over. Since women decided when and if a male attendant should be called, they maintained that measure of control. Additionally, Leavitt points out, women could accept or reject the advice or intervention the physician planned. As long as birthing women assembled "their women" as helpers and childbirth remained in the home, women retained some measure of control over the specifics of their birth experience.[19]

Those specifics were not confined simply to forceps, of course. Although forceps for live birth were the basic technological claim that physicians made in their effort to legitimize their presence at women's bedsides during birth, the larger claim was that birth was in fact a disease. Although many births might be uneventful just as many other diseases were, they might also be "preternatural" or abnormal and would need one of the therapies physicians offered. Women who chose physicians as attendants in eighteenth-century America, then, also might

---

[18] Donegan, *Women and Men Midwives*, pp. 141-57.
[19] Judith Walzer Leavitt, "'Science' Enters the Birthing Room: Obstetrics in America since the Eighteenth Century," *Journal of American History* 70 (1983): 281-304; and Leavitt, *Brought to Bed*.

be bled if their contractions stalled or given a tobacco enema if the bloodletting did not work. They might also take opium (in tincture form and known as laudanum) to ease the pain of their contractions.[20]

By the close of the eighteenth century, then, women were giving birth in America in a wider variety of ways than they had early in the century. In addition to the ways that varied from one ethnic group to another and from one geographic area of the country to another were added ways that differed according to whether one was wealthy and urban or not, since it was typically these latter women who engaged male physicians to attend their childbirths. Well into the nineteenth century these distinctions would remain, with a few exceptions. An increasing number of urban *poor* women would be attended by physicians as hospitals became part of the urban landscape and medical scene during the century; moreover, *more* women would have the childbirth experience of being attended by physicians as their numbers increased and successful practices came more and more to include (even depend upon) childbirth attendance.

ACCEPTANCE OF BIRTH INTERVENTION INCREASES

Women who chose physicians to attend them faced a widening array of interventive possibilities during the nineteenth century. Early in the century, ergot, a fungus which sometimes grows on rye grain and which, when picked at the right time, prepared properly, and administered in appropriate doses, can increase and intensify contractions, came into widespread use. Its use flowed like waves throughout the century, ebbing when charges were rife that it often caused tonic or sustained uterine contractions which resulted in stillbirth or maternal death, and flowing when such charges died down or a new method of more careful preparation offered better assurance of uniform results. By the end of the century, it was widely considered too dangerous to use during labor, and recognized as safe only to stop postpartum (after birth) hemorrhaging.[21] As was true with all therapies of the nineteenth and early twentieth centuries, however, use was never standard. What a physician would

---

[20] Janet Bogdan, "Care or Cure?: Childbirth Practices in Nineteenth Century America," *Feminist Studies* 4 (1978): 92–99.
[21] Janet Carlisle Bogdan, "Aggressive Intervention and Mortality," in Pamela S. Eakins, ed. *The American Way of Birth* (Philadelphia: Temple University Press, 1986), pp. 87–88.

choose as therapy depended upon with whom and when he had been apprenticed or received his (or her, after the middle of the nineteenth century) education, what kind of medical information he or she was exchanging and with whom, and what customs were usual in the community he or she was serving.[22]

Beginning at midcentury, and with physicians as attendants, women giving birth might experience another intervention—anesthesia. Given to allay childbirth pain, ether and chloroform sometimes helped and sometimes harmed the expectant mother and her fetus. Soon after both kinds of anesthesia came into use in the late 1840s, they began to be recognized as responsible for the undesirable side effects which often accompanied them; anesthesia could slow down the labor by interfering with the intensity of the contractions, or cause breathing difficulties for the newborn, for example. Though both ether and chloroform were recognized as potentially dangerous, women sometimes requested, even demanded, that they be used.[23]

Accompanying the increasing incidence and variety of interventions in physician-attended childbirths was the growing problem of birth accidents which left a new mother injured and often chronically ill or disabled. Birth canal injuries, tears in perineal tissue (the tissue between the vaginal and the anal opening), and acute and chronic infection unwittingly introduced by physicians' hands, equipment, or instruments became a common hazard expected when a physician was called upon to attend. Lacerations or tears were left to heal as they might, since suturing only created new and often worse problems for the new mother. Haphazard healing could result in chronic problems, too, some of which would make further normal or successful pregnancies very unlikely or impossible.[24]

The possibility of health-threatening outcomes that might result from a physician's intervention kept that aspect of physician attendance open for negotiation much as the use of anesthesia was. That women could and would negotiate the terms of their birth attendance indicates a definition of childbirth dramatically different from that held by their seventeenth-century sisters. Nineteenth-century women who took an

---

[22] Leavitt, *Brought to Bed*, pp. 143–51.

[23] Ibid., pp. 123–26. See also Sylvia D. Hoffert, *Private Matters: American Attitudes Toward Childbearing and Infant Nurture in the Urban North, 1800–1860* (Urbana: University of Illinois Press, 1989), pp. 82–94.

[24] Ibid., pp. 45–67; 142–50; Bogdan, "Intervention and Mortality," pp. 89–92.

active stance toward the specifics of their birth experience (or allowed
their attendants—family, friends, neighbors—to do so on their behalf
during the rigors of the childbirth itself), were not defining the particulars of the individual childbirth experience wholly as God's plan in
action, or God's judgement on the adequacy of their prayerful preparation for the event, as had many of their seventeenth-century sisters.
With individual variations, of course, they and their helpers and attendants were viewing childbirth itself as an event they could not only affect
but also over which they could expect to have some control.[25] Women
continued actively to participate in determining the terms of their childbirths, as Leavitt points out, as long as the home was the locus of
childbirth. When birth moved into the hospital, however, women lost
this power.[26] Without the coterie of support and advocacy represented
by the women gathered to care for the birthing woman and her household, alone and isolated in a hospital bed, unsure of the procedures *and*
the personnel, and increasingly drugged at some point before the baby
actually arrived, the expectant mother had little chance even to anticipate just what would happen, let alone affect the course of the birth.

THE DIFFERENCE RACE, ETHNICITY, AND CLASS MADE

Women who learned about methods of anesthesia administration or
whose friends and family helped them negotiate with the attending
physician about what steps could or should be taken next in the delivery
process tended to be, as I have mentioned, middle- and upper-status and
often urban women. Their birth experience is the one chronicled even in
current scholarship on the history of women's health and health care.
We are just beginning to understand something of how women of color,
foreign-born women, and those not wealthy enough to call in a physician
to attend them thought about and managed their childbirths.

Slavewomen were often cultivated as breeders by slaveholders in the
latter eighteenth and nineteenth centuries, and as such were encouraged
in frequent pregnancies. Births took place in their quarters with friends,

---

[25] Seventeenth-century women saw God's plan, His judgement, in the outcomes of a
   childbirth, even though they also called upon midwives whom they expected would
   ease the pain and help them through the hard work of travail. Such help might call for
   repositioning a fetus so it could make its way into the world, if the midwife were skilled,
   but help did not call for active interference or intervention in the process of birth.

[26] Leavitt, *Brought to Bed*, p. 107.

family, and neighbors helping out while the midwife oversaw the event. Though particular superstitions and beliefs about the best way to negotiate a pregnancy and birth might differ from their northern sisters— their basis was in African heritage, after all—the childbirth itself did not. Midwives were usually the most skilled among the many women on a plantation who knew about birth, and they were regularly called upon to attend not only other bondswomen, but also the plantation owner's wife and other local white women.[27] After slavery, these "grannies," as lay midwives were usually called in the South, continued to serve as the main childbirth attendants for women of color and not infrequently for white women as well. As spiritual as well as medical advisors, these lay attendants helped to maintain the traditional nature of childbirth in African-American communities throughout the South.[28] Well into the twentieth century—at first because they could not afford and/or did not wish to have medical help at their births, and later because they were not permitted to enter white hospitals even if they might have chosen to do so—African-American women of the South continued to give birth in traditional ways. In those ways, it is important to note, they fared as well or better than their medically attended white sisters.[29]

Childbirth retained much of its traditional aspect during the nineteenth and into the twentieth century in areas of the country other than the South, and among groups other than African-Americans. In Utah, for example, male doctors were frowned upon as childbed attendants among Mormons; Mormon women relied upon midwives until the close of the nineteenth century when the Church began to sponsor women to attend women's medical colleges in the East.[30] Women traveling West worked to create a comfortable birthing situation for themselves, one that included whatever women were in the traveling group as well as any close enough to be called.[31] Immigrant groups, both in cities and in rural

---

[27] Norton, *Liberty's Daughters*, pp. 31, 78–84; Deborah Gray White, *Ar'n't I a Woman?, Female Slaves in the Plantation South* (New York: W. W. Norton, 1987), pp. 94–118; 67–69.

[28] Linda Janet Holmes, "African American Midwives in the South," in Eakins, ed., *The American Way of Birth*, pp. 273–91.

[29] Neal Devitt, "The Statistical Case for the Elimination of the Midwife: Fact versus Prejudice, 1890–1935, (Part I)" *Women and Health* 2 (Spring, 1979): 169–79.

[30] Blanche E. Rose, "Early Utah Medical Practice," *Utah Historical Quarterly* 10 (1942): 14–32; Chris Rigby Arrington, "Pioneer Midwives," in Claudia Bushman, ed. *Mormon Sisters: Women in Early Utah* (Cambridge, MA: Emmaline Press, 1976), pp. 42–65.

[31] John Mack Faragher, *Women and Men on the Overland Trail* (New Haven: Yale University Press), pp. 139–40.

areas, arranged childbirth in as traditional ways as they were able. When rural women were able to find a countrywoman who was a midwife, they called her along with other countrywomen. Often, when family was far away, women had to settle for a neighbor or neighbors, or give birth alone. As the number of physicians grew during the nineteenth century and into the twentieth, they, too, were increasingly called in by rural women.

Both rural and urban immigrant women, however, often insisted on midwives. Custom—and not infrequently husbands—dictated female attendance at birth.[32] As especially Southern and Eastern European immigrant groups swelled the populations of many cities in the closing decades of the nineteenth and opening decade of the twentieth centuries, the number and availability of midwives increased. Despite immigrant midwives' often medical or midwifery training in European schools, and a record of success at least as good and often better than physicians' from one city to another, however, their availability did not last long. Pressure against these independent midwives from a growing urban reform and public-health movement and from a group of medical men determined to see obstetrics become a medical area whose practitioners could survive both financially and professionally, spelled the eventual elimination of the midwife from even urban immigrant women's bedsides. By the 1920s, independent midwives were a minor presence in all but the rural South. Women who might have called themselves midwives in an earlier day still attended women at home during birth, but they typically worked with a local physician.[33]

Certainly not all the immigrant and urban poor called upon independent or trained midwives during the nineteenth and into the twentieth century. Many gave birth with only family members and perhaps a neighbor present; many called upon whatever midwife or other helper they could afford or could find once labor began. Some gave birth alone. For the poor, and especially for the unmarried poor, finding help for

---

[32] Eugene Declerq, "The Nature and Style of Practice of Immigrant Midwives in Early Twentieth Century Massachusetts," *Journal of Social History* 19 (1985): 118; Elizabeth Ewen, *Immigrant Women in the Land of Dollars: Life and Culture on the Lower East Side, 1890–1905* (New York: Monthly Review Press, 1985), p. 131; Frances Kobrin, "The American Midwife Controversy: A Crisis of Professionalization," *Bulletin of the History of Medicine* 40 (1966): 354.

[33] Judy Barrett Litoff, *American Midwives, 1860 to the Present* (Westport, CT: Greenwood Press, 1978), p. 113; Neal Devitt, "The Statistical Case for the Elimination of the Midwife: Fact versus Prejudice, 1890–1935 (Part II)," p. 84; Declerq, "The Nature and Style of Practice," p. 125.

their childbirths could be a problem. Beginning in the first few decades of the nineteenth century, the married poor could sometimes find refuge in a lying-in hospital or secure assistance in their homes through the hospital's outpatient service; the unmarried poor were frequently fired if they became pregnant, stigmatized by prevailing moral codes as degraded or depraved, and forced to resort to the local almshouse. During the nineteenth century and into the twentieth, the number of hospitals and dispensaries grew as did the range of services they offered, the number of physicians and medical schools increased, and poor women living in or coming to cities to give birth enjoyed a better chance to secure help. Their need was often a boon to physicians and medical students whose need was "clinical material" that they could teach with, observe, and on which they could practice.[34]

CHILDBIRTH IN THE TWENTIETH CENTURY

For American women, twentieth-century childbirth has been largely an experience of increasing medicalization, hospitalization, and aliena- tion. Begun in the last century as physicians came more and more to be identified with normal and not just abnormal childbirths, childbirth's medicalizing continued and gathered momentum during the twentieth century's teens and twenties. Women were increasingly convinced by the assertions of social reformers that maternal and infant mortality were unacceptably high and could be lowered by taking advantage of medical attention during pregnancy and even by being hospitalized for childbirth. Reformers' urgings fit nicely into the efforts of obstetricians to gain recognition for their own work as worthy of specialty status within the medical profession. One of the ways obstetricians accomplished their goals was to press for the relegation of midwives to only the least accessible areas of the country and to the least valued segments of the population. Using both medical arguments and legal means, they saw to the rapid loss of midwife acceptability and availability among women for

---

[34] Virginia G. Drachman, "The Loomis Trial: Social Mores and Obstetrics in the Mid- Nineteenth Century," in Susan Reverby and David Rosner, eds. *Health Care In Amer- ica, Essays in Social History* (Philadelphia: Temple University Press, 1979), pp. 67–83; Nancy Schrom Dye, "Modern Obstetrics and Working-Class Women: The New York Midwifery Dispensary, 1890–1920," *Journal of Social History* 20 (Spring, 1987): 550, 556; Virginia A. Metaxsas Quiroga, "Female Lay Managers and Scientific Pediatrics at Nursery and Child's Hospital, 1854–1910," *Bulletin of the History of Medicine* 60 (1986): 197.

whom the midwife would formerly have been the attendant of choice. Midwives who did continue attending women in the twentieth century did so less and less openly as efforts to eliminate them from childbirth attendance gathered steam in the century's teens.[35] By the 1920s, childbirth had moved rather fully into the realm of disease, of pathology. For the next half century, pregnant and childbearing women would see themselves increasingly as medical patients whose chances for a safe birth were enhanced by the modern and the technological.

Hospitalization for childbirth increased from the 1920s onward as it became an attractive choice for a widening array of women.[36] Hospitals promised a safer and easier birth. Physicians could offer this safety and competence only in the hospital setting, they maintained, because only the hospital could provide the equipment and trained staff required. Leavitt describes how growing numbers, first of urban and then other middle- and upper-class women, turned to hospital birth as they became convinced that it was safer, on the one hand, and as they found it more and more difficult to arrange for a safe, convenient, and restful childbirth at home, on the other.[37] Childbirth was becoming a special event in the lives of most Americans and their families, as women gave birth less and less often.[38] Poor women who were unable to mount the expense of

---

[35] On the medicalization of childbirth, see Nancy Schrom Dye, "The Medicalization of Birth," in Eakins, ed. *The American Way of Birth*, pp. 33–43; on the elimination of midwives, see Kobrin, "A Crisis of Professionalization," and Devitt, "The Statistical Case for the Elimination of the Midwife," pp. 88–93.

[36] In 1935, 36.9% of births in America took place in a hospital; in 1950, it was 88%; by 1960, it was 96.9%. Neal Devitt, "The Transition from Home to Hospital Birth in the United States, 1930–1960," *Birth and the Family Journal* 4 (Summer, 1977): 47, 56.

[37] Leavitt, *Brought to Bed*, pp. 171–95. On the movement of childbirth into the hospital, see also Wertz and Wertz, *Lying-In*, pp. 132–77.

[38] The total fertility rate (or TFR—number of children born to a woman experiencing the average fertility for each year of her reproductive life) for white women fell from about 7 in 1800 to about 3.5 in 1900. It continued to fall during the first forty years of the twentieth century, to close to 2 births per woman in 1940. After the baby-boom years, 1946 to the early 1960s during which time the total fertility rate reached the level of 1900, 3.5, the rate declined again to its present rate of 1.9, below replacement level (2.1). Coale and Zelnick, *New Estimates of Fertility*, p. 36; Population Reference Bureau, *1989 World Population Data Sheet*.

Figures for nonwhites have been collected only since World War I and are available from 1920 onwards. Both TFRs follow similar paths, although the nonwhite TFR is consistently higher than the white rate. In 1920, for example, the rate among whites was 3.22; among nonwhites, 3.56; in 1960, the white TFR was 3.51, the nonwhite 4.24. In 1979, rates were 1.76 and 2.40. See "Fertility Tables for Birth Cohorts by Color: United States, 1917–1973," U.S. Department of Health, Education, and Welfare, National Center for Health Statistics, Rockville, MD, April, 1976; *Statistical Abstract of the United States*, 103rd Edition, Bureau of the Census, U.S. Department of Commerce, 1983.

a physician-attended hospital birth had access to the growing number of hospitals and wards attended by medical students-in-training or resident interns. The poor continued to be clinical material. Other women might engage one of the dwindling number of midwives resident in both urban and rural areas who were less likely than physicians to require payment at time of service and who would often take in-kind payment.

Mystification of childbirth deepened as the hospital rather than the home became its normal locus. Though childbirth had already become a mystery to women in many of its aspects by the 1920s, removing it from women's homes, as Judy Leavitt points out, took from women any say or control they had had over the conduct of birth in their domestic sphere. In the hospital they abrogated any semblance of control: "they put themselves . . . in the hands of obstetricians and medical institutions, . . . [and] their faith and their bodies . . . into the hands of science."[39] Women accepted the science claim of medical professionals and the medical claim of their physician attendants and later obstetricians: birth was a mystery of science inscrutable except to the medically trained. In exchange for their faith and trust, women felt that they suffered little at birth and enjoyed the safest childbirth possible. That probably neither of these beliefs was true is suggested by a variety of statistical compilations and studies of the issue over the course of this century.[40]

Signs of dissatisfaction with hospital childbirth and with predominantly male medical definition and control of the childbirth experience began to appear soon after the hospital became the usual site for giving birth. By the forties and fifties women were regularly expressing dismay at being so removed from their own births. Strapped down and drugged during labor and again during delivery, women awoke from childbirth with little or no memory of the experience. Looking for alternatives to this often alienating birth experience, women turned to European models of birth which suggested childbirth should be anticipated with joy, not fear, and could be accomplished with less pain, less drugging, and less of the medical and surgical management that had become characteristic of birth in American hospitals. In the late 1950s and early 1960s women turned to the natural-birth relaxation method advocated by Britisher Grantley Dick-Read, and later to the more active psychopro-

---

[39] Leavitt, *Brought to Bed*, p. 173.
[40] Bogdan, "Intervention and Mortality"; Devitt, "The Statistical Case for the Elimination of the Midwife"; Leavitt, *Brought to Bed*.

phylaxis of Ferdinand Lamaze's "prepared" childbirth during which women could expect to be "awake and aware."[41]

Women's efforts to reduce medical and technological control over their births by preparing themselves for a more active part have not proven transformative, however. These efforts to experience birth as less of a pathological process are occurring just while the technologies surrounding this life beginning event—from pre-pregnancy genetic and fertility counseling of the potential parents to the care of the high risk newborn—are expanding at a dizzying rate. Women's wish to gain some say in our own childbirths, to have access to the "natural" aspects of this basically normal process, then, is coming at a time when the medical perspective claims increasing access to the possible pathological pathways a childbirth might take. In the renewed resistance to what Adrienne Rich has called the "Theft of Childbirth," however, women have begun to question whether our own interests are being fairly represented in the quest for a safer birth—whether, in fact, our interests are represented at all. Women are seeking alternative paths to a safe and meaningful childbirth, some by negotiating less obtrusively managed medical births in hospital birthing rooms or birthing centers, others by choosing non-medical births at home or with lay midwives, and still others by re-examining the bases upon which the scientific understanding of birth rests. Such attempts to understand childbirth in ways new to American women of the 1980s, ways based on different combinations of medical knowledge and women's experience than were available in the past, may hopefully lead to a childbirth tradition that addresses the needs of all parties to a birth, whatever their social location, their expectations, and the specifics of their particular childbirth.[42]

---

[41] Wertz and Wertz, Lying-In, pp. 179–89; Leavitt, Brought to Bed, pp. 190–95; Barbara Katz Rothman, In Labor, Women and Power in the Birthplace (New York: W. W. Norton, 1982), pp. 30–32; and Shelly Romalis, "Natural Childbirth and the Reluctant Physician," in Shelly Romalis, ed., Childbirth: Alternatives to Medical Control (Austin, Texas: University of Texas Press, 1981), p. 86.

[42] Adrienne Rich, "The Theft of Childbirth," New York Review of Books, October 2, 1975.

• • • —————— • • •

5

RACE AS A FACTOR IN HEALTH

Edward H. Beardsley

One January morning in 1939 public health nurse Mattie Ingraham prepared to make the rounds of her black maternity clients in South Carolina's poor, rural Beaufort County. For Ingraham, a white, it would be a typical day. She would see seven of her regular patients, five of whom were in serious difficulty. Their problems, taken together, were a testament to the sad fortunes of Southern black women.

Sara was the first of the five. Her pregnancy was complicated by syphilis. Though Ingraham had referred her to a nearby clinic, Sara had missed several treatments because she did not like how the "shots" affected her. Susie, the second patient, also had syphilis, plus a kidney infection and high blood pressure. She had already had three stillbirths, and Ingraham feared that this time Susie herself might be a casualty. The third patient, Rosa, showed no complications yet, but she was unmarried and too young to be bearing a child. Her own mother had recently given birth, but that baby had died. Knowing Rosa's need for infant clothing, Ingraham urged her to use the little brother's garments. But Rosa refused, fearing that a dead child's clothing would bring her baby bad luck.

In the next cabin was Sadie, another unmarried juvenile. Sadie was facing her delivery virtually alone and without resources: her mother was severely ill, the mother's husband had a bad eye infection, and there was neither work nor government relief in sight. Finally, there was Rosalie, who had safely delivered her infant. But Rosalie was slovenly, her cabin was filthy, and the month-old child had already developed rickets. To Ingraham's despair, Rosalie had stopped giving her baby cod-liver oil because neighbors told her that the infant had already had too much.[1]

There were many reasons for the unpromising condition of the women on Ingraham's list—and of black women generally in the early twentieth century (about 75 percent of whom still lived in the South in 1940). First and foremost, Ingraham's patients were poor, which meant that they could not afford needed food or medical attention. Ingraham's work reflected government efforts to offer a public substitute for fee-for-service medicine, but such programs were a recent development and as late as 1940 met only the merest fraction of need. There were steps that poor women like Sara and Rosalie could take on their own to safeguard health, but a lack of education—often of literacy—prevented them from knowing of such possibilities (and often encouraged their opposite). Given the unsanitary, overcrowded conditions in which they lived, it was questionable if they could have effectively applied preventive knowledge in any case.

But to explain ill health of black women merely on the basis of economic and social deficits would be to miss its underlying cause. That cause was racism—and the segregation and discrimination that it invoked, not just in the South but wherever blacks took up substantial residence.

Although black women's health problems had some ties to their status as females (and bearers of children), in matters of health their racial status was a far greater determinant than their gender. In racist America, their blackness was their primary identification, subjecting them, the same as their men, to all the beliefs and practices of white supremacy. The consequences for health were as corrosive as they were inevitable. In the early 1900s, the view still had currency among educated Southerners that black women (and men) were psychologically and constitutionally unfit for freedom. Biologically speaking this meant that blacks were doomed to extinction. As a result, public health and medical expenditures on their behalf were deemed a waste of resources.[2] Among those who doubted the doomsday theory, it was "evident" that black people lived lives of such profligacy that applications of modern medicine would be likewise wasted. Later, as it became clear that the

---

[1] "The County Health Nurse," S.C. Writers' Project, file A-3-15, Jan. 31, 1939, South Caroliniana Library, Columbia.

[2] A discussion of the idea that the black race was dying out is found in James Jones, *Bad Blood: The Tuskegee Syphilis Experiment* (New York: Free Press, 1981), pp. 19–29.

black race was not dying out but multiplying, their very fertility became an argument—perhaps an unconscious one—for denying black women (and their infants) better maternal and obstetrical care. Otherwise they would overwhelm the "superior" race. For those public leaders who did not subscribe to racist beliefs and who were not unwilling to support measures of uplift in education, health, and employment, their political need to placate a harshly racist white public that saw blacks in simple demonic terms had the effect of strangling such altruism before it could draw breath.

Even after racism itself fell from fashion, thanks to the civil rights victories of the 1960s, its hard residue—poverty, lack of education, poor housing, and black feelings of powerlessness—would continue to shape the lives of many black women (and men). As a result, they would fail to realize the health gains that other, better-placed black females were enjoying by the 1960s.[3]

When one examines the relationship between racism and black female health in more detail, it becomes clear that for the twentieth century that history divided into three distinct epochs. First came the "era of denial," spanning the years 1900 to 1930. Those were the decades when racism had its harshest impact, not just in denying black women health care but also in locking a great proportion of them in positions of permanent disadvantage, long after the burden of racism had eased. Even while racism held sway, the "era of denial" gave way to an "era of inclusion," which extended from about 1930 to 1960. This was the period when Roosevelt's New Deal and later Truman's Fair Deal made available to poor whites and blacks of both sexes a striking variety and quantity of new health services. Though still delivered in segregated settings, services were now more equally distributed across racial lines than ever before. Finally, the most recent decades have seen black female health history enter a new phase, the "era of attempted restitution." Born out of the momentum of the civil rights movement and a renewed

---

[3] The black population, on average, has made substantial progress since the early twentieth century in terms of mortality reduction. For example, the general mortality rate among black females fell from 2,440 deaths per 100,000 of population in 1900 to 947 in 1960, a drop far greater than among white women, whose mortality fell by only 1,018 points. One disturbing note, however, was black women's slower relative progress: in 1900 their rate was 49 percent above white women, but by 1960 it was 54 percent higher. Two standard sources for data on black life expectancy and mortality are Robert Grove and Alice Hetzel, *Vital Statistics Rates in the United States, 1940–1960* (New York: Arno Press, 1976) and Bureau of the Census, *Vital Statistics Rates in the United States, 1900–1940* (Washington, D.C., 1943).

commitment to the "social gospel" on the part of many whites, the third era saw an abandonment of medical segregation and a national determination to close the health gap between the races. That the latter goal was not achieved was less a sign of failed commitment than of the depth and complexity of problems.

THE ERA OF DENIAL, 1900–1930

At the start of the century, white Americans' desire to improve the lives of black Americans—women and men—was virtually nonexistent. In part this was due to the popularity of the race-suicide idea (noted above), which owed its standing to an 1897 book, *Race Traits and Tendencies of the American Negro*, by insurance statistician F. L. Hoffman. Hoffman saw black vitality as *the* crucial aspect of the "Negro problem" and argued that of all races blacks showed the least ability to compete in the struggle for existence.[4] The bulk of Southern physicians, as well as many sociologists and others who studied the "Negro problem," agreed with him and doubted the wisdom of even trying to keep black women (and men) alive.

On the other hand, most of the South's public physicians came to doubt that dire forecast and tended to take a more environmentalist view of blacks' prospects. At a 1914 American Public Health Association meeting held in the South, Georgia health-officer William Brummer spoke for most of his colleagues when he said that while the Negro "is not a white man painted black . . . neither is he incapable of improvement over his present position." In fact, he said, "it would be just the same . . . with the white race if they lived in the same environment."[5] Though most public physicians were absolutely convinced of blacks' inherent shiftlessness, low intelligence, and love of carnal pleasure, they also agreed that with proper health education and training, black mortality rates could be lowered.

But such a plan was costly, and in the early twentieth century Southern legislatures were barely willing to spend tax dollars to protect the health of whites. Also, to have made special efforts to rid blacks of disease—even if that would have safeguarded whites—would have raised dark fears among white supremacists. As Columbia University econo-

---

[4] F. L. Hoffman, *Race Traits and Tendencies of the American Negro* (New York: Macmillan, 1896), pp. 148, 328.

[5] William Brummer, "The Negro Health Problem in Southern Cities," *American Journal of Public Health* 5 (March 1915): 188–89.

mist Frank Tannenbaum put it in the 1920s, whites were so fearful of being outbred by the more prolific blacks that "there would immediately arise . . . [a] pressure of public sentiment against any program . . . which would . . . cut down the death rate of the negro also."[6] Thus, until the 1930s and large federal health grants, blacks could count on little help from public health agencies.

In consequence, the great majority of black women in the North and in the South endured serious and multiple problems, many of them related to maternity. To begin with, black women got little care, professional or otherwise, during pregnancy. That was partly because care was largely unavailable. Even in the early 1900s white and black doctors practiced mostly in cities. Where access was not a barrier, money usually was, for black doctors expected to be paid just like white doctors. As a result, many black women dispensed with professional care, and partly in consequence they and their babies died in alarming numbers.

The greatest danger came at delivery. Following a long tradition reinforced by poverty, Southern black women commonly used midwives as birth-attendants, and the dangers were often great. No state effectively regulated its midwives until after World War II, and many of those birth-attendants, though surely well meaning, were not only ignorant of sanitary practice but lacked the competence to handle even minor problems. One Southern health officer lamented that tetanus, convulsions, hives, and colds appeared with disturbing frequency on infant death certificates filed by midwives.[7] But doctors were not the only ones to worry. Black women did, too. A 1920s Texas survey of black and Mexican-American women who used midwives found that many of the new mothers were also concerned about their attendants' lack of skills.[8]

In the rare event that a Southern black woman had a hospital delivery (as late as 1949 only 30 percent of them did), there was no assurance of safety. The hospital was nearly always a black-owned facility, which usually meant poor equipment and a less-than-efficient staff. In the early 1930s Northern black physician M. O. Bousfield inspected a number of Southern black hospitals. He found them less than adequate,

---

6   Quoted in Tannenbaum, "Race Theory and Negro Mortality," *Opportunity* 2 (March, 1924): 132.
7   C. E. Terry, "The Negro as a Public Health Problem," *Southern Medical Journal* 7 (1914): 461.
8   Judy Litoff, *The American Midwife Debate. Sourcebook on Modern Origins* (Westport, CT: Greenwood Press, 1986).

calling the Jacksonville, Florida, hospital "a dreary place to contemplate from the medical point of view."[9]

If blacks had to endure primitive conditions, it was not because better facilities did not exist. They did at many white hospitals, but segregation dictated that blacks could not use them. South Carolina black doctor L. W. Long recalled that as late as 1930 a white hospital might admit a black patient for emergency surgery, but he or she was sent home immediately afterwards, sometimes while still under anesthesia.[10] In the 1930s public hospitals in the South started admitting black patients to specially constructed segregated wards. But those quarters were only a little better, medically, than the black hospitals to which they were supposedly a "separate-but-equal" alternative. Also if the patient's physician was black, the latter could not enter the hospital but had to turn over his patient to a white doctor (often an intern). One rule of America's caste system was that to enjoy hospital privileges (or be appointed to medical boards and commissions), a physician must be a member of the local AMA affiliate. But until the 1930s in the North and the 1950s in the South, those societies were closed to black professionals.[11]

Problems of maternity were only the start of the black woman's troubled health odyssey—whether in North or South. A major killer of all blacks up to World War II was tuberculosis (TB), and though it generally struck more savagely at men than women, black females aged 15 to 34 had the highest mortality of all. Moreover, the disease infected black women four to five times more often than white.[12] Part of the reason was racial: having encountered the disease only when they encountered whites in the seventeenth century, black women and men had less resistance to TB and tended to fall prey to its deadliest form, miliary TB or "galloping consumption."[13]

---

9   M. O. Bousfield to Peter Marshall Murray, c. June, 1932, box 5, Peter Marshall Murray Papers, Moorland-Spingarn Research Center, Howard University. For data on the use of hospitals by black expectant mothers, see Edward H. Beardsley, *A History of Neglect. Health Care for Blacks and Mill Workers in the Twentieth Century South* (Knoxville: University of Tennessee Press, 1987), p. 287.
10 Beardsley, *A History of Neglect*, p. 36.
11 Ibid., pp. 79–80.
12 All comparisons of mortality by race are based on 1940 rates, drawn from Grove and Hetzel, *Vital Statistics Rates*. For TB see pp. 381–82.
13 For a discussion of black susceptibility to TB see Todd L. Savitt, *Medicine and Slavery: The Diseases and Health Care of Blacks in Antebellum Virginia* (Urbana: University of Illinois Press, 1978), pp. 42–43.

Although there would be no chemotherapy for TB until the 1950s, there was one sure, if drawn-out, cure in sanatorium care—but once again racism denied blacks equal access to it. In South Carolina a black sanatorium was not opened until five years after the white, and blacks had to raise part of its cost. Moreover, when Carolina blacks did begin to get attention, they got only a fraction of the number of beds needed. Even white children had more beds than black adults.[14]

That racism underlay such neglect was clearly apparent from one Georgia episode. In 1940 its state health officer tried to put ill-housed black patients on the unused top floor of the white sanatorium. But Governor Ellis Arnall vetoed the idea, even though whites would have no contact with or even see the blacks. Any mixing, Arnall argued, would be an awful mistake, for it would "play into the hands of those who would like to discredit our health work. . . ."[15]

Venereal disease was another major problem for black females, especially because of its contribution to morbidity. Syphilis particularly burdened the childbearing years, when rates climbed to fifteen times those of white women. Often black women were unknowing victims of diseased men, but the real innocents were the thousands of black fetuses who died each year as a result of the mother's infection.[16]

Death seldom occurred from gonorrhea, but morbidity among black women ranged up to five times that for syphilis. And if it did not take their lives, it often rendered them sterile. One surprising demographic trend of the 1867 to 1935 era was the sharp drop in black fertility, a decline far more precipitous than for whites. Historians differ over its chief cause, but gonorrhea was one likely culprit, as were deficient diets (causing a malformed pelvis) and unsanitary deliveries, which caused a high rate of puerperal infections.[17]

---

[14] Beardsley, A History of Neglect, pp. 14 and 136. The annual reports of the various state boards of health are a good source for year-to-year statistics on health problems of Southern blacks (especially TB). For example, see Annual Report, South Carolina Board of Health (1919), p. 73.

[15] Ellis Arnall to T. F. Abercrombie, Dec. 5, 1944, and Abercrombie to Arnall, Dec. 7, 1944, "Governor" file, box 27, Director's General Administrative Records, Georgia Board of Health Papers. This and other state archives contain a fund of primary information on public health work in the various states.

[16] Grove and Hetzel, Vital Statistics Rates, pp. 391–92.

[17] Reynolds Farley, Growth of the Black Population: A Study in Demographic Trends (Chicago: Markham Publishing Co., 1970), pp. 3–5; Phillips Cutright and Edward Shorter, "The Effects of Health on the Completed Fertility of Non-white and White U.S. Women from 1862 Through 1935," Journal of Social History 13 (1979): 191–97.

Another scourge of American black women that also contributed to high morbidity—and to death from other causes—was diabetes mellitus. Pre-1940 data are scanty, but current knowledge suggests that diabetes was a serious illness then, especially for women over 50. Today, black (as opposed to white) women have a major problem with diabetes because of their greater obesity. Assuming similar weight problems seventy-five years ago, black women, then, would have battled not only diabetes but all of its known sequela: blindness, heart disease, stroke, and kidney disease.[18]

Cardiovascular and renal diseases were by 1900 among the greatest killers of blacks. Though whites, too, had a high mortality from CVR diseases, the racial differential was staggering, as black women died four times more often than white. Obesity, stress, and poor diet were key causes, and contributing to them all was the ever-present factor of caste.[19]

Though it would not loom large in the mortality rolls until the mid-1920s, cancer quickly became another special cross for black women. Although females aged 35–54 of both races had a higher cancer mortality than males, black women again had the greater problem, dying more than twice as often as white women.[20]

Finally, there was the high rate of black female deaths from causes loosely labelled (in the pre-World War II era) as "ill-defined conditions." The Census Bureau category for unknown causes of death, it reflected the lack of physician care during final illness—perhaps the ultimate measure of medical deprivation. From this "cause" black females perished five or six times more often than white, and as late as 1940 "unknown causes" ranked even ahead of cancer as a leading cause of death among black women.[21]

It was such statistics that led black physician M. O. Bousfield to demand an accounting from the white health establishment. In 1934 Bousfield, director of Negro health for the Julius Rosenwald Fund, addressed the annual meeting of the American Public Health Association. In blunt language he asserted that one reason why black people

---

[18] Grove and Hetzel, *Vital Statistics Rates*, pp. 439–40; for relationships between obesity, diabetes, and other diseases see Alvin and Sandra Headen, "General Health Conditions and Medical Insurance Issues Concerning Black Women," *Review of Black Political Economy* 14 (1985–86): 189–90.

[19] Grove and Hetzel, *Vital Statistics Rates*, pp. 443–45.

[20] Ibid., pp. 396–97.

[21] Ibid., pp. 522–23.

were dying at high rates from mostly preventable illnesses was because American health officials simply did not know what the conditions were among black people. Partly, he conceded, ignorance was due to a lack of funds to mount programs among blacks. But racism was mostly to blame. It was inconceivable, Bousfield said, that any other factor could explain why health officers could "so complacently review, year after year, the unfavorable vital statistical reports of one-tenth of the population and make no special effort to correct [them]."[22]

One Southern state, whose record in preventive health work among blacks was not only typical but bore out Bousfield's analysis, was South Carolina. From 1908, when health work was put on a permanent footing, until the start of New Deal health funding, South Carolina did almost nothing to address the special health problems of its sizeable black population. Much blame could be levelled at state lawmakers, who had little interest in supporting such work. But equal fault surely lay on the shoulders of the state's public health establishment, and in the pre-World War II era that chiefly meant state health-officer James A. Hayne.

Hayne, who took charge in 1911, was a product of a South Carolina upbringing and education. He was also a typical representative of the white culture. That was not to say that he was a racist on the lines of Dixie political demogogues, but he was a white supremacist. To him the sick Negro, whom he blamed for the state's poor showing in the vital statistics, was an embarrassment, not a challenge. When he addressed racially identifiable problems, such as TB, it was largely to protect whites. He once confided to a national health meeting that "in my state 80 percent of the colored population are attended by midwives," which was "bad enough." Even worse was that "20 percent of the white population are also attended by the dirty, ignorant midwives."[23]

Hayne's bias was more apparent in his argument for state funding for malaria eradication. The seldom-fatal disease struck blacks two to four times as often as whites, but Hayne was interested only in the benefits of malaria control for the latter. One area of infestation was the state's heavily black coastal lowland. To Hayne, malaria had made that region unattractive to whites, but if it were curbed, "many Counties . . . which are now given over to negroes and negro tenants will be occupied by white people and the fertile soil of these counties properly utilized."[24]

---

[22] M. O. Bousfield, "Reaching the Negro Community," *American Journal of Public Health* 24 (1934): 209–15. This is an important source for understanding the subtle ways that racism affected the health of black people.

[23] Beardsley, *A History of Neglect*, pp. 142–43.

[24] Ibid., p. 143; also p. 19.

If state health agencies like South Carolina's generally proved an unwilling source of help for black women, that did not mean that they were ignored everywhere. A few foundations, such as the Rockefeller Foundation, the Rosenwald Fund, and the Duke Endowment, helped black women on a large scale. For example, the Duke Endowment, started in 1926 by North Carolina utilities titan James B. Duke, invested millions in the improvement of white and black hospitals and hospital care in the two Carolinas.[25]

But black women were not just *objects* of benevolent white attention, nor just *victims* of an unjust social order. They were also *actors* in the struggle for health improvement. Beginning with the formation in 1896 of the National Association of Colored Women (NACW) and continuing with a myriad of local efforts, black women—most of them middle class—showed a talent for organization and an eagerness to uplift their race, along a broad front. As one of the most pressing and basic problems, ill health of black women and children attracted a large share of the attention and energy of such groups. In many ways black volunteer work paralleled that of white women (who had started a half-century or so earlier): it involved primarily the middle class, and it was concerned chiefly with preserving the values of home and family. But in key respects it was different. Whereas white women were responding primarily to problems of their own gender and class, black women were filled with a mission to better their whole race. Moreover, black middle-class activists focused on aiding the black underclass, while white clubwomen were somewhat indifferent to problems of poor whites. As one black female reformer put it, *her* sisters strove "in behalf of the many incompetent," while white women sought chiefly to advance "the already uplifted."[26]

Two illustrations of the reform work of black females were the Neighborhood Union of Atlanta and the health work of Dr. Matilda A.

---

[25] See ibid., p. 46. on the Duke Endowment.

[26] Paula Giddings, *When and Where I Enter: The Impact of Black Women on Race and Sex in America* (New York: William Morrow and Co., 1984), pp. 93–102, esp. p. 98. In the same vein is Jacqueline Jones, *Labor of Love, Labor of Sorrow: Black Women, Work, and the Family from Slavery to the Present* (New York: Basic Books, 1985), p. 190 looks at middle-class black volunteerism in Northern cities. An excellent discussion of white female volunteerism is found in Carl Degler, *At Odds: Women and the Family in America from the Revolution to the Present* (New York: Oxford University Press, 1981), pp. 298–327. Although not chronicles on volunteerism, histories of black nursing are useful for their multiple focus on racism, medical matters, professionalism, *and* women. Two valuable works are Mary E. Carnegie, *The Path We Tread: Blacks in Nursing, 1854–1984* (Philadelphia: J. B. Lippincott, 1986); and Darlene Clark Hine, *Black Women in the Nursing Profession: A Documentary History* (NY and London: Garland Publishing, 1985).

Evans of Columbia, South Carolina. The Atlanta project, begun in 1908, was the inspiration of Lugenia Hope, the wife of Atlanta University president John Hope. Focused primarily on the health needs of black women and children, this federation of sixteen neighborhood groups gave special attention to much-neglected school and home sanitation and to TB. By 1911 the Union had created a settlement house, modelled on Jane Addams' Hull House, and by 1916, a medical clinic for indigents. In later years the Union's program expanded to include home nursing and mobile clinics. By the 1920s the organization was touching the lives of nearly three-fourths of Atlanta's black population.[27]

By contrast, the efforts of physician Matilda Evans were mostly a one-woman show. Yet they met equally pressing needs. Settling in Columbia at the turn of the century, Evans first sought to fill the gap in black hospital care. The three institutions that she established in the next ten years served not only blacks of South Carolina but those from adjoining states as well. In 1930, following a failed effort to create a statewide home-nursing program and several years of private practice, she launched the project for which she is best remembered, a clinic for expectant mothers, infants, and children. Aided by black businessmen and, eventually, state and local governments, the Evans Clinic was soon treating hundreds of patients daily. Though it ended with Evans's death in 1935, it revealed such a huge unmet need that when federal health funds came available in 1936, local health agencies were eager to put such work on a permanent basis.[28]

Besides the conscious efforts of women like Hope and Evans and of groups like the NACW, there was another, unintentional sort of self-help activity which advanced the health of millions of black women. That was the black migration to Northern cities, which began as a trickle around 1900 and swelled to a torrent by the end of World War I. Initially, and continuing until about 1930, rural blacks who went North experienced a decline in health (the one exception being expectant mothers, who registered a decline in mortality as early as 1920). For black infants, Northern death rates remained higher than Southern rural rates until about 1935.[29]

---

[27] On the Union see Gerda Lerner, "Early Community Work of Black Club Women," *Journal of Negro History* 59 (1974): 163; also *A History of Neglect*, pp. 104–5.

[28] Beardsley, *A History of Neglect*, pp. 83–85.

[29] Ibid., pp. 23–26. For a discussion of the overall impact of the Northward migration on black women see Jones, *Labor of Love, Labor of Sorrow*, chapter 5.

Reasons for the initial collapse in health were not hard to find. Like British industrial cities of the early 1800s, urban America in the early 1900s was not ready for the massive inflow of black migrants—or rather, the only ones ready were those white landlords, realtors, and others who benefitted from an unregulated immigration. One contemporary black physician noted that "just as soon as Negroes move into a neighborhood, . . . rents rise, promoting overcrowding, the sanitary standards are lowered, [and] garbage collections and street cleanings become fewer."[30] The shockingly high TB death rate among Northern black females was one measure (and result) of public neglect.

By 1930, however, Northern blacks were beginning to move ahead of their rural Southern cousins in mortality tables. Causes were multiple. For one thing there were more and better public health services to be found in Northern cities by then, as well as more black doctors. For their part black physicians found as many reasons to flee the South as their patients, so that by 1930 the black doctor-to-patient ratio in New York city was four times greater than that in South Carolina and Georgia (though it was just a fourth of New York's white ratio). Northern migrants were also better paid and housed by 1930, as illustrated by the higher average value of black residences in Philadelphia ($4,662), as compared to Columbia ($1,464).[31]

Another cause was the growing political power of Northern blacks—women and men—most of whom were voting for the first time. With the ballot came improvements in many areas, including health. The Harlem Hospital episode of the 1920s was instructive. A public facility with a black patient clientele, Harlem had at first an all-white professional staff. In the early 1920s, that arrangement was challenged by the addition of a black visiting physician and a black nurses' training school. Those changes raised a storm among white staff: some resigned and others began to express openly their contempt for their new colleagues.

The city's organized black doctors responded by charging white physicians with racism and blatant discrimination against black patients.

---

[30] Charles Garvin, "Negro Health," *Opportunity* 2 (1924): 341–42.

[31] Beardsley, *A History of Neglect*, pp. 26–28, 80–81. For a wealth of data on this and other socio-economic characteristics of black Americans in the early twentieth century, see Bureau of the Census, *Negroes in the United States, 1920–32* (Washington, D.C., 1935). Similar data from an earlier period (reaching back to the founding of the republic) is contained in Bureau of the Census, *Negro Population in the U.S., 1790–1915* (Washington, D.C., 1918).

Soon the issue erupted in the public press, forcing the city's Democratic machine—ever sensitive to new constituencies—to launch an inquiry. The upshot was the full integration of professional staff and administrative board, and the approval of plans for a major expansion, to permit the hospital to better care for the area's growing black population.[32]

THE ERA OF INCLUSION, 1930–1960

Such gains, however, were put in jeopardy by the onset of the Great Depression. By 1930, in every state, budget cuts had eliminated not just the remnants of earlier public health programs, but even basic protections, such as smallpox and typhoid immunizations. Hospitals also had to cut back, and those reductions fell most heavily on indigents. Eventually, the Depression even affected major private organizations, such as the Rockefeller Foundation and the Rosenwald Fund (which had supported the training of black doctors and nurses and helped get them on the staffs of Southern health agencies).[33]

Mounting black unemployment was the most disastrous consequence, for it threatened blacks' very survival. Whites lost jobs too, but black men and women (North and South) suffered most. Said a writer in *Opportunity*: blacks "are being forced off jobs to make places for unemployed whites . . . by intimidation, coercion, and murder."[34] In the rural South, blacks now lost what tenuous hold they had on the land: in one North Carolina county, by 1932, 42 percent of black tenant farmers had gone over two years without a cotton-growing contract.[35]

It was that sort of economic desperation that made New Deal relief programs a godsend to blacks, even though Southern states discriminated in the matter of wages. But work relief did more to promote health than furnish income. A basic belief of New Deal planners, expressed pointedly by relief-director Harry Hopkins, was that "conservation and maintenance of the public health is a primary function of government."[36] Thus, much relief went for projects designed to eliminate long-standing health risks and secure the nation's physical well-being. Federal Emergency Relief Administration funds paid to keep hospitals going, and when that proved too great a drain on resources, money was shifted

---

[32] Herbert Morais, *A History of the Afro-American in Medicine* (Cornwell Heights, PA: The Publisher's Agency, 1978), pp. 117–19.
[33] Beardsley, *A History of Neglect*, pp. 152–55.
[34] "Emergency Employment in Mississippi," *Opportunity* 10 (Oct., 1932): 3.
[35] "The New Deal and the Negro," Ibid 13 (July, 1935): 200–202.
[36] Quoted in Beardsley, *A History of Neglect*, p. 157.

to the hiring of black and white public health nurses, who addressed a multitude of problems. FERA, Civil Works Administration, and Public Works Administration money also went into malaria control. By World War II the South, the remaining infested area, had essentially banished that disease. Works Progress Administration school-lunch programs not only upgraded child stamina, but also gave jobs to food-service workers, a market to farmers, and a precedent for later food-supplement plans. Besides helping individuals, federal funds also put state and country boards of health back on their feet—to stay.[37]

But most relief projects were only meant to be a stop-gap. More important in terms of permanent health impact—especially in eliminating racial disparities—were New Deal reform measures. Among them the most far-reaching was the Social Security Act of 1935 (SS). Remembered chiefly for its aid to the elderly and unemployed, SS—with its shower of federal funds—also laid the foundation for the first truly national health program. But it did something else, particularly important to black women. It shifted health leadership from the states to Washington. For poor blacks and whites, that would prove crucial: there would now be an alternative (and augmented) source of health funding for such needs as nutrition and maternal and infant care, not tied to the race and class mentality of Southern state legislators, welfare directors, and even public health officers, who had often made race and social conformity preconditions for receiving health services.[38]

What SS meant for black women was best seen in the initiation of maternal and child-health services, provided by the thousands of prenatal, infant, and well-baby clinics set up after 1935—permanent clinics for urban areas and two-to-three-day travelling clinics for rural populations. Though open to both races (on a segregated basis), they became identified rather quickly in the South as Negro clinics, because black women took greater advantage of them. North Carolina's first clinics enrolled 11,000 black but only 2,000 white expectant mothers. Thereafter, the proportion of black patrons rose, attaining black-white ratios of ten or twelve to one by 1950. Actual numbers of black females seeking services grew too. By the early 1950s estimates were that virtually every expectant black woman in the South was making some use of

---

[37] Ibid., pp. 158–65.
[38] Roy Lubove, "The New Deal and National Health," *Current History* 72 (1977): 200, 225.

clinic services. Moreover, pregnant females were getting a higher quality of midwife care (thanks to new midwife licensing requirements) and getting that help earlier in their pregnancy.[39]

During World War II the federal health enterprise expanded beyond its base in SS to include a number of other programs benefitting black females. With the health of "American boys" at stake, there was a dramatic increase in funding for civilian VD work. Not only were there more treatment centers; by the end of the war, thanks to penicillin, that treatment was being reduced from many months to mere days, making it possible for the first time to hold patients in treatment programs.[40]

One war project aimed solely at women was the Emergency Maternal and Infant Care program (EMIC) of 1943, a response to the crowding of military families about the nation's training bases. Many of the women could not afford obstetric and pediatric services, and to avert a crisis, Congress voted massive funds to enable states to provide free hospital, maternal, and infant care to wives of servicemen in the first four pay grades. A side benefit was the upgrading of OB-GYN services, for local hospitals had to come up to standard to qualify for federal money. Black women were not singled out for help, but as their soldier-husbands were more concentrated in the lowest ranks, they enjoyed disproportionate assistance.[41]

EMIC (and the war) sparked one other federal initiative, the Hospital Survey and Construction Law (1946), popularly known as the Hill-Burton Act (H-B). Aimed at providing more hospitals and health clinics, H-B focused primarily on America's underserved rural areas. Requiring a two-to-one dollar match from the states (Southern states got off lighter), the law also made states survey their needs and set priorities before construction. By 1956, and the expenditure of hundreds of millions, H-B had made a difference, especially in the South. Of some 7,000 hospital projects (including additions to existing facilities), the South laid claim to half.[42]

H-B's one glaring defect was that it bolstered segregation, by allowing Southern states to build separate hospital wards for black patients—provided they got a proportional quantity of facilities, and services "of like quality." But if care was still segregated, at last in H-B facilities—

---

[39] Beardsley, A History of Neglect, pp. 167, 277.

[40] Ibid., pp. 173-4.

[41] Ibid., pp. 174-6; also James Conrad, "Health Services of the U.S. Children's Bureau, 1935-53," Ph.D. dissertation (Ohio State University, 1974): 99-114.

[42] Beardsley, A History of Neglect, pp. 177-84.

which comprised about one-third of all Southern hospitals—an attempt was made to apply it equally. A 1952 survey of H-B in Georgia reported that every facility served black patients and all offered a reasonable amount of indigent care.[43]

To say that black women were finally gaining access to primary medical services was not to say that they were moving forward on all fronts. Where Washington was not looking over the shoulders of those who controlled health services, it was business as usual. Thus, through the 1930s some white landlords charged black tenant families for food and other supplies meant to be free. Hard dealing was also done by public bodies. In 1936 Columbia's city council, without warning, fired a black physician hired in 1934 to care for black indigents. The council kept its two white doctors, however, even though both were over-worked. About the same time North Carolina required black domestics to furnish employers with medical proof that they had no contagious diseases. Raleigh's message was clear: if public care was unavailable, diseased black females would have to heal themselves.[44]

But the South had no monopoly on racism. Discrimination in the North was merely more subtle. At the end of World War II Chicago's 350,000 black citizens were still virtually shut out of the city's twelve private hospitals. Even black paying patients found only 315 general hospital beds open to them, near all provided by the city's two black-run hospitals and its one county facility. To satisfy minimum needs, a 1945 health survey found, black Chicagoans required 2,700 additional general beds, 1,800 of them for indigents.

When survey officials pressed private hospitals to reveal their actual admission policies, they all insisted that they did not discriminate, but none could prove it. One particularly dirty piece of business was the run-around given blacks with hospital insurance coverage. Their policies guaranteed full care in semiprivate rooms, but at the moment of admission, hospitals discovered that they only had private rooms free, thereby dodging guarantees and sending subscribers to the already crowded county hospital. Expectant black mothers were particularly victimized

---

[43] Ibid., pp. 178, 183–4, 257.

[44] Hewell Eason, "The Negro of North Carolina Forsakes the Land," *Opportunity* 14 (April, 1936): 116; Elaine Ellie, "Women of the Cotton Fields," *Crisis* 45 (Oct., 1938): 333; *Palmetto Leader* (May 16, 1936), p. 4; *Biennial Report of the North Carolina Board of Health* (1936–38), p. 57.

by Chicago racism: their own black hospitals often had no space for them, yet many maternity beds lay empty in white hospitals.[45]

Although public agencies were less apt to discriminate by this time, the racist mind-set was present there, too. In both North and South, blacks commonly complained of discourteous and demeaning treatment from white health staff, which led many to shy away from such agencies.[46]

Ironically, health setbacks also resulted when white professionals were "too good" to blacks. In 1956 Dr. Deborah Coggins, Florida's first female health officer, was fired by the Madison County commission for flaunting the race code. Her crime was to eat with a black woman in a public restaurant. The fact that her companion was one of her own field nurses did not matter. Nor did it matter that Coggins was beginning to address the serious health problems of poor black (and white) women. Although a number of influential moderates took her side, local commissioners, being political animals (and white supremacists), were more sensitive to *popular* feelings—and there was no doubt what those were. As one citizen told a hearing, "when we give one inch we are going to give the whole thing [away]. It's time to stand up and be white men, not jellybacks."[47]

THE ERA OF ATTEMPTED RESTITUTION

Episodes like the Coggins affair were best seen as rear-guard actions of a retreating white supremacy. Momentum was clearly on the side of race equality; and by 1970, owing to the successes of the civil rights movement, segregation and overt discrimination in health care had pretty much come to an end everywhere. Medical societies and schools were open to blacks, white doctors had removed "colored waiting room" signs, and local health agencies began to provide a quality of service indistinguishable by race—in part because a growing number of health professionals now had black faces, too.

But the major change was the integration of the nation's hospitals. This was the result not just of black citizen pressure but also of a key

---

[45] *The Chicago-Cook County Health Survey* (New York: Columbia University Press, 1949), pp. 612, 1076–78, 1082, 1106.

[46] Beardsley, A *History of Neglect*, p. 94.

[47] Quoted in Charlotte Downey-Anderson, "The Coggins Affair. Desegregation and Southern Mores in Madison County, Florida," *Florida History Quarterly* 59 (1980–81): 468; also see pp. 464–72.

1963 federal court case (closing the H-B segregation loophole), the 1964 Public Accommodations Act, and the 1965 Medicare Law, which mandated integration as the price of federal aid.[48]

With integration came major gains in black patient care. As noted above, that care had seldom been as good as white patients got. At one Southern hospital (an H-B facility), there was no X-ray equipment in the black wing. For X-ray examination or treatment, blacks not only had to be in serious condition but also had to be carried across an open court to the white wing.[49] Integration made such services routine. In addition, black cases now came under the review of the full hospital staff, not just one or two doctors of perhaps average-to-limited ability, as was often true in all-black hospitals or segregated wards. To enable the nation's poor to pay for that improved (but costly) care, Congress created Medicaid, whose aim was to give welfare clients the same high quality of care available to the affluent.[50]

But the new concern for health equality extended beyond the institutions of curative medicine. In 1967 it began to reach even into black homes. That year the nation was shocked to learn that ten million Americans, mostly blacks, but also many whites, Indians, and Latinos, were suffering from hunger and in many cases, clinical malnutrition. After months of denial by powerful Southern lawmakers and state health officers beholden to them, investigations proved that wide hunger did exist; and Congress, along with the U.S. Department of Agriculture, began to seek remedies. The USDA lowered the cash outlay for food-stamp purchase, Congress voted added millions for that program, and a nutritional project was begun for expectant mothers and children (WIC).[51]

Among sympathetic observers, hope rose that the health gap between white and black would soon be closed. But that did not happen: instead of closing in on white mortality and morbidity, by 1980 black progress had come to a halt, leaving black women with a death rate 60 percent above that of whites and black men with a rate 45 percent higher. For the 35 percent of blacks living near or below the poverty line, things were far worse.[52] Among that group, black women have

---

[48] Beardsley, A History of Neglect, chapter 11.

[49] Modjeska Simkins, interview, Oct. 10, 1978. Tape is available from the South Caroliniana Library, University of South Carolina.

[50] Beardsley, A History of Neglect, p. 271.

[51] Ibid, pp. 288–304. The standard and very solid history of the 1960s hunger issue is Nick Kotz, Let Them Eat Promises (Englewood Cliffs, NJ: Prentice Hall, 1969).

[52] Monroe Lerner and Odin Anderson, Health Progress in the US, 1900–60 (Chicago: University of Chicago Press, 1963), p. 121; Beardsley, A History of Neglect, p. 309.

borne the heaviest burden in recent decades, for they, far more often than black men, have been imprisoned in a trap of poverty. And as always, poverty lay at the base of many other causes of ill health: poor housing, bad nutrition, high levels of stress, little use of hospitals and doctors, and feelings of hopelessness and alienation that kept many black women from even trying to get help.[53]

Even had they tried, chances were that these black women, especially if they lived in the inner city, would have found few solutions. The urban medical establishment that had recently opened its arms to them was fast crumbling. Not only was its tax-base shrinking as whites departed for the suburbs but "white flight" also lured away physicians, leaving fewer and older doctors (plus deteriorating hospitals) increasingly unable to furnish the kind of quality services available in the suburbs.[54]

True, Medicaid was in place to provide at least second-rate services, but there were problems of diminishing returns there too, and not just for urban black women. Many states, including most in the South, set welfare cut-off levels so low that only a small percentage of those whom Medicaid aimed to help actually got free care. Moreover, Medicaid's fee schedule fell so far behind expected compensation that doctors of both races, in all parts of the country, increasingly rejected participation. For John Knowles of the Rockefeller Foundation, who had had high hopes for the program's viability, Medicaid proved an "abortion."[55]

If those problems were not enough, the lifestyle of many inner city black females put them at an added disadvantage. What handicapped them most was single parenthood. By the late 1970s around 30 percent of urban black families were headed by women. Some were alone because their husbands had died—one of every five black females (aged 45–54) was widowed, compared to only one of eleven whites—but most were raising children alone because their men had deserted or never

---

53 Selig Greenberg, *The Quality of Mercy. A Report on the Critical Condition of Hospital and Medical Care in America* (New York: Atheneum, 1971), pp. 115–16; Amara Ford, *Urban Health in America* (Oxford: Oxford University Press, 1976), pp. 103–4; Vern and Bonnie Bullough, *Poverty, Ethnic Identification, and Health Care* (New York: Appleton Century Crofts, 1972), pp. 54–56.

54 Eli Ginsburg et al., *Urban Health Services. The Case of New York* (New York: Columbia University Press, 1972), p. 103.

55 Beardsley, *A History of Neglect*, pp. 306–8; Dewey Gardner et al., "Factors Affecting Physician Participation in a State Medicaid Program," *Medical Care* 17 (Jan., 1979): 43–58; Knowles is quoted in Alex Gerber, *The Gerber Report. The Shocking State of American Medical Care* (New York: David McKay Co., 1971), p. 206.

married them.[56] And too many were teen mothers, with their own special health risks.

The net result of all those burdens was that the single black mother was often in bad health, more liable to heart disease, hypertension, and alcoholism than her married sister. And if medicaid was not available to help her, neither in many cases was private health insurance, as underwriters tended to look at the black mother's burdens and rate her as uninsurable.[57]

It was difficult to claim that racism underlay these later problems. After all, by 1987, 56 percent of black female and male wage-earners had made it to the middle class, a tribute to America's new openness, if not its change of heart. Yet if racism was not the explanation, its lingering effects clearly were, for the poorest third of black women (and men) had become so mired in the poverty and despair that were racism's legacy that no amount of civil rights legislation could free them. They were, in the words of British observer Godfrey Hodgson, "trapped without a ladder out of the flooded basement of American society."[58] In 1990, as in 1900, the challenge to that society (and to its white and black leaderships) remained the same: to help the nation's poorest blacks acquire the "ladders" needed to climb up to better life and health.

---

[56] "Motherhood in the Black Community," The Crisis 84 (Dec., 1977): 483; also Lerner and Anderson, Health Progress, p. 115.
[57] "Motherhood in the Black Community," p. 484.
[58] Godfrey Hodgson, America in Our Time (New York: Vintage Books, 1976), p. 462; also see "Black and White in America," Newsweek (Mar. 7, 1988), pp. 19–20.

ORTHODOX HEALTH CARE

6

HISTORICAL PERSPECTIVES ON WOMEN AND MENTAL ILLNESS

Nancy Tomes

The figure of the madwoman has had a perennial fascination for women, from the nineteenth-century novelists who used representations of the "madwoman in the attic" to explore their own pent-up feelings of rage and alienation, to the modern day feminists who see the female mental patient as the embodiment of what a sexist society does to assertive members of their sex. Feminists have linked madness and femininity, as Phyllis Chesler did in her ground-breaking 1972 book, *Women and Madness,* and Elaine Showalter reiterated recently by styling mental illness *The Female Malady* (1985). Critiques of male domination have often used the writings and experiences of talented women who struggled with mental illness, including Charlotte Perkins Gilman, Virginia Woolf, and Sylvia Plath, to explore the psychic costs of restrictive gender roles. In the realm of popular culture, films such as "Frances," which explored the actress Frances Farmer's tragic life, have dramatized the plight of women mental patients. More than any other medical specialty, psychiatry and psychiatric institutions have been the particular

Julia Epstein and Barbara Sicherman deserve a special acknowledgment for their helpful readings of an earlier draft of this paper. I would also like to thank Rima Apple, Joan Jacobs Brumberg, Gerald Grob, Allan Horwitz, Constance McGovern, and the members of the Rutgers University seminar on health care policy for their helpful comments. Finally, I would like to recall my participation in the Rutgers-Princeton Program in Mental Health Research (N.I.M.H. Grant PHS MH 16242) as an inspiration for my parallel reading of contemporary and historical trends.

target of feminist censure. In the burden of restrictive sex roles on the female spirit, the equation of female self-assertion with pathology, and the institutional abuse of women mental patients, feminists have seen the injustices of all women writ large.[1]

Yet, for all the heavy symbolic weight attached to the "madwoman," until very recently we have known little about the actual experiences of those women considered mentally ill by their society. Only in the last fifteen years have historians, literary critics, and social scientists systematically begun to study the influence of gender on the expression of and cultural response to emotional distress. Armed with new insights into the social definition of disease and the role of medical institutions in reinforcing larger social values, these scholars have challenged the conventional history of psychiatry as a value-free, gender-blind discipline. At the same time, their findings suggest the need to revise what might be termed the "Cheslerian thesis"—that is, the argument that a sexist society makes women more prone to mental illness and more likely to be committed to mental institutions than men—and also to pay more heed to class and other differences *among* women. This recent historical scholarship does not deny the reality of women's oppression or the influence of gender on psychiatric thinking, but rather provides a more complex rendering of the links between the female experience and mental illness.

My review of the historical literature will concentrate primarily on nineteenth-century conceptions and treatments of women's mental disorders, prior to the introduction of psychoanalysis, including both general histories of psychiatry and mental hospitals, and studies of specific mental disorders associated primarily with women, such as hysteria and anorexia nervosa.[2] The geographical focus will be limited chiefly to the United States, although I will at times refer to works on European psychiatry as they help illuminate the American experience.

---

[1] Sandra M. Gilbert and Susan Gubar, *The Madwoman in the Attic* (New Haven: Yale University Press, 1979); Phyllis Chesler, *Women and Madness* (New York: Doubleday and Co., 1972); Elaine Showalter, *The Female Malady: Women, Madness, and English Culture, 1830–1980* (New York: Pantheon, 1985).

[2] In order to keep this essay to a manageable length, I regrettably could not include the rich new literature on women, hysteria, and psychoanalysis. These topics stand in much need of a good critical review, which is forthcoming from Mark Micale in *The History of Science*. For a sample of some of the new writings, see Charles Bernheimer and Clair Kahane, eds., *In Dora's Case: Freud-Hysteria-Feminism* (New York: Columbia University Press, 1985).

CONTEMPORARY ISSUES AND THE HISTORIAN

Historical work on the gender-madness nexus is only part of a larger intellectual effort to understand the influence of gender on the experience of and cultural response to emotional distress. In the past fifteen years, scholars from both the biomedical and social sciences have shown that significant sex differences exist in the incidence and treatment of many mental disorders, and that those differences stem in large part from the sex-role socialization and social inequality of women. In its modeling of the linkages among psychological development, cultural context, and patterns of disease, this research suggests some useful insights for historians.[3]

Moreover, a working knowledge of contemporary trends provides a useful corrective to popular misconceptions, which date back to Phyllis Chesler's influential book, that women are more liable to be labelled mentally ill and committed to mental hospitals than are men. Recent research presents a much more complex picture: women are more likely than men to report emotional distress, but they do not suffer from higher rates of severe mental illness, or psychosis; neither do women outnumber men in mental hospital admissions.

Gender differences first appear in the perception of emotional distress itself: numerous studies have found that women report experiencing more anxiety and depression than men. Various explanations have been offered for this finding: that women experience more stress than men because of the role conflicts and social inequalities they face; that they experience no more stress, but are less able to cope with it, due to "learned helplessness" and external handicaps imposed by a discriminatory society; or that they report more distress solely because they are more willing to express feelings in general.[4]

---

[3] For good overviews of contemporary work in the field, see Marcia Guttentag, Susan Salasin, and Deborah Belle, eds., *The Mental Health of Women* (New York: Academic Press, 1980); Elizabeth Howell and Marjorie Bayes, *Women and Mental Health* (New York: Basic Books, 1981); Leonore Walker, ed., *Women and Mental Health Policy* (New York: Sage Publications, 1984); and Patricia P. Rieker and Elaine H. Carmen, *The Gender Gap in Psychotherapy* (New York: Plenum Press, 1984).

[4] Nancy F. Russo, "Women in the Mental Health Delivery System," in *Women and Mental Health Policy*, ed. Walker, p. 26; Ruth Cooperstock, "A Review of Women's Psychotropic Drug Use," in *Women and Mental Health*, ed. Howell and Bayes, p. 136.

While scholars concur that women report more emotional distress, they do not agree that women suffer more mental illness than men. To date, all efforts to determine the relative prevalence of mental disorders among the two sexes have been hampered by such serious methodological problems that their findings carry little conviction. What research *has* shown conclusively is that sex differences are strongest in the least serious, most poorly defined forms of mental illness, namely the neuroses and psychosomatic ailments. In contrast, the psychoses show few significant variations by gender. For example, schizophrenia, a disorder believed to have a large genetic or biological component in its etiology, affects roughly equal numbers of men and women. In other words, sex differences show up most strongly in the disorders most sensitive to cultural and social influences.[5]

Likewise, sex differences in treatment lessen as one moves from general practice and outpatient care to the specialty sector of inpatient hospital care. Women are more likely to seek help for their psychological problems, and outnumber men in outpatient and office-based services of all kinds. The vast majority are seen by general practitioners, who are more likely to prescribe drugs for them than for men presenting similar complaints. But contrary to popular belief, women are *not* more likely than men to be committed to mental hospitals. The latest available data on the use of psychiatric facilities, which covers the year 1980, shows roughly equal rates of admission, 52% male, 48% female.[6]

Increasingly, scholars have turned from efforts to ascertain which sex suffers more mental illness to focus instead on why men and women

[5] Noreen Goldman and Renee Ravid, "Community Surveys: Sex Differences in Mental Illness," in *The Mental Health of Women*, ed. Guttentag, et al., pp. 31–55; Deborah Belle and Noreen Goldman, "Patterns of Diagnoses Received by Men and Women," Ibid., pp. 21–30.

[6] Russo, "Women in the Mental Health Delivery System," p. 27; Cooperstock, "A Review," p. 138; Elaine H. Carmen, Nancy F. Russo, and Jean B. Miller, "Inequality and Women's Mental Health," in *The Gender Gap in Psychotherapy*, ed. Rieker and Carmen, p. 29; Deborah Belle, "Who Uses Mental Health Facilities?" Ibid., pp. 1–20. The 1980 data appear in N.I.M.H., *Mental Health, United States, 1987*, edited by Ronald W. Manderscheid and Sally A. Barrett, D.H.H.S. publ. no. (ADM) 87-1518 (Washington, D.C.: Superintendent of Documents, United States Government Printing Office, 1987), p. 93. Note that there are striking sex differences in the *type* of mental hospital used; the 1980 data show that men are much more numerous in state and county mental hospitals (65% to 35%), while women predominate in the psychiatric wards of general hospitals (55% to 45%) and in private mental hospitals (52% to 48%). On the issue of drug use, Cooperstock cites a 1977 study that found that women received 66% of all prescriptions for psychotropic drugs, 63% of all tranquilizers, and 71% of all antidepressants.

express psychological distress in such different ways. Simply put, epidemiological studies show that women tend to manifest psychological distress in depression; they outnumber men two to one in that category of illness. Men are much more likely to suffer from alcoholism, drug abuse, and personality disorders that involve the acting-out of distress, often in violent ways. This striking gender asymmetry in symptomology suggests that women are more likely to interpret their distress as signs of illness and be labeled "sick," while men deny the distress and exhibit it in behaviors such as drinking and fighting, which are labeled "bad."[7]

From an epidemiological perspective, depression best merits the distinction of being the "female malady" of the late twentieth century. Although still searching for a genetic or endocrinal predisposition to depression, most researchers agree that sociocultural factors account for the marked sex difference in its incidence. Their attempts to explain women's special vulnerability to depression are of particular interest to historians because of the way they model the links between the cultural devaluation of women, low self-esteem, and limited access to social resources. Contrary to popular assumptions that only affluent women have the "luxury" to become depressed, the disorder correlates highly with low income, low education, and other measures of powerlessness in modern society. Indeed, some scholars have argued that "the excess of psychological symptoms in women is not intrinsic to femaleness but to the conditions of subordination that characterize traditional female roles."[8]

The forms of medical treatment women have usually received may only exacerbate their problems of low self-esteem and dependency. As mentioned earlier, women are more likely than men to receive drug treatment, and if they are white, to have longer lengths of stay in psychiatric facilities. Psychotherapy may also be a mixed blessing: studies suggest that until very recently, therapists' unreflective sex-stereotypes often dictated their responses to women patients. A famous 1970 study of therapists' definitions of mental health showed that their very conception of normality was biased in favor of men; to be a healthy woman was by definition to deviate from the psychological norm. Sub-

---

[7] Goldman and Ravid, "Community Surveys," pp. 31–55; Belle and Goldman, "Patterns of Diagnoses," pp. 21–30; Carmen, Russo, and Miller, "Inequality," p. 22.

[8] Quote is from Carmen, Russo, and Miller, "Inequality," p. 26. See also their discussion on pp. 22–27; Deborah Belle, "Inequality and Mental Health," in *Women and Mental Health Policy*, ed. Walker, pp. 135–150; and Gerald Klerman and Myrna Weissman, "Depressions Among Women," Ibid, pp. 57–92.

sequent studies suggest that therapists often encouraged women struggling with the psychic and practical consequences of discrimination to
conform to their prescribed gender roles rather than question them. If
regaining mental health requires women to gain some insight into the
real disadvantages they suffer by virtue of their gender, then mental
health practitioners may not have done them much therapeutic service.[9]

While these contemporary studies of women and mental illness
reflect the specific problems of modern women, they can be used to
formulate a number of interesting problems for historical consideration.
First, they posit certain associations among gender roles, stress, and patterns of mental illness that may help historians decipher women's (and
men's) emotional experiences in the past. Second, they highlight the
importance of "medicalization," that is, the equation of distress with
disease, as a process shaping the perception and treatment of women's
psychological disorders. Third, they pose interesting questions about sex
differences in commitment and treatment patterns. In the essay that
follows, I will expand on each of these themes in turn.

SEX ROLES, STRESS, AND THE "CHOICE" OF SYMPTOM PATTERNS

Using historical data to comment on etiological and epidemiological
questions is necessarily a speculative enterprise. If social scientists, with
all their sophisticated survey methods, cannot answer many fundamental
questions about mental illness, historians, who must rely on far more
fragmentary sources, can hardly do better. Yet read in the context of
current debates about sex roles and stress, recent historical studies of
women's nervous ailments reveal significant continuity and change in
their psychological experience. While contemporary research often im-
plicates the post-World War II trend toward combining family and
work outside the home as the cause of high levels of distress among
women, the historical literature indicates that the sources of strain may
be more deeply rooted in the female experience.

---

[9] Carmen, Russo, and Miller, "Inequality," pp. 28–29; Russo, "Women in the Mental
Health Delivery System," p. 35; Inge Broverman, et al., "Sex-Role Stereotyping and
Clinical Judgments of Mental Health," in *Women and Mental Health*, ed. Howell and
Bayes, pp. 86–97. On gender-role stereotypes in therapy, see also Annette M. Brodsky
and Jean Holyroyd, "Report of the Task Force on Sex Bias and Sex-Role Stereotyping in
Psychotherapeutic Practice," in the same volume, pp. 98–112.

Certainly the nineteenth century, no less than the postwar period, was a period of enormous change in women's roles, as has been documented by many historical studies over the last two decades. The social and economic changes associated with industrialization, urbanization, and modernization transformed family life for both the middle- and working-classes. Among the more affluent, the traditional family economy gave way to a "cult of domesticity" in which women assumed new importance as the emotional, moral, and domestic arbiters of the household. Meanwhile, working-class women adapted traditional patterns of work and childrearing to accommodate new urban and industrial work opportunities. The transition was not an easy one for women of any class, and signs of strain abound in many aspects of their lives, from rising divorce rates to religious enthusiasm and reform agitation.[10]

Nineteenth-century women writers and male physicians agreed that as a result of these changes, women suffered from more physical and mental debility than their grandmothers. Whether they were indeed more sickly is impossible to say, but as Ann Douglas Wood argued in her influential 1973 article, "The Fashionable Diseases," it is significant that so many women apparently *thought* of themselves as sick and were encouraged to do so by the larger society. The phenomenon of the "nervous woman" involved two distinct but related processes, which we will consider in turn: the greater likelihood that women would consider themselves nervous, and the increased attention of the larger society, particularly the medical profession, to their "female complaints."[11]

Contemporary studies of women and stress point to one explanation for the nineteenth-century preoccupation with female nervous disease: that women were indeed experiencing heightened levels of anxiety as a result of the contradictory roles thrust on them by rapid social change. In her 1972 article, "The Hysterical Woman," Carroll Smith-Rosenberg made an elegant argument along these lines, paralleling, in more explicitly psychoanalytic terms, recent formulations of the association among

---

[10] For good surveys of nineteenth-century women's roles, see Kathryn Sklar, *Catharine Beecher* (New York: Norton, 1973); Mary Ryan, *Cradle of the Middle Class* (New York: Cambridge University Press, 1981); and Nancy Cott and Elizabeth Pleck, *A Heritage of Our Own* (New York: Simon and Schuster, 1979).

[11] Ann Douglas Wood, "The Fashionable Diseases," in *Clio's Consciousness Raised*, ed. Mary Hartman and Lois Banner (New York: Harper & Row, 1974), pp. 1–22. The article originally appeared in the *Journal of Interdisciplinary History* 4 (1973): 25–52.

low self-esteem, "learned helplessness," and depression. Smith-Rosenberg asserted that the apparent rise in the incidence of hysteria, a syndrome marked by debilitating emotional distress and sometimes bizarre psychosomatic symptoms, reflected at least in part the contradictions inherent in Victorian gender roles. On the one hand, nineteenth-century cultural norms for middle- and upper-class women encouraged them to be passive, emotional, and nurturant, thus allowing them to come to adulthood "with major ego weaknesses and with narrowly limited compensatory ego strengths"; on the other hand, the realities of their adult lives often included many difficult and unpredictable events, such as illness, financial reverses, and death of a loved one, which demanded emotional strength and self-reliance. Unprepared psychologically or otherwise to meet these demands, many women felt overwhelmed and frustrated; encouraged by prevailing social views to think of women of their class as "nervous" and "delicate," some chose, albeit unconsciously, to express that dissatisfaction by retreating into hysteria. As Smith-Rosenberg points out, the sick-role allowed a woman simultaneously to escape social demands and express her will, at the same time shielding her from punitive moral judgments.[12]

While Smith-Rosenberg's argument about nineteenth-century women is quite convincing, Michael MacDonald's work on women's mental disorders in early modern England suggests that historians must be careful not to assume that such role conflict and its resulting psychological distress were unique to industrializing society, or to affluent women. Analyzing the case records of a physician-astrologer, MacDonald found that two-thirds of his many patients complaining of mental distress were women; while both sexes suffered deeply from the unexpected ills of life, women were more distressed by them because of their greater powerlessness.[13]

The point here is not to claim that women endured more stress or powerlessness in the seventeenth century as opposed to the nineteenth or twentieth centuries. Rather the historical evidence might more modestly be read to suggest that the relationship among socialization, life

[12] Carroll Smith-Rosenberg, "The Hysterical Woman," *Social Research* 39 (1972): 652–78. Quote is from p. 677. This article is reprinted in Carroll Smith-Rosenberg, *Disorderly Conduct* (New York: Knopf, 1985).
[13] Michael MacDonald, *Mystical Bedlam* (New York: Cambridge University Press, 1981), pp. 36–40, 74, 84–5. He cites a contemporary observer, Thomas Wright, who wrote in 1604 that women's greater emotional travail resulted from their "unableness to resist adversities or any other injury offered." (p. 75)

experience, and emotional distress posited by contemporary theorists retains its explanatory power across several centuries, regardless of the social changes that have occurred in women's roles. Although more historical work needs to be done to confirm this point, it appears likely that these associations hold across class, race, and other social differences among women. When women with low self-esteem and limited access to social resources face stressful situations, especially ones that contradict their expected sex roles, they are likely to respond with emotional distress. The specific sex roles and social realities that interact to create this predisposition to emotional distress vary across time, as do the repertoire of sex-stereotyped symptoms available to express it, but the fundamental link between powerlessness and distress remains.

It is important to remember, too, that sex-role socialization patterned men's as well as women's responses to stressful situations. In light of contemporary debates, historians might well interpret the high rates of alcohol consumption and propensity to violence among nineteenth-century men as the functional analogues to female "nervousness."[14] In their studies of admissions to nineteenth-century mental hospitals, Ellen Dwyer and Constance McGovern found an interesting gender asymmetry; even allowing for the physician's bias in recording the cause of illness, it is apparent that female mental patients suffered more from melancholy or depression, while men succumbed more often to alcohol-related disorders or general paresis, the tertiary stage of syphilis. In the same vein, women's insanity was more likely to be attributed to interpersonal or family problems; men's insanity was more frequently attributed to "bad habits" such as alcoholism, sexual excess, and drug abuse. The nineteenth-century association between alcohol abuse and mental illness among men is especially striking.[15]

Thus the historical record supports the argument that sex-role socialization may have predisposed men and women to gender-specific

---

[14] On alcohol consumption, see W. J. Rorabaugh, *The Alcoholic Republic* (New York: Oxford University Press, 1979). On violence, see Richard M. Brown, *Strain of Violence* (New York: Oxford University Press, 1975).

[15] Ellen Dwyer, "A Historical Perspective," in *Sex Roles and Psychopathology*, ed. Cathy S. Widom (New York: Plenum Press, 1984), pp. 22–23, 39; Ellen Dwyer, "The Weaker Vessel: Legal Versus Social Reality in Mental Commitments in Nineteenth-Century New York," in *Women and the Law*, ed. D. Kelly Weisberg (Cambridge, MA: Schenkman Publishing Company, 1982), p. 96; Constance McGovern, "The Myths of Social Control and Custodial Oppression," *Journal of Social History* 20 (1986): 11; Nancy Tomes, *A Generous Confidence: Thomas Story Kirkbride and the Art of Asylum-Keeping* (New York: Cambridge University Press, 1984), p. 324.

reasons for and modes of expressing psychological distress. In a culture where the meaning of women's lives was closely bound up with personal relationships, disruptions of those relations—by illness or death, by economic need, or by family conflict—could become an enormous source of suffering. Of course, not all women who suffered disappointments in their personal lives automatically became ill. Rather the expectations and realities of personal relationships and family life loomed as a larger variable in their emotional lives than they did for men.

Using that insight, some of the most stimulating recent work focuses on the relationship between sex roles and symptom "choice" in the classic women's disorders of hysteria and anorexia nervosa. Joan Jacobs Brumberg's brilliant study of anorexia nervosa provides the best historical model to date for exploring the complex relationships among social context, sex roles, and disease symptomatology. Brumberg shows that anorexia nervosa emerged as a medical problem among adolescent girls from affluent families because of the conjunction of many powerful cultural forces in the late nineteenth century. Food refusal had traditionally afforded women a means of demonstrating piety, as in the case of the medieval Saint Catherine of Siena. But the shift from a religious to a scientific worldview gradually transformed food refusal "from a religious act to a pathological state." Simultaneously, changing middle-class standards of family life created an intense, indeed stifling, climate for adolescent girls; when denied other outlets of expression, some began to use "the appetite as voice." Brumberg posits that "middle-class girls, rather than boys, turned to food as a symbolic language, because the culture made an important connection between food and femininity, and because girls' options for self-expression outside the family were limited by parental concern and social convention." Her analysis demonstrates the specific cultural trends that combined to make food refusal a powerful but destructive mode of self-expression for adolescent girls in the late nineteenth century.[16]

Inevitably the metaphor of illness as "voice" leads to troublesome questions about what meaning historians should assign to the experience of insanity itself. If indeed women's social roles created particular vulnerabilities to mental illness, should their psychic disorders then be

---

[16] Joan Jacobs Brumberg, *Fasting Girls: The Emergence of Anorexia Nervosa as a Modern Disease* (Cambridge: Harvard University Press, 1988), p. 188. I put the word "choice" in quotations to underline the reality that the pattern of symptoms rarely involved a conscious or rational decision on the patient's part.

read as a form of protest against those roles? Some feminists have been tempted to see madness as a form of proto-feminism; there are those, for example, who liken modern day anorectics to hunger-striking suffragists.[17] But as Elaine Showalter warns in *The Female Malady*, "Such claims . . . come dangerously close to romanticizing and endorsing madness as a desirable form of rebellion rather than seeing it as the desperate communication of the powerless."[18]

In the nineteenth century it was a rare woman such as Charlotte Perkins Gilman who made the connection between restrictive gender roles and women's vulnerability to emotional distress. A talented artist and writer, she suffered a nervous breakdown soon after her first marriage and the birth of her daughter. In later years, Gilman came to see how her emotional illness stemmed from the devastating impact of her father's desertion on her too-dependent mother, who could barely nurture her children as a result. With only a fragile sense of self-worth, Gilman broke down in the face of the choice between career and marriage that Victorian society forced upon women of her generation. Her chilling autobiographical short story, "The Yellow Wallpaper," (1892) conveys the sense of low self-esteem and frustration that led to her mental collapse; it also describes how she suffered at the hands of the paternalistic neurologist S. Weir Mitchell, who tried a regimen of enforced bedrest and isolation to "cure" her of her longings for a different life.[19]

For the vast majority of nineteenth-century women, the connections between emotional distress and women's inequality, which Gilman articulated so well, appear to have remained hidden. In their discussions of women's illnesses, both Smith-Rosenberg and Brumberg stress the largely unconscious choice to be ill, and the enormous price the nineteenth-century woman patient paid for her assumption of the sick-role. As Smith-Rosenberg writes, "the hysteric purchased her escape from the emotional—and frequently—from the sexual demands of her life only at

---

[17] Brumberg, *Fasting Girls*, p. 37, mentions finding the anorectic/suffragist comparison in her readings of contemporary feminist literature.

[18] Showalter, *The Female Malady*, p. 5.

[19] Charlotte Perkins Gilman's story has been reprinted as *The Yellow Wallpaper* (New York: The Feminist Press, 1973). See also her autobiography, *The Living of Charlotte Perkins Gilman* (New York: Harper & Row, 1975; reprint of 1935 edition) for her account of her nervous breakdown. Showalter has an interesting discussion of Mitchell's rest cure and Gilman's fictional account of it in *The Female Malady*, pp. 138–44. See also Barbara Sicherman, "The Uses of A Diagnosis," *Journal of the History of Medicine* 32 (1977): 33–54, on the psychosexual dynamics of the rest cure.

the cost of pain, disability, and an intensification of women's passivity and dependence."[20]

From the personal accounts entered in asylum case-records, women suffering from emotional distress appear more broken by than in protest against their limited role in society. Such records document cases of middle-class women apparently made ill by physical inactivity, domestic heartbreaks, and dearth of meaningful work, as well as working-class women suffering the mental and physical consequences of chronic malnutrition, overwork, and too-frequent childbearing. These mentally ill women may not have seen themselves as victims of oppression, yet their ailments give a moving testimony to the strains and contradictions involved in the sex roles of the period.[21]

THE MEDICALIZATION OF MADNESS AND ITS IMPLICATION FOR WOMEN

A central theme in recent historical work on women and madness has been the process of medicalization, that is, the expansion of medical authority over a variety of human behaviors and conditions traditionally thought of in moral or religious terms. While historians cannot claim that people felt more or less distress in the past, they can confidently assert that the *range* of feelings and behaviors thought to indicate mental illness has dramatically increased over the last century, a trend that has extended medicine's authority largely at religion's expense. From the historian's perspective, the contemporary findings that women are more likely than men to perceive their psychological distress as symptoms of illness and seek medical help can be seen as the logical outcome of professional and intellectual developments of nineteenth-century medicine.[22]

In *The Female Malady*, literary critic Elaine Showalter has argued that this process of medicalization led to a "feminization" of madness.

---

[20] Smith-Rosenberg, "The Hysterical Woman," p. 671. See also Brumberg, *Fasting Girls*, esp. ch. 1. Brumberg notes that the body's biological response to prolonged starvation transforms the anorectic's original, voluntary decision not to eat into an involuntary inability to eat.

[21] I base these statements on my own readings of the Pennsylvania Hospital for the Insane case records, as well as the various works by Ellen Dwyer and Constance McGovern cited in these notes.

[22] For general discussions of the medicalization process, see Sicherman, "The Uses of A Diagnosis," and Andrew Scull, *Museums of Madness* (London: Allen Lane, 1979).

Analyzing cultural representations of insanity in literature and art, she shows how the eighteenth-century figure of the dangerous, raving madman gave way to the nineteenth-century figure of the young, romantic madwoman. Showalter then tries to show how this "gender asymmetry in the representational tradition" carried over into a "gendering" of medical discourse and practice: women soon outnumbered men in the new asylums being built for the insane, and male physicians came to believe that women were more liable to insanity than men. Even though men still suffered from it, insanity came to be seen as a "female malady."[23]

While Showalter's analysis of the cultural representations of madness is fascinating, her characterization of nineteenth-century medical thought and practice needs serious qualification. To be sure, the medicalization of madness made gender a central category of psychiatric diagnosis and treatment. But nineteenth-century physicians were less certain about which sex was more prone to mental illness than Showalter suggests. Moreover, women did not, in the United States at least, outnumber men as mental patients when all types of institutional care are considered.

Changing views of madness reflected a gradual but profound redrawing of the boundary lines between religion and madness in the nineteenth century. While a naturalistic conception of mental illness, as distinct from supernatural affliction or demonic possession, long predated the Enlightenment, medicine had only limited claims to be the "treatment of choice" for emotional distress in the seventeenth and eighteenth centuries. Colonial women (as well as men) interpreted their anxieties and fears in a spiritual context. In her study of insanity in colonial Massachusetts, Mary Anne Jimenez found that "melancholy arising from despair over the state of one's soul" was a common problem among women. This "spiritualization" of emotional distress probably continued into the nineteenth century, particularly among the middle-class women who became deeply involved with evangelical religious culture. In my work on an early mental hospital, I discovered a diary kept by one pious young woman, supposedly cured of religious melancholy by her hospital stay, which shows clearly how she regarded her feelings of despair as "sins." But gradually over the course of the nineteenth century, women were encouraged by physicians and the larger culture to "somaticize" their feelings of distress with the promise

---

[23] See Showalter, *The Female Malady*, especially the introduction and ch. 2, for the "feminization" argument. The quote is from p. 5.

that medicine, not religion, would provide the surer form of relief. This process began first among middle- and upper-class women, but soon included working-class women as well.[24]

In their accounts of two classic women's diseases, anorexia nervosa and hysteria, Joan Jacobs Brumberg and Jan Goldstein provide important explications of this medicalization process and its profound implications for the treatment of women's nervous disorders. Brumberg shows that in the nineteenth century, neurologists eager to discredit spiritual rationales for female food refusal and other pious behaviors waged a determined war against "fasting girls," young women who claimed to live miraculously without eating. So zealous did physicians become that in the case of Sarah Jacob, the "Welsh Fasting Girl," they staged an experiment in which she was literally starved to death to prove the point that no one could live without eating. In her work on hysteria, Goldstein goes a step further to posit an active campaign on the part of neurologists "to claim women for science," by teaching them to think of the symptoms of emotional distress as "medical conditions falling within the purview of the physician, rather than as moral failings or spiritual crises requiring the guidance of the priest."[25]

Given the way many physicians tried use their influence to restrict women's activities, it is not immediately apparent why the latter might have accepted this expansion of medical authority. Barbara Sicherman's excellent article, "The Uses of a Diagnosis" (1977), suggests some of the reasons why patients, male as well as female, may have welcomed a somatic interpretation of their nervous complaints. In an age of increasing respect for medical science, viewing emotional distress as the product of a disease process helped transform it into a condition that might be treated and eventually "cured." For women experiencing the mental and physical consequences of severe stress, Sicherman writes, the concept of "neurasthenia" or nervous exhaustion allowed them, as well as their physicians, to interpret "behavioral symptoms that some found morally reprehensible (an inability to work for no apparent cause, compulsive or phobic behavior, bizarre thoughts) as signs of illness rather than willfulness."[26]

---

[24] Mary Anne Jimenez, *The Changing Faces of Madness* (Hanover, NH: University Press of New England, 1987), p. 22; Tomes, *A Generous Confidence*, pp. 230–31.

[25] Brumberg, *Fasting Girls*, esp. pp. 61–100. Jan Goldstein, *Console and Classify: The French Psychiatric Profession in the Nineteenth Century* (New York: Cambridge University Press, 1987), pp. 322–77. Quote is from p. 374.

[26] Barbara Sicherman, "The Uses of a Diagnosis," p. 53.

Still, as Sicherman well understands, women paid a high price for this reassurance. The theories available to physicians to explain women's distinctive psychological problems also served admirably as rationales for limiting their participation in the larger society. In a series of classic articles on nineteenth-century medical theory, Charles Rosenberg and Carroll Smith-Rosenberg have explicated how medical and biological views of women "formed an ideological system rigid in its support of tradition, yet infinitely flexible in the particular mechanisms which could be made to explain and legitimate woman's role." Within the context of traditional explanations of illness, which portrayed disease as a condition that varied enormously from individual to individual, physicians believed that women as a group were especially vulnerable to diseases of the nervous and reproductive systems, which were thought to be in close sympathy. Their explanations for women's mental diseases frequently centered on disruptions of the reproductive system during the physiological "crises" of puberty, childbirth, and menopause.[27]

Using these theories, conservative physicians delivered proscriptive as well as clinical judgments: in the advice literature of the day, they frequently invoked insanity as a likely consequence if women transgressed the "laws of nature" and stepped outside their proper social roles. For example, in his influential 1878 treatise *Sex and Education*, physician Edward Clarke cited examples of adolescent girls who studied too hard during the physiological upheavals of puberty and succumbed as a result to insanity and even death.[28]

Of course, this same kind of medical "scare literature" existed for boys and men, who were threatened with insanity if they masturbated or overindulged in sex and liquor. And despite the universal belief in the greater fragility of the female nervous system, medical men did not necessarily agree that women were more liable to insanity than men.

---

[27] Charles Rosenberg and Carroll Smith-Rosenberg, "The Female Animal," in *No Other Gods*, ed. Charles Rosenberg (Baltimore: Johns Hopkins University Press, 1976), pp. 54–70. Quote is from p. 55. See also Carroll Smith-Rosenberg, "From Puberty to Menopause," in *Clio's Consciousness Raised*, ed. Hartman and Banner, pp. 23–37.

[28] Rosenberg and Smith-Rosenberg, "The Female Animal," esp. pp. 58–63; Edward Clarke, *Sex and Education* (Boston: Houghton, Osgood, 1878). Ellen Dwyer notes that physicians' prescriptive judgments about women's behavior did not necessarily carry over into clinical practice. For example, when Amariah Brigham was a physician in general practice, he wrote a tract strongly implicating overeducation as a source of women's nervous diseases. But once he became superintendent of the Utica asylum, he never cited overeducation as a cause of his female patients' illness, perhaps, Dwyer suggests, because he no longer needed to work so hard to attract an upper-class clientele. See Dwyer, "The Weaker Vessel." p. 93.

Many doctors thought that the biological disadvantage that women suffered on account of their reproductive physiology was more than countered by the special risks men faced by virtue of their participation in the modern world, such as the temptation to "bad habits" and the wear and tear of overwork and economic uncertainty. In other words, the two sexes experienced different stresses in their respective social roles that more or less balanced out one another. It is also important to remember that in the hierarchical thinking of the day, having a highly developed nervous system was a mark of evolutionary superiority. Thus to portray women as greater martyrs to mental disease than men had troublesome implications for the doctrine of male superiority.[29]

Given the demonstrable gender biases of nineteenth-century physicians, some scholars have been tempted to conclude that the whole theory of women's mental diseases evolved consciously and unconsciously as a means to control female sexuality and assertiveness. Showalter contrasts the "rather vague and uncertain concepts of insanity in general," to theories about women, which were "specifically and confidently linked to the biological crises of the female life cycle." Likewise, in "The Fashionable Diseases," Ann Douglas Wood suggests that medical theories might be viewed as the product of a "veiled but aggressively hostile male sexuality and superiority."[30]

While agreeing that nineteenth-century medicine was extremely gender-conscious, historians of medicine emphasize that its theories about women grew out of an ancient medical tradition that tied treatment to the patient's age, class, race, and residence, as well as gender. In "The Lady and Her Physician," Regina Morantz argues that in the context of this larger system of thought, the theory of women's diseases was not uniquely harsh, but rather quite consistent with medicine in general; she points out that male as well as female patients were subjected to moral judgments and painful procedures at the hands of their physicians. John Harley Warner's recent study of nineteenth-century medical practice, which explicates the importance of individual attributes such as gender in therapeutic thinking, bears out this point.[31]

---

[29] The best overview of medical thinking on gender and etiology is Dwyer, "A Historical Perspective." See esp. pp. 22–23. On nervousness as a mark of civilization, see John Haller and Robin Haller, The Physician and Sexuality in Victorian America (Chicago: University of Illinois Press, 1974), esp. pp. 5–43.

[30] Showalter, The Female Malady, p. 55; Wood, "The Fashionable Diseases," p. 9.

[31] Regina Morantz, "The Lady and Her Physician," in Clio's Consciousness Raised, ed. Hartmann and Banner, pp. 38–53; John Harley Warner, The Therapeutic Perspective (Cambridge: Harvard University Press, 1987).

Historical disagreement over the "male hostility" thesis is nowhere more evident than in discussions of the practice of gynecological surgery. In his account of nineteenth-century medicine, *The Horrors of the Half-Known Life* (1973), G. J. Barker Benfield claims that physicians performed ovariotomies and clitoridectomies to control or eradicate a female sexuality that they found enormously threatening. But historians who subsequently looked at case records of women patients encountered little evidence to support his argument. The majority of gynecological surgery performed by neurologists aimed simply at repairing the common injuries of childbirth, while asylum doctors rarely did gynecological exams, much less surgery. When they did, as Wendy Mitchinson shows in her study of gynecological surgery at the London, Ontario asylum, they were as much concerned about making a professional reputation for themselves as controlling their patients' sexuality. As for male patients, F. G. Gosling and Joyce Ray cite the drastic operations and local treatments applied to male patients' genitalia in this period as a sign that women were not being singled out for punishment. Likewise, Richard Fox found that 60% of the mental patients operated upon under California's liberal sterilization laws in the early twentieth century were men.[32]

Significantly, female doctors were recruited into asylum work largely to provide women patients with better gynecological care, suggesting that some motivation other than male hostility was at work. In her work on women and psychiatry, Constance McGovern suggests that in an age when gynecological injuries and infections were both extremely common and highly debilitating, women patients may have appreciated such care, which they could not have afforded otherwise; for example, she found that under Dr. Alice Bennett's direction, the Norristown, Pennsylvania asylum's extensive program of gynecological treatment was a major attraction for its largely working-class clientele. However, as McGovern realizes, it is difficult to assess from the available records how

---

[32] G. J. Barker-Benfield, *The Horrors of the Half-Known Life* (New York: Harper & Row, 1976); F. G. Gosling and Joyce Ray, "The Right to Be Sick: American Physicians and Nervous Patients, 1885–1910," *Journal of Social History* 20 (1986): 260–61; Gerald Grob, *Mental Illness and American Society, 1875–1940* (Princeton: Princeton University Press, 1983), pp. 122–23. Dwyer, "A Historical Perspective,' p. 29; Wendy Mitchinson, "Gynecological Operations on Insane Women: London, Ontario, 1895–1901," *Journal of Social History* 15 (1982): 467–84. On the treatment of men, see Gosling and Ray, "The Right to Be Sick," pp. 260–1; Richard Fox, *So Far Disordered in Mind: Insanity in California, 1870–1930* (Berkeley: University of California Press, 1978), p. 257.

much choice or consent women patients really exercised in receiving such treatment.[33]

Some of the confusion in characterizing medical attitudes toward women stems from inattention to specialization as a determinant of a doctor's outlook. Nineteenth-century physicians were by no means a monolithic group; the three specialties most likely to be called in to treat women with mental disorders—asylum doctors, neurologists, and gynecologists—all had very different intellectual and professional agendas. The oldest of the three groups was psychiatry or asylum medicine, as it was then called, which emerged as a separate specialty in the 1830s and 1840s with the rapid expansion of the mental hospital system. Asylum doctors dealt with the most severely disabled, psychotic patients who could no longer be cared for at home. While always eager to attract a higher class of patrons and patients, they had little difficulty filling beds. In the 1860s and 1870s, neurology and gynecology emerged as office-based specialties, catering primarily to a middle- and upper-class clientele suffering from milder mental ailments or "neuroses," as they came to be designated. These latter two groups produced a more innovative, sometimes radical, view of mental illness in general and women's disorders in particular.[34]

In their reviews of medical writings about women's insanity, historians have found, not surprisingly, that gynecologists were most likely to claim that reproductive disorders caused mental illness and to advocate surgical treatments for insanity. The larger medical profession tended to regard gynecologists such as Horatio Storer, who implicated uterine disease in all cases of female insanity, as dangerous extremists. Likewise, controversy dogged the few asylum doctors, including Alice Bennett, Richard Bucke, and Maurice Hobbs, who did perform gynecological surgery. Those doctors who dealt with the largest number of mentally ill women, namely the asylum doctors, did not focus obsessively on the reproductive system, and "were less likely than neurologists or gynecologists to lose sight of the role played by environmental stresses in producing insanity," according to Ellen Dwyer.[35]

---

[33] Constance McGovern, "Doctors or Ladies?" *Bulletin of the History of Medicine* 55 (1981): 99–101; McGovern, "The Myths of Social Control," pp. 12–13, 15.

[34] For general accounts of the growth of specialty competition in mental health care, see Grob, *Mental Institutions*, and Sicherman, "The Uses of a Diagnosis."

[35] Gosling and Ray, "The Right to Be Sick," p. 257; Dwyer, "A Historical Perspective," pp. 27–32 (quote is from p. 42); McGovern, "Doctors or Ladies?," pp. 99–101; Mitchinson, "Gynecological Operations," esp. pp. 472–74.

Recent studies of clinical practice also suggest that male doctors' moral judgments on their emotionally distressed women patients were far more subtle and complex than the original formulations of Barker-Benfield and Wood would suggest. On this point, a comparative perspective across both gender and class lines has been especially productive; as Gosling and Ray point out, most studies of women patients never systematically compare them to men suffering from the same mental disorder. Using published clinical studies of neurasthenic men and women, Gosling and Ray found that the physicians' negative moral judgments did not follow a simple gender dichotomy, but rather reflected the practitioner's assessment of the individual's moral responsibility for the illness: "Physicians sympathized most with those patients whom they perceived to be victims of overwork, primarily middle-class men and lower-class women." To a lesser degree, they excused women as a class because they were "biologically predisposed" to nervousness. They showed virtually no sympathy for "those believed to be guilty of vices such as sexual excess or other bad habits," usually working-class men.[36]

Apparently, asylum doctors shared the same prejudices against their male patients. At the Utica asylum, 20% of the men were supposedly ill as a result of "bad habits," compared to only 4% of the women. Similarly, in California court hearings, women were more likely to be labeled "good or intelligent" than men, and received negative moral judgments in only 6% of the cases, as opposed to 20% for their male counterparts. Dwyer found that asylum doctors showed considerable sympathy for overworked wives and mothers, especially those from the working classes. For example, despite his strong belief in the somatic origins of mental illness, John Gray, the influential superintendent of the Utica, New York asylum, cited the "travails of the poor," combined with too-frequent childbearing, as a most common cause of insanity among women. In one published report, he stated that maternity was directly or indirectly responsible for more female insanity than any other factor, and suggested that special social organizations be set up to assist new mothers and thus prevent this "cruelest form of neglect."[37]

---

[36] Gosling and Ray, "The Right to be Sick," p. 253.

[37] Dwyer, "The Weaker Vessel," pp. 94–95; Dwyer, *Homes for the Mad*, p. 90; Fox, *So Far Disordered*, pp. 153–57. The case of women committing crimes also supports this line of argument. Dwyer speculates that women criminals may well have been sent to mental hospitals instead of jails. The assumption of mental illness may thus have been used to excuse women's violent acts. See Dwyer, "A Historical Perspective," p. 37; Dwyer, *Homes for the Mad*, p. 90.

The evidence suggests that asylum doctors rarely saw mental disease as punishment for transgressions against femininty, but rather viewed it as the result of too little economic and social support for the difficult tasks involved in homemaking and childrearing. Never questioning the fundamental fairness of the gender division of labor, their paternalism nevertheless did not lead them to blame women patients for their plight. The "sick" versus "bad" dichotomy seems to have existed even in the nineteenth century.

WOMEN IN THE ASYLUM

Over the past two decades, the twin notions of disease as social construction and medicine as cultural authority have raised important questions about the uses of medical authority to control women's behavior. The power to label certain behaviors as "sick" or "bad" is clearly a vital aspect of maintaining social order in general and sex roles in particular. Nowhere are these issues of power and authority more clearly revealed than in the confinement of women in mental institutions. Following Phyllis Chesler, feminists have long assumed that asylums functioned as potent weapons against outspoken women: that acts of female defiance prompted institutionalization; that as a result, women outnumbered men as asylum patients; and that asylum treatment aimed at coercing them into a passive acceptance of their oppression. But recent studies based on actual case-records of women asylum patients have qualified this vision of the mental hospital, and render a more complex picture of women's experiences as mental patients.

Recent general histories of psychiatric institutions have emphasized the limitations on medical authority both within and outside the asylum. In its place, the family has come to play a much more central role in the asylum's history. Studies of public and private asylums alike have shown that relatives, not public officials or physicians, initiated the vast majority of commitment proceedings. In other words, physicians confirmed familial judgments that an individual was insane and needed hospital care. This realization has focused new attention on the step *prior* to medical intervention, namely the familial processes involved in commitment, and how they bore differently on women and men.[38]

---

[38] For a general overview of the revisionist position, see McGovern, "The Myths of Social Control," and Nancy Tomes, "The Anatomy of Madness: New Directions in the History of Psychiatry," *Social Studies of Science* 17 (1987): 358–71.

Familial definitions of what constituted insanity reflected and reinforced the larger social roles assigned men and women in the nineteenth-
century American society. As I have shown in my study of lay attitudes
toward insanity, family members often cited sudden or extreme devia-
tions from an individual's habitual behavior, including departures from
their normal sex roles, as evidence of mental disease—for example
women who ceased to care for their personal appearance, began to keep
house in bizarre fashion, or developed strong aversions to family and
friends. But it is important to stress that relatives did not automatically
label women mad because they transgressed the cult of domesticity;
there were many ill-kempt and unaffectionate women outside the asylum
walls. In the nineteenth century the category of "mental illness" was
usually reserved for an extreme state of mental alienation and inappropriate behavior that went far beyond mere eccentricity or unconvention-
ality. In studies of commitment patterns, neither Ellen Dwyer nor I
found much evidence that family members rushed to commit unruly
women at the first sign of eccentricity. Rather in the vast majority of
cases, relatives explored all other alternatives, then came to the decision
after a complex calculus of financial considerations, family resources,
and the patient's likelihood of benefit.[39]

Still, contested commitment cases exposed enough exceptions to
this generalization to create a widespread suspicion that asylums could
be used improperly by conniving relatives. By modern standards, nineteenth-century commitment laws were extraordinarily lax; as a rule,
families needed only to present certificates of insanity from one or more
"reputable" physicians to secure a relative's admission to the asylum. In
her study of New York State commitment laws, Dwyer did not find such
overt discrimination against women, yet posits that because women had
less power in general, they may have been less able to evade or manipulate the law. Richard Fox found in San Francisco that women brought to
the court's notice were less likely to convince the examiners to release
them, perhaps because they had a more difficult time defending themselves in public, or because the court officials were less sympathetic to
their arguments.[40]

The celebrated case of Elizabeth Packard is often cited to show how
lax commitment laws could be misused against women in cases of family

---

[39] Tomes, A *Generous Confidence*, pp. 101, 103. See also pp. 92–118; Dwyer, *Homes for the Mad* esp. pp. 86–98.
[40] Dwyer, "The Weaker Vessel," pp. 89, 101; Fox, *So Far Disordered*, pp. 103, 124.

conflict. Under the Illinois law, which allowed married women and invalids to be committed without any legal safeguards, Packard's clergy-man-husband committed her to the Illinois State Hospital in 1860, claiming she was a threat to her family. Packard insisted that her husband was punishing her for her unorthodox religious views. After three years in the asylum, she was released, whereupon she sued her husband for wrongful confinement and began a career of reforming commitment laws. As a result of her efforts, "Packard laws" guaranteeing patients more legal safeguards against wrongful commitment were passed in many states.[41] Packard's case was exceptional: Ronald and Janet Numbers' study of religious insanity found no evidence that patients were committed solely because of deviant religious views; as a rule, physicians were quite careful to distinguish pathology from heterodoxy. But the ill-defined boundaries between sane and insane behavior, coupled with the ease of commitment, virtually guaranteed that some cases of questionable commitment would occur in nineteenth-century asylums.[42]

In historical retrospect, these commitment controversies are exceedingly difficult to evaluate. Consider, for example, the case of Mary Todd Lincoln, Abraham Lincoln's widow. Using the same basic sources, historians Mark Neely and R. Gerald McMurtry defend her son Robert's decision to commit her to a private asylum, on the grounds that she threatened his life, while Jean Baker portrays her as merely a difficult, unhappy woman who was victimized by an unsympathetic son. The Lincoln case well illustrates how slippery judgments about mental status can be, then as now.[43]

There was one area, however, in which cultural standards of behavior unquestionably bore more heavily on women than men—sexuality. In cases where sexual behavior was mentioned as grounds for commitment, Fox found that women were considered sexually deviant solely on the grounds that they were promiscuous, whereas men had to commit

[41] For a thorough if uncritical account of Packard's career, see Myra Himelhoch and Arthur Shaffer, "Elizabeth Packard: Nineteenth-Century Crusader for the Rights of Mental Patients," *Journal of American Studies* 13 (1979): 343–75. Grob, *Mental Illness*, p. 47, cites the Illinois commitment law.

[42] Ronald Numbers and Janet Numbers, "Millerism and Madness," *Bulletin of the Menninger Clinic* 49 (1985): 289–320.

[43] Mark E. Neely and R. Gerald McMurtry, *The Insanity File: The Case of Mary Todd Lincoln* (Carbondale: Southern Illinois University Press, 1986); Jean H. Baker, *Mary Todd Lincoln* (New York: W. W. Norton, 1987), esp. ch. 11.

specific deviant acts to be considered abnormal. Similarly, Elizabeth Lunbeck has shown how early twentieth-century psychiatrists used the label "sociopath" to stigmatize working-class women whose sole "pathological" behavior was too much enthusiasm for heterosexual activity.[44]

Given the many cultural judgments involved in the commitment process, the rate at which women versus men were committed to the asylums becomes a social fact of some significance. If women tended to be hospitalized more frequently than men, it might suggest some special cultural concern about female madness. Elaine Showalter makes precisely that argument, contending that women outnumbered men in mental hospitals because madness was perceived as a "female malady." But in contrast to Showalter's characterization of English asylums, the American mental hospital does not seem to have become "feminized" in the nineteenth century.[45]

Ellen Dwyer has made the most systematic effort to assess the relative liability of women to be institutionalized. In late nineteenth-century New York, men comprised 45.2%, women 54.4% of all inmates in state mental hospitals, an imbalance that would seem to confirm Showalter's thesis. But looking more carefully at two institutions, the Utica and Willard asylums, Dwyer discovered an important trend: At Utica, which provided acute care for recent cases, the sex ratio of admissions was virtually equal, 50.8% men, 49.2% women. At Willard, a chronic care facility, the population was 56.3% female, many of them immigrant women. To explain these gender differences, Dwyer cites institutional factors: chronically ill women were more likely to get sent to a state hospital, while their male counterparts were more likely to be left in almshouses or jails.[46]

Other studies have found men to outnumber women in psychiatric facilities. According to Grob, the first reliable national surveys of institutional populations done in the early 1900s showed men to have higher rates of first admission. Likewise, Fox found men to have higher rates of

---

[44] Fox, *So Far Disordered*, p. 146; Elizabeth Lunbeck, "'A New Generation of Women'," *Feminist Studies* 13 (1987): 513–43. Lesbianism does not figure prominently in the stated reasons for commitment. Ellen Dwyer cites one fascinating case in which a woman assumed a man's name, dressed in male garb, and "married" a woman; she lived that way for years, and was only sent to the asylum when she became violent and erratic in her behavior. See Dwyer, "A Historical Perspective," p. 36.

[45] Showalter, *A Female Malady*, see esp. pp. 52–54.

[46] Dwyer, "The Weaker Vessel," pp. 88, 92; Dwyer, "A Historical Perspective," p. 41; Dwyer, *Homes for the Mad*, p. 86.

commitment to early twentieth-century California asylums. Census returns for 1900 to 1930 showed that women made up 49% of the total
population, but only 44% of the inmates of state hospitals. He also
found that immigrant men were more likely to be held in almhouses than
their female counterparts, who were sent on to the state hospital.[47]

While women do not seem to have been committed in disproportionate numbers to men, once admitted to the hospital, they were
subjected to therapeutic philosophies that legitimated sex differences in
both psychological and somatic treatments for insanity. Yet "[d]espite
their professed belief in the basic differences between the sexes," Dwyer
writes, "nineteenth-century doctors never attempted to develop psychiatric syndromes sufficiently sex-specific so as to justify radically distinct
systems of psychiatric treatment." Rather gender differences in treatment represented variations on the main lines of therapeutic intervention.[48]

Under the general philosophy of moral treatment, asylum physicians provided a regimen of daily activities that reflected class and gender
standards of the day. Men and women were treated in separate wards (in
some institutions, even in separate buildings) and allowed only closely
supervised contact with each other. Middle-class ladies did handiwork,
read carefully selected books and magazines, and took carriage rides,
while working-class women washed, sewed, and ironed. By virtue of
working indoors, unaffected by weather or darkness, Dwyer found that
working-class women put in longer hours on the ward than their male
counterparts, whose work took them out of doors.[49]

---

[47] Grob, *Mental Illness*, pp. 191–92; Fox, *So Far Disordered*, pp. 123–24, 131. Another
potentially revealing indicator of how gender affected perceptions of madness is the
duration of attack before commitment. But on this point, the available studies disagree:
Dwyer and McGovern found that given similar precommitment behavior, women were
hospitalized more quickly than men. Fox found the opposite, that women had been ill
longer than men before commitment. They all offer interesting reasons for their
findings, ranging from a different tolerance to female violence and disruptiveness in the
home to the availability of other relatives to care for the sick person. See Dwyer, *Homes
for the Mad*, p. 107; McGovern, "The Myths of Social Control," pp. 8, 15; Fox, *So Far
Disordered*, pp. 127–30.

[48] Dwyer, "A Historical Perspective," p. 25.

[49] Ibid., pp. 24–25; Dwyer, *Homes for the Mad*, pp. 133–34; Tomes, *A Generous Confidence*, pp. 201–3. As the members of the Rutgers health policy seminar pointed out to
me, patients spent many more hours with the ward attendants than they did with the
asylum doctors. Thus historians' almost exclusive focus on medical attitudes toward
gender roles should be broadened to consider how other staff members may have
treated male and female patients differently.

More interesting differences are evident in the medical treatment of the two sexes. One of the most significant findings, in light of the contemporary studies cited earlier, has to do with patterns of drug prescribing. Even in the nineteenth century, Constance McGovern has found that women patients received twice as many sedatives as male patients. Drug treatment correlated highly with social status; middle-class women and women committed by their families were more likely to be given drugs than poor or friendless women, indicating that families may have urged their use. Some of these sedatives may have been prescribed in place of physical restraints; McGovern found that violent women were more likely than men to be drugged instead of restrained.

Contrary to contemporary opinion, which tends to emphasize the negative aspects of drug use, McGovern argues that in the context of nineteenth-century psychiatry, the therapeutic use of sedatives may have helped rather than harmed women. In her sample of cases, women who were given drugs were discharged "recovered" more often than those who were not. She speculates that the drug may have acted as a placebo, increasing the patient's confidence in her doctor, and reinforcing his expectation of her improvement. Drug treatment, along with gynecological care, also necessitated more individual attention to the patient, which may have enhanced her chances for recovery.[50]

If benefit from hospital treatment is measured solely by the physician's perception of its outcome, women fared better than men. McGovern, Dwyer, and I all found that women were more likely to be discharged "cured" than men, while men were more likely to die in the asylum. These statistics defy easy generalizations about medical intent toward either sex. They might, for example, reflect the different forms of mental illness for which the two sexes were committed. At the Pennsyl-

---

[50] McGovern, "The Myths of Social Control," pp. 13–15. Jack Pressman's work on psychosurgery in the late 1940s and 1950s presents an even more striking example of the ambiguities inherent in the retrospective evaluation of medical treatments. Showalter, among others, has invoked the fact that women have outnumbered men as recipients of insulin shock, electroshock, and lobotomies, to argue for the "male hostility" thesis. But as Pressman shows, psychiatrists regarded somatic therapies as their most "progressive" forms of treatment. Why women more often than men were picked as the recipients of these new therapies is not at all clear. See Showalter, *The Female Malady*, p. 205; Jack Pressman, "Sufficient Promise: John F. Fulton and the Origins of Psychosurgery," *Bulletin of the History of Medicine* 62 (1988): 1–22; and Jack Pressman, "Uncertain Promise: Psychosurgery and the Development of Scientific Psychiatry in America, 1935–55," Ph.D. dissertation, University of Pennsylvania, 1986, esp. pp. 162–230.

vania Hospital for the Insane, 19% of the men and only 8% of the women were admitted with dementia, the most hopeless diagnosis. No doubt many of the male dementia cases were suffering from general paresis, an incurable organic disease, and therefore would derive little benefit from hospital care. At the same time, more women than men suffered from depression. Given our previous speculations about the origins of female depression in marital strain and overwork, asylum treatment, with its emphasis on nourishing food and rest, may well have helped in this condition, especially for working-class women.[51]

The whole concept of the "rest cure" takes on a different meaning when it is considered along class lines. Working-class women and middle-class ladies did not come to institutional care with the same experiences or needs. To a laborer's wife worn out from malnutrition, repeated childbearing, and physical abuse from an alcoholic husband, the idea of a "rest cure" may not have sounded so oppressive. In their surveys of asylum records, both Dwyer and McGovern found evidence that some women did regard the mental hospital as a refuge from overwork and physical abuse. "For single women facing a life of drudgery as domestic servants, for those without family support systems, or for those exhausted by the caretaking of an elderly parent or relative, the asylum could be benign, protective, and even more tolerant than the outside world," posits McGovern. As a result, some women resisted efforts to remove them from the hospital, pretending to be ill to prolong their stay. In her study of abbreviated "rest cures" for neurasthenia at the Massachusetts General Hospital, Barbara Sicherman found that working-class women (and men) responded positively to bedrest and overfeeding.[52]

The higher "cure" rates for women asylum patients may also reflect the fact that by virtue of their gender-role socialization, they made more compliant patients. I have attributed the confidence one nineteenth-century asylum doctor inspired in his women charges (one of whom he later married) in part to the resonance between the doctor/patient, male/female roles. Conversely, as Constance McGovern points out, "Men had difficulty playing the invalid role and adjusting to the asylum

[51] Tomes, A Generous Confidence, pp. 324, 326; McGovern, "The Myths of Social Control," pp. 8, 10; Dwyer, "A Historical Perspective," pp. 25, 39.
[52] Constance McGovern, "The Community, The Hospital, and the Working-Class Patient," Pennsylvania History 54 (1987): 25. See also McGovern, "Myths of Social Control," pp. 11–13; Dwyer, Homes for the Mad, pp. 11, 94; Sicherman, "The Uses of a Diagnosis," p. 52.

environment which called for passive behavior and unquestioning submission to authority." Whatever advantages men enjoyed in the outside world, once in the asylum, "gender and diagnostic stereotypes yielded few advantages for men patients."[53]

While McGovern's point is well taken, we might well question the assumption that gender and diagnostic stereotypes yielded women any real advantages, if "cure" consisted solely of learning to conform to the doctor's paternalistic assumptions. Moreover, for all the women who were discharged "cured," there were other women who did not find asylum life so benign. They complained, refused to eat, and escaped as protests against what they perceived to be a form of incarceration. But both extremes of compliance and rebellion demonstrate "considerable choice on the part of the so-called victims," McGovern notes. The multiple uses women made of nineteenth-century mental hospitals underline the need to rethink social-control explanations that "patients and their families were passive victims of state policies and institutional programs."[54]

At the same time, a note of caution about this "revisionist" view of women asylum patients needs to be sounded. While they were not passive victims, women's choices were nonetheless severely bounded by the class structure and paternalism of the larger culture, not to mention the mental disabilities they suffered. While asylum doctors expressed some sympathy for their female charges, they never questioned the fundamental wisdom of nineteenth-century gender roles, and always acted to reinforce them. The asylum functioned as society in microcosm, rewarding only those patients who could and would comply with the physician's definition of sanity. For those women who remained "unconverted" by the doctor's therapeutic ministrations, asylum paternalism offered cold comfort indeed, in the form of years of tedious confinement. Thus the *diversity* of women's institutional experiences within the larger context of this paternalistic system must always be kept at the forefront of historical analysis.

FURTHER DIRECTIONS FOR RESEARCH

As this essay demonstrates, recent historical studies have provided new insights into the influence of gender on the etiology, diagnosis, and

---

[53] Tomes, *A Generous Confidence*, p. 226; McGovern, "The Myths of Social Control," p. 11.
[54] McGovern, "The Myths of Social Control," p. 16.

treatment of mental illness. To encourage future work on the many interesting questions that remain, I would like to offer a few concluding thoughts on promising lines of methodology and research. The most convincing work has not relied only on medical texts about women and mental illness, but has paired theory with analysis of actual clinical records. Published sources simply do not provide sufficient information to serve as accurate guides either to medical practice or women's experience. In addition, medical conceptions of women's mental illnesses need to be interpreted within the context of larger professional and intellectual struggles, particularly the competition among medical specialties.

The most convincing generalizations about sex differences in medical theory and treatment are those grounded in a *comparative* perspective; if men are not included as a "control group," it is impossible to distinguish how women's experiences really differed from theirs.[55] The same argument applies to the role of class as a factor shaping patterns of women's mental illness. Working-class women not only comprised the majority of asylum patients, but evidently had a special claim on physician paternalism, and their experience must be considered apart from and compared to their middle-class counterparts. Last but not least, none of the studies to date have included race as a significant variable determining women's institutional experiences; this comparative dimension must be built into future research.

Attending carefully to gender, class, and race, scholars in the future might pursue a number of important issues suggested by the studies surveyed here. In order better to understand how the commitment process affected women and men differently, careful comparative studies of precommitment behavior are required. Likewise, we need some more convincing explanation, beyond the male hostility thesis, for the greater likelihood of women to receive somatic interventions, from sedatives to lobotomies. (Two works in progress, Constance McGovern's monograph on women and psychiatry and Jack Pressman's study of psychosurgery, are eagerly awaited in this regard.)

Given the current interest in women and depression, historians might well want to look more closely at that disorder. Unlike hysteria or

---

[55] Mark Micale's new work on Charcot's theory of male hysteria is an excellent example of how comparison across class and gender lines can enrich our understanding of psychiatric theory and diagnosis. See his "Jean-Martin Charcot and the Theory of Hysteria in the Male: An Essay on Gender, Mental Science, and Medical Diagnostics," forthcoming in *Medical History*.

anorexia nervosa, depression, apart from its postpartum form, was not perceived primarily as a woman's disease in the nineteenth century, despite the fact that women already outnumbered men in hospital admissions for that diagnosis. That physicians focused on hysteria as the most interesting woman's disease of the nineteenth century probably had more to do with the medical milieu of the period, in which diseases of the nervous system were "hot" intellectual and professional properties, than the clinical incidence of the disease. In any event, women and depression would seem to offer a fascinating topic for future historical exploration. Regrettably, Stanley Jackson's recent survey of the history of depression as a clinical concept hardly mentions gender.[56]

The medicalization of women's psychological distress also beckons as an important but still too-little understood process. To study this phenomenon, medical historians could profit by an examination of women's diaries and letters. By comparing women's responses to painful experiences such as illness and death over time, they might well detect important shifts in the language and symbols they used to discuss their emotional experiences, as well as clarify the role of medicine, whether through the medium of advice literature or the family physician, in fostering those shifts.

Let me conclude with another caution. Recent historical work has begun to reconsider certain assumptions about the gender-madness nexus, and to reject oversimplified notions of women's liability to mental illness and victimization at the hands of male physicians. This new approach has resulted in a much more complex reading of women's experience as mental patients. But in rewriting the history of women and madness, historians must be careful not to overromanticize their subjects. While the madwoman may not have been a helpless victim of male hostility, she nonetheless suffered the burden not only of madness but of gender, a fact that we cannot afford to forget.

---

[56] Stanley Jackson, *Melancholia and Depression* (New Haven: Yale University Press, 1986).

7

SURGICAL GYNECOLOGY

Judith M. Roy

The development of surgical gynecology introduced a new approach to health care for women. Beginning in the early nineteenth century, certain physicians proposed surgical procedures to investigate and cure pathological conditions of the female reproductive organs. As long as these organs remained hidden from view inside the body, both normal and abnormal functions elicited speculative and sometimes fanciful explanations. The Greeks, for example, attributed certain female illness to *hysteria*, i.e. "traveling womb."

The possibility of surgical access to the reproductive organs allowed direct observation of gynecological dysfunctions and more aggressive therapy by physicians. In 1809, surgeon Ephriam McDowell of Danville, Kentucky successfully removed an ovarian cyst weighing twenty-two pounds from the body of a woman who subsequently made a complete recovery. After performing three other ovariotomies with one fatality, McDowell argued for the relative safety of his abdominal surgery techniques. The operation could be attempted, he claimed, ". . . by any good anatomist, possessing the judgement requisite for a surgeon."[1]

McDowell's experiments in ovariotomy set the early precedent for gynecological surgery. Most of the medical community, however, rejected the procedure as too dangerous and an outrageous violation of female modesty. Further developments in the field languished until the 1850s when Alabama physician J. Marion Sims published his successful method of surgically repairing a common childbirth injury, vesico-

---

[1] Ephriam McDowell, "Observations on Diseased Overia," *The Eclectic Repertory and Analytical Review, Medical and Philosophical* IX (1819): 654.

vaginal fistula. Long or difficult labor caused a tear, or fistula, between the vagina and the bladder. Women so afflicted endured lifelong incontinence; the constant drip of urine from the vaginal opening resulted in severe skin irritations, odor, and social ostracism.[2]

Sims proved a consummate proselytizer of surgical treatments for a wide variety of female complaints. He relocated from Montgomery, Alabama to New York City in 1853 in order to gain influence and prestige in the medical community. By 1855, he succeeded in his efforts to open the first hospital devoted to the treatment of gynecological dysfunctions and disease, The New York Woman's Hospital. As the institution's chief medical officer, Sims positioned himself at the forefront of a new medical specialty.[3]

Initially, practitioners of the new specialty referred to themselves as "woman's doctors" in order to differentiate their field from obstetrics. By the 1870s, however, both the physicians and their patients used the more "scientific" term *gynecologist*. Over the next fifty years, the new "woman's doctors" extended the range of their operations from the repair of childbirth lacerations to uterine displacements and menstrual irregularities and ultimately to the "capital" operations of ovariotomy and hysterectomy. Gynecological therapeutics addressed every aspect of female health from puberty to menopause and beyond. The very construct of the specialty combined the influence of medical knowledge and the process of professionalization with societal definitions of acceptable gender roles. Gynecology adopted a specific medical technique, surgery, to attack specific dysfunctions of the female reproductive system. At the same time, practitioners incorporated a holistic view of patient health common to nineteenth-century medicine. Lifestyle and behavior, therefore, influenced gynecological functions. Women who overexerted themselves physically or mentally at puberty, who exposed themselves to cold weather while menstruating, or who lived a "frivolous" life of fashion and gossip irreparably damaged their reproductive systems. For

---

[2] J. Marion Sims, "On the Treatment of Vesico-vaginal Fistula," *American Journal of the Medical Sciences* 23 (Jan. 1852): 59–87.

[3] For details of Sims's move to the North and the founding of New York Woman's Hospital, see Sims, *The Story of My Life*, H. Marion Sims, ed., (New York: D. Appleton & Co., 1884) and Seale Harris, *Woman's Surgeon: The Life Story of J. Marion Sims* (New York: Macmillan Co., 1950). See also Deborah Kuhn McGregor, "Silver Sutures: The Medical Career of J. Marion Sims," Ph.D. dissertation, State University of New York at Binghamton, 1986.

gynecologists and their patients who internalized these beliefs, "correct" female behavior equaled "healthy" behavior and bad habits led to poor health.[4]

In light of the potential for insights into the physical life of women plus the cultural context of their medical care, the researcher is surprised to note the paucity of historical monographs on the subject of surgical gynecology. Over the last two decades, the literature on women's health-care issues increased dramatically. While subjects such as childbirth and women in the medical professions are well represented, a major study of women and gynecology has yet to appear.[5] A number of studies, how-ever, touch on gynecological issues as part of their discussion of other topics. In general, secondary literature on gynecology falls into one of three categories: (1) the standard medical histories that focus almost exclusively on medical developments with little social analysis, (2) the polemic arguments that view every aspect of gynecological surgery as overt misogyny, and (3) the approach that places concern for cultural influences on female health care within the context of the medical therapeutics of the day. The standard medical histories carry their narra-tive through to the mid-twentieth century but almost all the other works focus on the nineteenth century. Very little historical analysis exists for the period between the First World War and the social critiques of today's medical treatment of women. It is to be hoped that research will extend into the twentieth century as more scholars examine women's physical past.

MEDICAL HISTORIES

The standard medical histories outline the development of gynecol-ogy and are at times referred to as "great doctor" history. The authors identify the individual physicians responsible for each innovation in gynecological therapeutics. They mention controversy over competing medical theories, but couch the discussion in primarily medical terms

---

[4] Charles Rosenberg, "The Therapeutic Revolution," in *The Therapeutic Revolution*, Mor-ris Vogel and Charles Rosenberg, eds. (Philadelphia: University of Pennsylvania Press, 1979), pp. 5–9.
[5] For example, see Judith Walzer Leavitt, *Brought to Bed* (New York: Oxford University Press, 1986) and Regina Markell Morantz-Sanchez, *Sympathy and Science* (New York: Oxford University Press, 1985).

with little or no analysis of nonmedical components such as professionalization or gender roles.[6]

James Ricci, in his 1945 work *One Hundred Years of Gynecology*, went
beyond a simple listing of medical advances with occasional statements
of opinion and critical comment. For example, he attributed the beginning of gynecology as a medical specialty to an improvement in the status
of women during the nineteenth century. The rise in status led to
increased concern with female health problems and thus to a growing
market for medical services.[7] Even more unusual, Ricci castigated the
rapid increase in gynecological surgery during the 1870s and 1880s as an
era of "pelvic surgery gone wild."[8] Such pronouncements are rare,
however, leaving the reader with much information on chronological
development and medical detail but little understanding of the complex
external factors shaping medical therapeutics.

Unfortunately, the works mentioned above represent the bulk of
historical material on the subject of surgical gynecology generated by
physicians in recent decades, either in monograph form or in the medical
literature. One article, which appeared to mark the centenary of the
American Gynecological Society in 1976, discloses the element of self-
criticism that existed in the society in earlier years. The authors, Houston S. Everett, M.D., and E. Stewart Taylor, M.D., trace medical developments in gynecology as reflected in papers presented to the society
and pay tribute to illustrious Fellows. Their analysis, however, suggests
an element of self-criticism within the society. Several presidential addresses at the turn of the century cautioned against too frequent use of
surgery while J. Whitridge Williams took an even more caustic view of
the value of the society in his presidential address in 1914: Out of one
thousand and ten papers presented since 1876, "he concluded that only

---

[6] Theodore Cianfrani, *A Short History of Obstetrics and Gynecology* (Springfield, IL: Charles
     C. Thomas, 1960); J. M. Munroe Kerr, R. W. Johnstone, and H. Miles, eds., *Historical
     Review of British Obstetrics and Gynaecology, 1800–1900* (London: E. & S. Livingstone,
     1954); and James V. Ricci, *One Hundred Years of Gynecology, 1800–1900* (Philadelphia:
     The Blakiston Co., 1945) provide the basic information on medical developments in
     gynecology. See also Harvey Graham, *Eternal Eve: The History of Gynecology and Obstet-
     rics* (Garden City, NJ: Doubleday, 1951); Harold Speert, *Obstetrics and Gynecology
     Milestones: Essays in Eponymy* (New York: Macmillan Press, 1958); and Speert, *Pic-
     torial History of Gynecology and Obstetrics: Iconographia Gyniatrica* (Philadelphia: Davis,
     1973).
[7] Ricci, *One Hundred Years*, p. 3.
[8] Ibid., pp. 46–47.

forty-two were creditable and twenty-two were excellent."!⁹ His successor hastened to redress such a negative position the following year.

The most recent of the standard medical histories of gynecology
appeared in 1960. Written by physicians for physicians, these works did
not claim to be sophisticated historical analysis nor did they try to reach
a wide audience.[10]

MEDICAL HISTORY AS SOCIAL HISTORY

A completely different type of author and a potentially large audience emerged in the early 1970s. Beginning in the late 1960s, the
women's movement sensitized many academics to inequities in women's
role in society. Women's historians and feminist scholars in a variety of
other fields brought an entirely different perspective to women's physical past by interpreting the female patient/male physician relationship as
the patriarchial society writ small. Rejecting the old model of uncritical
praise for "scientific medical progress," the new studies emphasized
cultural biases as major factors in women's medical care.

Several early studies saw surgical gynecology as female victimization
by a sexist society with physicians exerting total control over helpless
women patients. Barbara Ehrenreich and Deirdre English reflect the
activism of the era by focusing on male power over female behavior in
two studies, *Complaints and Disorders: The Sexual Politics of Illness* and *For
Her Own Good: One Hundred Years of Experts' Advice to Women*. The ideal
Victorian woman displayed the characteristics of passivity, modesty, and
virtue coupled with devotion to family and domestic duties. In their
discussion of gynecological surgery, Ehrenreich and English claim female
behavior that deviated from this ideal threatened male sexual and/or
economic superiority. Physicians possessed a special ability to exert
control over women by defining any aberrant behavior as illness caused
by "the dictatorship of the ovaries."[11]

---

[9] Houston S. Everett, M.D. and E. Stewart Taylor, M.D., "The History of the American
Gynecological Society and the Scientific Contributions of its Fellows," *The Journal of
Obstetrics and Gynecology* 126 (Dec. 1976): 911, 908–19.

[10] A thorough review of the medical literature reveals that physicians, who are not, after
all, historians, tend to restrict themselves to chronological details of gynecological
development. For example, see H. A. Kelly, M.D., "Pre-1933 History of Gynecology
in Maryland, "*Maryland State Medical Journal* 29 (1980): 21–30, 81–83 and
P. E. Bordahl, M.D., "Tubal Sterilization: An Historical Overview," *Journal of Reproductive Medicine* 30 (1985): 18–24.

[11] Barbara Ehrenreich and Deirdre English, *Complaints and Disorders: The Sexual Politics of
Sickness* (Old Westbury, NY: Feminist Press, 1973); and *For Her Own Good* (Garden
City, NY: Anchor Books, 1979), p. 120 ff.

In his book, *The Horror of the Half-Known Life*, G. J. Barker-Benfield followed the villain/victim scenario and set forth a psychological profile of nineteenth-century gynecologists. According to Barker-Benfield, a basic element in nineteenth-century male identity was a need to "exclude and subordinate women."[12] A subconscious hostility and need to control women, therefore, existed within the psyche of every gynecologist. These men, either consciously or subconsciously, chose a medical specialty that allowed them to act out their sexual aggression toward women through surgery. In collusion with husbands and fathers, gynecologists performed unnecessary mutilating operations such as clitoridectomy and ovariotomy in order to control female behavior.[13]

This concept of women as defined by their reproductive organs became one of the most important components of the new work on women and health care. Ann Douglas Wood, quoting a medical professor of the 1870s, explained that to physicians it seemed "as if the Almighty, in creating the female sex, had taken the uterus and built up a woman around it."[14] For gynecologists, even more than other practitioners, the conviction that the uterus and ovaries dominated all other body functions legitimated gynecology as a specialty and extended the scope of their therapies.

According to accepted nineteenth-century medical theory, the female generative system affected all other parts of the body through its contact with the sympathetic nervous system. Thus headaches, nervous complaints, or dyspepsia could be caused by menstrual difficulties or a retoverted uterus. Gynecologists urged women to consult them for any illness since as specialists they possessed expertise in treating the organs ultimately responsible for the symptoms. This perception of female illness increased the potential clientele for gynecologists; one scholar suggested these physicians rejected previously existing effective treatments in favor of the more costly surgical innovations.[15] By implication, gynecologists misused their medical knowledge in order to enhance their

---

[12] G. J. Barker-Benfield, *The Horrors of the Half-Known Life* (New York: Harper and Row, 1976), p. 129.

[13] Ibid.

[14] Ann Douglas Wood, "'The Fashionable Diseases': Women's Complaints and Their Treatment in Nineteenth-Century America," in *Women and Health in America*, Judith Walzer Leavitt, ed. (Madison: University of Wisconsin Press, 1984), pp. 222–38. (originally published in *The Journal of Interdisciplinary History* IV (1973): 25–52).

[15] Patricia Branca, *Silent Sisterhood* (New York: Science History Publications, 1977), pp. 62–63.

professional standing and ultimately control female behavior. This argument, however, overestimates the level of knowledge and training available to nineteenth-century physicians. Further, the researcher must avoid the underlying assumption that early gynecologists would be able to discern the "correct" medical approach amongst a host of competing ideas. In the world of nineteenth-century medicine, therapeutic efficacy was decided more on personal opinion and observation in individual practices than by any sort of controlled scientific study. The patient, therefore, depended on the individual skill of his or her physician in choosing the best treatment from a large menu of conflicting medical ideas. Since the profession lacked any standardized requirements for education and training, a well-meaning doctor might choose a useless or harmful therapy but the mistake would stem from a lack of knowledge and not necessarily from hostility towards female patients.

The studies referred to above provided an invaluable stimulus to research on women's physical past. Feminists used an analysis of gender roles to interpret the medical care available to women and focused on cultural rather than strictly medical components. In a landmark article, however, Regina Markell Morantz cautioned against an oversimplification of the medical history of women. Unless the treatment of women's diseases in the past is put in the context of the medical therapeutics of the day, the scholarship suffers from a "presentism" that labels woman as victim without exploring the complexities of the medical/cultural interaction.[16] In addition, an article by Gail Pat Parsons offers evidence of harsh medical treatments for nineteenth-century men, showing that gender alone did not dictate choice of therapy.[17] A number of recent works on the history of women and medicine reflect the type of approach advocated by Morantz, reevaluating the status of the physicians, the doctor/patient relationship, and the surgical procedures themselves.[18]

---

[16] Regina Markell Morantz, "The Perils of Feminist History," in *Women and Health in America*, pp. 239–45; (first published in *The Journal of Interdisciplinary History* IV [1973]): 649–60).

[17] Gail Pat Parsons, "Equal Treatment For All: American Medical Remedies for Male Sexual Problems: 1850–1900," *Journal of the History of Medicine and Allied Sciences* 32 (1977): 55–71. For an analysis of contemporary differences in treatment for women and men, see Lois M. Verbrugge and Richard P. Steiner, "Physician Treatment of Men and Women Patients" in *Medical Care* 19 (1981): 609–32.

[18] Examples of this work are: Virginia G. Drachman, *Hospital with a Heart: Women Doctors and the Paradox of Separatism at the New England Hospital, 1862–1969* (Ithaca: Cornell University Press, 1984); Gloria Moldow, *Women Doctors in Gilded-Age Washington: Race, Gender, and Professionalization* (Urbana: University of Illinois Press, 1987); and Martha H. Verbrugge, *Able-Bodied Womanhood: Personal Health and Social Change in Nineteenth-Century Boston* (Oxford: Oxford University Press, 1988).

MEDICAL SPECIALIZATION

Gynecology did not develop as a medical specialty in a vacuum. During the last half of the nineteenth century, American medicine struggled with numerous changes in professional status and structure. One of the most controversial issues faced by the medical community was the spread of specialization and the field of gynecology reflected the general trends in this process.

Charles Rosenberg, in his article "Between Two Worlds," claims that by 1879 specialism was "the major institutional change in American medical practice."[19] Physicians identifying themselves as specialists in such fields as neurology, ophthalmology, and orthopedic surgery, among others, contributed disproportionately to the medical journals and formed national associations. The growing numbers and prominence of such specialists fueled extensive debate over the boundaries of specialized practice. In particular, the "ordinary physician" faced a double threat from the trend: losing patients to doctors claiming expertise in one area or to specialists who continued "to serve as general practitioners and thus competitors."[20]

Despite the variety of opinions and considerable opposition, specialization steadily increased its appeal for ambitious members of the medical community. Both Rosenberg and sociologist Paul Starr discuss the professional, economic, and social factors which encouraged this development. Basically, a combination of long-term economic struggles and accelerated urbanization of medical institutions stimulated new approaches to success in the medical marketplace. Ambitious doctors flocked to urban centers for the opportunity to affiliate with prestigious teaching hospitals. Along with increased opportunities, however, came increased competition. This competition in turn stimulated the growth of specialization since the specialist gains a partial advantage by giving up services producing the lowest returns in favor of those producing the highest.[21]

Rosemary Stevens adds to the complexity of the discussion of medical specialization by considering the nature of a specialty as an idea.[22] She points out that the definition of specialization remained fluid

---

[19] Charles Rosenberg, "Between Two Worlds," in *Centenary of Index Medicus, 1879–1979*, John B. Blake, ed. (Bethesda, MD: U.S. Department of Health and Human Services, N.I.H. Publication no. 80-206B, 1980), p. 7.

[20] Ibid.

[21] Paul Starr, *The Social Transformation of American Medicine* (New York: Basic Books, 1982), pp. 76–77, 81–92.

[22] Rosemary Stevens, "The Changing Idea of a Medical Specialty," *Transactions and Studies of the College of Physicians of Philadelphia* 5 (1980): 159–77.

until the 1930s, with no one standardized set of criteria. In the 1890s the word "specialty" could stand for an avocation or special interest on the part of a doctor in general practice as well as exclusive concentration in a field. Some practitioners described themselves as specialists, while others, such as pediatric pioneer Abraham Jacobi, rejected the appellation even when colleagues dubbed them specialists due to their particular skills and knowledge. Even the self-proclaimed specialists differed in their definitions of the same field. Many gynecologists viewed their specialty as a particular set of surgical skills and therapies. Yet for Dr. Kate Hurd Mead, a specialty in obstetrics and gynecology represented her interest in social reform and all aspects of infant and maternal welfare. During her years of practice from the 1880s to the 1920s, Mead campaigned for legislation to provide funds for maternal and child welfare services. To her, gynecology stood for the special relationship between women physicians and women patients rather than surgical cures for female complaints.[23]

Specialization, therefore, remained a controversial issue throughout the last half of the nineteenth century. Proponents of general medicine criticized the trend on economic grounds—fear of competition. In addition, some critics predicted the loss of a holistic approach to medicine when the physician treated a specific disease rather than the entire individual. Even specialists themselves disagreed over definitions and qualifications for a given field. Inexorably, however, specialization attracted growing numbers of doctors through competitive advantages and the importance of "scientific expertise" in medicine by the close of the nineteenth century.[24]

GYNECOLOGISTS: EDUCATION AND STATUS

Some intriguing information about the progress of gynecologists as specialists emerges from a few studies which focus on this field. First, throughout the nineteenth century practitioners of gynecology suffered from a lack of education and status. Lawrence D. Longo describes the emergence of gynecology as a medical specialty separate from obstetrics at mid-century and the appalling lack of training available in the field for the next fifty years. Eli Van de Warken, a prominent professor of

---

[23] Ibid., pp. 160, 163–65.
[24] Ibid., pp. 174–77.

obstetrics, told a meeting of the AMA in 1888 "that in 66 of 109 medical colleges gynecology either was taught by an ill-trained obstetrician or not taught at all. . . . American medical students scarcely encountered it."[25] The reference to obstetricians as instructors in gynecology is significant since the practice of gynecology remained separate from obstetrics well into the twentieth century; a survey taken in 1912 revealed only 13 out of 120 schools with closely allied gynecology and obstetrics departments. Gynecology was a surgical specialty, while obstetrics was not. Without specialized training, woman's doctors had adapted general surgical techniques to the treatment of female complaints on an ad hoc basis in private practice. Significant improvements in education in the field did not appear until the 1920s and 1930s.[26]

With few exceptions, therefore, gynecologists entered practice with weak or inadequate training in their specialty. Further, as a relative newcomer gynecology possessed lower status than more established areas of medicine such as obstetrics and the elite ranks of general practice. A number of works explore "The Fall and Rise of the American Medical Profession"[27] in general but we have a few tantalizing hints of the particular situation of woman's doctors.

Gynecologists faced censure from other physicians and from the general public. As we have seen from the general discussion of specialization above, general practitioners feared the loss of women patients to "experts" in curing female complaints. The fluid nature of specialty designation exacerbated such fears since the medical profession as a whole lacked effective means of control over qualifications for specialty practice until the 1930s.[28] Physicians also equated specialization with quackery since earlier in the century "only charlatans advertised specialized cures."[29]

---

[25] Lawrence D. Longo, "Obstetrics and Gynecology," in *The Education of American Physicians*, Ronald L. Numbers, ed. (Berkeley: University of California Press, 1980), pp. 205-25.

[26] Ibid., pp. 221-25. For information on the gradual integration of gynecology with obstetrics in the 1920s and 1930s and application of surgical techniques to obstetrics, see Pamela S. Summey and Marcia Hurst, "Ob/Gyn on the Rise: The Evolution of Professional Ideology in the Twentieth Century - Part II," *Women and Health* 11 (1986): 103-22.

[27] See Ronald Numbers, "The Fall and Rise of the American Medical Profession," in *Sickness and Health in America*, Judith Walzer Leavitt and Ronald L. Numbers, eds. (Madison: University of Wisconsin Press, 1985), pp. 185-96.

[28] Starr, *Transformation*, pp. 81-87, 224-25.

[29] Sarah Stage, *Female Complaints* (New York: W. W. Norton & Co., 1979), p. 77.

In her study of the development of obstetrics and gynecology in Boston, Edna Manzer indicated that such inauspicious beginnings influenced the type of men adopting the specialty of gynecology. Comparing the membership of the separate Obstetrical Society with that of the Gynecological Society in 1884 revealed interesting differences in background and success. Members of the Obstetrical Society came from relatively affluent families while the gynecologists came from less wealthy backgrounds. Twenty-seven out of twenty-eight Obstetrical Society members graduated from college compared with only seven out of twenty-seven members of the Gynecological Society. All but one member of the Gynecological Society lived outside Boston proper; almost all the obstetricians lived within the city. Finally, few gynecologists participated in the most prestigious Boston medical societies though most obstetricians listed such affiliations. For the gynecologist, therefore, starting practice at a greater disadvantage than his obstetrical colleague, the practice of specialized medicine offered a larger opportunity for professional and social advancement.[30] Aspiring doctors without funds for a college education or an upper-middle-class background found gynecology an "open" field where their advancement would not be blocked by an established group with "superior" economic and class advantages. The gynecologists in Manzer's study, however, would not be unaware of the professional and economic differences between themselves and their obstetrical colleagues. By advancing the status of gynecology as a medical specialty, a practitioner could rise above socioeconomic disadvantages and enter the professional and social world of the medical elite.

Biographies of two leading gynecologists of the nineteenth century buttress Manzer's findings. Both J. Marion Sims and his British colleague Robert Lawson Tait came from backgrounds of genteel poverty and consciously struggled to enter the realm of the medical elite.[31] Much work remains to be done, but early evidence points to even greater feelings of defensiveness on the part of woman's doctors than in more established physicians. Historian Peter Gay maintained that "physicians of the nineteenth century did not rise above the common humanity; they

---

[30] Edna Manzer, "Woman's Doctors: The Development of Obstetrics and Gynecology in Boston, 1860–1900," Ph.D. dissertation, Indiana University, 1979, pp. 131–35.

[31] For biographical information on Sims and Lawson Tait, see Harris, *Woman's Surgeon* and John Shepherd, *Lawson Tait: Rebellious Surgeon* (Lawrence, KS: Coronado Press, 1980).

felt themselves dependent on the good will of their fellows and their society.''[32] Because the medical community adopted a superior attitude towards the fledgling specialty, gynecologists pursued professional and social acceptance very aggressively.

EARLY CRITICISM

The particular nature of gynecological therapeutics elicited criticism and suspicion from the lay community as well as the medical world. The extreme concern of Victorian society for the purity and modesty of middle-class women called the very practice of gynecology into question. Reformer Catharine Beecher expressed grave misgivings about the propriety of gynecological examinations by male physicians in her 1855 publication *Letters to the People on Health and Happiness*. Beecher thought innocent women risked immoral advances by unscrupulous men during the course of a procedure "performed with bolted doors and curtained windows, and with no one present but patient and operator.''[33] Another woman, a suffragist, warned of an "unclean army of gynecologists.''[34]

The criticisms voiced by these women reflected widely held beliefs in women as moral guardians and sexual innocents. As Martha Verbrugge points out, middle-class women interested in improving female health struggled to balance the need for knowledge about their bodies with the requirements of Victorian respectability. For many women reformers, female physicians offered the ideal compromise: treatment for sex-specific health problems without the threat to female modesty posed by a male doctor.[35] For the ordinary woman, a visit to the gynecologist was a courageous act. After all, she must discuss "indelicate" body functions and reveal parts of her body she had been taught to hide from all but a husband.

If reformers such as Catharine Beecher feared an assault on female modesty, the competitors of "regular" physicians offered alternative forms of therapy. In particular, proponents of hydropathy—the water cure—"proffered . . . moderate remedies utilizing water and changes in

---

32 Peter Gay, *The Education of the Senses*, vol. 1 of *The Bourgeois Experience: Victoria to Freud* (New York: Oxford University Press, 1984), p. 316.
33 Catharine Beecher, in *The Roots of Bitterness*, Nancy F. Cott, ed. (New York: E. P. Dutton & Co., 1972), p. 268. See also Stage, *Female Complaints*, pp. 78–79.
34 Stage, *Female Complaints*, p. 78.
35 Verbrugge, *Able-Bodied Womanhood*. Ch. 3 discusses the conflict middle-class women felt when participating in study groups to learn more about female physiology.

personal habits" in place of harsh drugs or surgery.[36] Susan Cayleff examines hydropathic views on female disease in her book *Wash and be Healed*. Hydropaths redefined female physiological processes as natural and nonpathological, stressing prevention through healthy living and gentle intervention when problems arose.[37] As Cayleff and others point out, however, hydropathy peaked as a health movement by the end of the 1860s.[38] Thus, the attraction of the water cure declined just as gynecological surgery began its most active period.

As techniques in anesthesia, antisepsis, and asepsis improved, gynecological surgery increased dramatically in the years after 1870. Even before surgeons implemented antiseptic procedures, the use of anesthesia transformed the nature of general surgery and promoted gynecological surgery in particular. Most recent research concentrates on anesthesia during childbirth, but Martin Pernick presents broader concepts of cultural attitudes towards women and pain. Nineteenth-century medicine believed in the greater physical frailty of women. Women felt pain with much more severity than men and with graver consequences to their sensitive nervous systems. Without anesthesia, most women could not withstand the type of surgery needed to repair childbirth injuries or to remove an ovarian cyst. In addition, male physicians considered women ideal candidates for anesthesia because unconsciousness protected female modesty from the shame of exposure during gynecological surgery. An increase in all kinds of gynecological surgery followed the use of anesthesia, including experimental procedures such as "normal" ovariotomy, but Pernick points out that the proportion of experimental operations was relatively small compared to the overall growth in surgery.[39]

Anesthesia vastly enhanced the appeal of gynecology to women patients by adding freedom from pain to promises of quick, permanent

---

[36] Susan E. Cayleff, *Wash and Be Healed* (Philadelphia: Temple University Press, 1987), p. 16.

[37] Ibid., ch. 2, pp. 53–54.

[38] Ibid., Conclusion. For a discussion which focuses on hydropathy as applied to pregnancy and birth, see Jane Donegan, *Hydropathic Highway to Health* (Westport, CT: Greenwood Press, 1986).

[39] Martin Pernick, *A Calculus of Suffering* (New York: Columbia University Press, 1985), pp. 174–75, 212–14. An article which deals almost exclusively with obstetrical anesthesia is Mary Poovey, "'Scenes of An Indelicate Character': The Medical 'Treatment' of Victorian Women," in *The Making of the Modern Body*, Catherine Gallegher and Thomas Laqueur, eds. (Berkeley: University of California Press, 1987), pp. 137–68. See also John Duffy, "Anglo-American Reaction to Obstetrical Anesthesia," *Bulletin of the History of Medicine* 38 (1964): 32–44.

cures. Many potential patients suffered from chronic conditions or childbirth injuries which caused severe debilitating pain. Edward Shorter presents a litany of misery endured by women with perineal lacerations, prolapsed uteri, and pelvic infections. Among lifelong effects of unrepaired childbirth injuries were pelvic and back pain, pressure, fecal or urinary incontinence. With a prolapsed uterus, the uterus descends into the vaginal cavity and in severe cases falls out of the vagina to hang between the thighs. The women found it difficult to stand or walk for any length of time. Venereal disease also took its toll on female health when the infections passed through the uterus into the Fallopian tubes. The resulting pelvic inflammatory disease caused infertility and severe abdominal pain.[40]

Some women would endure anything, even unanesthetized surgery, to gain relief. Many others, however, would avoid treatment out of fear of additional pain. Is it any wonder that women sought help from gynecologists who offered them cures while "asleep," without terrifying suffering?

ATTITUDES OF WOMEN PHYSICIANS

Early studies implied a gender difference in nineteenth-century opinions of gynecological surgery. Male doctors endorsed it while female physicians rejected it. Physician Elizabeth Blackwell emerged as the major spokeswoman for the view that the surgery mutilated women who were victims of male medical experimentation.[41] A recent book by Regina Markell Morantz-Sanchez mentions other women practitioners who criticized irresponsible surgery on the female reproductive system, and the leading role played by women doctors during the 1890s in challenging the theory of ovarian disease as the cause of insanity in women.[42]

Morantz-Sanchez and others, however, disprove a facile assumption of total opposition to surgical gynecology by female physicians. A letter

---

[40] Edward Shorter, *The History of Women's Bodies* (New York: Basic Books, 1982), pp. 255–75.
[41] Stage, *Female Complaints*, pp. 79–82.
[42] Morantz-Sanchez, *Sympathy and Science*, pp. 221–22. See also Virginia G. Drachman, "Gynecological Instruments and Surgical Decisions at a Hospital in Late Nineteenth-Century America," *Journal of American Culture* 3 (1980): 660–72 for female physicians who perform gynecological surgery at the woman-run New England Hospital for Women.

written in 1888 by Dr. Mary Putnam Jacobi cautioned Elizabeth Blackwell against ignoring the legitimate and necessary uses of surgical treatments, such as removing diseased fallopian tubes.[43] Morantz-Sanchez found many women prided themselves on their ability in the operating theater, a finding reiterated in a study of the Blackwell Medical Society of Rochester, New York, by Ellen More. When compared with male members of the Rochester Pathological Society at the turn of the century, More found that "In their training, therapeutics, and approach to clinical science, . . . Rochester's female regulars were virtually indistinguishable from their contemporaries in the Pathological Society."[44] In gynecological cases, the women actually reported more instances of surgical treatment in the minutes of their society than the men did in their reports.[45] It is unclear whether this difference meant the women physicians were more willing to operate than the men or if the choice of reports to the respective societies simply reflected a greater interest in women's diseases within the Blackwell Society.

We still await specific studies of the relationship of female practitioners to surgical gynecology, as supporters, as critics, and as outsiders struggling to gain access to the field. Clearly, some women physicians, such as Mary Putnam Jacobi, supported the proper use of gynecological surgery. The all-woman medical staff at the New England Hospital for Women performed gynecological operations regularly during the last quarter of the nineteenth century.[46] Yet men continued to dominate the field to an overwhelming degree. Did male prejudice keep women medical students from training in gynecological surgery? Did women choose more nurturing, idealistic ways to practice medicine and reject the more "scientific" and impersonal modes such as surgery? In what ways did the attitudes of female doctors towards surgical treatment change over time? Not only must the above questions be answered but their interaction must be examined and traced in individual careers. No single, simplistic explanation will suffice. Based on evidence to date, the conclusions drawn by Morantz-Sanchez on the attitudes of women doctors vis-a-vis their male counterparts stand as a model for any medical specialty. While women physicians might have more sensitivity towards women's

[43] Stage, *Female Complaints*, p. 82.
[44] Ellen More, "The Blackwell Medical Society and the Professionalization of Women Physicians," *Bulletin of the History of Medicine* 61 (1987): 603–28, 614.
[45] Ibid., p. 616.
[46] Drachman, *Hospital*, pp. 85–87.

issues, their medical opinions "tended to reflect professional and scientific trends and their divergences among themselves often appeared to be similar to those of male doctors."[47]

Current research, then, delineates the scope of criticism against gynecologists and their specialty during the nineteenth century on both moral and professional grounds. Other studies look at particular procedures, such as ovariotomy, examining the interactions involved on a more specific and detailed level. The literature concentrates on nineteenth-century surgery with very little data available on twentieth-century developments such as hysterectomy, but the work begins to create the outlines of gynecological practice.

SEXUAL SURGERY

One of the most controversial types of operation was the removal of healthy reproductive organs in order to cure some disease or problem in another part of the body. Historians used the term "sexual surgery" to describe such a procedure, which included clitoridectomy (removal of the clitoris) and öophorectomy or Battey's operation (excision of healthy ovaries). The medical logic for this kind of surgery grew out of the belief that the female reproductive organs affected the totality of a woman's physical and mental health. Taken to a logical extreme, individual practitioners proposed clitoridectomy and öophorectomy as treatment for nervous conditions and even insanity.

The "clitoridectomy craze" began in London in the 1860s and was discredited before it took hold to any great extent in the United States. The American medical press followed the progress of this treatment with great interest, however, and it represented the desire of practitioners in both countries for a "cure-all" operation for female complaints. Briefly, a London surgeon, Isaac Baker Brown, concluded that female "nervous complaints" including hysteria, epilepsy, and insanity stemmed from secret masturbation. Clitoridectomy stopped self-abuse and thus restored the women to good health.

After several years of self-publicized "success" with the operation, public and medical opinion began to turn against Baker Brown. In 1866 he faced charges of operating without the consent of patients or their families and also performing clitoridectomy on women institutionalized for insanity. The downfall of Baker Brown served as a warning to

---

[47] Morantz-Sanchez, *Sympathy and Science*, p. 22.

American physicians and prevented widespread use of clitoridectomy in the United States.[48] By the 1870s, however, American gynecology developed its own form of sexual surgery, öophorectomy. Devised by Robert Battey of Georgia, this procedure removed healthy ovaries in order to induce menopause artificially.

Lawrence Longo traced the progress of öophorectomy in his article "The Rise and Fall of Battey's Operation: A Fashion in Surgery."[49] Battey observed the cessation of many chronic female complaints when patients reached menopause. Gynecologists already knew ovariotomy gave great relief to women by removing diseased ovaries and ovarian cysts. Battey carried the principle one step farther in removing healthy ovaries in order to cure problems elsewhere in the reproductive system. Longo defends Battey's motivation for attempting to bring about menopause prematurely since from the beginning Battey recommended the surgery only as a last desperate measure when all other treatment failed. Unfortunately, the guidelines presented by Battey as indications for the surgery opened the way to future abuses. Candidates for the operation suffered from protracted physical and mental distress associated "with monthly nervous and vascular perturbations." They also could be victims of insanity or epilepsy brought on by uterine disease.[50]

While Battey himself warned against indiscriminate use of the operation, others attempted to use it as a panacea for women suffering from pelvic pain, dysmenorrhea, hysteria, or convulsive disorders. Once antiseptic and aseptic techniques reduced mortality rates for abdominal surgery during the 1880s, Longo explained, öophorectomy attracted many gynecologists as a new cure-all to offer their patients. Longo believes the 1906 estimate of 150,000 normal ovariotomies exaggerated the numbers at least tenfold but that it would be impossible to calculate the exact total. Whatever the numbers, they were large enough to attract criticism by eminent gynecologists such as T. Adis Emmet of New York and W. Spencer Wells of London by the mid-1880s.[51]

---

[48] John Duffy, "Masturbation and Clitoridectomy. A Nineteenth-Century View," *Journal of the American Medical Association* 186 (1963): 246–48. For a more detailed discussion, see Andrew Scull and Diane Favreau, "The Clitoridectomy Craze," *Social Research* 33 (1986): 243–60.

[49] Lawrence D. Longo, "The Rise and Fall of Battey's Operation: A Fashion in Surgery," *Bulletin of the History of Medicine* 53 (1979): 244–67. For a Canadian perspective, see Wendy Mitchinson, "Gynecological Operations on Insane Women: London, Ontario, 1895–1901," *Journal of Social History* 15 (1982): 467–84.

[50] Longo, "Rise and Fall," p. 249.

[51] Ibid., pp. 264–67.

Intraprofessional critiques could damage the reputation of Battey's operation but adverse public opinion would destroy its credibility. As with Isaac Baker Brown and clitoridectomy, gynecologists believed in a direct connection between uterine and ovarian functions and insanity in women. A number of practitioners progressed from the individual treatment of middle- and upper-class women for physical conditions to the surgical treatment of women suffering from mental disorders.

Andrew Scull and Diane Favreau detail the expansion of Battey's operation as a cure for insanity in an article on sexual surgery for psychosis.[52] Initially barred from asylums by skeptical superintendents jealous of their own professional standing, gynecologists began operating on middle- and upper-class patients with symptoms of hysteria or nervous complaints. By the 1890s, however, some advocates of öophorectomy gained positions in state asylums and had the chance to test their theories on institutionalized women. Only a few asylums adopted the procedure and the doctors performed a relatively small number of operations but the experiments drew attention and publicity. Ironically, the experimental surgery began in asylums just as medical evidence against normal ovariotomy gained acceptance. Throughout the 1890s the medical elite increasingly disparaged the operation and when its use on insane women attracted attention, a public outcry against "castrating" helpless women completed the downfall of Battey's operation.

Both Longo and Scull and Favreau stress the importance of professional ambitions and rivalries in the spread of Battey's operation and its demise. Each article also demonstrates gynecology's sensitivity to public criticism and to any suggestion of impropriety or cruelty towards women. Scull and Favreau concluded that the interplay of lay and medical stereotypes of women, especially the centrality of female reproductive functions, made women particularly vulnerable to radical sexual surgery techniques. At the same time, physicians based their social and professional standing on their claims to act in the female patient's best interest and as paternalistic protectors of women.[53] The evidence marshaled by Scull and Favreau from medical literature and asylum records reveals how fear for their public reputation influenced doctors' medical judgement. By the end of the nineteenth century, new scientific knowledge contradicted the medical logic which supported Battey's operation.

---

[52] Andrew Scull and Diane Favreau, "A Chance to Cut is a Chance to Cure," *Research in Law, Deviance, and Social Control* 8 (1986): 3–39.

[53] Ibid., p. 26.

It can be argued, however, that negative public opinion created an even stronger motive for abandoning öophorectomy. A significant amount of time elapsed between the publication of the latest findings in physiology, pathology, and anatomy and the application of this information to the daily practice of the average physician. Public criticism, on the other hand, forced doctors to reject a controversial therapy or face the immediate consequence of fewer patients and lower income. At the very least, the combination of new medical knowledge and adverse public reaction relegated Battey's operation "to a collection of crackpots and cranks" by the end of the nineteenth century.[54]

GYNECOLOGY AND VENEREAL DISEASE

Surgery to reposition the uterus remained one of the most frequently performed gynecological procedures throughout the nineteenth century. Often such surgery attempted to relieve chronic pelvic pain, painful menstruation, heavy bleeding, or sterility. Unfortunately, physicians did not realize many of these symptoms resulted from the effects of sexually transmitted disease, especially gonorrhea.

Until 1879, when Albert Neisser of Germany identified the gonococcus as the infecting agent, physicians could not diagnose gonorrhea with any accuracy. Since women often presented no symptoms in the early stages of the disease the infection passed unchecked through the womb to the Fallopian tubes and peritoneal cavity. In 1872 Emil Noeggerath tried to convince American physicians of a "latent" period for gonorrhea in men, when men were asymptomatic but still could infect their wives. Many doctors, however, believed gonorrhea to be endemic in women and a relatively trivial problem.

By the turn of the century, medical research revealed the serious cost to women in infertility and chronic invalidism. Effective medical treatment came with the advent of the sulfa drugs in the 1930s but in the meantime major gynecological surgery such as salpingectomy (removal of the Fallopian tubes) or hysterectomy offered the only relief.[55] Surgery

---

[54] Ibid., p. 27. Part of the new medical knowledge consisted of changes about female insanity and/or hysteria. See Ilza Veith, *Hysteria: The History of a Disease* (Chicago: University of Chicago Press, 1965).

[55] Stage, *Female Complaints*, pp. 82–4; The most comprehensive coverage of the topic of venereal disease in the United States since the late nineteenth century is Allan Brandt, *No Magic Bullet* (New York: Oxford University Press, 1985), pp. 3–31. See also Edward Shorter, "Women's Diseases Before 1900," in *New Directions in Psychohistory*, Mel Albin, ed. (Lexington, MA: D.C. Heath and Co., 1980), pp. 183–208.

succeeded where all else failed, removing the site of infection. Without treatment, many women endured an unending cycle of illness and acute pelvic pain. It is significant that 50% of the women admitted to the Mount Sinai Hospital gynecological service between 1883 and 1894 suffered from pelvic infections.[56] Gynecological surgery offered these women the chance to return to a normal life.

HYSTERECTOMY AND BREAST CANCER

In 1989 about 650,000 women will have had hysterectomies in the United States, a rate of seven per one thousand women. Hysterectomy is the second most common surgical procedure in America and is the subject of heated debate over "necessary" and "unnecessary" operations. Critics caution against doctors motivated by greed or too casual an attitude toward removing the female reproductive organs. Much disagreement exists among physicians and patients alike over appropriate indications for hysterectomy.[57] No historical studies, however, analyze the development of this much-utilized operation.

The primary reason for this important gap in the research is the overwhelming concentration on the nineteenth century to date. As Edward Shorter pointed out, excision of the uterus for uterine cancer only became possible after the advances made in abdominal surgery during the 1890s.[58] The phenomenal increase in the number of hysterectomies, therefore, occurred during the twentieth century. One recent article on obstetrics and gynecology since 1920 largely ignores gynecological surgery but does mention several medical studies from the 1940s and 1950s that indicate professional concern over the misuse of the operation. One 1946 study claimed as many as one-third of all hysterectomies were questionable, and in 1957 critics objected to the large number of routine postmenopausal hysterectomies.[59] The controversy over the indications for hysterectomy existed long before the present decade but we lack information on the medical, professional, and social factors which encouraged hysterectomy as the treatment of choice in non-life-threatening cases.

---

56 Shorter, *Women's Bodies*, p. 278.
57 Mary E. Guinan, M.D., "Women's Health: Three Cheers For Elective Hysterectomy."
    Journal of the American Women's Medical Association 44 (1989): 97–98. See also C. L.
    Easterday, D. A. Grimes, and J. A. Riggs, "Hysterectomy in the United States,"
    Obstetrics and Gynecology 62 (1983): 203.
58 Shorter, *Women's Bodies*, p. 247.
59 Summey and Hurst, "Ob/Gyn on the Rise," pp. 103–22, 105.

Surgical treatment for breast cancer suffers from the same scholarly neglect as hysterectomy. Gynecologists shared the concern over the frequency of breast cancer in women, often making the initial diagnosis even though general surgeons usually performed mastectomy. Our available sources on the historical aspects of the disease primarily limit themselves to narrative accounts of changes in the type of surgery. Dr. James O. Robinson presents a comprehensive overview of treatments from the first amputations of cancerous breasts by the Greeks through the development of radical mastectomy by William Halsted in 1882 and the modified surgery with radiation and chemotherapy offered today. Rose Kushner covers much of the same material in less technical terms in her book *Alternatives: New Developments in the War on Breast Cancer*.[60]

Kushner introduces another element for consideration in understanding the therapeutics for breast cancer: the propensity of women throughout the ages to delay treatment until the cancer was well advanced. A study cited by Edward Shorter in *The History of Women's Bodies* revealed that of 356 women admitted to London's Middlesex Hospital for breast cancer between 1805 and 1933, 68% had ulceration of the breast.[61] Why did women wait so long? Kushner quotes a current medical textbook which attributes delay to false modesty and female vanity.[62] While vanity might play a significant role, a woman's very real fear of disfigurement, horrific pain, and ultimately death influenced her reaction on discovering a lump in her breast. Shorter offers a hint of this fear with evidence from eighteenth-century Europe. Women avoided breastfeeding their infants, even though this meant higher infant mortality, because of a "folkloric belief that lactation caused breast cancer."[63] As with hysterectomy, the existing research on women and breast cancer only begins to ask the many questions that need answers.

FUTURE ISSUES

Even for the nineteenth century, important areas of surgical gynecology remain unexplored. Practitioners surgically repositioned the uterus and reshaped the vagina and cervix to treat menstrual dysfunction or

---

[60] James Robinson, M.D., "The Treatment of Breast Cancer Through the Ages," *The American Journal of Surgery* 151 (1986): 317–33 and Rose Kushner, *Alternatives: New Developments in the War on Breast Cancer* (New York: Warner Books, 1984), ch. 3. See also Daniel de Moulin, *A Short History of Breast Cancer* (Boston: Nijhoff Press, 1981).
[61] Kushner, *Alternatives*, p. 57; Shorter, *Women's Bodies*, p. 244.
[62] Kushner, *Alternatives*, p. 57.
[63] Shorter, *Women's Bodies*, p. 244.

infertility. What combination of medical logic and cultural assumptions prompted the development of these therapies and patient acceptance of them? At what point did patients accept gynecologists as "experts" and how did that change the doctor/patient relationship?

We also need to consider the effect the development of surgical gynecology had on medical practice in general. For example, surgical treatments for female disease moved into the ranks of general practitioners and even some sectarians. At the height of the craze for ovariotomy, eminent gynecologist Thomas Adis Emmet protested "the indiscriminate manner in which this operation is being done all over the country, and by anyone."[64] What motivated such wholesale adoption—professional competition, patient demand, medical conviction, or a complex combination of all three?

Other gynecological procedures found an application far removed from the original intent. The details of the eugenics movement are tangential to the focus of this chapter but eugenicists appropriated gynecological techniques to "improve" human stock. During the 1890s surgeons developed tubal ligation as a necessary form of birth control for women who could not deliver a child vaginally—the risk of tubal ligation being much less than that of a cesarean delivery. Early in the twentieth century both women and men deemed "inferior" by virtue of "mental feebleness" (or poverty, race, or ethnic group) underwent surgical sterilization. This extension of Social Darwinism culminated in the horrifying perversions carried on in Nazi death camps.

At its most benign, eugenics used hereditarian principles to advocate birth control in order to ensure the "survival of the fittest." Linda Gordon even found a feminist element in the early years of the movement which argued for women's right to limit births and refuse husbands their sexual privileges. Antifeminist, conservative eugenicists dominated the movement in the twentieth century, however, and resorted to surgical sterilization.[65] How did this campaign differ from the use of Battey's operation on institutionalized women? What cultural, socioeconomic

---

[64] Thomas Adis Emmet, "Pelvic Inflammations: Or Cellulitis Versus Peritonitis," *Transactions of the American Gynecological Society* 11 (1886): 101–11.

[65] For a full investigation of eugenics, see Daniel J. Kevles, *In the Name of Eugenics* (New York, 1985). Chapter 7 is especially pertinent. See also Mark H. Haller, *Eugenics* (New Brunswick, NJ: Rutgers University Press, 1963); Kenneth M. Ludmerer, *Genetics and American Society* (Baltimore: The Johns Hopkins University Press, 1972); and Robert N. Proctor, *Racial Hygiene: Medicine Under the Nazis* (Cambridge: Harvard University Press, 1988).

factors shaped public reaction to sexual sterilization? How did gynecologists respond to this use of the surgery (mainly performed by nonspecialists)? The answers to such questions await future studies.[66]

At any point in history, how did societal perceptions of the female role influence diagnosis and treatment? How did the woman's perception of herself dictate the presentation of her symptoms and her psychological as well as physical response to gynecological surgery? Recent medical evidence shows a decline in negative psychosomatic symptoms and depression following hysterectomy. This is due to the weakening of the link between reproductive capability and female identity.[67] Today women have roles in addition to motherhood. The preliminary work on issues in surgical gynecology shows us how important it is to address complex social, psychological, and medical relationships when interpreting the history of health care for women.

[66] Linda Gordon, *Woman's Body, Woman's Right* (New York: Penguin Books, 1977), pp. 109–15, 126–35.

[67] Carol Nadelson, M.D.; Malkah Notman, M.D.; and Elizabeth Ellis, M.D., "Psychosomatic Aspects of Obstetrics and Gynecology," *Psychosomatics* 24 (Oct. 1983): 871–84. Nadelson et al. also point out that the strong identification of women as mothers in the 1950s led gynecologists to diagnose infertility and painful menstruation as psychosomatic symptoms brought on by ambivalence towards childbearing (p. 871). For another view of how cultural attitudes alter medical treatment, see S. E. Bell, "Changing Ideas: The Medicalization of Menopause," *Social Science of Medicine* 24 (1987): 535–42.

THE PROFESSIONALIZATION OF OBSTETRICS: CHILDBIRTH BECOMES A MEDICAL SPECIALTY

Charlotte G. Borst

Writing in 1902 about the development of the specialty of obstetrics, Barton Cooke Hirst, a Philadelphia physician, claimed that during the previous decade, no branch of medicine had "displayed such a remarkable development . . . [and] no other specialty . . . promises such development in the next ten years."[1] Dr. Hirst's optimism was probably premature. By the second decade of the twentieth century, even in Boston, New York, Philadelphia, Baltimore, and Chicago, there were twenty to thirty surgeons for every obstetrician, and outside of these centers, there were almost no well-qualified obstetrical specialists.[2] About one-half of all births in 1910 were attended by midwives, and most of the doctors who attended births were general practitioners, not obstetric specialists.

Though obstetrics did not show remarkable development within the ten years foreseen by this Philadelphia physician, by the late 1950s and

---

[1] Barton Cooke Hirst, "The Future of Obstetrics as a Specialty in America," *American Medicine* 3 (1902): 815. I wish to thank Lawrence Longo for directing me to this article and several other historical articles cited throughout the chapter.

[2] H. P. Newman, "The Relation of Preventive Medicine to Gynecology," *Surgery, Gynecology, and Obstetrics* 29 (1919): 557–60. In 1911, there were no obstetric specialists at all in Cleveland. (A. H. Bill, "Newer Obstetrics; Presidential Address," *American Journal of Obstetrics and Gynecology* 23 [1932]: 155–64).

1960s it had become an important and powerful field in medicine. Most parturient women delivered their babies in hospitals, attended by obstetrical specialists.[3] Nonspecialist physicians and others who delivered babies usually found their maternity practices governed by obstetricians.

Obstetrics struggled to achieve respect and recognition in the same years that medicine in the United States was rebuilding its professional institutions and striving to achieve legal protection for its services. As one historian explains, reforms in medical education and medical licensing "reflected a movement toward the strengthening of professional status and the consolidation of professional authority."[4] This process of professionalization also explains the development of medical specialties like pediatrics and obstetrics. Both freestanding professions and medical specialties established occupational institutions to control recruitment and practice, structured markets for the delivery of services, and competed among themselves for status and resources. Their emergence served as a means for collective upward mobility.[5]

By the 1960s, the assumption by obstetrical specialists of the majority of deliveries had had a profound impact on the experiences of birthing women, but historians of the field disagree as to the exact consequences. This essay reviews the literature that has addressed the development of obstetrics. However, this literature is not as voluminous as in other areas of women's health history. While there are a few articles that directly address the history of obstetrics, most of the scholarship concerning the growth of this specialty comes either from inside studies by physicians or incidentally from histories of childbirth.[6]

One of the reasons for the dearth of research on the history of obstetrics may be the fact that the professionalization process for obstetrics differed from that of other medical specialties. Indeed, for much of the first half of the twentieth century, there was no agreement on what constituted an obstetrical specialist. Though later analyses would concentrate on the relationship between the specialty and technological

---

[3] In 1968, 68% of all births were attended by an obstetrician. This percentage rose to 81% by 1977. (National Institutes of Health and the U.S. Public Health Service, *Cesarean Childbirth* NIH Publication No. 82-2067 [U.S. Department of Health and Human Services, 1981], p. 80).

[4] Paul Starr, *The Social Transformation of American Medicine* (New York: Basic Books, 1982), p. 81.

[5] Sidney A. Halpern, *American Pediatrics: The Social Dynamics of Professionalism, 1880–1980* (Berkeley: University of California Press, 1988), pp. 4–9.

[6] Interested readers are directed to chapter 4 in this handbook, "Childbirth in America, 1650 to 1990" by Janet Carlisle Bogdan.

innovations, many early twentieth-century leaders believed that the development of obstetrics as a specialty did not conform to models that linked organizational complexity with technological innovations. As Henry P. Newman, a leading physician in the field, reported in 1919, obstetrics did not grow out of a new medical science or technology, nor was it concerned with "finding a new disease."

In his attempts to delineate boundaries for obstetrics, Newman also noted that the work of obstetrics was divided among many types of physicians. "Everyone is doing, has always done, obstetrics," Newman remarked.[7] General practitioners in 1900 cared for and delivered many pregnant women, and these family doctors argued that obstetrics was an integral part of their overall practice. In fact, the very lack of professional recognition and respect for obstetrics as a specialty meant that general surgeons or gynecologists performed most obstetrical surgery because it was generally agreed that most obstetricians were "entirely incompetent to perform any obstetric operations."[8]

Given this early attitude, it is ironic that by the 1980s many obstetrical specialists found themselves accused not of a lack of surgical skill, but of using operative obstetrics to shorten or to conclude a birth when more traditional methods may have sufficed.[9] Now, at the end of the twentieth century, it seems to many observers of the specialty that technological innovations and the development of skillful techniques have led physicians to intervene excessively in the birth process. Henry Newman may not have found a link between technology and the development of obstetrics as a medical specialty in the early decades of the twentieth century, but much of the contemporary analysis of obstetrics addresses the effect of technology on obstetrical practice and on the relationship between obstetricians and their women patients.

As I will discuss below, the great majority of the scholarship on the history of obstetrics has focused on the institutional structures established by early specialists and the debates by obstetricians about the need to claim exclusive domain over childbirth. Indeed, the relationship

---

[7] Newman, "The Relation of Preventive Medicine to Gynecology," p. 466.

[8] R. W. Holmes, "Graduate Education of Physicians in Obstetrics," *American Journal of Obstetrics and Gynecology* 21 (1931): 822.

[9] Helen Marieskind, *Women in the Health Care System: Patients, Providers, and Programs* (St. Louis: C. V. Mosby, 1980.) Marieskind attributes the dramatic rise in the cesarean section rate in part to the fact that residents in obstetrics are often trained to do surgical techniques and are not well trained to manage normal labors (p. 255). Quoted in Margot Edwards and Mary Waldorf, *Reclaiming Birth: History and Heroines of American Childbirth Reform* (Trumansburg, NY: Crossing Press, 1984), p. 125.

between physicians and other birth attendants has dominated the histories of obstetrics written by both physicians and their severest critics. Physician accounts of this history have tended to be quite laudatory. Citing the many technological and scientific achievements of twentieth-century obstetrics, they have pointed out the decrease in maternal mortality and concluded that the development of obstetric specialization has contributed in great part to saving the lives and health of parturient women. In contrast, as this essay will show, accounts of the development of obstetrics by nonphysician historians have noted that the growth of this medical specialty brought negative as well as positive aspects. They have argued that obstetricians have medicalized an important family event, and that these doctors have taken much of the control away from the birthing woman.

This essay's analysis of the history of obstetrics as a specialty draws out four major issues in the field. Several historians have examined the institutionalization of childbirth, which includes investigations of both the move from midwife to professional obstetrician as well as the move from the home to the hospital. Other work has focused on medical education for obstetrics, the role of technology, and the gender of the physician.

Harold Speert's *Obstetrics and Gynecology in America: A History* outlines the history of the rise of the specialty from the perspective of a practicing physician.[10] He follows the maturation of the specialty by tracing the rise of specialty journals and organizations and new innovations in science and technology. The triumph of science over ignorance, the rise of obstetrics included the banishment of midwives and the growth of medical education in obstetrics. Midwives, Speert argues, were ignorant, often illiterate and superstitious, and their practices were reflected in the maternal and infant mortality statistics. "Clearly needed by American mothers was protection from incompetence and superstition," he writes, and the replacement of midwives by obstetric specialists was an indication of the success of science.[11] The upgrading of obstetric education, including the addition of graduate residences in obstetrics, furthered the growth of the field.

As Speert points out, by the early twentieth century, the public was asking "who was a specialist rather than what was a specialist."[12] Special-

---

[10] Harold Speert, *Obstetrics and Gynecology in America: A History* (Chicago: American College of Obstetricians and Gynecologists, 1980).

[11] Ibid., p. 11.

[12] Ibid., p. 82.

ists in these years were self-defined, and there were no bodies, such as state licensing boards, to determine objectively what a practicing specialist ought to know. During World War I, the United States Council of Defense and later the Army established certain requirements and standards for most specialists. Indeed, the Army found that many self-styled specialists had little expertise in their field.[13] For many specialties, this government action prompted the establishment of boards that could persuade medical schools and hospitals to provide adequate facilities for specialty training and could approve qualified practitioners. Obstetrics and gynecology escaped the scrutiny of the Army, but by the late 1920s, leaders in the field, such as Walter T. Dannreuther of New York and John Osborn Polak of Brooklyn, suggested that the American Association of Obstetrics and Gynecology join with the American Gynecological Society and the American Medical Association Section of Obstetrics and Gynecology to sponsor the formation of a Board for Obstetrics and Gynecology. With Dannreuther as its president, the Board was established in 1930. Requirements for specialty approval included: three to five years of intensive training in both obstetrics and gynecology following an internship, demonstrated knowledge in both obstetrics and gynecology, experience in private practice, and assurance that one's practice would be limited to the specialty.[14]

There were other problems in addition to those surrounding licensing and specialization. Although many groups of practitioners had organized around the subject of obstetrics, none of them specifically evaluated a physician's obstetric training. Regional obstetrical societies dated back to the founding in 1861 of the Obstetrical Society of Boston.[15] However, these societies served as a forum for the presentation and discussion of clinical cases and topics of current interest; they did not attempt to

---

[13] See Rosemary Stevens, *American Medicine and the Public Interest* (New Haven: Yale University Press, 1971), pp. 127–28.

[14] Walter T. Dannreuther, "The American Board of Obstetrics and Gynecology: Its Organization, Function and Objectives," *Journal of the American Medical Association* 96 (1931): 797–98; Dannreuther, "Qualifications of Specialists; President's Address," *American Journal of Obstetrics and Gynecology* 25 (1933): 165–71; also Stevens, *American Medicine and the Public Interest*, pp. 200–204.

[15] B. E. Cotting, "Extracts from a Historical Sketch of the Obstetrical Society of Boston," *Boston Medical and Surgical Journal* 105 (1881): 475–77. A relatively complete listing of such societies to 1951 is given by W. D. Beacham, "American Academy of Obstetrics and Gynecology: First Presidential Address; history of American obstetrics and gynecology organizations and genesis of the American Academy," *Obstetrics and Gynecology* 1 (1953): 115–24.

determine their members' qualifications for practice. The American Medical Association's Section on Practical Medicine and Obstetrics (established in 1859) which later became the Section on Obstetrics and Gynecology, debated current therapeutic issues as well as the educational qualifications of physicians who were practicing obstetrics and gynecology. However, the Section focused its efforts on challenging its members to "help general practitioners to acquire experience in obstetrics and gynecology."[16] Two other groups, the American Gynecological Society and the American Association of Obstetrics and Gynecology, also devoted themselves to the study of women's diseases and maternity-related problems. However, neither of these groups ever sought or received the power to establish credentials for an obstetric specialist. Though the American Board of Obstetrics and Gynecology eventually assumed a significant role in determining the competence of practitioners who professed to be specialists, the Board was powerless to control the overall practice of obstetrics and gynecology by other licensed practitioners. Indeed, this lack of significant authority was demonstrated in 1951, with the formation of the American Academy (later College) of Obstetrics and Gynecology. As the last truly national organization of the "big four" specialties, it required for membership a minimum of five years of training or practice limited to obstetrics and/or gynecology, evidence of high ethical and professional standing, graduation from an accredited medical school, and membership in either the American or Canadian Medical Association.[17] Certified Board standing, however, was not a prerequisite for membership. Indeed, for several years, nonspecialists were encouraged to apply and some general practitioners interested in obstetrics and gynecology were admitted. This policy of not limiting fellowship to specialists caused considerable discord, not only within the Academy, but also with comparable specialty organizations.[18]

---

[16] J. C. Masson, "Trend of Present-day Medical Education," *Journal of the American Medical Association* 95 (1930): 765–66. The section concentrated its scientific efforts chiefly on the diseases of women, not obstetrics.

[17] The American College of Surgeons was established in 1913, The American College of Physicians in 1915, and the American Academy of Pediatrics in 1930. The requirement for membership in the AMA or the CMA subsequently was dropped because some state medical societies refused admission to black physicians. William F. Mengert, *History of the American College of Obstetricians and Gynecologists* (Chicago: American College of Obstetrics and Gynecology, 1971), pp. 1, 14–15.

[18] Ibid., p. 26.

In his outline of the growth of obstetric specialist organizations, Speert asserts that the significant factors in the reduction of maternal mortality were specialization in obstetrics and the establishment of the American Board of Obstetrics and Gynecology.[19] However, he does not address the lack of power these societies had in controlling who could be termed an obstetrical specialist. Because of his failure to confront this issue of power, Speert cannot point to a causal relationship between the development of specialist groups and the decline of maternal mortality. While it is true that maternal death rates fell significantly throughout the twentieth century, the decline preceded obstetrics' rise to power as a medical specialty and the prominent place of obstetricians in the birthing room. The maternal death rate in the first decades of the twentieth century hovered around 60 deaths per 10,000 live births, and dropped rapidly after the late 1930s. By 1950, around the date of the founding of the American Academy of Obstetricians and Gynecologists, the figure was less than 10 deaths per 10,000 live births.[20]

Theodore Cianfrani's *A Short History of Obstetrics and Gynecology* surveys the history of obstetrics from ancient times to the present, and like Speert, he too argues for a direct link between the discovery of scientific knowledge and the practice of obstetrics.[21] He maintains that technological innovations such as anesthesia and antibiotics, together with the expansion of research in endocrinology in the 1930s, drove the profession to achieve great results for the benefit of childbearing women. Though Cianfrani alludes to the relationship between midwives and the developing field of obstetrics, he is more concerned with the internal debates between obstetricians and general practitioners. Thus, he attaches significant importance to the ability of early obstetrical specialists to rise above the embarrassment and ridicule directed against them by most of the medical profession. Aside from the question of the diminution of maternal mortality, Cianfrani, like Speert, does not address the effect of the professionalization of obstetrics on childbearing women.

Lawrence Longo, like Cianfrani, is interested in the relationship between obstetrics and the rest of the medical profession. His work examines the growth of obstetric education within the medical curricu-

---

[19] Speert, *Obstetrics and Gynecology in America*, p. 146.
[20] Ibid., p. 147, figure 13.1.
[21] Theodore Cianfrani, *A Short History of Obstetrics and Gynecology* (Springfield, IL: Charles C. Thomas, 1960).

lum. In "Obstetrics and Gynecology"[22] Longo traces the gradual incor-
poration of formal obstetrics and gynecology into the medical school
curriculum. He sees the fifty-year period from about 1840 to 1890 as an
era of great achievements in the practice of obstetrics, including the
beginning of the use of anesthesia in childbirth and the elucidation of the
physicians' role in transmitting puerperal sepsis. However, none of these
developments had as much effect on the teaching of obstetrics as the
introduction of demonstrative midwifery in the mid-nineteenth century.
James Platt White's use in 1850 at the University of Buffalo's Medical
College of an actual laboring woman to demonstrate normal labor and
delivery paved the way for more medical students to actually witness a
childbirth.[23] But Longo finds little progress after the 1860s in the
teaching of obstetrics and in the development of new methodology for
the discipline.

Obstetrics suffered initially even at the Johns Hopkins Medical
School, an institution usually identified with promoting the scientific
basis of medical education in the United States. However, the school
acted as a significant catalyst for the development of obstetrics as a
specialty with John Whitridge Williams's creation in 1919 of the first
full-time department of obstetrics. Longo argues that students trained
under Williams formed a coterie of physician-academicians who left
Hopkins to form departments of obstetrics at other schools. Gradually
locating new departments across the country, these physicians helped to
diffuse the principles of medical education and specialty training first
laid down at Hopkins.[24] These academicians were also in the forefront of
the fight to establish a board and specialty journals for obstetrics, a point
that Longo does not explore.

William Ray Arney's history, *Power and the Profession of Obstetrics*,
analyzes the relationship between knowledge and practice.[25] His work is

---

[22] Lawrence D. Longo, "Obstetrics and Gynecology," in *The Education of American
Physicians: Historical Essays*, ed. Ronald L. Numbers (Berkeley: University of California
Press, 1980), pp. 205–25.

[23] Virginia Drachman explores this case and its effects on obstetrics teaching in greater
detail in "The Loomis Trial: Social Mores and Obstetrics in Mid-Nineteenth Century
America," in *Women and Health In America: Historical Readings*, ed. Judith Walzer
Leavitt (Madison: University of Wisconsin Press, 1984), pp. 166–74.

[24] Longo explores Williams's career in greater depth in "John Whitridge Williams and
Academic Obstetrics in America," *Transactions and Studies of the College of Physicians of
Philadelphia* 5 (3 no. 4) 1981: 221–54.

[25] William Ray Arney, *Power and the Profession of Obstetrics* (Chicago: University of
Chicago Press, 1982).

the most recent monograph to focus exclusively on the history of obstetrics. However his work also reflects the methodology and the present-day policy concerns of an academic sociologist. Arney critiques the physician-historians' interpretations of the history of obstetrics that I have just dealt with as well as feminist interpretations which will be discussed below. Linking the expansion of science and technology with the growth of this medical specialty, he argues, does not explain fully the tremendous rise to power of obstetrics, particularly after World War II. By the end of the 1940s, he points out, "the social development of the profession underwent a severe and probably irreversible disruption. . . . The discontinuity in development was more than a change in the rate of technological advance. Instead, the profession experienced (and was partly responsible for bringing about) a qualitative transformation in its mode of social control over women, pregnancy, and childbirth generally."[26]

This second transformation, Arney contends, involved a new logic and a new metaphor for the body that changed the conceptual basis of medicine. By the late 1940s, scientists no longer regarded the body as a machine made up of other machines. Instead, an ecological metaphor had replaced the old mechanical one. Doctors now regarded the human body as a system composed of other systems articulated at many points and levels. Arney traces this change and argues that it has been overlooked by both physician and feminist historians. While feminists have concentrated on the first transformation in obstetrics—the replacement of midwives by physicians—Arney maintains that the second transformation of obstetrics may be just as profound, and perhaps ultimately even more significant. This new obstetrics reconceptualized pregnancy as a process with a "trajectory"; that is, the normative course of pregnancy was understood, but it was also seen to be influenced by systems both within and without the body. All the events of a woman's life both before and after birth were understood to influence the way a woman could deliver a baby.

Medicine's change in metaphor, Arney maintains, influenced modifications in obstetrical technology and in the delivery of obstetrical services. The "technology of domineering control" moved to "a technology of monitoring, surveillance, and normalization."[27] Arney argues

---

[26] Ibid., p. 6.
[27] Ibid., p. 8.

that the social organization of birth, including the doctor-patient relationship, also changed. Birth was now something to be managed, rather
than to be either attended or dominated. All births and all pregnancies
were carefully controlled by a process of monitoring. This process of
monitoring meant that obstetrics became organized as a hierarchical
team. Doctors, Arney insists, were not necessarily always leaders of
these teams, but members who were responsible to the larger team
structure. The parturient woman was also part of this team, her fetus
now the chief concern of the obstetrician.

In his analysis of the ramifications of this process of change, Arney
departs from the conclusions of feminist historians to argue that physicians and their women patients cooperated in securing the power of
obstetrics over childbirth. By examining articles in the obstetrical specialty journals, he finds that obstetricians embraced the natural birth
movement, which had been started by women who wanted some say in
the conduct of their births. Arney contends that physicians introduced
procedures compatible with natural birth and "women joined the obstetrical project and helped bolster the control monitoring exerts over
childbirth. . . ."[28]

While physicians may have thought that they had elicited women's
cooperation, histories of childbirth that have included women's voices
have revealed that parturient women did not always want to cooperate
with obstetricians in monitoring their births. By disregarding the vast
literature generated by other members of the "obstetrical team," such as
nurses and mothers, Arney overlooks an important contradiction to his
thesis. Indeed, many women argued that monitors often led to undesirable interventions.[29]

While Arney maintains that there was a cooperative alliance between modern birthing women and their obstetricians, a number of
scholars interested in women's history have found this relationship
much less harmonious both in the past and in the present. By being
sensitive to gender, these historians have raised issues of the role of
women in this previously male-oriented scholarship. Unlike the physician-historians or Arney, however, the following historians have often
focused on the changing links between parturient women and their

---

[28] Ibid., p. 97. See also chapter 7, "Modern Women and Modern Obstetricians: The
Development of a Univocal Discourse," pp. 208–42.

[29] See, for example, Shelly Romalis, "Natural Childbirth and the Reluctant Physician," in
Childbirth: Alternatives to Medical Control, ed. Shelly Romalis (Austin: University of
Texas Press, 1981), pp. 73–74.

caregivers and not on the history of the profession itself. Rather than finding a linear, positive association between childbearing women and technological progress, feminist writers have found a complex and often contradictory relationship.

Like the physician-historians, many feminist historians have focused their attention on the relationship between midwives and the developing specialty of obstetrics in the early twentieth century. Frances Kobrin's pioneering article, "The American Midwife Controversy: A Crisis of Professionalization," asserts that "the decade from about 1908 began the contest between the increasingly self-conscious obstetrical specialist and his adversaries, the midwife and her advocates."[30] Kobrin points out the professional and economic difficulties faced by early twentieth-century obstetricians, and she argues that the "professional obstetricians" wanted to eliminate midwives for both economic and pedagogical reasons. These obstetricians saw midwives taking business away from physician birth attendants and from hospitals, leaving fewer obstetrics cases available for teaching. In addition, obstetric leaders worried about practicing doctors who felt that they were superior to midwives, in no need of improving their own skills. Though the number of midwives fell drastically by 1930, Kobrin acknowledges that their decline in the United States was not simply a "function of the maturity of the obstetric profession."[31] Instead, this decline was probably due to larger social changes, including the demand by childbearing women for better obstetrics, which had been a long-term goal of professional obstetricians.

Judy Barrett Litoff's *American Midwives, 1860 to the Present* expands Kobrin's argument.[32] Though her work is chiefly devoted to understanding the relationship between midwives and physicians in general, she devotes significant portions of her study to reviewing the status of obstetrics in the United States in the late nineteenth and early twentieth century.[33] She argues that physician leaders who aspired to upgrade the status of obstetrics sought to eliminate midwives as birth attendants. J. Whitridge Williams, Joseph B. DeLee, and others contended that midwives dragged down the general level of obstetrics among all physicians

---

[30] Frances Kobrin, "The American Midwife Controversy: A Crisis of Professionalization," *Bulletin of the History of Medicine* 40 (1966): 350.

[31] Ibid.

[32] Judy Barrett Litoff, *American Midwives, 1860 to the Present* (Westport, CT: Greenwood Press, 1978).

[33] Litoff, *American Midwives*, especially chapter 5, "The Early Twentieth-Century Midwife Debate: Opponents," pp. 64–90.

and degraded the position of the obstetrican. Abolishing these female birth attendants, it was felt, would free up more patients for teaching obstetrics and would raise the status of physicians who delivered babies.

Though Litoff gives a good account of the attitudes of obstetrical leaders at the turn of the twentieth century, her work really focuses on the decline of midwifery rather than the rise of obstetrics. Indeed, the rise of obstetrics is only one of several reasons for the decline of midwifery in the United States.[34] Because of her attention to midwifery, she is not able to explore the complex changes that were affecting the development of obstetrics as a medical specialty.

Women were both patients and practitioners of obstetrics in the late nineteenth and early twentieth century, and thus the issue of gender cuts across analyses of both groups. Though a great deal of attention has focused on midwives, no study has been devoted entirely to the examination of women doctors and the development of obstetrics. However, Regina Morantz-Sanchez devotes a portion of her larger study of women physicians to the place of women doctors in obstetrics. In her book, *Sympathy and Science: Women Physicians in American Medicine*,[35] Morantz-Sanchez depicts obstetrics, together with pediatrics and public health, as "feminine" medical specialties in the late nineteenth century. Because of discrimination against women doctors and because of nineteenth-century beliefs in women's "special" abilities, female doctors confined themselves to a few specialties like obstetrics and pediatrics where they could work with women and children and perhaps raise the moral tone of society.[36] Indeed, Dr. Rachel Bodley's 1880 survey found that most of the graduates of the Woman's Medical College of Pennsylvania were general practitioners with a heavy emphasis on obstetrics and gynecology.[37] Morantz-Sanchez finds in addition to the female medical colleges, the few women-run hospitals significantly contributed to women doctors' expertise in the field. These hospitals offered instruction that in many cases was far better than the training given to male physicians, and

---

[34] Litoff, *American Midwives*, pp. 139–42. Though physicians, many of whom were obstetric specialists, engineered the antimidwife campaign, Litoff sees other factors, such as lack of midwife training and organization and social and cultural changes, as equally valid explanations for the demise of midwifery in this country.

[35] Regina Markell Morantz-Sanchez, *Sympathy and Science: Women Physicians in American Medicine* (New York: Oxford University Press, 1985).

[36] Ibid., pp. 61–62.

[37] Bodley was Dean of the Woman's Medical College of Pennsylvania in 1880. Morantz-Sanchez, *Sympathy and Science*, p. 91.

they propelled some female physicians into the forefront of the field.[38] Dr. Anna E. Broomall, for example, the chair of Obstetrics at the Women's Hospital of Philadelphia in the 1880s, established a separate maternity hospital connected with the Woman's Medical College. She emphasized prenatal and postnatal care, and was one of the first doctors to emphasize the need for routine episiotomies.[39]

By the twentieth century, however, the professionalization of medicine, together with the new ideology of science and broader shifts in society, affected women physicians in several ways. Morantz-Sanchez argues that women's medical schools, which were underfunded and undercapitalized, could not make adjustments needed to keep up with innovations in medical education, and they were forced to close. Though some previously all-male medical schools did become coeducational, many of them admitted only a few women, and the number of women medical students dropped precipitously. In addition, most of the coeducational schools refused to appoint women as faculty, positions that promoted the development of leaders of the profession.[40] Morantz-Sanchez also maintains that the agenda of many women physicians differed from their male colleagues. Many women physicians found that the ideology of the liberal reform of the professions for the public good meshed with earlier nineteenth-century goals for training women doctors. Thus, women physicians found social reform movements particularly appealing, and they threw themselves enthusiastically into every aspect of progressive reform that touched on areas where they had been considered experts. Though Morantz-Sanchez does not analyze the connections between women doctors' work in social medicine and the development of obstetrics specialization, it is obvious from her study that these women doctors found public health campaigns that brought

---

[38] Virginia G. Drachman analyzes this process at the New England Hospital and finds that it led both to opportunities for women and to conflict. *Hospital with a Heart: Women Doctors and the Paradox of Separatism at the New England Hospital, 1862–1969* (Ithaca: Cornell University Press, 1984).

[39] One of her students later wrote that "Dr. Broomall was far ahead of her time in teaching obstetrics, and her students were greatly superior in mechanical skill to the young men who graduated from the universities during the eighties and nineties." Rachelle Yarros, "From Obstetrics to Social Hygiene," *Medical Women's Journal* 33 (November 1926): 306; quoted by Morantz-Sanchez, *Sympathy and Science*, pp. 169–70. Morantz-Sanchez notes the seeming contradiction of Broomall's contribution to obstetrics. She notes that attitudes toward childbirth by male and female physicians were often congruent (pp. 223–24).

[40] A survey at the turn of twentieth century of 912 teachers showed that only 27 were female, all in subordinate positions. Morantz-Sanchez, *Sympathy and Science*, p. 258.

medical care to women and children more to their taste than the promotion of the scientific development of obstetrics.[41] This movement, together with the low numbers of women physicians in the first five
decades of the twentieth century helps to explain why the development
of obstetrics as a specialty lacked women physicians' voices.

Several scholars have examined the development of obstetrics on its
own terms, mostly in articles rather than book-length studies. Pamela S.
Summey and Marsha Hurst, in "Ob/Gyn on the Rise: The Evolution of
Professional Ideology in the Twentieth Century," review the rise of
obstetrics and gynecology as a specialty from 1920 to the present.[42]
Using two specialist journals, American Journal of Obstetrics and Gynecology and Obstetrics and Gynecology (for the period after 1953), Summey
and Hurst delineate three periods of professional growth. Between 1920
and 1939, they argue, obstetrics and gynecology organized itself as a
professional discipline. The field established a definition for practice and
set boundaries that would help to characterize specialist obstetricians.
Summey and Hurst contend that the most important ramification of this
professional organization was the emergence of an activist ideology that
was asserted by the so-called "radicals" of the period. This activism has
persisted as the dominant ideology of the obstetrician/gynecologist. The
emergence of this radical stance, which advocated widespread intervention in labor, displaced the less interventionist "conservative" stance for
several reasons. First, the specialty was a union of obstetrics and the
surgical field of gynecology. The second related reason was the new
specialty's need to separate itself from general practice. As Summey and
Hurst explain, obstetricians felt that "any medical person could assist in
a delivery, but only the experienced specialist—the ob/gyn—could in-
terfere safely and successfully."[43] Though some conservative obstetricians challenged this activism on both economic and safety grounds,[44]
Summey and Hurst argue, "the activist ideology developed during the

---

[41] For an analysis of women physicians' work in reform, see Morantz-Sanchez, Sympathy
     and Science, chapter 10, "The Emergence of Social Medicine: Women's Work in the
     Profession," pp. 266–311.
[42] Pamela S. Summey and Marsha Hurst, "Ob/Gyn on the Rise: The Evolution of
     Professional Ideology in the Twentieth Century," Women and Health, part 1, 11(1)
     (1986): 133–45; part 2, 11(2) (1986): 102–22.
[43] Ibid., part 1, p. 138.
[44] Conservatives attacked radical intervention in childbirth, arguing that activist physi-
     cians were turning every obstetric case into an operative case, and that interventions
     could be used by physicians to serve their own purposes. Summey and Hurst, "Ob/
     Gyn on the Rise," part 1, p. 139.

1920s served as a foundation during the late 1940s and 1950s for an expansionist view of the ob/gyn's role of caring for women's entire reproductive system in all its physical and psychological aspects."[45]

In tracing the development of obstetrics and gynecology to the modern period, Summey and Hurst argue that by the early 1960s, the field had resolved its chronic identity crisis by redefining its relationship with its women patients. Instead of the profession being dependent upon women's views of their own medical needs, obstetrics and gynecology defined women as totally dependent upon them. Obstetrics and gynecology was seen now as a specialty that encompassed "all of the medical factors which have a bearing on the reproductive process."

Summey and Hurst agree with Arney's analysis that by the late 1960s and 1970s, obstetrics and gynecology had shifted its focus from management and procedures to monitoring and surveillance. They disagree strongly with Arney, however, about the outcome of this new technology for doctors and patients. Summey and Hurst maintain that the technological innovations that allowed this transformation created a new role for the obstetrician. Instead of focusing on the woman patient or even her reproductive system, the specialist doctors now concentrated their efforts on the fetus, ignoring many of the needs of parturient women.

Even as technological innovations like the new fetal monitors were causing changes in medicine in the 1960s and 1970s, obstetricians and gynecologists found themselves under attack from all sides. From within medicine, they faced the encroachments of other specialists and the disdain of medical students. From outside the field, obstetrics and gynecology faced the criticism of their women patients, who sought a redistribution of power between the gynecologist and the patient, and from the government and the press, who criticized the United States' relatively high infant mortality rate.

Obstetric leaders sought to meet the challenges to their authority, particularly those from within the profession, by becoming even more specialized and elitist. By 1968, for example, the ACOG closed its doors to generalists and made specialty board certification a qualification for membership. Many doctors felt that the field should even offer subspecialty training. By defining the specialty in terms of scientific expertise in very specific aspects of disease, the leaders believed that obstetrics and gynecology could meet the demands from within the profession and

---

[45] Ibid., part 2, p. 104.

from their government attackers. However, Summey and Hurst point out that these practitioners did not acknowledge the pressure from the women's movement. It was rare to find an article in the specialist journals expressing the woman's perspective on the medical management of her health. Specialists in obstetrics and gynecology ignored the growing body of literature outside the profession that "challenged the dominant paradigm of male ob/gyn's controlling women's reproductive system."[46]

Though specialists in obstetrics (and gynecology) have sought to establish a profession for themselves, Summey and Hurst argue that this goal has been confounded by two major contradictions. The first is due to the conflict between the field's two "parents," midwifery and surgery. The inherent philosophical differences between midwifery and surgery, the authors argue, led to the conflict between the philosophies of conservative and active obstetrics, the longest and bitterest conflict in the specialty. For reasons that the authors do not fully explore, the advocates of intervention won out, and their ideology of activism in obstetrics became the dominant one in the specialty. The second contradiction confounding obstetrics is related to the relationship between the field and its women patients. As Summey and Hurst argue, obstetrics and gynecology needs women in order to exist, but it must minimize its dependence upon the "second sex" in order to acquire status and power in the medical world. "In other words, ob/gyn's relation to women both defines and degrades it as a medical specialty."[47]

Summey and Hurst offer a pointed feminist critique of the history of obstetrics that is also somewhat sympathetic to the myriad professional problems faced by this developing medical specialty. However, their use of two specialty journals limits them to an analysis of the public pronouncements of obstetrical leaders. Thus they cannot explain how or why or even if other practicing obstetricians agreed with and followed their leaders. In addition, they do not explore one of their most interesting points—the development of obstetrics and its relation to science. They argue that obstetrical leaders, particularly those in the 1950s and 1960s, increasingly defined the specialty in terms of diseases. Indeed, obstetrics seemed to have an almost never-ending need for the scientific approbation that its practitioners hoped would delineate its expertise and its claim to hegemony. As J. I. Brewer, the President of ACOG,

---

[46] Ibid., part 2, p. 117.
[47] Ibid., part 2, p. 118.

wrote in 1970, "we have established a territory, a specialty of obstetrics
and gynecology. We have defined its scope and marked its borders. . . .
We recognize the territorial rights of others. We have struggled to
possess and defend this territory. As environmental changes occur we
make attempts to expand our territory. . . ."[48] Summey and Hurst argue
that this type of rhetoric demonstrates that leaders in the specialty have
ultimately been more interested in using science to carve out a base of
power than to answer problems posed by their women patients.

Judith Walzer Leavitt's work in the history of obstetrics goes
beyond the work of Summey and Hurst to analyze the role of science in
creating a professional discourse for obstetrics. In her article, "Joseph B.
DeLee and the Practice of Preventive Obstetrics,"[49] she explores the
relationship between the career of one important obstetrical leader and
the scientific milieu in which he operated. Leavitt argues that Joseph B.
DeLee used the language of prevention, as developed by the public
health movement of the late nineteenth and early twentieth centuries, in
a medically-directed prevention program for obstetrics. In forging a
union of practice and prevention, illustrated by both the Chicago Maternity Center and the prophylactic forceps operation, DeLee hoped to
improve the conditions for childbearing women and to help the cause of
the development of a specialty of obstetrics.

Joseph DeLee's life poses several contradictions for the historian, as
Leavitt acknowledges. He advocated substantial medical interventions
for labor and delivery that often put birthing women at greater risk from
associated complications than they might have been subjected to if labor
had progressed without interference. Yet DeLee's work is regarded as
important to medical progress because he made significant contributions
to obstetrics at a critical time in its development.[50] To understand these
contradictions, Leavitt argues, it is important to understand DeLee's
conception of the meanings of prevention.

When DeLee began his obstetrical practice at the end of the nineteenth century, over 25,000 American women were dying from child-
birth-related problems each year. As Leavitt explains, not all women
shared the same experience of childbirth, nor did the dead all die from

---

[48] J. I. Brewer, "Some Aspects of Behavior. Presidential Address," *American Journal of Obstetrics and Gynecology* 106 (1970): 957, quoted by Summey and Hurst, part 2, p. 115.

[49] Judith Walzer Leavitt, "Joseph B. DeLee and the Practice of Preventive Obstetrics," *American Journal of Public Health* 78 (1988): 1353–59.

[50] Ibid., p. 1353.

the same complications. DeLee, a firm believer in the power of science and public health to attack the high rates of infant and maternal mortality, felt that he had to develop a philosophy of prevention that would be relevant to all the situations in which women gave birth. Thus, the many forms that prevention could take were demonstrated by the prophylactic forceps operation, to be performed by skilled obstetricians in hospital settings for wealthy women, and the Maxwell Street Dispensary, an outpatient facility offering physician-assisted, noninterventive aseptic deliveries for poor Chicago women. As Leavitt argues, the two techniques DeLee advocated—watchful waiting and active intervention—"were both directed toward preventing the suffering, debility, and death associated with childbearing. . . . (T)hese techniques emphasized the medical model as the preferred route to maternal safety and, most important, they were prevention-oriented."[51]

DeLee's focus on prevention in a medical setting served two purposes for obstetrics. As Leavitt explains, the attention to prevention in medical practice gave "birthing women the safety of the new medicine at the same time as obstetricians were elevated to the status of surgeons."[52] DeLee envisioned the practice of obstetrics as preventive at heart. All doctors, not just public health physicians, could keep people from getting sick. At the same time, he believed that advocacy of his methods would contribute to the scientific and systematic practice of obstetrics. According to Leavitt, DeLee's optimism for the power of science and medicine was rooted in the social hopes of the early twentieth century when medicine held out the promise of improving the lives of all people. "That the result of all of these policies was to increase the medicalization of childbirth in the twentieth century was part of their prevention-oriented original intent and meanings; DeLee believed medicine (preventatively practiced) would rescue women from the dangers of childbirth."[53]

In her article "The Growth of Medical Authority: Technology and Morals in Turn-of-the-Century Obstetrics,"[54] Leavitt analyzes the debate about performing craniotomies (the surgical mutilation of the fetal head to permit vaginal extraction) to examine the growth of physician

---

[51] Ibid., p. 1358.
[52] Ibid.
[53] Ibid., p. 1359.
[54] *Medical Anthropology Quarterly* 1 (1987): 230–55.

power and obstetrical authority at the turn of the twentieth century. High forceps operations, the cutting of the pubic bone, and cesarean section gave physicians several available options in addition to craniotomy by the end of the nineteenth century for dealing with an extreme disproportion between the woman's pelvis and the size of her baby's head (cephlopelvic disproportion). But, as Leavitt explains, these new options ultimately became the weapon with which physicians found and gained control over decision making in the birthing room. Though physicians still delivered women in their homes, the technical nature of the details of these procedures limited the ability of the other parties involved to understand the nature of the problem and thus participate in determining its solution. Though husbands and even the clergy began to have a role in deciding whether the mother's or the fetus's life was more important, the new technology made it possible to consider fetal life as a viable option and provided physicians with the opportunity to wrest decision-making power away from its traditional place within the family. In tracing the ensuing debate in the medical journals, Leavitt finds that physicians increasingly began to claim medical authority over all decisions—moral, ethical, religious, social, economic, and even political—relating to childbirth. Physicians came to understand that indications for the new surgical procedures could be defined in medical and scientific terms, even though their risk to parturient women brought up new moral and social concerns. But Leavitt concludes that it was in these high-risk cases requiring surgical intervention that physicians found their first commanding voice in the birthing room. Over time they learned to use their new authority in all obstetric cases.

Judith Walzer Leavitt's analysis of the interaction between science and power in medicine points the way for further research in the history of obstetrics. While we have a good understanding of the chronology and the major institutional parameters that shaped obstetrics, more work like Leavitt's is needed to understand the meaning of science for Progressive-Era physicians and how it modeled the development of this important medical specialty. In addition, little work has focused on examining how the program set by obstetric's leaders was played out by both practicing physicians and academicians. Few studies of the development of obstetrics have analyzed the maternity work patterns of early twentieth-century physicians. Further studies might analyze, for example, the question of when and how prospective specialists limited their practice solely to obstetrics and gynecology. Some research suggests that there might have been differences among the women patients who went to specialist physicians.[55] Were these differences related to the economic circumstances of race and class or were there medical reasons—i.e., were these women at particular risk for a problem birth? In addition, we need to understand more about the development of academic obstetrics. For example, how did J. Whitridge Williams's program for a laboratory science for obstetrics translate to medical schools that were less well-funded than Johns Hopkins or that had different educational missions?[56]

As this essay has tried to show, the existing literature on the history of obstetrics demonstrates a wide range of political opinions about the development of this important women's medical specialty. Further research should show us the complex effects of this development.

---

[55] Judith Walzer Leavitt's *Brought to Bed: Childbearing in America* (New York: Oxford University Press, 1986) looks at the women patients who entered the hospital for their babies' births. Her work suggests that these women were predominantly upper- middle-class women who saw the hospital as a representative of science. See chapter 5, "Birth Moves to the Hospital," pp. 171-95.

[56] A recent dissertation examines some of these questions by analyzing groups of physicians in Wisconsin. See Charlotte G. Borst, "Catching Babies: The Change from Midwife to Physician-Assisted Childbirth, Wisconsin, 1870-1930" (Ph.D. dissertation, University of Wisconsin at Madison, 1989).

9

WOMEN'S REPRODUCTIVE HEALTH

Suzanne Poirier

Instead of being raised and educated by women who told them the truth about their bodies, the girls were taken from their villages and put in schools. . . . Instead of learning that once a month their bodies would become sacred, they were taught they would become filthy. . . . [T]hey were taught they were sick, and must bandage themselves and act as if they were sick.

—Anne Cameron, *Daughters of Copper Woman*[1]

Imani had once lived in New York . . . near the Margaret Sanger clinic, where she had received her very first diaphragm, with utter gratitude and amazement that someone apparently understood and actually cared about young women as alone and ignorant as she. . . . [S]he felt how close she was still to that earlier self. Still not in control of her sensuality, and only through violence and with money . . . in control of her body.

—Alice Walker, "The Abortion"[2]

These two quotations, one from an arrangement of legends from a women's society of Native Americans of the Northwest and the other from a contemporary short story, demonstrate the myriad issues contained in the story of women's reproductive health. I use the word *story* here deliberately, to imply not only events and people but also the feelings and beliefs that inform and motivate them. When the young girls in *Daughters of Copper Woman* (who had previously been taught

---

[1] Anne Cameron, *Daughters of Copper Woman* (Vancouver, B.C.: Press Gang Publishers, 1981), pp. 61–62.
[2] Alice Walker, "The Abortion," in *You Can't Keep a Good Woman Down: Stories by Alice Walker* (New York: Harcourt Brace Jovanovich, 1981), p. 69.

about menstruation and pregnancy by village "wise women") were sent to the church schools, the white, male priests taught them that the natural functions of their bodies were shameful and somehow sick. The "facts" being taught to these girls were shaped by others' attitudes about women and women's bodies. The separation of women from knowledge about their bodies is also evident in Alice Walker's short story: a young black married woman realizes that "violence and money" are necessary for her to (re)gain "control" of her body through an abortion. As she remembers her feelings on receiving her first diaphragm, Imani realizes how integral both contraception and abortion are to her own sense of "sensuality" and self—and how tenuous "still" is her control over both.

The story of women's reproductive health encompasses not only the history of scientific and medical knowledge and practice but also the history of law, religion, popular opinion, women's roles, sexuality, economics, and the lives of individual women. This review of the histories of women's reproductive health, then, will present a wide variety of voices. It includes methods and perspectives not only of historians but also of legal scholars, journalists, demographers, social scientists, and scientists. Furthermore, none of these historians of women's reproductive health will be, themselves, without feelings or beliefs shaped by their own experiences and personalities. Thus, though the scholars discussed below draw upon many of the same primary and secondary sources, all come to slightly different conclusions.

There is a double edge to most of the dilemmas that are discussed below. For example, many women worldwide have in the past wanted— and continue to want—a reliable method of birth control, whatever the risk. Yet reproductive technologies that offer hope or even life to some women threaten oppression or coercion to others. Emotions around all of these issues have always run high. This chapter was written during the time that the Supreme Court was deciding the case of *Webster v. Reproductive Health Services*, the most serious challenge to date of *Roe v. Wade*, the 1973 Supreme Court decision which acknowledged a woman's right to have an abortion. That the public does not yet agree on a vision or definition of women's reproductive health—that women themselves do not yet agree—is evident by this ongoing debate. Furthermore, that the issues in the abortion debate are essentially the same issues that were voiced in debates about birth control in the nineteenth century and are voiced in debates about the reproductive technologies of recent years, dramatically illustrates to us that history can be a window not only on the past but on the present and even the future.

I. EUGENICS

> We have, of course, made it our first business to train out, to breed
> out, when possible, the lowest types. . . . If the girl showing the bad
> qualities had still the power to appreciate social duty, we appealed to
> her, by that, to renounce motherhood.
>
> —Charlotte Perkins Gilman, *Herland*[3]

> These natural graces in the quadroon are often united with beauty of
> the most dazzling kind. . . . [Eliza, s]afe under the protecting care of her
> mistress, . . . had reached maturity without those temptations which
> make beauty so fatal an inheritance to a slave.
>
> —Harriet Beecher Stowe, *Uncle Tom's Cabin*[4]

An important thread that runs throughout the history of all areas of
women's reproductive health is the role of eugenics in the thinking of
both the makers and interpreters of that history. In its broadest sense,
eugenics is "a science which investigates ways to improve the genetic
condition of the human race."[5] Important here are the words *improve*,
which implies judgments of worth, and *genetic*, a reference to the science
of genetics, which has been little understood until fairly recently (more
will be said about both of these points later). Historians of eugenics
usually begin their story in England with Francis Galton, described by
historian Daniel J. Kevles as an "innocent of the future, [who] confidently equated science with progress."[6] Galton believed that selective
breeding of humans would give nature a boost forward in its own
process of evolution. At first he advocated state regulation of marriage
to ensure this progress, measuring worthiness to reproduce by one's
social eminence (members of Parliament, nobility, etc.). Finding little
popular support for his ideas, Galton eventually contented himself with
the hope that converts to eugenics would voluntarily adopt his reproductive guidelines. Galton supported his beliefs with numbers, collecting
statistics about whatever he studied, from sweet peas to criminals.

Galton's efforts, however rudimentary or naive they may seem
today, typify themes and methods that are often proposed to control
women's reproduction. The setting of standards of reproductive

---

[3] Charlotte Perkins Gilman, *Herland* (1915; reprint, New York: Pantheon, 1979), p. 82.
[4] Harriet Beecher Stowe, *Uncle Tom's Cabin* (1849; reprint, New York: Library of America, 1982), p. 22.
[5] Kenneth M. Ludmerer, *Genetics and American Society: A Historical Appraisal* (Baltimore: Johns Hopkins University Press, 1972), p. 2.
[6] Daniel J. Kevles, *In the Name of Eugenics: Genetics and the Uses of Human Heredity* (New York: Alfred A. Knopf, 1985), p. 3.

"worth" by self-appointed groups, the debate between regulation and voluntarism, the tendency to think of reproduction in terms only of married couples, and reasoning in terms of populations rather than individuals are all issues that have regularly informed the discussions of eugenicists, family planners, and population engineers. They usually regard women as one half of a heterosexual couple and a means to a larger, often nationalistic end. The rhetoric of eugenics has echoed throughout recent public discussion of "the population explosion," which essentially asserts that worldwide poverty and "over" population can be eliminated only by reducing the world population, most particularly the poor classes of the third world.[7]

Some of the utopian communities of the mid-nineteenth century embraced eugenics as a way to produce a "better" world or offer "better" opportunities to succeeding generations.[8] We hear such hopes echoed in the feminist utopian novel of Charlotte Perkins Gilman, *Herland*. Eugenics underpins the concept of "race suicide," the belief that certain groups of people, usually the more "refined" or "intelligent," were bringing about their own extinction either through weakening their reproductive systems or deliberately limiting the sizes of their families through contraception or abortion. In the late nineteenth century, "race suicide" became a clarion call of middle- and upper-class, primarily Nordic, whites who feared that their diminishing numbers would be engulfed by the unrestrained reproduction of less fully "evolved," "animalistic" lower classes, composed predominately of blacks and white Catholic immigrants.[9] (This attitude toward the lower class and nonwhite races pervaded the thinking even of many reformers, as the words of Harriet Beecher Stowe reveal.)

Historians of birth control in the United States have differed markedly in the relationship that they see between women and eugenics in the mid-nineteenth and early twentieth centuries. Nearly all of them recognize the race and class biases inherent in concerns about "race

---

[7] For discussions of overpopulation, see especially Ludmerer, *Genetics*; Linda Gordon, *Woman's Body, Woman's Right: A Social History of Birth Control in America* (New York: Grossman, 1976); and James Reed, *From Private Vice to Public Virtue: The Birth Control Movement and American Society Since 1830* (New York: Basic Books, 1978).

[8] Dolores Hayden, *Seven American Utopias: The Architecture of Communitarian Socialism, 1790–1975* (Cambridge: MIT Press, 1976).

[9] For definitions and discussions of the role of fears of "race suicide" on public and medical attitudes toward birth control and abortion, see especially Gordon, *Woman's Body*; and James C. Mohr, *Abortion in America: The Origins and Evolution of National Policy, 1800–1900* (New York: Oxford University Press, 1978).

suicide," but not all of them note a gender bias as well. Linda Gordon was one of the first historians to explore this connection, identifying women in general as an oppressed group and thus making a connection between women and other economically and socially disenfranchised groups.[10] These conditions made women in the nineteenth century vulnerable to the judgment of those eugenicists who often criticized women who went to college and/or into careers. Because these women frequently postponed or forewent marriage, they were seen as contributing to the demise of their race—and class. Gordon finds parallels in the politics and rhetoric of today's fears of a "population explosion" with the rhetoric and politics of the fears of "race suicide" a century earlier, and she urges caution when thinking about nationwide or worldwide plans of population control.[11] Other historians, however, convey a sense of urgency and offer a eugenic analysis of their own interpretations. For example, James Reed describes birth control as "a moral imperative in a crowded world," and C. Thomas Dienes concludes that "the new jurisprudence seeks to achieve a more efficacious 'social engineering' through law."[12] These interpretations of today's population issues often reflect views of women's reproductive health.

II. CONTRACEPTION

> You see, they were Mothers, not in our sense of helpless involuntary fecundity, forced to fill and overfill the land, but in the sense of Conscious Makers of People. Mother-love with them was not a brute passion, a mere "instinct," a wholly personal feeling; it was—a religion.
> —Charlotte Perkins Gilman, *Herland*[13]

> At this moment hundreds of women
> a few miles from here are looking
> for the same sign of reprieve, the red
> splash of freedom. .
> . . And some lesser number
> of women in other bedrooms and bathrooms
> see that red banner unfurl and mourn!
> Another month, another chance missed.
> —Marge Piercy, "The Watch"[14]

---

[10] Gordon, *Woman's Body.*
[11] Ibid., pp. 391–402.
[12] Reed, *Private Vice,* p. xiii; and C. Thomas Dienes, *Law, Politics, and Birth Control* (Urbana: University of Illinois Press), pp. 254, 300.
[13] Gilman, *Herland,* p. 68.
[14] Marge Piercy, "The Watch," in *Stone, Paper, Knife* (New York: Alfred A. Knopf, 1983), p. 56.

Central to the history of birth control has been the linkage in many people's minds between sexual intercourse and procreation. Recognizing the possibility of preventing conception or birth forces the further acknowledgement that sexual activity might exist for its own sake. This possibility joins the concept of birth control with concepts of women, sexuality, and the family. It encompasses issues of economics, law, medicine, and religion.

Before discussing the history of contraception, definitions—or a look at the range of possible definitions—are in order. Taken at its most literal, *birth control* is any means by which population increase is prevented. It encompasses abstinence, contraceptive chemicals and devices, abortion, and infanticide. Narrowed to apply only to sexual intercourse itself, it refers to the prevention of conception, and abortion and infanticide are usually dropped from the definition. Such a definition, however, is not entirely accurate. Intrauterine devices (IUDs) do not prevent conception; rather, they prevent the fertilized egg from attaching to the wall of the uterus. "Morning after" pills (referred to as postcoital contraceptives) also prevent attachment of the fertilized egg, as does the contraceptive pill itself.[15] In other words, most methods developed in the second half of the twentieth century are, technically, abortifacients. Similarly, some people refer to menstrual extraction (a self-care method of removing the uterine lining to eliminate menses or relieve cramps) as a contraceptive technique, although it may also remove a fertilized egg that has attached to the uterine lining.[16] Finally, although these narrower definitions of birth control usually encompass sexual activities between heterosexual couples that involve penetration of the vagina by the penis but avoid emission of semen in the vagina (such as coitus interruptus—withdrawal of the penis before ejaculation—or coitus reservadus—penetration without any ejaculation), discussions of birth control have, historically, not included male or female orgasm without penetration (i.e., masturbation), or homosexual activity in general. These activities deserve mention because historical studies often see sexual behavior and procreation as inseparable.

---

15 For a detailed description of the devices and methods of contraception in current use, see Susan Bell, "Birth Control," in *The New Our Bodies, Ourselves: A Book By and For Women*, The Boston Women's Health Book Collective (New York: Simon and Schuster, 1984), pp. 220–62.

16 Laura Punnett, "Women-Controlled Research," in *Birth Control and Controlling Birth: Women-Centered Perspectives*, ed. Helen B. Holmes, Betty B. Hoskins, and Michael Gross (Clifton, NJ: Humana Press, 1980), pp. 61–70.

Obviously, then, the term *birth control* has a variety of definitions. Although, popularly, *birth control* is generally understood to refer to contraception only, for the purposes of this paper, *birth control* will be used to encompass both contraception and abortion. The terms *contraception* and *abortion* shall be used when discussing specific devices or methods.

We do know that methods for preventing pregnancy have been used, with varying degrees of success, throughout time.[17] "Potions"— either magical, herbal, or chemical—have been a part of medical folklore from most ancient to most recent times, attesting to the efforts that have always been made (usually primarily by *women*[18]) to prevent conception. The most widely used method of contraception throughout world history has been coitus interruptus. Also in wide general use have been versions of the "rhythm method," the practice of abstaining from sexual intercourse during times of greatest female fertility—although the female fertility cycle was not accurately understood until 1924.[19]

The devices most frequently used in the past to prevent conception have been douches (water or other solutions which flush semen from the vagina and/or act as spermicide), barriers (obstructions of the cervix which prevented movement of sperm into the vagina), and pessaries (vaginal suppositories which were spermicides and/or barriers). All of these methods are still in use today as douches, spermicidal foams and jellies, vaginal sponges, diaphragms, and cervical caps.[20] The condom, originally designed for men but today often purchased by women, also has a centuries-long history, although it was probably used primarily as a guard against venereal infection until the eighteenth century.[21] Finally, sterilization of both men and women has long been used for contraception, gaining popularity as the methods and technology of surgery have advanced. Sterilization, however, also carries a history of association with programs of "negative eugenics," the practice of "breeding out" undesired characteristics by denying certain individuals the right to reproduce. In the nineteenth century, "the unfit" (criminals, the insane, the "feeble-minded," or prostitutes) who inhabited the country's jails,

---

[17] Norman E. Himes, *Medical History of Contraception* (Baltimore: Williams and Wilkins, 1936), p. xii.
[18] Gordon, *Woman's Body*, p. 26.
[19] Ibid., p. 45.
[20] Bell, *New Our Bodies*, pp. 220–62.
[21] Himes, *Medical History*, pp. 194–200.

hospitals, or asylums were often sterilized, without their consent or
sometimes even their knowledge.[22]

Birth control among the general public first gained popular attention
in the United States with growing concern about falling birth rates
among middle- and upper-class whites in the middle of the nineteenth
century. In 1863, Congress passed the Comstock Law, an anti-obscenity
law which defined contraception as obscene and forbade the use of the
mails to distribute information about it. Religious and state law also
acted, directly or indirectly, in the nineteenth century to keep the
methods of contraception out of the hands of the general public.
Whereas Jewish, Catholic, and Protestant laws were originally quite
open about abortion in the early months of pregnancy, they were unanimously opposed to contraception of every kind except abstinence,
usually citing God's condemnation of Onan for "spilling his seed upon
the ground" (used originally to argue against coitus interruptus, masturbation, and male homosexuality). The power of religion in the second
half of the nineteenth century must be viewed within the context of a
variety of phenomena: rapid industrialization, increased mobility, growing status of science and medicine, growing public acceptance of birth
control, and the emancipation of women. These events are presented by
historians of religion in a variety of causal relationships, but all analyses
reveal the weakening authority of religious law and the growing inclina-
tion of the public to separate the phenomena of sexual intercourse and
procreation.[23]

By the second half of the nineteenth century, contraception was a
cause for religious, political, and medical debate, often centering on the
concept of Voluntary Motherhood. *Voluntary Motherhood*, a term coined
by historian Linda Gordon,[24] refers to the belief that women should be
allowed to determine when they would bear children. Advocates of

---

[22] Philip Reilly, "The Surgical Solution: The Writings of Activist Physicians in the Early
Days of Eugenical Sterilization," *Perspectives in Biology and Medicine* 26 (1983): 637–56.

[23] Histories of religion which give the fullest account of religious law and its changes over
time can be found in David M. Feldman, *Birth Control in Jewish Law: Marital Relations,
Contraception, and Abortion as Set Forth in the Classic Texts of Jewish Law* (New York:
New York University Press, 1968); and John T. Noonan, Jr., *Contraception: A History of
Its Treatment by the Catholic Theologians and Canonists* (Cambridge, MA: Belknap Press,
1966). The history of the response of the Catholic church to "the Pill" is contained in
fullest detail in Dienes, *Law, Politics*; David M. Kennedy, *Birth Control in America: The
Career of Margaret Sanger* (New Haven: Yale University Press, 1970); and Thomas B.
Littlewood, *The Politics of Population Control* (Notre Dame: The University of Notre
Dame Press, 1977).

[24] Gordon, *Woman's Body*, pp. 95–115.

Voluntary Motherhood, frequently feminists, believed that motherhood was a valued, central role in women's lives. Some people exalted motherhood to a sacred calling, as we hear in the words of Charlotte Perkins Gilman at the start of this section. They usually recommended sexual abstinence to achieve their goals, however, and vigorously opposed any mechanical means of birth control because such devices could give license to promiscuity, especially prostitution. Similarly, they also almost unanimously opposed abortion.

Historians often offer different interpretations of the social and political dynamics behind the various arguments for Voluntary Motherhood. Gordon sees women's acceptance, or even advocacy, of women's domestic strengths and Voluntary Motherhood as evidence, in part, of their economic and political subordination. Daniel Scott Smith and Carl Degler, on the other hand, conclude that the glorification of the qualities of womanhood and motherhood reflects women's growing equality and autonomy within the Victorian family.[25] Finally, James Reed describes these phenomena but concludes that such ideas had little influence on the events of that time.[26]

Like the supporters of Voluntary Motherhood, Margaret Sanger and her colleagues believed that a woman could--should—have *control* of her body. Sanger chose the term *birth control* to emphasize that belief. Like the supporters of Voluntary Motherhood, Sanger opposed abortion, but she went further to search for a way to prevent conception without abstinence.[27] Sanger, a trained and practicing nurse, first became involved in birth-control issues through her work as a nurse in New York's slums. Her shocked reaction in the desperation of her poor patients and the refusal of physicians to teach them about contraception found ready sympathy in the circle of socialists and anarchists of which she and her husband were a part. Her friends supported her as she was arrested twice, first for sending information about contraception through the mails in 1912 and then for opening a clinic which fitted women with diaphragms in 1916.

---

[25] Carl N. Degler, *At Odds: Women and the Family in America from the Revolution to the Present* (New York: Oxford University Press, 1980); and Daniel Scott Smith, "Family Limitation, Sexual Control, and Domestic Feminism in Victorian America," in *Clio's Consciousness Raised: New Perspectives on the History of Women*, ed. Mary S. Hartman and Lois Banner (New York: Octagon Books, 1976), pp. 119–136.

[26] Reed, *Private Vice*, pp. 41–45.

[27] Sanger's own perspective on her work and motives can be found in her autobiography, *Margaret Sanger: An Autobiography* (1938; reprint Elmsford, NY: Maxwell Reprint Company, 1970).

Sanger's ties to this circle of friends weakened, however, and eventually broke as she increasingly distanced herself over the years from their "radical" causes and aligned herself with more conservative middle- and upper-class groups. Recent historians have debated the extent to which birth *control* was sacrificed as Sanger garnered support for her goals by advocating laws whereby "physicians only" could prescribe and fit diaphragms, by adopting the goals of the eugenicists for population control, and by turning to academic and pharmaceutical research centers for the development of a contraceptive pill. Scholars who most unreservedly praise Sanger's accomplishments, such as Reed, often share her eugenic outlook.[28] Emily Taft Douglas proclaims legislation in the 1960s, which finally opened the door to women's access to birth control, to be a "victory [that] assured a basic freedom by which mankind [sic] might rear a better race."[29] On the other hand, David Kennedy, who criticizes eugenics as a politically conservative cause, suggests that Sanger may have used the country's fears of overpopulation to hurry the acceptance of birth control and assure for herself "complete and exclusive control of the birth control movement."[30]

The history of contraceptive devices, too, has been variously interpreted. Different historians have focused on different structures within society. Norman E. Himes has written the medical/technical history of contraception cited most frequently by other writers on birth control.[31] James Reed places this technical history within the broader contexts of the histories of the profession and practice of medicine, business, and government.[32] Such a history moves considerably beyond Himes's subject, but its focus on public institutions that were shaped and controlled by men does not provide much information about women's activities or attitudes. Studies by Daniel Scott Smith and Carl Degler call attention to the changing shape and function of the American family.[33] Such histories call attention to the roles of women in the family and (as a corollary) the world beyond the family. Finally, Linda Gordon looks at medicine,

---

28 Reed, *Private Vice*, p. xiii.
29 Emily Taft Douglas, *Margaret Sanger: Pioneer of the Future* (Garrett Park, MD: Garrett Park Press, 1975), p. 261.
30 Kennedy, *Birth Control*, p. 106.
31 Himes, *Medical History*. A reprinting of this 1936 edition occurred in 1963, with an added preface by eugenicist Alan F. Guttmacher, who praises the book and heralds the dawn of "physiological mechanisms" for preventing pregnancy (New York: Gamut Press, 1963), p. xxix.
32 Reed, *Private Vice*.
33 Smith, "Family Limitation"; Degler, *At Odds*.

government, law, and the family in her history of birth control, adding to this her interests in the history of women's sexuality and economic status. Her decision to explore "the point of view of . . . women seeking sexual and reproductive self-determination" leads her to challenge the premises of all the above-mentioned institutions, public and private.[34]

Some histories of birth control are biographies of the major actors in the various birth-control movements.[35] Margaret Sanger receives the most attention; other figures in the birth-control campaign, though, have also captured historians' interest and imagination. Some historians, particularly British ones, praise "the remarkable Emma Goldman,"[36] observing that Sanger "borrowed much—more than she later cared to admit—from Emma Goldman."[37] Mary Ware Dennett, an early associate of Sanger, with whom Sanger split when the National Birth Control League opposed Sanger's decision to seek "physician only" laws, is less vividly presented;[38] she deserves fuller attention. The major financial contributor to the development of "the Pill," philanthropist Catherine McCormick, has been vividly depicted with her eccentric dress and manner.[39] The tribulations and triumphs of the birth-control physicians have also been recorded: Robert Latou Dickinson, the first physician to devote a major part of his life to fight actively in the birth-control campaign; Gregory Pincus ("Pinky"), the physician-scientist-entrepreneur of "the Pill"; and John Rock, the Catholic physician who worked on the oral contraceptive and publicly answered Catholic attacks against it.[40]

---

[34] Gordon, *Woman's Body*, p. 42.

[35] For an analysis of these different birth-control movements within the context of the feminism and its history, see Linda Gordon, "The Struggle for Reproductive Freedom: Three Stages of Feminism," in *Capitalist Patriarchy and the Case for Socialist Feminism*, ed. Zillah R. Eisenstein (New York: Monthly Review Press, 1979), pp. 107–32.

[36] Clive Wood and Beryl Suitters, *The Fight for Acceptance: A History of Contraception* (Aylesbury, England: Medical and Technical Publishing Company, 1970), p. 183.

[37] Peter Fryer, *The Birth Controllers* (1965; reprint New York: Stein and Day, 1966), p. 204. Goldman also discusses her work for birth control in her autobiography, *Living My Life* vol. 2 (1931; reprint New York: Dover, 1970), pp. 553–70.

[38] The most complete portraits of Dennett appear within the pages of Dienes, *Law, Politics*; Gordon, *Woman's Body*; Kennedy, *Birth Control*.

[39] McCormick is most fully presented by Loretta McLaughlin, *The Pill, John Rock, and the Church: The Biography of a Revolution* (Boston: Little, Brown and Company, 1982); and Reed, *Private Vice*.

[40] See especially Reed, *Private Vice*, and Kennedy, *Birth Control*, on Dickinson. For Pincus, see M. C. Chang, "Development of the Oral Contraceptive," *American Journal of Obstetrics and Gynecology* 132 (1978): 217–19; and Oscar Hechter, "Homage to Gregory Pincus," *Perspectives in Biology and Medicine* 11 (1968): 358–70. The fullest portrait of Rock is provided by McLaughlin, *The Pill*.

Other scholars have interpreted demographic data of human fertility, family size, and population change in the United States. Numbers, though, like other information, can be widely interpreted. For example, although the smaller family sizes that were often reported among wealthier classes in the late nineteenth century were cited at the time as evidence of "race suicide," we recognize now that all racial groups were having fewer children. Discrepancies in the rate of decreasing fertility suggests to today's analysts that wealthier people had more access to efficacious methods of birth control, not that no birth control was being practiced among the poor. Demographers are particularly interested in the numbers and spacing of children in a family, age of the mother at the time of her child(ren)'s birth(s), education of parents, size and livelihood of their community, and religious ties. Some of these studies grew out of the ongoing eugenic interest in rate of growth of populations[41] and reflect the belief, dating back to Francis Galton, that explanations of social or biological conditions may lie in statistics. Only very recently have demographers begun to identify (or perhaps include) single as well as married mothers in their studies or to identify racial groups among their numbers. Some recent studies go beyond numbers to speculate on changing needs or values that motivated couples to limit their families even before a recognized birth-control movement[42] or to consider such influences on additional pregnancies as sex of the child.[43] Degler's study of the family and women's roles in the family uses both statistics and qualitative historical materials, thus gaining further insight into both his subject and his resources.[44]

These demographic data demonstrate that the Comstock Law was not totally effective. Although the law was finally overturned in 1938, state laws that had been written in the aftermath of the Comstock Law,

---

[41] Representative studies include Louise Kantrow, "Philadelphia Gentry: Fertility and Family Limitation among an American Aristocracy," *Population Studies* 34 (1980): 21–30; Warren C. Sanderson, "Quantitative Aspects of Marriage, Fertility and Family Limitation in Nineteenth Century America: Another Application of the Coale Specifications," *Demography* 16 (1979): 339–58; and Frank Sweetser and Paaro Piepponen, "Postwar Fertility Trends and Their Consequences in Finland and the United States," *Journal of Social History* 1 (1967): 101–18.

[42] Representative of these kinds of studies are Douglas L. Anderton and Lee L. Bean, "Birth Spacing and Fertility Limitation: A Behavioral Analysis of a Nineteenth Century Frontier Population," *Demography* 22 (1985): 169–83; and Deborah Dawson, Denise J. Meny, and Jeanne Clare Rielley, "Fertility Control in the United States before the Contraceptive Revolution," *Family Planning Perspectives* 12 (1980): 76–86.

[43] Representative are Douglas M. Stone and Chu-Fe Lee, "Sex of Previous Children and Intentions for Further Births in the United States, 1965–1976," *Demography* 20 (1983): 353–67.

[44] Degler, *At Odds*.

also forbidding birth control, remained on the states' books much longer. In 1965, *Griswold v. Connecticut* granted women access to information about birth control on the grounds that the decision to practice birth control was protected by an individual's right to privacy. Similar cases followed in other states over the next ten years.[45]

The challenge that finally forced states to reexamine their versions of the Comstock Law came with the release to the U.S. market of a contraceptive pill in the early 1960s. The paradox of *birth control* in Sanger's original sense of the term being so closely linked to a male scientific and medical community is heightened by the ironic fact that initial scientific research on anovulant drugs was actually undertaken in connection with infertility in women.[46] This research grew out of the same scientific enthusiasm over endocrinology which also produced DES (diethylstilbestrol), a synthetic hormone used to prevent both miscarriage in pregnant women (a use for which it was ineffective) and postcoital contraception (a "morning after pill"), for which it is still being used.[47] Some scientists were, in fact, aware of the contraceptive actions of the drugs they were developing but strove to downplay or even omit that information in their reports.[48]

Much of the medical rhetoric about the use of contraceptive drugs and devices focuses not on "safety" but on "risk," with physicians, scientists, and population planners often judging that prevented pregnancies outweigh the potential side effects of the contraceptives.[49] This

---

[45] The most detailed explorations of the relationship between state and national legislative and court systems in the years between the Comstock Law and *Griswold v. Connecticut* are given by Dienes, *Law, Politics*; and Kennedy, *Birth Control*.

[46] Histories of the science of the development of anovulant drugs are presented by Chang, "Development of the Oral Contraceptive"; Joseph W. Goldzieher, "Estrogens in Oral Contraceptives: Historical Perspectives," *Johns Hopkins Medical Journal* 150 (1982): 165–69; Joseph W. Goldzieher and Harry W. Ruden, "How the Oral Contraceptives Came to be Developed," *JAMA* 230 (1974): 421–25; and McLaughlin, *The Pill*.

[47] Scientific discussions of the development of DES are provided by Roberta J. Apfel and Susan M. Fisher, *To Do No Harm: DES and the Dilemmas of Modern Medicine* (New Haven: Yale University Press, 1984), pp. 11–58; Diana B. Dutton, "DES and the Elusive Goal of Drug Safety," in *Worse than the Disease: Pitfalls of Medical Progress* (New York: Cambridge University Press, 1988), pp. 31–90; and Howard Ulfelder, "The Stilbestrol Disorders in Historical Perspective," *Cancer* 45 (1980): 3008–11.

[48] Chang, "Development of the Oral Contraceptive"; and McLaughlin, *The Pill*, pp. 119–40.

[49] Representative of these arguments, offered at the time of the most heated debate over the side effects of the drugs are Celso-Ramon Garcia and Edward E. Wallach, "Biochemical Changes and Implications Following Long-Term Use of Oral Contraception," in *Fertility and Family Planning: A World View*, ed. S. J. Behrman, Leslie Corsa, Jr., and Ronald Freedman (Ann Arbor: University of Michigan Press, 1969), pp. 252–92; and Belita Cowan, "Ethical Problems in Government-Funded Contraceptive Research," in *Birth Control and Controlling Birth*, ed. Holmes, et al., pp. 37–46.

desire for an efficacious means of contraception, plus the sense of political and economic urgency felt by many of the scientists involved in early anovulant research, led to testing the drugs by methods whose accuracy and ethicality both came under question.[50] The testing of the first anovulant drugs on poor Puerto Rican women is treated variously by historians, often depending on their own position on eugenics and world population control. Thus, although Reed observes that it "might be argued" that such tests were wrong, he goes on to comment that Puerto Rico provided an "ideal" population to test, ideal largely because of the Puerto Rican women's eagerness to receive a contraceptive pill of any kind.[51] Gordon, on the other hand, discusses the economic and political influences of "informed consent" and the discrimination inherent in all governmental programs of population control because of those influences.[52]

The lines between volunteerism and coercion become vague under such conditions. Gordon and Reed both report the entry of the U.S. government into family planning programs during the Depression. These programs were provided primarily to poor women and urged the most invasive of contraceptive measures (i.e., sterilization). Such programs often draw a fine (if even perceptible) line between providing women with a service they desperately want and coercing them into decisions that they cannot freely make. There is today recurring evidence of unconsented-to sterilizations of women, usually poor women of color, on charges of mental "deficiency" or reproductive irresponsibility.[53] The recent use of Depo-Provera (a contraceptive injection often called "the Shot") raises similar issues.[54]

---

50 Gordon, Woman's Body, pp. 336–38; Reed, Private Vice, p. 364; and Paul Vaughan, The Pill on Trial (New York: Coward-McCann, 1970), pp. 38–49.

51 Reed, Private Vice, pp. 347, 359–60.

52 Gordon, Woman's Body, pp. 398–402.

53 See Angela Y. Davis, "Racism, Birth Control and Reproductive Rights," in Women, Race and Class (New York: Random House, 1981), pp. 202–21; Adelaida R. Del Castillo, "Sterilization: An Overview," in Mexican Women in the United States: Struggles Past and Present, ed. Magdalena Mora and Adelaida R. Del Castillo. Occasional Paper no. 2 (Los Angeles: University of California Los Angeles, Chicano Studies Research Center Publications, 1980), pp. 65–70; Claudia Dreifus, "Sterilizing the Poor," in Seizing Our Bodies: The Politics of Women's Health, ed. Claudia Dreifus (New York: Random House, 1977), pp. 105–20; Helen Rodrigues-Trias, "Sterilization of Abuse," Women Health 3 (May–June 1978): 10–15; and Sandra Serrano Sewell, "Sterilization Abuse and Hispanic Women," Birth Control and Controlling Birth, ed. Holmes, et al., pp. 121–24.

54 The following three articles in Holmes, et al., eds., Birth Control and Controlling Birth raise these issues: Marie M. Cassidy, "Depo-Provera and Sterilization Abuse Overview," pp. 97–100; Gena Corea, "The Depo-Provera Weapon," pp. 107–16; and Carol Levine, "Depo-Provera: Some Ethical Questions about a Controversial Contraceptive," pp. 101–6.

The abuses or potential for abuse of sterilization notwithstanding, sterilization of both men and women ranks today as the most popular voluntary method of birth control. The other most widely used forms of contraception in the United States are contraceptive pills and intrauterine devices (IUDs).[55] These forms are the most effective ones, but they also have the greatest frequency of adverse side effects. Gordon has noted differences in methods of birth control, with some giving control to men, others to women, and others cooperative in their technique.[56] Research in contraceptive methods in the past twenty years has, paradoxically, given women methods that they can "control," but undercut that control by making physicians the distributors of those methods. In addition, the control of research agendas by (primarily white male) scientists gives consumers little voice about which forms of contraception will be developed.[57] Inadequate funding for the development and testing of such relatively noninvasive methods as cervical caps or vaginal sponges[58] stands in stark contrast to the strong medical support for the IUD, anovulant drugs, and contraceptive injections such as Depo-Provera.

The history of many of these new methods has been or is being played out in the courts or governmental agencies as well as the laboratory or physician's office. Historians of "the Pill," intrauterine devices (namely the Dalkon Shield), and DES (for its effects on both the daughters of its users and the users as well) often tell of the hurried and inadequate testing, the downplaying of serious side effects, and the reluctance of physicians, drug companies, and/or government officers to respond to the discovered dangers until pressured by women who have been harmed by those drugs or devices.[59]

---

[55] Linda E. Atkinson and Jacki Ans, "Status of Contraceptive Technology Development," *Birth Control and Controlling Birth*, ed. Holmes, et al., pp. 55–60.

[56] Gordon, *Woman's Body*, p. 28.

[57] For a discussion of this phenomenon and its implications for future research, see Carol C. Korenbrot, "Value Conflicts in Biomedical Research into Future Contraceptives," in Holmes, et al., eds., *Birth Control and Controlling Birth*, pp. 47–53.

[58] Ibid., pp. 50–51; and Bell, *The New Our Bodies*, pp. 230–31.

[59] Medical and legislative struggles around oral contraceptives are the focus of Dienes, *Law, Politics*; McLaughlin, *The Pill*; and Vaughan, *The Pill on Trial*. The history of DES touches several facets of women's health in its use as a "morning after" pill, to prevent miscarriage (which it did not do), and as a therapy during menopause. The struggles to stop these uses of DES are documented and analyzed by Apfel and Fisher, *To Do No Harm*; Susan Bell, "A New Model of Medical Technology Development: A Case Study of DES," in *Research in the Sociology of Health Care, Vol. 4: The Adoption and Social Consequences of Medical Technologies*, ed. Julius A. Roth and Sheryl Burt Ruzek (Greenwich, CT: JAI Press, 1986), pp. 1–32; and Dutton, "DES," pp. 31–90.

The "double edge" of reproductive issues is seen not only in the rhetoric of "risk versus safety" but also in the acknowledgment that many women themselves advocated—and continue to advocate—methods of birth control that may be harmful. Part of the problem stems from a lack of concern for consumers but also important is the great need of some women for birth control regardless of the risks.

III. ABORTION

> . . . oh, what I say, how is the truth to be said?
> You were born, you had body, you died.
> It's just that you never giggled or planned or cried.
> Believe me, I loved you all.
> Believe me, I knew you, though faintly, and I loved, I loved you
> All.
> —Gwendolyn Brooks, "The Mother"[60]

> In 1971, in Chicago, it cost what you could afford.
> Triscuit and apricot nectar included along with
> Tetracycline and para-cervical block,
> The deed, a claim back to our own "property,"
> a term which men have carved deeper and hold older
> than any love they may say they have for our children,
> For us.
> Life begins in the taking hold of it: this
> is the song.
> —Linnea Johnson, "A Participant Historian Sings"[61]

The history of abortion shares many issues with the history of contraception. Women's efforts in the twentieth century to repeal or modify abortion laws voice many of the same arguments for a woman's right to control her body as were heard in earlier arguments for "Voluntary Motherhood" and birth control.[62] Moreover, the open practice of contraception emphasized the belief that pregnancy could and should be planned, making abortion an even more readily acceptable option to many women. Legal and social acceptance of both abortion and contraception have also been closely tied to other, larger movements. While contraception is seen as an issue whose acceptance was inextricably tied to fears of world overpopulation in the 1960s, the liberalization of

---

60 Gwendolyn Brooks, "The Mother," *Selected Poems* (New York: Harper & Row, 1963).
61 Linnea Johnson, "A Participant Historian Sings," unpublished poem, excerpted by permission of the author.
62 Gordon, *Woman's Body*; and Mohr, *Abortion*.

abortion law is generally viewed as equally inextricably tied to the women's movement. Finally, as contraception came increasingly to be placed in the hands of physicians, so abortion, as allowed in *Roe v. Wade*, has become more exclusively than ever the province of medicine.

Abortion has been recognized as a widely practiced form of birth control throughout history.[63] In most Western religions, abortion was not necessarily forbidden. Jewish law has traditionally said that a mother's life takes precedence over that of the fetus.[64] Protestant clergy usually held with the Biblical concept of "quickening," which viewed abortion as serious but not criminal in the early stages of pregnancy.[65] There is some disagreement among historians of Catholic law over very early doctrine regarding abortion, but distinctions based on stage of pregnancy may also have originally existed there as well.[66]

Early U.S. physicians tended to follow temporal guidelines similar to the concept of quickening, often calling abortion in the first trimester a miscarriage, and using the term "criminal abortion" to apply to artificial termination of a pregnancy only after quickening.[67] Physicians play an important role in the legal history of abortion, as state legislation beginning in the mid-1880s not only made most abortions illegal, but also made illegal any abortions not performed by physicians. Although the first abortion laws were passed with the expressed desire of protecting women from the hazards of abortions performed by nonphysicians, these laws also have close connections with the rising influence of the American Medical Association, efforts of the medical profession to establish the specialty of obstetrics-and-gynecology, concerns of "social purists" regarding prostitution and obscenity, and fears of "race suicide" among the white middle and upper classes upon realizing that the majority of abortions were being sought by women of their own social strata.[68]

---

[63] Gordon, *Woman's Body*, p. 4; Himes, *Medical History*, p. 4.

[64] Feldman, "Abortion: Jewish Perspectives," *Encyclopedia of Bioethics* 1 (New York: Macmillan, 1978): 5.

[65] James B. Nelson, "Abortion: Protestant Perspectives," *Encyclopedia of Bioethics* 1:14–15.

[66] The historical and textual details of the argument are most fully presented by John Connery, *Abortion: The Development of the Roman Catholic Perspective* (Loyola University Press, 1977); and Noonan, *Contraception*.

[67] Carroll Smith-Rosenberg, "The Abortion Movement and the AMA, 1850–1880," in *Disorderly Conduct: Visions of Gender in Victorian America* (New York: Alfred A. Knopf, 1985), 217–44.

[68] Mohr, *Abortion*; Smith-Rosenberg, "Abortion Movement."

Thus, the history of abortion becomes largely a story of access—medically, legally, and economically. Abortions have occurred throughout time, yet nearly all legal abortion procedures today are available only from physicians and are performed in medical clinics or hospitals. That abortion is a *procedure* that often requires anesthetic has probably reinforced a sense that only physicians can or should perform abortions. The development, however, of menstrual extraction (a suction method of removing the menses which can also remove early fetal material) by women's self-help groups in the early 1970s[69] and the experiences of the women of "Jane," an abortion collective in Chicago in which women learned and taught each other how to perform abortions[70] challenge those assumptions. Now, with the oral drug RU486, popularly called "the abortion pill," arguments about the medical complexity of abortion are further challenged.[71]

The use of this abortion-inducing drug in Europe and the efforts to prevent its use in the United States and other countries challenges not only the medical system but the legal and regulatory systems that are also involved in controlling access to abortion, a process that actually began soon after the abortion laws of the nineteenth century went into effect. As the acceptability of abortion before quickening faded, these laws permitted abortion if the life of the mother was threatened, but physicians alone were given the power to judge when an abortion was necessary, or when an abortion that had been performed was not of a "criminal" nature. Thus, physicians became both the medical and moral arbiters of abortion. There have been some rather paradoxical results of this situation. For one thing, physicians and others who performed abortions were prosecuted under these laws, making a woman who sought an abortion a victim of a crime rather than an actor in it.[72] Moreover, such laws also limited a woman's identity to that of receptacle for the fetus. Some historians have also interpreted this process as a reflection of the fear men have always felt toward women's childbearing powers.[73]

---

[69] Punnett, "Women-Controlled Research"; and Jill Wolhandler with Ruth Weber, "Abortion," *New Our Bodies*, p. 295.

[70] Jane [pseud.] "Jane," *Voices* (serialized June through November 1973). *Voices* was a short-lived radical paper in Chicago.

[71] Thomas G. Maggio, "Politics in the Drug-development Process: The Case of Mifepristone," "Commentary" in *American Journal of Hospital Pharmacy*, 46 (1989): 133–36.

[72] Eva R. Rubin, *Abortion, Politics, and the Courts: Roe v. Wade and Its Aftermath*. Revised ed. (New York: Greenwood Press, 1987), p. 35.

[73] Smith-Rosenberg, "Abortion Movement," pp. 239–40.

Not surprisingly, most histories of abortion become histories of policy or law. They view the events that led to the legalization of abortion as the story of the gradual unraveling of the resulting consensus between medicine, government, and religion.[74] As abortion moved into the twentieth century, it became apparent that properly performed abortions were seldom life threatening. Consequently, the argument of abortion as a health risk became increasingly hollow.[75] To increase the availability of abortion, some medical professionals began to broaden the definition of "threat" to the physical life of a mother to include her psychological life, then her physical and psychological "health," and finally (in the wake of the possibility of fetal deformities from Thalidomide and a rubella outbreak in the 1960s) the quality of the prospective child's life and the psychological and economic impact of that life on the mother. Hospital abortion boards created in the 1950s often exhibited highly visible differences in attitudes and practices among both physicians and hospitals regarding abortion, as some hospitals adopted widely divergent formal and informal policies regarding the permissibility of and criteria for abortion.[76] These differences further demonstrated the weakened consensus of medical opinion.

In the 1960s several new groups promoted abortion reform, most notably the Association for the Study of Abortion (ASA), an educational group composed largely of physicians and other professionals, and the National Association for Repeal of Abortion Laws (NARAL), a lobbying group of citizens. Other grass-roots and professional groups worked primarily for reform of individual state laws. These groups included the American Law Institute, which wrote a "model" abortion law in 1959, and the National Organization for Women, which was active on both the local and national levels throughout the campaign

---

[74] See Nanette J. Davis, *From Crime to Choice: The Transformation of Abortion in America* (Westport, CT: Greenwood Press, 1985); Kristin Luker, *Abortion and the Politics of Motherhood* (Berkeley: The University of California Press, 1984); and Mohr, *Abortion*.

[75] Mohr, *Abortion*, p. 250.

[76] The causes and effects of forming abortion boards in hospitals are discussed by Davis, *Crime to Choice*; and Luker, *Abortion and the Politics of Motherhood*. Similar considerations of hospital policy following the liberalization of abortion laws after *Roe v. Wade* are raised in articles such as Michael S. Goldstein, "Creating and Controlling a Medical Market: Abortion in Los Angeles after Liberalization," *Social Problems* 31 (1984): 514–29; Charles A. Johnson and Jon R. Bond, "Policy Implementation and Responsiveness in Nongovernmental Institutions: Hospital Abortion Services after *Roe v. Wade*," *Western Political Quarterly* 35 (1982): 385–405; and Kathleen Kemp, Robert A. Carp, and David W. Brady, "The Supreme Court and Social Change: The Case of Abortion," *Western Political Quarterly* 31 (1978): 19–31.

for new abortion laws.[77] By 1973, in fact, abortion laws had already been liberalized to varying degrees in several states, most markedly in New York and California.[78] In 1973, in the case of *Roe v. Wade*, the Supreme Court decided that abortion for any reason during the first trimester of pregnancy was solely a matter between a woman and her physician; no state intervention was permitted. During the second trimester, the state could regulate conditions under which an abortion is performed, and during the third trimester the state could forbid an abortion unless the woman's life or health was at stake. The main argument presented in *Roe v. Wade* was the same argument for right-to-privacy that was the focus in the contraception decision of *Griswold v. Connecticut*.

The grounds on which *Roe v. Wade* were argued has been a continuous source of debate. Kristin Luker, for example, holds that the nineteenth-century medical and legal arguments served largely to divert attention from the fundamental issue of abortion, the question of personhood. She says that in *Roe v. Wade* feminists demanded that that question be directly addressed: "By making a claim that women had a *right* to abortion, they challenged the medical profession's control of the abortion decision. In so doing, they brought to the surface the philosophical issues that had remained latent for so long: the value and meaning of the embryo."[79] Although Luker sees this strategy as courageous and commendable, other historians do not see personhood as the main issue of abortion. Eva R. Rubin, for example, argues that because *Roe v. Wade* echoed the same line of argument as was followed in *Griswold v. Connecticut*, the 1973 decision skirted the "real" moral issue of abortion. For her the issue is gender inequality, and she concludes that "the decision restructured the dispute itself," paving the way to the "fetal politics" of today.[80] Nanette J. Davis concludes that the vocal feminist support of abortion has served to impede widescale acceptance or allowance of abortion, a conclusion also suggested by Judith Blake in her frequently cited survey of changing public opinion about abortion.[81] Davis says, "Using abortion as a power wedge, the women's liberation

[77] Marian Faux, *Roe v. Wade: The Untold Story of the Landmark Decision That Made Abortion Legal* (New York: Macmillan, 1988), pp. 102, 111, 225–26.

[78] Lawrence Lader, *Abortion II: Making the Revolution* (Boston: Beacon Press, 1973).

[79] Luker, *Abortion and Politics of Motherhood*, pp. 90–91.

[80] Rubin, *Abortion, Politics and the Courts*, p. 187.

[81] Nanette J. Davis, *Crime to Choice*; and Judith Blake, "Elective Abortion and Our Reluctant Citizenry: Research on Public Opinion in the United States, " in *The Abortion Experience: Physiological and Medical Impact*, ed. Howard J. and Joy D. Osofsky (Hagerstown, MD: Harper & Row, 1973), pp. 447–67.

movement took a dramatic leap foward. But in creating this paradox . . . established groups said No."[82]

Differing analyses of the abortion controversy in general reflect historians' views of the existing social and political fabric of the United States. For example, while James C. Mohr recognizes the anti-feminism of many physicians in the nineteenth century and generally describes abortion as the pawn of medicine and government, he would not, ultimately, reject those institutions.[83] Barbara Milbauer, on the other hand, is skeptical of the ability of public institutions to serve individual freedom. Observing "how fragile the rights of individuals are," she describes how legislative actions since *Roe v. Wade* have "continuously whittled away at the woman's bodily autonomy."[84] Historians who urge a renegotiation of existing public institutions (and/or attitudes) tend to argue along the lines of Rosalind Pollack Petchesky that "[w]e have to struggle for a society in which responsibility for contraception, procreation, and childbearing is no longer relegated to women primarily; and, at the same time, we have to defend the principle of control over our bodies and our reproductive capacities."[85]

With the exception of that of New York City's notorious abortionist of the late nineteenth century, Madame Restell,[86] the history of abortion is a curiously faceless one. Lawrence Lader, the founder of the NARAL, however, offers often lively descriptions of the people he has met during his years as an abortion activist.[87] A recent history of the events leading to, surrounding, and following *Roe v. Wade* by Marion Faux[88] presents a narrative history which gives the most extensive portraits of Norma ("Roe") McCorvey and her attorneys Linda Coffee and Sarah Waddington to date, but still no booklength biographies have appeared.

For one thing, many of these women, including Sherri Finkbine, who fought to receive an abortion after receiving Thalidomide during her pregnancy in the early 1960s, have acted out of personal exigency.

---

[82] Davis, *Crime to Choice*, p. 128.
[83] Mohr, *Abortion in America*, pp. 257–59.
[84] Barbara Milbauer in collaboration with Bert N. Obrentz, *The Law Giveth: Legal Aspects of the Abortion Controversy* (New York: Atheneum, 1983), p. 54.
[85] Rosalind P. Petchesky, *Abortion and Woman's Choice: The State, Sexuality, and Reproductive Freedom* (Boston: Northeastern University Press, 1985), p. 3.
[86] Allan Keller, *Scandalous Lady: The Life and Times of Madame Restell, New York's Most Notorious Abortionist* (New York: Atheneum, 1981).
[87] Lader, *Abortion II*.
[88] Faux, *Roe v. Wade*.

Some of them essentially allowed or created their "case" to test the limits of existing law. The attorneys who argued these cases have not risen to (nor have they sought) public prominence as did Margaret Sanger. Some women or groups of women, such as the illegal abortion collective "Jane," have only recently been willing to make their history known.[89] Approaches to abortion reform or repeal have often been collective efforts, undertaken by organizations for whom abortion is only one of several interests.[90] In short, it is probably too soon to know how much and what aspects of the "personal" history of abortion will eventually emerge or what shape it will take.

Many historians of abortion approach their subject through the social sciences. They tend to draw their information about abortion in the nineteenth century from secondary sources,[91] focusing the bulk of their own studies on field observations or political analyses of more recent events. Some of them use descriptive, anthropological methods of the social sciences. Thus, in addition to formally identified oral histories of women's abortion experiences,[92] we find historical documents in Carol Gilligan's interviews with women about their decision to have or not to have an abortion, Barbara Katz Rothman's interviews of women regarding their abortion decisions in connection with amniocentesis, and Kristin Luker's interviews with women choosing "not to contracept" in California as a result of the liberalization of abortion laws in that state in 1967.[93]

The quantitative tools of the social scientists, however, continue to be used. Demographers approach abortion from two major angles: the nature and extent of change in the institutions that offer abortions and

---

[89] Pauline Bart, "Seizing the Means of Reproduction: An Illegal Feminist Abortion Collective—How and Why It Worked." Paper presented to American Sociological Association, annual meeting, Chicago, Illinois, September 1977; and Sheryl Burt Ruzek, The Women's Health Movement: Feminist Alternatives to Medical Control (New York: Praeger, 1978), p. 25.

[90] The work of these different groups is presented by Faux, Roe v. Wade; Lader, Abortion II; Luker, Abortion and the Politics of Motherhood; and Rubin, Abortion, Politics, and the Courts.

[91] Mohr's Abortion in America and Gordon's Woman's Body, Woman's Right are most often cited by the other scholars noted in this review.

[92] Diane Sands, "Using Oral History to Chart the Course of Illegal Abortions in Montana," Frontiers 7 (1983): 32–37.

[93] Carol Gilligan, In a Different Voice: Psychological Theory and Women's Development (Cambridge: Harvard University Press, 1982); Barbara Katz Rothman, The Tentative Pregnancy: Prenatal Diagnosis and the Future of Motherhood (New York: Viking Press, 1986); and Kristin Luker, Taking Chances: Abortion and the Decision Not to Contracept (Berkeley: University of California Press, 1975).

the characteristics of the women receiving abortions in the years since *Roe v. Wade*. Studies by health-care providers usually focus on changes in number of services performed,[94] while studies by political scientists tend to look at the relationship between hospitals (or hospital decision-makers) and the communities they serve.[95]

Many of these studies directly or indirectly document the problems that poor women, many of whom are women of color, have faced in obtaining an abortion, especially since the subsequent restrictions of *Roe v. Wade*.[96] *Maher v. Roe* (1977) forbade the use of federal funds for performing abortions, a decision given further legislative force in the congressional "Hyde Amendment" of 1980. In July 1989, the Supreme Court handed down a decision that supported opponents of abortion in *Webster v. Reproductive Health Services*. In a controversial prologue to its case, Webster stated that life begins at conception. The case itself argued to prohibit the granting of federal funds to any public institution that advocates or performs abortions and placed stricter requirements on abortions performed in clinic rather than in hospital settings. This case poses a major challenge not only to *Roe v. Wade* but also to the earlier decision in the birth control case *Griswold v. Connecticut* because a woman's right to privacy is a major point of contention.[97] Moreover, the decision can have ramifications for contraception since most recently developed contraceptive devices actually remove a fertilized egg from the

---

[94] A collection of papers of this nature has been made by Howard Osofsky and Joy D. Osofsky, *The Abortion Experience*.

[95] Examples of these kinds of studies include Susan B. Hansen, "State Implementation of Supreme Court Decisions: Abortion Rates since *Roe v. Wade*," *Journal of Politics* 42 (1980): 372–95; Charles A. Johnson and Jon R. Bond, "Policy Implementation and Responsiveness in Nongovernmental Institutions: Hospital Abortion Services after *Roe v. Wade*," *Western Political Quarterly* 35 (1982): 385–405; Kathleen A. Kemp, Robert A. Carp, and David Brady, "The Supreme Court and Social Change: The Case of Abortion," *Western Political Quarterly* 31 (1978): 19–31; and Petchesky, *Abortion and Woman's Choice*.

[96] See Willard Cates, Jr., "Abortion Attitudes of Black Women," *Women Health* 2 (November–December 1979): 3–9; Michael W. Combs and Susan Welch, "Blacks, Whites, and Attitudes Toward Abortion," *Public Opinion Quarterly* 46 (1982): 510–20; Littlewood, *Politics of Population Control*; and J. Mayone Stycos, "Some Minority Opinions on Birth Control," in *Population Policy and Ethics: The American Experience*, ed. Robert M. Veatch (New York: John Wiley and Sons, 1977), pp. 169–96.

[97] A bibliography of the current coverage of *Webster v. Reproductive Health Services* is obviously impossible here. Two good overviews of the arguments that have appeared in the popular press are Eloise Salholz and Ann McDaniel, "The Battle over Abortion," *Newsweek* (May 1, 1989): 28–32; and a printing of the text of closing arguments in the New York *Times*, "High Court Asks Sharp Questions in Abortion Case" (April 27, 1989): 1, 14–16.

uterus. Requiring viability testing of fetuses at twenty weeks of gestation and providing full life-support equipment for those abortions place further financial, bureaucratic, and emotional obstacles between a woman and an abortion. Although the Supreme Court justices did not, in their decision, go on to overturn *Roe v. Wade*, cases coming before that court in subsequent months will offer such opportunities. In addition, the *Webster* decision has generated similar bills in the legislative bodies of most states. Clearly, the story—or drama—is still unfolding.[98]

Thus the lines between contraception and abortion, both medically and politically, remain blurry. The issues being debated today are little different from the arguments heard in the struggles for Voluntary Motherhood or birth control in either the early or middle decades of the twentieth century.

IV. REPRODUCTIVE TECHNOLOGIES

> I could stay here in the warm pocket
> that precedes shock, unlike those women
> who don't feel their own faces
> anymore. They walk from room to room
> in the four perfect chambers
> of their own hearts. . . .
> Listen as they mouth the name of the child
> that was meant to be, while around them
> silence widens, and the depths.
> —Judith Skillman, "Written on Learning of Arrhythmia in the Unborn Child"[99]

> On the ultrasound screen my child curled
> in his own fluid orbit, less real
> than any high-school-textbook tadpole
> used to symbolize birth, till the nurse
> placed a white arrow on his heart flicker:
> a quick needle of light. .
> . . He is all sweetness,

---

[98] This chapter was actually written while *Webster v. Reproductive Health Services* was being argued in April, 1989. Because of the rapidity with which events are evolving, I have made no attempt, other than to note the decision in July, to bring the situation up to date with specific court cases or state bills, with the admission that any attempt to be up-to-date here is impossible.

[99] Judith Skillman, "Written on Learning of Arrhythmia in the Unborn Child," in *Sutured Words: Contemporary Poetry about Medicine*, ed. Jon Mukand (Brookline, MA: Aviva Press, 1988), p. 231.

mouth smudged against the clear silk
that envelopes him, webbed hands that reach
and retreat as a cat tests water.
—Mary Kerr, "Soft Mask"[100]

Technically, the devices and mechanical methods of contraception and abortion are *reproductive technologies*, but this term is more usually applied to methods or procedures used to achieve or maintain pregnancy. The methods for achieving pregnancy include artificial insemination, which is the injection into a woman's vagina of sperm from her chosen partner or from an anonymous donor; in vitro fertilization, the union of egg and sperm outside of and then reimplanted into a woman's uterus; or surrogacy, the bearing of a child for one woman by another woman, usually through artificial insemination by the contracting woman's partner.[101] Reproductive technologies also include various means for maintaining or monitoring pregnancy. Earlier in this century, DES was considered a means of maintaining pregnancy by preventing miscarriages. Current technologies for monitoring pregnancy include amniocentesis, alpha-fetoprotein tests (for neural tube defects), and sonography, which check a fetus by, respectively, sampling the pregnant woman's amniotic fluid, sampling her blood, or "photographing" the fetus by sound waves.[102]

All of these technologies were originally developed to help either infertile or "subfertile" women or men, or to identify couples carrying genetically lethal or "disabling" traits (such as Tay-Sach's disease, spina bifida, or Down's Syndrome—raising further debates on the nature and definition of *disability*). The possibility of aborting a fetus that carries any of these "genetic markers" underlies the rationale for monitoring technologies. Moreover, recent technological development provides ways to abort fetuses selectively in the multiple pregnancies that often result from fertility drugs. The issues surrounding reproductive technologies seem almost ironic corollaries to the history of debates about birth control. The separation of sexual intercourse from procreation fostered more open attitudes toward birth control; now technologies enable procreation *without* sexual intercourse. Birth-control advocates insist that women should *not* be forced to bear children; proponents of reproductive technology profess that women and men have the right to

---

[100] Mary Kerr, "Soft Mask," *Sutured Words*, p. 230.
[101] A table of these technologies and their definitions appears in Mary Thom, "Dilemmas of the New Birth Technologies," *Ms.* (May 1988): 70–76.
[102] Descriptions of these technologies are given in Jane Pincus with Norma Swenson and Bebe Poor, "Pregnancy," *The New Our Bodies*, pp. 355–59.

become parents when they want—and to become parents of the genetic *kind* of children they want.

Dissimilar though they may seem, all of these technologies share some common elements. For example, the medical profession has played a major role in both defining and creating the procedures, which are closely tied for access and regulation to the legal system as well. All of the technologies can provide either opportunity or despair, as demonstrated by the two poems which open this section. These technologies raise questions about the rights versus the responsibilities of women. Close connections exist between these technologies and sexual mores, as artificial insemination and surrogacy raise questions about "accepted" sexual behavior and the meaning of motherhood, and the monitoring and screening technologies raise the possibility of abortion. It is not surprising, therefore, that religious or other moral arbiters have also been active commentators on these procedures and activities.

Histories of reproductive technology are still few and brief. The single exception is artificial insemination, an extension of animal "husbandry" practices that have long been in existence. J. Marion Sims, the "father" of gynecology, abandoned attempts at artificial insemination in the 1860s, judging it to be immoral.[103] Medical professor William Pancoast reportedly impregnated a married woman with the sperm of "the best looking member of the class" in 1884, an action subsequently condemned by his peers.[104] This general approbation of artificial insemination notwithstanding, these events sound two familiar themes in the history of reproductive technology. First, although the procedure was performed for the "medical problem" of female infertility, the procedure itself was one designed for "breeding" (i.e., eugenic) purposes. Second, the first recorded procedures were performed by physicians on married, presumably heterosexual, women.

Two developments, one socio-legal and the other scientific, have been crucial for the development and use of the variety of reproductive technologies that we find today. One of them is the liberalization of abortion laws; the other is the development of genetics.[105] In contrast to eugenics, whose roots are mathematical, genetics originated in the bio-

---

[103] Wilfred J. Finegold, *Artificial Insemination*, 2nd ed. (Springfield, IL: Charles C. Thomas, 1976).

[104] A. T. Gregoire and Robert C. Mayer, "The Impregnators," *Fertility Sterility* 16 (1965): 130–34.

[105] The information on the history of genetics is drawn from Ludmerer, *Genetics and American Society*.

logical sciences with Gregor Mendel, who, like Galton, studied the presence of traits carried from one generation of plant or animal life to the next. The *process* of transmission, however, rather than the fact or results of it, was of most interest to geneticists, who did not, at least originally, translate their observations into normative social policy or programs. The degree of certainty to which they could identify or trace the process of transmission, however, was minimal, until the discovery of the structure of genes in the DNA molecule and the subsequent linking of certain genes to certain traits; then the opportunities of genetics not only to detect but to effect changes in people's genetic makeup became clear.

The eugenic implications of the application of genetic information became equally clear. References to genetic counseling as "the New Eugenics"[106] suggest values and goals regarding who shall reproduce what on the part of those professionals who test, interpret, and advise the people who come to them. This posture represents a step that many scientists say they do not—or will not—take. Although some of the early (and even more recent) geneticists were or are members of eugenic societies, most geneticists, notes genetics historian Kenneth Ludmerer, have viewed themselves as separate from eugenicists. They see the medical sciences as "an ideologically neutral field" which enables most of them to "distinguish between research in human genetics and applications thereof, and . . . demand that any application be critically considered from both a scientific and ethical point of view."[107] Other geneticists are more skeptical, seeing the need for the ethical consideration of the applications of scientific research but not certain that scientists are necessarily the ones most able to make that evaluation.[108]

As more specific information about genetic structures has become available and methods of alternative fertilization have become more sophisticated (and more imaginative), concerns about the fetus have grown and questions about the pregnant woman's autonomy resurface. As in the days of Voluntary Motherhood, many feminists now see reproductive technologies subordinating women—either individually or collectively—to the unborn next generation. Some historians of genetics and geneticists themselves have noted the psychological burden when a

---

[106] Ibid., p. 175.
[107] Ibid., pp. 169, 173.
[108] See Garland Allen, "Genetics, Eugenics and Class Struggle," *Genetics* 79 (1975 Suppl): 29–45; Kevles, *Name of Eugenics*; and J. K. Sherman, "Synopsis of the Art of Human Semen Banking," *Fertility and Sterility* 24 (1973): 397–412.

decision about abortion needs to be made.[109] Barbara Katz Rothman's *The Tentative Pregnancy* documents this process, and other feminist writers use evidence of past medical and social sexism to warn of misogynistic potentials in today's new technologies.[110]

The "double edge" of new opportunities also appears. Public interest (of both women and men) has generally supported the development of genetic knowledge and its related technologies, but with that knowledge and technology has also come regulation. In the case of surrogacy, the obligation of a woman to give up a child that she has carried, even if she has contracted to do so, has already come to trial, and a narrative account of the Whiteheads and Sterns (the two couples involved in that case), as well as portraits of other women and men involved in surrogacy agreements, has recently appeared.[111] Access of poor, unmarried, and/or lesbian women to these services (which are often not reimbursed by health insurance and are very expensive) again raises issues of "gatekeeping" by the medical, legal, and legislative establishments.[112] Most of the social, moral, and legal complexities of these technologies are only now being "discovered," but the debates echo those of previous generations, couched this time in the language of donors and genomes.

V. CONCLUSION

Women's reproductive health is a concept that is at once individual and collective. Reproductive health is inextricably intertwined with considerations of reproductive rights and reproductive choice. The persistence of the issues of access, autonomy, and relative worth sound through past, present, and even future policy and practice. The preceding discussion, of necessity, has been in many instances a cursory one. It

[109] Kevles, *Name of Eugenics*, p. 298; and Curt Stern, "The Domain of Genetics," *Genetics* 78 (1974): 21–33.

[110] Gena Corea, *The Mother Machine: Reproductive Technologies from Artificial Insemination to Artificial Wombs* (New York: Harper & Row, 1985); *Reproductive Technologies: Gender, Motherhood, and Medicine*, ed. Michelle Stanworth (Minneapolis: University of Minnesota Press, 1987); and Mary Anne Warren, *Gendercide: The Implications of Sex Selection* (Totowa, NJ: Rowman and Allanhead, 1985).

[111] Lori Andrews, *Between Strangers: Surrogate Mothers, Expectant Fathers, and Brave New Babies* (New York: Harper & Row, 1989). An overview of the legal status of surrogate motherhood has been written by Martha A. Field, *Surrogate Motherhood* (Cambridge: Harvard University Press, 1988).

[112] Francie Hornstein, "Children by Donor Insemination: A New Choice for Lesbians," in *Test Tube Women*, ed. Rita Arditti, Renate Direlli Klein, and Shelley Minden (Boston/London: Pandora Press/Routledge Kegan Paul, 1984), pp. 373–81; and *Reproductive Technologies*.

runs the danger of oversimplifying not only the history of women's reproductive health but also the interpretations of the historians. That medical, legal, and social concepts are so much a part of the history of women's reproductive health reinforces the importance of having scholars from many disciplines study the history of and ongoing debates about reproductive technologies. Furthermore, it is important to recognize that a subject so emotionally charged and intimate will call forth the personal beliefs and emotions of those who write as well as those who read—and those who create—its history.

10

. . . ——————— . . .

INSTITUTIONALIZING WOMEN'S HEALTH CARE IN NINETEENTH- AND TWENTIETH-CENTURY AMERICA

Joan E. Lynaugh

Contemporary historical scholarship on women and health tells us about female illness and treatment, it describes caretakers and advisers, and explores sometimes conflicting ideas about health, illness, and the power of medicine. It raises vital questions of control, oppression, reform, belief, and the meaning of health. If we agree with anthropologist Mary Douglas, however, that institutions shape both the meaning of events and the nature of what happens, we realize that until we learn more about the actual settings for care, we are still only on the edge of understanding the history of women's health care in America.[1] Sites where women sought, received, and gave care reveal much about health, illness, and caretaking; they also usefully mirror the social context in which they existed. Historians are now reporting the results of their studies of these institutions, why they were created, what was done in them, and how they help to understand the history of women. This essay surveys these recent historical studies; it will describe this body of work,

---

[1] Mary Douglas, *How Institutions Think* (Syracuse: Syracuse University Press, 1986). Mary Douglas's work provides the crucial sociological framework for considering the relationship between institutions and social thought. She analyzes the effect that institutions have on classifying and recognizing information; it is this interpretive function that makes comprehension of women's institutions so important to women's history.

review persistent themes developed by scholars, and suggest some neglected or less-developed areas yet to be explored.

First we should recall that most assistance received by the sick and
injured, by pregnant women, by dependent children and the elderly, and
by incapacitated mentally ill people always was, and is, mainly given by
their families in their homes. Among the many sweeping changes of the
nineteenth century, however, was the creation of alternatives to complete reliance on family or servant care at home. Institutions giving care
to the sick on a temporary or long-term basis included hospitals, clinics,
asylums, rest homes, and sanitaria of various kinds. In addition to these
new physical locations for care, other organizations developed. These
provided temporary assistance to the sick person's family in the patient's
own home or substituted in situations where the family failed to provide
care. Though this essay focuses on history of caregiving institutions
separate from the domestic residence, I will also review recent scholarship on home care which illuminates complex and fundamental debates
about who should be cared for, and, whether that care should be given in
the domestic residence or in a specialized institution.[2]

BACKGROUND

The historiographic account of institutionalization of the health care
of women is set in the context of several transitions. First, over the last
two hundred years, some of the work of care was gradually reallocated
from the home and family to certain institutions and professionals.
Second, these public or voluntary institutions exchanged a mission
originally confined to poor, infectious, insane, or solitary persons for a
more general social role of healer and personal caregiver during times of
illness or dependence. By the second decade of the twentieth century
institutionally based health care was offered to a broad spectrum of
American society. The creation of both a middle class and a working
class with disposable income who sought or were forced by circumstance
to find an alternative to "do-it-yourself" care in their own homes is at
the heart of these changes. Criticisms of institutions as morally dangerous, restrictive in access or services, or too expensive, form part of the

---

[2] Although the debate over home care versus institutional care has a long history, it is
important to recognize that hospitals and clinics often tried to expand their services into
the home. For a variety of logistical and economic reasons these efforts were ephemeral
in most cases.

context. Also in transition were the vision of self and the aspirations of women who were patients, caregivers, and managers in these settings.

The places where women could turn for care were shaped by at least three forces: the philosophies of their founders, social and cultural pressures on the institution, and the economic resources supporting them. For the founder or caregiver the institution variously represented the actualization of a religious mission, a place to practice or learn a profession, a place to earn a living, or an opportunity to act out a vision of benevolence or social reform. For the recipient of care the institution also represented various meanings: a shelter of last resort, a socially determined alternative to self or family care, a place of access to medical technology and cure, or one alternative for care among many from which she could make a choice.

Beginning nearly two hundred years ago the growth of women's health-care institutions was driven by rapidly spreading industrialization and urbanization. The first manifestations of this phenomenon were scattered lying-in and maternity hospitals and home-care projects of benevolent women and concerned physicians. Efforts by the Ladies Benevolent Society of Charleston, South Carolina in 1813, and by physician Joseph Warrington in Philadelphia in 1833, for instance, attempted to improve the care of isolated women during labor and delivery; each sent helpers and provisions into the women's homes.[3]

Other reformers of the first half of the nineteenth century also responded to the health-care problems of urban life through benevolence and charity directed to families in their own homes. The old almshouses developed hospital services, but for most patients they were an option of last resort. Women often refused almshouse care to avoid its stigma. Women who did give birth in the city almshouses ran great risks of infection and neglect. Even those admitted to the rare voluntary hospital that provided maternity care, as did the Pennsylvania Hospital of Philadelphia, were at risk. The Pennsylvania Hospital eventually shut down its lying-in wards because it could not prevent recurrent episodes of puerpural fever. Reformers who sent trained women into the homes of the poor to help with childbirth recognized the importance of avoiding institutionalization. Voluntary hospitals remained relatively scarce

---

[3] For the Ladies Benevolent Society and Joseph Warrington see Anne Austin, *History of Nursing Source Book* (New York: G. P. Putnam's Sons, 1957), pp. 333–36, 330–31; and Joseph Warrington, *The Nurses Guide: Containing a Series of Instructions to Females Who Wish to Engage in the Important Business of Nursing Mother and Child in the Lying-In Chamber* (Philadelphia: N.p. 1839).

until after the Civil War; the lying-in wards that did exist were periodi-
cally plagued with puerpural fever. Judy Litoff, Judith Leavitt, and
William Williams all provide useful overviews of this era, which explain
the pressures that eventually inspired institutional reform.[4]

In spite of these early problems, dispensaries, clinics, and hospitals
won out over home care as the dominant community strategies for
conveying health services. Historian George Rosen has suggested that the
Dispensary for the Infant Poor, opened in 1769 in London, was the
forerunner of the dispensary system widely adopted in the nineteenth-
century United States.[5] Clinics and dispensaries were intended to serve
the sick poor in ameliorative but economic ways. They provided information, drugs, and treated wounds. Women sought assistance from
dispensaries for a variety of ailments or for care during labor and
delivery of their children. Founded primarily as a service to the poor,
these dispensaries and clinics and their successor, the neighborhood
health center, never attracted a paying clientele. Throughout most of the
nineteenth century very few middle-class people would have considered
any choice other than care at home; they paid their own physician to
visit there or they "doctored" their own illnesses using family lore or
domestic guidebooks.[6]

---

[4] Judith Leavitt, Brought to Bed, Child Bearing in America, 1750–1950 (New York and
Oxford: Oxford University Press, 1986)); Judy Litoff, American Midwives 1860 to the
Present (Westport, CT: Greenwood Press, 1978); and William H. Williams, America's
First Hospital: The Pennsylvania Hospital, 1751–1841 (Wayne, PA: Haverford House,
1976). Judith Leavitt classifies women seeking maternity care into four groups: the
institutionalized, the traditionalists, the integrationists, and the privileged. Traditional-
ists relied on family, friends and local midwives; they were probably safer. Leavitt,
Brought to Bed, pp. 76–83.

[5] Rosen's essay on hospitals offers a panoramic overview of institutional care. See George
Rosen, "The Hospital," in From Medical Police to Social Medicine (New York: Science
History Publications, 1974), pp. 274–303.

[6] The best overviews of the dispensary movement are: George Rosen, "The First Neighborhood Health Center—Its Rise and Fall," in Sickness and Health in America—Readings
in the History of Medicine and Public Health, ed. Judith Leavitt and Ronald Numbers
(Madison: The University of Wisconsin Press, 1978), pp. 185–200; and Charles Rosenberg, "Social Class and Medical Care in Nineteenth Century America: The Rise and Fall
of the Dispensary," Journal of the History of Medicine 29 (January, 1974): 32–54. See also
Michael Davis and Andrew Warner, Dispensaries, Their Management and Development. A
Book for Administrators, Public Health Workers, and all Interested in Better Medical Service
for the People (New York: Macmillan, 1918) for a complete discussion of the twentieth
century version of the dispensary idea; and Nancy Schrom Dye, "Modern Obstetrics
and Working-Class Women: The New York Midwifery Dispensary, 1890-1920,"
Journal of Social History 20 (Spring 1987): 549–64. Self-care ideas are reviewed in essays
collected in Medicine Without Doctors, Home Health Care in American History, ed. Guen-

Debilitating illnesses and injuries beyond the scope of dispensary care forced the poor into hospitals, rare in the eighteenth century but proliferating in urban centers during the nineteenth century. The Pennsylvania Hospital, founded in 1751 by Benjamin Franklin, was the first, and for a long time, the only successful effort to establish a general hospital in the United States. Franklin lays out an agenda of benevolence with the practical goal of returning the sick to productive, self-sustaining life in his justification for his hospital.

> . . . observing the distress of such distempered poor . . . how difficult it was for them to procure suitable lodging, and other conveniences . . . , and how expensive the providing good and careful nurses . . . many must suffer greatly, and some probably perish that might otherwise have been restored to health and comfort, and become useful to themselves, their families and the publick for many years after.[7]

GENERAL STUDIES OF HOSPITALS AND WOMEN IN THE UNITED STATES

Beginning with the publication of Morris Vogel's 1980 study *The Invention of the Modern Hospital*, a series of histories focusing on the hospital have appeared.[8] These recent hospital histories respond to Rosen's charge to examine the hospital as an integral part of its commu-

---

ter B. Risse, Ronald Numbers, and Judith Leavitt (New York: Science History Publications, 1977). Charles Rosenberg provides a detailed analysis of the role of domestic or self-care in his "Medical Text and Social Context: Explaining William Buchan's *Domestic Medicine*," *Bulletin of the History of Medicine* 57 (1983): 23–42. A facsimile of one of the popular self-help books of the time recently published is John C. Gunn, *Gunn's Domestic Medicine—A Facsimile of the First Edition with an Introduction by Charles Rosenberg* (Knoxville: University of Tennessee Press, 1988).

7 Benjamin Franklin, *Some Account of the Pennsylvania Hospital Printed in Facsimile, with an Introduction by I. Bernard Cohen* (Baltimore: The Johns Hopkins Press, 1954), p. 3.

8 Vogel's work led a series of hospital studies. Morris Vogel, *The Invention of the Modern Hospital: Boston 1870–1930* (Chicago: University of Chicago Press, 1980); David Rosner, *A Once Charitable Enterprise: Hospitals and Health Care in Brooklyn and New York, 1885–1915* (Cambridge: Cambridge University Press, 1982); Harry F. Dowling, *City Hospitals, The Undercare of the Underprivileged* (Cambridge: Harvard University Press, 1982); Jon M. Kingsdale, "The Growth of Hospitals: An Economic History in Baltimore," (Ph.D. dissertation, University of Michigan, 1981); Joan Lynaugh, *The Community Hospitals of Kansas City, Missouri, 1875–1915* (New York: Garland Publishing, 1989); Vanessa Gamble, "The Negro Hospital Renaissance: The Black Hospital Movement, 1920–1940" (Ph.D. dissertation, University of Pennsylvania, 1987); Charles Rosenberg, *The Care of Strangers—The Rise of America's Hospital System* (New York: Basic Books, 1987); Rosemary Stevens, *In Sickness and In Wealth—American Hospitals in the Twentieth Century* (New York: Basic Books, 1989); and Diana Long and Janet Golden, eds. *Hospitals and Communities: A Contemporary Institution in Historical Perspective* (Ithaca: Cornell University Press, 1989).

nity rather than as a temple of science or as an isolated, neutral entity—
viewpoints that had characterized the field until the late 1960's.[9]
Vogel's book looks at Boston's hospitals during the era of rapid
hospital growth, between 1870 and 1930. He demonstrates the growing
impact of physician influence on the services given in hospitals and
explores the political roles hospitals came to play in the city. He clarifies
both increasing public reliance on hospitals for care and the eventual
choice by the middle class of the hospital alternative over home care.
David Rosner, in his examination of Brooklyn hospitals, closely analyzes
the economics of these new enterprises. He illustrates the economic
forces that altered the original benevolent mission of voluntary hospitals; charity was replaced by an emphasis on curative services which
generated revenue from paying patients. Jon Kinsdale also focuses on
hospital economics in his Baltimore study. His work validates and
broadens Rosner's description of the fiscal exigencies which influenced
hospital decision-makers.

Harry Dowling's account of America's municipal hospitals traces
the often discouraging story of underfunded, graft-ridden city institutions. Most large cities supported hospital services for the poor throughout this era but, as Dowling and others demonstrate, these crucial
services were vulnerable to political pressures which undermined their
quality and ultimately their survival. Left with the burden of care for the
chronically ill, the destitute, social outcasts, and the insane—few of
whom were accepted by the voluntary hospital system—municipal hospitals had few defenders when city budgets grew tight. The quasi-public
role of the voluntary, community hospitals described by Joan Lynaugh
and the black hospitals in Vanessa Gamble's work, illustrates the important place of local, ethnic, religiously, or racially oriented hospitals in the
life of Americans.

This series of studies, many journal articles, and works now in
progress testify to the power and fascination the hospital has for historians. Publication of Charles Rosenberg's The Care of Strangers (1987) and
Rosemary Stevens' In Sickness and In Wealth (1989) culminates this
series, but by no means exhausts the subject. Rosenberg's study of
American hospitals unravels the complexity and variety of interpreta-

---

[9] Rosen, From Medical Police, p. 274. There are dozens of internally created histories of
individual hospitals which tend to glorify the institution, its founders, and its benefactors. Rosen and historian Richard Shryock encouraged historians to turn their attention
to medical history in general and hospital history in particular.

tions of the institution. He examines the hospital in the context of its time and place and interprets its rapid growth. Most of all, *The Care of Strangers* attends carefully to the constant exchange between the institution and the environment around it, thus conveying the reality of the hospital as an institution reflecting its society. Rosemary Stevens brings the history of hospitals to the present time. She chronicles the uneasy, complex interaction inherent in a system which relys on not-for-profit, voluntary hospitals to provide equitable public service. She assesses the late twentieth-century hospital in the light of American values and politics. Together Rosenberg and Stevens provide an excellent background of research and analysis for scholars interested in women's health-care institutions.

Although Dowling, Lynaugh, and Rosenberg pay specific attention to women caregivers and, to a lesser extent, to women as patients, their works do not focus on women's health-care settings or women as agents of hospital reform in a systematic way. In fact, in some of the studies of hospitals, the omission of women as managers, caregivers, and patients is hard to understand since primary sources tell us women were there. Thus, some of the recent history of hospitals reveals as much about the invisibility of women in American history as it does about the history of health care.

Historians who unfettered themselves from traditional subjects and sources in health-care history discovered the possibilities inherent in uncovering the story of women who, in many cases, led new nineteenth-century approaches to health care. This developing picture of settings where women might expect to obtain care during childbirth or illness should be considered in the light of studies of the general benevolent and reform movements of the nineteenth century.

Fortunately for health-care historians, there is a solid base of scholarship investigating nineteenth-century women and assessing their reform work, their ideology, and their over all imprint on events. Carroll Smith-Rosenberg in particular probes the complexities and ambiguities of the "domestic sphere"; she examines its ideology and how women saw themselves and each other.[10] Nancy Cott and Kathryn Sklar allowed women of the early part of this century to speak for themselves: of their

---

[10] Carroll Smith-Rosenberg, *Religion and the Rise of the American City: The New York City Mission Movement 1812–1870* (Ithaca: Cornell University Press, 1971); and Smith-Rosenberg's collected work, *Disorderly Conduct: Visions of Gender in Victorian America* (New York: Alfred A. Knopf, 1985). Also see Barbara Berg, *The Remembered Gate: Origins of American Feminism* (New York: Oxford University Press, 1978).

work, their beliefs, and the world they lived in. This work provides a rich background against which the founders, managers, and, to some extent, the clients of early women's health-care institutions can be visualized.[11]

Much of these scholars' work, however, is based on the letters and journals of white, Protestant women. These sources are silent on the enterprises and experiences of Catholic and immigrant women. In work that begins to fill this gap, Mary Ewen identifies and describes the orders of religious women who were working out their own version of benevolence and reform. The essays collected by Janet James in *Women in American Religion* take us further toward understanding the aspirations and changes experienced by women from diverse ethnic, religious, and geographic vantage points. Especially useful are those by Mary Ryan, Barbara Welter and James's own overview essay, "Women in American Religious History."[12]

In more recent work, Mary Ryan and Nancy Hewitt carry this understanding forward in their detailed analyses of specific communities in upstate New York, which outline the charitable, ideological leadership of women against their own cultural background. This closer look makes it possible to see distinctions and differences among the reformers and founders of new institutions.[13] Lori Ginsberg's 1985 dissertation, "Women and the Work of Benevolence," follows changing ideology from 1820 to 1885; she finds a transition from domestic, benevolent femininity to a growing preference for professionalized institutional settings for good works.[14]

---

[11] Nancy Cott, *The Bonds of Womanhood: 'Women's Sphere' in New England, 1780–1835* (New Haven: Yale University Press, 1977); and Kathryn Kish Sklar, *Catharine Beecher: A Study in American Domesticity* (New York: W. W. Norton and Company, 1976). Also see Ann M. Boylan, "Women in Groups: An Analysis of Women's Benevolent Organizations in New York and Boston, 1797–1840," *Journal of American History* 71 (December, 1984): 497–523.

[12] Mary Ewen, *The Role of the Nun in Nineteenth Century America* (New York: Arno Press, 1978); Janet Wilson James, ed., *Women in American Religion* (Philadelphia: University of Pennsylvania Press, 1980).

[13] Mary Ryan, *Cradle of the Middle Class: The Family in Oneida County, N.Y. 1790–1865* (New York: Cambridge University Press, 1981); Nancy Hewitt, *Women's Activism and Social Change: Rochester, N.Y., 1822–1872* (Ithaca: Cornell University Press, 1984).

[14] Lori D. Ginsberg, "Women and the Work of Benevolence: Morality and Politics in the Northeastern United States, 1820–1885," (Ph.D. dissertation, Yale University, 1985). Ginsberg's chapters on the Civil War and its aftermath also offer a helpful synthesis of this pivotal period leading up to the era of extensive hospital-building. Regina Kunzel examines the transition from an ideology of benevolence to professionalism and the disappointments of the professionalization strategy in "The Professionalization of Benevolence: Evangelicals and Social Workers in the Florence Crittenden Homes, 1915 to 1945," *Journal of Social History* 22 (1988): 21–43.

WOMEN'S HEALTH-CARE INSTITUTIONS

Scholars focusing on women and health care are beginning to delineate the relationship between women's lives and their work in institutions. A chronologically organized survey of health-care historians' work gives some sense of how this field is developing.

Regina Markell Morantz-Sanchez offers the most sophisticated analysis to date of women's roles as health protectors; her work spans the gamut from women's self-help programs to the women in mainstream American medicine. Her *Sympathy and Science* in particular discusses the professional issues faced by women physicians in their relationship to hospitals.[15] Jane B. Donegan's 1986 account of the antebellum popularity of hydropathy is a strong example of analysis of early health-care institutions in their own context. Donegan and more recently Susan Cayleff document the institutions developed by hydropaths to serve their clientele. Hydropathy and other medical sects fit well into the aspirations of women to play out their new role as promoters and guardians of the family health.[16]

Water-cure institutions, many of which were directed by women, served an upper- and middle-class clientele. Though their greatest popularity had passed by the time of the Civil War, some survive to the present day by adapting and broadening their scope of services.[17] Women who practiced as hydropaths or who ran hydropathic institutions did not confine their services to other women. It appears that direct care was segregated by sex but the separatism that was to characterize some women's institutions played no particular part in the goals and dreams on the "Hydropathic Highway to Health."[18]

---

[15] Regina Markell Morantz, "Nineteenth Century Health Reform and Women: A Program of Self-Help," in *Medicine Without Doctors, Home Health Care in American History*, ed. Guenter Risse, Ronald Numbers, and Judith Leavitt (New York: Science History Publications, 1977), pp. 73–93; and Regina Markell Morantz-Sanchez, *Sympathy and Science: Women Physicians in American Medicine* (New York: Oxford University Press, 1985). See chapter 2 for women as guardians of family health.

[16] Jane B. Donegan, "*Hydropathic Highway to Health*" *Women and Water-Cure in Antebellum America* (Westport, CT: Greenwood Press, 1986); Susan Cayleff, *Wash and Be Healed: The Water-Cure Movement and Women's Health* (Philadelphia: Temple University Press, 1987); and William Rothstein, *American Physicians in the 19th Century: From Sects to Science* (Baltimore: The Johns Hopkins University Press, 1972). Rothstein's overview introduces sectarian medicine in the nineteenth century, in which women played a significant role.

[17] For instance, the Clifton Springs Hydropathic Institute of upstate New York was first a sanitarium, then an alcoholic retreat, and now a hospital.

[18] Donegan and Cayleff see this somewhat differently. Cayleff argues that hydropathic institutes were female retreats while Donegan underscores the attractiveness of hydropathy to both sexes.

Virginia Metaxas Quiroga, on the other hand, examines institutions run by women for women in her studies of institutions for childbirth and child care.[19] The New York Asylum for Lying-In Women, for example, was supported by philanthropic women aiming to "furnish comfortable accommodations and skillful medical care to reputable married females who desire an asylum during the period of their confinement."[20] The Asylum, which dated from 1823, relied on patients to care for each other at first, then hired nurses. The women who resorted to institutions such as this were, in Judith Leavitt's terms, "the poorest of urban women" who had no support or recourse except public or private charity.[21] Following the pattern established by the earliest home-care charities, the women who managed the New York Asylum intended that their charity toward the married, respectable, poor woman would save her from the degrading and dangerous experience of maternity care at Bellevue or some other almshouse. As Quiroga makes clear, some women who created care institutions for other women felt justified in restricting their charity to those who met their moral standards. The goals of maintaining class and morality barriers transcended mere gender solidarity or benevolence among these particular institution-builders.

The debate between advocates of care at home versus institution-builders is also illustrated here. Quiroga's analysis of the conflicts between Dr. Abraham Jacobi and the lady managers at New York Nursery and Children's Hospital is a nineteenth-century version of the perennial and very contemporary debate that pits institutional strategies against decentralized care at home.[22] Jacobi believed every effort should be made to return infants and their mothers to their own homes, while the lady managers believed the infants would be better off under the protection of their institution. Their argument forecast the frequent professional-lay and male-female conflicts over institutional control which would appear throughout the century and beyond.

---

[19] Virginia A. Metaxas Quiroga, "Female Lay Managers and Scientific Pediatrics at Nursery and Childs Hospital, 1854–1910," *Bulletin of the History of Medicine* 60 (1986): 194–208; and Quiroga, "Poor Mothers and Babies: A Social History of Childbirth and Child Care Hospitals in Nineteenth Century New York City" (Ph.D. dissertation, SUNY at Stony Brook, 1984).

[20] Virginia A. Metaxas Quiroga, "Culture and Class Conflict at the New York Asylum for Lying-In Women, 1823–1850," unpublished paper presented at Sixth Berkshire Conference, 1984, p. 1.

[21] Leavitt, *Brought to Bed*, p. 73.

[22] Quiroga, "Female Lay Managers," *Bulletin* pp. 196–98.

The New England Hospital for Women, founded in 1862, became part of the burgeoning hospital movement of the latter part of the century and one of the many separate institutions for women that characterized the nineteenth-century women's movement. The hospital's goals were: care of sick women by women, clinical training of women physicians, and training of nurses to care for the sick. Virginia G. Drachman's *Hospital with a Heart, Women Doctors and the Paradox of Separatism at the New England Hospital, 1862–1969* describes its founder and physicians in the context of their setting; by this means she partially illuminates their institution. Her biographic approach, however, of necessity relegates the hospital and its story to the background.[23] Biographies of women so tightly identified with their institutions are needed; we come to know hospital-founder Marie Zakrzewska, her colleagues, and her times. We understand more of how she and they shaped events; equally as instructive, we see how they, in turn, were shaped by circumstance.

Drachman is interested in the costs of the strategy of separatism to the institution, its founders, and their successors. Her account reveals the paradox of the separatist strategy: exclusiveness enabled control by women but may have cut them off from resources essential to full development of their institutions. It is not altogether clear, however, that the problems of the New England Hospital stemmed only from feminist separatism. They may have been partially due to the remarkable longevity of Zakrzewska's leadership which risked inbreeding and obsolescence in times of very rapid change and growing dominance of men physicians. At any rate the New England Hospital story depicts an institution with a highly focused mission. It is an important case study of a hospital that reflected the goals of its founders' feminist ideology to an extent that inhibited its competitiveness in a rapidly expanding hospital system.[24]

We can conclude that a small segment of the existing scholarship on hospital history, exemplified by Drachman and Quiroga, points the way

---

[23] Virgina Drachman, *Hospital with a Heart, Women Doctors and the Paradox of Separatism at the New England Hospital, 1862–1969* (New York: Cornell University Press, 1984). See also Virgina Drachman, "Female Solidarity and Professional Success: The Dilemma of Women Doctors in Late Nineteenth Century-America," *Journal of Social History* 15 (1982): 607–19.

[24] See Estelle Freedman, "Separatism as Strategy: Female Institution Building and American Feminism, 1870–1930," *Feminist Studies* (Fall, 1979): 512–29 for a paper focused on the separatism question. Also see Freedman, *Their Sister's Keepers: Women's Prison Reform in America, 1830–1930* (Ann Arbor: University of Michigan Press, 1981) for an excellent discussion of institution-building after the Civil War.

toward an arena of promising investigation of institutions created by women for women. Both authors offer examples of sensitive scholarship in the specialized area of all-female health-care projects; Jane Donegan and Susan Cayleff remind us of the special impact of sectarian health-care institutions. From their work a picture emerges of the rapidly changing ways American women were trying to cope with intimate and sometimes frightening personal experiences, such as illness and child-birth, outside their domestic residences. Women institution-builders tried, in their various ways, to control and direct this transition.

In the United States the most explosive growth in hospital-building began in the late 1870s and 1880s. Thousands of new institutions responded to care demands from city and town dwellers, an increasing proportion of whom were prepared to pay for care. These citizens constituted a different clientele than the occupants of the almshouse hospitals and charity hospitals of earlier times.[25] The concept of the hospital was expanded to offer personal health care to a wider spectrum of the community.

Organized and managed by churches, benevolent societies, physicians, and ethnic groups, the new community hospitals imitated their clients' homes in design and atmosphere. During the early phases of this epoch of hospital-building only adult men and women requiring medical treatment or surgery were admitted. By the turn of the twentieth century, however, some general community hospitals admitted children and maternity patients. After 1880 the idea of the hospital as the appropriate place to be sick and to receive treatment slowly began to be accepted across a wide spectrum of American society. Beyond this, the last decades of the nineteenth century witnessed the beginnings of the delegation of what was once every woman's work, that is, care of the sick and injured, to a special occupational group called trained nurses. (See chapter 18 in this volume.)

Women were caregivers and care recipients in all of these community institutions. Ownership and managerial influence by women, however, was most significant in the small- and medium-sized (50 to 150 bed) hospitals. Much of the historical work done on hospitals has focused on large teaching hospitals, almshouses, or those founded specifically for care of women.[26]

---

[25] For accounts of this transition see Rosenberg, *Care of Strangers*, chapter 4; Vogel, *The Invention of the Modern Hospital*, chapter 5; and Lynaugh, *The Community Hospitals of Kansas City*, chapter 2.

[26] See notes 8, 19, and 23.

The impact of women as founders and managers of the numerous general community hospitals that dotted the American landscape by 1900 is just now being explored. Edward Atwater discusses this perspective in his study of affluent community matrons and religious orders of nuns who established and controlled community hospitals in small and medium-sized New York State towns between the 1880s and World War I.[27] Atwater's work reveals the pivotal role of women leaders in community health care. Their local institutions offered care to both men and women, though maternity services usually were not available until after 1900. After that time, however, hospital growth was importantly affected by admission of women for gynecological care and obstetric services. The "Worthy Enterprises" described by Atwater also were involved in a kind of religious competition or separatism which led many small upstate New York towns to support both a "Protestant" hospital managed by lay women leaders of the town, and a Roman Catholic hospital run by nuns.[28]

It may well be that the necessary ingredients of educated, self-confident women with both access to money and control of their workplace helps explain the success of the small town women benefactors and nuns Atwater writes about. Women who founded and/or supervised general community hospitals have not drawn much concentrated attention yet except from Atwater. Karen Buhler-Wilkerson, however, studied the upper-class women who invented the visiting nurse societies of the late nineteenth century.[29]

---

[27] Edward Atwater, "This Worthy Enterprise—The Development of General Hospitals in Upper New York State," in Hospitals and Communities: A Contemporary Perspective, ed. Diana Long and Janet Golden (Ithaca: Cornell University Press, 1989). See also Atwater, "Rochester's Early Hospitals," The Bulletin of the Rochester Academy of Medicine (January 1975): 29–38; and David Lovejoy, "The Hospital and Society: The Growth of Hospitals in Rochester, N.Y. in the Nineteenth Century," Bulletin of the History of Medicine 49 (1975): 536–55, for a discussion of the influence of public opinion and charity policy on institutional expansion.

[28] Other studies dealing with the founding of general community hospitals by religious and ethnic groups are Gail Farr Casterline, "St. Joseph's and St. Mary's: The Origins of Catholic Hospitals in Philadelphia," Pennsylvania Magazine—History and Biography 108 (1984): 289–314; and Joan Lynaugh, "From Respectable Domesticity to Medical Efficiency: The Changing Kansas City Hospital, 1875–1915," in Hospitals and Communities. See also note 36.

[29] Karen Buhler-Wilkerson, "False Dawn: The Rise and Decline of Public Health Nursing, 1900–1930," (Ph.D. dissertation, University of Pennsylvania, 1984), and Buhler-Wilkerson, "False Dawn: The Rise and Decline of Public Health Nursing in America, 1900–1930" in Nursing History—New Perspectives, New Possibilities, Ellen Condliffe Lagemann, ed. (New York: Teachers College Press, 1983), pp. 89–106.

Acting on reform impulses and marshalling the aid of benefactors of both sexes, women in late nineteenth-century cities organized and financed bands of nurses to intervene in homes where illness or childbirth and poverty combined, requiring help from outsiders. Buhler-Wilkerson chronicles both the zenith and decline of these organizations between 1890 and 1930; she takes a close look at the conflict between the altruistic motives of visiting nurse-society leaders and the financial stability of their organizations. Using board minutes and budgets she traces the creation of their institutions, documents their work, and witnesses their reluctance to participate on a competitive basis in the health-care environment of post-World War I America. Looking at this issue from a different perspective, Diane Hamilton's insightful study of visiting nurse societies and the Metropolitan Life Insurance Company further demonstrates the discrepancy between the benevolent, altruistic goals of the women leaders and the business-oriented demands of insurance executives.[30]

Atwater's small town matrons, Buhler-Wilkerson's ladies, and the mostly unstudied founders and managers of children's hospitals, sanitariums, and small health clinics invested their efforts in what turned out to be the mainstream of institutional health care. Their leadership in these enterprises, however, faded by the second decade of the twentieth century as male hospital managers and physicians increased their control over health-care institutions. Thus, though gender segregation, according to Drachman, lead to institutional isolation, the women working in gender integrated health-care settings had a different problem as their control weakened when the institutions grew in size and importance. Existing studies shed some light on why women lost power but the complex ideological, economic, political, and scientific factors affecting twentieth-century institutions call for more study.[31]

---

[30] Diane Hamilton, "Faith and Finance: The Evolution of the Metropolitan Life Insurance Company's Visiting Nurse Service (1909–1953)," (Ph.D. dissertation, University of Virginia, 1986), and Hamilton, "Faith and Finance," *Image: Journal of Nursing Scholarship* 20 (Fall, 1988): 124–27.

[31] *Transactions*, which annually reported meetings of the American Hospital Association, reveals that more than 50% of hospital superintendents were women in 1915, but this proportion began to fall in the 1920s. Primary sources reveal women at work in a wide variety of health-care enterprises. Women physicians, nurses, and others established settings for care as yet under-described in the secondary literature. There are examples indicating that research is developing in this field. See Marion Hunt, "Women and Childsaving: St. Louis Children's Hospital 1879–1979," *Bulletin of the Missouri Historical Society* 36 (1980): 65–79. The sanitarium movement in tuberculosis care attracted

Throughout this entire period another almost invisible group of American women was building services and institutions. In a fascinating scholarly exploration of the significant and pervasive role of nuns in developing health-care institutions, Marta Danylewycz explored the uncloistered religious career in the context of women's work and culture. Danylewycz carries the theme of institution-building into this neglected area by searching out the story of women creating settings for health care under the auspices of their own religious organizations. The Sisters of Misericorde, a Canadian group of religious women, founded in 1848, specialized in the care of unmarried mothers and abandoned infants. The chosen work of the group, their interest in caring for "sinners," made it difficult for them to garner support and secure the needed financial base for their work. Danylewycz chronicles their tortuous route to institutional stability. She describes the melding of this ". . . peculiar assortment of middle-aged widows, older spinsters, and young women into a cohesive community . . ," arguing that the appeal of the convent rested in the freedom it offered from familial obligations and the expression it gave to women's intellectual and vocational aspirations.[32] On the other hand, she asserts, religious communities also had a functional role as French-Canada's solution to the problem of redundant women. This is a provocative and fascinating glimpse into an important area of women's history and institution-building.[33]

As Charles Rosenberg points out, Catholics opened 154 hospitals by 1885 in the United States; this was more than all the hospitals in existence in the late 1860s.[34] Virtually all these hospitals were managed

---

women as proprietors. Barbara Bates, "'Searching for Blackberries': Consumptives and Their Caretakers, 1876–1938," (work in progress), examines women's roles in this area. The often strained relationship between women nurses and various twentieth-century health institutions is described in Barbara Melosh, *The Physician's Hand* (Philadelphia: Temple University Press, 1982), chapters 3 and 5; and Susan Reverby, "The Search for the Hospital Yardstick: Nursing and the Rationalization of Hospital Work," in *Health Care in America: Essays in Social History*, ed. Susan Reverby and David Rosner (Philadelphia: Temple University Press, 1979), pp. 206–24. See Paul Starr, *The Social Transformation of American Medicine* (New York: Basic Books, 1982) for discussion of the growing importance of hospitals and economic change in health care.

[32] Marta Danylewycz, *Taking the Veil, An Alternative to Marriage, Motherhood, and Spinsterhood in Quebec, 1840–1920* (Toronto: McClelland and Stewart, 1987), pp. 80, 84.

[33] See also Freedman, note 24. Vicinus's work on women in England includes an in-depth discussion of redundant women. Martha Vicinus, *Independent Women: Work and Community for Single Women, 1850–1920* (Chicago: The University of Chicago Press, 1985), pp. 3–6.

[34] Rosenberg, *Care of Strangers*, p. 111.

and staffed by members of female religious orders. Although new work is beginning to recognize their contributions, very little is known of their attitudes toward care of women, their services, or their results.[35] Given the dimensions of organized religious women's involvement in health care and their recent openness to scholars it is probable that more historians will join Mary Ewen, Marta Danylewycz and Patricia Tarbox in probing this fruitful arena of research.[36]

OPPORTUNITIES FOR STUDY

Overall, these studies look at the goals, motives, achievements, and failures of the lay, religious, or professional women who founded and led institutions or projects. They explore the strategy of separatism, and analyze collaboration or tensions between lay benefactors and professionals. Most of the studies, excepting that of Diane Hamilton, do not focus on the fiscal basis of the institution, its actual management, or the development of technology. So far, little comparative work between women's institutions and others helps us to understand the "meaning" of these institutions in their own community context.

Thus, this overview of scholarship on settings for health care and women suggests new opportunities for research. Autobiographical accounts by some reformers involved in community health issues, such as Jane Addams, Lillian Wald, Jospehine Baker, and Margaret Sanger, reveal the negotiations and tensions in the struggle between hospitals, physicians, clinics, public health officials, and, of course, the public, over what care would be provided, where, and to whom.[37] Patient-care

---

[35] Mary Ewen, "Removing the Veil: The Liberated American Nun," in *Women of Spirit,* ed. Rosemary Ruether and Eleanor McLoughlin (New York: Simon and Schuster, 1970), pp. 257–59, offered an early insight on this field. For a recent exploration see Mary P. Tarbox, "The Origins of Nursing by the Sisters of Mercy in the United States: 1843–1910" (Ed.D. dissertation, Columbia University Teachers College, 1986).

[36] Judith Moore studied religious women and hospitals in England. Her "A Zeal for Responsibility—The Struggle for Professional Nursing in Victorian England, 1868–1883" (Athens: University of Georgia Press, 1988) traces conflicts between nuns and physicians over institutional control.

[37] A sample of these autobiographies includes Jane Addams, *Twenty Years at Hull House* (New York: Macmillan, 1910), and *The Second Twenty Years at Hull House, September 1909 to September 1929* (New York: Macmillan, 1930); Frederick Howe, *Confessions of a Reformer* (New York: Quadrangle/The New York Times Book Co., 1967) [originally published by Charles Scribner's Sons, 1925]; Lillian Wald, *The House on Henry Street* (New York: Holt, Rinehart and Winston, 1915); Mary Brackinridge, *Wide Neighborhoods, A Story of the Frontier Nursing Service* (New York: Harper and Brothers, 1952); Margaret Sanger, *Margaret Sanger: An Autobiography* (New York: Norton, 1938); and S. Josephine Baker, *Fighting for Life* (New York: Macmillan, 1939).

records, physicians' and nurses' accounts, public records, and the growing professional literature of the time will support comprehensive study of institutional and extra-institutional care for women. The mid-twentieth-century dominance of the general, acute care hospital over all other care choices for women and the associated decline of other forms of care is an instructive historical event.

Today's demands for a new balance between in-home care and hospital care should prompt historians' interest in previous efforts to carry health care into the home. Now 175 years in the past, the earliest home-care experiments and their institutional sequelae, though documented, await the detailed study they deserve. Studies of the type previewed in Patricia O'Brien's brief article linking the reform aspirations of educated, affluent women to the wage earning needs of working-class women and the professional control goals of a slowly developing medical profession will help. O'Brien's account of antebellum Philadelphia health reform assembles what seem to be the vital ingredients to institutional development in women's health care. Similarly, Nancy Schrom Dye, in her essay on the Frontier Nursing Service, uses data on home based services to illuminate the strategies, both successful and failed, employed by twentieth-century reformers. Here the coalition is between affluent Mary Breckinridge and nurse-midwives.[38] In these enterprises, as in Drachman's *Hospital with a Heart*, there is a certain continuity of reformers and professionals seeking to do important work, and, at least temporarily, sharing compatible perceptions of a social problem.

As women became more and more involved in the industrial work force, their health in that setting also became an issue. The story ranges from exclusion from certain jobs for health reasons to examples of both economic opportunity and health exploitation. Women were involved as reformers, caregivers, and workers seeking better conditions. Although industrial health reformers like Alice Hamilton are fairly well known, much remains to be explored in this complex field. More and

---

[38] Patricia O'Brien, "'All A Woman's Life Can Bring': The Domestic Roots of Nursing in Philadelphia, 1830–1885," *Nursing Research* 36 (1987): 12–17; and Nancy Schrom Dye, "Mary Breckinridge, The Frontier Nursing Service, and the Introduction of Nurse-Midwifery in the United States," in *Women and Health in America*, ed. Judith Leavitt, (Madison: University of Wisconsin Press, 1984), pp. 327–43. Karen Buhler-Wilkerson's new work, "Home Care the American Way: An Historical Analysis," (paper presented at the International Community Health Nursing Conference, The Netherlands, March, 1989), begins to examine the forces that supported or inhibited home-care availability.

more the fact of where American women work determines not only their health risks but the nature and availability of their health care through work-related insurance.[39]

With some notable exceptions, in much of this history the missing ingredient is the recipient of care. Whether it is the poor and parturient woman of antebellum Philadelphia or the domestic servants, aged women, women with terminal illnesses, exhausted women, the mentally ill women, the women who feared pain and death in childbirth, or the women who hoped for cure through medicine or surgery, it is the patients, so difficult to study, who lend a richer dimension to the history of institutions. Work by Regina Morantz-Sanchez, Sue Zschoche, Judith Leavitt and Constance McGovern illustrates the clarity added when the recipient of care is restored to the historical story.[40]

While participation of women as care recipients during this long and sweeping cultural change is understudied, understanding the participation of women as principal caregivers and institution-builders, though helped by the recent work outlined here, still requires broader and deeper investigation, especially in certain neglected areas.

For instance, the care of the aged, though an acknowledged social obligation and a subject of intense twentieth-century debate, is nearly a

---

[39] Ruth Heifetz, "Women, Lead, and Reproductive Hazards: Defining A New Risk," in *Dying For Work: Worker's Safety and Health in Twentieth-Century America*, ed. David Rosner and Gerald Markowitz (Bloomington: Indiana University Press, 1987), pp. 160–74. For an account by the leading woman reformer in occupational health see Alice Hamilton, *Exploring the Dangerous Trades* (Boston: Little, Brown, 1943).

[40] Regina Markell Morantz and Sue Zschoche, "Professionalism, Feminism, and Gender Roles: A Comparative Study of Nineteenth-Century Medical Therapeutics," *Journal of American History* 62 (1980): 568–88. Judith Leavitt in *Brought to Bed* weaves the story of women at childbirth throughout, but see especially chapters 1, 3, and 4. Although the subject of mental health is dealt with elsewhere in this volume, some studies from that area integrate patients into the story in highly useful ways. See, for instance, Constance McGovern, "Doctors or Ladies?" *Bulletin of the History of Medicine* 51 (1981): 99–101; McGovern, "The Myths of Social Control and Custodial Oppression: Patterns of Psychiatric Medicine in Late Nineteenth-Century Institutions," *Journal of Social Medicine* 20 (1986): 3–23; and McGovern, "The Community, the Hospital, and the Working-Class Patient: The Multiple Uses of Asylum in Nineteenth-Century America," *Pennsylvania History* 54 (1987): 17–33; Ellen Dwyer, *Homes For the Mad: Life Inside Two Nineteenth-Century Asylums* (New Brunswick: Rutgers University Press, 1987); Gerald Grob, *Mental Institutions in America: Social Policy to 1875* (New York: Free Press, 1973); and Grob, *Mental Illness and American Society 1875–1940* (Princeton: Princeton University Press, 1983). See also Nancy Tomes, *A Generous Confidence: Thomas Story Kirkbride and the Art of Asylum Keeping, 1840–1883* (Cambridge: Cambridge University Press, 1984) for interactions between families and institutions. Nancy Schrom Dye's paper (see note 6) also clarifies the relationships between the institution and the patient.

blank slate historiographically.[41] Public provisions for the destitute aged ranged from almshouse to mental institution, but, for the majority, responsibility for care primarily rested in the private sector. Asylums, homes, and institutes for the aged began to appear before the Civil War as supplements to family care and as refuges for those elderly who found themselves with no kin. Women figured prominently in this story, both as recipients of care (since women live longer than men) and, as caregivers and institution-builders. Carole Haber points out, in her work on institutionalizing the elderly, that women were the first subjects of attention when reformers began to develop homes for the aged.[42] Her account is a good place to gain an overview of the issues surrounding care of the frail aged. The advent of Social Security in 1935, coupled with a steadily increasing lifespan, set off an explosion of development of what are now called nursing homes. Now that there are approximately 18,000 nursing homes in the United States and considering that 90% of their residents are women, historians of women should pay more attention.

The ferment in health care in the twentieth century, particularly since World War II, has so far incited modest response from historians interested in women's health. Though Susan Reverby and David Rosner challenged historians in 1979 to provide "an essential tool for analyzing current health problems [through creating] a sense of their origins and the possibilities to affect change," few monographs based on recent twentieth-century events have yet appeared.[43]

An explanation of this reluctance may be found in the sheer size of the task, the immediacy of the present events, and the difficulty of achieving distance or detachment. As Alan Brinkley notes in his 1984 *Daedalus* essay, the speed of social change is daunting; twentieth-century history is further complicated, he says, by the politicized, interdependent world we live in, which forces the social historians who do most of this

---

[41] For histories of aging see W. Andrew Achenbaum, *Old Age in the New Land, The American Experience Since 1790* (Baltimore: The Johns Hopkins University Press, 1978), and David Hackett Fischer, *Growing Old in America* (Oxford: Oxford University Press, 1978). More useful for settings where the elderly receive care is Carole Haber, *Beyond Sixty-Five, The Dilemma of Old Age in America's Past* (Cambridge: Cambridge University Press, 1983). An excellent overview of the public's response to the needs of the aged is Michael B. Katz, "Poorhouses and the Origins of the Public Old Age Home," *Milbank Memorial Fund Quarterly* 62 (1984): 110–40.

[42] Haber, *Beyond Sixty-Five*, pp. 82–107.

[43] Susan Reverby and David Rosner, eds. *Health Care in America—Essays in Social History* (Philadelphia: Temple University Press, 1979), p. 12.

research to enter the not-so-comfortable world of political history.[44] Study of women's institutions in recent decades is also affected by the fact that modern women routinely negotiate two worlds, those of home and work. These women are struggling to integrate their domestic lives, influenced by traditional female roles and expectations, with their professional lives, where standards of achievement are set according to long-established male formulas. Thus modern women's institutions are populated by women acting out new, rather tentatively developed amalgams of roles.

But historians seeking to understand the interacting relationships between women's health-care experiences and the settings in which they occur do have a rich opportunity for exploration in the exciting period of the post-Eisenhower years. For instance, in her dissertation and a subsequent policy text, *Women in the Health System*, Helen Marieskind offers a highly useful compendium of facts and figures to aid historians attempting to sort out the many factors and aspects of women's health in the twentieth century.[45] The persistence, popularity and expansion of Planned Parenthood Clinics, what could be called the post-Sanger history of birth-control services, and the evanescent career of the 1970s women's health-care clinics await more study from an institutional standpoint. Better told is the effort to move the experience of birth away from the sterile, physician-dominated operation which it became earlier in the century; an account of this transition is in Barbara Katz Rothman's assessment of childbirth reforms in the twentieth century.[46]

All these more recent social experiments are generously documented and await the scholar. As the century closes, and pressures to cope with society's demands for health services escalate, it will be more and more important that we have the benefit of detailed historical analysis of the events of recent years. And, as we pay historical attention to the influence of institutions on the behavior of patients and their caretakers, we

[44] Alan Brinkley, "Writing the History of Contemporary America: Dilemmas and Challenges," *Daedalus* 113 (Summer, 1984): 121–41.

[45] Helen Marieskind, "Gynecological Services: Their Historical Relationship to the Women's Movement With Recent Experience of Self-Help Clinics and Other Delivery Modes" (Ph.D. dissertation, University of Michigan, 1976); and Marieskind, *Women in the Health Care System: Patients, Providers, and Programs* (St. Louis: The C. V. Mosby Company, 1980).

[46] Barbara Katz Rothman *In Labor: Women and Power in the Birthplace* (New York: Norton, 1982).

will improve our understanding of how institutions and their inhabitants shape each other.[47]

Finally, scholars studying the settings in which women receive health care need to attend to the financial mechanisms by which that care is delivered and paid for. The voluntary, charitable organizations of the last century, sometimes aided by a stingy public purse, found the money to supplement payments individuals made for care. Budgets were always marginal; debt was always a problem. Minute-books of boards responsible for health-care institutions before the advent of insurance readily reveal their preoccupation with fiscal matters.

As far as women's institutions are concerned, however, the historiographic account is sparse. Perhaps it is because the financial management of women's institutions was subsumed in their voluntary, benevolent structure, or because historians have been more interested in relationships, power struggles, and ideas. Whatever the reason, only a few students of the subject have paid much attention to money matters in women's institutions.[48] This omission leaves a giant gap which gets worse with time. For, as health care increasingly came to be seen both as useful and revenue-producing in the years after World War I, some types of services had a fair price attached but others did not. Charles Rosenberg describes the thinking through which the price attached to hospital care became medicalized; that is, medical diagnosis became the means by which the value of care was accounted. Shelter, nurturance during illness, or even moral improvement no longer counted as reasons for hospital admission. Promise of cure through physicians' services attracted paying patients to hospitals.[49] Institutional leaders nearly always chose to keep their institutions solvent, which led them to make decisions that improved income. The effect, of course, was to drastically narrow the scope of care thought appropriate in health settings by restricting services to persons with curable health problems. We still

---

[47] Criticisms of services and settings include Suzanne Arms, *Immaculate Deception: A New Look at Women and Childbirth in America* (Boston: Houghton Mifflin, 1975); Sheryl Burt Ruzek, *The Women's Health Movement: Feminist Alternatives to Medical Control* (New York: Praeger Publishers, 1978); and Gena Corea, *Man-Made Women, How Reproductive Technologies Affect Women* (London: Hutchinson, 1985).

[48] Diane Hamilton's study is an important exception to this. Her focus is not on hospitals, however.

[49] Rosenberg, *Care of Strangers*, pp. 174–75. For criticism of the change in scope of hospital work see David Rosner, "Social Control and Social Service: The Changing Use of Space in Charity Hospitals," *Radical History Review* 21 (1979): 183–97.

know little about choices women's institutions made or what bearing those choices may have had on their future. We do know that the marriage of medical diagnosis and dollar value has a narrowing effect on care-availability, which continues in our private and public insurance programs.

If anything, the relevance of health care financing to women's health grows even more important in the late twentieth century. Some would argue that cost has become the only relevant factor in recent health-care decision making. The advent of health insurance, government programs for the poor and the elderly, and prepaid health "maintenance" organizations are crucial to the nature and availability of health care for women. The debates over access to health care will preoccupy Americans for the rest of the century. We need to understand them in historical perspective.

CONCLUSION

We need to improve and extend our historical analysis of women's health-care settings because institutions both implement a point of view and authorize certain sets of relationships and products. They are the sites where personal and intellectual aspirations are played out. They also serve the sick and injured, the needy, and the dependent who still seek shelter and succor. We need better comprehension of how they fit or failed to fit in American society at certain points in time.

Institutional history is in the classic tradition, as Sally Kohlstedt notes, since it "provide[s] a vantage point from which to view the connections between ideology and operation," but, she cautions, we can only use the institutional tendency to remember and retain the past effectively if we remember that institutions sometimes conveniently forget their past.[50] Our modern American health-care system is huge, fragmented, and uneven. We can not be surprised if its history is still too small and too shallow to be satisfying. At the same time, as this essay shows, there are excellent examples of institutional studies; they provide

---

[50] Sally Kohlstedt, "Institutional History," in *Historical Writing On American Science*, ed. Sally Kohlstedt and Margaret Rossiter (Baltimore: The Johns Hopkins Press, 1985), p. 36. For an excellent essay on contemporary perspectives on hospitals that proves Kohlstedt's point, see Rosemary Stevens, "'A Poor Sort of Memory': Voluntary Hospitals and Government Before the Great Depression," *Milbank Memorial Quarterly* 60 (1982): 551–84. Stevens's latest work *In Sickness and in Wealth: American Hospitals in the 20th Century* details this debate in the larger context of the latter part of the century.

illustrations of how fruitful this genre can be. They are vital to historians looking more deeply at women's health-care settings.

It is clear that a significant agenda of historical scholarship still needs to be worked through. Settings where women obtain care and assure care for others may reveal, when examined, clearer comprehension of that "autonomy with connectedness" speculated on by Susan Reverby in her recent monograph on nursing.[51] Health care is, after all, bound up in a complex array of questions about altruism, self-determination, gender issues, and, most profoundly, survival and death. The settings where women take the lead have much to tell us as we grope our way toward a more equitable and a more civil future.

---

[51] Susan Reverby, *Ordered To Care: The Dilemma of American Nursing, 1850–1945* (Cambridge: Cambridge University Press, 1987), p. 207.

PICTORIAL
ESSAY

· · · ———— · · ·

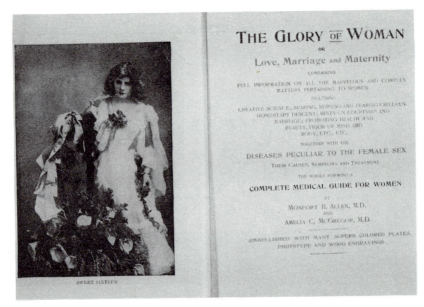

THE GLORY OF WOMAN
OR
Love, Marriage and Maternity
CONTAINING
FULL INFORMATION ON ALL THE MARVELOUS AND COMPLEX
MATTERS PERTAINING TO WOMEN
INCLUDING
CREATIVE SCIENCE; BEARING, NURSING AND REARING CHILDREN;
HEREDITARY DESCENT; HINTS ON COURTSHIP AND
MARRIAGE; PROMOTING HEALTH AND
BEAUTY, VIGOR OF MIND AND
BODY, ETC., ETC.
TOGETHER WITH THE
DISEASES PECULIAR TO THE FEMALE SEX
THEIR CAUSES, SYMPTOMS AND TREATMENT
THE WHOLE FORMING A
COMPLETE MEDICAL GUIDE FOR WOMEN
BY
MONFORT B. ALLEN, M.D.
AND
AMELIA C. McGREGOR, M.D.
EMBELLISHED WITH MANY SUPERB COLORED PLATES,
PHOTOTYPE AND WOOD ENGRAVINGS

Illus. 1: As in this 1896 publication, domestic medical guides typically combined contemporary physiological understanding with moral imperatives for good health and happiness.

In caring for their health and that of their families women could find assistance from many sources. A multitude of home health manuals written by physicians and laypersons enjoyed wide circulation in the nineteenth century and continue to be popular today. In the twentieth century governmental agencies and schools promoted health and nutrition instruction for girls and women.

Illus. 2: The Wisconsin Department of Health provided information for mothers at local health centers in the 1930s. (Source: State Historical Society of Wisconsin, WHi[X3]45122.)

Illus. 3: High school girls in Lake Geneva, Wisconsin, November 1934, received recreation instruction as part of a project of the federal work-relief program in the state. (Source: State Historical Society of Wisconsin, WHi[X3]45121.)

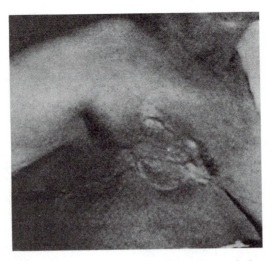

Illus. 4: Breast cancer was treated surgically even before the development of anesthesia and asepsis in the last century. Surgeons refined the procedures considerably in the late nineteenth century, by which time physicians used recently discovered x-rays to treat inoperable carcinoma. (Source: Sinclair Tousey, *Medical Electricity and Rontgen rays* [Philadelphia: W.B. Saunders, 1910].)

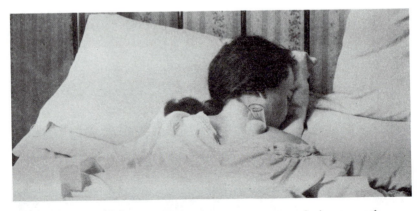

Illus. 5: Before the advent of chemotherapy, cupping was a standard treatment for tuberculosis patients into the twentieth century. Patients also were often moved to a sunny, open-air environment, such as a mountain sanitarium or roof-top living quarters. (Source: Albert Philip Francine, *Pulmonary Tuberculosis: Its Modern and Specialized Treatment* [Philadelphia: J. B. Lippincott, 1906].)

Breast cancer and tuberculosis were two important health problems for women in the nineteenth and twentieth centuries.

As the number of hospitals grew from the last third of the nineteenth century through the twentieth century, the scope and locus of medical practice changed.

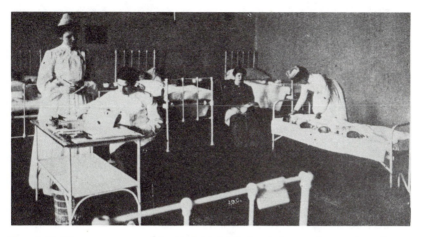

Illus. 6: Birthing women entered hospitals in rapidly increasing numbers in the early decades of the twentieth century. Flower Hospital tended mothers and newborns in the same ward. (Source: William Harvey King, *History of Homeopathy and its Institutions in America* [New York: Lewis Publishing, 1905].)

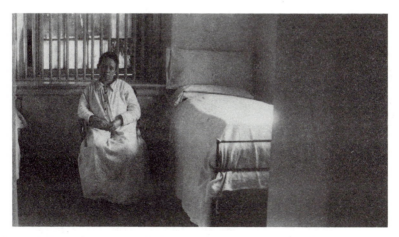

Illus. 7: Bellevue Hospital, New York, was an important center for the care of the mentally ill. This rare photograph shows a woman seated in a private room of Bellevue's Insane Pavilion in the 1890s. (Source: Edward G. Miner Library, George W. Corner History of Medicine Room, University of Rochester School of Medicine and Dentistry.)

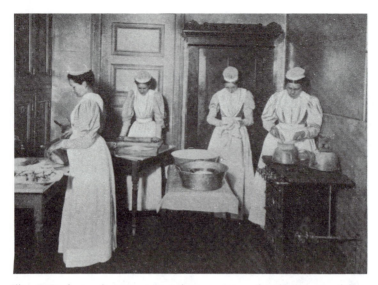

Illus. 8: Professional nursing attracted many women after the opening of the first nursing schools in this country in 1873. These schools were typically part of a hospital, and nursing students performed most hospital services, caring for the patients as well as housekeeping chores. Here students prepare meals in the diet kitchen of the Mt. Sinai Training School for Nurses, New York, 1898. (Source: Jane Hodson, *How to Become a Trained Nurse: A Manual of Information in Detail* [New York: William Abbatt, 1898].)

Slowly in the nineteenth century opportunities began to open for women who wanted to become professional health-care providers, though women continued to face significant obstacles throughout the twentieth century.

Illus. 9: Women wanting to be physicians had three options: the handful of women's medical colleges that opened in the nineteenth century, the few regular or allopathic men's medical schools that agreed to admit women, or the more welcoming schools of sectarian medical practitioners such as homeopaths and eclectics. Female and male students study together in this biological laboratory at the Boston Medical College in 1905. At this time the school trained homeopathic physicians. (Source: William Harvey King, *History of Homeopathy and its Institutions in America* [New York: Lewis Publishing, 1905].)

Illus. 10: At the turn of the century, new medical sects such as osteopathy and chiropractic offered additional options for women in medicine. Here Dr. Lora B. Riley makes an adjustment for Dr. Frannie Cline. (Source: Joe Shelby Riley, *Science and Practice of Chiropractic with Allied Sciences* [Washington, DC (?): 1919].)

ALTERNATIVE MEDICAL CARE

· · · ———— · · ·

11

WOMEN AND SECTARIAN MEDICINE

Naomi Rogers

In late nineteenth-century America Millie Chapman, a homeopath, warned her audience that "I should weary you by mentioning the long list of names of women living to-day" who were successful homeopathic physicians, "loving, devoted" wives, and "willing, faithful" mothers. Myra Merrick of Cleveland, for example, had graduated in 1852 with the "honors of her class" in medicine, yet "shrinking from public work or notoriety," she had "performed faithfully the home duties of a mother, and at the same time accomplished a mountain of medical work, and to-day is a martyr to the profession."[1] Samuel Hahnemann, the founder of homeopathy whose laws Chapman believed were "the only sure guide for prescribing remedies known to scientific medicine," she described as a man who was "encouraged and his labors increased tenfold, by a great woman, Madame Hahnemann." It was thus fitting that Hahnemann's American disciples had welcomed women physicians

---

I would like to thank Rima Apple, Sue Lederer, Rona Rogers, Jason Rosenstock, and John Harley Warner for their helpful suggestions and criticisms.

[1] Millie J. Chapman, *Women in Medicine* (N.p., n.d.[1880s?]) pp. 2–3. Myra King Merrick, a student of eclectic Lydia Folger Fowler, graduated from the Eclectic Medical College in Rochester in 1852, and helped to found Cleveland's Homeopathic Hospital and Medical College; see Esther Pohl Lovejoy, *Women Doctors of the World*, (New York: Macmillan, 1957), pp. 14–15. Chapman's other examples included Phoebe J. B. Waite, dean of the homeopathic Woman's Medical College in New York, Harriet J. Sartain of Philadelphia and Caroline Winslow of Washington. Chapman, born in Pittsburgh in 1845, graduated from Cleveland Homeopathic Medical College in 1874; see William Harvey King, ed., *History of Homeopathy and Its Institutions in America*, vol. 4 (New York: Lewis, 1905), p. 37.

since "his greatest success was accomplished by woman's aid." Still, unlike the Hahnemanns, most medical women, "like a greater number of men, have lived, labored, and died without being known or remembered beyond the limited circle they served." For, Chapman reminded her audience, "not every one can be a Grace Roberts or a Julia Holmes Smith, an Adaline Church or an Emily Pardee, but many others are equally eminent in the locality they bless."[2]

Despite Chapman's plea, most sectarian women have been all but invisible to historians. Who, we wonder, were Roberts, Smith, Church and Pardee? Consider a recent study of a battle between regulars and homeopaths at the University of Michigan's medical school during the 1870s.[3] In most of the photographs that accompany the article we see women among the classes of homeopathic students, watching a surgical operation, participating in an eye clinic, listening to a lecture. They seem to be integrated in their class, not in some separate part of the lecture theater.[4] Yet in the text their presence is ignored.

Sectarian women practitioners have been doubly neglected, by their gender and by their medical affiliation. Although historians have long remarked on the appeal of sectarian medicine among women, the depth and nature of this appeal, both for female practitioners and patients, remain largely obscure.[5] The link between women and sectarian medicine nonetheless raises some important analytical questions. These include the meaning and significance of the medical professional culture for women; the shifting associations between medical sects and the women's rights movements; the attraction for patients of a medicine that defines health and healing in broad, perhaps socially challenging

---

[2] Chapman, *Women in Medicine*, pp. 4, 3, 5. Homeopathy was an alternative medical system based on the law of similars (that like cures like) and infintessimals (that a drug increases its potency as it is diluted).

[3] Catherina M. Arnott, "An Airing of Reputations: Homeopaths vs. Allopaths at the University of Michigan," *Michigan History* 68 (1984): 40–47.

[4] Arnott, "An Airing," pp. 41, 44, 46. Homeopath women have gained some attention. A similar photograph is part of historian Rima Apple's pictorial essay which lies at the center of Judith Leavitt's *Women and Health* collection. Apple has drawn readers' attention to a lecture room at Hahnemann Medical College in Philadelphia, where women students, scattered through the hall, were not segregated from their male colleagues; Rima D. Apple, "Pictorial Essay," in *Women and Health in America*, ed. Judith Walzer Leavitt, (Madison: University of Wisconsin Press, 1984), p. 294.

[5] The sectarian divisions within the American medical profession in the nineteenth century "caused some confusion among medical women." Richard Shryock, "Women and American Medicine," [1950] in Shryock, *Medicine in America: Historical Essays* (Baltimore: Johns Hopkins Press, 1966), p. 188.

terms; the implications and meaning of science for women practitioners and patients; and the transformation of American medicine, regular and sectarian.

HISTORIANS AND SECTARIAN MEDICINE

Once examined by historians interested in the quaint and colorful, sectarian medicine by the early 1970s was taken more seriously as regular medicine came under increasing attack. The medical establishment was criticized for its reductionalism, medicalization of ordinary behavior, alienation from patients, and its sexism, classism, and racism. Alternative therapies and theories drawn from nonwestern and folk medical traditions initially intrigued members of the youth movement, and later gained wider acceptance. More recently we have also seen a growing popular interest in magic and mysticism related to healing, such as New Age medicine.[6] The women's movement, the self-help holistic movement, animal welfare activists, and environmentalists have all contributed to popular and scholarly interest in alternatives to mainstream American medicine.[7]

Historians and sociologists too began to reinterpret American medicine of the past. They examined the shortcomings of regular medical education and practice in the early and mid-nineteenth century, and suggested that sectarian critics as well as farsighted regulars had helped to transform medical therapy, particularly the regular profession's use of calomel, bloodletting, and alcohol.

Gradually this interest in the organizations and practices of regular physicians shifted to the sectarians themselves, although this scholarly work remains uneven. The Thomsonians, for example, cited by every historian of nineteenth-century medicine as a significant group of medical populists, still lack a complete, detailed history.[8] Historians, and especially medical sociologists, were intrigued by the Thomsonians' anti-

---

[6] See Jeffrey S. Levin and Jeannine Coreil, "'New Age' Healing in the U.S.," *Social Science & Medicine* 23 (1986): 889–97; James B. Whorton, *Crusaders for Fitness: The History of American Health Reformers* (Princeton: Princeton University Press, 1982), pp. 331–49.

[7] See, for example, Preston L. Schiller and Jeffrey S. Levin, "Is Self-Care a Social Movement," *Social Science & Medicine* 17 (1983): 1343–52.

[8] See Alex Berman, "The Impact of the Nineteenth Century Botanico-Medical Movement on American Pharmacy and Medicine," (Ph.D. thesis, University of Wisconsin, 1954); and Berman, "The Thomson Movement and Its Relation to American Pharmacy and Medicine," *Bulletin of the History of Medicine* 25 (1951): 405–28, 519–38. See also Daniel J. Wallace, "Thomsonians: The People's Doctors," *Clio Medica* 14 (1980): 169–86.

professional and anti-elitist strains, and linked the sect with nineteenth-century social and medical movements such as Jacksonian reform and anti-rationalism.[9] Sociologist Joseph Kett has argued that Thomsonianism gained popular support because, at a time when obstetricians were pushing laywomen out of traditional folk practices and midwifery, it offered women an opportunity to regain their place as legitimate domestic healers.[10] Scholars stressed the sect's criticisms of elite medical knowledge, the interactions between lay and elite medical thought and practice, and patients' shifting expectations of their medical advisors, but rarely examined in detail Thomsonian practitioners and proponents.[11] Female advocates of the sect, whether patients or practitioners, have remained mostly hidden.

Homeopaths, the followers of Samuel Hahnemann, have attracted more historical attention, perhaps because their professional organizations seemed more like those of the orthodox profession.[12] The decline of homeopathy by the early 1900s has been used as an example of the role played by scientific medicine in consolidating the authority of the regular profession. In one study of American homeopathy, Martin Kauf-

[9]   Paul Starr, for example, found in Thomsonians a nineteenth-century "medical counter culture." Paul Starr, The Social Transformation of American Medicine (New York, Basic Books, 1982) p. 54.

[10] Joseph F. Kett, The Formation of the American Medical Profession: The Role of Institutions, 1780–1860, (New Haven: Yale University Press, 1968) pp. 107, 117–18, 120; see also John B. Blake, "Women and Medicine in Ante-Bellum America," Bulletin of the History of Medicine 39 (1965): 107–8. Most historians have acknowledged few specific early female practitioners in sectarian medicine, other than Thomson's claim to have first trained with a female folk healer, an "old lady named Benton." See Martin Kaufman, American Medical Education: The Formative Years, 1765–1910, (Westport: Greenwood Press, 1976) p. 64.

[11] Starr has seen this sect reflecting the "dominant authority" of regular medical theory in Social Transformation, p. 92. Martin Kaufman, Homeopathy in America: The Rise and Fall of a Medical Heresy (Baltimore: Johns Hopkins Press, 1971) has linked Thomsonian theory to Galen and humoral theory, p. 19; see also Kett, Formation of American Medical Profession, p. 178; Ronald L. Numbers, "Do-it-yourself the Sectarian Way," in Medicine without Doctors: Home Health Care in American History ed. Guenter B. Risse, Ronald L. Numbers, and Judith Walzer Leavitt, (New York: Science History, 1977) pp. 49–72.

[12] Like Thomsonianism it has been considered an important part of the history of American medicine, but the history of homeopathy remains rather disjointed. Harris Coulter's multivolume study, still the most detailed available, is unfortunately defensive and somewhat evangelical. See Harris L. Coulter, Divided Legacy: A History of the Schism in Medical Thought, 3 vols. (Washington, D.C.: McGrath, 1973). For one detailed case study see Naomi Rogers, "The proper place of homeopathy: Hahnemann Medical College and Hospital in an age of scientific medicine," Pennsylvania Magazine of History and Biography 108 (1984): 159–201.

man argued that although in the mid-nineteenth century homeopaths were perhaps more "scientific" than regulars, by 1900 homeopathy had become out-of-date, pursuing a therapeutic context that was fast disappearing.[13] Later writers, drawing from his work, developed the "legitimate complexity" view of regular medicine. Unlike Kaufman, Paul Starr, for example, accepted that the complexity of medical knowledge and the professionalization of medicine after the 1890s led to the decline of homeopathy.[14] Kaufman briefly examined the antagonism expressed by male regulars to female sectarians, but the relations between male and female homeopaths, noted by Millie Chapman, were not discussed.[15]

This interest in sectarian medicine has forced scholars to define the relationship between sect and science. Historians' investigations of American sects have usually ended with the successful integration of bacteriology and other new sciences into regular medicine by 1900. Thus, scientific medicine has been seen as the gatekeeper for the end of sectarianism, or at least of legitimate sectarian critics. In 1972 sociologist William Rothstein urged historians to consider the ways the marketplace and popular demand shaped the transformation of nineteenth-century American medicine, but his tendency to judge the theory and practice of sectarians with presentist eyes weakened his work. During the nineteenth century, he argued, before what he termed medically valid therapy and objective scientific standards, both regulars and irregulars were sectarian; that is, they practiced nonscientific therapies. The regular profession, in this model, only achieved its ascendence with the abandonment of sectarian practices for those that were scientifically valid and

---

[13] Kaufman, *Homeopathy*, pp. 86, 185, 183. Kaufman urged "present and future medical sectarians" to learn from the history of homeopathy, a history, he believed, which is "to a large extent the history of every unorthodox sect." See Kaufman, *Homeopathy*, p. ix. See also a review of Kaufman by Walter I. Wardwell, "Orthodoxy and Heterodoxy in Medical Practice," *Social Science & Medicine* 6 (1972): 759–63.

[14] Paul Starr, *Social Transformation*, p. 97.

[15] Moses B. Pardee, a regular physician, was expelled from the Fairfield County Medical Society, Connecticut, in 1878, for consulting with his wife, Emily Pardee, a homeopath; Kaufman, *Homeopathy*, p. 90. See also Kaufman's brief comments on women homeopaths in the 1930s and 1950s; *Homeopathy*, pp. 179–80. Although the editor of the most recent study of irregular medicine in America has argued that "Women have always played a significant role in the genesis and growth of unorthodox medicine," [Gevitz, "Preface," p. viii] his collection contains no systematic examination of gender and sectarianism other than Susan Cayleff's study of hydropathy; see Norman Gevitz, ed., *Other Healers: Unorthodox Medicine in America* (Baltimore: Johns Hopkins University Press, 1988). For an unusually detailed study of women homeopaths, see Kristin Mitchell, "Women and Homeopathy in Nineteenth-Century America," (B.A. essay, Yale University, 1989).

convincing to the lay public. Implicitly, both homeopaths and regulars had this option, and only regulars took it. The new sciences of the 1890s, Rothstein argued, nullified the rationale for sectarianism, an explanation that casts those who support medical alternatives in this century as quacks.[16]

New approaches in the history and sociology of science have started to undermine these approaches. Sociologists of science have urged historians to become more critical of their view of science as an objective body of knowledge.[17] A few medical historians have developed a new analytical definition of therapeutic efficacy, and by implication, scientific validity. Charles Rosenberg, developing the insights of such anthropologists as Mary Douglas, argued that the nineteenth-century therapies "worked" in the view of both doctors and patients. These therapies, he urged, should be analyzed in terms of their meanings to contemporaries, not by present-day standards.[18]

In order to understand the appearance of sects such as osteopathy and chiropractic after the 1880s, historians have started to explore new ways to examine the relationship between sect and science. Sectarian medicine, after all, did not simply decline with the rise of scientific medicine, although clearly the sources of sectarians' popular support and intellectual authority have changed. Sectarians, sociologist Norman Gevitz has recently argued, unlike folk healers who base their practice on traditional cultural beliefs or religious healers who demand conversion and faith, believe their principles are universal and can be tested experimentally. That is, to some extent, sectarians share and adopt the methods and assumptions of orthodox medicine. Further, a successful medi-

---

[16] William G. Rothstein, *American Physicians in the Nineteenth Century: From Sects to Science* (Baltimore: Johns Hopkins University Press, 1972), pp. 21, 23, 24. Rothstein argued that in the nineteenth century homeopathy "did not attack the science in regular medicine; it attacked the sect in regular medicine," p. 169.

[17] See, for example, Barry Barnes and Steven Shapin, eds., *Natural Order: Historical Studies of Scientific Culture* (Beverly Hills: Sage, 1979); Harry Collins, *The Changing Order: Replication and Induction in Scientific Practice* (Beverly Hills: Sage, 1985); and Roy Wallis, ed., *On the Margins of Science: The Social Construction of Rejected Knowledge* (University of Keele: Sociological Review Monograph '27, 1979). For a study of women as subjects and researchers see Elizabeth Fee, "Nineteenth-Century Craniology: The Study of the Female Skull," *Bulletin of the History of Medicine* 53 (1979): 415–33.

[18] Charles E. Rosenberg, "The Therapeutic Revolution: Medicine, Meaning, and Social Change in Nineteenth-century America," *Perspectives in Biology and Medicine* 20 (1977): 485–506. See also John Harley Warner, *The Therapeutic Perspective: Medical Practice, Knowledge and Identity in America, 1820–1885,* (Cambridge: Harvard University Press, 1986); and J. Warren Salmon, "Introduction," in Salmon, ed., *Alternative Medicines: Popular and Policy Perspectives* (New York: Tavistock Publications, 1984), pp. 2–7.

cal sect must maintain a certain inflexibility in principle and a belief in the importance and uniqueness of the sect, and retain the ability to control sectarian institutions and keep medical power separate from the regular profession.[19] This, he has shown, American osteopaths were largely able to achieve. As Gevitz's study of osteopaths suggests, twentieth-century sectarians are not simply self-serving quacks.[20] The rise in interest of the American lay public and the medical profession in acupuncture during the early 1970s inspired scholars to investigate the history of similar alternative practices.[21] But even these histories of recent sects mostly focus on organizational and professional developments, rather than on patients, practitioners, or practice.

Although scholars have tended to define a medical sect by the character of its lay supporters, the ethnic, class, or gender background of sectarian followers have rarely been examined in detail. To explain the rise of osteopathy in the 1890s, for example, recent historians have pointed to the needs of rural communities and continuing populist distrust of elite medical knowledge.[22] But these insights remain untested. Still, although much of the history of American sectarian medicine has remained limited to intellectual and institutional history, some historians have begun to investigate sectarian medicine for rather different reasons than their predecessors. Interested in the array of resources available to patients, they have drawn finely detailed pictures of a medical arena in which regulars and sectarians competed, practiced, and

---

[19] Norman Gevitz, "Sectarian Medicine," JAMA 257 (March 1987): 1636–40. The relationship between sectarian medicine and religious beliefs is an important and complex one, but it lies outside the boundaries of this paper. Certainly Christian Science, for example, was in its early years treated as a medical sect by the regular medical profession, but within two decades had ceded the medical model to regulars, spurred by the vilification they received at the hands of doctors and medical examiners. I am grateful for Sue Lederer's suggestions on this point. See also Chapter 13 in this volume.

[20] Norman Gevitz, The D.O.s: Osteopathic Medicine in America (Baltimore: Johns Hopkins University Press, 1982).

[21] Some authors have argued that sectarian popularity reflects a crisis of confidence in the medical profession, and challenges the role of regular profession as the sole arbiter of what constitutes acceptable health care; see Robert Schwartz, "Acupuncture and Expertise: A Challenge to Physician Control," The Hastings Center 11 (1981): 5–7. See also Joseph A. Kotarba, "American Acupuncturists: The New Entrepreneurs of Hope," Urban Life 4 (1975): 149–77; John S. Haller, "Acupuncture in Nineteenth Century Western Medicine," New York State Journal of Medicine 73 (1973): 1213–21.

[22] Elizabeth Barnaby Keeney, Susan Eyrich Lederer, and Edmond P. Minihan, "Sectarians and Scientists: Alternatives to Orthodox Medicine," in Ronald L. Numbers and Judith Walzer Leavitt, Wisconsin Medicine: Historical Perspectives (Madison: University of Wisconsin Press, 1981), pp. 59–64.

worked with each other—therapy and principle at times rigid and defining, at times flexible. They have urged colleagues to integrate this new approach to orthodox and fringe medicine so that both can be considered in a dynamic social whole.[23] Turning from focusing solely on sectarian leaders, their journals and texts, on the development of formal organizations, and particularly on the reactions of leading elite regular practitioners, these scholars, increasingly influenced by the new social history, offer a new integration of women's and medical history—one that studies patients and ordinary practitioners, and thus reconsiders the role of women in American medicine.

WOMEN'S HISTORY AND SECTARIANISM

Until recently the history of sectarian women has been virtually defined as a study of women and medical education. Within this focus scholars in the 1970s have explored the role of gender in medical professionalism, the special place of women practitioners, and, to a lesser extent, women's attitudes to and critiques of science. In a passionate study Mary Walsh attacked the pattern of sexual discrimination she traced within the regular medical establishment over the last two hundred years. Walsh claimed that women physicians have been denied social and political equality through systematic discrimination by their male colleagues who limited women's access to professional opportunities. She sympathetically portrayed the leading women physicians of the late nineteenth century as pragmatic fighters who accepted the structure and content of regular medicine, were vehemently proscience, and as ambitious for personal and professional power as they were interested in improving the health of their sisters.

Walsh was careful not to attack "irregular women healers," for she argued that most nineteenth-century women had few options other than irregular medical training, and "in an age when there were few medically valid theories available, no one had a monopoly on medical truth." Nevertheless, she concentrated on those women who sought to attend regular medical institutions, and who "identified with the standardized therapies."[24] Understandably, then, Walsh was sympathetic to regular

---

[23] See Numbers and Leavitt, eds., *Wisconsin Medicine*; Risse, Numbers, and Leavitt, *Medicine without Doctors*; and W. F. Bynum and Roy Porter, eds., *Medical Fringe and Medical Orthodoxy 1750–1850* (London: Croom Helm, 1987), "Introduction," pp. 1–4.

[24] Mary Roth Walsh, *Doctors Wanted No Women Need Apply: Sexual Barriers in the Medical Profession, 1835–1975* (New Haven: Yale University Press, 1977), p. xvii.

women's attacks on irregulars. The New England Hospital Medical Society, the first female medical society, founded in 1878, excluded graduates from homeopathic and other irregular schools for "the women hoped that by not confusing the issue of women's competence with the sectarian controversies in the profession at large, they would advance the cause of women more directly."[25] Walsh criticized the chauvinistic behavior of male irregulars at two institutions ostensibly supportive of women physicians, Samuel Gregory's Female Medical College, and Boston University, the history of whose homeopathic medical department she believed was "an archetypal betrayal" of the struggle for women's medical education.[26] However, Walsh emphasized that the decline in irregular sects such as homeopathy did not explain women physicians' failure to maintain their earlier momentum. By 1900, she suggested, women had made substantial inroads into regular medicine; their subsequent professional decline she blamed on the discrimination of elite medical educators through most of this century.

A more powerful influence on the history of women and medicine has been the rise of the feminist health movement since the late 1960s. This approach, influenced by feminists more concerned with difference than equality, has led to an even more critical eye on the medical establishment, and a different kind of history. Women activists set up health clinics to provide (then illegal) abortion and contraceptive services, which reflected their growing suspicions not only of medical institutions, but also of the content of medical knowledge. Feminists also formed self-help groups, encouraging laywomen to learn to understand and examine their own bodies without the control of a physician. Increasingly critical of the technology and science of reproduction, many women became fervent supporters of noninterventionist childbirth techniques and alternative attendants such as midwives. At the same time, proponents of the counterculture and the holistic health movements encouraged a nostalgic view of health and healing in the past, urging Americans to regain their lost health by returning "back to nature." Spurred by a faith in preventive medicine, many Americans rediscovered diet and exercise as the means to healthful living, and began growing herbs for domestic healing, rejecting a meat-based diet, and baking their

---

[25] Ibid., pp. 83–4, 104.
[26] Ibid., pp. 195–99.

own bread with an almost Grahamesque concern for wholewheat flour.[27]

This antiestablishment position encouraged scholars to seek healers in the past who had maintained a similar critique of regular medicine. Using expansive definitions of health and healing, feminists in and out of academia studied forgotten women healers, such as witches and midwives.[28] In this version of the past, sectarians and critics of regular medicine became not cranks or quacks but insightful critics of the relations between medicine and society, medical therapy and science, and women's inequal position in society.

Two influential studies of women and health were undertaken by feminists Deirdre English and Barbara Ehrenreich, later expanded into their 1978 work *For Her Own Good*. These authors redefined the boundaries of medical history to include women patients and reformers as well as practitioners, and dwelt on the limitations of the regular profession and medical science.[29] In their polemical analysis of the "sexual politics of health" they tended to stereotype female reformers and healers as fervent feminist critics of the authority and theories of the regular profession, and paid limited attention to the intellectual and social history of American physicians. But they did take seriously sectarian critiques of medicine, and linked sectarianism with the women's rights and health-reform movements of the past as well as the present.

Historians of irregular medicine began to speculate on the meaning of unorthodoxy to women practitioners. In the early 1970s feminist scholars debated the depiction of Victorian women and their doctors, the role of the male medical profession, and the attitude of female medical reformers to science and to the profession. Harriot Hunt, one of the earliest women physicians in America, became a particular target, seen as either sectarian critic or early professional physician. Ann Douglas Wood based her argument, which saw woman victimized by male

[27] Sylvester Graham was a prominent health reformer in the mid-nineteenth century, who argued that health could be maintained by attention to personal hygiene and diet, and discouraged eating of meats and refined flour.
[28] For a brief overview, see Helen Marieskind, "The Women's Health Movement," *International Journal of Health Services* 5 (1975): 217–23; Sheryl Burt Ruzek, *The Women's Health Movement: Feminist Alternatives to Medical Control* (New York: Praeger, 1978).
[29] Barbara Ehrenreich and Deirdre English, *Complaints and Disorders: The Sexual Politics of Sickness* (Old Westbury, NY: The Feminist Press, 1973); Ehrenreich and English, *Witches, Midwives and Nurses: A History of Women Healers* (Old Westbury: The Feminist Press, 1972); Ehrenreich and English, *For Her Own Good: 150 Years of the Experts' Advice to Women* (New York: Doubleday/Anchor Press, 1978).

physicians and male science, in part around Hunt, whom she portrayed as fervently critical of the regular profession and its unscientific therapies. Hunt, she argued, believed that both male doctors and husbands encouraged the ignorance and dependence of their patients and wives.[30] In a critical response Regina Morantz used Wood's argument about Hunt to discuss the "perils of feminist history." Morantz contended that Hunt was, rather, a supportive therapist, whose attitudes to science and morality were shaped by her culture, not a scientist but someone who nonetheless sought professional recognition and scientific education. Thus, Hunt embraced eclectic medicine and health reform as a way to critique the health and morals of her society, and found it also offered her professional opportunities as a lecturer.[31] Walsh, similarly, later argued that Hunt was neither antiprofessional nor, despite her training with English botanic practitioners, antiscience. She portrayed her as a physician yearning to be accepted into the regular establishment, as exemplified by her attempts to enter Harvard Medical School, but the victim of sexist discrimination and professional neglect. Walsh argued that Hunt did not reject science; science rejected her.[32]

More recently, in one of the most sophisticated studies of women and medicine, Regina Morantz (now Morantz-Sanchez) has tried to integrate the sectarian and regular experiences of women physicians in American history. Although her book *Sympathy and Science* urges historians to reinterpret the professionalization of American medicine, the role of gender in shaping medicine's ideology, and practitioners' diverse understandings of science in medicine, recent studies of American medical education have remained remarkably untouched by her work.[33]

---

[30] Ann Douglas Wood, "'The Fashionable Diseases': Women's Complaints and their Treatment in Nineteenth-Century America," [1973] in Judith Walzer Leavitt, ed., *Women and Health in America* (Madison: University of Wisconsin Press, 1984), pp. 231-32.

[31] Regina Markell Morantz, "The Perils of Feminist History," [1973] in Leavitt, ed., *Women and Health in America*, pp. 241-44; see also Blake, "Women and Medicine," p. 113. Eclecticism was a term used to describe irregulars who drew from a broad range of therapies and theories, particularly from botanical practice.

[32] Walsh, *Doctors Wanted*, pp. 25-26.

[33] See also Regina Markell Morantz, "The 'connecting link': The case for the woman doctor in 19th-Century America," in Judith Walzer Leavitt and Ronald L. Numbers, eds., *Sickness and Health in America: Readings in the History of Medicine and Public Health* (Madison: University of Wisconsin Press, 1978), pp. 117-28. Compare, for example, Kenneth M. Ludmerer, *Learning to Heal: The Development of American Medical Education* (New York: Basic Books, 1985) and William G. Rothstein, *American Medical Schools and the Practice of Medicine: A History,* (New York: Oxford University Press, 1987). See also Walsh's comments on Kaufman, *Homeopathy* and Rothstein, *American Physicians*, in *Doctors Wanted*, p. xi, fn. 5.

Yet, like other historians of American medicine, Morantz-Sanchez has retained an ambivalence to the significance of women sectarians. She admitted that there were more sectarians among women doctors than men, but, like Walsh, justified her focus on women regulars, arguing that by the end of the nineteenth century over three-quarters of women doctors were regulars, a curiously anachronistic reason. These women regulars, she wrote, were "the only individuals who commanded much respect from the orthodox professionals, who were, by the 1980s, rapidly gaining ascendency."[34] Yet women's historians, including Morantz-Sanchez herself, have urged that women's history, particularly feminist history, maintain its own standards of significance, not necessarily gained from history's victors.

SECTARIAN WOMEN AND PROFESSIONAL IDENTITY

Women sectarians' stories have been mostly left out of women's medical history, even by feminist historians anxious to show how women's rights activists supported womens' medical education. The history of the early years of the Woman's (then Female) Medical College of Pennsylvania in Philadelphia is one example. In 1850 its Quaker founders, including Hannah Longshore and her brother-in-law Joseph, found it difficult to find male regular supporters and finally chose eclectically oriented physicians as the first faculty members. Joseph Longshore himself spurned heroic medicine and turned to homeopathy. Thus, the first class of the college, as some medical historians have pointed out, was trained by irregulars.[35] In 1853 two physicians on the faculty who advocated eclecticism, Longshore and Abraham Livezay, were asked to resign, and were replaced by regular women physicians. The men then opened a coeducational eclectic school, and Hannah Longshore left her faculty position at the Female Medical College and joined the new Penn

---

[34] Regina Markell Morantz-Sanchez, *Sympathy and Science: Women Physicians in American Medicine* (New York: Oxford University Press, 1985), pp. 394–95, fn. 7. Morantz-Sanchez, for example, excluded sectarian women's colleges from a quantified study of women's schools without explanation, in *Sympathy and Science*, p. 245. Walsh does include homeopathic schools in her table of women's medical colleges, *Doctors Wanted*, p. 180. Rothstein, *American Physicians*, noted that in 1900, 12% of all homeopathic physicians were women, but this information is not explored in his text, pp. 300–301, fn. 5.

[35] Morantz-Sanchez, *Sympathy and Science*, p. 59; Frederick C. Waite, "American Sectarian Medical Colleges Before the Civil War," *Bulletin of the History of Medicine* 19 (1946): 159.

Medical University as an instructor.[36] What happened? What was different about their approach? Why did it so disturb the founders and supporters of the college? These questions remain unanswered. Similarly, historians of the women-run New England Hospital for Women and Children in Boston have noted that the hospital's physicians refused to admit women homeopaths to residency positions, but have not examined the struggle there, or the possible differences of opinion among the hospital's feminist supporters.[37]

Sectarian schools clearly played an important role for women interested in formal medical training. The eclectic Penn Medical University in Philadelphia, for example, graduated at least one hundred women between 1853 and its demise in 1881. Russell Trall's hydropathic college in New York similarly attracted numbers of women students in the 1850s and 1860s.[38] The earliest formal education of American women practitioners, historians have long acknowledged, took place in irregular colleges.[39] The last half of the nineteenth century saw the establishment of as many sectarian as regular women's medical schools. As late as Abraham Flexner's 1910 report, one of the three remaining women's medical colleges was irregular, the homeopathic Women's Medical College and Hospital in New York City.[40] Nineteenth-century sectarian

---

[36] Lovejoy, *Women Doctors of the World*, pp. 29–30. See also Morantz-Sanchez's brief account, *Sympathy and Science*, pp. 76–77. Sarah Adamson Dolley, too impatient to wait for the regular Philadelphia college to open, left the city to attend an eclectic school in Syracuse (p. 397, fn. 33). See also Shryock, "Women in American Medicine," pp. 188–89; Blake, "Women and Medicine," pp. 115–17. Gulielma Fell Alsop, *History of the Women's Medical College, Philadelphia, Pennsylvania, 1850–1950* (Philadelphia: J. B. Lippincott, 1950) omits this aspect of the college's history.

[37] Morantz-Sanchez, *Sympathy and Science*, pp. 73, 296–97, fn. 25; Virginia Drachman, *Hospital with a Heart: Women Doctors and the Paradox of Separatism at the New England Hospital, 1862–1969* (Ithaca: Cornell University Press, 1984), p. 233, fn. 64.

[38] Waite, "American Sectarian Medical Colleges," pp. 161, 166; Blake, "Women and Medicine," pp. 114, 116–17. The National Eclectic Association endorsed coeducation in 1855.

[39] Frederick C. Waite, "Dr. Lucinda Susannah (Capen) Hall: The First Woman to Receive a Medical Degree from a New England Institution," *New England Journal of Medicine* 210 (1934): 644–47. Before June 1852, twenty women had graduated from six American medical schools: Geneva (regular), Central (eclectic), Syracuse (eclectic), Female Medical College of Pennsylvania (regular), Western Homeopathic and Western Reserve (homeopathic). For the support male eclectics offered women practitioners see Ronald L. Numbers, "The Making of an Eclectic Physician: Joseph M. McElhinney and the Eclectic Medical Institute of Cincinnati," *Bulletin of the History of Medicine* 47 (1973): 160, 162.

[40] Morantz-Sanchez, *Sympathy and Science*, p. 65; Abraham Flexner, *Medical Education in the United States and Canada* (New York: Carnegie Foundation for the Advancement of Teaching, Bulletin '4, 1910), pp. 160, 271. This school still lacks a detailed history, but

schools more often adopted coeducational policies, long before most regular schools, and continued them even after regular schools had ended coeducational experiments. Still, male sectarians were at times reluctant to welcome women as students or colleagues, as the case of Cincinnati's Pulte Medical College shows.[41]

Historians have little explored the reasons that mid-nineteenth-century women were attracted to sectarian colleges, apart from their open admission policies. Regina Morantz-Sanchez and Gloria Moldow have noted that the first generation of women doctors (those graduating between 1850 and 1870) was made up of a significant number, perhaps a majority, of women trained as sectarians who had women patients seeking female sectarian doctors.[42] In Victorian America both regular and sectarian female physicians urged women patients to choose practitioners of the same gender for reasons of modesty and empathy gained through shared experience. In fact, Morantz-Sanchez has argued that the "challenge posed by sectarian medicine to older concepts of professionalism worked in favor of women."[43] Conscious that the opinions of regular and sectarian women sometimes differed, she has carefully tried to distinguish them in her work. Yet who were these women? What happened to them? Why did the next generation turn away from sectarian training? The issue of why sectarian colleges were more open to coeducation also remains unresolved. Why did sectarians continue to defend this practice against the separatist policies of regular schools until the last quarter of the nineteenth century?

The attitude of women towards the questions of formal training and professionalization has an ambiguous legacy, historians Gloria Moldow and Virginia Drachman have recently argued. Their studies of women doctors in the mid- and late nineteenth century show that the fervent

see Leonard Paul Wershub, *One Hundred Years of Medical Progress: A History of the New York Medical College Flower and Fifth Avenue Hospitals* (Springfield, IL: Charles C. Thomas, 1967), pp. 148–54. The women's college was founded in 1863, the hospital in 1869.

41 William Barlow and David O. Powell, "Homeopathy and Sexual Equality: The Controversy over Coeducation at Cincinnati's Pulte Medical College, 1873–1879," [1981] in Leavitt, *Women and Health in America*, pp. 422–28. During the 1890s Chicago, New York, and Philadelphia had no regular schools open to women; see Walsh, *Doctors Wanted*, p. 182.

42 Morantz-Sanchez, *Sympathy and Science*, p. 31. Of fifty identifiable women physicians in Edward T. and Janet Wilson James, eds., *Notable American Women 1607–1950: A Biographical Dictionary* (Cambridge, MA: Belknap Press, 1971), ten were clearly graduates from a sectarian school, and the majority of these graduated before 1880. Most of the regular graduates, however, were second-generation, graduating between 1880 and 1900.

43 Morantz-Sanchez, *Sympathy and Science*, p. 31.

emulation of regular male medical models by a new scientifically oriented generation of women doctors paradoxically stripped these women
of their supportive institutions and professional networks.[44]

   In a finely detailed study of around two hundred women doctors
and medical students in Washington, D.C. between 1870 and 1900,
Moldow found similar professional aspirations among both homeopathic women and their regular sisters.[45] Caroline Brown Winslow, for
example, a homeopath educated in Cleveland, helped to found the
Homeopathic Free Dispensary, the National Homeopathic Hospital, and
the Washington chapter of the national homeopathic association.[46] Male
and female homeopaths together established the National Homeopathic
Medical College in the 1890s, a financially marginal institution which
only lasted three years.[47]

   Like Morantz-Sanchez, Moldow argued that the later generation of
women doctors—both homeopaths and regulars—wanted to become
physicians for financial and professional reasons, and were less interested in questions of women's rights. Homeopathic female advocates,
however, had only limited power in determining the direction of homeopathy. A new hospital, for example, was to be established in memory of
President Garfield, a supporter of homeopathy whose family physician
was a woman homeopath. Female supporters of homeopathy, who were
members of the hospital board, were unable to convince regular

---

44 Drachman, *Hospital with a Heart*; Gloria Moldow, *Women Doctors in Guilded Age*
    Washington: Race, Gender, and Professionalization (Urbana: University of Illinois Press,
    1987). For an insightful discussion of the links between professionalization in the
    nineteenth century and women's culture, work, and family, see Joan Jacobs Brumberg
    and Nancy Tomes, "Women in the Professions: A Research Agenda for American
    Historians," *Reviews in American History* 10 (1982): 275–96.
45 She found that women made up 20% of the city's homeopaths; Moldow, *Women*
    Doctors, p. 12.
46 Moldow, *Women Doctors*, pp. 135–41. Women homeopaths were members of the
    national body as early as 1869 but Massachusetts women homeopathic students
    struggled to gain membership in their state homeopathic societies; *Doctors Wanted*,
    pp. 162, 196–97. For a detailed study of the homeopathic education of women in
    Cleveland, a city which graduated over two hundred homeopathic women and only
    sixty-four regular women between 1852 and 1914, see Frederick C. Waite, *Western*
    Reserve University Centennial History of the School of Medicine (Cleveland: Western
    Reserve University Press, 1946), pp. 325–30. In 1919 Martha L. Bolger, Portsmouth's
    first woman doctor and a homeopath, was denied entrance to the regular medical
    society, yet she worked alongside her regular male colleagues at the local hospital;
    J. Worth Estes and David M. Goodman, *The Changing Humors of Portsmouth: The*
    Medical Biography of an American Town, 1623–1983 (Boston: Francis C. Countway
    Library of Medicine, 1986), pp. 111–12. Bolger was granted honorary membership in
    1952.
47 Moldow, *Women Doctors*, p. 54.

members that homeopaths should be permitted to practice alongside regulars. Still in need of clinical facilities, the city's homeopathic community established a dispensary, but was never able to raise sufficient funds for a hospital.[48]

Unlike Walsh's study, which implied that women became homeopaths because regular institutions were closed to them, Moldow has found at least seven women who switched from orthodox to homeopathic medicine between 1870 and 1885.[49] The issue of converts raises problems for historians who have assumed that formal training defines a practitioner, without also examining practice. Moldow's study is sensitive to the ways that gender and race have defined the experiences of medical women, but she has offered little explanation of why she found no black women homeopaths.[50] Nor has she explicitly considered the role of the homeopathic community in shaping the reactions of male regulars to their female colleagues. The threat of the appeal of sectarian medicine to both patients and practitioners may have led male regulars in Washington to try to woo women regulars away from homeopathy and contributed to the pressure to grant them membership in the city's medical societies.[51]

Moldow's work makes her readers ache for detailed biographies of women sectarians. Scattered in the historical literature there are a couple of brief studies of some of the most famous practitioners, such as Lydia Folger Fowler. Fowler was the second woman in America to graduate from a medical school, and the first to hold an academic position. Her

---

[48] Ibid., pp. 77–79. See also Kaufman, Homeopathy, p. 73, on Garfield's support for homeopathy. Coulter, Divided Legacy: Science and Ethics in American Medicine, 1880–1914, claims that Edson was not Garfield's family physician but that she did attend him after he was shot; p. 321, fn. 60. For a brief study of another homeopathic hospital fight involving men and women, regulars and homeopaths, see Waite, Western Reserve, pp. 242–45, 321–22. Cleveland homeopaths, however, did manage to establish their own hospital in 1879, which retained its homeopathic title for thirty years.

[49] Moldow, Women Doctors, p. 80. These included Grace Roberts and Caroline Burghardt.

[50] See Darlene Clark Hine, "Co-Laborers in the Work of the Lord: Nineteenth-Century Black Women Physicians," in Ruth J. Abram, ed., "Send Us A Lady Physician": Women Doctors in America, 1835–1920 (New York: W. W. Norton & Co., 1985) pp. 108, 116–17, for a brief discussion of Susan Smith McKinney Steward (1848–1919) who graduated from the homeopathic New York Medical College for Women in 1870 and practiced in New York City. Steward was an activist in black women's rights and worked at the Brooklyn Women's Homeopathic Hospital.

[51] Moldow, Women Doctors, p. 107. Alexander Wilder, in his evangelistic history of eclecticism, History of Medicine (New Sharon, ME: New England Eclectic Publishing Co., 1901) p. 580, argued that the regular Geneva Medical College only opened its doors to Elizabeth Blackwell as a response to her acceptance from the nearby Eclectic Medical Institute.

chroniclers have mostly argued that her practice and identification with irregular medicine was forced upon her. Frederick Waite urged that Fowler deserved a place in American medical history "although she was connected with sectarian medicine."[52] Another writer believed that "regardless of her championship of eclecticism, hydropathy, and homeopathy, Lydia Folger Fowler meets a significant place in American medical history."[53] But the lives and careers of these women have remained largely shrouded. Susannah Hall, another early medical graduate, practiced midwifery and opened a hydropathic health resort in the 1860s and 1870s.[54] Jane Donegan has traced some of the graduates of Russell Trall's hydropathic institute during the 1850s, with some success.[55] Even a brief examination of sectarian biographical texts, such as a contemporary's history of homeopathy, suggests that, as Millie Chapman assumed, women practitioners were a significant part of irregular medicine.[56] Without further detailed studies we cannot yet explain the appeal of sectarian medicine, nor the career paths of these physicians, and options they did or did not take.

Some sectarian women did become self-conscious professionals. Richard Shryock, for example, noted that women sectarians had formed national organizations some years before regular women did—women

---

[52] He believed that her ability, industry, and personal charm "combined to make a career that measures up to the best traditions of American medical women." See Frederick C. Waite, "Dr. Lydia Folger Fowler: The second woman to receive the degree of Doctor of Medicine in the United States," *Annals of Medical History*, n.s.4 (1932): 290–97. Fowler graduated in 1850 from Samuel Gregory's Female Medical College. She was appointed Professor of Midwifery and Diseases of Women and Children at the eclectic Central Medical College from 1851 to 1852. She practiced in New York City, and also taught at Russell Trall's Hygeio-Therapeutic College in the 1860s. See also Lovejoy, *Women Doctors of the World*, p. 18: "Her standing as a physician and as a medicosocial writer and lecturer was advantageous while she lived and worked, but prejudice has placed her at a disadvantage historically. Professionally speaking, eclectic medicine and phrenology are too heavy a handicap even for a Folger."

[53] Madeleine B. Stern, "Lydia Folger Fowler, M.D.: First American woman professor of medicine," *New York State Journal of Medicine* 77 (1977): 1137–40. "Dr. Fowler's endorsement of the unconventional aspects of medicine may arouse disdain among those who are inclined to overlook the opposition of the regular profession to women physicians of the nineteenth century," p. 1139. Hydropathy was a health-reform movement based on the theory of the healing powers of water.

[54] Waite, "Susannah Hall," pp. 644–47. Hall studied at Gregory's Female Medical College and graduated with a certificate of proficiency before the school received a state charter. She received her M.D. from the eclectic Worcester Medical Institution in 1852.

[55] Jane B. Donegan, *"Hydropathic Highway to Health": Women and Water-Cure in Antebellum America* (Westport: Greenwood Press, 1986) pp. 171–73.

[56] King, *History of Homeopathy*, vol. 4.

homeopaths in 1904 and women osteopaths in 1914, the latter a year before the founding of the regular Medical Women's National Association. Millie Chapman herself was president of the Women's Homeopathic Medical Association of Pittsburgh, and vice-president of the American Institute of Homeopathy.[57] As these sectarian women sought professional approbation, were they rejecting a previous antiprofessional sectarian model? Sectarian medicine also provided women doctors with alternative career paths. Female supporters of homeopathy played a key role in the decision of Boston University to select homeopaths to run their newly formed medical school in 1873.[58] Some women sectarians became teachers in sectarian schools. Others, sometimes with limited formal training, founded and practiced in irregular institutions such as water-cure establishments.[59]

Clearly, sectarian medicine, both its theory and its practice, attracted women practitioners and patients. Yet some became dissatisfied. What was the lure of regular medical training? In the 1870s Oregon eclectic Bethenia Owens-Adair felt that her unorthodox training was hindering her career and returned to the University of Michigan for a regular degree.[60] Sarah Adamson Dolley later claimed that her own eclectic training was an accident, and that she had not known the Central Medical College was sectarian until she arrived on campus.[61] Do their actions suggest the declining appeal of sectarian practice? shifting public attitudes? a new meaning of science among women doctors?

Morantz-Sanchez has suggested that the history of women physicians in the nineteenth century cannot be understood without an examination of the ideological conflicts between pioneer physicians such as Elizabeth Blackwell and those more oriented to the new sciences such as Mary Putnam Jacobi.[62] These two generations fought over their perspectives of women's role in society and medicine, symbolized by separatist women's

[57] Shryock, "Women and American Medicine," p. 189; King, *History of Homeopathy*, vol. 4, p. 37.
[58] A group of Boston women regulars, including Zakrewska, opposed the merger of Boston University with Gregory's College; see Walsh, *Doctors Wanted*, p. 71.
[59] See Numbers, "Do-It-Yourself the Sectarian Way," in Risse, Numbers, and Leavitt, *Medicine Without Doctors*, pp. 64–68.
[60] Morantz-Sanchez, *Sympathy and Science*, pp. 67–68. In the 1880s homeopathy was popular among the middle class; see Lovejoy, *Women Doctors of the World*, p. 107. For a brief survey of women sectarians on the West Coast, pp. 106–9.
[61] Ellen More, "The Blackwell Medical Society and the Professionalization of Women Physicians," *Bulletin of the History of Medicine*, 61 (1987): 609, fn. 15.
[62] See Morantz-Sanchez, *Sympathy and Science*, chapter 7.

education, and the role of interventionist and experimental science. Both generations, it appears, shared a low opinion of sectarian medicine. Yet was their scorn necessarily a sign of a forward-looking scientific approach?

Consider the story of Clemence Lozier. Lozier trained at an eclectic college, and then founded the New York Medical College and Hospital for Women in 1863, a homeopathic institution which lasted over fifty years.[63] In her twenty-five-year term as dean Lozier saw over two hundred women graduate.[64] Her work was supported by suffragist Elizabeth Cady Stanton, a fervent proponent of sectarian medicine.[65] Lozier's school was only a few blocks away from Elizabeth Blackwell's New York Infirmary, which was a direct competitor for women students. One historian has argued that the "distance between those small institutions was the gulf between sectarian and orthodox medicine."[66] Elizabeth Blackwell, a feminist supporter, rejected interventionist medical science and eschewed the germ theory; yet the regular doctors at her Infirmary refused applicants too clearly associated with suffrage and the health-reform movement—women with very short hair, for example, or wearing a Bloomer costume. Morantz-Sanchez has termed Blackwell's opposition to homeopathic women a "hard-headed assessment" of the proper professional path for women in medicine.[67]

These conflicts between regular and sectarian women appear to have occurred just as women's rights activists such as Susan B. Anthony were starting to distance themselves from the radical wings of social reformers, rejecting dress reformers and free love advocates. Post-pioneer regular physicians, the second generation, rarely embraced active feminism. Did they also reject the close relationship between women's rights activists and irregular medicine? Sectarian women seem to have continued their commitments to feminism longer. Susan Edson, for example, a graduate of an eclectic school in Cincinnati, treated President Garfield's family, and helped to establish the National Women's Suffrage Association. Caroline Winslow, inspired by hydropath Rachel

---

[63] See Walsh, *Doctors Wanted*, p. 206.

[64] Morantz-Sanchez, *Sympathy and Science*, p. 46.

[65] Ibid., p. 46; Lovejoy, *Women Doctors of the World*, pp. 63–68. Lozier (1813–1888) was president of the New York Woman's Suffrage Society, the National Woman's Suffrage Association, and the Women's American Temperance League; King, *History of Homeopathy*, vol. 4, pp. 325–26.

[66] Lovejoy, *Women Doctors of the World*, p. 64. Morantz-Sanchez noted that male regulars urged Blackwell to found a regular women's school after her residents were turned down by regular male schools, as the appearance of a homeopathic women's medical college disturbed them; *Sympathy and Science*, p. 66.

[67] Morantz-Sanchez, *Sympathy and Science*, pp. 73–74.

Gleason, attended both eclectic and homeopathic colleges, and helped to found the American Association of University Women. Susan B. Anthony's physician was homeopath Julia Holmes Smith.[68]

In the mid-nineteenth century, relations between regulars and sectarians in some circles were not as severe as some of these examples suggest. John Harley Warner has shown in his study of regulars and homeopaths in antebellum America that, whatever their professions' rhetoric, in practice doctors of the old and new schools worked together, and sometimes employed one another's therapies, despite the strong link between therapeutic loyalty and professional identity.[69] Martha Verbrugge, in a study of nineteenth-century Boston, noted that the Ladies' Physiological Institute invited both regulars and sectarians to speak.[70] Moldow, similarly, found regular and homeopathic women working on committees together, particularly on issues relating to women's rights.[71] We await, however, a detailed historical exploration of the relationship between these competing sects, and the role feminism may have played in transforming and perhaps transcending professional antagonisms.

An analysis of the behavior of ordinary physicians may change our understanding of their feelings about sectarianism, but historians of women physicians have tended to focus on the rhetoric of women leaders concerned with rigid orthodoxy, particularly by those who became leaders in their field such as Marie Zakrzewska, Elizabeth Blackwell, and Mary Putnam Jacobi. What did these women fear? Were their attacks on sectarian women a sign of their shaky relations with the regular male establishment? Morantz-Sanchez argued that "the founding of sectarian institutions that admitted women students exacerbated al-

[68] Moldow, *Women Doctors*, pp. 135, 136, 208, fn. 2. Smith was an active homeopathic professional, and also the first woman trustee of the University of Illinois; King, *History of Homeopathy*, vol. 4, pp. 228–29. See also the career of suffragist reformer and homeopath Martha Ripley in Winton U. Solberg, "Martha G. Ripley: Pioneer Doctor and Social Reformer," *Minnesota History* 39 (1964): 1–17.

[69] John Harley Warner, "Medical Sectarianism, Therapeutic Conflict, and the Shaping of Orthodox Professional Identity in Antebellum American Medicine," in Bynum and Porter, *Medical Fringe and Medical Orthodoxy*, pp. 242–43.

[70] Martha H. Verbrugge, *Able-Bodied Womanhood: Personal Health and Social Change in Nineteenth-Century Boston* (New York: Oxford University Press, 1988), pp. 57, 92. She suggests that the group seemed indifferent to the marginal status of irregulars (p. 58). Members of Rochester's Blackwell Medical Society had "cordial but distant" relations with women irregulars, worked together to raise money for a future medical missionary, and granted an honorary membership to a regularly trained hydropath, Cordelia Greene; see More, "The Blackwell Medical Society," pp. 609, 622.

[71] Moldow, *Women Doctors*, pp. 145–46.

ready bitter feelings in the regular profession regarding allegations of poorly trained men."[72] Clearly, many regularly trained women tried to separate themselves from attacks by male regulars of women physicians' low standards, poor training, and their popular association with hydropaths, abortionists, and other morally and professionally suspect practitioners. Did sectarian women such as Owens-Adair and Dolley also seek to separate themselves from less professionally respectable sectarians?

Certainly, women doctors also found that sectarian men could be just as exploitative and dismissive. Boston health entrepreneur Samuel Gregory, for example, clearly exploited the women who enrolled at his Female Medical College in the 1850s and 1860s. Morantz-Sanchez has remarked on the glee of women regulars in the 1870s when his college merged with Boston University's homeopathic medical department. Although women students remained loyal to Boston University even as the popularity of homeopathy declined and fewer students applied, in its 1918 reorganization administrators chose to ignore women students, whose numbers dropped from one-third of the graduating class to under 10% by the 1930s.[73]

WOMEN, SCIENCE, PRACTICE, AND HEALTH REFORM

Implicit in the attacks of sectarian medicine by regular women physicians was a definition of not only the proper woman professional but the kind of medicine she should be practicing. One historian has reminded us of the relationship regular male doctors assumed between science and social truth, and the socially defined role of male doctor and female patient.[74] Sectarians' promotion of coeducation seemed to undermine this link between Victorian culture and medical professionalism. However, historians have tended to focus on professional rhetoric rather than the content of sectarian science. Few studies have examined the practice or knowledge of women sectarians; Moldow, for example, seems clearly uninterested in the intellectual content of her women practitioners' work. Morantz-Sanchez remains one of few medical historians to have considered the relation between female culture and medical

---

[72] Morantz-Sanchez, *Sympathy and Science*, p. 69.
[73] Ibid., p. 399, fn. 58; Walsh, *Doctors Wanted*, pp. 195–99.
[74] Susan E. Cayleff, *Wash and Be Healed: The Water-Cure Movement and Women's Health* (Philadelphia: Temple University Press, 1987), pp. 9–11.

science.[75] Yet a detailed study of the sectarian critique of the content of regular medicine could bring women's and medical history closer to the history of science, particularly with insights from recent work on the concept of feminist science.[76]

American historians have become interested in the historical dimensions of contemporary concerns with fitness and popular health. They have explored the history of physical education, patent medicines, hydropathy, and other health reforms, with a particular emphasis on their attractions for women. These topics have allowed scholars to bring together the interests and approaches of medical and women's history. Often not medical historians, these scholars have defined health broadly, and been less interested in the professionalism themes that still dominate much history of American medicine. The study of women as patients and consumers of health care has found an active historical audience. Some historians, accepting the notion of conflicting generational changes between groups of health reformers, have been more critical of the meaning of science in medicine, the role of women's rights, and whether health reform was necessarily progressive. They have tried to integrate this topic into broader studies of American culture and women's history.[77]

Susan Cayleff's study of hydropathy, *Wash and Be Healed*, is the one of the most ambitious of these, and one of the few studies that has taken seriously the intellectual content of a sectarian movement. She placed hydropathy within regular medicine, looking at both practices and rhetoric. Hydropathy, she argued, was distinguished from regular medicine by its therapeutic ideology; it rejected certain practices such as heroic drugging, but it retained a traditional conception of the body and environment. In fact, some hydropaths even continued their own version of

---

[75] See for example Morantz-Sanchez, *Sympathy and Science*, pp. 184–202; and also the recent suggestion by John Harley Warner, "Science in Medicine," *Osiris*, 1 (1985): 37–58.

[76] See, for example, Ruth Bleier, ed., *Feminist Approaches to Science* (New York: Pergamon, 1986); and Sandra Harding and Jean O'Barr, eds., *Sex and Scientific Inquiry* (Chicago: University of Chicago Press, 1987).

[77] For an early approach suggesting that the health-reform critique improved regular medical practice and public health, see Richard Harrison Shryock, "Sylvester Graham and the Popular Health Movement, 1830–1870," in Shryock, *Medicine in America* pp. 111–22. For one of the few major studies which examines the intellectual and social history of a major woman health reformer, see Ronald L. Numbers, *Prophetess of Health: A Study of Ellen G. White* (New York: Harper & Row, 1976).

therapeutic excesses. Hydropathy was clearly linked to other sects, such as Thomsonianism, homeopathy, and phrenology, although Cayleff did not explore these connections in detail.[78] The sect's success, she suggested, indicated a broad popular rejection of interventionist medical therapy. And hydropathy was especially appealing to women due to its less rigid sense of gender and class division.[79]

Cayleff's study focused on the relation of hydropathy to orthodox medicine. She found hydropaths offered an articulate critique of regular medical care and Victorian social relations, particularly the doctor-patient relationship.[80] But her approach to the question of orthodoxy is disappointing; like Rothstein, she considered regular medicine in the nineteenth century as a sect, but defined it simply as a competitive medical theory. Her view of science, similarly, is that it offered medicine "detachment."[81]

Nonetheless, her study offers a partial model for historians of American culture, women, and medicine. It suggests ways to explore the relations between sectarian and orthodox medicine beyond simply examining women's medical education. In the 1850s, for example, Elizabeth Blackwell became a patient in a water-cure establishment. Yet, unlike other social feminists, Blackwell did not embrace the therapy or its principles in her own career.[82] Another interesting issue Cayleff raised was the ambivalence expressed by sectarian writers about sex-segregated medical education. The *Water Cure Journal*, for example, argued that separate women's medical schools were "unnatural and

---

[78] Cayleff, *Wash*, pp. 7, 8, 12. See also Marshall Scott Legan, "Hydropathy in America: A Nineteenth Century Panacea," *Bulletin of the History of Medicine* 45 (1971): 267–80; John B. Blake, "Mary Gove Nichols: Prophetess of Health," *Proceedings of the American Philosophical Society* 106 (1962): 219–34; Kathryn Kish Sklar, "All hail to pure cold water," *American Heritage* 26 (1974); 64–69, 100–101; and Harry B. Weiss and Howard R. Kemble, *The Great American Water-Cure Craze: A History of Hydropathy in the United States* (Trenton: Past Times Press, 1967).

[79] Cayleff, *Wash*, pp. 8, 9–11. Almina Rhodes Dean, trained at Philadelphia's Woman's Medical College, founded a sanitarium employing hydropathic therapies and her own "Vacuum Technique"; Ellen J. Smith, "Institutions: Wide and Fruitful Fields," in Abram, *"Send Us A Lady Physician*, pp. 193–96.

[80] Cayleff, *Wash*, pp. 5, 18.

[81] Ibid., pp. 6, 53. Morantz-Sanchez has argued that by 1900 most water-cure women were regulars (regularly trained?); *Sympathy and Science*, p. 154.

[82] Cayleff, *Wash*, p. 69; Blake, "Women and Medicine," p. 103, suggested that Blackwell's experience made her dissatisfied with both regular and sectarian therapies. Whorton, *Crusaders for Fitness* pp. 108–10, notes Blackwell's links with Christian physiology.

unphysiological," although the editor defended Philadelphia's Female Medical College when it came under allopathic attack.[83]

Jane Donegan has estimated that between one-fifth and one-third of hydropathic practitioners were women. She has argued that the question of therapeutics was at the heart of sectarian medicine. Her study of hydropathy suggests even more strongly that it was a viable health alternative for patients whereas regular medicine was dangerous, distasteful, and ineffective.[84] In their examinations of hydropathic practice both Donegan and Cayleff have relied mostly on prescriptive and descriptive literature rather than case records. Cayleff has suggested that women hydropaths were often eager to adopt the methods and advances of scientific medicine. One woman hydropath, for example, who had graduated from the University of Michigan, employed radium therapy. Some water-cure institutions promoted the use of other sectarian and regular therapies; Elmira, for example, promised clients both homeopathy and electrotherapy in the 1860s.[85] Yet both Donegan and Cayleff have argued that the therapeutics issue led to the sect's decline. Hydropaths, they suggested, lost public credibility because they refused to endorse regular scientific practices such as vaccination and vivisection. Thus, scientific medicine and its model of expert knowledge helped to defeat hydropathy as a distinctive sect. Their studies, however, still blur the relationship between a nineteenth-century sect and the rise of scientific medicine, perhaps because they have not fully confronted the multiple meanings of science for patients and practitioners. What, after all, was the science of hydropathy?

More intriguing are Cayleff and Donegan's suggestions of alternative role-models for women interested in medical careers, an approach which may lead us to reassess the influence of the great women regular doctors. Eminent nineteenth-century sectarian women, in addition to those discussed by Millie Chapman, such as Rachel Gleason and Mary Gove

---

[83] Cayleff, *Wash*, p. 71. Allopathy is a term rather misused by recent scholars. It was initially used by homeopaths to denigrate the practice of regulars, who, homeopaths argued, based their therapies on difference rather than "like cures like." Subsequently other irregulars adopted the term to attack regular critics, but, as many regulars aptly noted, it is an inaccurate and simplistic description of regular practice or theory.

[84] Donegan, *Hydropathic Highway*, p. 194, xiv. Sarah Stage, in her study of Lydia Pinkham, similarly stressed the lack of safe, effective treatments which were economically feasible, in *Female Complaints: Lydia Pinkham and the Business of Women's Medicine* (New York: W. W. Norton & Co., 1979), p. 10.

[85] Cayleff, *Wash*, pp. 93–94, 103. The importance of examining case records has recently been shown in a study of regular medicine; see Warner, *The Therapeutic Perspective*.

Nichols, went beyond private practice and became lecturers and activists. Donegan has stressed that Gleason, who graduated from an eclectic medical college in 1851 and became a well-known hydropath, proved an "outstanding model woman."[86] Further, many of these women practiced in husband-and-wife teams—the Shrews, Tralls, Nichols, Gleasons, and Jacksons.[87] The implications of these alternative professional models need to be explored more fully. Was sectarian medicine, perhaps, based more commonly on a domestic model of household work?

FUTURE DIRECTIONS

To understand the appeal and meaning of sectarian medicine, historians must turn more closely to the patient's perspective, as well as that of the ordinary practitioner. Diaries, letters, and case notes are difficult to find, but some have survived. Harvey Green has examined the diary of Almira MacDonald, who in the 1870s went to "Mrs. Greenleaf" for electrotherapy after hearing a lecture on the subject by "Mrs. French."[88] Gloria Moldow has found the diary of Julia Green, a Washington homeopath and active clubwoman whose records suggest that one-quarter of her patients were charity cases. Morantz-Sanchez has been able to explore the private lives of women doctors through an extensive study of manuscript collections, including the papers of both regular and sectarian women physicians. Anna Manning Comfort, for example, who graduated from the homeopathic Women's Medical College in New York, faced discrimination and professional hardship as an intern at Bellevue Hospital.[89]

Popular literary works also have been undervalued, though Walsh has reminded us that many nineteenth-century novelists were fascinated by the women doctor as a literary figure.[90] Perhaps the most famous of

---

[86] Donegan, *Hydropathic Highway*, p. 46. For a discussion of this interest in the lifestyle of women professionals, see Brumberg and Tomes, "Women in the Professions," p. 281.
[87] Cayleff, *Wash*, p. 72.
[88] Harvey Green, *Fit for America: Health, Fitness, Sport and American Society* (New York: Pantheon, 1986), p. 167.
[89] Moldow, *Women Doctors*, pp. 128, 144, 158; Morantz-Sanchez, *Sympathy and Science*, pp. 164, 412 fn. 52, 214, 420 fn. 24. Comfort's papers are at Syracuse University. See also More, "Blackwell Society," for her use of Sarah Adamson Dolley Papers, p. 620 fn. 44. See also a brief reference to the papers of Frances Janney, a young Ohio homeopath, Barlow and Powell, "Homeopathy and Sexual Equality," p. 428 fn. 16.
[90] Walsh, *Doctors Wanted* p. 181 discussed James' quite positive portrayal of Prance. The relationship between sectarianism and popular culture can only be briefly mentioned here. Note that when British secret agent James Bond found himself prisoner in a sanatorium, one of his tormenters was a "ravishing female osteopath"; see Ian Fleming, *Thunderball* [1961], cited by E. S. Turner, *Taking the Cure* (London: Michael Joseph, 1967), p. 273.

these is Mary Prance, in Henry James' *The Bostonians* (1886).[91] In Prance, a homeopathic physician, James found an appropriate character for his satirical look at the faith healers and suffrage activists of 1870s Boston. Prance is a "plain, spare young woman, with short hair and an eye-glass; she looked about her with a kind of near-sighted deprecia- tion." A sailor and a fisherwoman, Prance has few feminine qualities; "spare, dry, hard, without a curve, an inflection or a grace, she seemed to ask no odds in the battle of life and to be prepared to give none."[92] James' portrayal suggests that the link between sectarian medicine and women's rights was stronger from the patient's perspective than from the doctor's. Unlike her feminist friends, Prance does not "care for great movements," and believes in neither the superiority of women nor men, for "'there is room for improvement in both sexes. Neither of them is up to the standard.'" But Prance treats a suffragist patient with homeo- pathic medicines, for, as her patient acknowledges, "'it's generally agreed now to be the true system.'"[93]

Another fictional woman homeopath, the central character in Eliza- beth Stuart Phelps's *Doctor Zay* (1882), has received some historical attention. Ann Douglas Wood has called this doctor a "superwoman," the epitome of the independent and self-sufficient female physician Blackwell and others dreamed of.[94] Dr. Zay's first male patient, Waldo Yorke, is comforted by her homeopathic therapies even as he is initially horrified by her gender, for "he recognized the familiar tumbler and teaspoon of his infancy." His mother, a Boston intellectual and suffrage supporter, would, he believed, "never have been able to bear it, if I had died under the other treatment."[95] If no superwoman, this doctor, a "Vassar girl" who pursued her medical education in New York and then Europe, is certainly an assured professional with a well-developed sense of morality and compassion.[96]

---

[91] Henry James, *The Bostonians* [1886] (New York: New American Library, 1979). In her study of health reform Vebrugge has shown that Boston was a center for reform and dissension, and sectarian proponents of many kinds; see her *Able-Bodied Womanhood*.

[92] James, *The Bostonians*, pp. 23, 31–32.

[93] Ibid., pp. 33, 295.

[94] Wood, "The Fashionable Diseases," pp. 233–34.

[95] Elizabeth Stuart Phelps, *Doctor Zay* [1882] (New York: Feminist Press, 1987), pp. 40, 39. For rather different pictures of women regulars, see Sarah Orne Jewett, *A Country Doctor* [1884] (New York: New American Library, 1986); and Annie Nathan Meyer, *Helen Brent, M.D.: A Social Study* (New York: Cassell, 1892).

[96] Phelps, *Doctor Zay*, pp. 77, 79. Grace Breen, a homeopath who also trained in New York, is the central figure in W. D. Howells, *Dr. Breen's Practice* (Boston: James R. Osgood & Co., 1882).

The story of sectarian medicine and women in American history may always remain a fragmented one. Yet we must also ask, why is it important to try to piece it together? Sectarian medical schools clearly provided important opportunities for nineteenth-century women interested in studying medicine. An analysis of sectarian medical education can offer a way to look at the history of regular medical education comparatively, without necessarily having to judge their relative merits, but in order to seek the meaning and significance of, for example, formal training and professionalization for both doctors and patients. This story, then, can illuminate a new side of the transformation of American medicine, the complexity of the ideology of social feminism, and the diverse meanings of science for practitioners and patients.

Women practitioners and patients found sectarian medicine appealing, but why did many shift from sects emphasizing domestic healing to those involving formal medical training? By the late nineteenth century the lay public had begun to seek self-conscious professionals like homeopaths and osteopaths rather than self-help groups such as Thomsonians. Perhaps women embraced their role as populist reformers, redefining themselves not simply as domestic healers but as participants in the professionalizing culture of American medicine. At the same time, there were clearly tensions between the ideology of self-help, the individual in control of her own health, and the proper role of the trained professional. The ambiguity of the self-help elements of hydropathy suggests that this transformation was more gradual and complex than previous historians of regular American medicine may have assumed.

Did medical sects offer a distinct reconceptualization of the proper roles of men and women, particularly the definition of a proper Victorian physician? How were gentlemen and ladies to be respectably educated? Morantz-Sanchez has noted that health reformers welcomed women practitioners at sectarian institutions, and derided regulars for their conservatism not just in practice but also concerning women's rights.[97] But the issue of coeducation in regular and sectarian education is still largely unexamined. Why were eclectics, homeopaths and osteopaths at least initially supportive of women practitioners? Did their support alter with the professionalization of regular and irregular medicine in late nineteenth-century America? At the same time, sectarian women established their own separatist institutions—schools, dispensaries, hospitals—sometimes as direct competitors of regular separatist

---

[97] Morantz-Sanchez, *Sympathy and Science*, p. 46.

ones. What happened to these institutions? Women regulars worried that they were linked professionally and by the lay public with quacks and abortionists ("doctresses"). How did sectarian women professionals try to distinguish themselves? What, then, was the meaning of professionalism for a woman eclectic or homeopath?

Sectarians have generally been portrayed as social activists, challenging society's beliefs about health, fitness, diet, and dress, as well as regular medical theories and therapies. But we lack detailed studies of the content of sectarian ideology, the interplay between mainstream and alternative therapies and ideas. Historians have found clear links between social feminist reforms and sectarian partisanship, particularly among women homeopaths and hydropaths. Women sectarians became reformers and entrepreneurs, conscious of the power of their sisters as consumers and patients and even as potential fee-paying students. Feminists in nineteenth-century America saw health reform as a significant part of the women's rights movement. The founders of the American Vegetarian Society, for example, included Susan B. Anthony and Amelia Bloomer. Their expansive definition of health has only recently been studied, mostly by feminists investigating the sexual politics of health. Yet Moldow's and Morantz-Sanchez's insights about the rejection by second generation women doctors of feminist activism and sectarianism have yet to be fully explored. What were the reasons for the declining appeal of these sects for both women practitioners and patients? How can we explain the appearance and continuation of new sects in the late nineteenth century, such as osteopathy and chiropractic? In the 1890s, Gevitz has noted, an osteopathic college assured prospective women students that "the science of osteopathy appeals to women who desire a noble, uplifted work."[98] What was the special appeal of this new kind of science to women?

And what about practice? What did it mean, choosing a sectarian practitioner? To explain the appeal of sectarian medicine we need a historical understanding of the expectations of patients and ordinary practitioners, their attitudes to science, and the function of their therapies. A focus on practice may also offer historians a way of examining the difficult relationship between training and professional identity.

---

[98] "The Science of Osteopathy," [1897] cited in Gevitz, *The D.O.'s*, pp. 44–45. For reference to one modern female quack, who in the 1940s popularized a black box that was supposed to cure breast cancer and pneumonia, see James Harvey Young, "Device Quackery in America," *Bulletin of the History of Medicine* 13 (1965): 154–62.

Perhaps a detailed study of male and female converts to irregular practice will illuminate the popular and professional meaning of sectarian medicine, how ordinary doctors saw themselves and were seen by the lay public and their professional colleagues. If, as some historians have suggested, therapeutics played a key role in defining one's professional identity, what then did it mean to change therapies?

Historians of American medicine have been influenced increasingly by the theoretical sophistication of anthropologists and sociologists investigating contemporary alternative therapeutic systems during the last decade or so. Our field still lacks, however, historical studies of twentieth-century sects such as acupuncture and chiropractic. These studies will have to deal with the problem of sectarian medicine in the post-germ-theory years. Perhaps this focus on recent medical sects will enable us to gain greater perspective on the appeal of scientific medicine. Certainly, scholars need more thoughtful models of the definition of sectarian, so that the popularity of sects after 1900 is not dismissed as quackery or superstition.

I have called for more detailed histories of individual sectarian practitioners and institutions; this may sound like a return to an older style of "great women" history. But, as recent historical work has shown, personal and institutional biographies need not be narrow and Whiggish. Aside from a growing interest in female and minority medical practitioners, social historians have begun to explore extraordinary institutions placed in their social and intellectual contexts. Perhaps sectarian medicine in the nineteenth century had no Hopkins equivalent, but what of now-forgotten, longlasting sectarian schools? The New York homeopathic Women's Medical College and Hospital, after all, was the second-last women's medical school in America; even Dr. Zay appears to have attended it.

The influence of the recent feminist movement has inspired scholars to examine the relationship between women as practitioners and women as patients in the present and in the past. Our critical view of the defining ideology of scientific medicine has helped to shape historical studies of regular medicine in America. But sectarian medicine has remained largely untouched. Medical historians' emphasis on the nineteenth century, and Morantz-Sanchez's critical insights into the shifting attitudes of pioneer and second-generation women doctors towards science have begun to alter our understanding of medical professionalism and practice. But what of the third generation? Who were the Roberts, Smiths, Churches and Pardees of the last eighty years? What has being a sectarian practitioner meant to them? Certainly, the meaning of donning a sectarian mantle has altered significantly from an antebellum woman hydropath to a woman osteopath of the 1980s. This topic, further, may allow us to examine the dynamics of race and ethnicity as well as gender in shaping American medicine. Many Jewish students facing anti-Semitism in the 1920s and 1930s chose to pursue the study of medicine in osteopathic schools. More detailed studies of sectarian medicine may allow us to recover forgotten experiences of ordinary and exceptional women who sought a certain freedom in training, practice and health care.

12

SELF-HELP AND THE PATENT MEDICINE BUSINESS

Susan E. Cayleff

A HISTORICAL OVERVIEW OF THE LITERATURE

Efforts to control health and increase longevity have a long history. Through diet, shamanism, medicinal plant use, application of remedial agents, and healing rituals, people have sought to stem the tide of disease and preserve health. Domestic medications and patent medicines both fall within this tradition of self-help doctoring, as does the oral transmission of self-help remedies.

The advocates of self-medication have been a varied lot with a wide range of motives. Upper-middle class women, disillusioned recipients of radical and/or unsuccessful treatments by the medical profession, commonfolk and ethnic minorities who rejected the dominant world view inherent in the orthodox physician-patient model, rurally isolated people and the poor who did not have geographic or economic access to orthodox medicine, and social reformers have all sought control and knowledge of their bodies. The appeal of self-help cuts across class, gender, and regional lines.

Ironically, women—who have administered most home–based cures across eras and cultures—have often been ignored in the historical literature on self-help and in more recent interpretive scholarship. De-

I would like to thank Annette Dutton of San Diego for her invaluable research assistance during the preparation of this essay. This paper was supported in part by a San Diego State University Affirmative Action grant.

spite some notable exceptions, even sources that are otherwise sensitive to issues of social inequality and conflict fail to address gender issues.

This historiographical essay seeks to accomplish several tasks: to place domestic self-help and patent medicines within their cultural contexts; to review the available primary and secondary literature while highlighting their contributions and omissions; to expand the definition of self-help to account for ethnic, racial, and regional diversities; to insert gender as a category of analysis; and to chart directions for future study. The second portion of the essay examines patent medicine's use, promotion, and marketability among women. The final section examines contemporary self-help literature. Suggestions for future scholarship are interspersed throughout.

Self-Help Medicine and Women: The Literature

The popularity of domestic self-help medications in America can be traced to existing cultural and economic conditions. In early America, domestic medicine was largely informed by oral tradition and was an integral part of women's household responsibility. Treating the sick and preparing medicinal remedies was a vital component of women's central function in the domestic economy, as well as an extension of her caretaking role. Buoyed by cultural values of self-sufficiency and suspicious rejection of expertise, domestic medicine's popularity was also aided by the recognition of "indirect costs" associated with a physician's services. Transportation costs and a day's lost work, in addition to the fee for service, often made the summoning of a physician financially burdensome and thus unlikely.[1]

From its inception, medical self-help for women also encompassed caring for the health of her family. As written sources emerged on the topic, this crucial link was not always acknowledged. But in the daily lives of most Americans, self-help and women's administration to the sick were synonymous.

Although physician-authored manuals were more common, self-help guidebooks were often written by lay people in the eighteenth century. The more popular manuals offer valuable insight into the directives and values extant in domestic medicine. In 1742 Mrs. E. Smith's *The Compleat Houswife*—the first cookbook in America—was published. Its combination of medicinal as well as food recipes became typical of a large number of books by both women and men in the

---

[1] Paul Starr, *The Social Transformation of American Medicine*, (New York: Basic Books, 1982), pp. 65–67.

seventeenth and eighteenth centuries. Smith's book provides recipes for the cure of specific diseases and conditions using herbal and distilled drugs, many with a high alcoholic content. *The Maternal Physician,* written by An American Matron (1818; reprinted 1972), is another lay-authored text addressing women as the caretakers of others.[2]

Among eighteenth-century self-help manuals authored by physicians, the most reprinted was Dr. William Buchan's 1772 publication, *Domestic Medicine: or a Treatise on the Prevention and Cure of Diseases by Regimen and Simple Medicines* (reprinted 1985). Buchan argues that it is the physician's duty to enlighten the public with basic medical knowledge in order to protect patients against quackery and help the poor who cannot afford to see a doctor. Yet while he criticizes the medical profession and believes most people can care for themselves,[3] Buchan is not an advocate of medicine without doctors: "We do not mean that every man should become a physician. This would be an attempt as ridiculous as it is impossible."[4] The goal of increasing the lay public's medical knowledge is to enhance their trust and faith in physicians and to dispel quackery. Thus his emphasis is on simple "domestic medicine" through proper diet, exercise, fresh air, and cleanliness. His text explains the symptoms and causes of diseases and medicines for treatment, and includes chapters on chronic and acute conditions and childhood diseases. Women's conditions, such as childbirth, menstruation, pregnancy, and barrenness, are discussed separately.

Charles Rosenberg's excellent interpretive essay "Medical Text and Social Context: Explaining William Buchan's Domestic Medicine" (1983) describes Buchan's popularity, audience, belief in the body's ability to heal itself, desire to limit the boundaries of lay practice and define physicians' roles, innovations, dismissal of charms and magic, and creation of a subgenre in medical literature that was copied by many.[5] Clearly, Buchan views nostrum- and device-makers and irregular physicians as his and his patients' mutual enemies. He advocates a finite amount of patient self-help; ultimate authority and knowledge is still

---

[2] Other England-based written sources preceded both of these: John B. Blake, "The Compleat Housewife," *Bulletin of the History of Medicine* (Spring 1975): 30–31; and An American Matron, *The Maternal Physician,* (1818).

[3] Starr, *Social Transformation,* pp. 32–33.

[4] William Buchan, M.D., *Domestic Medicine: a Treatise on the Prevention and Cure of Disease by Regimen and Simple Medicines,* (London: 1772; reprint, New York: Garland Publishing, 1985), p. xix.

[5] Charles E. Rosenberg, "Medical Text and Social Context: Explaining William Buchan's Domestic Medicine," *Bulletin of the History of Medicine,* 57, no. 1 (1983): 22.

invested in the physician. In contrast, John Wesley's *Primitive Physic* (1747), widely reprinted in the eighteenth century, denounced doctors much more vehemently than did Buchan and fostered the belief that commonfolk were capable of treating their illnesses.[6]

John C. Gunn's *Domestic Medicine, or, Poorman's Friend* (1830; reprinted 1986) was the leading antebellum guide book in America, surpassing Buchan, and was in its 68th printing by 1920. The book, "phrased in 'plain language, free from doctor's terms,' and aimed at 'families in the Western and Southern States,' . . . promised to reduce the practice of medicine, 'to principles of common sense'."[7] Like others in this genre, Gunn is sensitive to people's traditional ways of life. And, like other physician-authors, he hails the use of simple language, the virtue of simplicity in all medical matters, faith in common people's wisdom, hygienic practices, herbal plant use, listening to the body and nature, and knowledge through experience. He also criticized and condemned medical practitioners, while prescribing (like Buchan) "heroic" therapeutics.[8] Gunn's manual is particularly attuned to women's concerns and role in domestic medicine. He advocates women's education since they are the childrearers, empathizes with the boredom of domestic life, and promotes sexuality for both women and men as a strengthener in marriage. Other ideas of his uphold more traditional views of women. His text also devotes separate sections to childbirth and the diseases of women and children. Taken together, these primary sources point out that a homemaker's duties included preparing medicines and treating serious and minor illnesses.

Several interpretive texts provide strong theoretical frameworks in which to place domestic medicine, although they often lack gender analysis. Paul Starr's *The Social Transformation of American Medicine* (1982) discusses the persistent popularity of domestic medicine and the effect of indirect costs on Americans' medical self-sufficiency. Another source, John Duffy's *The Healers: The Rise of the Medical Establishment* (1976), also places self-help within a broader cultural context. In the chapter entitled, "The Irregulars, Folk Medicine, and Self-Medication," Duffy argues that the increase in the number of orthodox physicians led

---

[6] Starr, *Social Transformation*, p. 33.

[7] John C. Gunn, *Domestic Medicine, or, Poorman's Friend* (1830); Facsimile of the First Edition with an introduction by Charles Rosenberg, *Domestic Medicine*, (Knoxville: University of Tennessee Press, 1986), p. iii.

[8] Gunn, *Domestic Medicine*, Introduction; and Starr, *Social Transformation*, p. 34.

to the decline in home and folk medicine. This interpretation assumes that "American" is synonymous with dominant European cultural groups who are urban, and able to purchase health care. For some groups (e.g., slaves, Native Americans, and pioneers), the increase in orthodox physicians affected their health practices far less.[9]

An example of regional and social differences can be seen in Royce McCrary's "The Use of Home Medical Books in Ante-Bellum Georgia: A Letter by John MacPherson Berrien" (1975) which appeared in the *Journal of the Medical Association of Georgia*.[10] This 1849 letter demonstrates the prevalence of domestic medicine in the antebellum South. Berrien describes Southern plantation owners' consultation of the texts for treating sick slaves. This source and others like it reveal regional patterns. State medical and local historical journals prove a rich source for oral histories, home medical recipe books, and personal correspondence.

Secondary texts that are particularly sensitive to the role of women as advocates, consumers, and self-help doctorers, include E. G. Gartrell's "Women Healers and Domestic Recipes in 18th Century America: The Recipe Book of Elizabeth Coates Paschall" (1987). Fellman and Fellman's *Making Sense of Self: Medical Advice Literature in Late Nineteenth-Century America* (1981) surveys the genre and places it amidst cultural aspirations, fears, and values. Despite a number of internal contradictions, texts like those Gartrell and Fellman and Fellman describe counseled moderation and self-control as the way to order and determine one's own life and to control the social environment. The latter text is particularly sensitive to the advice offered to women and how it affected sex-role expectations. Martha Verbrugge's *Able-Bodied Womanhood: Personal Health and Social Change in Nineteenth-Century Boston* (1988) expands upon the way middle-class women combined self-help medicine and personal improvement as a means of exerting order and direction on their lives. Verbrugge argues that both the

---

[9] John Duffy, *The Healers: The Rise of the Medical Establishment* (New York: McGraw-Hill, 1976); Joseph F. Kett, *The Formation of the American Medical Profession; The Role of Institutions, 1780–1860* (New Haven: Yale University Press, 1968); and Richard H. Shryock, *Medicine in America; Historical Essays*, (Baltimore: The Johns Hopkins University Press, 1966).

[10] Royce McCrary, ed., "The Use of Home Medical Books in Antebellum Georgia: A Letter by John MacPherson Berrien," *Journal of the Medical Association of Georgia* 64 (May 1975): 137.

definition of health for women and the proper means of achieving it changed as the nineteenth century progressed.[11]

Much self-help literature focused on diet and those food reformers who altered it. Since women prepared most food, their role in this regard was crucial. So argues Stephen Nissenbaum in *Sex, Diet, and Debility in Jacksonian America: Sylvester Graham and Health Reform* (1980) when discussing Graham's influence on culinary reform, circa 1830s. In Graham's view, women were vital to diet reform and their role as bakers, nurturers, and family caretakers was central to the family's—and the nation's—well-being. James C. Whorton's *Crusaders for Fitness: The History of American Health Reformers* (1982) focuses on the mid-nineteenth-century dietary reformers who promoted vegetarianism and justified it with religious, physiological, and cultural ideals. As Whorton notes, the constitution of the American Physiological Society appealed directly to women as guardians of the nation's health: "to no individuals, after all, is this subject (physiology) of more immediate importance than to mothers and housewives. In the education of a household, it is indispensable; and cannot be useless in the preparation of our food, especially bread."[12] These themes are also discussed in Regina Morantz's "Making Women Modern: Middle-Class Women and Health Reform in America" (1977).[13] Morantz maintains that a strong physiology for women was seen as the key to a better society, as well as a vehicle for women to modernize. If women were weak, they would be unable to do their work of managing the home, bearing and educating healthy children, and guiding all to a better society. As a result of these beliefs, health reform contributed to womens' domestic authority and social influence.

Scholars pursuing the ties between self-help and diet reform are encouraged to survey cook books, recipe anthologies (often group efforts by women, such as co-parishoners), and dietary regimens advo-

---

11 E. G. Gartrell, "Women Healers and Domestic Recipes in 18th Century America: The Recipe Book of Elizabeth Coates Paschall," *New York State Journal of Medicine* 87 (January 1987): 23; Anita Clair and Michael Fellman, *Making Sense of Self: Medical Advice Literature in Late Nineteenth-Century America* (Philadelphia: University of Pennsylvania Press, 1981); and Martha H. Verbrugge, *Able-Bodied Womanhood: Personal Health and Social Change in Nineteenth-Century Boston* (New York: Oxford University Press, 1988). See also Guenter B. Risse, Ronald L. Numbers, and Judith Walzer Leavitt, eds., *Medicine Without Doctors* (New York: Science History Publication, 1979).

12 Stephen Nissenbaum, *Sex, Diet, and Debility in Jacksonian America; Sylvester Graham and Health Reform* (Westport, CT: Greenwood Press, 1980).

13 Regina Markell Morantz, "Making Women Modern: Middle-Class Women and Health Reform in America," in *Women and Health in America*, ed. Judith Walzer Leavitt (University of Wisconsin Press, 1984), pp. 346–58.

cated by sects and utopian communities. But, although the work of reformers like Graham insisted on women's importance, we have yet to learn the extent to which women were involved in the *organized* nineteenth-century diet reform movement(s). Studying records of formal vegetarian societies, communities, and other groups will help to answer this kind of question.

The Importance of Ethnic and Regional Diversity

Ronald Numbers, in "The History of American Medicine: A Field in Ferment" (1982), argues that the new focus in the history of medicine ought to be on diet, housing, and personal hygiene. The author of this article adds to Numbers's criteria the need for an understanding of ethnic and regional diversity among American people's folk beliefs to move us closer to that goal.[14]

Self-healing means radically different things to people of different cultural backgrounds. Wayland Hand's edited collection *American Folk Medicine: A Symposium* (1976) provides an eclectic group of essays that address the broad and varied persistence of medicinal folklore and self-medication among Native, black, and Hispanic Americans and regional subgroups. Similarly, Wilbur H. Watson's *Black Folk Medicine: The Therapeutic Significance of Faith and Trust* (1984) points out the integration of magic with self-help practices. Both address women's roles as practitioners and patients, regional variations, and the use of magic *as* medicine (a partnership strongly denied by Buchan and other early physician-authors). Regional factors (among others) are also addressed by James Cassedy in explaining domestic medicine's appeal. In "Why Self-Help . . . ?" (1977) Cassedy includes the appeal of having access to one's own medicines, and of relying upon one's own resources, such as books and family members, for information; convenience; inclusion of family or familiar social habits; geographical isolation; cost of medical care; and inadequacies of the medical profession in supply or performance. Cassedy confines his discussion to the members of dominant European cultural groups, yet many of the features also motivate other cultural groups. Among non-Anglo-centric sources, these practices are usually referred to as folk medicine. In folk medicinal practices it is the *system* of healing, not the healer alone, that in several instances provides

---

[14] Ronald L. Numbers, "The History of American Medicine: A Field in Ferment," *The Promise of American History*, ed. Stanley L. Kutler and Stanley N. Katz, *Reviews in American History* 10:4 (Baltimore: The Johns Hopkins University Press, December 1982): 245–64.

guidance in self-help methods by providing a framework of prayers, beliefs in supernatural forces, fetishes, cooking instructions, and other at-home remedies that the afflicted person must actively utilize *after* consulting the shaman/healer. (This is quite different from, for example, a chiropractor. In this instance the patient does not go home and continue to manipulate her own spinal column). Saunders and Hewes in "Folk Medicine and Medical Practice" (1969) discuss how scientific medical beliefs are adjusted and fitted into folk belief systems and self-help practices. Historians of medicine must recognize that *two different belief systems are operating simultaneously* when researching members of these groups.[15]

In the United States, folk belief systems and self-doctoring have relied on a mix of indigenous beliefs and orthodox medicine. Three sources of exceptional value address blacks' use of self-help medicine: Todd Savitt's *Medicine and Slavery: The Diseases and Health Care of Blacks in Antebellum Virginia* (1978); Watson, cited above, which highlights the roles played by older women and their kinship groups in the practice of folk medicine; and Bethel Ann Power's "The Use of Orthodox and Black American Medicine" (1982), which points out southern blacks' use of folk remedies to cure illnesses. According to Powers, healing methods include home remedies via herbal and/or patent medicines, and patients use one or more of three types of folk doctor (the healer, the fortuneteller, or the hoodoo doctor), all of whom treat serious and ordinary illnesses, give counsel, and remove hexes. These methods are congruent with the patients' world view. While they are practiced by both sexes, questions arise about what status black women healers hold within their communities. Studying oral testimonies found in folklore collections would illuminate this question.[16]

Native American culture also relies heavily upon self-help and domestic medicine. Excellent overviews are found in Virgil Vogel's

---

[15] Lyle Saunders and Gordon Hewes, "Folk Medicine and Medical Practice" in *The Cross-Cultural Approach to Healing Behavior*, ed. L. Riddick Lynch (Rutherford: Fairleigh Dickinson University Press, 1969), pp. 402–8; Wayland Hand, ed., *American Folk Medicine: A Symposium* (Berkeley: University of California Press, 1976); Wilbur H. Watson, ed., *Black Folk Medicine: The Therapeutic Significance of Faith and Trust* (New Brunswick: Transaction Books, 1984); and James Cassedy, "Why Self-Help . . . ?" in *Medicine Without Doctors*, ed. Guenter B. Risse, Ronald L. Numbers, and Judith Walzer Leavitt (New York: Science History Publications, 1977).

[16] Todd Savitt, *Medicine and Slavery: The Disease and Health Care of Blacks in Antebellum Virginia* (Urbana: University of Illinois Press, 1978); Watson, *Black Folk Medicine*; and Bethel Ann Powers, "The Use of Orthodox and Black American Folk Medicine," in *Advances in Nursing Science* (April, 1982), p. 35.

American Indian Medicine (1970), Carolyn Niethammer's *Daughters of the Earth: The Lives and Legends of American Indian Women* (1977), and Virginia Scully's *A Treasury of American Indian Herbs: Their Lore and Their Use For Food, Drugs, and Medicine* (1980). These texts explain the cultural context for specific self-help medicines, and discuss the use of foods prepared and administered by women as medicine. As in black culture, magic is a recognized part of the doctoring and healing process. Helen Jaskowski's rich essay, "'My Heart Will Go Out': Healing Songs of Native American Women" (1981), describes North American Indian culture in which medicine women, women's medicine societies, and special ceremonials for women use poetry and song to cure disease and restore health to the individual and the community. This essay is valuable for its emphasis on women's role as healer as well as patient and the *communal* (vs. privatized) context in which self-help occurs.[17]

Self-help methods also flourish among Hispanic Americans, with much variety occurring among subgroups. As Alan Harwood points out in "The Hot-Cold Theory of Disease: Implications for Treatment of Puerto Rican Patients" (1971), foods, medicines, and illnesses are thought of as "hot" or "cold" by some Puerto Ricans and must be countered by opposites. (Thus "hot" foods cure "cold" diseases, and "cold" foods cure "hot.") Naturally, this requires that women as food-preparers know the list of ailments, foods, and appropriate "counter-combinations" of the two. Like many self-help methods, this approach is also used in conjunction with orthodox medicine.[18]

Among Mexican-Americans the use of *curanderos*, or folk healers, is prevalent. *Curanderos/as* are discussed in detail by J. Dennis Mull and Dorothy S. Mull in "Residents' Awareness of Folk Medicine Beliefs of Their Mexican-American Patients" (1981); E. Ferol Benavides' "The Saints Among the Saints: A Study of Curanderismo in Utah" (1973); and George Agogino and Bobbie Ferguson's "Curanderismo: The Folk

---

[17] Virgil Vogel, *American Indian Medicine* (Norman: University of Oklahoma Press, 1970); Carolyn Niethammer, *Daughters of the Earth: The Lives and Legends of American Indian Women* (New York: Collier Books of Macmillan Publishing Company, 1977); Virginia Scully, *A Treasury of American Indian Herbs: Their Lore and Their Use for Food, Drugs and Medicine* (New York: Crown Publishers, 1980); and Helen Jaskowski, "'My Heart Will Go Out': Healing Songs of Native American Women," *International Journal of Women's Studies* 4, no. 2 (1981): 118.

[18] Alan Harwood. "The Hot-Cold Theory of Disease: Implications for Treatment of Puerto Rican Patients," *Journal of the American Medical Association* 216, no. 7 (May 17, 1971): 1153.

Healer in the Spanish Community" (1983).[19] *Curanderos/as* are believed by their communities to be conduits for a deity's, or a spirit's, healing; they combine herbal remedies, prayer, and religious rituals that, while begun by the healer, are continued through domestic self-help.

Women play a central role in this system as providers and recipients. Further, female patients tend to be diagnosed with sex-role appropriate ailments such as fright ("susto") and shame. This makes it ironic that "This lore (or curing) is handed down from generation to generation, from mother to daughter."[20] Further research on women's role as *curanderas*, their generational teaching of one another, and the consequent reinforcement of sex roles is needed.

These ethnically diverse folk practices with their self-help components have a number of things in common: oral transmission, a world view congruent with the patient's, a belief in the supernatural (at times involving charms and magic), and either a "calling" to heal or apprenticed learning. Women supply the "prescriptions" within their homes through remedies, food preparation, or prayers; diagnosticians and patients are both women and men. Studies by physician-authors and/or historians address many of these factors, but others omit adequate discussion of gender issues and the supernatural. Does underestimating the importance of gender roles and magic in these systems distort their meaning and efficacy?

Just as ethnic and racial differences affect the type and nature of medicinal self-help, so does regional diversity. The nature and extent of self-help in pioneer or rural settings differs tremendously from that in an urban area. Madge Pickard and R. Carlyle Buley's *The Midwest Pioneer; His Ills, Cures, & Doctors* (1945–46) is considered a leading source on domestic medicine during the nineteenth century. It provides brief, nontechnical accounts of pioneer medicine in the Middle West. The authors trace ailments in different regions, people's explanations of disease origin, and pioneers' classifications of diseases. By providing testimonies of the sick, they meticulously chronicle the experiences of

---

[19] J. Dennis Mull and Dorothy S. Mull, "Residents' Awareness of Folk Medicine Beliefs of Their Mexican-American Patients," *Journal of Medical Education* 56 (1981): 520; E. Ferol Benavides, "The Saints Among the Saints: A Study of Curanderismo in Utah" *Utah History Quarterly* (Fall 1973): 373; and George Agogino and Bobbie Ferguson, "Curanderismo: The Folk Healer in the Spanish-Speaking Community," in *The Masterkey. Indian Lore History* (1983), pp. 101–6.

[20] Benavides, *Utah History Quarterly*, p. 381.

both illness and doctoring. This text has an invaluable seventeen-page bibliography as well.

As Phyllis M. Japp argues in "Pioneer Medicines: Doctors, Nostrums and Folk Cures" (1982), pioneers, by necessity or choice, diagnosed and treated their own health problems using purchased medicines or folk cures. Domestic medical manuals reinforced their belief that treating ordinary ills fell within the range of their abilities and that physicians should be distrusted, a theme also developed in Pickard and Buley's *The Midwest Pioneer* and elsewhere. Japp points out women's role as well, noting that "Housewives advised each other on medical matters," using treasured almanacs, family recipes, and word of mouth.[21] She discusses the communal value placed on health and the ability to work, which contrasts sharply with the late nineteenth-century dominant European-stock upper-middle class's tolerance for infirmity among women. The importance of health suggests at least one reason that nonwhites and rural people would use self-help for staying well.[22]

To research geographic perspectives, scholars are well advised to consult state and regional folklore journals. This entails crossing disciplinary bounds not previously traversed by historians of medicine, but ready for exploration nonetheless. Tom Waller and Gere Killion in "Georgia Folk Medicine" (1972) provide a list of self-help methods used for chronic and acute conditions. These cures reflect Indian, European, and African influences, and although it lacks analysis, the article recounts traditions worthy of historical study. No mention is made of women, yet one suspects it was the women who were administering the folk cures to their families. Oral histories would illuminate these practices.[23]

Patent Medicines and Women: The Literature

While the dominant theme of domestic medical guides between 1740 and 1860 was a challenge to professional expertise through the

---

[21] Phyllis M. Japp, "Pioneer Medicines: Doctors, Nostrums, and Folk Cures," *Journal of the West* (July 21, 1982): 19; and Madge Evelyn Pickard and R. Carlyle Buley, *The Midwest Pioneer; His Ills, Cures, & Doctors* (New York: Schuman, 1945).

[22] Bernard Herman, "Folk Medicinal Recipes in Nineteenth-Century Farm Journals," *Pennsylvania Folklife* 25, no. 4 (1976): 16; and D. Yoder, "Advertisements of Urban Healers," *Pennsylvania Folklife* 27, no. 3 (1978): 94.

[23] Tom Waller and Gere Killion, "Georgia Folk Medicine," *Southern Folklore Quarterly* (1972): 71. Also see, Gordon Wilson's two-part study, "Talismans and Magic in Folk Remedies in the Mammoth Cave Region," *Southern Folklore Quarterly* (1966): 192; "Swallow it or Rub It On: More Mammoth Cave Remedies," *Southern Folklore Quarterly* (1967): 296; and John Q. Anderson, ed., *Texas Folk Medicine: 1,333 Cures, Remedies, Preventives and Health Practices* (Austin: The Encino Press, 1970).

assertion that families could care for themselves, these texts also expanded the perimeters of medical involvement.[24] They created a climate favorable to later acceptance of professional authority.

Both Starr and Kett mark 1860 as a turning point in domestic medicine. Starr notes Americans' increasing ability to buy manufactured commodities due to an economic shift from household manufacturing to factory production as well as improved transportation, which lessened previously problematic indirect medical costs. Kett notes that "by 1860 patent medicines were serving many of the functions of domestic practitioners of colonial times."[25]

As in oral and written domestic medicine traditions, patent medicine promotions appealed to women as the family doctors. And yet, as numerous historians have documented, a distinct new group of chronically frail and infirm female patients (largely middle and upper-middle class, from dominant European cultural groups) elicited medical concern, illness-labelling, and therapeutics. These female sufferers were particularly targeted by purveyors of patent medicines, a fact noted by Pickard and Buley in "Nirvana in Bottles: Drugs and 'Patents'" in *The Midwest Pioneer*, which discusses the numerous medications for women's "nervous debility and female obstructions." The height of popularity for patent medicines, 1865 to 1900, is portrayed by most sources as a transitional era from home-doctoring and folk remedies to prescription drugs and professionalized medicine. This period spawned the "medicine show," which led in turn to questions about public gullibility and business ethics, and finally to governmental regulations.[26] Women's use and promotion of patent medicines is best understood within this cultural context.

One of the most important events of the period was Samuel H. Adams's 1905 serial exposé in *Collier's* and *The National Weekly* of what he called the "Great American Fraud"—nostrum medicine.[27] Adams's exposé alerted people to the dangers of self-diagnosis and patent medicine. It included a chapter on "Female Weakness" cures and further demonstrated women's particular vulnerability to the remedies, and

---

[24] Starr, *Social Transformation*, pp. 36–37.
[25] Kett, *Formation of the American Medical Profession*, p. 164.
[26] E. L. Smith, *Patent Medicine: The Golden Days of Quackery* (Lebanon, PA: Applied Arts Publishers, 1963); and Kay Deuner, *Patent Medicine Picture* (Tombstone, AZ: Tombstone Epitaph, 1968); and p. 4.
[27] Samuel Hopkins Adams, *The Great American Fraud* (Chicago: Press of the American Medical Association, P. F. Collier and Son, 1905).

eventually led to the 1906 Pure Food and Drug Act that controlled the labelling of patent medicines and their fraudulent claims. The Harrison Narcotic Act of 1915 regulated the sale of narcotics, their alcohol content, advertising, and fraudulent claims. It also banned narcotics in medications for children and the sale of abortifacients.[28] This era of regulation, 1906 to the 1950s, saw medical special interest groups and consumers turn towards the federal government to control the claims and distribution of patent medicines.

Among the best secondary sources focusing on the American use of self-dosage medicines is James Harvey Young's *The Toadstool Millionaires: A Social History of Patent Medicines in America Before Federal Regulation* (1961). Young's text and Kay Deuner's *Patent Medicine Picture* (1968) are valuable for the distinctions they draw between patent and proprietary medicines (the term "patent medicine," while a misnomer, is commonly used for "proprietary"). Young's work is especially useful, charting the history of proprietary medicines from the early 1700s—when patented brands, imported from England, appeared in the colonies—through the first production of nostrums during the Revolution, to the "big-scale patent medicine makers, (circa early 1800s) who blazed a merchandising trail."[29] Young also chronicles the development of retail druggists, the medicine shows of 1880 to 1900, and Adams's 1905 exposés, concluding with descriptions and accounts of the June 1906 Pure Food and Drug Act, after which "the concept of control over proprietary remedy promotion was firmly written into national policy."[30]

Many sources provide solid overviews of the popularity and tactics of the medicine shows.[31] Because of women's function as entertainers and consumers, such histories often pay attention to gender issues. As medicine-show entertainers (e.g., burlesque dancers or fortunetellers), women were used to entice a listening audience,[32] so that, as Young discusses in *Toadstool Millionaires*, (fraudulent) "cures" would be affected. Arrell M. Gibson's "Medicine Show" (1967), for example,

---

[28] James Harvey Young, *American Self-Dosage Medicine: An Historical Perspective* (Lawrence, KS: Coronado Press, 1974), p. 419.
[29] James Harvey Young, *The Toadstool Millionaires: A Social History of Patent Medicines in America Before Federal Regulation* (Princeton: Princeton University Press, 1961), p. 42.
[30] Young, *Toadstool Millionaires*, p. 244.
[31] Secondary literature focusing upon the hyperbole and persuasive skills of patent medicine hawkers include: E. L. Smith, *Patent Medicine*, and Japp, *Pioneer Medicines*.
[32] Arrell M. Gibson, "Medicine Show," *American West* (1967), p. 39.

argues that slow sales, competition from resourceful pioneer women who developed their own family remedies, and inroads from an emerging medical profession forced early drug peddlers to use entertainment to promote their medicines.[33] Even more important, sales pitches were often directed at sufferers of "women's diseases" and at women as the caretakers of family health.

Few sources discuss the relationship among women, infirmity, and patent medicines. Because it was part of the domestic self-help tradition, women's attraction to and use of patent medicines was not "new." What *was* new was the notion of infirmity and frailty among leisured women and the size of the competitive marketplace claiming relief for their ills. Young's "From Hooper to Hohensee" (1986) details colonists' use of pills for female ailments, and although he provides no analysis of the connection between gender, illness, and patent medicines, the chronicling of these early nostrums remains valuable.[34] David L. Dykstra, in "The Medical Profession and Patent Proprietary Medicine During the Nineteenth Century" (1955), also discusses early twentieth-century opponents of patent medicines, many of whom pointed to the dangers encountered by women nostrum-users.[35]

Two sources do provide exceptional analysis of the connection among patent medicines, gender, and infirmity. Samuel J. Thomas's "Nostrum Advertising and the Image of Woman as Invalid in Late Victorian America" (1982) argues that nostrum advertising mirrored and perhaps helped to sustain the stereotype of women as inherent invalids. Thomas notes the correlation between the increased use of nostrums and the rise of "consumption" among women, poor dietary

---

[33] Gibson, *American West*, pp. 34–39, 74–79. For information on the appeal of medicine shows see: Martin Kaufman, "'Step Right Up, Ladies and Gentlemen,' Patent Medicines in 19th-Century America," *American History Illustrated* 16, no. 5 (1981): 38–45; James Harvey Young, "From Hooper to Hohensee: Some Highlights of American Patent Medicine Promotion," *Journal of the American Medical Association* 204, no. 1 (April 1, 1968); L. A. Arata, "Nostalgia: The Medicine Show," *Journal of the Indiana State Medical Association* (June 1980): 353; and Elsie H. Booker and Curtis Booker, "Patent Medicines Before the Wiley Act of 1906," *North Carolina Folklore Journal* 18, no. 3 (1970): 130.

Interpretive sources also focus upon the advertising and marketing techniques which included the use of an Indian, who, to Europeans, represented all that was mystical, nobel, and trustworthy. See: Howard G. Wilcox, "Redskin Remedies: Contributions of the American Indian to Patent Medicines," *Michigan Medicine* (May 1974).

[34] Young, "From Hooper to Hohensee," *Journal of the American Medical Association*, p. 100.

[35] David L. Dykstra, "The Medical Profession and Patent Proprietary Medicine During the Nineteenth Century," *Bulletin of the History of Medicine* 29 (1955): 413.

habits, the stresses associated with the sexual biases of the day, and the idle, bored, and hypochondriacal aspects of leisured womanhood. Sarah Stage's *Female Complaints: Lydia Pinkham and the Business of Women's Medicine* (1979) provides the most comprehensive analysis of women and patent medicines. It is the sole book-length source focusing on a woman as the *producer* of nostrums as well as on women as consumers. Stage provides a thorough biography of Pinkham, intertwined with the success of her Vegetable Compound. The author views Pinkham's success in terms of the popular concern with women's health in the late nineteenth century, the ways the medical profession and patent medicine manufacturers defined and treated female complaints, and the emergence of national advertising and distribution markets. She avoids portraying women as hapless victims, arguing that women took patent medicines as an alternative to orthodox treatments they believed to be unsafe. Pinkham's advertising, Stage argues, played a key role in that it reflected women's popular discontent with professionalized medicine, especially gynecology. As Stage writes, "With the doctor suspect, self-dosing became a logical and inexpensive substitute."[36]

The demise of patent medicines through regulations (1892 to the 1950s) and the motives of competing interests are discussed by James Harvey Young in *American Self-Dosage Medicines: An Historical Perspective* (1974).[37] Young also charts the major legislative acts limiting patent medicines and the actions and reactions of competing interests (druggists, muckrakers, politicians, etc.). Although he foregrounds the social tensions and struggles among newly professionalized groups seeking to secure dominant status, Young's scholarship does not address gender issues. But it does suggest many related questions: were female muckraking journalists particularly drawn to this issue? Was regulation a "woman's issue" as well as a professional one? Was there any resistance, by women as consumers, to the regulations?

---

[36] Sarah Stage, *Female Complaints: Lydia Pinkham and the Business of Women's Medicine* (New York: W. W. Norton, 1979), p. 27; and Samuel J. Thomas, "Nostrum Advertising and the Image of Woman as Invalid in Late Victorian America," *Journal of American Culture* 5, no. 3 (Fall 1982): 104. Also see: Dorothea D. Reeves, "Come All for the Cure-All: Patent Medicine, Nineteenth-Century Bonanza," *Harvard Library Bulletin* 15 (1967): 253–72.

[37] James Harvey Young, *American Self-Dosage Medicines: An Historical Perspective* (Lawrence, KS: Coronado Press, 1974); Dykstra, *The Medical Profession and Patent Propriety*; and Bryan E. Boatman, "On American Nostrum Making and Quackery," *Journal of the Oklahoma State Medical Association* 75 (January 1982): 3.

Consumers at the turn of the century were urged to educate themselves as further protection against "dangerous and fraudulent remedies" that constituted an $80 million-a-year industry.[38] It is likely that much of this self-education fell to women as caretakers of their families. Thus the popular health journal, *Hygeia*, edited by Dr. Morris Fishbein, began in 1923 and was devoted to attacking patent medicines (along with cults and antivivisectionists) while educating the public. Four years later, Fishbein published *The New Medical Follies*, an exposé of the cults and quacks then rampant. Primary among them were beauty treatments, weight loss, and dietary fads, all three involving women as vulnerable subjects. In 1933 Arthur Kallet and F. J. Schlink published *100,000,000 Guinea Pigs: Dangers in Everyday Foods, Drugs and Cosmetics*. By 1937 it had been reprinted thirty-two times, signalling the public's enthusiastic reception. This text played a key role in rallying consumers and helped secure the passage of the 1938 Food, Drug and Cosmetic Act.[39]

Two secondary sources from the 1950s, James Cook's *Remedies and Racket: The Truth About Patent Medicines Today* (1958) and Stewart H. Holbrook's *The Golden Age of Quackery* (1959), are valuable for posing a question about people's capacity to medicate themselves. This question reflects the near-total reversal of cultural attitudes towards self-medication: by the 1950s, people were no longer their own doctors, but rather patients in the hands of trained experts.[40]

During this transition from self-doctoring to patient-recipient, the use of narcotics reached alarming proportions. David T. Courtwright in *Dark Paradise: Opiate Addiction in America before 1940* (1982) explores women's addiction to patent medicines and pure narcotics and details their devastating effects.[41] Studies like this one suggest that addiction might have had effects on debates over women's participation in other spheres—such as higher education. Work remains to be done on possi-

---

[38] Stewart H. Holbrook, *The Golden Age of Quackery* (New York: MacMillan, 1959), p. 12.

[39] Morris Fishbein, M.D., *The New Medical Follies: An Encyclopedia of Cultism and Quackery in the United States, with Essays on the Cult of Beauty, the Craze for Reduction, Rejuvenation, Eclecticism, Bread and Dietary Fads, Physical Therapy, and a Forecast as to the Physician of the Future* (New York: Boni and Liveright, 1927); and Arthur Kallet and F. J. Schlink, *100,000,000 Guinea Pigs: Dangers in Everyday Foods, Drugs and Cosmetics* (New York: Grosset and Dunlap, 1933; 32nd printing October 5, 1937).

[40] James Cook, *Remedies and Rackets: The Truth About Patent Medicines Today* (New York: W. W. Norton, 1958); and Stewart H. Holbrook, *The Golden Age of Quackery* (New York: Macmillan, 1959).

[41] David T. Courtwright, *Dark Paradise: Opiate Addiction in America Before 1940* (Cambridge: Harvard University Press, 1982).

ble connections between women's narcotics use and the movement for physical education for girls and women, as well as changes in family size or the frequency of divorce.

Questions about professionalism, autonomy, and gender are also suggested by work on women's relationship to patent medicine. Did the "modern woman" now turn to a privatized physician-patient relationship instead of patent medicines? Did the patent-medicine debate mask more profound questions of who should doctor women and the family? Who continued to use unorthodox nostrums *despite* their regulation, and why? Finally, since self-help medicines were originally created in the home *by* women, then "taken over" by proprietary salesmen, and later, by the pharmaceutical industry, what did this loss of female influence (circa 1860–1910) mean to women's ability to control their own and their families' health? These questions would benefit from oral histories taken from those familiar with self-doctorers between 1900 and 1940, the period of patent medicine's decline.

Since so few of them examine gender issues in any detail, it is not surprising that few sources adequately explore *why* the patent medicines were so popular among women. A notable exception is James Cassedy's excellent essay "Why Self Help? Americans Alone with Their Diseases, 1800–1850" (1984). This essay addresses all of self-help medicine and provides some insight into its appeal. Among those sources that discuss patent medicine exclusively, its popularity is attributed to a variety of causes. It was, among other things, a justifiable source of alcohol for women, it reinforced appropriate upper-middle-class sex roles that linked infirmity with femininity, and instilled in women a sense of bodily self-control. But as insightful as these theories are, further study is needed. Were these "elixirs of life" in the tradition of panacea cures fostered by sectarian medicine advocating self-doctoring? Were nostrum users also sectarians? In late nineteenth-century America, as mobility and isolation increased, it is possible that this type of self-doctoring provided a sense of continuity and control. In addition, concocting and administering remedies had long been (and continues to be) an identifiable part of women's care-taking role. Did the *purchase* of mass-produced nostrums signify an increasingly modern, class-distinct, and consumer-oriented adaptation to this expected role? Here, the roles of organizations like the Women's Christian Temperance Union and women's magazines of the period need further exploration. Sales records of nostrum manufacturers, testimonial letters written by women consumers, trade cards (with due caution taken for hyperbole), advertisements in women's magazines, excerpts from extant private paper collec-

tions, and case studies of addiction in turn-of-the-century medical journals would further illuminate these questions.

Another area ripe for exploration is the bottles themselves as historical sources. References to gender, ailment, region, and the invocation of
Indian women as "sage-healers" can be found on labels, embossments of
bottles, trade cards, and packing paper, as Leland May discusses in
"Collecting Patent Medicine Bottles" (1987), printed for antique collec-
tors and hobbyists. Likewise, the 1897 Sears, Roebuck Catalogue (1976)
contains a several-page spread of patent medicines, elixirs, capsules,
tinctures, pills, granules, etc., listed under the "Drug Department."
Alongside them are morphine-based products and hypodermic syringes
(also available for over-the-counter purchase before regulation). Catalogues like this reveal the accessibility of products, their contents, their
specific appeal to women by age and region, manufacturers' origins and
their claims, and relative affordability. Here, as elsewhere, gender analysis must be introduced by the scholar.[42]

SELF-HELP AND PATENT MEDICINES: THE MODERN ERA

With the reemergence of the self-help medicine movement, literature from the modern era, 1960 to the present, now asks "who is in
control of your health?" Here, considerable overlap occurs between
nonprescription drugs and self-help medicine. The hallmark of the contemporary self-help movement is the belief that the choice of systems,
practitioners, and methods is ours. As numerous scholars have noted,
the 1960s marked a turning point in the reemergence of medical self-
help which, in previous decades in the dominant culture, was suppressed
through legislation and a cultural preference for professionalism. As part
of a larger cultural questioning of authority and expertise, self-care in
health was revived as a social critique, emphasizing humaneness, cost,
efficiency, and effectiveness of professional medical care.[43] Very few
interpretive sources exist for this era, yet one primary document of
particular value places the material in a theoretical context: Lowell S.

---

[42] Leland May, "Collecting Patented Medicine Bottles," *Antiques and Collecting Hobbies* 91
(January 1987): 22; and Fred L. Israel, ed., 1897 *Sears Roebuck Catalogue* (New York:
Chelsea House, 1976).
[43] Alexander Schmidt, M.D., "Opening Remarks," *Self-Medication: the New Era . . . A
Symposium: Condensation of Papers and Discussions* (Washington, D.C.: Sponsored by the
Proprietary Association, 1980).

Levin's *Self-Care: Lay Initiatives in Health* (1975). Its varied approach and strong annotated bibliography help frame the material in a historical context.[44]

Many sources point out the link between feminism and self-help. In the 1970s the women's movement increased public consciousness about health by focusing attention on the quality of care received by women in a male-dominated medical care system. As a result, self-observation, self-examination, and women's clinics flourished. Demands for self-care increased because of women's dissatisfaction with biotechnical medicine, as well as better education, the availability of more technical information through the media, increased reliance on personal judgement, and greater isolation of individuals. Interesting parallels exist with an earlier historical epoch, as Regina Markell Morantz describes the 1850s in "Nineteenth-Century Health Reform and Women: A Program of Self-Help" (1977). Then, as in the 1970s, "health reform was one means by which many women articulated their feminism." Further, women gained self-control in a rapidly changing social environment, and it "offered to countless women a means of coping with an imprecise, undependable, and often hostile environment."[45] In both eras women's bonds with relatives and neighbors weakened, with reading materials offering a sense of commonality that helped bridge that gap. Of course, the eras have many differences, but the similarities reinforce the idea that there is a relationship between bodily self-care and personal and political emancipation.

Women's activism in the self-help movement fueled its development throughout modern society. A recent survey (1987) conducted by the American Board of Family Practice surmised that nearly half of the American population uses a medical reference book at home to help diagnose family health problems.[46] Further, in 1980 the Proprietary Association (manufacturers of over-the-counter [OTC] medications) estimated there were 500,000 mutual aid groups—ranging from Alcoholics Anonymous to an organization of parents with mentally-imparied

---

[44] Lowell S. Levin, *Self-Care: Lay Initiatives in Health* (New York: Prodist, 1979). This book is the publication of Proceedings of the First International Symposium on the Role of the Individual in Primary Health Care, Copenhagen, Denmark, 1975.

[45] Regina Markell Morantz, "Nineteenth-Century Health Reform and Women: A Program of Self-Help" in *Medicine Without Doctors*, ed. Guenter B. Risse, Ronald L. Numbers, and Judith Walzer Leavitt (New York: Science History Publications, 1977), pp. 73–93, specifically p. 81.

[46] "Heal Thyself?" *The Wall Street Journal*, October 22, 1987, p. 41. Respondents answered "Sometimes" 23%, "Frequently" 20%.

children—representing 15 million people. There is a mutual aid group representing nearly every disease category listed by the World Health Organization (WHO).[47] These groups are formed in answer to *gaps* in professional services,[48] and as supplements to some existing services. As a result of this burgeoning interest, since 1977 a self-care and personal health-enhancement market has developed. Self-care or fitness books account for 23% of the nonfiction hardcover bestsellers, generating $500 million in sales annually.[49] It would be interesting to investigate whether there were nineteenth-century equivalents of AA and similar self-help groups, and if so, what women's relationship to them was. And much remains to be asked about current "personal enhancement" literature, including who now constitutes an "expert."

An excellent interpretive source that puts these cultural and historical issues in perspective is Robert Crawford's essay, "Individual Responsibility and Health Politics in the 1970s" (1979). He focuses on the impetus from the women's movement, the overmedicalization of women's health, and the costs and promotion of good health. He credits these factors and "more individual responsibility for our own health" with the recent explosion of self-help medicine,[50] tracing Americans' shifting demands to include both affordable health care and prevention of disease. Self-help medicine, Crawford notes, addresses both of these needs. Future scholarship ought to trace the historical development of the notion of "individual responsibility" for health, an idea whose importance has been addressed in the field of medical ethics.

Like their predecessors Buchan and Gunn, a significant percentage of the present orthodox medical profession views limited self-medication as a vital component of health care.[51] Within medical circles, self-help is defined on a continuum that ranges from the proper use

---

[47] Lowell S. Levin, "Self-Medication: The Social Perspective," *Self-Medication: The New Era*, (Washington, D.C.: Proprietary Association, 1980), pp. 48–50.

[48] Lowell S. Levin, "Mutual Aid Groups: Annotated Bibliography," *Self-Medication: The New Era* (Washington, D.C.: Proprietary Association, 1980), pp. 135–40. The bibliography relies upon literature from the fields of social work, social science, nursing, mental health, and rehabilitation.

[49] Lori Andrews, "Take Good Care of Yourself: Health Care Is Coming Out of the Doctor's Office and into the Home," *Parents Magazine* (July 1984), p. 43. Andrews quoted John Fiorillo, President of the Health Strategy Group, within the article.

[50] Robert Crawford, "Individual Responsibility and Health Politics in the 1970s," in *Health Care in America: Essays in Social History*, eds. Susan Reverby and David Rosner, (Philadelphia: Temple University Press, 1979), p. 264.

[51] Alexander Schmidt, M.D., "Opening Remarks," *Self-Medication: The New Era* (Washington, D.C.: Proprietary Association, 1980).

of non-prescription medication for relief of symptoms and conditions not requiring professional attention[52] to near-total patient self-sufficiency. Most patient self-care, however, is encouraged with an eye towards supplementing rather than usurping the trained physician's role.

In fact, recent (1970s) studies by governmental agencies argue that consumer health education "must now be recognized as a top priority in the national commitment to health promotion."[53] Individual physicians also emerge as champions of limited patient self-care.[54] In this genre, Morris Fishbein's, *Modern Home Remedies and How to Use Them* (1966) argues the maximum protection provided by federal and state laws, along with a high level of consumer sophistication, makes self-treatment via OTC home remedies safe and practical. (Among remedies appropriate for home use, Fishbein includes aspirin, antacids, laxatives, vitamins, weight-control drugs, cough and cold remedies, etc.) He cautions, though, that "People should not, of course, attempt to treat themselves for any serious condition."[55] Other physicians and auxiliary health care professionals advocate "bibliotherapy": physician-recommended reading materials for a patient.[56] Given these limits, it would be interesting to ask whether medical personnel have ever argued for total patient *dis*engagement from orthodox medicine.

Many contemporary observers see the acceptance of self-help remedies as a sign of a shift in the physician-patient relationship: "We used to have the doctor-patient relationship. Now we have the provider-consumer relationship, an economic or bureaucratic model, not a professional one, offering many perspectives and options that were not there before."[57]

As in the heyday of patent medicines, consumer protection agencies and private organizations (e.g., the FDA, the Consumers' Union, etc.)

---

[52] Ibid.

[53] The studies by the Task Force on Health Promotion and Consumer Health Education, sponsored by the National Institutes of Health and the American College of Preventive Medicine, agree that since individual behavior and lifestyles are major factors in health status, consumer health education "must now be recognized as a top priority in the national commitment to health promotion." See Crawford, *Health Care in America; Essays*, p. 263.

[54] Yvonne Horn, "M.D. Turns Editor to Teach Medical Self Care," *American Medical News* (February 13, 1987), p. 33.

[55] Morris Fishbein, M.D., *Modern Home Remedies and How to Use Them* (New York: Doubleday, 1966), p. 11.

[56] Robert L. Edsall, et al., "An Antidote to Medical Misinformation," *Patient Care* 20 (February 15, 1986): 117.

[57] Levin, *Self Medication; The New Era*, p. 50; and William E. Blundeli, "When the Patient Takes Charge," *Wall Street Journal*, April 24, 1987.

have become the watchdogs of OTC medication and devices. Helpful sources on this topic are primary ones, since interpretive studies have not yet been written. Wallace F. Janssen's "The Gadget Quacks," which appeared in the *FDA Consumer* (1977), traces the "gadget quackery" that gained popularity in the 1930s to the 1950s. But it is also possible to read these gadgets as reflecting the consumer's opinion of what diseases and concerns were most in need of additional attention. This kind of focus on the consumer's perspective can be found in Warren Schaller and Charles Carroll's *Health Quackery and the Consumer* (1976), which analyzes the consumer's role in health maintenance—the focus of the Report of the President's Committee on Health Education in 1973. The authors argue that an informed and motivated consumer is the key to enhanced personal health care and to decreased consumer vulnerability to health quacks. Also oriented toward consumers is the much reprinted *Consumer Reports The Medicine Show: Some Plain Truths about Popular Remedies for Common Ailments* (1961), a guide to OTC drugs ranging from dandruff, anti-aging, and sun products to acne, mouth odor, and tooth decay treatments. This text seeks to dispel drug advertisers' misrepresentations.[58]

The Medicine Show anticipated the acknowledged watershed work in modern self-care literature: *Our Bodies, Ourselves*, originally published in 1971 by the Boston Women's Health Book Collective. This woman-centered guide emphasizes prevention, holistic health, the *sharing* of responsibility between patients and practitioners, and teaches women self-help techniques. It is a clear incursion into the professional domain of medicine, and has become a prototype for other texts, manuals, guides, and reference books on the health needs, risks, and status of women (and others) in America. The authors decry the "condescending, paternalistic, judgemental and non-informative" treatment they received from medical doctors.[59] The *New Our Bodies, Ourselves* (1984) is almost twice the length of the original and includes several new topics. "Health" is defined even more broadly in this new edition, and now includes every aspect of physical well-being and communal/global relationships. The text's goals are social and political as well as medical, strikingly similar

[58] Wallace F. Janssen, "The Gadget Quacks," *FDA Consumer* (February 1977), p. 5; Warren E. Schaller and Charles R. Carroll, *Health, Quackery and the Consumer* (Philadelphia: W. B. Saunders, 1976); and Consumer Reports eds., *The Medicine Show: Some Plain Truths About Popular Remedies for Common Ailments* (Mount Vernon, NY: Consumers Union, 1961).

[59] Boston Women's Health Book Collective, *Our Bodies, Ourselves: A Book By and For Women*, 2nd ed. (New York: Simon and Schuster, 1976), p. 11.

to nineteenth-century health reformers, who also defined health all-inclusively.

Like its nineteenth-century antecedents, *Our Bodies, Ourselves* created a new health-care genre and opened the floodgates for other books that dealt specifically with women's health.[60] Similar "know-your-body" texts address family health and contain subsections on women's health, usually organized according to the female life cycle.[61] Other books are aimed at children.[62] What is noteworthy about these texts is their early emphasis on self-sufficiency and consumer self-protection.

Women have also generated self-help literature warning one another of biased medical care[63] and unnecessary surgeries.[64] Texts by women also teach self-help techniques to other women *after* a hysterectomy or mastectomy.[65] It would be interesting to know whether there are historical precedents for these aspects of women-centered self-help.

In fact, the sea of self-help literature is so vast and the claims so all-inclusive that a 1988 *New York Times* article spoke of "Coping with Self-Help Books." Some of the claims, the article states, border on the

---

[60] Books addressing women include: Christine Ammer, *The A to Z of Women's Health: A Concise Encyclopedia* (New York: Facts on File, 1983); Emrika Padus, *The Women's Encyclopedia of Healing and Natural Healing* (Emmaus, PA: Rodale Press, 1981) [Padus is the senior editor of *Prevention Magazine*]; and Linda Holt and Melva Weber, *The American Medical Association Guide of Womancare* (New York: Random House, 1981). This text is jointly authorized by women doctors in conjunction with the AMA.

[61] Books addressing family health include: Mike Samuels, M.D. and Hal Bennett, *The Well Body Book* (New York: Random House, 1973); Tom Ferguson, *Medical Self-Care: Access to Health Tools* (New York: Summit Books of Simon and Schuster, 1980); and Donald M. Vickery, M.D. and James F. Fries, *Take Care of Yourself: A Consumer's Guide to Medical Care* (Reading, MA: Addison-Wesley, 1987).

[62] One of the best books available addressing children's health, written for children is: Linda Allison, *Blood and Guts: A Working Guide to Your Own Insides* (Boston: Little Brown and Co., 1976). Also see Ellen Austin, Julia Stone, and John C. Richards, *The Parents' Medical Manual* (Englewood Cliffs: Prentice Hall, 1978).

[63] Willie Pearson, Jr. and Maxine L. Clark, "The Mal(e) Treatment of American Women in Gynecology and Obstetrics," *International Journal of Women's Studies* 5, no. 4 (September–October, 1982): 348; Diane Scully, *Men Who Control Women's Health: The Miseducation of the Obstetrician-Gynecologist* (Boston: Houghton-Mifflin, 1980); and Christine Webb, *Feminist Practice in Women's Health Care* (New York: John Wiley and Sons, 1986).

[64] Mary E. Davis, "A Consumer's Guide to Hysterectomy," *Medical Self Care* (Summer 1983), p. 33; Paula Dranov, "Do You Need These Operations?" *Health* 18 (June 1986): 24; Amy Mereson, "Surgery Women Should Think About Twice," *McCalls* 114 (July 1987): 139; and Rachel Lynn Palmer and Sarah K. Greenberg, M.D., *Facts and Frauds in Woman's Hygiene* (New York: Vanguard Press, 1936).

[65] Susanne Morgan, *Coping With a Hysterectomy* (New York: Dial Press, 1982).

fantastic, and the therapies are often untested.[66] The author cautions that publishers produce what people expect: instant cure and success. He does not denounce the books' value, but cautions once again, "Consumer beware!"—a theme developed twenty years ago by James Harvey Young in *The Medical Messiahs: A Social History of Health Quackery in Twentieth-Century America* (1967).[67]

DIRECTIONS FOR FUTURE SCHOLARSHIP

Despite the increase in self-care manuals, however, few contemporary sources address the toll this insistence on greater health-care responsibilities will take on women. Women are already taxed with domestic and paying jobs, yet "self-help" often actually means "women's help." As Illona Kichbush of WHO points out, "adding the role of 'doctor' might be overwhelming."[68] The "cost of caring" for women needs further study and analysis, a task well begun by Hilary Graham in "Providers, Negotiators, and Mediators: Women as the Hidden Carers" (1985).[69]

In addition to self-help literature, home medical tests are presented by their proponents as useful for screening, diagnosing, and monitoring.[70] Studies show that women conduct breast self-examination and treat pregnancy-related health problems without doctors and medicines at a higher rate than other groups treat themselves.[71] This makes issues related to home-testing especially important for women, and their desirability for particular groups, such as older and poor women, remains to be studied.[72]

A sizeable number of Americans have revolted against orthodox

---

[66] Michael DeCourcy Hinds, "Coping with Self-Help Books," *New York Times* 137 (January 16, 1988): L33.

[67] James Harvey Young, *The Medical Messiahs: A Social History of Health Quackery in Twentieth-Century America* (Princeton: Princeton University Press, 1967).

[68] Lori Andrews, "Take Good Care of Yourself," *Parents Magazine*, (June 1934), p. 47. Illona Kichbush of the World Health Organization is quoted within this article.

[69] Hilary Graham, "Providers, Negotiators, and Mediators: Women as the Hidden Carers," in *Women, Health and Healing*, eds. Ellen Lewin and Virginia Olesen (New York: Tavistock, 1985).

[70] Keith Sehnert, M.D., "Medical Tests You Can Perform at Home," *Consumers Digest* (March–April 1987), p. 61; and Amy Mereson, "New At-Home Diagnoses: Over the Counter Detection Kits Offset Soaring Medical Costs," *Science Digest* (March 1985), p. 16.

[71] Charles Pergola, "New Insights On How the Public Practices Self-Medication," *American Druggist* (May 1984), p. 104.

[72] Sehnert, *Consumers Digest*; Pergola, *American Druggist*; Dixie Farley, "Do It Yourself Medical Testing," *FDA Consumer* (February 1986): 22; and Brent Filson, "Self-Testing Kits Replace House Calls," *Consumers Digest* (March–April 1985): 11, discuss the FDA's and Proprietary Association's watchdog postures on home medical tests.

medicine and have disengaged themselves from virtually all aspects of it. These people, too, rely on self-help or "holistic" medicine and "new" practitioners. A holistic approach defines health comprehensively, as the meshing of mind, spirit, and body within an environmental and cultural context.[73] Texts in this genre embrace therapies and theories as diverse as biofeedback, herbalism, dream, nutritional, and music therapy, homeopathy, manipulative therapies (osteopathy, Rolfing, chiropractic, etc.), Oriental therapies, and exercise/movement therapies.[74] In nineteenth-century America, many of these methods were considered sectarian, but more recently they have been redefined as holistic. Whether these therapies seek to complement or replace orthodox methods varies from group to group, although most see the differences between holistic and orthodox medicine as irreconcilable.

Given the apparent rise in self-treatment and alternative therapies, the response of contemporary physicians also needs analysis. Are they likely to form partnerships with their consumers/patients to improve the latter's satisfaction with biotechnical health care? If not, to what extent will educated middle- and upper-class people experience the same two-tiered health care that culturally distinct minorities have known, where herbalism or rituals are "prescribed" at home, insulin or pencillin at the physician's office?

The current self-help movement also raises larger theoretical and ethical questions. For example, what is the effect of the individualistic approach implicit in self-help medicine? Would communal and social responsibility for improved health be a more just and feasible approach? Can members of nondominant groups benefit from self-care as it is now conceptualized, if their housing, nutrition, education, and income are all substandard? Where does personal initiative end and societal responsibility begin, and how can the two be reconciled? Many of these questions have particular implications for women as well, raising issues about the way contemporary gender roles define not only the traditional health-care system, but the administration of self-care. For example, does

---

[73] Jack LaPrata, *Healing: The Coming Revolution in Holistic Medicine* (New York: McGraw-Hill, 1978), pp. 1–2.

[74] Leslie J. Kaslof, *Wholistic Dimensions in Healing: A Resource Guide* (Garden City, NY: Doubleday, 1978); Michael C. and Lynda J. Moore, *The Complete Book of Holistic Health* (Englewood Cliff, NJ: Prentice-Hall, 1983); and Mike Samuels, M.D. and Hal Zina Bennett, *Well Body, Well Earth: The Sierra Club Environmental Health Sourcebook* (San Francisco: Sierra Club, 1983), p. 229, which urges healing the planet as part of healing ourselves. See also, Brian Inglis and Ruth West, *The Alternative Health Guide* (New York: Alfred A. Knopf, 1983), which discusses herbal medicine, homeopathy, manipulative therapies, exercise/movement, etc.; see the Table of Contents.

modern self-help medicine necessitate a critique of traditional sex roles so that men might become co-equal carers of others?

The marketing of self-care products has also meant that the aged are targeted by the self-help mail-order business.[75] As income decreases, senior citizens and retirees look for less costly options to hospital care. Is self-help via mail-order remedies a desirable way to meet their needs? Is self-care a reasonable goal for the aged? Can history illuminate these questions for us?

The role of contemporary women physicians needs further study. Do they appraise health more comprehensively and communicate more sympathetically with patients? Early studies indicate this is so.[76] Does this mean they might be better "teachers" of self-help than male physicians? If so, what are the implications of this?

How does the definition of self-help vary cross-culturally? In ethnic communities it has a group appearance, while in dominant European cultural groups it has developed as a set of tasks done in isolation. What does group support lend to the healing process?

The history of the numerous disease-specific self-help groups needs serious study by trained scholars. Are women-only groups (focused around mastectomy, menopause, pregnancy, hysterectomy, etc.) organized differently than groups like Alcoholics Anonymous? Is there an efficacious difference between communal and individualist approaches?

Finally, is our present obsession with wellness a manifestation of larger "social insecurities," as historians suggest might be the case with nineteenth-century analogies? Is our emphasis on a seemingly limitless level of health and productivity emblematic of desirable cultural values? What has happened, over time, to those who are overweight, aged, handicapped, mentally impaired, or defective at birth? Most of the contemporary sources consulted presume that physical near-perfectability *is* possible, desirable, and attainable. Is that a reasonable standard? How does our cultural emphasis on wellness through self-help affect our ability to cope with terminal illness, old age, and death? How have we responded—and how will we respond—as a community to those women and men who "fall short" of this ideal of self-improvement through healthful regimens?

---

[75] Arnold Fishman, "The Health Products Market," *Direct Marketing* 49 (April 1987): 80.

[76] Carol S. Weisman and Martha Ann Teitelbaum, "Physician Gender and the Physician-Patient Relationship: Recent Evidence and Relevant Questions," *Social Science and Medicine* 20, no. 11 (Great Britain, 1985): 1119–27.

13

CHARISMATIC WOMEN AND HEALTH: MARY BAKER EDDY, ELLEN G. WHITE, AND AIMEE SEMPLE MCPHERSON

Jonathan M. Butler and Rennie B. Schoepflin

I. COMPARISONS AND CONTRASTS

The three women in this study were "unorthodox" with respect to both religion and medicine. None of them found easy acceptance within traditional religious establishments and, therefore, all three assumed charismatic roles within movements of their own making. Moreover, their self-made religions were each distinguished by a health emphasis that diverged from contemporary medicine. While marginal figures in relation to both religious and medical communities of their times, these three women came to occupy a central place in the spiritual and physical lives of vast numbers of their adherents. They also left literary and institutional legacies that continue to exert, to varying degrees, a cultural impact wider than their own circle of believers. Through the founding of three distinctly American denominations—the Christian Scientists, the Seventh-day Adventists, and the International Church of the Foursquare Gospel—Mary Baker Eddy, Ellen G. White, and Aimee Semple McPherson, respectively, transformed a position of weakness into one of inordinate strength and influence.[1]

---

[1] For a cross-cultural study by a social anthropologist that explores the interrelationship between charisma, women, illness, and healing, see I.M. Lewis, *Ecstatic Religion: An Anthropological Study of Spirit Possession and Shamanism* (New York: Penguin Books, 1971).

The notion that they lifted themselves from weakness to strength lends itself to something of a double entendre. For each of their religious systems integrated health ideas and practices designed to restore physical vigor and well-being in others. These women placed their charismatic imprimatur on a particular health reform or healing tradition. Eddy shifted from homeopathy, with its principle of "like curing like" and its use of diluted doses of medicine, to embrace a style of mind cure built on her distinctive understanding of the mind-body relationship and her confidence that she had recovered the healing techniques of Jesus. White, on the other hand, saw God's healing accomplished through hydropathy, or the "water cure." Spurning the evils of drugs and lauding the benefits of water and other natural remedies, she called for a twice-a-day dietary regimen of fruits, grains, nuts, and vegetables. For both these women, their religious sects had incorporated key elements of medical sects of their times. However, McPherson, as an evangelistic healer, drew upon none of the "science" of the health reformer. Her Pentecostal tradition traced itself to eighteenth-century German Pietism, which claimed that New Testament miracles had not ceased with the end of the apostolic age. Believers could expect physical healing as surely as they looked for spiritual salvation. Thus, along with "speaking in tongues," divine healing identified the Pentecostals.[2]

An historiographical survey of the varied emphases on health of these three charismatic women provides an important glimpse into the longstanding interrelationship of religion, women, and health. Their biographers have touched upon issues of importance in this area to recent social and cultural historians, and a comparative look at their lives renders their insights all the more revealing. Students of these women have looked into their inner biographies, for example, where illness and vocation intertwine.[3] They also have examined the way in which these figures projected their health views and practices not only on their

---

[2] For an overview of the three traditions of health reform or healing embodied in these three women, see the following three essays: Rennie B. Schoepflin, "The Christian Science Tradition," in *Caring and Curing: Health and Medicine in the Western Religious Traditions*, ed. Ronald L. Numbers and Darrel W. Amundsen (New York: Macmillan Publishing Company, 1986), pp. 421-46; Ronald L. Numbers and David R. Larson, "The Adventist Tradition," in *Ibid.*, pp. 447-67; Grant Wacker, "The Pentecostal Tradition," in *Ibid.*, pp. 514-38.

[3] Biographers have often concerned themselves with the ways in which ill health influences individuals. George Pickering deals with illness in the lives of several nineteenth-century figures, including Florence Nightingale, Elizabeth Barrett Browning, and Eddy. See his *Creative Malady* (New York: Oxford University Press, 1974).

immediate religious communities but on generations of believers that have followed. Naturally, coming to terms with what is known about these women exposes pockets of misinterpretation and lack of information about their lives as well.

Eddy (1821-1910) gave birth to Christian Science when, with her spontaneous recovery from a severe injury, she "discovered" that reality is wholly spiritual and evil a mere illusion. After nearly a decade of teaching, healing, and writing, she published the first edition of *Science and Health* (1875), her textbook on mind healing. She then chartered the Massachusetts Metaphysical College in 1881 to train practitioners in her system of Christian Science healing. But her movement grew slowly until, in 1892, she established a central church organization in Boston identified as the Mother Church. Six years later she founded the Christian Science Publishing Society which advanced worldwide evangelism by way of the printed word, including notably *The Christian Science Monitor* (1908). In the last two decades of her life, her church's membership exploded nearly sevenfold to exceed 55,000. Now, an undisclosed number of Christian Scientists meet in about 3,000 local churches throughout the world, with the vast majority of them in the United States, Great Britain, and West Germany. While they remain a small, distinctive group, their system of thought resonates among more popular manifestations of mind cure, New Thought and positive thinking in the wider culture.[4]

White (1827-1915) overcame both an invalid childhood and a crisis in faith over William Miller's failed prophecies on the world's end to

---

[4] For a fairly reliable introduction to Christian Science during Mary Baker Eddy's lifetime, see nonmember Norman Beasley's *The Cross and the Crown: The History of Christian Science* (New York: Duell, Sloan and Pearce, 1952); Beasley's *The Continuing Spirit: The Story of Christian Science Since 1910* (New York: Duell, Sloan and Pearce, 1956) traced the story to the mid-twentieth century. The two most important Christian Science historians studied their tradition within the context of American religious and cultural history, in Stephen Gottschalk's *The Emergence of Christian Science in American Religious Life* (Berkeley: University of California Press, 1973), and Robert Peel's, *Christian Science: Its Encounter with American Culture* (New York: Henry Holt and Company, 1958). The best work on Eddy and Christian Science during her lifetime is Peel's three-volume biography, *Mary Baker Eddy* (New York: Holt, Rinehart, Winston, 1966-1977). Charles S. Braden imposed scholarly order on the chaos of America's many mind-healing sects in *Spirits in Rebellion: The Rise and Development of New Thought* (Dallas: Southern Methodist University Press, 1963); Donald Meyer interpreted Christian Science and mind cure in terms of pop psychology in his influential *The Positive Thinkers: A Study of the American Quest for Health, Wealth and Personal Power from Mary Baker Eddy to Norman Vincent Peale* (New York: Doubleday, 1965; reissued under a slightly revised title in 1980).

cofound the Seventh-day Adventist church in 1863 with her husband, James White. The Victorian couple assumed complementary roles in the movement, with Ellen a visionary, exhorter, and devotional writer and her husband an organizer, entrepreneur, and theologian. Drawing upon a series of spectacular public visions, the prophet produced a flood of letters, pamphlets, and books which her husband published with a steam press the impoverished couple acquired in the mid-1850s. After a number of severe illnesses to herself and her family, White received a vision in 1863 that Adventists should give up meat, alcohol, tobacco, tea, and coffee, shun drug-dispensing doctors and rely instead on natural remedies. She then urged the establishment in 1866 of the Western Health Reform Institute in Battle Creek, followed by a medical school, the College of Medical Evangelists (now Loma Linda University), in southern California. Through her travels and her extensive writings on a whole range of Christian topics, White inspired her church's world missionary outreach enhanced by an Adventist network of schools, sanitariums, and health food factories. As a result, Seventh-day Adventists have grown from seventy-five thousand members in 1900 to a church of over five million today (with roughly 85% of them ouside the United States). In contrast to the Christian Scientists, however, Adventists seem less known than their numbers warrant.[5]

---

[5] While there is not yet a standard history of Seventh-day Adventists, a concise and reliable introduction to the movement may be found in a collection of essays by Gary Land, ed., *Adventism in America: A History* (Grand Rapids, MI: William B. Eerdmans Publishing Company, 1986); Adventist history is surveyed as well in a college-level textbook by Richard W. Schwarz, *Light Bearers to the Remnant* (Mountain View, CA: Pacific Press Publishing Association, 1979); for an interpretive look at Adventism, past and present, see Malcolm Bull and Keith Lockhart, *Seeking a Sanctuary: Seventh-day Adventism and the American Dream* (New York: Harper & Row, 1989); a valuable reference work, which contains numerous historical sketches of individuals and institutions, beliefs and practices of the denomination, is Don F. Neufeld, ed., *Seventh-day Adventist Encyclopedia*, rev. ed. (Washington, D.C.: Review and Herald Publishing Association, 1976); for a brief historical summary of the movement, see Mircea Eliade, ed., *The Encyclopedia of Religion* (New York: Macmillan Publishing Company, 1987), s.v. "Seventh-day Adventism," by Ronald L. Numbers and Jonathan M. Butler. Like Seventh-day Adventists as a whole, Ellen White has been somewhat neglected by historians. This trend began to change with a critical study of her as a health reformer in Ronald L. Numbers, *Prophetess of Health: A Study of Ellen G. White* (New York: Harper & Row, 1976); Ronald D. Graybill explored her domestic life as a wife and mother as it related to her prophetic career in "The Power of Prophecy: Ellen G. White and the Women Religious Founders of the Nineteenth Century" (Ph.D. dissertation, Johns Hopkins University, 1983); for a wealth of information on White, albeit uncritically slanted, see the six-volume official biography by her grandson Arthur L. White, *Ellen G. White* (Washington, D.C.: Review and Herald Publishing Association, 1981-86).

McPherson (1890-1944) overcame personal tragedies and conflicts, scandals and lawsuits to found the International Church of the Four-square Gospel. After the death of her beloved first husband, a Pentecostal missionary to China named Robert Semple, she launched her own career as a Pentecostal evangelist and healer. In 1917 she established a periodical, *The Bridal Call*, by which she maintained a continuous bond with her followers and on which she later based her national organization. After several years of transcontinental evangelistic campaigns, she settled in Los Angeles. By January 1, 1923, she opened the Angeles Temple, with a seating capacity of 5,000, and exposed herself to a much wider public. But both her resulting celebrity and notoriety should not detract from her impressive institutional accomplishments. Her Foursquare Gospel empire included a radio station, an Echo Park Evangelistic Association for the publication of magazines and books, as well as L.I.F.E. Bible Colleges, whose graduates served as ordained ministers, evangelists, and missionaries of her Foursquare Gospel message. The "foursquare" in McPherson's message represented the four elements of Pentecostal belief in a Jesus who saves, baptizes, heals, and comes again. Today the Foursquare Gospel church ranks as one of the three or four most distinguished branches of the Pentecostal or Holiness churches, with a world membership of about one-and-a-half million (with less than 15% in the United States and most in Latin America).[6]

---

[6] McPherson deserves better in the way of a biography than she has gotten. The most thorough study of her, albeit limited by its exercise in iconoclasm, is the double biography of both McPherson and her mother Ma Kennedy by Lately Thomas, *Storming Heaven: The Lives and Turmoils of Minnie Kennedy and Aimee Semple McPherson* (New York: William Morrow and Company, 1970); the same author investigated the most scandalous event of her career in *The Vanishing Evangelist: The Aimee Semple McPherson Kidnaping Affair* (New York: Viking Press, 1959); the vantage point of the two books is evident from the fact that "Lately Thomas," itself a pseudonym, dedicated *Storming Heaven* to Faith and Fable, and *The Vanishing Evangelist* to Folly. A somewhat more sympathetic slant on the alleged kidnaping may be found in Nancy Barr Mavity, *Sister Aimee* (Garden City, NY: Doubleday, Doran & Co., 1931); a popular study of her, but tantamount to historical fiction, is that of Robert Bahr, *Least of All Saints: The Story of Aimee Semple McPherson* (Englewood Cliffs, NJ: Prentice-Hall, 1979); the best overview of McPherson's life, however, which might well serve as the abstract for a balanced biography, is that of William G. McLoughlin, Jr., "Aimee Semple McPherson: 'Your Sister in the King's Glad Service,'" *Journal of Popular Religion* 1 (1967): 193-217; for brief biographical and historical sketches on her and her church, see Stanley M. Burgess and Gary B. McGee, eds., *Dictionary of Pentecostal and Charismatic Movements* (Grand Rapids, MI: Zondervan Publishing House, 1988), s.v. "McPherson, Aimee Semple," and "International Church of the Foursquare Gospel (ICFG)," both by Cecil M. Robeck, Jr.; the same author discusses McPherson in Robeck, "The Use of Biography in Pentecostal Historiography," *Pneuma: The Journal of the Society for Pentecostal Studies* 8 (1976): 77-80.

Noting that Eddy, White, and McPherson were all women who founded sects with a health emphasis suggests only the barest introduction to the profound parallels between them. Even the briefest of summaries invites further reflection. In Eddy's and White's nineteenth century, but scarcely less so in McPherson's 1920s and 1930s, the options for talented, ambitious women outside the home were conspicuously curtailed. By being born as late as 1890, McPherson enjoyed some advantages over the other two women, but even she was 30 years old before the nineteenth century, in a cultural sense, had ended. At any rate, whatever social advances were made by women as a whole from the nineteenth through the first half of the twentieth centuries, these three women in particular form case studies of disenfranchisement. Like so many of their sisters, they were disenfranchised in a number of ways. Society offered them confinement in the home. The churches relegated them to the pew. Medicine wanted them as no more than patients. But each of these women remarkably overcame such social and cultural obstacles. If preordained to oversee the home, they would extend their self-made church-homes to "mother" vast families of followers. If denied a formal place among mostly male clergy, they would claim more direct access to the divine as charismatic women. And if they could not practice orthodox medicine as taught in regular medical schools, they would embrace the health reform or heterodox healing available to them.[7]

Both their ill health and poor educations restricted their opportunities in society. None of them ever seemed to enjoy lasting good health. For much of their childhoods, Eddy and White were virtually invalids. Religious anxiety and physical sickness prevented Eddy from obtaining any more than a smattering of formal education, although she did receive some tutoring from her oldest brother. White likewise knew a spiritually troubled childhood but it was her physical disabilities which limited her to about three grades of schooling. Neither ill as a child nor undereducated like Eddy or White, McPherson managed to reach high school but never completed it. All three women suffered severe physical and psy-

[7] For a general introduction to the topic of women and religion within the context of culture and society, see Barbara Welter, *Dimity Convictions: The American Woman in the Nineteenth Century* (Athens, OH: Ohio University Press, 1976), esp. Chapter 6, "The Feminization of American Religion: 1800-1860"; Nancy F. Cott, *The Bonds of Womanhood: "Woman's Sphere" in New England, 1780-1835* (New Haven: Yale University Press, 1977); and Ann Douglas, *The Feminization of American Culture* (New York: Alfred A. Knopf, 1977).

chological problems while in the throes of vocational conflict. Eddy's fall and serious head injury preceded her discovery of Christian Science. After years in a childhood sickbed following a traumatic head injury of her own, White resisted the call to prophesy. Questioning its divine origin, she was struck dumb for twenty-four hours. McPherson, too, resisted what she felt sure was a divine call and as a result experienced a nervous breakdown. Moreover, as they embarked on their religious careers, all three women claimed their health improved. In fact, however, they remained chronically ill as adults. Like so many Victorian women, Eddy and White complained openly of health problems throughout their lives, and yet both lived into their late eighties. McPherson, on the other hand, seemed healthier but died at only 54. While founders of health-conscious sects, their own illnesses to some extent belied their health views. Yet without their ill health they might never have become so preoccupied with the health of others. The irony of health reformers or healers who were nagged by personal illnesses is like later psychiatrists with their own psychological problems. T.S. Eliot's reference to the latter as "wounded surgeons" might apply as well to the women in this study.[8]

If society offered little promise to them outside the home, none of these women fulfilled conventional ideals of marriage and domesticity either. Eddy's first husband, George Glover, a successful builder in South Carolina, died after seven months of marriage, leaving her pregnant. In deep depression and unable to care for her young son, she left him permanently with his nurse and her husband in order to pursue a literary career. She then married a ne'er-do-well dentist, Daniel Patterson, who soon deserted her. Nearly twenty-five years later, having established her own church, she married Asa Gilbert Eddy, a converted sewing machine salesman, who vied for no share of her church leadership.

In her late teens, Ellen Harmon, as a young visionary, married twenty-five-year-old James White, an erstwhile Millerite evangelist and

8 For a brief comparative sketch of Eddy and White that covers their health and education, see Ronald L. Numbers and Rennie B. Schoepflin, "Ministries of Healing: Mary Baker Eddy, Ellen G. White, and the Religion of Health," in *Women and Health in America: Historical Readings*, ed. Judith Walzer Leavitt (Madison: University of Wisconsin Press, 1984): 376-89. Lately Thomas thoroughly discusses McPherson's illnesses and her educational level in *Storming Heaven*, esp. pp. 2-37. Donald Meyer points up the irony of Victorian women who complained about health problems and nevertheless lived so long in *The Positive Thinkers* (New York: Doubleday, 1965), p. 30; T.S. Eliot's provocative term "wounded surgeons" is cited in Lewis, *Ecstatic Religion*, p. 184.

school teacher. He became her manager, editor, and publisher. But their combined efforts in nurturing a fledgling Adventist movement allowed little time for the care of a growing family. As a result, the first two of their four sons were left for several years in the care of others. For much of their marriage, however, Ellen assumed a subordinate role of wife and mother while her husband nearly eclipsed her as a church leader. The balance of power then tipped in her favor toward the end of James's life, causing considerable marital strife between the strong-willed twosome. But after James's death in 1881, White blossomed as a church matriarch.

McPherson's three marriages each represented a different phase of her career. Her first and only happy marriage, to Robert Semple, came after her conversion to his Pentecostal faith. Her second marriage, to Harold McPherson, a wholesale grocery businessman, was a casualty of her itinerant evangelistic career. Her last husband, David Hutton, a choral singer, refused to be "married to Angelus Temple." McPherson saw mixed results not only as a wife but as a mother. While her son Rolf accepted her mantle of leadership, her daughter Roberta grew permanently estranged from her.[9]

While denied access to the corridors of real power in society, and at the same time frustrated by the more vicarious influence of homemakers, these women created their own subcultures over which they exercised a blend of raw political power and motherly nurture. Their titles implied no more than their nurturing side. Eddy was designated Mother by Christian Scientists. And although White was Sister White to Seventh-day Adventists, as a widow she assumed the more expansive role of her church's mother. McPherson, for her part, approved the diminutive appellation of Sister Aimee. But notwithstanding their homely labels, all three women came to dominate highly authoritarian religious organizations which predicated membership on personal loyalty to them. This is not to say there could never be serious challenges to their authority. In 1888 discontent and disaffection decimated Christian Science leadership and reduced its membership by one-third, but Eddy radically restructured the church and its publications under her control. In the same year, doctrinal disputes pervaded Adventist leadership, and by 1891

---

[9] For the domestic side of these women, Eddy's marriages are discussed in Peel, *Mary Baker Eddy*, 1, pp. 66-70, 109-12, 140-45, 174-87, 200-203; 2:18-23, 63-75; White's relationship to her husband is analyzed in Ron Graybill, "The Power of Prophecy," pp. 25-53; Lately Thomas provides the easiest access to McPherson's marriages in *Storming Heaven*, pp. 10-15, 36-37, 205-18, 225-46, 255-74, 344-45.

White had taken refuge in Australia, where she remained for a decade. But in a triumphal return in 1901 she oversaw a recasting of the church, both doctrinally and organizationally, in her image. McPherson walked away from her newly built empire in 1926 by apparently staging her own "kidnaping." She had disappeared off a California beach, apparently drowned, but turned up a month later in Mexico with the story that she had been kidnaped. This prompted rumors of an affair between McPherson and a former employee, and criminal charges against her for obstruction of justice and suborning perjury. But despite the scandal, she returned to her church's headquarters to battle for absolute control of Angelus Temple against her own mother, who felt betrayed by her daughter's scandal. By any standard, Eddy, White, and McPherson successfully positioned themselves as the matriarchs of important American sects. But their achievement cannot be construed as an unequivocal expression of feminism, unless qualified as domestic feminism. They did less to challenge a patriarchal society than to parlay the often feminine preoccupation with health care into an enduring social and religious legacy.[10]

Despite the obvious historical importance of these three religious founders, however, their place among historians is not entirely secure. At best the historiography on Eddy, White, and McPherson is uneven. In terms of sheer volume of historical work on them, Eddy has prompted by far the most, with White running a distant but respectable second, and McPherson a rather poor third. Much of this history, especially in the case of Eddy and White, had been written by insiders to their religious traditions. This poses a special problem for the critical readers of authorized biographies who hope to benefit from the often considerable wealth of information therein without falling prey to the bias, half-truths, and blatant untruths which may accompany apologetics. Among religious biographers, the fact that there are insiders implies there are outsiders as well. The very insularity of a religious tradition which leads to the canonization of its founder at the same time can provoke an

---

[10] On Eddy see Peel, *Mary Baker Eddy*, volumes 1 and 2; for White see, in addition to his six-volume biography, Arthur L. White's, *Ellen G. White: Messenger to the Remnant*, rev. ed. (Washington, D.C.: Review and Herald Publishing Association, 1969); Thomas fills in this aspect of McPherson's story in his *Storming Heaven* and *Vanishing Evangelist*. More general approaches to gender and culture, which provide a background for discussion of these three religious figures, include Mary Kelley, *Private Woman, Public Stage: Literary Domesticity in Nineteenth-Century America* (New York: Oxford University Press, 1984) and Carroll Smith-Rosenberg, *Disorderly Conduct: Visions of Gender in Victorian America* (New York: Oxford University Press, 1985).

iconoclasm either within or beyond the community. History-writing on Eddy and White especially has been marked by polarization between insiders and outsiders.[11] It has not helped that the private papers of both prophets are housed in closed archives, with Eddy's materials only selectively penetrable to the secular historian while the White documents are becoming somewhat more accessible. Mcpherson, on the other hand, who lived out even the most personal and sordid aspects of her life on the front pages of the nation's newspapers, left a relatively modest collection of family papers. As an historical subject, then, she has been generous from the outset, but by now seems to have given away all her best secrets. Taking the three women together, however, plenty of important historical analysis remains to be done, beyond a voyeur's glimpse of the curious parallels between them. For in the ways their lives and careers both compare and diverge, Eddy, White, and McPherson still have much to reveal on the interplay of women, health, and religion.[12]

II. MARY BAKER EDDY

From Mark Twain's contemptuous reflections of 1907 and Georgine Milmine's serial exposé in McLure's Magazine (1907-08) to the rudimentary psychohistory of Edwin Franden Dakin's Mrs. Eddy: The Biography of a Virginal Mind (1929), many authors interested in Christian Science have allowed the looming presence of Mary Baker Eddy to dominate their work.[13] Beyond their often unflattering accounts of the founder, however, these early critics staked out much of the terrain

---

[11] For the best illustrations of the whole spectrum of historical perspectives on the three founders, Robert Peel's Mary Baker Eddy was an insider's view, Ronald Numbers's Prophetess of Health was a work on White by an insider in transit to the outside, and Lately Thomas's Storming Heaven looked in on McPherson from the outside.

[12] Of these three women, only Eddy and White have invited enough historical discussion to warrant historiographical essays. Some of the literature on Eddy is reviewed in Raymond J. Cunningham, "Christian Science and Mind Cure in America: A Review Article," Journal of the History of the Behavioral Sciences 11 (1975): 299-305; the best introduction to the historical debate on White may be found in Donald R. McAdams, "Shifting Views of Inspiration: Ellen G. White Studies in the 1970s," Spectrum 10 (March 1980): 27-41.

[13] Mark Twain, Christian Science (New York: Harper and Bros., 1907); Milmine's McClure's articles, vol. 28, no. 2 (December 1906) to vol. 31, no. 2 (June 1908), reappeared as The Life of Mary G. Baker Eddy and the History of Christian Science (New York: Doubleday, Page & Company, 1909): Edwin Franden Dakin, Mrs. Eddy: The Biography of a Virginal Mind (New York: Charles Scribner's Sons, 1929).

mined by future historians and social scientists. Milmine and her sub-sequent editors (including Willa Cather) probed Eddy's intellectual sources, described her eccentric behavior, documented the often conten-tious nature of her flock, and wryly noted the material well-being of many of her idealist followers.[14]

Often as an alternative to Christian Scientists' simple trust in Eddy's divine inspiration, scholars before and after Dakin have found them-selves drawn to a variety of psychological and medical models to under-stand her personality.[15] In his classic biography Dakin refused the label of saint or sinner, choosing instead human terms and psychiatric models to paint a picture of "her glamorous rise from the lot of a simple country girl to a position of unique eminence and wealth."[16] Dakin wrote of Eddy's delusions of grandeur and persecution, bouts of hysteria, and sexual tensions, and highlighted the numerous physical and mental illnesses that plagued her throughout her life.[17] Fifty years later, Julius Silberger, Jr., a psychoanalyst in private practice, looked more systemati-cally and with keener insight into Eddy's struggles with the conflicting urges that manifested themselves in physical symptoms, ambivalent feel-ings about men, and troublesome nightmares.[18] Eschewing medical jar-gon and aware that society and culture may be as important as the mind in understanding a person, Silberger concluded in his generous psycho-biography that Eddy "was able to exemplify in her own personality the

---

[14] Many of these themes were repeated and expanded in Ernest S. Bates and John V. Dittemore, *Mary Baker Eddy, The Truth and the Tradition* (New York: A. A. Knopf, 1932).

[15] Authors before and after Dakin who have examined the mind of Eddy include Stefan Zweig, *Mental Healers: Anton Mesmer, Mary Baker Eddy, Sigmund Freud* (Garden City, NY: Garden City Publishing Co., 1932); Gail Thain Parker, "Mary Baker Eddy: New Thought Parodied," chapter in *Mind Cure in New England: From the Civil War to World War I* (Hanover, NH: University Press of New England, 1973), pp. 109-29; George Pickering, *Creative Malady: Illness in the Lives and Minds of Charles Darwin, Florence Nightingale, Mary Baker Eddy, Sigmund Freud, Marcel Proust, Elizabeth Barrett Browning* (London: George Allen and Unwin, 1974); F. E. Kenyon, "Mary Baker Eddy, Founder of Christian Science: The Sublime Hysteric," *History of Medicine* (London) 6 (Autumn-Winter 1975): 29-46; John K. Maniha and Barbara B. Maniha, "A Comparison of Psychohistorical Differences Among Some Female Religious and Secular Leaders," *The Journal of Psychohistory* 5 (1978): 523-49; Janice Klein, "Ann Lee and Mary Baker Eddy: The Parenting of New Religions," *The Journal of Psychohistory* 6 (1979): 361-75.

[16] Edwin Franden Dakin, *Mrs. Eddy: The Biography of a Virginal Mind* (New York: Blue Ribbon Books, 1930), p. vii.

[17] For examples see Ibid., pp. 35, 147, 171, 314-16.

[18] Julius Silberger, Jr., *Mary Baker Eddy: An Interpretive Biography of the Founder of Christian Science* (Boston: Little, Brown and Company, 1980).

contradictions that characterized her era [such as, "proper" public roles for women, medical efficacy and contradictory definitions of disease, and rural-urban tensions] and to utilize those very contradictions in building her own success."[19]

In contrast to the work of such critics, Christian Science hagiographers created triumphalist accounts of Eddy and her movement that drew unquestioningly from Eddy's own writings and reminiscences, including her 1891 autobiography, *Retrospection and Introspection*.[20] Prototypical of such efforts was Sibyl Wilbur's uncritical and often plodding *Life of Mary Baker Eddy* (1908), whose inspirational and ethereal Eddy, devoid of earthly influences, stood for years as the church's semi-official image.[21] Wilbur reported unquestioningly that Eddy's childhood "voices" were the voice of God and related how God led the young invalid untainted through encounters with the evils of spiritualism, hydropathy, and Quimby's "mesmerism." The worshipful tone of Wilbur's narrative only solidified believers' love, admiration, and trust for their spiritual founder.

Before the 1950s, much of the historiography of Eddy and her movement reflected a polarization of opinion between critics and believers and allowed images of Eddy's personality to dominate an understanding of Christian Science and its place in American culture. Under the influence of a new generation of social historians and sociologists, scholars shifted their focus from Eddy to the beliefs and practices of Christian Scientists and the structure of their organizations.[22]

In his programmatic study of American religious cults, *These Also Believe* (1949), Charles Braden presented a Christian Science without Eddy at the center.[23] Of greater interest to Braden were the intellectual roots of Eddy's teachings, the institutionalization of her movement, and the beliefs and practices of Christian Scientists. Subsequent social scientists identified healing as a key motivation for conversion to Christian

---

19 Ibid., p. 11.
20 Mary Baker Eddy, *Retrospection and Introspection* (Boston: W. G. Nixon, 1891).
21 Sibyl Wilbur, *The Life of Mary Baker Eddy* (New York: Concord Publishing Company, 1908). For other such uncritical works, see Lyman P. Powell, *Mary Baker Eddy: A Life Size Portrait* (New York: The Macmillan Company, 1930) and Norman Beasley, *Mary Baker Eddy* (New York: Duell, Sloan, and Pearce, 1963).
22 To gain a sense of the centrality of healing to a Scientist's life, see *A Century of Christian Science Healing* (Boston: The Christian Science Publishing Society, 1966).
23 Charles Samuel Braden, "Christian Science," chapter in *These Also Believe: A Study of Modern American Cults and Minority Religious Movements* (New York: The Macmillan Company, 1949), pp. 180-220.

Science, used the church as a case study of the secularization of a religious movement, analyzed the urban characteristics of Christian Science, or studied the health practices of contemporary believers.[24] Bryan Wilson's *Sects and Society* (1961) and Charles Braden's *Christian Science Today* (1958) dealt with the routinization of Eddy's authority through the organization of the Christian Science church and institutions such as the Christian Science Publishing Society and the Board of Directors of the Mother Church.[25] They also described and critically examined the healing practices of Christian Science practitioners and their relationship to the medical profession and the law. Although still important sources, many of their observations and conclusions regarding healing have been subsequently modified by religious historian Walter Wardwell and historian of medicine Rennie Schoepflin. Ronald Numbers and Schoepflin compared and contrasted Eddy with Ellen White in order to reveal the ways in which these two influential women "found their social niche at the intersection of medical and religious reform."[26]

Just as social historians shifted their attention from Eddy to the organization and institutions of Christian Science, so cultural historians concentrated more on Eddy's cultural context and the influence of

---

[24] R. W. England, "Some Aspects of Christian Science As Reflected in Letters of Testimony," *The American Journal of Sociology* 59 (1954): 448-53; Harold W. Pfautz, "Christian Science: A Case Study of the Social Psychological Aspect of Secularization," *Social Forces* 34 (1956): 246-51; Harold W. Pfautz, "A Case Study of an Urban Religious Movement: Christian Science," in *Contributions to Urban Sociology*, ed. Ernest W. Burgess and Donald J. Bogue (Chicago: University of Chicago Press, 1964), pp. 284-303; Arthur Edmund Nudelman, "Christian Science and Secular Medicine" (Ph.D. dissertation, University of Wisconsin, 1970); see also Harold W. Pfautz, "Christian Science: The Sociology of a Social Movement and a Religious Group" (Ph.D. dissertation, University of Chicago, 1954).

[25] Bryan Wilson, *Sects and Society: A Sociological Study of the Elim Tabernacle, Christian Science, and Christadelphians* (Berkeley: University of California Press, 1961), especially chapters 6-10, pp. 121-215; Charles S. Braden, *Christian Science Today: Power, Policy, Practice* (Dallas: Southern Methodist University Press, 1958).

[26] Walter I. Wardwell, "Christian Science Healing," *Journal for the Scientific Study of Religion* 4 (Spring 1965): 175-81; Schoepflin, "The Christian Science Tradition," in *Caring and Curing*, ed. Numbers and Amundsen, pp. 421-46; the Christian Scientists responded to Wardwell in David E. Sleeper, "Comments on Wardwell's 'Christian Science Healing'," *Journal For The Scientific Study of Religion* 5 (1966); 296-98. For three other views of the relationship between practitioners and the medical profession, see Margery Fox, "Conflict to Coexistence: Christian Science and Medicine," *Medical Anthropology* 8 (1984): 292-301; Thomas C. Johnsen, "Christian Scientists and the Medical Profession: A Historical Perspective," *Medical Heritage* 2 (January/February 1986): 70-78; and Robert Peel, *Health and Medicine in the Christian Science Tradition* (New York: Crossroad Publishing Company, 1988).

Christian Science on American culture than on her personality. Historian Robert Peel studied Christian Science vis-à-vis transcendentalism in *Christian Science: Its Encounter with American Culture* (1958) and concluded that they represented "related but distinct" intellectual traditions.[27] Charles Braden looked for similar cultural parallels and found them in the plethora of late nineteenth-century mind-healing movements that collectively became New Thought.[28] In *The Positive Thinkers* (1965) Donald Meyer concluded that Christian Science attracted many followers because of the power over self that it and similar pop psychologies from Dale Carnegie to Oral Roberts offered to Americans.[29] Believing that Christian Science can best be understood by examining its religious teaching, Christian Scientist and historian Stephen Gottschalk traced its movement from the fringes of American religious life into its mainstream in *The Emergence of Christian Science in American Religious Life* (1973).[30] Other cultural historians have examined the spiritualist context for Christian Science, its attraction as a popular religion that offered "solution to the problem of the emotional dissatisfactions of everyday life," and the way more established American denominations experienced a renaissance of faith healing in response to Christian Science.[31]

After these extended cultural and social excursions beyond Eddy, it was not accidental that the Christian Scientist Robert Peel, for whom Mary Baker Eddy had always remained a spiritual guide, returned to an examination of Eddy in his scholarly three-volume biography, *Mary Baker Eddy* (1966-1977).[32] Building on the social theory of sects, Peel divided Eddy's life into three crucial phases—"prophetic" discovery, struggle for legitimacy, and routinization of authority—and crafted a

---

[27] Peel, *Christian Science*.
[28] Braden, *Spirits in Rebellion*.
[29] Meyer, *The Positive Thinkers*.
[30] Gottschalk, *The Emergence of Christian Science*.
[31] R. Laurence Moore, "The Occult Connection? Mormonism, Christian Science, and Spiritualism," in *The Occult in America: New Historical Perspectives*, ed. Howard Kerr and Charles L. Crow (Urbana: University of Illinois Press, 1983), pp. 135-61; R. Laurence Moore, "Christian Science and American Popular Religion," chapter in *Religious Outsiders and the Making of Americans* (New York: Oxford University Press, 1986), pp. 105-27; Raymond J. Cunningham, "The Impact of Christian Science on the American Churches, 1880-1910," *The American Historical Review* 72 (1967): 885-905; and Raymond J. Cunningham, "The Emmanuel Movement: A Variety of American Religious Experience," *American Quarterly* 14 (1962): 48-63.
[32] Peel, *Mary Baker Eddy*. In some ways the goals of Peel's work had been anticipated in the less scholarly work of Hugh A. Studdert Kennedy, *Mrs Eddy: Her life, Her Work and Her Place in History* (San Francisco: The Farallon Press, 1947).

narrative of her within that framework. Although Peel willingly put the best face on the many troublesome episodes of Eddy's career, he obliterated the myth of a changeless Eddy and replaced it with a picture of a creative and adaptive woman influenced by homeopathy, Quimbyism, and the woman's movement and firmly grounded in the intellectual and cultural traditions of New England.[33]

III. ELLEN G. WHITE

In Ellen White's case, historiographical developments have occurred roughly in reverse order from the chronological sequence of her life. At first historians noted her legacy of Seventh-day Adventist hospitals, sanitariums, a medical school, and the career of her most notable protégé, John Harvey Kellogg, M.D. Then, just over a decade ago, the attention shifted to the prophet herself as the prime mover of Adventism's health empire, with a full-blown biography of her as a health reformer. Once examined as a "prophetess of health," more recent studies have probed her health as a prophet, whose chronic illnesses began more than twenty-five years before she launched her career in health reform.

Ronald L. Numbers, a historian of science who had written *Prophetess of Health: A Study of Ellen G. White* (1976), and his wife Janet S. Numbers, a clinical psychologist, compiled a chronology of eleven single-spaced pages on White's "physical complaints and psychological disturbances."[34] The historian and psychologist then coauthored an

---

33 We still lack a sophisticated analysis of the evolution of Eddy's thought that systematically examines the various editions of *Science and Health*. For simple documentation of change, see [Alice L. Orgain], *Distinguishing Characteristics of Mary Baker Eddy's Progressive Revisions of Science and Health and Other Writings* (New York: Rare Book Company 1933) and William Dana Orcutt, *Mary Baker Eddy and Her Books* (Boston: The Christian Science Publishing Society, 1950). Charges of Eddy's plagiarism surfaced in Horatio W. Dresser's defense of Quimby's originality; see Dresser, ed., *The Quimby Manuscripts Showing the Discovery of Spiritual Healing and the Origin of Christian Science* (New York: Thomas Y. Crowell Co., 1921); a defense of Eddy against such charges may be found in Thomas C. Johnsen, "Historical Consensus and Christian Science: The Career of a Manuscript Controversy," *The New England Quarterly* 53 (1980): 3-22.
34 Ronald L. Numbers and Janet S. Numbers, comps., "Ellen G. White: A Chronology of Physical Complaints and Psychological Disturbances," Madison, WI, n.d. (Typewritten.) The Numbers's chronology was by no means exhaustive, as a reading of Arthur White's six-volume biography indicates. While seeking to minimize references to the prophet's weak health, as he stated in *Ellen G. White: The Lonely Years, 1876-1891*, p. 150, White nevertheless considerably amplified on the visionary's illnesses. To take one volume as an example, see his *Ellen G. White: The Early Years, 1827-1862*, pp. 55, 66, 88, 91-92, 111, 115, 133-35, 146, 159, 162, 164, 292-93, 334, 371-72, 414, 432-33.

article on White's opinions in regard to the causes and cures of mental illness. They found her ideas on mental health to have been deeply rooted not only in the Bible and nineteenth-century American culture but in her own experience.[35] Dubbed by contemporaries the "weakest of the weak," White liberally revealed her medical history, after the pattern of other Victorian women, in testimonies, letters, and autobiographical accounts. Following her shattering accident at about ten years of age when she was struck on the nose by a stone, White reported over the years on everything from nosebleeds to rheumatic pains. The Numberses recounted her "complaints of lung, heart, and stomach ailments, frequent 'fainting fits' (sometimes as often as once or twice a day), paralytic attacks (at least five by her mid-40s), pressure on the brain, and breathing difficulties." They found that at least once a decade from her teens through middle age she expected to die from disease. Suffering profound anxiety and depression, she described a two-week period of "extreme sickness," in which her "mind wandered" and she became "strangely confused."[36]

The Numberses avoided a diagnosis of White's psychological condition. Several physicians, however, were not as reticent to take on the prophet as a "patient." In a paper for the American Academy of Neurology, Dr. Gregory Holmes and Dr. Delbert Hodder concluded that the head trauma of White's childhood accident led to temporal lobe epilepsy. Her visions were therefore partial complex seizures, while many other aspects of her personality and behavior (such as hypermoralism, hypergraphia, sobriety, guilt, paranoia) were further symptomatic of the partial-complex seizure patient.[37] In an exhaustive article, Dr. Molleurus Couperus delved more deeply into White's biography as well as the

[35] Ronald L. Numbers and Janet S. Numbers, "The Psychological World of Ellen White," *Spectrum* 14 (August 1983): 21-31.
[36] Ibid., p. 23. Her period of mental distress followed the Millerite disappointment, which apparently left a number of her spiritual brothers and sisters in a similar state; for a discussion of Millerism and insanity that mentions White's experience, see Ronald L. Numbers and Janet S. Numbers, "Millerism and Madness: A Study of 'Religious Insanity' in Nineteenth-Century America," in *The Disappointed: Millerism and Millenarianism in the Nineteenth Century*, ed. Ronald L. Numbers and Jonathan M. Butler (Bloomington: Indiana University Press, 1987), pp. 92-117. Ronald Graybill combined psychological and anthropological perspectives in his analysis of White's visions in "The Power of Prophecy," pp. 84-112; for a psychohistorical glimpse of White, see Bernadine L. Irwin, "A Psychohistory of the Young Ellen White: A Founder of the Seventh-day Adventist Church," (Ph.D. dissertation, United States International University, 1984).
[37] An abstract of this argument appeared in Gregory Holmes and Delbert Hodder, "Ellen G. White and the Seventh-day Adventist Church: Visions or Partial Complex Seizures?" *Journal of Neurology* 31 (1981): 160-61; a fuller treatment of the subject for a lay

neurological literature on temporal lobe epilepsy to corroborate the Holmes-Hodder findings.[38]

Psychohistory on White has remained in its infancy, however, and has had nothing close to the impact of Ronald Numbers's social biography of her as a health reformer. Prior to this book White had been a neglected figure alongside other indigenous American religious founders like Joseph Smith, Mary Baker Eddy, or Charles Taze Russell. No more appreciated for her contributions to health care than for those to millenarianism and social welfare, child nurture and education, she certainly warranted the effort by Numbers "neither to defend nor to damn but simply to understand."[39] In concentrating on the health-reform aspect of White's wide-ranging career, Numbers pursued two objectives: first, to discover the extent of her indebtedness to contemporary health reformers; and second, to show the degree to which her health messages developed and changed from 1863 to her late years.

In arguing for a derivative prophet, Numbers countered the hagiographic tradition within Adventism, which saw White as an original, a *tabula rasa*, whose utterances on health put her years ahead of her time. Instead, he placed the prophet against a colorful backdrop of Grahamites, vegetarians, homeopaths, hydropaths, Thomsonians, phrenologists, sexual theorists, and dress reformers. He likewise identified the Adventists who had preceded her in the temperance cause such as Larkin B. Coles, Joseph Bates, John Andrews, and John P. Kellogg.[40] In short, the prophet received her health vision in June of 1863, an afterthought (by several decades) in the history of American health reform. Although she claimed divine inspiration for her views, Numbers suggested a more

---

audience may be found in Hodder, "Visions or Partial-Complex Seizures?" *Evangelica* 2 (November 1981): 30-37. Attributing White's visions to epilepsy is not altogether new. Dudley M. Canright, an ex-Adventist evangelist and erstwhile friend of the prophet, did so in his *Life of Mrs. E.G. White* (Cincinnati: Standard Publishing Company, 1919), pp. 170-88. Adventist apologist Francis D. Nichol rebutted Canright by arguing that White's visions and other personality traits were inconsistent with either grand mal or petite mal seizures; for this argument consult *Ellen G. White and Her Critics* (Washington, D.C.: Review and Herald Publishing Association, 1951), pp. 26-86. Hodder conceded that White did not suffer from the epilepsy Nichol described, but the physician dismissed this as an explanation because Nichol had been unaware (as everyone was in the 1950s) of partial-complex seizures; see "Visions or Partial-Complex Seizures?" p. 31.

38 Molleurus Couperus, "The Significance of Ellen White's Head Injury," *Adventist Currents* 3 (June 1985): 17-33. For a critique of this position, see Donald I. Peterson, "Did Ellen White Really Have Seizures?" Loma Linda University Heritage Room, 1985. (Typewritten.)

39 Numbers, *Prophetess of Health*, p. xi.

40 Ibid., pp. 48-76.

immediate source by demonstrating the basic similarities in concept between White and other health reformers. While he never termed her a plagiarist as such, he pointed out close literary parallels between White and earlier writers.[41]

In tracing the development of White's health ideas, Numbers also dismantled the myth of a changeless and unerring prophet. He found that in 1849 the visionary condemned consultation with physicians as a denial of faith, while in the 1860s she criticized the excesses of faith healing and recommended physicians on occasion. In 1867 she initiated her campaign for dress reform but abandoned it as a lost cause by 1875. In the 1890s she modified her arguments for supporting a vegetarian diet. And her early protests against masturbation and sexual excesses in marriage that evoked the familiar "vital force" principle disappeared in her comprehensive health volume *Ministry of Healing* (1905). In making his case, Numbers judiciously allowed the prophet to speak for herself, albeit within the historical framework an historian can provide. In the process, however, White's foibles, self-contradictions, and more bizarre health notions proved readily apparent.[42] In Adventist historiography on Ellen White and her health care legacy, Numbers's book served as a watershed. Before *Prophetess of Health*, the best survey on health reform among Adventists was the triumphalist study of Dores E. Robinson, White's personal secretary and grandson-in-law.[43] Two less reverent

---

[41] See, for example, ibid., pp. 162-63, 232n.

[42] A provocative chapter along these lines is "Short Skirts and Sex," ibid., pp. 129-59. The debate within Adventism over Numbers's book was intense and prolific. Much of the discussion revolved around whether good history could be written about White without presupposing her supernatural inspiration. While such a parochial cast to the argument limited its significance for a wider public, an extensive historical critique did surface apart from theological concerns. The official Adventist response to *Prophetess of Health* was the multi-authored work by The Staff of the Ellen G. White Estate, *A Critique of the Book Prophetess of Health* (Washington, D.C.: Ellen G. White Estate, 1976); Gary Land critically reviewed the White Estate publication in "Faith, History and Ellen White," *Spectrum* 9 (March 1978): 51-55. The most valuable exchange on Numbers's book appears in "Ellen White and Health," *Spectrum* 8 (January 1977): 2-36; see especially the comments by Fawn Brodie, Ernest Sandeen, and Numbers himself. My discussion of the Numbers book above first took shape in my review of *Prophetess of Health: A Study of Ellen G. White*, by Ronald L. Numbers, in *Church History*, 47 (1978): 243-44.

[43] Robinson, *Story of Our Health Message: The Origin, Character, and Development of Health Education in the Seventh-day Adventist Church*, 3rd ed. (Nashville: Southern Publishing Association, 1965). The following two biographies bore on the health story: Godfrey T. Anderson's study of an Adventist pioneer who preceded White in health reform in *Outrider of the Apocalypse: Life and Times of Joseph Bates* (Mountain View, CA: Pacific Press Publishing Association, 1972); and that of a leading administrator of the Adventist medical school in Merlin L. Neff, *For God and C.M.E.: A Biography of Percy Tilson Magan* (Mountain View, CA: Pacific Press Publishing Association, 1964).

treatments from non-Adventists were Gerald Carson's entertaining *Cornflake Crusade* and Ronald Deutsch's exposé, *The Nuts Among the Berries*, both of which devoted several chapters to White, Kellogg, and Battle Creek.[44] Richard Schwarz provided a fresh explanation for the rift that developed between White and Kellogg and the physician's resulting loss to the church.[45] After *Prophetess of Health*, Adventist authors fell into "nativist" reactions in which they reiterated aspects of a tradition rendered obsolete by Numbers's research.[46] By 1979, however, Schwarz had produced a college-level textbook on Adventist history which incorporated the new health story and probably ensured its inclusion as the new orthodoxy for Adventists.[47] Now, as more than a decade has passed since Numbers's historiographical explosion among Adventists, composure has long since been restored. The Adventist health story, including White's part in it, can now be told with the historian's detached appreciation. Two excellent examples of this may be found, first, in a chapter by Numbers himself and David Larson on the Adventist health tradition in a volume on health and medicine among Western religions. The second is the popular introduction to Adventists in *Seeking a Sanctuary* which offers an insightful account of the prophet and her health ideas.[48]

---

[44] Gerald Carson, *Cornflake Crusade* (New York: Rinehart & Co., 1957), pp. 71-146; Ronald W. Deutsch, *The Nuts Among the Berries*, rev. ed. (New York: Ballantine Books, 1967), pp. 43-84.

[45] Schwarz produced an excellent dissertation on "John Harvey Kellogg: American Health Reformer" (Ph.D. dissertation, University of Michigan, 1964); his published biography, however, catered to an Adventist audience by glossing over controversial aspects of his argument. Fortunately, Schwarz rectified this shortcoming with his more candid essay on "The Kellogg Schism: The Hidden Issues," *Spectrum* 4 (Autumn 1972): 22-29; Schwarz surveyed much of the same ground in "The Perils of Growth, 1886-1905," in Gary Land, ed., *Adventism in America*, pp. 95-138.

[46] They include Richard A. Schaefer, *Legacy: the Heritage of a Unique International Medical Outreach* (Mountain View, CA: Pacific Press Publishing Association, 1977), pp. 16-25; and George W. Reid, *A Sound of Trumpets: Americans, Adventists, and Health Reform* (Washington, D.C.: Review and Herald Publishing Association, 1982), esp. pp. 96-114; for more sophisticated apologetics on the Adventist health story, see the handsome coffee-table volume *The Vision Bold: An Illustrated History of the Seventh-day Adventist Philosophy of Health*, ed. Warren L. Johns and Richard H. Utt (Washington, D.C.: Review and Herald Publishing Association, 1977).

[47] Schwarz, *Light Bearers*, esp. pp. 104–17, 314–24.

[48] Ronald L. Numbers and David R. Larson, "The Adventist Tradition," in *Caring and Curing*, ed. Numbers and Amundsen, pp. 447-67; Bull and Lockhart, *Seeking a Sanctuary*, especially chapter 10 on "The Science of Happiness." In the same category as the above titles is the book in progress by Roy Branson on *Health and Medicine in the Adventist Tradition* (New York: Crossroad Publishing Company, forthcoming).

IV. AIMEE SEMPLE MCPHERSON

Much less has been written on Aimee Semple McPherson and healing than on either Ellen White or Mary Baker Eddy and their health concerns. Although the sensational practice of healing gained McPherson early attention, the Pentecostal evangelist earned such notoriety in other ways that even her role as a healer was overshadowed. Scholars have studied her as a public speaker, but the resulting speech dissertations have failed to examine the speaker as healer.[49] The less scholarly tack of the popular biography, on the other hand, has practically ignored McPherson not just as a healer but as a religious figure altogether.[50] Lately Thomas, whose *Storming Heaven* has provided the most complete biography to date of the evangelist along with her mother Ma Kennedy, nevertheless has left readers with a severely limited portrait of her. For by the time Thomas had combed through her personal imbroglios, legal entanglements, and scandals—especially her alleged kidnaping—there seemed little time to portray her adequately as a Pentecostal healer. But this hardly means that nothing can be learned from Thomas about McPherson and health. Both her own illnesses and her response to others' ills found their way into his story, if only as a subplot. Unlike the historiography on Eddy and White, however, McPherson's biography remains largely in narrative form unexploited by various interpretive perspectives. It is necessary here, then, to review her story as it has been told by Thomas and other biographers in order to encourage more penetrating analysis of it.

To this point, the matter of McPherson's personal health has drawn neither the psychohistorian concerned with the function of illness in a life and career nor the sociologist or anthropologist who brings comparative studies to bear on women, illness, and religious vocation. Without

---

[49] An extensive rhetorical analysis of McPherson has been done by Kenneth Howard Shanks, "An Historical and Critical Study of the Preaching Career of Aimee Semple McPherson," (Ph.D. dissertation, University of Southern California, 1960); for sociological and rhetorical perspectives, see Todd Vernon Lewis, "Charismatic Communication and Faith Healers: A Critical Study of Rhetorical Behavior," (Ph.D. dissertation, Louisiana State University and Agricultural and Technical College, 1980); see also Lawrence L. Lacour, "A Study of the Revival Method in America: 1920-1955, with Special Reference to Billy Sunday, Aimee Semple McPherson, and Billy Graham," (Ph.D. dissertation, Northwestern University, 1956); and William Ferdinand Fahrner, "The Persuasive Techniques of Aimee Semple McPherson," (M.A. thesis, University of Redlands, 1949).

[50] These have included Thomas's *Storming Heaven* and Robert Bahr's *Least of All Saints*.

the drawbacks of such methodological "baggage," but also without benefit of the "provisions" carried in it, as it were, Thomas trekked through the autobiographies, sermons, interviews, and copious news stories which make up the McPherson materials. Regardless of his limitations of perspective, he clearly saw the way in which serious illness accompanied the woman's intense vocational crisis.[51] Resigning herself to a housewifely role in a second but failing marriage, she fell gravely ill both physically and psychologically. She complained of "heart trouble," "hemorrhages," and an "intense nervousness" which made the slightest sound or light unbearable. While she came to view her illnesses as the supernatural punishments of God for denying her call to the ministry, she left herself in the hands of earthly physicians who performed several operations on her (including probably a hysterectomy).[52] Reportedly on her hospital deathbed, she resolved to preach the Gospel. With her marriage finished and her children left with their grandmother, McPherson found that her rededication to the ministry had finally brought physical and spiritual relief. Her vocation had functioned as a form of self-therapy. Since returning to the ministry, she later claimed, "I have hardly known an ache or pain from that day to this."[53]

McPherson had clearly exaggerated, for she experienced a number of illnesses throughout her career that might be described as "creative maladies." That is, if illness occasioned her return to the ministry, a

---

[51] Her reminiscence may be found in two of her autobiographies: *This Is That: Personal Experiences, Sermons and Writings* (Los Angeles: Echo Park Evangelistic Association, 1923), pp. 73-79; and *Aimee Semple McPherson: The Story of My Life* (Waco, TX: Word Books, 1973), pp. 74-75; historians have reported her story in Thomas's *Storming Heaven*, pp. 12-13; Shanks, "An Historical and Critical Study," p. 17; and Joel Whitney Tibbets, "Women Who Were Called: A Study of the Contributions to American Christianity of Ann Lee, Jemima Wilkinson, Mary Baker Eddy and Aimee Semple McPherson," (Ph.D. dissertation, Vanderbilt University, 1976), pp. 217-20.

[52] This juxtaposition of the divine and the human in McPherson's world view conforms to what Grant Wacker discovered in twentieth-century Pentecostalism. He concluded that the modern movement "reveals a very other-worldly supernaturalism and very this-worldly pragmatism still locked in a curiously compatible marriage that has lasted longer than anyone can quite remember. . . . Another way of putting it is to say that under the canopy of a first-century cosmology, divine healing rituals and high-tech hospitals have proved to be equally functional devices for getting along in the real world." Grant Wacker, "The Pentecostal Tradition," in *Caring and Curing*, ed. Numbers and Amundsen, p. 531. Perhaps another illustration of Wacker's point from McPherson's personal life is the fact that the healer evidently sought out plastic surgeons for cosmetic surgery.

[53] *This Is That*, p. 77; Tibbetts, "Women Who Were Called," pp. 217-20.

series of ailments similarly served to sustain her at opportune moments in her career.[54]

Without making much of the coincidence of personal crisis and ill health, Thomas amply documented McPherson's scandals, litigation, and broken relationships. He also reported a number of instances in which McPherson retreated from a crisis by as little as a swoon or as much as prolonged hospitalization, even surgery. When her third husband faced a breach-of-contract charge from a former girlfriend, Aimee, who appeared to have been the real target, experienced a complete breakdown and was carried from hospital to hospital throughout the trial. After a heated mother-daughter quarrel in which Aimee broke Ma Kennedy's nose, it was *Aimee* who fell ill. And when her daughter Roberta brought suit against her and succeeded, Aimee collapsed and had to be hauled from the courtroom. Laying aside her chronic physical setbacks, her series of ruptured personal relationships (such as her permanent estrangement from Roberta), suggests a rich vein for the psychohistorian. But to whatever degree her physical problems may be explained in psychological terms, her death was not a suicide as some assumed. The coroner ruled the cause of death as an accidental overdose of barbiturates together with a "kidney ailment."[55]

Turning from McPherson's personal ill health to her ministry of healing others, most of her biographers have allowed her notoriety as a public figure to eclipse her more serious role as a Pentecostal evangelist and healer. Only in the context of her Holiness-Pentecostal tradition can her career be fully appreciated.[56] In his book *Theological Roots of Pente-*

---

[54] In his argument on the relation of illness and the creative personality, George Pickering could as easily have added Aimee Semple McPherson to his list in *Creative Malady*.

[55] Thomas made numerous references to McPherson's personal health in *Storming Heaven*, pp. 162, 173, 225-26, 230, 236, 238, 257, 262, 308, 322, 336; he dealt with her death on pp. 339-47.

[56] For an introduction to Pentecostalism, see Vinson Synan, *The Holiness-Pentecostal Movement in the United States* (Grand Rapids, MI: William B. Eerdmans, 1971); a most valuable bibliographical essay on healing revivalism, especially its obscure primary sources, may be found in David Edwin Harrell, Jr., *All Things Are Possible: The Healing and Charismatic Revivals in Modern America* (Bloomington: Indiana University Press, 1975), pp. 240-54; on Pentecostalism as a worldwide phenomenon, see Walter J. Hollenweger, *The Pentecostals: The Charismatic Movement in the Churches*, trans, R.A. Wilson (Minneapolis: Augsburg Publishing House, 1972); the best, if highly critical, study of Pentecostalism in the United States is Robert Mapes Anderson, *Vision of the Disinherited: The Making of American Pentecostalism* (New York: Oxford University Press, 1979); for a more sympathetic look at the movement's theological heritage, see Donald W. Dayton, *Theological Roots of Pentecostalism* (Metuchen, NJ: The Scarecrow Press, 1987).

costalism, Donald W. Dayton did much to dignify that tradition by seeing it as a complex and cohesive system of thought. He discounted simplistic descriptions of Pentecostalism which equate it with nothing more than "speaking with tongues." In its place, he characterized Pentecostal belief as made up of four elements (referred to at the outset of this essay)—salvation, healing, baptism of the Holy Spirit, and a second coming of Christ outlook. In a bibliographical note, Dayton commented, "My analysis of the four-fold character of Pentecostal thought is original, but relies heavily on the writings of Aimee Semple McPherson, the founder of the International Church of the Foursquare Gospel, for clues to this analysis."[57] Dayton's purpose was to show the inner logic of Pentecostal thought, not to describe the movement in social terms. But his findings should alert students of McPherson to an understanding of her career as a healer within a broad and viable theological framework.

Perhaps the most glaring weakness in studies of McPherson has been the failure to appreciate her as a healer. To some degree, Pentecostal historiography in general has suffered the same problem; historians have neglected divine healing within the tradition. In his article on health within Pentecostalism, Grant Wacker attributed this lapse to "a certain loss in historical memory." In reconstructing the primitive Pentecostalism between 1900 and 1930, out of which McPherson's career arose, Wacker agreed with David Edwin Harrell that the central focus of the movement was supernatural healing. "The common heartbeat of every service," Harrell wrote of a somewhat later period, "was the miracle—the hypnotic moment when the Spirit moved to heal the sick and raise the dead." Wacker found that Pentecostal writers, somewhat uniquely, concentrated on the special gifts of healing in 1 *Corinthians* 12 and the "Great Commission" in *Mark* 16:17-18. Since God always responded to the prayer of faith, if illness persisted in the life of a believer it must have been due to impurity or shallowness of faith. Only truly converted and Spirit-filled believers were exempted from ill health. From the beginning, Pentecostals saw a difference between the corporate gifts of healing, which resided in the collective church, and the personal gifts of healing that remarkable individuals possessed. Early Pentecostals emphasized the value of corporate-church healing while, by the end of the

---

[57] Dayton, *Theological Roots of Pentecostalism*, pp. 15-33, 183; he found her writings on these themes conveniently collected by Raymond L. Cox, *The Four-Square Gospel* (Los Angeles: Foursquare Publications, 1969).

1920s, Pentecostals were acknowledging the demonstrably capable healing, to the point of minor celebrity status, of such evangelists as Fred F. Bosworth, Smith Wigglesworth, Charles S. Price, and McPherson.[58]

McPherson's theological tradition, although a neglected aspect of her story, is not the whole story. One historian has stood out in his effort to view the evangelist against her social, cultural, and religious backdrop. The noted historian of American revivalism, William G. McLoughlin, Jr., published an article in 1967 on McPherson for the *Journal of Popular Culture* which might well have provided an interpretive framework for any subsequent biography.[59] Notwithstanding his care in reconstructing a historical setting for the evangelist, McLoughlin still placed McPherson's personal story in the forefront (the place to which she had gravitated in her lifetime). That is, McLoughlin did not allow McPherson the healer to be upstaged by other aspects of her social biography. In telling her story, he noted the fact that she became a healer after observing someone with a broken ankle healed. She and her mother then adopted self-styled nursing uniforms in the pulpit to connect faith healing with angelic purity. McPherson healed the wife of a gypsy chief of a tumor and thereby received the personal and financial support of gypsies throughout the world, including their handsome donations to the building of her famed Angelus Temple in Los Angeles. She claimed to have made cripples walk, the blind see, all kinds of sick people well, and she pointed to a room adjacent to her stage, filled with discarded crutches, wheelchairs, and other hygienic paraphernalia, as dramatic testimony of her success.[60] Without a sense of her social and religious context, however, McPherson's story as a healer may appear as little more than the tawdry spectacle of "Sister Aimee, the Barnum of reli-

---

58 Grant Wacker, "The Pentecostal Tradition," *Caring and Curing*, ed. Numbers and Amundsen, esp. pp. 520-27; the David Harrell quotation appeared in *All Things Are Possible*, p. 6.

59 McLoughlin, "Aimee Semple McPherson," pp. 193-217. Unfortunately, Thomas's *Storming Heaven* appeared in 1970 without either citing McLoughlin in his notes or apparently benefiting from his short but insightful article.

60 McLoughlin, ibid., pp. 198, 202, 206, 212. Surprisingly limited reference to her as a healer may be found in other works about her. See Thomas, *Storming Heaven*, pp. 20-21; Joel Whitney Tibbets, "Women Who Were Called," pp. 208, 226, 339; Yeol Soo Eim, "The Worldwide Expansion of the Foursquare Church," (Ph.D. dissertation, Fuller Theological Seminary, 1986), pp. 26-29. In her autobiography, Aimee allowed that in Melbourne, Australia, she downplayed healing because of the kind of use made of it by revivalists who had preceded her to the city. "There were many precious instances of divine healing in answer to prayer," she commented, "but the Lord gave me a very definite check about emphasizing the ministry because healing had been unduly exploited prior to our revival," *The Story of My Life*, p. 116.

gion." McLoughlin resisted such a distortion by measuring her against the morals and religion, technology and media that marked the "Roaring Twenties." Moreover, he reached further back than her immediate decade to place her in the Pietist-Pentecostalist-Fundamentalist tradition. Unlike her popular biographers, McLoughlin took McPherson seriously as a religious figure who spoke the language of a particular religious tradition, albeit in her own compelling accent.[61]

McPherson's health legacy included the sustained commitment to healing within the church which she founded, but this involved more than healing in the narrow sense.[62] McPherson thrust her church, from its outset, into a wide range of activity from the usual Sunday schools, Bible classes, and choirs, to dramatic productions, a magazine, a Bible college, a network of social services, and far-flung missionary establishments.[63] In this vast enterprise, McPherson had supplied the charisma, and Ma Kennedy, a tight-fisted business manager, had kept order, but the charismatic demanded and secured control of the organization. Vivian Denton, a Bible student who sought to succeed Aimee, was soundly rebuffed by the evangelist.[64] McPherson chose instead to pass the mantle to her son, Rolf, who carried on the organization with none of her charismatic flare. Indeed, unlike Eddy or White, McPherson sustains today no more than a minimal influence on the church she originated.[65]

V. WOMEN RELIGIOUS LEADERS AND HEALTH: A MODEL FOR STUDY

A historiographical review of the work on the health interests of these three female religious figures involves more than an annotated bibliography. It seeks rather to point up the strengths and weaknesses of past historical efforts and to chart areas of prospective investigation. Future historians should strike a healthy balance between the need to recognize the unique religious and medical contributions of these

---

[61] McLoughlin, "Aimee Semple McPherson," pp. 195, 203-4; see also Tibbetts, "Women Who Were Called," pp. 36-38; an effort to understand McPherson as an early media personality appears in David L. Clark, "'Miracles for a Dime'—From Chautauqua Tent to Radio Station with Sister Aimee," *California History: The Magazine of the California Historical Society* 57 (1978): 354-63.

[62] The growth of McPherson's church is documented in partisan terms by Yeol Soo Eim, "The Worldwide Expansion."

[63] McLoughlin, "Aimee Semple McPherson," pp. 209, 212.

[64] Thomas, *Storming Heaven*, pp. 128-66, 280.

[65] Tibbetts, "Women Who Were Called," pp. 342, 345-46.

women, and the imperative to understand the broad influences that the culture of their times had upon them. We must attend to their roles as innovators while remembering that they also reflected their times. Similarly, scholars should explore more subtly the dynamic relationship that existed within their movements between themselves and their followers, for that relationship created, and continues to evolve, the social definitions of prophetic authority that have outlived each woman. Finally, contemporary issues, such as feminism, psychology, anthropology, or literary criticism, which continue to influence historians' philosophy or methodology, will further foster innovative insights into the lives of these women.

Many historians have studied Eddy, White, and McPherson, three women who found social and personal success through religions of health, in near isolation from their social, cultural, or intellectual contexts. Most typical of such isolationist views have been works by hagiographers, detractors, and psychobiographers.

Because Eddy, White, and their believers were so convinced of their divinely inspired messages and attributes, they downplayed the importance of "earthly" influences upon their revelations, bridled at any suggestion of significant doctrinal change over time, and believed that a prophet always obeys her own teaching. Illnesses and spectral voices signalled a divine call or the visitation of the devil; God imparted the power to overcome and the spiritual discernment to move forward "in truth." The reverent hagiographies that buttressed such beliefs severely underestimated the human influences on Eddy and White; yet, through such works one gains insight into the nature of religious belief. In studying the sources of such "otherworldly" admiration the historian must not underestimate the charismatic power of these women nor neglect to analyze seriously the culture that allowed followers to see their power as supernatural.

Although McPherson did not sustain the importance for later generations of believers that Eddy and White did for their adherents, she nevertheless commanded the kind of importance as a religious leader to make herself the target of iconoclasts in much the way Eddy and White were. While such unflattering accounts may never convince believers that their prophet is a fraud, they tend to underscore a leader's humanity. Biographer Fred Kaplan does well to remind us, however, that "it is possible for unpleasant people who are small in various ways other than in their artistic genius to produce great art. Art and morality have no necessary connection."[66]

---

[66] Fred Kaplan, "The Real Charles Dickens, or The Old Animosity Shop," *The New York Times Book Review*, October 12, 1988, p. 15.

Only Eddy, and to a lesser extent White, have received sophisticated analyses by psychiatrists, physicians, and psychohistorians. From partial complex siezures to clinical hysteria, "scientists" have tried, in the words of anthropologist Kenelm Burridge, to tell us what went on in their brains, but they "can tell us little about the *minds* of the participants or what their thoughts" were.[67] Scholars rarely have used psycho-physiological tools in a balanced way that avoids distortion of past world views and rejects scientific reductionism. Psychobiography can easily become what author and critic Joyce Carol Oates called "pathography." "Its scenes are sensational, wallowing in squalor and foolishness" and lead "a reader to ask, 'How did a distinguished body of work emerge from so undistinguished a life?'"[68] Given our distance from the "patients" and our limited information about them, the historian's goal should not be to determine truth or error, mental health or illness, but to understand the psychological dimensions of the women's successful work and to translate the past into a modern vocabulary.[69]

Cultural and social historians, sensitive to the ways context defines individuals, have created the best work to date on these three women. Numbers on White; Braden, Peel and others on Eddy; and the short article by McLoughlin on McPherson, provide models for future historians. Each author has recognized that times bind an individual and create boundaries for her beliefs and actions. Attitudes toward illness and inner voices, antagonism toward physicians and organized medicine, and confidence in therapeutic nihilism or sectarian and religious healers must all be seen as part of the cultural ferment that surrounded these women. But a person, especially a charismatic, can supersede her times. With just such recognition, these model studies have revealed women who built a symbiotic relationship between their worlds and their personalities in which culture influenced but did not determine their beliefs and actions. Each woman transcended her culture by establishing movements, organizations, and institutions that outlived her and extended her personal influence beyond a particular time and place. Before the work of

---

[67] Kenelm Burridge, *New Heaven New Earth: A Study of Millenarian Activities* (New York: Schocken Books, 1969), p. 119.

[68] Joyce Carol Oates, review of *Jean Stafford: A Biography*, by David Roberts, In *The New York Times Book Review*, October 23, 1988, p. 3.

[69] The forthcoming psychobiography of Mary Baker Eddy by Robert David Thomas, author of *The Man Who Would Be Perfect: John Humphrey Noyes and the Utopian Impulse* (Philadelphia: University of Pennsylvania Press, 1977), draws heavily on Eddy materials in the Archives of the Mother Church and undoubtedly will replace Silberger's *Mary Baker Eddy*.

Numbers, Peel, Braden, and McLoughlin such social frameworks were seen through the dominant eyes of the leader, often resulting in a skewed picture of the interactive relationship between leader and followers.[70] Now we have begun to see the more dynamic interaction among followers, leader, and society that created adaptive extensions of the prophets' visions.

Doubtless growing out of the increased interest among historians in women's studies, the most distinctive historiographical trend during the last decade has been a new or renewed interest in several religious founders as women. The authors of both dissertations and articles have used an analysis of Eddy, White, and McPherson to gain insight into the public role of women in American culture.[71] Among the three figures, Eddy once again has generated the most substantial historiography in this area. Historians have concluded, for example, that Eddy institutionalized sentimental womanhood, used a rhetoric that "had ideological roots in the burgeoning woman's movement of the late nineteenth century," and fashioned religious doctrines that appealed to women.[72] Others have used Eddy, White, and McPherson as examples of the way in which women successful in a man's world accommodated themselves to the traditional female roles of mother and wife.[73] Clearly, a feminist appraisal of any one of these women would benefit from the cross-pollinization of a comparative approach.

---

[70] For a general development of this social understanding of prophetic charisma, see Bryan R. Wilson, *The Noble Savages: The Primitive Origins of Charisma and Its Contemporary Survival* (Berkeley: University of California Press, 1975); Wilson applied his approach to Christian Science in *Sects and Society: A Sociological Study of the Elim Tabernacle, Christian Science, and Christadelphians* (Berkeley: University of California Press, 1961), esp. pp. 121-215.

[71] See for example Penny Hansen, "Woman's Hour: Feminist Implications of Mary Baker Eddy's Christian Science Movement, 1885-1910" (Ph.D. dissertation, University of California, Irvine, 1981); Margery Q. Fox, "Power and Piety: Women in Christian Science" (Ph.D. dissertation, New York University, 1973).

[72] Gail Parker, "Mary Baker Eddy and Sentimental Womanhood," *The New England Quarterly* 43 (1970): 3-18; Gage William Chapel, "Christian Science and the Nineteenth Century Woman's Movement," *Central States Speech Journal* 26 (1975): 142-49; Mary Farrell Bednarowski, "Outside the Mainstream: Women's Religion and Women Religious Leaders in Nineteenth-Century America," *Journal of the American Academy of Religion* 48 (1980): 207-31; see also Jean A. McDonald, "Mary Baker Eddy and the Nineteenth-Century 'Public' Woman: A Feminist Reappraisal," *Journal of Feminist Studies in Religion* 2 (1986): 89-111.

[73] Graybill dealt with Eddy as well as White in "The Power of Prophecy"; Tibbets covered both Eddy and McPherson in "Women Who Were Called," pp. 204-263, 363-434 passim.

What should the future bring? It must bring new attention to Aimee Semple McPherson as a healing charismatic and a closer examination of her religious and American contexts. For each of the women future research should refocus on the unifying presence of the woman herself as a key to an integrative-historical biography. This does not mean that historians should resurrect the character worship or assassination of an earlier time. Rather, they should transform the passive analysis of a woman and her times into the active recreation of a flesh-and-blood figure who reported divine encounters, creatively molded a body of thought, absorbed and yet transformed her culture, wrote and preached, and organized movements and established institutions that continue to draw strength from her creative energies. The tools developed by religious and medical anthropologists and members of the "history-of-religions" movement can help us recognize that these women were not just oddballs who established fringe movements.[74] They stand on their own as culturally significant individuals who represent the spirit of their times.

---

[74] Contemporary history of religions as a discipline has been defined by Mircea Eliade in, among his numerous works, *The Sacred and the Profane* (New York: Harcourt, Brace and World, Harvest Books, 1959); Jerald C. Brauer called for an application of the history-of-religions perspective to American religious history in his essay "Changing Perspectives on Religion in America," in *Reinterpretation in American Church History*, ed. Jerald C. Brauer (Chicago: University of Chicago Press, 1968), pp. 1-28; a significant attempt to answer Brauer's call is the college text by Catherine L. Albanese, *America: Religions and Religion* (Belmont, CA: Wadsworth Publishing Company, 1981); Albanese commented on Eddy and White, (but her discussion of Pentecostalism did not include McPherson) in pp. 104-7, 146-55; for an example of the application of cultural anthropology to Christian Science see Lucy Jayne Kamau, "Systems of Belief and Ritual in Christian Science" (Ph.D. dissertation, University of Chicago, 1971).

Social and Political Dynamics of Women's Health Concerns

14

· · · · · ·

KNOWLEDGE AND POWER: HEALTH AND PHYSICAL EDUCATION FOR WOMEN IN AMERICA

Martha H. Verbrugge

How do Americans learn about health? Today, our sources of information are countless. The general media, for instance, both instruct and entertain: television programs feature "the disease of the week"; books, magazines, and newspapers startle readers with the latest trends in medicine; advertisements marshal scientific "facts" to hype products. In schools around the country, youngsters take classes in health and practice physical skills in "gym." Adults join health clubs or visit community centers, where they learn the basics of nutrition and exercise. Voluntary associations and public-interest groups rally concern for health through newsletters and political activism. Government agencies, from the local to federal level, alert citizens about public-health risks and how to avoid them. (The 1988 mass distribution of a bulletin about AIDS from the Surgeon General's office is a striking example.) In a culture preoccupied with fitness, advice about health is ubiquitous.

Perhaps many Americans assume that such a phenomenon is new, that health information was more limited in earlier days. Although the media and messages have varied over time, popular instruction in health has always been evident in our society. For generations, an assortment of Americans has guided the country's men, women, and children toward physical well-being.

The history of health education and physical education has always interested professionals in those fields who wanted to trace the evolution of their discipline. During the past two decades, with the growth of the social history of medicine and the sociology of knowledge, the broad topic of health education has attracted the attention of other scholars as well. This essay reviews historical studies about health education and physical education for women in America. It discusses recent research examining how women have learned the principles and habits of health throughout American history.

The boundaries of this essay are important to note at the outset. First, *education* here means instruction that is supervised and systematic; it involves direct and regular contact between some type of teacher and learner, whose common goal is the transmission of knowledge and skills. Thus, "education" excludes ways in which a woman might learn about health informally, for instance through medical care or recreational activities. Second, the essay covers *health and physical education*, ranging from the principles of human anatomy and physiology to practical training in hygiene, exercise, and sports. Those subjects appear to be natural allies, since each addresses the development and care of the body, but in reality such topics are often segregated: school curricula have different classes in health education and physical education; the two fields have become distinct professions; researchers have written separate histories of popular physiology, exercise, and public health. While in some contexts those divisions are useful, they complicate the job being assumed in this essay: there are few unifying questions or perspectives in the literature. Third, this chapter focuses on *institutions*, meaning formal agencies such as schools and organizations. Histories of medical advice literature are thus not considered. Finally, the essay is concerned with instruction for or by *women*, that is, institutions serving females, exclusively or in part, and women who taught about health in some formal setting.

Several books provide new readers with a quick introduction to some of the subjects (and shortcomings) in this area.[1] To date, however,

---

[1] Stephanie Lee Twin, *Jock and Jill: Aspects of Women's Sports History in America, 1870-1940* (Ann Arbor: University Microfilms International, 1985), offers a good overview. Two anthologies reflect the diversity of topics (and unevenness of research) in the field: Reet Howell, ed., *Her Story in Sport: A Historical Anthology of Women in Sports* (West Point, NY: Leisure Press, 1982); and Earle F. Zeigler, ed., *A History of Physical Education and Sport in the United States and Canada (Selected Topics)* (Champaign, IL: Stipes Publishing, 1975).

no single review essay or bibliography adequately covers the field.[2] This chapter opens with a discussion of general issues in the history of health and physical education for women. Two subsequent sections deal with more specialized topics: schools (both secondary and collegiate) and voluntary organizations. An overall assessment and prospectus conclude the essay.

CULTURE, GENDER, AND BODY

The fundamental purpose of health education is clear: to convey theoretical and practical information about the human body, its organization, functioning, and healthy development. For girls and women, such instruction usually covers the female life cycle, from menstruation to

---

[2] One related essay is June A. Kennard, "The History of Physical Education," *Signs* 2 (Summer 1977): 835-42. Literature reviews in the history of recreation and sports, though helpful, tend to focus on the male experience; until recently, sports historians paid scant attention to girls and women, and reviews in the field have followed suit. See Melvin L. Adelman, "Academicians and Athletics: Historians' Views of American Sport," *Maryland Historian* 4 (Fall 1973): 123-37; Melvin L. Adelman, "Academicians and American Athletics: A Decade of Progress," *Journal of Sport History* 10 (Spring 1983): 80-106; Stephen Hardy, "The City and the Rise of American Sport: 1820-1920," *Exercise and Sport Sciences Reviews* 9 (1981): 183-219; and Steven A. Riess, "Sport and the American Dream: A Review Essay," *Journal of Social History* 14 (December 1980): 295-303. Both of Adelman's essays bring up the paucity of histories about female recreation and sports. Finally, numerous bibliographies in women's studies and in physical education and sports will lead scholars to sources beyond the ones mentioned in this discussion. Useful bibliographies in women's studies include Jill K. Conway, *The Female Experience in Eighteenth- and Nineteenth-Century America: A Guide to the History of American Women* (New York: Garland Publishing, 1982); Katherine Fishburn, *Women in Popular Culture: A Reference Guide* (Westport, CT: Greenwood Press, 1982); V. F. Gilbert and D. S. Tatla, comps., *Women's Studies: A Bibliography of Dissertations, 1870-1982* (Oxford: Basil Blackwell, 1985); Cynthia E. Harrison, ed., *Women in American History: A Bibliography*, 2 vols. (Santa Barbara: ABC-CLIO, 1979-85); Catherine R. Loeb, Susan E. Searing, and Esther F. Stineman, *Women's Studies: A Recommended Core Bibliography, 1980-1985* (Littleton, CO: Libraries Unlimited, 1987); and Esther Stineman, *Women's Studies: A Recommended Core Bibliography* (Littleton, CO: Libraries Unlimited, 1979). In the area of physical education and sports, readers might consult Bonnie Gratch, Betty Chan, and Judith Lingenfelter, comps., *Sports and Physical Education: A Guide to Reference Resources* (Westport, CT: Greenwood Press, 1983); Mary L. Remley, *Women in Sport: A Guide to Information Sources* (Detroit: Gale Research, 1980); and Earle F. Zeigler, Maxwell L. Howell, and Marianna Trekell, *Research in the History, Philosophy, and International Aspects of Physical Education and Sport: Bibliographies and Techniques* (Champaign, IL: Stipes Publishing, 1971). Two guides about women's health are Belita Cowan, *Women's Health Care: Resources, Writings, Bibliographies* (Ann Arbor: Anshen Publishing, 1977), and Sheryl K. Ruzek, *Women and Health Care: A Bibliography with Selected Annotation* (Evanston, IL: Program on Women, Northwestern University, 1975; addendum, 1976).

pregnancy to menopause. Health educators also impart the value of personal and sexual hygiene, nutrition, and exercise. Cultivating good physical skills and habits is, more particularly, the job of physical educators, who supervise games, sports, and other recreational activities. Whether theoretical or applied, such lessons carry the mark of science. Americans who teach their fellow citizens about health and exercise often cast their work in biological and medical terms.

Health and physical education, though, are not collections of supposedly neutral, scientific facts. As with any form of education, they bear a "hidden curriculum."[3] Health and physical education encourage certain values, attributes, activities, and physiques, which owe as much to cultural preferences as to biological imperatives. In particular, health and physical education help socialize Americans into femininity and masculinity. They identify gender boundaries, that is, the physical, psychological, and social barriers that purportedly separate girls from boys and women from men.

The theme of socialization has been a prominent one in recent sociological and psychological research about women's health. It is especially common in critiques of athletics.[4] Scholars have observed that American culture endorses certain sports as "feminine" (those requiring grace and dexterity) and others as "masculine" (those involving more strength and endurance). Girls and women who stray over the boundary are stigmatized, and learn either to suppress or to flaunt their womanhood.[5] Some writers have stressed the political import of such stereotyp-

[3] See Ann Diller and Barbara Houston, "Women's Physical Education: A Gender-Sensitive Perspective," in Women, Philosophy, and Sport: A Collection of New Essays, ed. Betsy C. Postow (Metuchen, NJ: Scarecrow Press, 1983), pp. 256-58.

[4] The following sources are especially useful: Mary A. Boutilier and Lucinda SanGiovanni, The Sporting Woman (Champaign, IL: Human Kinetics, 1983), chapters 3-6; Jan Felshin, "The Dialectic of Woman and Sport," in The American Woman in Sport, Ellen W. Gerber et al. (Reading, MA: Addison-Wesley, 1974), pp. 179-210; M. Ann Hall, ed., "The Gendering of Sport, Leisure, and Physical Education," special issue, Women's Studies International Forum 10 (1987): 333-465; Dorothy V. Harris, ed., Women and Sport: A National Research Conference, Penn State Health, Physical Education and Recreation Series, no. 2 (University Park: The Pennsylvania State University, 1972), part 3; Janice Kaplan, Women and Sports (New York: Viking Press, 1979); Carole A. Oglesby, ed., Women and Sport: From Myth to Reality (Philadelphia: Lea & Febiger, 1978), chapters 4-7; and "Women and Sport," in Sport and American Society: Selected Readings, comp. George H. Sage, 2nd edition (Reading, MA: Addison-Wesley, 1974), pp. 285-340. The challenges of being black and female are addressed in Tina Sloan Green et al., Black Women in Sport (Reston, VA: AAHPERD Publications, 1981).

[5] For example, see Boutilier and SanGiovanni, The Sporting Woman, pp. 106-10, and pp. 93-130 in general.

ing. Helen Lenskyj, for example, argues that sports contribute to men's control over women's bodies and sexuality; male-dominated culture enforces patriarchy and heterosexuality by confining women athletes to feminine (i.e., "inferior") activities and proscribing masculine and/or lesbian (i.e., "deviant") traits.[6]

What happens when women define their own health and physicality? Many commentators have posited a natural link between feminism and the women's health movement. They have asserted that self-knowledge, unlike received knowledge, is innately affirming and that control over one's own body is both symbol and substance of liberation.

Those premises certainly underlie the modern women's health movement. When *Our Bodies, Ourselves*, a guide to self-knowledge and self-help, was first issued in 1973, it quickly became the bible of feminist health advocates. The authors shared with readers the joy of discovering and governing their own health:

> Finding out about our bodies and our bodies' needs, starting to take control over that area of our life, has released for us an energy that has overflowed into our work, our friendships, our relationships with men and women, for some of us our marriages and our parenthood. . . . Learning to understand, accept, and be responsible for our physical selves, we are freed of some [negative] preoccupations and can start to use our untapped energies. Our image of ourselves is on a firmer base, we can be better friends and better lovers, better *people*, more self-confident, more autonomous, stronger, and more whole.[7]

Women activists predict an equally liberating result when feminism permeates the structure and values of athletics in America. Wilma Scott Heide, for example, believes that the "values revolution" implicit in feminism can transform sport as domination into "sport as fun, as play, as one vital method to grow and know one's power to be humane."[8]

The work of feminist scholars and women's health advocates has raised two focal questions for historians of health and sports: first, what

---

[6] Helen Lenskyj, *Out of Bounds: Women, Sport and Sexuality* (Toronto: Women's Press, 1986).

[7] The Boston Women's Health Book Collective, *Our Bodies, Ourselves: A Book By and For Women* (New York: Simon and Schuster, 1973), pp. 2, 3. Two recent analyses also note the empowering effects of the women's health movement: Helen I. Marieskind, *Women in the Health System: Patients, Providers, and Programs* (St. Louis: C. V. Mosby, 1980), pp. 284-311, and Sheryl Burt Ruzek, *The Women's Health Movement: Feminist Alternatives to Medical Control* (New York: Praeger Publishers, 1978), pp. 27-64 and passim.

[8] Wilma Scott Heide, "Feminism for a Sporting Future," in *Women and Sport: From Myth to Reality*, ed. Oglesby, p. 202.

is the relationship of health and physical education to gender socialization, and second, is there a basic synergy between women's physical
freedom and social empowerment?

Most historians have addressed the former issue. For example, some
have demonstrated how cultural norms about gender have been embedded in scientific models of health and sickness.[9] The classic example
is the Victorian cult of female frailty; framed in medical terms, the
equation between womanhood and ill health was powerful ammunition
in nineteenth-century debates about female education, work, and exercise. Other scholars have begun examining the role of physical education
and sports in preserving the separate spheres that American society
delineated for men and women. Roberta J. Park, a professor of physical
education, has argued that "sporting and recreative activities . . . helped
to define and reinforce prevailing concepts of *gender*." In particular, she
continues, "nineteenth-century sport came to be forcefully and graphi-
cally depicted as the 'natural' province of males; hence, sport contributed substantially to establishing and maintaining ideologies about the
proper sphere of women."[10] In the late 1800s and early 1900s, female
athletes who overstepped the bounds of normalcy met ambivalence: was
this "Third Sex" deviant or progressive?[11] Sociologists and historians
alike now perceive such questions to be cultural, rather than biological
ones. Among researchers, the dialectic between gender and society has
become a commonplace idea.

The issue, then, is how the interplay between social ideology and
female behavior is regulated. More specifically, who has disseminated
ideas about women's health and what have their motives been? Have the
ideologies and intentions of health education been different when men

---

[9] Some of the most recent contributions have been collected in Judith Walzer Leavitt,
     ed., *Women and Health in America: Historical Readings* (Madison: University of Wiscon-
     sin Press, 1984). Other noteworthy discussions include Harvey Green, *Fit for America:
     Health, Fitness, Sport and American Society* (New York: Pantheon, 1986); John S. Haller,
     Jr. and Robin M. Haller, *The Physician and Sexuality in Victorian America* (Urbana:
     University of Illinois Press, 1974); Carroll Smith-Rosenberg, *Disorderly Conduct: Vi-
     sions of Gender in Victorian America* (New York: Alfred A. Knopf, 1985), pp. 182-216;
     and Martha H. Verbrugge, *Able-Bodied Womanhood: Personal Health and Social Change
     in Nineteenth-Century Boston* (New York: Oxford University Press, 1988).
[10] Roberta J. Park, "Sport, Gender and Society in a Transatlantic Victorian Perspective,"
     in *From 'Fair Sex' to Feminism: Sport and the Socialization of Women in the Industrial and
     Post-Industrial Eras*, ed. J. A. Mangan and Roberta J. Park (London: Frank Cass, 1987),
     p. 59.
[11] See Twin, *Jock and Jill*, p. 215, and pp. 175-220 in general; and Donald J. Mrozek,
     "The 'Amazon' and the American 'Lady': Sexual Fears of Women as Athletes," in *From
     'Fair Sex' to Feminism*, ed., Mangan and Park, pp. 282-98.

and women controlled it? One answer emerges in a series of articles by Patricia A. Vertinsky, a professor of education and physical education, who examines the role of health reformers, doctors, and physical educators in perpetuating gender-specific models of health in the nineteenth and early twentieth centuries.[12] Recreation, sexual mores, myths about menstruation, and standards of female physique, she maintains, were vehicles of social control, curbing improper values and behavior among women. Though physical education had some liberating effects, its main objective and consequences in American history, Vertinsky contends, have been conservative. Many of her protagonists are men who, for social and professional reasons, had a vested interest in maintaining traditional gender roles. In a more radical analysis, Helen Lenskyj specifies men's concerns by exploring how the model of frail, heterosexual womanhood protected male supremacy, physically and socially.[13]

Other scholars have focused on women who challenged cultural expectations about their health and physicality. During the nineteenth and twentieth centuries, women's gains in education, employment, and political and legal rights were paralleled by physical liberation (physiological instruction, healthy clothes, less restricted exercise and recreation).[14] Feminists—from health reformers in the 1800s to physical edu-

---

[12] Listed chronologically, Vertinsky's essays include "The Effect of Changing Attitudes Toward Sexual Morality Upon the Promotion of Physical Education for Women in Nineteenth Century America," in *Her Story in Sport*, ed. R. Howell, pp. 165-77; "God, Science and the Market Place: The Bases for Exercise Prescriptions for Females in Nineteenth Century North America," *Canadian Journal of the History of Sport and Physical Education* 17 (May 1986): 38-45; "Exercise, Physical Capability, and the Eternally Wounded Woman in Late Nineteenth Century North America," *Journal of Sport History* 14 (Spring 1987): 7-27; and "Body Shapes: The Role of the Medical Establishment in Informing Female Exercise and Physical Education in Nineteenth-Century North America," in *From 'Fair Sex' to Feminism*, ed. Mangan and Park, pp. 256-81.

[13] Lenskyj, *Out of Bounds*, pp. 11-71.

[14] Several works trace developments in female exercise and sports in the context of major social changes during the nineteenth and twentieth centuries. See Twin, *Jock and Jill*, and Park, "Sport, Gender and Society in a Transatlantic Victorian Perspective," in *From 'Fair Sex' to Feminism*, ed. Mangan and Park, pp. 58-93. An older study is Doris Paige Watts, "Changing Conceptions of Competitive Sports for Girls and Women in the United States from 1880-1960" (Ed.D. dissertation, University of California, Los Angeles, 1960). It is worth noting that histories of games and recreation in America, though technically outside the scope of this essay, have described similar changes (albeit with less sophistication). Descriptions of female recreation may be found in Reet Howell, ed., *Her Story in Sport*, especially articles contributed by the volume's editor (pp. 35-43, 70-79, and 87-95) and one in collaboration with Maxwell L. Howell (pp. 154-64).

cators and athletes in the 1900s—spearheaded that movement for physical freedom. Early birth-control advocates, for instance, regarded body politics, more than electoral politics, as the primary focus of the women's movement in America. Other Victorian women discovered how physical activity engendered confidence and self-knowledge. (A delightful example is the story of Frances Willard, leader of the Women's Christian Temperance Union, and her progress as a bicycle rider.[15]) Some historians, then, have found evidence of a vital connection between the feminist movement and women's physical independence.[16]

The overall argument in recent scholarship has considerable validity. Knowledge *is* power: whoever controls health and physical education helps set the boundaries of gender. Thus, conservative and progressive groups have struggled to define and govern women's physicality throughout American history. Women's autonomy has grown, in part, because of their knowledge and independence in the physical realm.

At the same time, that interpretation is oversimplified. It adopts an outdated analysis of women's history: victimized by a repressive society, courageous women fought for and won their rights; the historian exposes the villains and celebrates the victors. In recent years, that scenario has given way to more sophisticated models in women's studies. Historians and sociologists now regard the interaction of gender and culture as more dynamic and more complex than was once perceived. For instance, women grappled with and transformed the very notion of "womanhood" while struggling for their civil rights; far from being smooth, their journey involved ambivalence, disagreements, and compromises about women's place in society.

The implication for the historiography of health and physical education is evident. As some researchers in the field have recognized, a simple

15 See Frances E. Willard, *A Wheel Within a Wheel; How I Learned to Ride the Bicycle* (1895), excerpted in *Out of the Bleachers: Writings on Women and Sport*, ed. Stephanie L. Twin (Old Westbury, NY: The Feminist Press; New York: McGraw-Hill, 1979), pp. 103-14.
16 Among histories of physical education and sport, two clear-cut examples of this thesis are Roberta J. Park, " 'Embodied Selves': The Rise and Development of Concern for Physical Education, Active Games and Recreation for American Women, 1776-1865," *Journal of Sport History* 5 (Summer 1978): 5-41 (and condensed in *Her Story in Sport*, ed. R. Howell, pp. 44-56); and Marianna Trekell, "The Effect of Some Cultural Changes Upon the Sports and Physical Education Activities of American Women, 1860-1960," in *History of Physical Education and Sport in the United States and Canada*, ed. Zeigler, pp. 155-66.

typology of male as oppressor and female as victim and rebel is no longer adequate.[17] We must ask precisely *who* has controlled health and physical education in America, *what* the content (intellectual and ideological) of that knowledge has been, and *how* power over health instruction has been gained and exercised. In particular, we need to know about women's experiences as they managed their own health education and physical activity. A logical source of case studies is the history of institutions where hygiene and exercise have been taught.

HEALTH EDUCATION AND PHYSICAL EDUCATION IN SCHOOLS

Much of the work (both early and recent) in the history of health and physical education has focused on schools, private and public, secondary and collegiate. The results have been mixed: although numerous details about individual schools have been compiled, the quality of research and analysis in the field has been uneven. The following discussion identifies the primary conclusions that have emerged in the literature, and suggests issues that future researchers might address.

During the nineteenth century, American females gained access to secondary and then collegiate education. One controversy that engaged advocates and opponents alike was student health. Would intense intellectual study jeopardize girls' physical well-being? In fact, was it possible to enhance, not merely protect, female health during formal education? Those questions led many schools (especially private ones) to prescribe physiological instruction and/or supervised exercise for female students during the 1800s and 1900s.[18]

Several factors influenced the content and purpose of curricula in health and physical education. One was the educational vision of a school—what the founders, administrators, and staff regarded as healthy womanhood and what measures they chose to promote it. Another factor was the range (usually limited) of resources, facilities, and faculty

---

[17] Two good examples of revisionist work are Twin, *Jock and Jill*, and "Introduction," in *Out of the Bleachers*, ed. Twin, pp. xv-xli. See also Paul Atkinson, "The Feminist Physique: Physical Education and the Medicalization of Women's Education," in *From 'Fair Sex' to Feminism*, ed. Mangan and Park, pp. 38-57. Atkinson describes how nineteenth-century female educators subverted the tools of oppression (for example, the ideology of women's frailty and the practices of body measurement) for their own purposes.

[18] An old, but still useful overview is Thomas Woody, *A History of Women's Education in the United States*, 2 vols. (New York: Science Press, 1929; reprint ed., New York: Octagon Books, 1966), II: 98-136.

in health and physical education. Finally, social ideologies impinged on curricular decisions; what knowledge and skills were deemed appropriate for women at a given time and place, and would a school accommodate or challenge cultural expectations?

With few exceptions, those same matters have defined historical research in the field. Studies about individual institutions follow a predictable pattern: they trace changes in the objectives and systems of school exercise (from light gymnastics in the nineteenth century to sports and dance in the twentieth century); they discuss how social judgments about women's abilities and temperament affected school programs, especially athletics; they describe educators' concerns about competitive sports for girls and their search for alternatives; and they chronicle slow increases in facilities and staff members devoted to health and physical education (from sadly limited to fairly adequate, with coed institutions often lagging behind female schools). Those points are invariant in the historical literature—regardless of institution (public or private; secondary or collegiate) or time period (nineteenth or twentieth century) or geographical region.

The least developed subject is physical education for girls in public and private secondary schools. Several case studies about cities or regions are available, as are some accounts of girls' athletics in high schools.[19] Literature about physical education and sports for collegiate

---

[19] Some information about girls in Northeastern academies is found in Roxanne Albertson, "Sports and Games in Eastern Schools, 1780-1880," in *Sport in American Education: History and Perspective*, ed. Wayne M. Ladd and Angela Lumpkin (Washington, D.C.: American Alliance for Health, Physical Education, Recreation and Dance, 1979), pp. 19-32. Albertson has also studied private girls schools in the South; see "School Physical Activities for [Southern] Antebellum Females," in *Her Story in Sport*, ed. R. Howell, pp. 369-79. Developments in one Midwestern city are considered in Margaret Lee Driscoll, "The History of Physical Education for Girls in the Public Schools of Cincinnati, Ohio" (Ed.D. dissertation, University of Cincinnati, 1966). The following describe interscholastic and intercollegiate athletics in particular sports: Jan Beran, "The Story: Six-Player Girls' Basketball in Iowa," in *Her Story in Sport*, ed. R. Howell, pp. 552-63; Mary Ellen Hanson, "Competition vs. Recreation in the Early Development of Women's Basketball, 1891-1922" (paper delivered at the Midyear Conference of the Special Interest Group: Research on Women in Education, American Educational Research Association, Tempe, Arizona, November 3, 1983; copy acquired from EDRS); and Paula Welch, "Interscholastic Basketball: Bane of Collegiate Physical Educators," in *Her Story in Sport*, ed. R. Howell, pp. 424-31. J. Thomas Jable, "The Public Schools Athletic League of New York City: Organized Athletics for City Schoolchildren, 1903-1914," in *Sport in American Education*, ed. Ladd and Lumpkin, pp. ix-18, mentions activities for girls. Barbara N. Noonkester, "The American Sportswoman from 1900-1920," in *Her Story in Sport*, ed. R. Howell, pp. 178-222, also includes some information about interscholastic sports; for example, see pp. 185-92 on baseball and basketball.

women is far more plentiful. Typically, researchers focus on a particular school or region and cover standard topics: curricular developments and requirements; battles and compromises over intercollegiate athletics; gradual improvements in exercise costumes, equipment, and facilities; growth in the number and qualifications of personnel; and governance of physical education and sports, locally and nationally.[20]

The usual result of such research is a descriptive chronology. Authors relate *what* changes were made in physical education, but relatively little about *who* controlled the decisions, *how* judgments were reached and implemented, and *why* certain options were pursued and others were forsaken. Why, for example, were girls' interscholastic athletics less restricted than women's intercollegiate sports?[21] Moreover, why did most colleges and universities, despite their many other differences,

---

[20] Programs in the Northeast are covered in Dorothy S. Ainsworth, *The History of Physical Education in Colleges for Women: As Illustrated by Barnard, Bryn Mawr, Elmira, Goucher, Mills, Mount Holyoke, Radcliffe, Rockford, Smith, Vassar, Wellesley and Wells* (New York: A. S. Barnes and Company, 1930); Dorothy S. Ainsworth, "The History of Physical Education in Colleges for Women (U.S.A.)," in *History of Physical Education and Sport in the United States and Canada*, ed. Zeigler, pp. 167-80; Joanna Davenport, "The Eastern Legacy - The Early History of Physical Education for Women," in *Her Story in Sport*, ed. R. Howell, pp. 355-68; Mary-Lou Squires, "Sport and the Cult of 'True Womanhood': A Paradox at the Turn of the Century," in *Her Story in Sport*, ed. R. Howell, pp. 101-6; and Verbrugge, *Able-Bodied Womanhood*, pp. 139-61, about Wellesley College. Regarding schools in the South, see Angela Lumpkin, "Women's Physical Activity at the First State University - An Uphill Struggle," in *Sport in American Education*, ed. Ladd and Lumpkin, pp. 117-29, on the University of North Carolina, and Mildred Marie Usher, "A History of Women's Intercollegiate Athletics at Florida State University from 1905-1972" (Ph.D. dissertation, Florida State University, 1980). Midwestern institutions are discussed in Educational Transitions Committee of the Midwest Association of College Teachers of Physical Education for Women, *A Century of Growth: The Historical Development of Physical Education for Women in Selected Colleges of Six Midwestern States* (Ann Arbor: Edwards Brothers, 1951); Althea Heimbach, "Women's Physical Education in Milwaukee," *Historical Messenger* [of the Milwaukee County Historical Society] 25 (1969): 63-67; June F. Kearney, "The History of Women's Intercollegiate Athletics in Ohio, 1945-1972," in *Her Story in Sport*, ed. R. Howell, pp. 460-71; Nancy Struna and Mary L. Remley, "Physical Education for Women at the University of Wisconsin, 1863-1913: A Half Century of Progress," *Canadian Journal of the History of Sport and Physical Education* 4 (1973): 8-26; and Phyllis Kay Wilke, "Physical Education for Women at Nebraska University, 1879-1923," *Nebraska History* 56 (Summer 1975): 192-220. For an example from the Far West, see Roberta J. Park, "History and Structure of the Department of Physical Education at the University of California [Berkeley], With Special Reference to Women's Sports," in *Her Story in Sport*, ed. R. Howell, pp. 405-16. One of the few pieces that compiles information from various regions is Betty Spears, "The Emergence of Women in Sports," in *Women's Athletics: Coping with Controversy*, ed. Barbara J. Hoepner (Washington, D.C.: American Association for Health, Physical Education, and Recreation, 1974), pp. 26-42.

arrive at identical solutions for women's physical education? Were there no significant local variations in social ideology, institutional politics, or educational philosophy?

In lieu of detailed analyses, the historical explanations are general and routine: institutional constraints and social norms restricted women's physical activities in schools during the 1800s; in the twentieth century, students and faculty members sought, with some success, women's rights in the gym and on the playing field. Many studies simply relate what improvements were attained.

Some scholars, however, have raised the next logical question: what did "women's rights" actually mean to female students and teachers? The issue is vital and intriguing. In most instances since the mid-nineteenth century, physical education has been sex-segregated: women have taught other females, and men have taught other males. Moreover, during the twentieth century, female physical educators established an independent network of professional organizations and governance structures. To some extent, then, the character of women's physical education in America has reflected the knowledge and power of female teachers, not merely institutional politics and social ideologies. What version of "women's rights" did that cohort of teachers and coaches promote?

The answer seems universal, irrespective of region or institution: female physical educators neither pursued nor gained full "equality" for their students; though pressing for facilities and opportunities that matched those of male students, female teachers viewed men's sports as philosophically flawed and physically dangerous; they created a "separate, but equal" zone of female athletics that reconciled play and womanhood. (Insisting, for example, that men's competitive sports were too violent, women physical educators made basketball and other games "safe" for female athletes. Regarding intercollegiate contests as too elitist and too intense, they invented such substitutes as the "Play Day," in which competing teams were comprised of students from various schools. That system dominated women's collegiate sports during the late 1920s and 1930s.)

Most histories of female sports in the twentieth century now describe the ambivalent views and separatist strategies of women physical

[21] One scholar to raise the question is Welch, "Interscholastic Basketball: Bane of Collegiate Physical Educators."

educators.[22] Ellen W. Gerber's work is especially noteworthy.[23] Gerber examines the philosophical basis for women's opposition to intercollegiate sports in the 1920s and 1930s, and demonstrates how they cultivated the money, power, and organizations required to control its development. Another perspective is offered by Stephanie Lee Twin, who contrasts the relative conservatism of female educators with the more radical stance of American sportswomen. Although both groups championed women's exercise and can be labeled "feminist," their disagreements made a broad, unified campaign for female athletics in the early 1900s impossible.[24]

Such work reminds us that the relationship between feminism and physical independence is *not* a formulaic one. Proponents of female exercise certainly contributed to women's physical freedom: they redefined American ideas of able-bodied womanhood and made new opportunities in recreation and sports available to women. Yet, the views of female physical educators perpetuated the concept of innate gender differences and their separatist strategy, however productive, was costly. The result, some observers say, was an athletic ghetto—one in which the concerns of women prevailed, but the resources, publicity, and prestige accorded men's sports were sorely absent.[25] The legacy—both intellectual and institutional—of early female physical educators has been con-

---

[22] Typical examples are Judy Jensen, "Women's Collegiate Athletics: Incidents in the Struggle for Influence and Control," *Arena Review* 3 (May 1979): 13-24; Mary Lou Remley, "Women and Competitive Athletics," *Maryland Historian* 4 (Fall 1973): 88-94; and Laura Robicheaux, "An Analysis of Attitudes Toward Women's Athletics in the U.S. in the Early Twentieth Century," *Canadian Journal of the History of Sport and Physical Education* 6 (May 1975): 12-22.

[23] See Ellen W. Gerber, "The Controlled Development of Collegiate Sport for Women, 1923-1936," *Journal of Sport History* 2 (Spring 1975): 1-28 (and reprinted in *Her Story in Sport*, ed. R. Howell, pp. 432-59); also, Ellen W. Gerber, "Collegiate Sport," in *The American Woman in Sport*, Gerber et al., pp. 48-85. Another useful piece is Ronald A. Smith, "The Rise of Basketball for Women in Colleges," *Canadian Journal of the History of Sport and Physical Education* 1 (December 1970): 18-36.

[24] See Twin, *Jock and Jill*, pp. 208-15, 221-75, and *Out of the Bleachers*, ed. Twin, pp. xxiii-xxxiv.

[25] In recent decades, the status of women's athletics has improved due to federal legislation, including Title IX of the 1972 Higher Education Act, women's participation in the Olympics, and the growth of women's professional sports. Although such developments have increased the public visibility and financial support of women's athletics, they have not yet corrected all the disparities between men's and women's sports at the amateur or professional level. See Elizabeth R. East, "Federal Civil Rights Legislation and Sport," in *Women and Sport: From Myth to Reality*, ed. Oglesby, pp. 205-19, and Patricia Huckle, "Back to the Starting Line: Title IX and Women's Intercollegiate Athletics," *American Behavioral Scientist* 21 (January/February 1978): 379-92.

siderable, yet our understanding of their work and lives is far from complete.

There are numerous biographical sketches of individual administrators and teachers in health and physical education.[26] (Most subjects, however, are white; information about black women in the field is scarce.[27]) Some fascinating autobiographies are also available.[28] Several scholars have described the professional organizations and governance structures that female physical educators established in the twentieth century.[29]

---

[26] Biographical material appears in a wide range of sources: anthologies about physical education, biographical dictionaries, professional journals and institutional publications, and innumerable master's and doctoral theses. The items are far too numerous to list here. As a start, readers might consult "Biographical Sketches of Early Leaders," *Journal of Health, Physical Education and Recreation* 31 (April 1960): 37 and 108; 50; 51 and 110; Janice Williams Carkin, "A Study of Five Women in the Field of Physical Education Who Have Been Recipients of the Gulick Award Up to 1950" (Ed.D. dissertation, Stanford University, 1952); Ellen W. Gerber, *Innovators and Institutions in Physical Education* (Philadelphia: Lea & Febiger, 1971); Madge Marie Phillips, "Biographies of Selected Women Leaders in Physical Education in the United States" (Ph.D. dissertation, State University of Iowa, 1960); "Pioneer Women in Physical Education," *Research Quarterly*, supplement, vol. 12 (October 1941): 615-703; entries under "Physical Education" in *Notable American Women: The Modern Period*, ed. Barbara Sicherman and Carol Hurd Green (Cambridge: The Belknap Press of Harvard University Press, 1980). Few book-length biographies are available. One is Betty Spears, *Leading the Way: Amy Morris Homans and the Beginnings of Professional Education for Women*, Contributions in Women's Studies, no. 64 (New York: Greenwood Press, 1986). Homans directed the Boston Normal School of Gymnastics, a prominent training school in physical education, from its opening in 1889 to 1918. Group profiles of female graduates of the Boston Normal School of Gymnastics may be found in Betty Spears, "Success, Women, and Physical Education," in *Women as Leaders in Physical Education and Sport*, ed. M. Gladys Scott and Mary J. Hoferek (Iowa City: University of Iowa Press, 1979), pp. 5-19, and Verbrugge, *Able-Bodied Womanhood*, pp. 162-91.

[27] Sources include Leon N. Coursey, "Anita J. Turner: Early Black Female Physical Educator," *Journal of Health, Physical Education and Recreation* 45 (March 1974): 71-72; Leon N. Coursey, "Pioneer Black Physical Educators: Contributions of Anita J. Turner and Edwin B. Henderson," *Journal of Physical Education and Recreation* 51 (May 1980): 54-56; and Armstead A. Pierro, "A History of Professional Preparation in Physical Education in Selected Negro Colleges and Universities to 1958," in *History of Physical Education and Sport in the United States and Canada*, ed. Zeigler, pp. 255-71. Profiles of contemporary physical educators and athletes are available in Green et al., *Black Women in Sport*, pp. 15-48.

[28] For example, see Mabel Lee, *Memories of a Bloomer Girl, 1894-1924* (Washington, D.C.: American Alliance for Health, Physical Education, and Recreation, 1977), and its sequel, *Memories Beyond Bloomers (1924-1954)* (Washington, D.C.: American Alliance for Health, Physical Education, and Recreation, 1978); and Lilian Welsh, *Reminiscences of Thirty Years in Baltimore* (Baltimore: The Norman, Remington Co., 1925). Lee taught at the University of Nebraska, and Welsh was associated with Goucher College.

[29] Quick overviews are found in *The American Woman in Sport*, Gerber et al., pp. 68-85, and Jensen, "Women's Collegiate Athletics."

This area should be a research priority in coming years, and two quite different approaches might prove fruitful. First, more sophisticated studies of women physical educators at individual schools would be valuable. Scholars need to move beyond public materials (such as college catalogues and professional publications) and begin mining more private sources (such as institutional records, faculty minutes, and personal correspondence and diaries). We need more detailed accounts of how institutions reached curricular decisions in physical education, and of the role and experiences of female administrators and teachers, in particular. Second, no one, to date, has undertaken a comprehensive analysis of women in American physical education. The field awaits a systematic survey of their backgrounds, career patterns, personal lives, educational philosophies, and professional activities. That collective story, moreover, needs to be placed in the larger context of American social history and the maturation of physical education as a profession. Other historians have conducted exciting research on women scientists, doctors, and nurses in America; one can hope that similar work on female physical educators will be forthcoming.

Quite absent from this discussion has been the topic of health education (human anatomy, physiology, and hygiene). Although histories of physical education typically note schools' requirements and coursework in health, few researchers have concentrated on the subject. One general survey, by Richard K. Means, chronicles health education programs in American private and public schools, colleges, and normal schools.[30] Means describes how the philosophy and structure of curricula changed over roughly two hundred years (late 1700s to the 1960s), and how health education developed as a distinct profession. Although Means does not specifically mention curricula for females, some evidence exists that public schools designed different programs for boys and girls.[31] A recent study by John C. Burnham offers an original look at the popularization of science and health in the United States through various agencies (the media, schools, and voluntary associations).[32]

---

[30] See Richard K. Means, *A History of Health Education in the United States* (Philadelphia: Lea & Febiger, 1962).

[31] For example, see Martha H. Verbrugge, "Fitness for Life: Female Health and Education in Nineteenth-Century Boston" (Ph.D. dissertation, Harvard University, 1978), pp. 308-22. Verbrugge discusses the different requirements and curricula in physiology for boys and girls in the Boston public schools during the mid-1800s.

[32] John C. Burnham, *How Superstition Won and Science Lost: Popularizing Science and Health in the United States* (New Brunswick: Rutgers University Press, 1987).

Burnham describes major shifts in the format, content, and purveyors of health education, but does not identify gender as one of the variables that affected the field.

There is considerable room, then, for historians to explore the development of health education for girls and women in American schools. The dynamics of knowledge and power might serve well as a starting point: what did coursework in health include or exclude, who made curricular decisions, and what was their "hidden curriculum" for student values and behavior?

HEALTH AND PHYSICAL EDUCATION IN VOLUNTARY ORGANIZATIONS

Voluntary organizations have been the mainstay of the modern women's health movement. Lists of women's health clinics, collectives, and associations during the last twenty years are lengthy.[33] Their activities have been equally diverse: dissemination of health information to women; political activism and lobbying to further women's interests; and providing alternative medical services and/or training women in self-help care. Among the groups emphasizing education, two of the more enduring and influential are the Boston Women's Health Book Collective and the National Women's Health Network in Washington, D.C.

Did similar organizations exist before the 1970s? Did earlier generations of women form groups to promote health and physical education? Students and scholars will have some difficulty finding the answer. Information is widely scattered and not readily visible. Detailed studies about private associations that specialized in health and physical education are rare. Therefore, readers must sift through the histories of organizations that had more general interest, or through social histories of American medicine and public health in search of relevant information. Instead of an inclusive survey, the following discussion indicates some current topics in the field and areas of future research.

During the 1800s and early 1900s, various female associations undoubtedly taught their members or other women about health. Hints of programs related to medicine and hygiene appear throughout contem-

---

[33] For a general discussion of organizations and their strategies, see Ruzek, *The Women's Health Movement*, pp. 143-80. For representative lists of groups, see Ibid., pp. 241-65, and Ruzek, *Women and Health Care: A Bibliography with Selected Annotation*, pp. 50-53.

porary reports and historical summaries of women's groups. Developing full accounts of those activities, though, has been difficult. Physiological lecture clubs, for instance, were a vital component of nineteenth-century health reform. Although social historians of medicine frequently refer to such groups, the apparent dearth of primary materials has limited research in the area. Martha H. Verbrugge's in-depth study of the Ladies' Physiological Institute of Boston and Vicinity (founded in 1848 and still extant) gives us a rare glimpse at the concerns that led urban, middle-class women to study health and hygiene in the company of other ladies.[34] Other women's societies addressed the needs of urban workers. In the late 1800s, the Women's Educational and Industrial Union in Boston (and later, Buffalo), for example, hoped to improve the health of local working girls and women through practical lectures and advice.[35] In some cities, settlement homes and working girls' clubs may have offered similar services. The history of child health organizations extends from the early twentieth century to the present. In the 1910s, Little Mothers' Clubs taught girls the basic principles of infant care; since 1956, the La Leche League has given new mothers the information and support needed to breastfeed their babies.[36] Finally, some women's organizations have attempted to reach young children by shaping school curricula. Perhaps the most familiar example is the successful campaign of the Women's Christian Temperance Union in the late nineteenth century to mandate temperance instruction in public schools around the country.[37]

---

[34] See Verbrugge, *Able-Bodied Womanhood*, pp. 49-96. Research about female health lecturers in the nineteenth century is another source of information about physiological clubs. For example, see John B. Blake, "Mary Gove Nichols, Prophetess of Health," *Proceedings of the American Philosophical Society* 106 (June 1962): 219-34, and Sally Gregory Kohlstedt, "Physiological Lectures for Women: Sarah Coates in Ohio, 1850," *Journal of the History of Medicine and Allied Sciences* 33 (January 1978): 75-81.

[35] See Karen J. Blair, *The Clubwoman as Feminist: True Womanhood Redefined, 1868-1914* (New York: Holmes & Meier Publishers, 1980), p. 81 and pp. 73-91 passim, and R. B. Jennings, "A History of the Educational Activities of the Women's Educational and Industrial Union from 1877-1927" (Ed.D. dissertation, Boston College, 1978), pp. 52-59.

[36] See Rima D. Apple, *Mothers and Medicine: A Social History of Infant Feeding, 1890-1950*, Wisconsin Publications in the History of Science and Medicine, no. 7 (Madison: University of Wisconsin Press, 1987), pp. 101-3, 177-78.

[37] See Ruth Bordin, *Woman and Temperance: The Quest for Power and Liberty, 1873-1900* (Philadelphia: Temple University Press, 1981), pp. 135-38; Andrew McClary, "The WCTU Discovers Science: The Women's Christian Temperance Union, Plus Teachers, Doctors and Scientific Temperance," *Michigan History* 68 (January/February 1984): 16-22; and Norton Mezvinsky, "Scientific Temperance Instruction in the Schools," *History of Education Quarterly* 1 (March 1961): 48-56.

Much of the research on those topics reflects the new historiography of women's voluntary organizations. For decades, scholars discounted such clubs and omitted them from historical narratives. As sources of knowledge and power, though, women's groups have held considerable importance, for both members and the larger culture. Beyond simply resurrecting female societies, historians are now examining their meaning in the private and public lives of members: what interests and needs brought women to clubs? how did membership affect their self-perceptions and relationships? what roles and attributes did women's groups foster? what social influence did they exert?[38] The relationship between knowledge, power, and feminism may be a key question as scholars continue studying women's organizations, including those with health-related programs. Some curious gaps in the literature, in fact, need to be filled. Little work has been done on some well-known educational organizations, such as the Young Women's Christian Association, the Girl Scouts of America, and the Camp Fire Girls.[39]

We know even less about private groups that have encouraged physical education and exercise among women. Although the history of recreation and sports has flourished in recent years, few scholars have asked about groups that included women or served a female population. The reasons for such neglect have been both valid and questionable.

Private gymnasia and health spas, for instance, are one means by which Americans have learned to exercise. Records about the owners and clients of such businesses, though, are rare, and historical studies have been necessarily limited.[40]

As seen in the previous section, private and public schools have been an important agency of physical education for girls and women. From the outset, voluntary groups have tried to influence what activities were offered. During the post-Civil War decades, for example, the *Turnverein*, a cultural and gymnastics association for German immigrants, was instrumental in gaining physical education programs for public

---

[38] Verbrugge, *Able-Bodied Womanhood*, pp. 67-69, reviews the historiography of women's organizations, including those involved in health reform.

[39] In-house histories, of course, have chronicled the stories of these organizations. Relatively little information, however, can be found in the professional historical literature. Brief mention is made in Twin, *Jock and Jill*, pp. 155-56.

[40] One brief example is Robert Knight Barney, "Mary E. Allen: Thought and Practice in 19th Century American Gymnastics," *Journal of Physical Education and Recreation* 51 (April 1980): 82, 84-86. Information about therapeutic retreats run by medical sects, such as hydropaths, is more prevalent; see chapter 11 in this volume.

schools in the Midwest and California.[41] In the twentieth century, labor organizations became involved in promoting recreation, including physical activities for schoolchildren.[42] The research does not indicate in what way, if any, concerns about girls' health motivated the organizations.

Another advocate of exercise in America has been amateur sports clubs, which originated in cities during the mid-nineteenth century. (Such groups are worth noting, even though they were not strictly "educational" and, therefore, fall outside the scope of this essay.) Since women's athletic clubs were relatively uncommon in the 1800s, most histories concentrate on groups for men.[43] Several scholars have chronicled organizations that supported amateur sports and recreation among girls and women, especially in the twentieth century.[44]

Finally, in the early 1900s, the parks and playground movement advocated public recreational areas, so that city dwellers could exercise outdoors. According to most authors, the primary leaders of the movement were male and their main objective was to prepare urban boys, especially immigrant youth, for proper manhood and citizenship.[45] Galen Cranz, a professor of architecture, demonstrates, however, that the policymakers and designers who planned urban parks also had an agenda for women.[46] During the second half of the nineteenth century, for example, they anticipated that women's presence would help civilize parks, thereby allowing respectable families to use them in safety. In the early twentieth century, Cranz continues, parks were intended to social-

---

[41] See William A. Stecher, "Influence of the American Turnerbund on Gymnastics in the Public Schools," in *A Brief History of the American Turnerbund*, Henry Metzner, rev. ed. (Pittsburgh: National Executive Committee of the American Turnerbund, 1924), pp. 34-37, and Robert Knight Barney, "German Turners in America: Their Role in Nineteenth Century Exercise Expression and Physical Education Legislation," in *History of Physical Education and Sport in the United States and Canada*, ed. Zeigler, pp. 111-20.

[42] See Arthur Weston, "The Contributions of Labor Leaders to Physical Education," in *History of Physical Education and Sport in the United States and Canada*, ed. Zeigler, pp. 93-99.

[43] For example, see Stephen Hardy, *How Boston Played: Sport, Recreation, and Community, 1865-1915* (Boston: Northeastern University Press, 1982), pp. 127-46, and Melvin L. Adelman, *A Sporting Time: New York City and the Rise of Modern Athletics, 1820-70* (Urbana: University of Illinois Press, 1986), which analyzes primarily men's recreation.

[44] An example is Merrie A. Fidler, "The Establishment of Softball as a Sport for American Women, 1900-1940," in *Her Story in Sport*, ed. R. Howell, pp. 527-40.

[45] Recent histories and review essays include Dominick Cavallo, *Muscles and Morals: Organized Playgrounds and Urban Reform, 1880-1920* (Philadelphia: University of Pennsylvania Press, 1981); Hardy, *How Boston Played*, pp. 65-106; Adelman, "Academicians and American Athletics," pp. 84-88; and Hardy, "The City and the Rise of American Sport," pp. 206-10.

[46] Galen Cranz, "Women in Urban Parks," *Signs* 5, suppl. (Spring 1980): S79-S95.

ize males and females alike; space was sex-segregated and "the equipment, the games, and the rules of the games all reflected sex-role differentiation."[47] Other scholars have also noted the creation of playground
activities for girls and the involvement of women reformers in the
playground movement.[48]

Obviously, readers in this area face a wide range of sources and
topics. One might argue that such diversity is useful, if not necessary:
voluntary organizations are eclectic institutions, and no common goal or
function binds them together. (One has trouble, for instance, envision-
ing a study that connects lecture clubs, the *Turnverein*, and the Girl
Scouts.) In all likelihood, case studies will continue to be the norm in
this field.

On the other hand, less specialized work might also assume a role. If
scholars frame more general questions about health and physical education, then comparative histories and comprehensive surveys might
emerge. If we ask, quite simply, how clubs helped popularize health or
exercise in America, then rather disparate institutions become allies.
Natural combinations for research might develop around the type of
knowledge being disseminated (for example, sex education or supervised
recreation), or the audience being addressed (by age, race, or class).

The contributions of voluntary groups to health and physical education are not as well understood as the history of school programs is. That
is not surprising; the difficulty of researching private organizations can
be substantial. Nevertheless, such work is crucial to the study of how
American females learned about health. The topic will become even
more valuable as scholars explore the full range of women's organizations, including those based outside the Northeast and within rural,
black, or working-class populations.

CONCLUSIONS AND PROSPECTS

The history of health and physical education for women is a curious
field. On the one hand, significant information has been collected over
the years. Important questions about the relationship between education, physical activities, and female socialization have been raised. On

---

[47] Ibid., p. S88.
[48] See Twin, *Jock and Jill*, pp. 152-54, and Patricia Mooney Melvin, "Building Muscles
      and Civics: Folk Dancing, Ethnic Diversity and the Playground Association of Amer-
      ica," *American Studies* 24 (1983): 89-99 (which describes the work of Elizabeth Bur-
      chenal, the leading figure in the folk dance movement).

the other hand, the quality of work has been uneven. Although some literature incorporates recent approaches in women's studies and the social history of medicine, the methods and analyses of most research look outdated. The field appears to be full of problems and full of promise.

To date, much of the research has been conducted by professional health educators and physical educators, who have brought their special insights and expertise to the field.[49] Attuned to the evolution of their disciplines and to contemporary issues in health and physical education, these researchers will identify many productive areas for further research. There are also numerous opportunities for professional historians with various interests—in physical education and sports; medicine and public health; women and gender. One can expect them, in particular, to bring the latest methods and perspectives of historical scholarship to bear on this field.

Several areas deserve particular attention. First, histories of physical education in schools are plentiful in number, but limited in scope. They have emphasized certain types of institutions and people: schools in the Northeast and, to some extent, the Midwest; secondary schools and colleges; educators and students who, apparently, were white, urban, and middle- or upper-class. There has been a serious neglect of other groups: Southern and Western institutions; primary-age children; working-class women; and women of color. We also know relatively little about physical education for girls and women outside the school system: in gymnasia, in supervised playgrounds, in recreational clubs.

In the area of health education, even more gaps need to be filled. Few historians have examined school requirements and coursework in physiology and hygiene, at any level of education or through varied curricula (including biology and home economics). The role of women's voluntary organizations (and associations with mixed membership) in popularizing health also warrants further study. The time is especially ripe because scholars are devising new frameworks for analyzing private female clubs.

In both physical education and health education, more rigorous research about the formulation, dissemination, and effects of knowledge

---

[49] Other reviewers have noted this pattern as well. See Adelman, "Academicians and American Athletics," n. 49, p. 97, and Boutilier and SanGiovanni, *The Sporting Woman*, n. 7, p. 22. The one exception is research about women's organizations, where scholars from women's studies and the social history of medicine predominate.

is required. If education is, innately and by design, a form of socialization, we need to understand precisely who educated women about health; what their goals were; what models of healthy womanhood inspired (or scared) them; and what information and programs they chose (and did not choose) to provide. Until recently, most researchers dealt only superficially with those questions. Moreover, we should focus on the many women who served as health and physical educators: school teachers, college professors and coaches, staff members at YWCA's and gyms, social workers, public health nurses, and so forth. What models of healthy womanhood did they teach and practice when holding the reins of knowledge and power? To what extent has a natural synergy developed between physical freedom and feminism?[50]

Finally, most research has focused on educators, not their audience; on the construction of knowledge, not its impact; on its dissemination by experts, not its transformation by users. Scholars should be more mindful of a compelling lesson from women's history and social history: expert advice and popular behavior may not match. Women's personal choices about health may have differed from what schools and other institutions taught them. What did females think it meant to "look like a girl," "act like a girl," and "play like a girl"? For generations, American women have learned about and exercised their bodies, but, for the most part, we have not heard their voices in the history of health and physical education.

---

[50] Ten years ago, for example, a "sports-minded" scholar raised a provocative question: if feminists and women athletes are natural allies, why does such distrust and misunderstanding separate them today? See Hollis Elkins, "Time for a Change: Women's Athletics and the Women's Movement," *Frontiers* 3 (1978): 22-25.

15

• • • ────── • • •

WOMEN'S HEALTH
AND PUBLIC POLICY

Molly Ladd-Taylor

The twentieth century witnessed the transformation of women's and children's health from a private family responsibility into a matter of national policy. In the first decades of the century, the growing number of female and child wage-earners and the high rate of infant and maternal deaths persuaded reformers that they needed to take drastic action to ensure the health of women and children—and the future of the nation. They enacted special labor laws to protect the health of women workers and established federally funded maternal and infant health services. Yet by the end of the 1920s, physicians' opposition to "state medicine" converged with the long-standing distrust of the federal government to challenge the idea that health care should be universally available and to limit American public health services to the poor.

Scholars have as yet paid little attention to the history of women's health and public policy, but it is a promising area for research in which much work needs to be done. Women played a key role in the creation of the American public health system as activists, health professionals, and the primary consumers of health care. However, the separation between women's history and scholarship on public health has left historians with only a partial explanation for the development of the public health system. For example, Daniel Fox's study of British and American health policy ignores the female pioneers in preventive health care and does not discuss maternal and infant services, one of the largest and most successful components of the public health system.[1]

Three themes have marked the history of women's health policy in the United States. First, most laws regarding women's health have been concerned with their role as mothers or potential mothers. Because women bear children and have been chiefly responsible for raising them, policymakers have tended to see women as family members, rather than as individuals, and to equate women's concerns with those of their children. At the same time, women activists have often justified their political activities on the basis of their maternal duties; they claimed that women had a special responsibility to create a more caring society for their children. Not questioning women's responsibility for child care, early twentieth-century reformers thought that the nation needed women's natural empathy and morality to balance the competitive world of men. Distressed by high infant and maternal death rates and frightened by immigration and the prospect of "race suicide," they determined that protecting (white) women's reproductive health should be an essential task of government.[2]

A second feature of women's health policy in the United States concerns the limited nature of the American welfare system. Unlike other industrialized nations, the United States has no national health-care system, maternity insurance, or family allowance. The American "semiwelfare" state is constrained by the ideologies of self-help and states' rights, by racial and ethnic diversity, and by the traditional distrust of a strong federal government. Although the government has funded numerous studies showing the relationship between poverty and illness, it has rarely provided direct aid to the needy. Most federally financed health programs have been marked by striking differentiation at the local level and have been oriented toward education rather than material assistance.[3]

[1] Daniel M. Fox, Health Policies Health Politics: The British and American Experience 1911-1965 (Princeton: Princeton University Press, 1986).

[2] For a more detailed analysis of the ideology of motherhood, see Molly Ladd-Taylor, "Mother-Work: Ideology, Public Policy and the Mothers' Movement, 1890-1930," (Ph.D. dissertation, Yale University, 1986).

[3] Michael B. Katz, In the Shadow of the Poorhouse: A Social History of Welfare in America (New York: Basic Books, 1986) and James T. Patterson, America's Struggle Against Poverty 1900-1980 (Cambridge: Harvard University Press, 1981) are two overviews of American welfare history. See U.S. Department of Labor, Children's Bureau, Causal Factors in Infant Mortality: A Statistical Study Based on Investigations in Eight Cities (Washington, D.C.: Government Printing Office, 1925) for an example of a government study showing the relationship between poverty and illness.

The third theme in women's health history is the persistent opposition of organized medicine to publicly funded health-entitlement programs. Indeed, the American Medical Association's hostility to "state
medicine" is arguably the principal reason for the limited nature of the
U.S. public health system. The AMA lobbied vigorously against national
health insurance, and it opposed the 1921 Sheppard-Towner Act, the
first federal welfare measure, which provided matching funds to the state
for infant and prenatal clinics. Dominated by male specialists engaged in
private practice, the AMA viewed preventive health services for women
and children as a threat to doctors' incomes and control over the health-
care system. Today, women's health policy continues to show the influence of the medical lobby. Most public health services reinforce the
authority of physicians, provide treatment based on high technology
rather than basic preventive care, and are available only to those who
cannot afford private medical care.[4]

PROTECTIVE LABOR LEGISLATION

The enactment of special laws for women workers in the late nineteenth century was the first important instance of government intervention into women's health.[5] Although protective laws grew out of labor's
long-standing efforts to shorten the workday and improve workers'
lives, most union leaders had abandoned legislative efforts to secure a
shorter workday for men by the turn of the century. The primary
impetus for protective laws then came from women's organizations, such
as the Women's Trade Union League and the National Consumers'
League, who were convinced that industrial conditions had a harmful
influence on women's health and were frustrated with the difficulty of

---

[4] See Ronald L. Numbers, *Almost Persuaded: American Physicians and Compulsory Health
Insurance* (Baltimore: Johns Hopkins University Press, 1978); Lloyd C. Taylor, *The
Medical Profession and Social Reform 1885-1945* (New York: St. Martin's Press, 1974);
James G. Burrow, *Organized Medicine in the Progressive Era* (Baltimore: Johns Hopkins
University Press, 1977); Paul Starr, *The Social Transformation of American Medicine*
(New York: Basic Books, 1982).
[5] On protective legislation, see Alice Kessler-Harris, *Out to Work: A History of Wage-
Earning Women in the United States* (New York: Oxford University Press, 1982), chapter
7, and her "Protection for Women: Trade Unions and Labor Laws," in Wendy
Chavkin, ed., *Double Exposure: Women's Health Hazards on the Job and at Home* (New
York: Monthly Review Press, 1984), pp. 139-54; Judith Baer, *The Chains of Protection*
(Westport, CT: Greenwood Press, 1978); Ann Corinne Hill, "Protection of Women
Workers and the Courts: A Legal Case History," *Feminist Studies* 5 (Summer 1979);
Ronnie Steinberg, *Wages and Hours: Labor and Reform in Twentieth-Century America*
(New Brunswick, NJ: Rutgers University Press, 1982).

organizing young factory workers. Protective legislation was also supported by male unionists, politicians, and the courts. Although they
were genuinely concerned about women's horrible working conditions,
these men supported protective laws primarily because they thought that
women were weaker than men and that their place was in the home. The
Massachusetts Supreme Court upheld the first maximum-hours law for
women and children in 1876. By 1925, all but four states limited
women's working hours; eighteen regulated rest periods and meal times;
sixteen prohibited night work, and thirteen states had a minimum wage
for women workers.[6]

Women activists' attitudes toward protective legislation have fluctu-
ated with the changing economy and ideas about woman's role. Both
female and male advocates of protective legislation idealized motherhood and emphasized women's position in the family. As an editorial in
the *Woman Citizen* put it, "The great mass of women . . . believe that the
most important function of woman in the world is motherhood, that the
welfare of the children should be the first consideration, and that because of their maternal functions women should be protected against
undue strain."[7] By the 1920s, however, some feminists began to oppose
protective laws as being paternalistic and discriminatory. Led by the
militant National Woman's Party (NWP), they applauded the 1923
Supreme Court decision, *Adkins v. Children's Hospital*, which invalidated
a minimum-wage law for women, and introduced an Equal Rights
Amendment, which would overturn all sex-based laws. The NWP opposition to hard-won protective labor laws angered proponents of the
legislation, such as National Consumers' League director Florence Kelley, and bitterly divided feminists.[8]

Just as early twentieth-century feminists were divided over the issue
of protective labor laws, scholars have also disagreed about whether sex-
based laws benefited women workers or discriminated against them.
Those who oppose protective legislation stress the benefits that male
trade unionists received from laws that kept women from competing

[6] Edward Clark Lukens, "Shall Women Throw Away Their Advantages?" *American Bar
     Association Journal* (October 1925). Woman's Rights Collection 744, Arthur and Eliza-
     beth Schlesinger Library on the History of Women in America, Radcliffe College,
     Cambridge, MA (hereafter referred to as SL).
[7] Gertrude Foster Brown, "Editorially Speaking," *Woman Citizen*, (July 1926): 24. Wom-
     en's Rights Collection 744, SL.
[8] On the debate over the ERA, see Nancy F. Cott, *The Grounding of Modern Feminism*
     (New Haven: Yale University Press, 1987), chapter 4.

for "men's" jobs. For example, Ann Corrine Hill argues that special laws for women "legitimated rather than challenged the second-class position of women in the American labor force" and were "more often a curse than blessing." Economist Heidi Hartmann sees them as evidence of collusion between capitalists and working-class men whose interests converged in the maintenance of patriarchy and the exclusion of women from high-paying jobs.[9]

Recent scholarship on gender and the welfare state challenges the view that protective laws were imposed on women workers. Historians Kathryn Kish Sklar and Linda Gordon, among others, see health and welfare policy as the product of struggle between reformers and working-class women. Instead of studying how welfare programs were imposed on women, they examine women's own contributions to the development of the welfare system. For example, Sklar argues that a cross-class coalition of women led by Kelley was chiefly responsible for an 1893 Illinois antisweatshop bill which regulated child labor and mandated an eight-hour day for women workers. According to Sklar, the law benefited women workers by allowing them to move from sweatshops into larger, unionized factories where they had better working conditions and received higher wages. She maintains that the Illinois law had the support of women unionists and the parents of child workers, and describes protective laws as "gender-specific reforms that served class-specific goals."[10]

Scholars today find the assumption that all women will become mothers to be one of the most troubling aspects of protective legislation. Many agree with Judith Baer that justifying differential treatment of women on the basis of permanent biological differences sets a dangerous precedent for sex discrimination in employment. For example, the Supreme Court rejected protection for men because it interfered with freedom of contract, but supported labor laws for women because they were considered "fundamentally weaker" than men. The principle of

---

[9] Hill, "Protection of Women Workers and the Courts," pp. 248, 271; Heidi Hartmann, "Capitalism, Patriarchy, and Job Segregation by Sex," *Signs: Journal of Women in Culture and Society* 1 (Spring 1976): 137-69. See also Eileen Boris and Peter Bardaglio, "The Transformation of Patriarchy: The Historic Role of the State," in Irene Diamond, ed., *Families, Politics, and Public Policy: A Feminist Dialogue on Women and the State* (New York: Longman, 1983), pp. 70-93.

[10] Kathryn Kish Sklar, "Hull House in the 1890s: A Community of Women Reformers," *Signs: Journal of Women in Culture and Society* 10 (Summer 1985): 658-77; Linda Gordon, *Heroes of Their Own Lives: The History and Politics of Family Violence* (New York: Viking, 1988).

differential treatment was established in the landmark case *Muller v. Oregon* (1908), in which the Court upheld an Oregon law limiting women's workday to ten hours. Oregon's attorney Louis Brandeis presented the Court with evidence that long hours were dangerous to women's health. The famous "Brandeis brief"—written largely by the attorney's sister-in-law Josephine Goldmark of the National Consumers' League—illustrates both the willingness of reformers to base social policy on biological difference and the important, but largely invisible, role women played in policy formation. Convinced by Brandeis's argument, the Court concluded, "Woman's physical structure and the performance of maternal functions place her at a disadvantage. . . . As healthy mothers are essential to vigorous offspring, the physical well-being of woman becomes an object of public interest and care in order to preserve the strength and vigor of the race." According to Baer, the Court's failure to distinguish between permanent biological differences, and temporary political and economic conditions (such as lower wages) that might have warranted special protection for women, set a precedent for later opinions that justified sex discrimination because of biology.[11]

Reformers and jurists saw protective legislation as a legitimate public health measure and a solution to the "problem" of wage-earning women precisely because it improved women's working conditions while affirming their domestic role. Yet although laws which reduced women's hours and regulated their working conditions probably did remedy the worst abuses against factory workers, they also made it more difficult for women to enter traditionally male—and higher paying—jobs. Moreover, as historian Alice Kessler-Harris has persuasively argued, by defining women primarily as mothers, special laws for women ensured that they would remain secondary workers in the paid labor force.[12]

The idea that the health of women workers needed special protection lost some of its force after the 1920s, as women remained in the labor force longer, entered "men's" jobs in greater numbers, and won political rights, such as suffrage, that previously had been denied them. The Depression offered the first major challenge to state protective laws; the sheer magnitude of the crisis necessitated a federal labor policy. In 1938, Congress enacted the Fair Labor Standards Act, which implemented minimum wages and maximum hours for both male and female

[11] Baer, *The Chains of Protection*, pp. 10-11.
[12] Kessler-Harris, *Out to Work*, p. 212.

workers, thereby establishing the concept of universal protection. By the 1970s, the dramatic increase in the number and proportion of full-time women workers, and the rise of the feminist movement, challenged the rationale for protective labor laws for women: that women were biologically weaker than men and that their place was in the home. Women's organizations and trade unions, initially the chief proponents of protective labor legislation, joined together to oppose protective labor legislation and to support the Equal Rights Amendment.[13]

Today few special laws for women workers remain on the books. Maximum-hour and minimum-wage laws now cover both sexes, and Title VII of the 1964 Civil Rights Act, which bans discrimination in employment on the basis of sex, race, color, religion, and national origin, makes most other restrictions illegal. Most of the remaining restrictions continue to focus on the issue of motherhood, emphasizing the dangers of exposure to radiation, chemicals, and nuclear materials to the female reproductive system. As in the past, these laws ignore any potential danger to the male reproductive system, and generally apply only to high-paying "men's" jobs. Predominantly female jobs, like nursing, which also expose women to dangerous chemicals, are usually excluded from restrictive rules.[14]

Given the ideological emphasis on protecting mothers in the 1910s and 1920s, it is significant that the majority of nonwhite women workers (whose high birth rate many policymakers considered a cause for concern) were left unprotected by women's labor laws. Agricultural and domestic labor—the largest employment categories for women, and ones in which women of color were most likely to be employed—were exempted from protective legislation. Although politicians and reformers idealized motherhood, they ignored and even condemned real mothers who did not conform to white middle-class ideals. Indeed, the same years which saw the enactment of labor laws to protect the health of potential mothers saw the spread of legislation designed to curtail the reproduction of "undesirables." Between 1907 and 1917 sixteen states enacted laws providing for the sterilization of the dependent poor, criminals, the feeble-minded, and other people allegedly unfit to have children. By 1932 twenty-seven states had sterilization legislation, al-

---

[13] Hill, "Protection of Women Workers," pp. 257-71.
[14] See Jeanne Mager Stellman, "Protective Legislation, Ionizing Radiation and Health: A New Appraisal and International Survey," *Women & Health* 12, no. 1 (1987): 105-25, and Judith A. Scott, "Keeping Women in Their Place: Exclusionary Policies and Reproduction," in Chavkin, ed., *Double Exposure*, pp. 180-95.

though only 12,145 people had been sterilized under the laws. An analysis of these laws, which have largely been ignored by historians of women, could add to our understanding of race, gender, and health policy.[15]

MATERNAL AND INFANT HEALTH CARE

The belief that the health needs of women and children were identical marked legislation designed to combat infant mortality, as well as protective labor laws. In the 1910s and 1920s, the United States had one of the highest infant and maternal death rates in the western world. In 1910, between 124 and 158 infants out of every 1,000 live births in the U.S. birth-registration area (where statistics were collected) died before they were one year old. Approximately six white—or eleven black—women died for every 1,000 live births; countless others suffered painful and debilitating injuries. These appalling death rates, combined with a belief in childhood innocence and an optimistic faith in science and medicine, made "baby-saving" a priority among reformers in the first decades of the twentieth century.[16]

For many years, historians portrayed Progressive-Era child-saving campaigns either as a humanitarian attempt to help the needy or as a pernicious effort by elite reformers to impose their values on the poor. However, scholars have recently begun to see health reform as the product of interaction between reformers and recipients. Examining the role of (mostly female) recipients, as well as reformers, in the development of health and welfare policy, they analyze women's efforts to

---

[15] Daniel J. Kevles, *In the Name of Eugenics: Genetics and the Uses of Human Heredity* (New York: Alfred A. Knopf, 1985); Mark Haller, *Eugenics: Hereditarian Attitudes in American Thought* (New Brunswick, NJ: Rutgers University Press, 1963); Rudolph J. Vecoli, "Sterilization: A Progressive Measure?" *Wisconsin Magazine of History* (Spring 1960): 191. See also Linda Gordon, *Woman's Body Woman's Right* (New York: Penguin, 1976), and Rosalind Pollack Petchesky, *Abortion and Woman's Choice: The State, Sexuality, and Reproductive Freedom* (Boston: Northeastern University Press, 1985), chapter 2.

[16] Henry Hibbs, Jr., *Infant Mortality: Its Relation to Social and Industrial Conditions* (New York: Russell Sage Foundation, 1916), p. 5; Bureau of the Census, U.S. Department of Commerce, *Historical Statistics of the United States, Colonial Times to 1970*, pt. 1 (Washington, D.C.: Government Printing Office, 1975): 57; Children's Bureau, U.S. Department of Labor, *Maternal Mortality* Bureau Publication no. 158 (Washington, D.C.: Government Printing Office, 1926): 37.

construct a "maternalist" state that protected the health of women and children.[17]

Women of all regions and economic groups participated in the fight against infant mortality. Physicians, nurses, and social workers joined clubwomen, settlement residents, and other female volunteers to establish infant and prenatal clinics, distribute pure milk to the needy, and run educational programs for mothers. In 1908, the remarkable physician S. Josephine Baker was appointed director of the new Bureau of Child Hygiene of the New York Department of Health, the nation's first tax-supported child-health agency. Under Baker's leadership, the agency distributed pamphlets on hygiene, dispensed pure milk and advice through infant health stations, organized classes for mothers on the care of babies, and trained and regulated midwives. In thirteen years, the number of infant deaths dropped from one in seven to one in fourteen. By 1923, forty-eight states had bureaus of child hygiene, all but three of them headed by women. The activities of these state agencies were modeled on the prenatal and maternal education programs pioneered by voluntary organizations such as the Boston Women's Municipal League; in turn, they served as the model for the 1921 Sheppard-Towner Maternity and Infancy Act.[18]

The most significant organization in the maternal and child-health movement was the federal Children's Bureau, established in 1912 as a division of the Department of Commerce and Labor. The first federal agency to be headed and staffed primarily by women—eight years before they won the vote—the Children's Bureau operated as the women's branch of the federal government in the 1910s and 1920s. Directed by former Hull House resident Julia Lathrop, the first woman to head a government agency, the Bureau was originally conceived as a research

---

17 The humanitarian perspective includes Walter Trattner, *From Poor Law to Welfare State: A History of Social Welfare in America*, 2nd ed. (New York: Free Press, 1979). Anthony Platt, *The Child-Savers: The Invention of Delinquency* (Chicago: University of Chicago Press, 1969), is an example of the social control thesis. Recent work that challenges those interpretations includes Linda Gordon, "Family Violence, Feminism and Social Control," *Feminist Studies* 12 (Fall 1986): 453-78, and her "Child Abuse, Gender, and the Myth of Family Independence: Thoughts on the History of Family Violence and Its Social Control, 1880-1920," *New York University Review of Law & Social Change* 12 (1983-1984): 523-37.

18 S. Josephine Baker, *Fighting for Life* (New York: Macmillan, 1939), pp. 135, 201; J. Stanley Lemons, *The Woman Citizen: Social Feminism in the 1920s* (Urbana: University of Illinois Press, 1973), p. 166; Ladd-Taylor, "Mother-Work," chapter 5.

agency designed to "investigate and report . . . upon all matters pertaining to the welfare of children and child life among all classes of our
people." Despite its small staff of fifteen and initial appropriation of
only $25,640, the Children's Bureau published and distributed child-
rearing advice, spearheaded a nationwide campaign to register births,
and undertook a series of investigations into the causes of infant mortality.[19]

Notwithstanding the pivotal role the Children's Bureau played in the
history of women's health and public policy, no recent books have been
published on the agency. However, two excellent dissertations by Nancy
Pottishman Weiss and Robyn L. Muncy place the Bureau at the intersection of the reform impulse of Progressive Era women and the development of the female professions. Noting the influence of Hull House on
the politics and style of the federal agency, Weiss and Muncy argue that
the women of the Children's Bureau developed and administered a
child-welfare policy based on what they considered to be uniquely
female values. In the process, they created new careers for themselves
and carried the reform movements of the Progressive Era into the
1930s.[20]

The enactment and administration of the 1921 Sheppard-Towner
Maternity and Infancy Act was the high point of the Bureau's activities
and the culmination of the Progressive women's health movement. "Of
all the activities in which I have shared during more than forty years of
striving," declared National Consumer's League secretary Florence Kelley, "none is, I am convinced, of such fundamental importance as the
Sheppard-Towner Act."[21] Lathrop designed the bill, which was sponsored by Texas Senator Morris Sheppard and Iowa Congressman Horace
Towner, and endorsed by every major women's organization. The first
"women's" bill to pass after suffrage and the first federal social welfare

[19] Law establishing the Children's Bureau, quoted in Children's Bureau, U.S. Department
   of Labor, *Prenatal Care*, Publication no. 4 (Washington, D.C.: Government Printing
   Office, 1913): 2. On the Children's Bureau, see Molly Ladd-Taylor, "Mothers, Child
   Welfare, and the State: Women and the Children's Bureau," in Nancy Schrom Dye and
   Noralee Frankel, eds., *Women in the Progressive Era* (Lexington: University of Kentucky
   Press, forthcoming); and Jacqueline Parker and Edward M. Carpenter, "Julia Lathrop
   and the Children's Bureau: The Emergence of an Institution," *Social Service Review* 55
   (March 1981): 60-76.
[20] Nancy Pottishman Weiss, "Save the Children: A History of the Children's Bureau,
   1903-1918" (Ph.D. dissertation, University of California at Los Angeles, 1974);
   Robyn L. Muncy, "Creating a Female Dominion in American Reform, 1890-1930,"
   (Ph.D. dissertation, Northwestern University, 1987).
[21] Quoted in Lemons, *The Woman Citizen*, p. 155.

measure, Sheppard-Towner passed Congress by a wide margin and was signed into law by President Harding on November 23, 1921. It appropriated $1,480,000 for fiscal year 1921-22 and $1,240,000 for the next five years to be distributed as matching funds to the states for information and instruction on nutrition and hygiene, prenatal and child-health conferences, and visiting nurses for pregnant women and new mothers. The law required states to pass special legislation before they could receive funds, it forbade outright financial aid or medical care, and it explicitly stated that government agents could not enter a home uninvited. Despite these restrictions, the American Medical Association and conservative groups lobbied against the measure, defeating the Children's Bureau's efforts to renew appropriations in 1926. A compromise allocated funds for two more years, but repealed the law itself on June 30, 1929.[22]

Historians have set their examinations of the Sheppard-Towner Act in three contexts. In the first major study of the bill, J. Stanley Lemons analyzed it as an example of the persistence of Progressivism in the 1920s. Next, Sheila Rothman portrayed it as an experiment in a female-run public health system that, ironically, led to the privatization of health care and the demise of female authority in the public health field. More recently, scholars have examined the bill as an example of women's efforts to expand federal authority in health and welfare.[23]

While many historians assume that the Sheppard-Towner Act simply imposed middle-class childrearing methods on the poor, I see the bill largely as the result of the needs and demands expressed by working-class and farm mothers to the Children's Bureau staff. Utilizing the letters working-class and farm women wrote to the Children's Bureau in the 1910s and 1920s, I argue that ordinary mothers had a profound influence on the Children's Bureau staff, and thus played an indirect but significant part in the formation of the Sheppard-Towner Act. For example, Lathrop was deeply moved by her lengthy correspondence with a pregnant Wyoming woman who lived sixty-five miles from a

---

[22] Lemons, *The Woman Citizen*, chapter 6. Molly Ladd-Taylor, "Protecting Mothers and Infants: The Rise and Fall of the Sheppard-Towner Act," in Susan Reverby and Dorothy O. Helly, eds., *Beyond Dichotomy: Public and Private Spheres in Historical Perspective* (Ithaca: Cornell University Press, forthcoming).

[23] J. Stanley Lemons, "The Sheppard-Towner Act: Progressivism in the 1920s," *Journal of American History* 55 (March 1969): 776-86; Sheila Rothman, *Woman's Proper Place: A History of Changing Ideals and Practices, 1870 to the Present* (New York: Basic Books, 1978), pp. 136-53; Ladd-Taylor, "Protecting Mothers and Infants."

doctor and was "so worried and filled with perfect horror at the prospects ahead. So many of my neighbors die at giving birth to their children." The Children's Bureau chief sent money for a layette, arranged for a public health doctor to visit, and designed a bill to provide other expectant mothers with medical and nursing care. In my view, the readiness of the Children's Bureau staff to send money for food, clothing, and health care out of their own pockets to the mothers who wrote them led to strong grassroots support among women for the agency. By 1918, more than eleven million women assisted in the Bureau's research projects, helped it run health clinics, and distributed copies of Bureau publications to their families and friends.[24]

Historians analyzing the defeat of the Sheppard-Towner Act have sought to explain the declining effectiveness of the women's health lobby. Lemons has argued persuasively that most politicians initially backed Sheppard-Towner more out of fear of the potential power of the female voter than out of commitment to the program. Yet Congressmen intimidated by the woman's vote when Sheppard-Towner was passed in 1921 knew by 1926, when its funding was running out, that women did not vote as a bloc.[25] This fact, combined with the conservative political climate and the disarray of the postsuffrage women's movement, reduced the effectiveness of the maternal and child health lobby.

Sheila Rothman's explanation of the bill's defeat, which focuses on its cooptation by the male medical establishment, has until recently been the interpretation favored by feminist scholars. Rothman argues that Children's Bureau supporters initially viewed Sheppard-Towner as a step toward a woman-controlled maternal and infant health system, and successfully resisted efforts to transfer its administration from the female-run Bureau to the medically-run Public Health Service. Yet, she maintains, women's enthusiasm for Sheppard-Towner services led doctors to incorporate preventive health examinations into their private medical practices and to improve obstetrical training in medical and nursing schools. At the same time, male physicians replaced women in the top positions in the state bureaus of child hygiene. According to Josephine Baker, all but three of the forty-eight state directors of child-

---

[24] Molly Ladd-Taylor, *Raising a Baby the Government Way: Mothers' Letters to the Children's Bureau 1915-1932* (New Brunswick, NJ: Rutgers University Press, 1986), pp. 18, 49; and her "Protecting Mothers and Infants." Grace Abbott, "Ten Years' Work for Children," *North American Review* 218 (August 1923): 189-200. For the contrasting view, see Muncy, "Creating a Female Dominion," chapter 4.

[25] Lemons, *The Woman Citizen*, p. 157.

welfare programs had been women when Sheppard-Towner began in 1922; by 1939 three-quarters of them were men.[26]

A third factor in the defeat of the maternity bill was, as I have argued elsewhere, the inability of Sheppard-Towner supporters to sustain a grassroots women's health movement in the states. Although women continued to support Sheppard-Towner throughout the decade, its enactment inevitably led to less active support. Moreover, political obstacles in some states made it difficult to provide effective services, while the tension between the Children's Bureau's dual role of service-provider and leader of a political campaign for child welfare limited the agency's ability to use Sheppard-Towner services to strengthen the lobby for maternal and child welfare.[27]

After the defeat of the Sheppard-Towner Act, the women's movement ceased making federally funded maternity and infancy care a central demand. Although some states continued their health programs after the withdrawal of federal funds in 1929, they received little public attention. For the most part, the issue of maternal and child welfare was left to health professionals, women in government, and the poor who were affected by the programs. Much more research needs to be done on this development. Among the questions to consider are the impact of the Depression on the political priorities of women activists; the role women in government played in the development of public policy; the growing influence of the medical profession; and the political impact of declining infant and maternal mortality rates among the middle class.[28]

Despite the absence of a strong women's health movement, Progressive reformers such as Grace Abbott, the Children's Bureau chief during the Sheppard-Towner years, continued to lobby for federal child-health programs. In 1935 they won a great victory, when some provisions of the Sheppard-Towner Act were restored and expanded in Title V of the Social Security Act. Congress mandated federal support for children

---

[26] Rothman, *Woman's Proper Place*, pp. 142-53; Baker, *Fighting for Life*, p. 201. For a similar analysis, which emphasizes the conflict between female and male views of professionalism, see Muncy, "Creating a Female Dominion," p. 178. Although Weiss does not discuss the Sheppard-Towner Act directly, she too emphasizes the growing influence of the male medical establishment. See Nancy Pottishman Weiss, "Mother: the Invention of Necessity: Dr. Benjamin Spock's *Baby and Child Care*," *American Quarterly* 29 (Winter 1977): 519-27.

[27] Ladd-Taylor, "Protecting Mothers and Infants."

[28] For a positive assessment of women's contributions to social welfare policy in the 1930s, see Susan Ware, *Beyond Suffrage: Women in the New Deal* (Cambridge: Harvard University Press, 1981).

through four programs: aid to dependent children; a maternal and child-welfare program modeled on the Sheppard-Towner Act; welfare services for homeless, neglected and delinquent children; and an entirely new Crippled Children's Services. Yet in contrast to the Sheppard-Towner Act, which distributed literature and opened clinic doors to middle-class as well as poor women, the Social Security Act was directed only to the needy who could not afford private medical care.[29]

Ironically, federally funded maternal and child-health services expanded in the 1930s and 1940s, just as grassroots interest in maternal health policy declined. In contrast to Sheppard-Towner, there was little direct agitation for—or opposition to—the children's provisions of the Social Security Act. Conservatives and the medical establishment who defeated Sheppard-Towner were too alarmed about the prospect of national health insurance, unemployment compensation, and old-age pensions to actively oppose the children's sections of the Social Security Act. Moreover, women's organizations, which played such an important role in Sheppard-Towner, had only an auxiliary role in the design and administration of the Social Security Act.

Sadly, women's success at getting the government to fund and administer the child-health services they initiated seems to have led to their loss of control over the services. By placing programs for children in the mainstream of social welfare policy, the Social Security Act raised the status of child welfare work and increased the opportunities for professional advancement, thus encouraging men to enter the field. Although individual women in government and the health professions continued to play an important role in the development and administration of child-health services, it was male professionals—not women—who came to dominate child-health policy.[30]

Despite the increase in federal monies allocated to maternity care since the defeat of the Sheppard-Towner Act, subsequent health policies received little attention from scholars or the general public. Yet, accord-

[29] See William M. Schmidt, "The Development of Health Services for Mothers and Children in the United States," *American Journal of Public Health* 63 (May 1973): 419-27; Lela B. Costin, *Two Sisters for Social Justice: A Biography of Grace and Edith Abbott* (Urbana: University of Illinois Press, 1983), pp. 221-26; Dorothy Brandbury, "The Children's Advocate: The Story of the U.S. Children's Bureau 1903-1946," n.d., vol. 2, p. 372, Martha May Eliot Papers, SL.

[30] Ladd-Taylor, "Mother-Work"; Muncy, "Creating a Female Dominion." For a related analysis, see Estelle Freedman, "Separatism as Strategy: Female Institution Building and American Feminism, 1870-1930," *Feminist Studies* 5 (Fall 1979): 512-29. See also Cott, *The Grounding of Modern Feminism*; and Ware, *Beyond Suffrage*.

ing to Joan Mulligan (virtually the only scholar to study women's health policy after 1929), they share many of the features of the Sheppard-Towner and Social Security Acts. Like the children's sections of the Social Security Act, the emergency maternity and infant-care program established during World War II was enacted with little public attention. Indeed, EMIC—the nation's largest public health-care program until that time—was the product of existing laws, rather than new legislation. The Children's Bureau staff designed the program, which employed the 1884 Military Dependents Act (stipulating that families of servicemen were entitled to medical assistance), Title V of the Social Security Act, and ten appropriation bills to provide federal funds for the medical costs of pregnancy and the first year of infancy.[31]

According to Mulligan, the war made it possible for the Children's Bureau to create a national health payment plan for low-income women and children, without presenting new legislation to Congress—and to circumvent some of the traditional restrictions against the expansion of federal power. In contrast to other welfare programs, EMIC did not have a residency requirement and did not require states to provide matching funds, ostensibly because of the transient nature of the recipient population. Moreover, recipients were not means-tested; women married to men in all noncommissioned ranks were entitled to assistance, and no check on marital status was made.

Despite their differences, EMIC resembled Sheppard-Towner in two important ways. First, the program was based on the assumption that men financially supported the family while women cared for the children. Indeed, women serving in the military were excluded from the program! The Bureau justified EMIC more as a way to maintain military morale than as a necessary health service. It claimed that military efficiency would be increased if servicemen knew that their families were taken care of while they were at war.[32]

---

[31] Joan E. Mulligan, "Pregnant Americans, 1918-1947: Some Public Policy Notes on Rural and Military Wives," Women & Health 5(4) (Winter 1980): 23-38; Martha M. Eliot and Lillian R. Freedman, "Four Years of the EMIC Program," Yale Journal of Biology and Medicine 19 (March 1947): 621-35. See Joan E. Mulligan, "Three Federal Interventions on Behalf of Childbearing Women: Sheppard-Towner, EMIC and 1963 Maternal-Child Health Amendments," (Ph.D. dissertation, University of Michigan, Ann Arbor, 1976).

[32] Mulligan, "Pregnant Wives," pp. 33-34. Similar justifications were used to support the expansion of public daycare during World War II. See Sonya Michel, "American Women and the Discourse of the Democratic Family in World War II," in Margaret Randolph Higgonet, et al., eds., Behind the Lines: Gender and the Two World Wars (New Haven: Yale University Press, 1987), pp. 154-67.

Second, EMIC was a further step in the professionalization of health care. The Children's Bureau wanted to raise the standards of maternity care by limiting government payments to hospitals with established obstetrical units and to physicians who graduated from AMA-approved medical schools. However, Congress saw the agency's attempt to impose federal licensing standards on medical care as a violation of states' rights. Over the Bureau's objection, it voted to provide funds to all health-care providers, including midwives, chiropractors, and osteopaths, who provided medical care to pregnant women. Despite the Bureau's defeat on the question of medical standards, EMIC increased the percentage of physician-attended hospital deliveries among white women from 55% to 92.8% of all births, and from 23% to 57.9% among nonwhites. Many historians rightly point out that the decline in midwife-attended births and the rise in hospital deliveries took childbirth out of women's control, but the improvement in hospital standards that occurred under EMIC (such as limiting patients to one per bed) saved many lives.[33]

In six years, EMIC provided care to 1.1 million mothers and 180,000 infants, and maternal deaths dropped dramatically. In 1940, 37.6 white, or 77.4 nonwhite, women were dying for every 10,000 live births; ten years later the death rate had dropped to 8.3 among whites and 22.6 among women of color. Although it is impossible to determine to what extent the decline was due to EMIC, it was, as Mulligan observes, an impressive achievement for a country at war. After EMIC ended in 1947, Congress passed a series of amendments to the Social Security Act which expanded government activities and appropriations for maternal and infant care. The 1963 Maternal-Child Health Amendments to the Social Security Act allocated funds for maternity care in order to prevent mental retardation, most of which went to demonstration projects and research. In 1965 Congress further amended the Social Security Act to establish the Medicaid program. Administered by the states, Medicaid pays for medical services to the poor, including prenatal care, childbirth costs, and (in some states) abortion.[34]

---

[33] Ibid., pp. 30-31. Judith Walzer Leavitt, *Brought to Bed: Childbearing in America 1750-1950* (New York: Oxford University Press, 1986) is a sensitive analysis of women's loss of control over childbirth. Government regulation of midwifery also limited women's birth options. See chapter 17 in this volume.

[34] Mulligan, "Three Federal Interventions on Behalf of Childbearing Women"; Richard W. Wertz and Dorothy C. Wertz, *Lying-In: A History of Childbirth in America* (New York: Free Press, 1977), p. 219; Patterson, *America's Struggle Against Poverty*, pp. 153, 164-66.

As in the past, the most comprehensive public health program for women today provides assistance only to women who are mothers. The Special Supplemental Food Program for Women, Infants and Children (WIC), a 1972 amendment to the Child Nutrition Act of 1966, is a 1.5 billion dollar program serving three million women and children. Administered by the Food and Nutrition Service of the Department of Agriculture, WIC provides milk, cheese, cereal, and infant formula to supplement the diet of pregnant and lactating women, and children under four years old. There are strict eligibility requirements; food is available only to those whom health professionals determine to be at "nutritional risk" because of inadequate income and nutrition. Yet despite its limitations, WIC is one of the most effective health programs operated by the federal government. According to a 1985 study, fetal death rates dropped by one-third and the number of premature births declined 15-25% among the poorly educated and low-income women participating in the program.[35]

Despite the absence of scholarship on WIC, it is clear that it suffers from the same limitations that have characterized the other programs discussed in this essay. First, WIC continues to see women only as part of the mother-child dyad; food and health services are available only to expectant or nursing mothers. Second, WIC continues to promote the professionalization of health care; studies of the program find that participants are more likely to use medical services than they had before. Third, there is tremendous local variation in its administration. Although WIC is funded by the federal government, it is administered by state health departments or Native American tribes, and must be sponsored by local health agencies or clinics. Thus, while there are long waiting lists for participation in some areas, the WIC program operates below capacity in others.[36] A fourth similarity between WIC and other federally funded women's health programs is that it is underfunded and has had to struggle to survive. WIC was enacted in 1972, but no WIC projects were funded until 1974, when Congressional pressure and a lawsuit forced the Department of Agriculture to comply. Moreover, the Reagan administration repeatedly tried to cut the WIC program during the 1980s, although its efforts to do so were blocked by Congress.

---

[35] *New York Times* January 30, 1986, B9:1; Mary Alice Caliendo, *Nutrition and Preventive Health Care* (New York: Macmillan, 1981), pp. 569-76.

[36] Caliendo, *Nutrition and Preventive Health Care.*

According to a 1988 report by the Children's Defense Fund, WIC reaches fewer than half of those eligible for it.[37]

Much research needs to be done about WIC, Medicaid, and other maternal health services, which have a tremendous impact on the nation's health-care system and the health of individual women. We need to investigate the operation of health policies among different racial and ethnic groups; we need to know how recipients have responded to the programs; and we need to explore the relationship between public health services and the medicalization of health care. For example, how have public health policies contributed to the substitution of modern medical care for alternative therapies and traditional healing? What technologies have been used on recipients, and to what effect?

The inadequate maternal and child health-care system in the United States today is the product of the medical opposition to "state medicine," the unwillingness of politicians and voters to spend federal dollars on public health programs, and the absence of a strong women's lobby for prenatal and infant care. Because federally funded maternal and infant care is directed toward the poor (in contrast to programs, like Social Security, which benefit middle-class voters), it is often stigmatized as charity and cut off from mainstream political support. Moreover, most members of feminist organizations are covered by private health insurance, have access to prenatal care, and have a low infant mortality rate, and they have not considered public funds for maternal and infant care to be an urgent women's issue.

CONCLUSION

While the Progressive Era women's movement campaigned to improve the health of women as mothers, the feminist health movement of the 1960s and 1970s sought to distance itself from motherhood. Some feminist health activists promoted "natural" childbirth and the rights of midwives, but the majority have concentrated their energies on defending women's right to birth control and abortion. They lobbied to change abortion laws, to defend the 1973 Supreme Court decision Roe v. Wade, and to oppose the 1976 Hyde Amendment to Title XIX of the Social Security Act, which prohibits federal funding for abortions. A

---

[37] Ruth Sidel, *Women and Children Last: The Plight of Poor Women in Affluent America* (New York: Penguin, 1986), pp. 151-53; Children's Defense Fund, "A Call for Action to Make Our Nation Safe for Children: A Briefing Book on the Status of American Children in 1988," pp. 4-5, 20-21.

number of groups also fought against the forced sterilization of poor women. Fighting for reproductive freedom—the right to choose when and if to have children—feminist health activists challenged the idea that motherhood was woman's primary destiny.[38]

By the 1970s, the "protection of motherhood" had become the refrain not of women reformers seeking government funds for maternal and child welfare, but of New Right conservatives who sought to overturn liberal abortion laws and dismantle the welfare state. According to sociologist Kristin Luker, the most significant difference between pro-life and pro-choice activists centers on definitions of motherhood. While pro-choice activists consider motherhood to be one of several roles available to women, pro-life reformers—like most women in the early twentieth century—view childrearing as woman's duty and ultimate fulfillment.[39] Yet there is a crucial difference. While Progressive reformers envisioned a maternalist state that would protect women and children from the domination of men, most anti-abortion activists of the 1970s and 1980s oppose a strong central government and defend the patriarchal family.

Economic and demographic changes have reshaped women's health policy in the twentieth century. The falling birth rate, the decline in infant and maternal deaths, and the increasing number of wage-earning women have made motherhood less central to women's lives than it was earlier in the century. At the same time, the stigma of federal welfare programs—and their failure to provide reasonable assistance—have kept feminists from making maternity insurance and federally funded health services central to their agenda. In contrast to women reformers of the Progressive Era, most health activists in the 1970s and 1980s are skeptical about the ability (and desirability) of the federal government to safeguard women's health.[40]

Much research remains to be done on the history of women's health and public policy. Although we know a great deal about the political

---

[38] On the different political orientations of various segments of the women's health movement, see Elizabeth Fee, "Women and Health Care: A Comparison of Theories," in *Women and Health: The Politics of Sex in Medicine* (Farmingdale, NY: Baywood Publishing Co., 1983), pp. 17-34.

[39] Kristin Luker, *Abortion and the Politics of Motherhood* (Los Angeles: University of California Press, 1984), especially chapter 8.

[40] Feminists concerned about new reproductive technologies are an important exception. See, for example, Robyn Rowlan, "Motherhood, Patriarchal Power, Alienation and the Issue of 'Choice' in Sex Preselection," in Gena Corea, *Man-Made Women* (London: Hutchinson, 1985).

history of some reforms, such as protective legislation and the Sheppard-Towner Act, we need to know more about how they affected women's health. We need to investigate local variation in health policies and programs; we need to compare U.S. health policy with that of other nations, and we need to know more about the history of health programs, such as sterilization laws, that affect mostly women of color. We also need to examine the effect of women's health policy on private medical care. How, for example, have government programs that fund research and technology affected the birth choices—and health—of middle-class as well as poor women?[41] The relationship between gender, race, and class in the formation of health policy should be a major focus of future research. We need greater knowledge about the history of public policies affecting women's health if we are to create a more fair and humane system of health care and a healthier population.

---

[41] Wertz and Wertz, *Lying-In*, pp. 201-28.

16

• • • • • •

WOMEN'S TOXIC EXPERIENCE
Anthony Bale

In our century, so filled with novel forms of fear and death, what I term "the toxic experience" has become part of the everyday world of many Americans. Most people are aware that they inhabit a world filled with toxic threats and people claiming to have been gravely injured by them. Some live with the awareness of "toxic time bombs" ticking away in their "human guinea pig" bodies. Some become sick and die. All live with a quiet fear of a modern world filled with potent, hidden toxic dangers. An environment that once seemed benign later appears to have caused cancer or other illness or to have placed people at risk. A work environment or ingested substance produces birth defects or cancer in a child. Suffering and confused people search for meaning for their misfortune, connecting it with an environment they have come to regard as toxic, malignant, and threatening. Science and the state become involved in interpreting and managing the situation. Victims become the object of public attention: some sympathetic commentators dramatize their plight, while others ridicule them as hysterics or frauds. The victims become organized; some come to see their misfortune as not part of "nature," but rather as a continuing wrong inflicted upon them by corporate and/ or governmental negligence of such magnitude that it amounts to a form of homicide. Victims may have the opportunity to present their cases before juries, seeking compensation for themselves and punitive damages to prevent future corporate crime.

This chapter is the first synthesis of the disparate material on women's experience with toxic environments in twentieth-century America. It examines the vast, previously ignored story of toxic assaults on women's bodies and well-being in numerous forms and historical contexts, as well as the efforts at redress. This story only became socially visible in

411

the 1970s when the conjunction of such events as the 1971 discovery
that the widely used synthetic estrogen DES (diethylstilbestrol) was a
transplacental carcinogen; the discovery of widespread danger from
toxic chemicals in hazardous waste sites like Love Canal; widespread
concern and conflict over dioxin by Vietnam veterans and many other
groups; the Karen Silkwood case; and the extensive, highly publicized
litigation by asbestos victims, atomic veterans, and residents downwind
of atomic tests helped reveal a massive phenomenon of toxic victimization and search for justice in the courts.

Clearly this massive phenomenon had a history, one that is only
slowly becoming known. Alongside the increasing public recognition of
a toxic world, growing feminist consciousness in the early 1970s produced explorations of women's particular victimization and forms of
activism. By 1977 the revival of interest in women's occupational health
had produced Jeanne Stellman's popular synthesis; that same year Barbara and Gideon Seaman published their feminist book aimed at a
popular audience on the turbulent recent experience with toxic contraceptive technologies.[1]

This chapter connects some of the numerous historical reconstructions of women's experiences into a survey of an important part of
modern life. There are five distinct types of reconstructions of the past
involved here. First, individual victims construct meaningful accounts
that link their current distress to past environmental conditions and
exposures. The second occurs when, through epidemiological studies,
scientists reconstruct past environmental and exposure conditions, linking them to patterns of risk and illness. The third reconstruction results
from inquiries before state investigatory bodies such as congressional
committees and jury trials, which retrace the circumstances leading to
the creation of an environmental problem. This last is particularly
important in a study of the American experience, since the United States
is unique in the extent of its toxic tort inquiries into corporate misconduct. American personal injury litigation provides an extensive public
tribunal in which the circumstances of latent injuries, often developed
over years or decades, are reconstructed and translated into fault and
money before juries and judges within a set of rules that restrict what
constitutes both acceptable discourse and compensable injuries.

---

[1] Jeanne Mager Stellman, *Women's Work, Women's Health* (New York: Pantheon, 1977);
   Barbara Seaman and Gideon Seaman, *Women and the Crisis in Sex Hormones* (New York:
   Rawson Associates, 1977).

Accounts by victims of toxic substances and leaders of their organizations, by journalists and filmmakers, and by historians and other social scientists constitute a fourth form of historical reconstruction. These accounts are often highly sympathetic to victims, juxtaposing a suffering innocent person and/or group to a corporation and/or government with a long pattern of misconduct. The victims search the past for causes of their bodily suffering, then attempt to redress the injustice of the past by presenting their historical case before juries, agencies of the state, and the court of public opinion. Finally, this chapter itself represents a fifth form of historical reconstruction: a synthesis of some of the disparate accounts of the numerous toxic episodes involving women in this century. Many of these reconstructions mine the past with an eye to the future: they attempt to draw lessons that might help create a balance between the activities of corporations and the government and the health of Americans. They look to prevent the future toxic disasters that the record of the past indicates may be developing invisibly around us, even as we attempt to cope with toxic disasters bequeathed from the past.

Women's experiences with a toxic world have encompassed a diversity of roles. Women have encountered it as both victims and advocates, as workers, as community residents, as mothers, as patients, as wives and widows, as scientists and other creators of knowledge. This chapter focuses on the most socially visible manifestation of their toxic experience: episodes of disability and death involving recognizable groups that have achieved a measure of public recognition and redress. The steady creation of victim groups in the United States throughout the first sixty years of the twentieth century reached a crescendo in the 1970s that continued through the 1980s. Their linked stories are part of a coherent historical phenomenon involving women's attempts to understand, control, and be compensated for their toxic experience.

WORK

In 1912 Congress banned the use of phosphorus in the match industry, which had a 40% female labor force, two years after John B. Andrews of the American Association for Labor Legislation had published an exhaustive study of the industry.[2] Andrews presented detailed case descriptions of agonized young women, often teenagers, with rotting

---

[2] John B. Andrews, "Phosphorus Poisoning in the Match Industry in the United States," *Bulletin of the Bureau of Labor*, no. 86 (January, 1910): 31–146.

jaws leading occasionally to their starvation. An outbreak in the 1920s of phosphorus necrosis of the jaw among young women making fire-works evoked a comparably detailed and horrifying report by Emma F. Ward of the U.S. Bureau of Labor Statistics, helping lead to the end of their manufacture.[3] Recent commentators have concentrated on the legislative and medical aspects of the control of phosphorus disease in America.[4] This is in contrast to Bonnie Gordon's complex study of French women match-workers' successful union organizing and their role in ending the use of phosphorus there in 1898.[5] Whereas in France the ban came largely from the organized efforts of women workers who skillfully gained public support by dramatizing issues such as supposed miscarriages and stillbirths from phosphorus exposure, the ban in the United States was largely the result of the efforts of social reformers. Gordon's fine study of the interplay of community, family, and union-organizing with a struggle over toxic substances has no counterpart for any comparable group of American women workers. Typically, in his-torical studies of groups of American women workers, a toxic work environment may be discussed as part of working conditions, but it is not the focal point of the research.[6]

Two complementary publications began the modern inquiry into women's toxic work environments. Elizabeth Beardsley Butler's 1909 contribution to the Pittsburgh Survey described the unhealthy gaseous and dusty work environments in numerous industries where women worked. A year earlier Alice Hamilton, then living in Hull House, reviewed the largely European literature on toxic hazards to women

---

[3] Emma F. Ward, "Phosphorus Necrosis in the Manufacture of Fireworks and in the Preparation of Phosphorus," *Bulletin of the United States Bureau of Labor Statistics*, no. 405 (May 1926): 1–44.

[4] Alton Lee, "The Eradication of Phossy Jaw: A Unique Development of Federal Police Power," *The Historian* 29 (November 1966): 1–21; Jean Spencer Felton, "Phosphorus Necrosis—A Classical Occupational Disease," *American Journal of Industrial Medicine* 3 (1982): 77–120.

[5] Bonnie Gordon, "Phossy-Jaw and the French Match Workers: Occupational Health and Women in the Third Republic" (Ph.D. dissertation, University of Wisconsin, 1985). On phosphorus disease in the British match industry, see Lowell J. Satre, "After the Match Girls' Strike; Bryant and May in the 1890s," *Victorian Studies* 26 (Autumn 1982): 7–31.

[6] Beverly W. Jones, "Race, Sex, and Class: Black Female Tobacco Workers in Durham, North Carolina, 1920–1940, and the Development of Female Consciousness," *Feminist Studies* 10 (Fall 1984): 441–51.

workers.[7] Hamilton, later revered as "the matriarch of industrial medicine," was soon to embark on the field investigations of lead poisoning
that were to make her the leading industrial physician of the day.[8] Her
long career—she died in 1970 at the age of 101—has been the object of
continual interpretation. A 1920s biographer lauded Alice Hamilton as
an exemplary woman who had applied "feminized" values learned at
home and extended through her Hull House contacts to unravel the
toxic hazards of modern industry better than any of her male contemporaries. She saw farther, argued Elizabeth Shapley Sergeant, because she
had learned to express her emotions "in the rigorous terms of science."[9]
Hamilton continued to reflect on her career throughout her life, drawing
lessons on the reduction of industrial hazards, and she remains of
interest to scholars today.[10] Jacqueline Karnell Corn explores Hamilton's
mid-1920s opposition to the Equal Rights Amendment, which would
have nullified protective labor laws.[11] A recent history dissertation examines her investigations of the dangerous trades, while the 1984 publication of a thick collection of her letters sparked a wider feminist
audience's interest in the personal aspects of her pursuit of a pathbreaking scientific and Harvard-faculty career.[12]

---

[7] Elizabeth Beardsley Butler, *Women and the Trades: Pittsburgh, 1907–1908* (New York:
Russell Sage, 1909; reprint, Pittsburgh: University of Pittsburgh Press, 1984); Alice
Hamilton, "Industrial Diseases, With Special Reference to the Trades in Which
Women are Employed," *Charities and the Commons*, September 5, 1908, pp. 655–59.

[8] J. S. Felton, "Home at Hadlyme," *Journal of Occupational Medicine* 11 (Feburary 1969):
91; Alice Hamilton, "Women in the Lead Industries," *Bulletin of the United States
Bureau of Labor Statistics*, no. 253 (February 1919): 5–38.

[9] Elizabeth Shapley Sergeant, "Alice Hamilton, M.D.: Crusader for Health in Industry,"
Harper's, May 1926, p. 770.

[10] Alice Hamilton, "Nineteen Years in the Poisonous Trades," *Harper's*, October 1929,
pp. 580–91; Alice Hamilton, "Healthy, Wealthy—if Wise—Industry," *Industrial Medicine* 7 (January 1938): 46–54; Alice Hamilton, *Exploring the Dangerous Trades* (Boston:
Little, Brown and Company, 1943; reprint Boston: Northeastern University Press,
1985); Alice Hamilton, "Forty Years in the Poisonous Trades," reprinted lecture given
April 1, 1948, *American Journal of Industrial Medicine* 7 (1985); Alice Hamilton,
"A Woman of Ninety Looks at Her World," *Atlantic Monthly*, September 1961,
pp. 51–55; Jean Spencer Felton, "Alice Hamilton, M.D.—A Century of Devotion to
Humanity," *Journal of Occupational Medicine* 14 (February 1972): 106–10.

[11] Jacqueline Karnell Corn, "Alice Hamilton, M.D., and Women's Welfare," *New England Journal of Medicine* 294 (February 5, 1976): 316–18.

[12] Angela Nugent Young, "Interpreting the Dangerous Trades: Workers' Health in America and the Career of Alice Hamilton, 1910–1935" (Ph.D. dissertation, Brown University, 1982); Barbara Sicherman, *Alice Hamilton: A Life in Letters* (Cambridge: Harvard
University Press, 1984).

In 1916, Alice Hamilton shifted her interest from the lead trades to the newly expanded munitions industries. During the early years of World War I, toxic jaundice due to TNT poisoning in the British munitions industry created a crisis in the availability of women workers to fill munitions shells. Antonia Ineson and Deborah Thom have shown how a combination of medical and managerial solutions helped to end the crisis and secure worker compliance. Hamilton and other physicians appointed by the War Labor Board could do little to combat what she termed "a sort of joyous ruthlessness" that seized American industry during the war. Hamilton's numerous investigations, Sergeant wrote, had revealed "the abyss of insecurity on which our pleasant and comfortable material American civilization rests." Familiar objects, such as houses and motor cars, "which seem points of stability on this whirling planet are really points of acute danger for the lives that produce them."[13]

Hamilton's revelation of the disease risks embedded in the products enjoyed by the prosperous classes was joined by the startling revelation of danger from the miraculous new radioactive substance, radium. The highly public agony of New Jersey radium dial painters—afflicted with necrosis of the jaw and other ailments caused by radium inhaled from the air and ingested by pointing with their mouths the brushes used for radium paint—alerted the world to the health risks of internal radiation. These women workers have been the objects of continual interest and reinterpretation. For Harrison Martland, the medical hero of the story, their misfortune provided the occasion for a triumph of science; this view was echoed fifty years later by William Sharpe when he described the episode as "a classic in occupational carcinogenesis."[14] Katherine Schaub, one of the dial painters involved in a lawsuit that received worldwide attention, chronicled her life in a magazine article: wartime work as a dial painter at age 15; problems with her jaw; Martland's

---

[13] Antonia Ineson and Deborah Thom, "T.N.T. Poisoning and the Employment of Women Workers in the First World War," in Paul Weindling, ed., *The Social History of Occupational Health* (London: Croom Helm, 1985), pp. 89–107; Hamilton, "Nineteen Years in the Dangerous Trades," p. 584; Sergeant, "Alice Hamilton, M.D.: Crusader for Health in Industry," pp. 169–70.

[14] Harrison S. Martland, "Occupational Poisoning in Manufacture of Luminous Watch Dials," Part 1, *New England Journal of Medicine* 92 (February 9, 1929): 466–73; Harrison S. Martland, "Occupational Poisoning in Manufacture of Luminous Watch Dials," Part 2, *New England Journal of Medicine* 92 (February 16, 1929): 552–59; William D. Sharpe, "The New Jersey Radium Dial Painters: A Classic in Occupational Carcinogenesis," *Bulletin of the History of Medicine* 52 (Winter 1978): 560–70.

diagnosis of radium poisoning; a long fight for compensation, leading to
fame and a large settlement; spending all the settlement; her futile
pursuit of health; and, finally, her faith in God. Coupled with Sharpe's
remarkable piece drawing on Schaub's medical records through her
death by cancer at age 30, the case is perhaps the most compelling in the
entire women's occupational health literature.[15] (In 1935, a federal court
reviewed the history of knowledge of the hazards from ingested radium
and concluded that the employer had not fraudulently concealed existence of the radium hazard in 1924, when it was, in the court's view,
unknown to science. The decision thus provided no basis for reinstating
the many suits barred by the New Jersey statute of limitations.[16])

In the late 1950s, the dial painters had become "A Most Valuable
Accident," since it was hoped that continuing medical studies conducted
on them by the Argonne National Laboratory might shed light on the
new threat of ingested Strontium 90 fallout from atomic bomb tests.[17]
The government's epidemiological reconstruction of radiation doses and
illness patterns produces its own reconstitution of the women's experience. At the same time, Congress has tried to uncover the hidden
history of unethical experiments—including the use of elderly people as
unwitting nuclear calibration devices—as part of the radium studies.[18]
Recent commentators have focused on the behind-the-scenes role of a
network of women advocates, including Alice Hamilton and the leader
of the National Consumers' League, Florence Kelley, who engaged in a
struggle both to open up a debate on the cause of the dial painters'
illnesses and to achieve justice. Roger Cloutier, Claudia Clark, and
Angela Nugent have all examined the struggle between this women's
reform network and a radium company seeking to generate its own
science as part of a cover-up. Nugent argues that the women's network
largely won, but in the process they helped to enhance the influence of

---

[15] Katherine Schaub, "Radium," *Survey Graphics*, May 1, 1932, pp. 138–40; William D.
   Sharpe, "Radium Osteitis with Osteogenic Sarcoma: The Chronology and Natural
   History of a Fatal Case," *Bulletin of the New York Academy of Medicine* 47 (September
   1971): 1059–82.
[16] *La Porte v. United States Radium Corporation*, 13 F.Supp. 263 (D.New Jersey 1935).
[17] Daniel Lang, "A Most Valuable Accident," *New Yorker*, May 2, 1959, pp. 49–92.
[18] James H. Stebbings, Henry F. Lucas, and Andrew F. Stehney, "Mortality From Cancers
   of Major Sites in Female Radium Dial Workers," *American Journal of Industrial Medicine* 5 (1984): 435–59; U.S. Congress, House Committee on Energy and Commerce,
   American Nuclear Guinea Pigs: Three Decades of Radiation Experiments on U.S. Citizens,
   Report by the Subcommittee on Energy Conservation and Power, November 1986
   (Washington, D.C.: Government Printing Office).

scientific specialists. My own work recasts the radium dial sage as a toxic tort story that prefigures many later such episodes.[19]

While Florence Kelley lived at Hull House she was instrumental in the passage of an 1893 antisweatshop law in Illinois; for the next four years Kelley served vigorously as the state's chief factory inspector, the first of many prominent U.S. women reformers active in the early twentieth century whose outlook was shaped by investigating the conditions of women workers.[20] Rosner and Markowitz have shown that the movement for occupational health and safety in the first two decades of this century was part of a broad multi-class and multi-interest reform movement involving many women's organizations working on a variety of interrelated issues. The Workers' Health Bureau, three radical New York City women who began actively organizing around occupational health in the early 1920s, has recently been rediscovered by historians. Its attempts to harness science for the class struggle involving "war between workers' bodies and profits" came into conflict with the more conservative approach of the mainstream labor leadership, resulting in the Bureau's demise in 1928.[21]

---

[19] Josephine Goldmark, *Impatient Crusader: Florence Kelley's Life Story* (Urbana: University of Illinois Press, 1953); Roger J. Cloutier, "Florence Kelley and the Radium Dial Painters," *Health Physics* 39 (November 1980): 711–15; Claudia Clark, "Physicians, Reformers and Occupational Disease: The Discovery of Radium Poisoning," *Women & Health* 12 (1987): 147–67; Angela Nugent, "The Power to Define a New Disease: Epidemiological Politics and Radium Poisoning," in David Rosner and Gerald Markowitz, eds., *Dying for Work: Workers' Safety and Health in Twentieth-Century America* (Bloomington: Indiana University Press, 1987), pp. 177–91; Tony Bale, "A Brush with Justice: The New Jersey Radium Dial Painters in the Courts," *Health/PAC Bulletin* 17 (November 1987): 18–21. The radium poisoning of women dial painters in Illinois in the 1930s has not received much attention. The best single source is Carol Langer's 1987 feature-length documentary film, "Radium City."

[20] Kathryn Kish Sklar, "Hull House in the 1890s: A Community of Women Reformers," *Signs* 10 (Summer 1985): 658–77. Kelley's British counterparts, the early women factory inspectors who, as did she, began work in 1893, made vigorous efforts to improve women's working conditions, but they were unable to make the issue of women's occupational health of major importance to the government. Helen Jones, "Women Health Workers: The Case of the First Women Factory Inspectors in Britain," *Social History of Medicine* 1 (August 1988): 165–81; Mary Drake McFeely, *Lady Inspectors: The Campaign for a Better Workplace, 1893–1921* (New York: Basil Blackwell, 1988).

[21] David Rosner and Gerald Markowitz, "The Early Movement for Occupational Safety and Health, 1900–1917," in Judith Walzer Leavitt and Ronald L. Numbers, eds., *Sickness & Health in America*, 2d ed. (Madison: University of Wisconsin Press, 1985), pp. 507–21; David Rosner and Gerald Markowitz, "Safety and Health on the Job as a Class Issue: The Workers' Health Bureau of America in the 1920s," *Science & Society* 48 (Winter 1984–1985): 466–82; Angela Nugent, "Organizing Trade Unions to Combat Disease: The Workers' Health Bureau, 1921–1928," *Labor History* 26 (Summer 1985): 423–46.

The Women's Bureau of the U.S. Department of Labor picked up part of the women's occupational health flame lit by the earlier movement, but its research and advocacy has not been studied. Throughout the 1920s, the Bureau produced a steady stream of information on women's unhealthy working conditions. A 1927 report containing numerous vivid cases documented widespread accidental poisoning among women working in industry and the small amounts of money available to them through workers' compensation.[22] The Bureau continued its investigations into the 1930s with reports such as a study of the serious problem of benzene poisoning in the New Hampshire shoe industry, and, most impressively, a series of reports by Margaret T. Mettert that summarized the existing information on the occurrence of occupational diseases and efforts at prevention.[23] Another important 1930s development with ties to the earlier reform movement was the Division of Labor Standards in the Department of Labor started by its secretary, longtime reformer Frances Perkins.[24] In 1940 Alice Hamilton reported to the Division on a new type of poisoning among women workers: a form of psychosis produced by carbon disulphide exposures in the rayon industry.[25]

In the early 1940s an outbreak of sarcoidosis of the lung occurred among predominantly women workers at a Massachusetts flourescent light plant. In response to industry pressure, scientists at the state's Division of Occupational Medicine suppressed publication of a paper on possible occupational origins of the illness; however, a later employee of the Division, Dr. Harriet Hardy, proceeded with an investigation that

---

[22] "Industrial Accidents to Women in New Jersey, Ohio, and Wisconsin," *Bulletin of the Women's Bureau*, no. 60 (1927): 1–316.

[23] Agnes L. Peterson, "A Survey of the Shoe Industry in New Hampshire," *Bulletin of the Women's Bureau*, no. 121 (1935): 1–100; Margaret Thompson Mettert, "State Reporting of Occupational Disease," *Bulletin of the Women's Bureau*, no. 114 (1934): 1–99; Margaret T. Mettert, "Summary of State Reports of Occupational Diseases with a Survey of Preventive Legislation 1923 to 1934," *Bulletin of the Women's Bureau*, no. 147 (1936): 1–42; Margaret T. Mettert, "Occurrence and Prevention of Occupational Diseases Among Women 1935 to 1938," *Bulletin of the Women's Bureau*, no. 184 (1941): 1–46.

[24] David Rosner and Gerald Markowitz, "Research or Advocacy: Federal Occupational Safety and Health Policies During the New Deal," *Journal of Social History* 18 (Spring 1985): 365–81; Gerald Markowitz and David Rosner, "More Than Economicism: The Politics of Workers' Safety and Health, 1932–1947," *Milbank Quarterly* 64 (Fall 1986): 331–54; Gerald Markowitz and David Rosner, eds., *"Slaves of the Depression": Workers' Letters About Life on the Job* (Ithaca: Cornell University Press, 1987).

[25] Alice Hamilton, "Occupational Poisoning in the Viscose Rayon Industry," *Bulletin of the Division of Labor Standards*, no. 34 (1940): 1–79.

helped identify beryllium as the cause. (Hardy, a friend of Alice Hamilton, has spent a lifetime studying beryllium disease and reflecting on its lessons. Successful lawsuits were brought in the 1950s and 1960s by women who contracted beryllium disease through washing their husbands' contaminated work clothes, and by women living in proximity to beryllium plants.) The 1940s also saw the beginning of successful suits against makers of household products, such as carbon tetrachloride carpet cleaner, for failure to warn of reasonably foreseeable uses that could lead to severe poisoning.[26]

Helping to spearhead a resurgence of interest in occupational health issues, movements for compensation of black lung and brown lung diseases, both with considerable participation from women, were prominent events of the late 1960s and 1970s.[27] Sociologist Barbara Ellen Smith has used numerous interviews with participants to chart the course of the black lung movement and the active role wives, widows, and women lay advocates played within it.[28] In the mid-1970s, a movement arose among southern textile workers for compensation of byssinosis or brown lung disease.[29] Here again, women took an active part in winning compensation, this time for their own illnesses.

The massive asbestos-disease disaster has touched the lives of millions of women, but there is no account that focuses on their experience.

---

[26] Craig Zwerling, "Salem Sarcoid: The Origins of Beryllium Disease," in David Rosner and Gerald Markowitz, eds., *Dying for Work: Workers' Safety and Health in Twentieth-Century America* (Bloomington: Indiana University Press, 1987), pp. 103–18; Harriet L. Hardy, "Beryllium Poisoning—Lessons in Control of Man-Made Disease," *New England Journal of Medicine* 273 (November 25, 1965): 1188–99; Harriet L. Hardy, "Risk and Responsibility: A Physician's Viewpoint," *New England Journal of Medicine* 293 (October 16, 1975): 801–6; Harriet L. Hardy, *Challenging Man-Made Disease* (New York: Praeger, 1983); *Maize v. Atlantic Refining Co.*, 41 A.2d 850 (Pa. 1945).

[27] Brit Hume, *Death and the Mines: Rebellion and Murder in the United Mine Workers* (New York: Grossman Publishers, 1971); Bennett M. Judkins, *We Offer Ourselves as Evidence: Toward Workers' Control of Occupational Health* (Westport, CT: Greenwood Press, 1986).

[28] Barbara Ellen Smith, "History and Politics of the Black Lung Movement," *Radical America* 17 (March–June 1983): 89–109; Barbara Ellen Smith, "Too Sick to Work, Too Young to Die," *Southern Exposure* 12 (May–June 1984): 19–29; Barbara Ellen Smith, *Digging Our Own Graves: Coal Miners and the Struggle over Black Lung Disease* (Philadelphia: Temple University Press, 1987).

[29] Mimi Conway, *Rise Gonna Rise: A Portrait of Southern Textile Workers* (Garden City, NY: Doubleday, 1979); Janet M. Bronstein, "Brown Lung in North Carolina: The Social Organization of an Occupational Disease" (Ph.D. dissertation, University of Kentucky, 1984); Richard Guarasci, "Death by Cotton Dust," in Stuart L. Hills, ed., *Corporate Violence: Injury and Death for Profit* (Totowa, NJ: Rowman & Littlefield, 1987), pp. 76–92.

New Yorker writer Paul Brodeur's *Outrageous Misconduct* documents the way plaintiffs' lawyers used the suits of asbestos-insulation workers to create a legal remedy and evidence of corporate negligence sufficient to win huge punitive damages awards from the asbestos industry, and my 1983 article looks at the experience of those insulation workers' widows in seeking compensation.[30] These women had to handle complex legal proceedings during the disorienting period following their husbands' deaths; they faced the additional burden of knowing they were at risk of contracting cancer from asbestos brought home on their husbands' clothes, and that their sons and other relatives in the trade might also become afflicted.

During the 1920s, the assumption that women were more vulnerable than men to disease and reproductive damage from toxic substances, notably lead, figured in the various debates over protective legislation and the Equal Rights Amendment. Kessler-Harris argues that, with the defeat of the ERA and the Depression conditions of the 1930s, women workers and many women's groups, such as the Women's Bureau, turned their attention to occupational disease. The resurgence of feminism and interest in women's occupational health in the 1970s focused considerable attention on corporate policies excluding women from jobs involving contact with toxic substances, principally lead, that might impair their reproductive capacity or damage the fetus.[31] Employers either could not or would not make the workplace clean enough to remove the risk, which also existed for men. Sociologist Donna Randall has studied the controversy involving exclusionary policies begun at an Idaho lead smelter in 1975. Women took different courses of action in response to such exclusion: some became sterilized in order to keep their jobs; others filed a sex-discrimination suit.[32] In 1979, the more widely

---

[30] Paul Brodeur, *Outrageous Misconduct: The Asbestos Industry on Trial* (New York: Pantheon, 1985); Tony Bale, "Breath of Death: The Asbestos Disaster Comes Home to Roost," *Health/PAC Bulletin* 14 (May–June 1983): 7–21.

[31] Alice Kessler-Harris, "Protection for Women: Trade Unions and Labor Laws," in Wendy Chavkin, ed., *Double Exposure: Women's Health Hazards on the Job and at Home* (New York: Monthly Review Press, 1984), pp. 139–54; Patricia Vawter Klein, "'For the Good of the Race': Reproductive Hazards from Lead and the Persistence of Exclusionary Policies toward Women," in Barbara Drygulski Wright, ed., *Women, Work and Technology* (Ann Arbor: University of Michigan Press, 1987), pp. 101–17.

[32] Donna M. Randall and James F. Short, Jr., "Women in Toxic Work Environments: A Case Study of Social Problems Development," *Social Problems* 30 (April 1983): 409–24; Donna M. Randall, "Women in Toxic Work Environments: A Case Study and Examination of Policy Impact," in Laurie Larwood, Ann H. Stromberg, and Barbara A. Gutek, eds., *Women and Work*, Volume 1 (Beverly Hills: Sage Publications, 1985), pp. 259–81.

publicized exclusionary policy and sterilizations at a West Virginia chemical plant among lead-exposed pigment workers drew further attention to this conflict between women's rights to equal employment opportunities and employers' efforts to infringe on these rights in order to limit their own legal liability. The emerging women's occupational health movement's interest in exclusionary policies, similar to the earlier debate, can be seen in a 1979 historical paper by Vilma Hunt, a leading movement scientist, and Wendy Chavkin's anthology on women's occupational health.[33]

Women work in a myriad of occupations and settings where, like men, they only understand dimly, at best, their risks of illness from toxic hazards. Their need for money may force them to assent to serious risks of which they are aware, while compensation remedies allow little financial recovery for an occupational disease. An article of mine examines the legal framework for risk acceptance and compensation among workers in the tort system prevailing before passage of the first workers' compensation laws in the 1910s. A few women were able to recover money in lawsuits for occupational diseases acquired under conditions where the employer failed to warn them of latent risks, such as those involving knowledge of chemistry, that a worker could not reasonably be aware of on her own. Dorothy Nelkin and Michael Brown present women in a wide variety of occupations speaking about how they perceive and respond to risks of toxic illness. Women workers' sense of their occupational risks are also embedded in broader social movements. Roberta Lessor traces the effects of the civil rights, women's, and occupational health movements on flight attendants' heightened sense of their collective health risks and occupational interests. In a recent set of articles, I look at the occupational disease claims that women brought into the workers' compensation and tort systems through 1960. Such claims reflect the broad range of everyday occupational disease patterns, but, as Jeanne Stellman has shown, represent only a small fraction of presumed toxic illness among female-dominated occupations.[34]

---

[33] *Oil, Chemical & Atomic Workers v. Am. Cyanamid Co.*, 741 F.2d 444 (1984); Mary Gibson, *Workers' Rights* (Totowa, NJ: Rowman & Allenhead, 1983); Vilma R. Hunt, "A Brief History of Women Workers and Hazards in the Workplace," *Feminist Studies* 5 (Summer 1979): 274–85; Wendy Chavkin, ed., *Double Exposure.*

[34] Anthony Bale, "Assuming the Risks: Occupational Disease in the Years Before Workers' Compensation," *American Journal of Industrial Medicine* 13 (1988): 499–514; Dorothy Nelkin and Michael S. Brown, *Workers at Risk: Voices from the Workplace* (Chicago: University of Chicago Press, 1984); Roberta Lessor, "Social Movements, the Occupational Arena and Changes in Career Consciousness: The Case of Women Flight

We still know very little about women's responses to their risks of toxic illness in the workplace. The history of American women's toxic experience at the workplace is only vaguely outlined: one can see a story here, but much remains to be done in providing more details, their context, and an overall interpretation.

ENVIRONMENT

Historian James Whorton notes that "the chemical artificiality of the modern industrial environment, and the dangers this portended, was a subject that began to attract considerable medical comment by the 1920s."[35] In 1936, A. Benson Cannon, a Columbia professor of dermatology, observed: "Within the past few years not only scientific publications but popular magazines, books, newspapers, and radio have brought to the notice of the general public the risks of poisoning from arsenic contained in various foods, candies, tobaccos, in cosmetics, in paints, wall-paper, and dyed clothing—to cite only a few examples."[36] Cannon described cases of men and women with high arsenic blood levels and severe symptoms suggestive of chronic arsenic poisoning derived, among other routes of exposure, from fruit sprayed with the leading pesticide of the time, lead arsenate. Whorton's important *Before Silent Spring* recounts the controversy over the health effects and regulation of pesticide residues in food before the 1940s, when DDT, "the atomic bomb of insecticides," replaced arsenical compounds.

Rachel Carson's best-selling *Silent Spring*, published initially in the *New Yorker* a month after the thalidomide birth-defects story broke, alerted the public to the environmental and health dangers of the synthetic insecticides she termed "elixirs of death." *Silent Spring* drew on the climate created by the most prominent toxic issue of the time, concern over the health effects of radioactive fallout from atomic testing. For

---

Attendants," *Journal of Occupational Behaviour* 5 (January 1984): 37–51; Roberta Lessor, "Consciousness of Time and Time for the Development of Consciousness: Health Awareness Among Women Flight Attendants," *Sociology of Health & Illness* 7 (July 1985): 191–213; Anthony Bale, "'Hope in Another Direction': Compensation for Work-Related Illness Among Women, 1900–1960," Parts 1 & 2, *Women & Health*, 15(1) (1989): 81–102, 15(2) (1989): 99–115; Jeanne Mager Stellman, "The Working Environment of the Working Poor: An Analysis Based on Workers' Compensation Claims, Census Data and Known Risk Factors," *Women & Health* 12 (nos. 3&4, 1987): 83–101.

[35] James Whorton, *Before Silent Spring: Pesticides and Public Health in Pre-DDT America* (Princeton: Princeton University Press, 1974), p. 176.

[36] A. Benson Cannon, "Chronic Arsenical Poisoning: Symptoms and Sources," *New York State Journal of Medicine* 36 (February 15, 1936): 220.

424   WOMEN, HEALTH, AND MEDICINE IN AMERICA

historian Thomas Dunlap, Carson's most influential idea was her rejection of the notion that people could control nature: "It is in this call for a new attitude toward nature, for a new recognition of the possible destructive effects of man's actions on the environment, that *Silent Spring* made its greatest contribution to the environmental movement." Dunlap's book traces the controversy and litigation that led to ban of DDT in 1972. Vera Norwood shows how Carson constructed a picture of nature as a home and family.[37]

Beginning in the mid-1950s, a series of environmental pollution disasters in Japan received worldwide attention. Best known was the horrible methylmercury poisoning in the area of Minamata City. Cases of severe neurological and emotional symptoms, followed by blindness and stiffness of the joints, and leading at times to death, occurred among men and women of that small fishing community; fetuses absorbed mercury from pregnant women, thereby protecting their mothers, while themselves developing severe, sometimes fatal, conditions. Patricia D'Itri and Frank D'Itri place the Minamata story and worldwide episodes of mercury contamination in the context of the many uses of the substance throughout history, and the attempts to control it. In 1973 a fire retardant containing polybrominated biphenyl (PBB) was inadvertently used as an animal feed by farmers in Michigan. Many animals died, some farmers became ill, and the poison spread throughout the Michigan food chain to the point where mothers became concerned about their own breastmilk containing PBB. The full story of this disaster, comparable to the Japanese ones, has been told elegantly by investigative reporter Joyce Egginton in her book *The Poisoning of Michigan*.[38]

The Michigan episode and Allied Chemical's pollution of the James River and Chesapeake Bay with its pesticide Kepone were only a prelude

---

37 Rachel Carson, *Silent Spring* (Boston: Houghton Mifflin, 1962); Ralph H. Lutts, "Chemical Fallout: Rachel Carson's *Silent Spring*, Radioactive Fallout, and the Environmental Movement," *Environmental Review* 9 (Fall 1985): 211–25; Thomas R. Dunlap, *DDT: Scientists, Citizens, and Public Policy* (Princeton: Princeton University Press, 1982), p. 113; Vera L. Norwood, "The Nature of Knowing: Rachel Carson and the American Environment," *Signs* 12 (Summer 1987): 740–60.
38 Frank K. Upham, "Litigation and Moral Consciousness in Japan: An Interpretive Analysis of Four Japanese Pollution Suits," *Law & Society Review* 10 (Summer, 1976): 579–619; Patricia A. D'Itri and Frank M. D'Itri, *Mercury Contamination: A Human Tragedy* (New York: John Wiley & Sons, 1977); Joyce Egginton, *The Poisoning of Michigan* (New York: W. W. Norton, 1980); Michael R. Reich, "Environmental Politics and Science: The Case of PBB Contamination in Michigan," *American Journal of Public Health* 73 (March 1983): 302–13; Sherry Lynn Hatcher, "The Psychological Experience of Nursing Mothers Upon Learning of a Toxic Substance in Their Breast Milk," *Psychiatry* 45 (May 1982): 172–81.

to a much larger toxic poisoning episode that gripped the country's attention in late 1978: Love Canal and the subsequent discovery of hazardous waste dumps throughout the country. Incredible as it seemed, the plight of several hundred families in Niagara Falls, New York, living near the enormous Love Canal toxic waste dump, was not an isolated case. Rather, they were simply the most visible of many such families who soon became aware of health threats from similar waste sites. By 1980 Michael H. Brown, a Niagara Falls journalist who began writing about Love Canal in the summer of 1977, had published an influential book that vividly portrayed a nationwide crisis. Two Love Canal books published in 1982 added to the story. Adeline Levine's sociological account showed the difficulties the Love Canal Homeowners Association and its leader, Lois Gibbs, had in dealing with the politically charged scientific debate surrounding the health impact on residents. Gibbs, whose story was made into a television movie and who went on to head a national organization aiding citizens' groups fighting hazardous wastes, published her own account of how an ordinary woman helped build an organization of other "blue-collar, middle class Americans" in which the women did most of the work fighting for justice. Journalist Paula Di-Perna skillfully wove the personal story of another leader, Anne Anderson of Woburn, Massachusetts, into a sweeping analysis of the discovery of cancer clusters by ordinary citizens and the difficulty of establishing that environmental exposure, rather than chance variation, was the cause. Anderson had the satisfaction of seeing a Harvard study confirm her suspicion that the cluster of childhood leukemia cases she had uncovered, which included, not untypically in these situations, her own son, was connected to polluted water from a toxic dumpsite.[39]

All across the country, citizens' groups, often led by women, were uncovering clusters of illness and reproductive harm and organizing against hazardous waste in their communities. Some, like Maine's Cathy Hinds, followed Lois Gibbs in making the transition from a local, anxious resident of a home near a toxic dump to a national leader of the

---

[39] Michael R. Reich and Jacquelin R. Spong, "Kepone: A Chemical Disaster in Hopewell, Virginia," *International Journal of Health Services* 13 (1983): 227–46; Michael H. Brown, *Laying Waste: The Poisoning of America by Toxic Chemicals* (New York: Pantheon, 1981); Adeline Gordon Levine, *Love Canal: Science, Politics and People* (Lexington, MA: Lexington Books, 1982); Lois Marie Gibbs, *Love Canal: My Story* (Albany: State University of New York Press, 1982); Lois Marie Gibbs, "Community Response to an Emergency Situation: Psychological Destruction and the Love Canal," *American Journal of Community Psychology* 11 (April 1983): 116–25; Paula DiPerna, *Cluster Mystery: Epidemic and the Children of Woburn, Mass.* (St. Louis: C. V. Mosby, 1985).

grassroots, antitoxics movement. Nicholas Freudenberg's *Not in Our Backyards!* describes much of this activity and draws political lessons from organizing successes, while psychologist Michael Edelstein's work examines psychological, family, and community organizing aspects of this new social movement.[40] By the mid-1980s, some of these toxic waste sites had become the object of sweeping judicial inquiries. A Tennessee federal judge exhaustively reviewed the history of Velsicol Chemical's notorious dump near Toone, Tennessee, in a book-length opinion, awarding large compensatory and punitive damages for physical and emotional suffering to a representative group of plaintiffs in a class action suit. Specifically, the court concluded that, because it knew of the dangers and continued to maintain and use the dump even after being warned by several state and federal agencies, Velsicol's actions constituted the kind of grossly wanton and willful disregard of health sufficient to justify a large punitive damages award.[41]

Seveso, Italy; Agent Orange; 2,4,5-T; Love Canal; Alsea, Oregon; Times Beach, Missouri; Jacksonville, Arkansas: these names resonate through the mid-1970s and 1980s, linked together with the fearsome substance dioxin. The 1976 explosion at a chemical plant near Seveso, Italy, scattered a toxic cloud containing dioxin over the town and introduced many people around the world to the dangers of this extremely potent animal carcinogen. Thomas Whiteside's *New Yorker* series presented to a large American audience this latest episode of what he termed "herbicidal adventurism." In 1977, Maude DeVictor, a benefits counselor at a Veterans Administration office in Chicago, began to connect some of the unusual illnesses she was seeing among Vietnam veterans with their exposure to the dioxin-contaminated defoliant Agent Orange.

---

[40] Jason Berry, "The Poisoning of Louisiana," *Southern Exposure* 12 (March/April 1984): 16–23; "Cathy Hinds," in Anne Witte Garland, *Women Activists* (New York: The Feminist Press, 1988), pp. 89–105; Nicholas Freudenberg, *Not in Our Backyards!: Community Action for Health and the Environment* (New York: Monthly Review Press, 1984); Nicholas Freudenberg and Ellen Zaltzberg, "From Grassroots Activism to Political Power: Women Organizing Against Environmental Hazards," in Wendy Chavkin, ed., *Double Exposure*, pp. 246–72; Michael R. Edelstein and Abraham Wandersman, "Community Dynamics in Coping with Toxic Contaminants," in Irwin Altman and Abraham Wandersman, eds., *Neighborhood and Community Environments* (New York: Plenum Press, 1987), pp. 69–112; Michael R. Edelstein, *Contaminated Communities: The Social and Psychological Impacts of Residential Toxic Exposure* (Boulder, CO: Westview Press, 1988).

[41] *Sterling v. Velsicol Chemical Corp.*, 647 F.Supp. 303 (W.D.Tenn. 1986). For a resident's viewpoint, see Nell Grantham, "'Together We Can Do It': Fighting Toxic Hazards in Tennessee," *Southern Exposure* 9 (Fall 1981): 42–47.

A March, 1978, Chicago television documentary on DeVictor's findings helped set in motion the public controversy and litigation surrounding the use of Agent Orange in Vietnam.[42]

The discovery of large quantities of dioxin at Love Canal and other toxic dumps in Niagara Falls and around the country added to growing concern about this widespread, possibly deadly substance. In 1975, journalist Carol Van Strum's children were sprayed with herbicides while they were swimming in an Oregon river deep in the forest. In *A Bitter Fog* she wrote about the militant struggle against herbicide use in the Pacific Northwest. Alsea, Oregon, resident Bonnie Hill's informal study of miscarriages among women in her area helped lead to the 1979 emergency ban of the dioxin-contaminated herbicide, 2,4,5-T—also a major constituent of Agent Orange. Van Strum's account of these citizens' movements underlines the transformations of ordinary people that enabled them to carry on the vision and work Rachel Carson began in *Silent Spring*. Investigative journalist Cathy Troost deepened the herbicide story by concentrating on Dow Chemical, a major producer of the chemicals. Her powerful book juxtaposes Dow's growth and arrogance with the condition of people who brought the company into court after being sprayed with 2,4,5-T or being exposed to DBCP, a chemical that produced sterility in male chemical workers. In 1983, the town of Times Beach, Missouri, was abandoned because of dioxin contamination. Journalist Liane Casten has recently reported on the plight of Jacksonville, Arkansas, residents who have lived with dioxin levels in their soil 200 times higher than those at Times Beach. In their books on the still-inconclusive scientific debate over the human health effects of dioxin, Alastair Hay and Michael Gough review numerous incidents of human exposure to it and the studies generated from them.[43]

---

[42] Thomas Whiteside, *The Pendulum and the Toxic Cloud: The Course of Dioxin Contamination* (New Haven: Yale University Press, 1979); Fred A. Wilcox, *Waiting for an Army to Die: The Tragedy of Agent Orange* (New York: Vintage paperback, 1983); Peter H. Schuck, *Agent Orange on Trial: Mass Toxic Disasters in the Courts* (Cambridge: Harvard University Press, 1986); Wilbur J. Scott, "Competing Paradigms in the Assessment of Latent Disorders: The Case of Agent Orange," *Social Problems* 35 (April 1988): 145–61.

[43] Carol Van Strum, *A Bitter Fog: Herbicides and Human Rights* (San Francisco: Sierra Club Books, 1983); Cathy Troost, *Elements of Risk: The Chemical Industry and Its Threat to America* (New York: Times Books, 1984); Liane Clorfene Casten, "A Town Is Being Poisoned," *Nation*, March 19, 1988, pp. 370–72; Alastair Hay, *The Chemical Scythe: Lessons of 2,4,5-T and Dioxin* (New York: Plenum Press, 1982); Michael Gough, *Dioxin, Agent Orange: The Facts* (New York: Plenum Press, 1986).

Two recent books reconstruct the experience of residents living downwind from atomic bomb tests in the 1940s and 1950s. Along with the familiar pattern of community women doing their own epidemiological study to document cancer clusters, and the emergence of citizens' organizations with active female participation, the "downwinders" began litigation in the federal courts that produced a dramatic verdict on their behalf and a book-length historical reconstruction of the circumstances of their injuries. Although this ruling was overturned on appeal, on the grounds that the government could not be held liable for discretionary activity of the Atomic Energy Commission, the downwinders' ongoing quest for justice for the callous indifference shown by the government for their lives and well-being is just one of the many toxic victim dramas involving women to command public attention in the late 1970s and 1980s.

Several controversies have involved electromagnetic fields and microwaves, possible hazards not well understood by science. Violent protests against high-voltage powerlines in Minnesota in the late 1970s were part of a struggle over energy policy and the quality of the rural environment that also had significant female participation and health implications.[44]

Beginning in 1961, when Women Strike for Peace led fifty thousand women around the country in a strike against nuclear testing, American women have played a central role in the antinuclear movement, including the large movement in the 1970s and 1980s against nuclear power. More likely than men to identify themselves as antinuclear, women participated in the movement in great numbers. The survivors of Karen Silkwood, the antinuclear movement's leading martyr, won a punitive damages jury-award against her employer, Kerr-McGee, providing public vindication of her claims that its plutonium fuel rod facility needlessly endangered workers and the public. Many women were in explicitly femininst local groups that asserted a connection between their roles as nurturers and protectors of children, their feminist consciousness, and their opposition to the destructive patriarchical nuclear power technology. Mary Sinclair, whose seventeen-year fight contributed greatly to

[44] Howard Ball, *Justice Downwind: America's Atomic Testing Program in the 1950's* (New York: Oxford University Press, 1986); Philip L. Fradkin, *Fallout: An American Nuclear Tragedy* (Tucson: University of Arizona Press, 1989); *Allen v. United States*, 588 F.Supp. 247 (D.Utah 1984); Barry M. Casper and Paul David Wellstone, *Powerline: The First Battle of America's Energy War* (Amherst: University of Massachusetts Press, 1981).

preventing the opening of a nuclear power plant in Dow Chemical's hometown, Midland, Michigan, acknowledged that her crusade often generated considerable hostility towards her husband, as well as herself, but: "We both felt this work of mine was just another part of parenting our children." The nuclear power industry responded to the women's antinuclear movement by organizing its own women's pronuclear movement, emphasizing the supposed economic benefit to women of a high-tech, high-energy economy. But the American antinuclear movement has been haunted by images of the Japanese atomic bomb survivors who, through their own organizations, existence, and moral example speak more powerfully about the nuclear age than do all the official claims—in the midst of continual foul-ups—that this fearsome power is in technically and morally reliable hands.[45]

Women's participation in a grassroots movement against environmental health hazards has not yet received much study. Neither Samuel Hays's history of recent environmental politics nor James Patterson's cultural history of twentieth-century America's response to cancer has much to say about it.[46] Such historical studies largely explore the attitudes and conduct of policy elites and images from the mass media, thereby leaving it to activists and sympathetic journalists to tell the tales of these self-proclaimed "ordinary women" confronting big corporations, big science, and big government to win important victories. The upsurge of such citizens' movements in the late 1970s was both a broad, populist response to environmental assaults, and an attempt by women to attach meaning to their fears and pain. It constituted a mass women's environmental health movement within a broader popular struggle. In part it represented an attempt by grass roots activists to link, in Frances

---

[45] Amy Swerdlow, "Ladies' Day at the Capitol: Women Strike for Peace Versus HUAC," *Feminist Studies* 8 (Fall 1982): 493–520; Richard Rashke, *The Killing of Karen Silkwood* (New York: Penguin, 1981); Dorothy Nelkin, "Nuclear Power as a Feminist Issue," *Environment* 23 (January/February 1981): 14–20, 38–39; "Mary Sinclair," in Anne Witte Garland, *Women Activists* (New York: The Feminist Press, 1988): 75–87; Lin Nelson, "Promise Her Everything: The Nuclear Power Industry's Agenda for Women," *Feminist Studies* 10 (Summer 1984): 291–314; Janet Bruin and Stephen Salaff, "Never Again: The Organization of Women Atomic Bomb Victims in Osaka," *Feminist Studies* 7 (Spring 1981): 5–18.

[46] Samuel P. Hays, *Beauty, Health, and Permanence: Environmental Politics in the United States, 1955–1985* (Cambridge: Cambridge University Press, 1987); James T. Patterson, *The Dread Disease: Cancer and Modern American Culture* (Cambridge: Harvard University Press, 1987). On the earlier campaigns to preserve forests and limit the use of feathers from wild birds on hats, see Carolyn Merchant, "Women of the Progressive Conservation Movement, 1900–1916," *Environmental Review* 8 (Spring 1984): 57–85.

Farenthold's words, "nurturance-activism-feminism"; in part it also represented a self-conscious attempt to elaborate an eco-feminist understanding of woman's relationship to the earth. Both the scope and shape of that movement, and its relationship to other women's movements, including active women's environmental movements in Europe, await historical synthesis.[47]

PHARMACEUTICAL

Since the early 1960s, American women have experienced a steady stream of adverse reproductive and health effects from pharmaceuticals and contraceptives. As a result, women have also been involved in extensive organization and litigation over injuries inflicted by negligent pharmaceutical companies. The opening shot in this extensive litigation battle was the worldwide scare concerning the teratogenic sedative thalidomide, which produced limb defects, colloquially termed "seal limb," in children of women who took it during pregnancy. Dr. Frances Kelsey of the Food and Drug Administration withheld the drug from the U.S. market until the William S. Merrell Company could satisfy her concerns about side effects from peripheral neuritis. While approval was delayed, Kelsey learned of European reports of the teratogenic effects, thus sparing this country numerous cases that would otherwise have resulted. *Washington Post* investigative reporter Morton Mintz, who broke the story in 1962, and a team from the *Sunday Times* of London have documented how elements of the international pharmaceutical industry reacted with irresponsible slowness to adverse drug-reaction reports and participated in a cover-up. There were far fewer cases in the United States, where the drug was used only in limited research studies, than in many other countries; the only thalidomide birth-defect suit tried before a jury was a California case that produced a judgment against Merrell in 1971 of $2.5 million ($1 million in punitive damages).[48]

---

47 Frances T. Farenthold, "Introduction," in Anne Witte Garland, *Women Activists*, p. xxii; Carolyn Merchant, "Earthcare: Women and the Environment," *Environment* 23 (June 1981): 6–13, 38–40; Abby Peterson and Carolyn Merchant, "'Peace with the Earth': Women and the Environmental Movement in Sweden," *Women's Studies International Forum* 9 (1986): 465–79.

48 Morton Mintz, *The Therapeutic Nightmare* (Boston: Houghton Mifflin, 1965); The Insight Team of *The Sunday Times* of London, *Suffer the Children: The Story of Thalidomide* (New York: Viking Press, 1979); Richard E. McFadyen, "Thalidomide in America: A Brush with Tragedy," *Clio Medica* 11 (July 1976): 79–93; Max Sherman and Steven Strauss, "Thalidomide: A Twenty-Five Year Perspective," *Food Drug Cosmetic Law Journal* 40 (October 1986): 458–66.

A fuller picture of the industry's potential for criminal conduct was revealed when Merrell's anticholesterol drug MER/29 was pulled off the market only a month after the company withdrew its application to market thalidomide in the United States. Several Merrell scientists pleaded no-contest to criminal charges that they fraudulently misrepresented animal experiments and falsified information submitted to the FDA, including data showing adverse reproductive effects. Extensive litigation resulting from cataracts and other MER/29 injuries involved a network of lawyers around the country and helped set a pattern for later drug litigation. MER/29 was a form of molecularly altered synthetic estrogen; the battle over this criminally marketed drug marked the first litigation skirmish in the controversy over those hormones.[49]

"Cancer of the vagina is rare, occurring as epidermoid carcinoma in women over the age of 50 years."[50] Thus Arthur Herbst and his Harvard colleagues began their historic and chilling 1971 report. Their case-control study had determined that an unusual cluster of vaginal cancer among women in their teens and early twenties was likely to have been caused by the widely used synthetic estrogen diethylstilbestrol (DES), taken by their mothers during pregnancy. Prescribed in the late 1940s and early 1950s for women with high-risk pregnancies, this hormone was held out to women as a magical gift from medicine in the strong postwar cultural climate urging them to have children. DES not only had no measurable benefit, but it caused cancer, cervical and vaginal abnormalities, adverse reproductive outcomes in daughters, and possibly caused abnormalities in sons as well.[51] This continuing, astonishing tragedy, involving thousands of families across generations, has been the occasion for considerable anguish, reflection, organization, and litigation.

Sociologist Susan Bell has shown how menopause became medicalized around 1941, when a conjunction of interests between drug manufacturers, physicians and scientists, and the Food and Drug Administration led to FDA approval for the use of DES among menopausal women

---

[49] Mintz, *Therapeutic Nightmare*; Ralph Adam Fine, *The Great Drug Deception* (New York: Stein and Day, 1972); Paul D. Rheingold, "The MER/29 Story—An Instance of Successful Mass Disaster Litigation," *California Law Review* 56 (January 1968): 116–48.

[50] Arthur J. Herbst, Howard Ulfelder, and David C. Poskanzer, "Adenocarcinoma of the Vagina: Association of Maternal Stilbestrol Therapy with Tumor Appearance in Young Women," *New England Journal of Medicine* 284 (April 22, 1971): 878.

[51] David A. Edelman, *DES/Diethylstilbestrol—New Perspectives* (Lancaster, England: MTP Press, 1986).

despite strong evidence from animal studies that it was carcinogenic. Estrogen-replacement therapy for menopausal women remains the object of continuing debate amidst reports of a possible cancer link. While the American women's health movement has been skeptical, viewing the therapy as another form of medicalization and indiscriminate use of dangerous hormones, its British counterpart has been actively urging more widespread use of it there.[52]

In 1947, manufacturers of DES received FDA approval for an additional use, preventing miscarriages, although the evidence that it was effective for that purpose was weak. In *Daughters at Risk*, the story of the useless marketing of DES for high-risk pregnancies is counterposed to the anguish of vaginal cancer-victim Anne Needham, whose personal injury trial resulted in an $800,000 verdict in her favor, although it was later overturned. Joyce Bichler's moving account describes her own vaginal cancer, her growing awareness of its cause, and the partial redemption through a large jury verdict against Eli Lilly in 1979; it places her personal struggle in the context of the substantial network of DES Action organizations that had grown up around the country. When she heard a New York jury's verdict awarding her $500,000—on the grounds that Lilly could reasonably have foreseen her cancer risk in 1953 when her mother took the drug—Bichler embraced her lawyer. "It was the moment of my life. I had won. I had survived."[53]

Robert Meyers's *D.E.S.: The Bitter Pill* remains the best overall account of the origins of the DES disaster and responses to it. Psychiatrists Roberta Apfel and Susan Fisher explore the various traumas experienced by mothers, daughters, and physicians in the DES tragedy. Their book does not answer the question focused on by all the diverse groups they have addressed: Who was responsible for this scandalous disaster? Rather, they argue that the DES scandal is "intrinsic to the structure of

---

[52] Susan E. Bell, "Changing Ideas: The Medicalization of Menopause," *Social Science & Medicine* 24 (1987): 535–42; Susan E. Bell, "A New Model of Medical Technology Development: A Case Study of DES," in Julius A. Roth and Sheryl Burt Ruzek, eds., *Research in the Sociology of Health Care*, Volume 4 (Greenwich, CT: JAI Press, 1986), pp. 1–32; Patricia A. Kaufert and Sonja M. McKinlay, "Estrogen-Replacement Therapy: The Production of Medical Knowledge and the Emergence of Policy," in Ellen Lewin and Virginia Olesen, eds., *Women, Health, and Healing: Toward a New Perspective* (New York: Tavistock, 1985), pp. 113–38; Frances B. McCrea and Gerald E. Markle, "The Estrogen Replacement Controversy in the USA and UK: Different Answers to the Same Question," *Social Studies of Science* 14 (February 1984): 1–26.

[53] Stephen Fenichell and Lawrence S. Charfoos, *Daughters at Risk: A Personal D.E.S. History* (Garden City, NY: Doubleday, 1981); Joyce Bichler, *DES Daughter* (New York: Avon, 1981), p. 186.

modern medicine," produced by medicine's perhaps overzealous pursuit of new knowledge and techniques to improve the quality of life.[54]

The search for responsibility and compensation continues in the courts. DES daughters have been burdened by problems involving the statute of limitations and by difficulties in proving which of the approximately 300 manufacturers of the product did the harm in a particular case. Many have tried to claim damages for their emotional distress from being at risk, so far with little success. Legal obstacles have prevented many cases from reaching juries. By the spring of 1983, 642 suits had been filed against Eli Lilly, the largest manufacturer of DES, yet by 1982 only 2 negligence suits against the company had gone to trial, with Lilly winning in one and losing in the Bichler case. Reviewing the legal labyrinth that DES daughters faced in the courts, Harlan Abrahams and Bobbee Joan Musgrave concluded that this reflected male dominance of the medical and legal professions: "'Women's problems' simply do not occupy a place of importance in the scheme of legal things."[55] Health risks to DES daughters have proven to be less than first feared; Herbst now estimates that no more than 1 in 1,000 of them developed the characteristic form of vaginal or cervical cancer. And the legal climate for DES lawsuits is somewhat improved over that of a decade ago, even as new DES situations continue to be brought into court. Thus, a California jury in 1986 had to choose between a 29-year-old plaintiff's claim that his mother's ingestion of DES caused him to be mistakenly raised as a girl for the first 14 years of his life and to develop testicular cancer, or, as the jury decided, that his cancer and pseudohermaphroditism were due to other causes. A 1986 settlement by Lilly and Squibb involved a particularly complicated case: a child who developed total blindness, allegedly from complications of premature birth, apparently produced by his mother's incompetent cervix, which was caused in turn by his grandmother's ingestion of DES.

Oral contraceptives began to be sold in the United States in 1960, and by the end of the decade popular books by Barbara Seaman and Paul Vaughan presented substantial evidence from the medical literature on harmful health effects from these combinations of synthetic hormones.

---

[54] Robert Meyers, *D.E.S.: The Bitter Pill* (New York: Seaview/Putnam, 1983); Roberta Apfel and Susan M. Fisher, *To Do No Harm: DES and the Dilemmas of Modern Medicine* (New Haven: Yale University Press, 1984).

[55] Thomas F. Campion, "DES and Litigation: The First Ten Years," *The Review of Litigation* 2 (Spring 1982): 171–96; Harlan S. Abrahams and Bobbee Joan Musgrave, "The DES Labyrinth," *South Carolina Law Review* 33 (May 1982): 663–711.

The premature rush to market the Pill has produced an extensive, continuing litigation battle over the pharmaceutical industry's duty to warn physicians and patients of the harmful effects of its products.[56] Many early appellate decisions found the warnings of excessive clotting in the package inserts sufficient as a matter of law to dismiss suits against the manufacturers, often overturning a plaintiff's verdict in a lower court.[57] Other courts upheld lower court verdicts or ordered new trials for cases summarily dismissed for lack of legal grounds by lower court judges.[58] In 1981, for instance, a federal court upheld a New Hampshire verdict awarding $700,000 to Judith Brochu, a 27-year-old oral contraceptive user who suffered a severe stroke. The jury apparently was impressed with evidence that Ortho Pharmaceutical's warnings to physicians in 1971 did not mention British studies indicating that oral contraceptives with lower estrogen content would have been just as effective, while presenting less risk of cerebral thrombosis.[59]

In 1984 the Supreme Court of Kansas upheld a $4.75 million verdict (including $2.75 million in punitive damages) for Carol Wooderson against Ortho in a suit involving malignant hypertension caused by oral contraceptives that resulted in the failure and loss of her kidneys.[60] The opinion noted evidence of the many articles in the medical literature in 1976 linking oral contraceptives with Wooderson's condition; indeed, twenty-one cases of her condition had been reported, but the company made no mention of adverse effects on renal functioning in its package insert. As in *Brochu*, the judge in *Wooderson* noted that the package insert downplayed British reports on the safety and efficacy of the higher dose products that Wooderson took—products that Ortho continued to push, presumably to bolster its competitive position. Courts in several states have begun to hold that manufacturers of oral

---

[56] Barbara Seaman, *The Doctors' Case Against the Pill* (New York: Avon, 1969); Paul Vaughan, *The Pill on Trial* (London: Weidenfeld and Nicolson, 1970); Marshall S. Shapo, *A Nation of Guinea Pigs* (New York: The Free Press, 1979); Joyce Barrett, "Product Liability and the Pill," *Cleveland State Law Review* 19 (September 1970): 468–79.

[57] *Leibowitz v. Ortho Pharmaceutical Corp.*, 307 A.2d 449 (Pa. 1973); *Lawson v. G.D. Searle & Company*, 356 N.E.2d 779 (Ill. 1976); *Chambers v. G.D. Searle & Co.*, 441 F.Supp. 377 (1975); *Dunkin v. Syntex Laboratories, Inc.*, 443 F.Supp. 121 (1977); *Goodson v. Searle Laboratories*, 471 F.Supp. 546 (1978).

[58] *McEwen v. Ortho Pharmaceutical Corporation*, 528 P.2d 522 (Or. 1974); *Mahr v. G.D. Searle & Co.*, 390 N.E.2d 1214 (Ill. 1979); *Ortho Pharmaceutical Corp. v. Chapman*, 388 N.E.2d 541 (Ind. 1979).

[59] *Brochu v. Ortho Pharmaceutical Corp.*, 642 F.2d 652 (1981).

[60] *Wooderson v. Ortho Pharmaceutical Corp.*, 681 P.2d 1038 (Kan. 1984).

contraceptives have a duty to warn consumers directly, not simply to warn the physician acting as a "learned intermediary." These courts have reasoned that unlike most other prescription drugs, it is the patient rather than the physician who usually elects to use oral contraceptives. Furthermore, women often take them for a long period of time between visits to the doctor, making it imperative that they have complete information about risks.[61]

The Dalkon Shield intrauterine device (IUD), launched with great fanfare in 1971 by the A.H. Robins Company as a safe alternative to the Pill, was withdrawn from the market in 1974 after reports of numerous cases of adverse side effects and deaths. Massive evidence of Robins's greed and cover-up helped fuel litigation that produced large punitive damages awards against the company, driving it into bankruptcy court in 1985. Books by Morton Mintz and Susan Perry and Jim Dawson present the victims' case. Robins's pattern of continual deceit and callousness was summarized at length by the Colorado Supreme Court when it upheld a $6.2 million punitive damages award in the case of Carrie Palmer, who suffered a life-threatening septic abortion with a resulting hysterectomy from using the Dalkon Shield. The most famous Dalkon Shield document, federal judge Miles Lord's searing 1984 personal rebuke of three top Robins executives and plea for them to recall their product from women still wearing it, presents a powerful picture of corporate and personal immorality, particularly in the document's annotated form, which lays out the case against Robins and the executives. Numerous networks of Dalkon Shield victims have sprung up around the country, and many of them have been heavily involved in the complex bankruptcy proceedings. Litigation is also proceeding against G.D. Searle's Cooper-7 IUD and Ortho Pharmaceutical's Lippes Loop.[62]

Litigation that began in 1980 over toxic shock syndrome has resulted in several large awards against makers of high-absorbency tam-

---

[61] Teresa Moran Schwartz, "Consumer Warnings for Oral Contraceptives: A New Exception to the Prescription Drug Rule," *Food Drug Cosmetic Law Journal* 41 (July 1986): 241–56.

[62] Morton Mintz, *At Any Cost: Corporate Greed, Women, and the Dalkon Shield* (New York: Pantheon, 1985); Susan Perry and Jim Dawson, *Nightmare: Women and the Dalkon Shield* (New York: Macmillan, 1985); *Palmer v. A.H. Robins Co., Inc.*, 684 P.2d 187 (Colo. 1984); "The Dalkon Shield Litigation: Revised Annotated Reprimand by Chief Judge Miles W. Lord," *Hamline Law Review* 9 (February 1986): 7–51; Sheldon Engelmayer and Robert Wagman, *Lord's Justice* (Garden City, NY: Doubleday Anchor, 1985); Guerry R. Thornton, Jr., "Intrauterine Devices: Malpractice and Product Liability," *Law, Medicine & Health Care* 14 (1986): 4–12.

pons, including $10 million punitive damages awards against Johnson & Johnson and International Playtex. Judges and juries were impressed by the companies' failure to test their products properly in the face of adverse reports, and, in Playtex's case, continuing to misrepresent a superabsorbent product it knew to be harmful.[63]

Numerous lawsuits have been filed against the suspected teratogen Bendectin, widely prescribed between 1956 and 1983 for women with morning sickness. A number of suits have been tried involving children with limb defects. Although the plaintiffs have won a few jury verdicts, including a huge punitive damages award in the District of Columbia, Merrell Dow has won most of them and has been extremely successful in its appeals, even to the point of having a large jury award overturned.[64] In 1985, a federal court upheld a large jury award against Ortho Pharmaceutical's spermicide as a teratogen in a limb-defect case, although the jury and appeals court's judgment that the spermicide was the legal cause of the injury has been bitterly contested by segments of the medical community.[65] Evidence that emerged in early 1988 indicating that Hoffman LaRoche's Accutane, a powerful drug for acne, was responsible for numerous birth defects gave new promise for litigation that had met with little success since its beginning in 1982.[66]

The Accutane story is only the latest of many linking corporate misconduct by the pharmaceutical industry and dubious conduct by segments of the medical profession with reproductive harm to women. Marshall Clinard and Peter Yeager found that in the mid-1970s, only the oil and automobile industries were as likely as the pharmaceutical industry to be cited by federal authorities for violations of the law. Australian sociologist John Braithwaite has written a brilliant examination of the causes of, and possible remedies for, criminal conduct by the industry.

---

[63] Tom Riley, *The Price of a Life: One Woman's Death from Toxic Shock* (Bethesda, MD: Adler & Adler, 1986); Sanford L. Weiner, "Tampons and Toxic Shock Syndrome: Consumer Protection or Public Confusion?," in Harvey M. Sapolsky, ed., *Consuming Fears: The Politics of Product Risks* (New York: Basic Books, 1986), pp. 141–58; Mark B. Hutton et al., "Tampons and Toxic Shock Syndrome," *Trial* 24 (February 1988): 54–59; *West v. Johnson & Johnson Products, Inc.*, 220 Cal.Rptr. 437 (1985); *O'Gilvie v. International Playtex, Inc.*, 821 F.2d 1438 (10th Cir. 1987).

[64] *Oxendine v. Merrell Dow Pharmaceuticals, Inc.*, 506 A.2d 1100 (D.C.App. 1986); *Richardson By Richardson v. Richardson-Merrell, Inc.*, 821 F.2d 1438 (10th Cir. 1987).

[65] *Wells by Maihafer v. Ortho Pharmaceut.*, 615 F.Supp. 262 (D.C.Ga. 1985); James L. Mills and Duane Alexander, "Teratogens and 'Litogens'," *New England Journal of Medicine* 315 (November 6, 1986): 1234–36.

[66] Diane Acker Nygaard, "Accutane: Is the Drug a Prescription for Birth Defects?," *Trial* 24 (December 1988): 81–83.

As the collection *Adverse Effects* illustrates, there is now an international women's network tracking the connections between the international industry's products and the schemes of population-control advocates. Much of the story of the interplay between American women's attempts to control their reproduction and the questionable conduct of the pharmaceutical industry and government regulators has been uncovered in the various inquiries surrounding the episodes discussed in this section. However, no attempt has been made to put all this together into a coherent story. Similarly, although the growing concern with reproductive outcomes has produced several books for a popular audience, there is no scholarly history of the modern political controversy over teratogenicity.[67]

CONCLUSION

This review of women's experience with the toxic environment has touched on only a few prominent episodes. Left unexamined, for example, are the familiar antidepressants, barbiturates, and carbon monoxide which together account for significant numbers of suicidal and accidental deaths among women. I have looked at neither the epidemic of "chemical hypersensitivity" among women in the Silicon Valley electronics industry and around the country, nor the continuing carnage from household cleaning products, nor the longstanding controversy concerning outbreaks of alleged mass psychogenic illness among women with possible toxic exposures.[68] Rather, I have examined the growing concern with a toxic environment that began to be constructed in the

---

[67] Marshall B. Clinard and Peter C. Yeager, *Corporate Crime* (New York: Free Press, 1980); John Braithwaite, *Corporate Crime in the Pharmaceutical Industry* (London: Routledge & Kegan Paul, 1984); Kathleen McDonnell, ed., *Adverse Effects: Women and the Pharmaceutical Industry* (Toronto, Ontario: Women's Educational Press, 1986); Christopher Norwood, *At Highest Risk: Protecting Children from Environmental Injury* (New York: Penguin, 1980); John Elkington, *The Poisoned Womb: Human Reproduction in a Polluted World* (New York: Penguin, 1986).

[68] Suzanne M. Froede et al., "An Analysis of Toxic Deaths, 1982 to 1985, Pima County, Arizona," *Journal of Forensic Sciences* 32 (November 1987): 1676–93; Amanda Spake, "A New American Nightmare?" *Ms*, March 1986, pp. 35–42, 93–95; "Cleaning Solutions and Compounds," *Negligence Compensation Cases Annotated* 54 (Wilmette, IL: Callaghan & Company, 1986): 266–389; Halley S. Faust and Lawrence H. Brilliant, "Is the Diagnosis of 'Mass Hysteria' an Excuse for Incomplete Investigation of Low-Level Environmental Contamination?," *Journal of Occupational Medicine* 23 (January 1981): 22–26; Michael J. Colligan and Lawrence R. Murphy, "A Review of Mass Psychogenic Illness in Work Settings," in Michael J. Colligan, James W. Pennebaker, and Lawrence R. Murphy, eds., *Mass Psychogenic Illness: A Social Psychological Analysis* (Hillsdale, NJ: Lawrence Erlbaum, 1982), pp. 33–52.

early part of this century, that took its distinctly contemporary form in
the 1940s and 1950s, and that produced an avalanche of illness and
resistance in the 1970s and 1980s. I have tried to look at this phenomenon as a whole, seen through the prism of diverse, significant, historical
reconstructions of important episodes. I hope that this first attempt at
characterizing the historical sweep of women's experiences with the toxic
environment in twentieth-century America will help open up an examination of events that have so far been treated only episodically, as
isolated stories, rather than being seen as connected to each other both
by common underlying social processes creating toxic risks, and by
women's continual efforts to understand and control their environments, bodies, and misfortunes.

    Several themes bear repeating as topics for further study. Numerous
ways of reconstructing the past figure prominently in the various controversies facing women in the American toxic environment. We know
very little about how these forms of knowledge of the past are produced
and how they interact in the discourse and conflicts surrounding toxic
episodes. Disentangling the layering of time periods becomes important
here: the world constructed in the 1940s and 1950s, when corporations
had a relatively free hand to apply science and manipulate the environment as they chose, became manifest on women's bodies; in the 1970s
and 1980s this became the object of major reinterpretation through
scientific and journalistic investigations and high-stakes tort litigation
when the women's, environmental, and other social movements created
a contesting view of the proper balance among corporate and governmental activity, the environment, and women's health. Connecting
women's suffering to aspects of this earlier world produced extensive
evidence of corporate and governmental misconduct that constitutes a
powerful critique of the moral basis of production, consumption, community life, and the government's protection of its citizens.

    Similarly, we know little about the early network of women who
studied and advocated on this issue, or about organizations such as the
Women's Bureau. Nor has there been much work on the continuities
and discontinuities between this early movement and the women's occu-
pational/environmental/reproductive health movement(s) that became
prominent in the 1970s. It would be helpful to know more about the
links between segments of this movement, particularly among grassroots
leadership. The personal transformations involved in individuals becoming aware of and fighting against corporate and governmental power,
manifest as illness, risks, and fear, is another topic worthy of study.

Above all, the historical evolution of women's consciousness of the toxic experience needs to be critically assessed. The various ways in which women experience and interpret their bodies—reading social relations transmitted through toxic environments in their own bodies—have a history tied into that of the socially constructed physical world in which women lived, and the forms of knowledge and organization open to them in seeking to alter it. The characteristic modern experiences of anxiety and fear, of being at risk, of confronting emblematic conditions such as cancer and limb defects, evolved together with particular environments, movements, and organizational forms for attaining some measure of insight and justice. In a world of nuclear nightmares and a myriad of other real and imagined toxic threats, women have tried to achieve some measure of retribution and redress. In a world of powerful toxic threats controlled by corporations with criminal propensities and a compliant government, women have attempted to use the moral force of their innocent suffering to appeal to juries and the broader public for the creation of a just balance between power, production, and people. Through publicly reconstructing past social relations implicated in their own and their children's present misfortune, through bearing witness to the past by their attempt to symbolically redress their suffering, women have tried to prevent the creation of future victims of the toxic world currently being built. These important stories are dimly visible in this review of the experience with the toxic environment by women who, through critically encountering their threatening world, came better to know it, and themselves.

HEALTH CARE PROVIDERS

· · · —————— · · ·

17

MIDWIVES AND HISTORY

Judy Barrett Litoff

During the fall of 1964, a twenty-one-year-old sociology major at the University of Pennsylvania, struggling to combine the rigors of academic life with the everyday realities of raising a two-year-old, enrolled in Charles Rosenberg's course on the History of Medicine. As she pondered the question of a paper topic, this young mother turned to the subject of childbirth and discovered that the question of the role and status of the American midwife had been all but ignored by professional historians. Narrowing her focus to the early twentieth-century "midwife debate," she wrote a paper which, two years later, was to be published in the *Bulletin of the History of Medicine* as "The American Midwife Controversy: A Crisis of Professionalization." The publication of this pioneering article brought new visibility to the nearly forgotten midwife and played a major role in shaping midwifery studies during the next two decades. However, this was the only time that the author, Frances E. Kobrin, entered the domain of the historian, choosing instead to pursue a career in sociology.[1]

Prior to the publication of "The American Midwife Controversy," information on the history of American midwives was largely confined

---

[1] Frances E. Kobrin, "The American Midwife Controversy: A Crisis of Professionalization," *Bulletin of the History of Medicine* 40 (1966): 350–63. The significance of this article is underscored by the fact that it has been reprinted in two recently published anthologies: Judith Walzer Leavitt, ed., *Women and Health in America* (Madison: University of Wisconsin Press, 1984), pp. 318–26 and Judith Walzer Leavitt and Ronald L. Numbers, eds., *Sickness & Health in America: Readings in the History of Medicine and Public Health* (Madison: University of Wisconsin Press, 1985), pp. 197–205. Frances E. Kobrin Goldscheider received the Ph.D. degree in demography from the University of Pennsylvania in 1971. She is currently a Professor of Sociology at Brown University.

to medical and obstetrical histories which emphasized the important strides made by medical science in improving the health care of parturient women. This "march-of-medical-progress" approach singled out physicians such as William Chamberlen, William Smellie, Ephraim McDowell, J. Marion Sims, Ignaz Semmelweis, and Oliver Wendell Holmes for special praise. At best, the authors of these works avoided the subject of midwifery. More frequently, however, they spoke disparagingly of midwives, typically characterizing them as "ignorant" and "superstitious." As an example, Theodore Cianfrani, author of *A Short History of Obstetrics and Gynecology* (1960), described the typical midwife as "a person of inferior education" for whom "relics, charms, and incantations comprised her armamentarium, in the main."[2]

There had been occasional theses, articles, and even book-length investigations that sought to present a more even-handed portrayal of midwifery. However, these works were often difficult to locate and were not usually considered to be major contributions. Probably the most significant of these early midwifery studies was Marie Campbell's *Folks Do Get Born* (1946), an examination of the practices of traditional black "granny" midwives from Georgia. This work was of special significance as it related a number of "story sketches" in the words of the midwives themselves. A similar study of black midwives from Mississippi, which provided accounts of midwife meetings and transcriptions of midwife songs, was written by James H. Ferguson and published in the *Journal of the History of Medicine* in 1950. Two additional works on southern lay midwives included "The 'Granny' Midwife: Changing Roles and Functions of a Folk Practitioner" (1961) written by a team of sociologists headed by Beatrice Mongeau and "Lay Midwifery in Southern Appalachia" (1966) by K. Asgood, D. L. Hochstrasser, and K. W. Deuschle. An informative discussion of midwifery in South Carolina, based largely on the records of the South Carolina board of health, was written by Mary Evelyn Leith and appeared in 1948.[3] Four other early works about

[2] Theodore Cianfrani, *A Short History of Obstetrics and Gynecology* (Springfield, IL: Charles C. Thomas, 1960), p. 131. Other "march-of-medical-progress" books include Irving S. Cutter and Henry R. Viets, *A Short History of Midwifery* (Philadelphia: W. B. Saunders Company, 1964); Harvey Graham, *Eternal Eve: The Mysteries of Birth and the Customs that Surround It* (London: Hutchinson and Co., 1960); Findley Palmer, *The Story of Childbirth* (New York: Doubleday, Doran and Co., 1934); and Herbert Thoms, *Chapters in American Obstetrics* (Springfield, IL: Charles C. Thomas, 1933).
[3] Marie Campbell, *Folks Do Get Born* (New York: Rinehart & Co., 1946; reprint, New York: Garland Publishing, 1985). James H. Ferguson, "Mississippi Midwives," *Journal of the History of Medicine* 5 (1950): 85–95. Beatrice Mongeau, Harvey L. Smith and Ann

American midwifery were Helen Marie Fedde's master's thesis at the University of Kentucky, "A Study of Midwifery with Special Reference to Its Historical Background, Its Present Status, and a Consideration of Its Future in the United States" (1950); Claire Noall's biographical sketches of Mormon midwives who practiced in Utah during the late nineteenth and early twentieth centuries (1942); M. Theopane Shoemaker's study of the origins and development of nurse-midwifery in the United States (1947); and Mary Breckinridge's autobiography, *Wide Neighborhoods: A Story of the Frontier Nursing Service* (1952).[4]

Much valuable information may be gleaned from these initial investigations. However, none of these studies provided the historical and theoretical framework necessary for fully understanding the complex phenomenon of American midwifery. In fact, what distinguished Frances Kobrin's article from these earlier works was her ability to relate the early twentieth-century "midwife debate" to the larger issue of medical professionalization.

After analyzing the relevant articles published in the leading medical periodicals of the day, Kobrin concluded that the early twentieth-century "midwife debate" revolved around two fundamentally different approaches to childbirth and midwifery. At one extreme were those physicians, many of whom were obstetricians, who emphasized the potential dangers of childbirth and who believed that the health of American mothers and infants would be most directly benefitted by the development of obstetrics as a recognized medical specialty. Individuals

---

C. Maney, "The 'Granny' Midwife: Changing Roles and Functions of a Folk Practitioner," *American Journal of Sociology* 66 (1961): 497–505. K. Osgood, D. L. Hochstrasser, and K. W. Deuschle, "Lay Midwifery in Southern Appalachia," *Arch. Environ. Health* 12 (1966): 759–70. Mary Evelyn Leith, "The Development of Midwife Education in South Carolina, 1918–1946" (M.A. thesis, Yale University, 1948).

4 Helen Marie Fedde, "A Study of Midwifery with Special Reference to Its Historical Background, Its Present Status, and a Consideration of Its Future in the United States" (Master's thesis, University of Kentucky, 1950). Claire Noall, "Mormon Midwives," *Utah Historical Quarterly* 10 (1942): 84–144. M. Theopane Shoemaker, *History of Nurse-Midwifery in the United States* (Washington, DC: Catholic University Press of America, 1947; reprint, New York: Garland Publishing, 1985). Mary Breckinridge, *Wide Neighborhoods: A Story of the Frontier Nursing Service* (New York: Harper & Brothers, 1952; reprint, University Press of Kentucky, 1981). Information on colonial and early national midwives may also be found in Claire Elizabeth Fox, "Pregnancy, Childbirth and Early Infancy in Anglo-American Culture, 1675–1830" (Ph.D. dissertation, University of Pennsylvania, 1966). Another early study of Mormon midwifery is Juanita Brooks, "Mariah Huntsman Leavitt: Midwife of the Desert Frontier," in *Forms Upon the Frontier*, Austin Fife, Alta Fife, and Henry H. Glassie, eds. (Logan: Utah State University Press, 1989), pp. 119–31.

who identified with what Kobrin labeled the "professional" approach to childbirth favored the outright abolition of midwives. At the other end of the spectrum were public health advocates who generally viewed childbirth as a normal physiological condition and were cognizant of the impracticality of finding satisfactory replacements for midwives, who, as late as 1910, attended approximately 50% of all births. This "public health" approach to childbirth called for the creation of training and regulatory programs for midwives modeled after the relatively successful programs already established in England and Europe.

In her final analysis, Kobrin studiously avoided a monocausal explanation for the eventual triumph of the "professional" approach to childbirth and the resultant precipitous decline in the number of midwife-attended births. "Despite the potential obstetric superiority of obstetricians over midwives," wrote Kobrin, "the triumph of the former was probably due most to the fact that the circumstances debated in this period changed radically." Noting that the "professionalization process was very sensitive to external conditions and attitudes," Kobrin contended that the near demise of the midwife during the early years of the twentieth century was related to a number of factors over which the obstetrician had little control. These included the significant decrease in immigration after World War I, the decline in the birth rate during the 1920s, and the growing public demand from reform-minded women for improved obstetrical care.[5]

Although other historians have enlarged upon and refined the arguments presented by Kobrin, the basic contours of her article remain intact. Indeed, "The American Midwife Controversy" serves as the standard introduction to modern midwifery studies.

Not until the decade of the 1970s, as the resurgence of feminism and renewed interest in the history of women began to take root, was the full significance of Kobrin's research recognized. Reducing her "professional" vs. "public health" approach to childbirth and midwifery to an almost static model, several writers concluded that the midwife was the victim of an elite, misogynous medical establishment. In a widely circulated pamphlet, *Witches, Nurses, and Midwives* (1973), Barbara Ehrenreich and Deirdre English portrayed American obstetricians as self-serving individuals who "had no real commitment to improved obstetrical care," and who systematically sought to outlaw midwifery in order to gain a monopoly over this potentially lucrative field of practice.

---

[5] Korbin, "The American Midwife Controversy," pp. 362–63.

G. J. Barker-Benfield made much the same point, arguing that the "campaign against midwives was an expression of the struggle to establish the male specialty of obstetrics and gynecology."[6] Other writers who depicted midwives as victims of a sexist medical system were Joan M. Jensen, Adrienne Rich, and Ann H. Sablosky.[7] Yet these authors not only exaggerated the unanimity with which medical practitioners sought to eliminate the midwife, they sometimes distorted the facts. For example, in their efforts to demonstrate that a powerful and misogynous medical establishment was responsible for the decline of midwifery, they erroneously reported that many states, responding to intense pressure from the medical profession, enacted laws making midwifery illegal.[8] In actuality, the only state to outlaw midwifery during the early years of the twentieth century was Massachusetts.

Less polemical in tone was Neal Devitt's 1979 article, "The Statistical Case for Elimination of the Midwife." Concentrating on the 1890–1935 era, Devitt examined the medical literature of this period in order to determine whether physicians were justified in calling for the abolition of midwifery. He found that the infant and maternal mortality rates of the midwife were equal to or even lower than that of the average general practitioner and concluded that while physicians often wrote about the "midwife problem," the more fundamental issue facing the medical profession was how to reduce the nation's alarmingly high infant and maternal mortality rates. However, most physicians were not willing to address this very complex issue and preferred to concentrate on what

---

[6] Barbara Ehrenreich and Deirdre English, *Witches, Midwives, and Nurses: A History of Women Healers* (Oyster Bay, NY: Glass Mountain Pamphlets [1973]), p. 32. G. J. Barker-Benfield, *The Horrors of the Half-Known Life: Male Attitudes Toward Women and Sexuality in Nineteenth-Century America* (New York: Harper & Row, 1976), p. 71.

[7] Joan M. Jensen, "Politics and the American Midwife Controversy," *Frontiers* 1 (Spring 1976): 19–33. Adrienne Rich, *Of Woman Born: Motherhood as Experience and Institution* (New York: W. W. Norton, 1976), pp. 136–41. Ann H. Sablosky, "The Power of the Forceps: A Comparative Analysis of the Midwife—Historically and Today," *Women and Health* 1 (1976): 10–13. The British sociologist Ann Oakley also argues that midwives were the victims of a misogynous medical system. See, for example, Ann Oakley, "Wisewoman and Medicine Man: Changes in the Management of Childbirth," in *The Rights and Wrongs of Women*, ed. Juliet Mitchell and Ann Oakley (Middlesex, England: Penguin, 1976); Ann Oakley, *Woman Confined: Towards A Sociology of Childbirth* (New York: Schocken, 1980); and Ann Oakley, *The Captured Womb: A History of Pregnant Women* (Oxford: Basil Blackwell Publisher, 1984).

[8] Ehrenreich and English, *Witches, Midwives, and Nurses*, p. 32. Barker-Benfield, *The Horrors of the Half-Known Life*, p. 63. Sablosky, "The Power of the Forceps," p. 11. Jensen, "Politics and the American Midwife Controversy," p. 20.

was to them the more pertinent question of "the expansion of the profession and the elimination of midwifery."[9]

Other scholars turned to the question of the changing role of the midwife in the pre-Civil War era. In an award-winning article, "'On the Importance of the Obstetrick Art': Changing Customs of Childbirth in America, 1760–1825," published in the *William and Mary Quarterly* in 1977, Catherine M. Scholten investigated the forces responsible for the gradual replacement of midwives, who had held a virtual monopoly on the field of midwifery in the colonial era, by physicians among urban, well-to-do women in the late eighteenth and early nineteenth centuries. She attributed this shift to a number of complex factors including the formal medical education of physicians and the evolution of scientific obstetrics, the desire of women for safer childbirth, the utility of obstetrics in building up a physician's practice, and the many social changes associated with urbanization.

Although Scholten devoted considerable attention to a discussion of the decline of midwifery, she was not satisfied with simply portraying the midwife as a victim of unavoidable circumstances. In fact, one of the most significant features of this article was Scholten's description of the actual world of the colonial midwife. She demonstrated that the midwife was a highly esteemed member of the community who not only assisted at childbed but also offered advice on a number of gynecological problems. Aided by female friends and relatives of the parturient woman, the midwife's major function was to provide moral support and encourage-

---

[9] Neal Devitt, "The Statistical Case for the Elimination of the Midwife: Fact Versus Prejudice, 1890–1935," *Women and Health* 4 (Spring 1979); 81–96 [part 1] and 4 (Summer 1979): 169–86 [part 2]. The quotation appears on p. 185. A very good comparative analysis of the infant and maternal mortality rates of midwives and physicians, which substantiates the findings of Devitt, is Joyce Antler and Daniel M. Fox, "The Movement Toward a Safe Maternity: Physician Accountability of New York City, 1915–1940," *Bulletin of the History of Medicine* 50 (1976): 569–95. Several contemporary surveys also found that the record of physicians was not equal to that of midwives. See, for example, Ransom S. Hooker, *Maternal Mortality in New York City: A Study of All Puerperal Deaths, 1930–1932* (New York: The Commonwealth Fund, 1933), pp. 32–33, 186, 209, 214; *Medical Care for the American People: The Final Report of the Committee on the Costs of Medical Care* (Chicago: University of Chicago Press, 1932), pp. 122–27; Louis S. Reed, *Midwives, Chiropodists and Optometrists: Their Place in Medical Care* (Chicago: University of Chicago Press, 1932), pp. 4, 13–16, 20, 22; and White House Conference on Child Health and Protection, *Fetal, Newborn, and Maternal Morbidity and Mortality* (New York: The Century Company, 1933), pp. 18, 217–218. The autobiography of S. Josephine Baker, one of the leading proponents of the trained and regulated midwife, also contains relevant information. See S. Josephine Baker, *Fighting For Life* (New York: Macmillan Company, 1939), especially pp. 113–16.

ment while waiting for nature to take its course. She might offer the laboring woman spirits or mulled wine, and sometimes she examined the cervix in order to assess the progress of labor. But her chief duty remained that of comforting the woman during the long and often arduous hours of labor.[10]

The significance of Scholten's research was highlighted when "'On the Importance of the Obstetrick Art'" won the *William and Mary Quarterly* award for the best article published in its 1977 volume. Unfortunately, Scholten's tragic death in 1981 cut short her promising career. At the time, she was completing a larger work on childbearing in American society which was posthumously published in 1985.[11]

The practices of nineteenth-century midwives were analyzed by Janet Bogdan in a 1978 article on changing approaches to childbirth in nineteenth-century America. Relying largely on midwifery manuals and the diaries and letters of women of the period, Bogdan discovered that the nineteenth-century midwife, like her colonial counterpart, relied largely on a noninterventionist approach to childbirth. However, she also noted that the increasing frequency with which physicians served as birth attendants resulted in a situation whereby women's childbirth experiences varied greatly according to the attendant they chose. If the parturient woman chose a midwife, her experience would "include comfort and encouragement laced with herb teas" while the woman who called on a physician would, most likely, experience an interventionist approach to childbirth which involved the use of instruments and drugs to "ease, hurry, slow down, or otherwise manipulate the process."[12]

At about the same time that these articles appeared, two other scholars were working on book-length treatments of American midwives. These studies, one by Jane B. Donegan and the other by Judy Barrett Litoff, both of which were published in 1978, provided an historical survey of American midwifery from colonial times to the present.[13]

---

[10] Catherine M. Scholten, "'On the Importance of the Obstetrick Art': Changing Customs of Childbirth in America, 1760–1825," *William and Mary Quarterly* 34 (1977): 426–45.

[11] Catherine M. Scholten, *Childbearing in American Society: 1650–1850* (New York: New York University Press, 1985).

[12] Janet Bogdan, "Care or Cure? Childbirth Practices in Nineteenth Century America," *Feminist Studies* 4 (June 1978): 92–99. The quotation appears on p. 97.

[13] Jane B. Donegan, *Women & Men Midwives: Medicine, Morality, and Misogyny in Early America* (Westport, CT: Greenwood Press, 1978; paperback edition 1985). Judy Barrett Litoff, *American Midwives, 1860 to the Present* (Westport, CT: Greenwood Press, 1978; paperback edition 1985). Information on the history of American midwives may

Donegan's book, *Women & Men Midwives: Medicine, Morality, and Misogyny in Early America*, presented an overview of American midwifery before the Civil War. Focusing her attention on the early years of the nineteenth century, Donegan was particularly concerned with exploring the seeming paradox of the growth of man-midwifery in an age which placed increasing emphasis on feminine modesty.[14] She determined that while many physicians supported midwifery in the name of preserving decency and morality in the lying-in chamber, proponents of man-midwifery were more persuasive in their efforts to convince American women that the skill and expertise of medical men necessitated that they cast aside their concerns about the "delicacy of the sexes." Although charges of immodest procedures and "meddlesome midwifery" would continue to be issued by opponents of man-midwifery, the proponents of the "new obstetrics" had succeeded in winning over large numbers of middle- and upper-class women by the eve of the Civil War. Donegan's examination of the subtleties and complexities of the nineteenth-century man-midwifery debate was especially illuminating. Moreover, her sensitive but balanced portrayal of early American midwives served as an important corrective to the commonly held view that they were ignorant, slovenly relics of a bygone era.[15]

Judy Barrett Litoff's survey of American midwifery after the Civil War, *American Midwives, 1860 to the Present*, complemented the work of

---

also be found in Richard W. Wertz and Dorothy C. Wertz, *Lying-In: A History of Childbirth in America* (New York: The Free Press, 1977). For a good discussion of British midwifery, consult Jean Donnison, *Midwives and Medical Men: A History of Interprofessional Rivalries and Women's Rights* (New York: Schocken Books, 1977). Also useful is Thomas Rogers Forbes, *The Midwife and the Witch* (New Haven: Yale University Press, 1966). On midwifery in Newfoundland, Canada, see Janet McNaughton, "Traditional Prenatal Care of Newfoundland Women," unpublished paper presented at the Women's Studies Programme, Memorial University of Newfoundland, 1988. For an important cross-cultural analysis of midwifery, see Lucile F. Newman, Guest Editor, Special Issue on Midwives and Modernization, *Medical Anthropology* 5 (Winter 1981).

14 On this same subject, see Jane B. Donegan, "Man Midwifery and the Delicacy of the Sexes," in *"Remember the Ladies": New Perspectives on Women in American History*, ed. Carol V. R. George (Syracuse: Syracuse University Press, 1975).

15 A very good summary of the major arguments presented in *Midwives & Medical Men* may be found in Jane B. Donegan, "'Safe Delivered,' but by Whom? Midwives and Men-Midwives in Early America," in *Women and Health in America*, Judith Walzer Leavitt, ed. (Madison: University of Wisconsin Press, 1984). An M.A. thesis which examines many of the same issues addressed by Donegan is Susan Cayleff, "The Eradication of Female Midwifery" (M.A. thesis, Sarah Lawrence College, 1978). A recent work which is highly critical of the work of midwives is Edward Shorter, *A History of Women's Bodies* (New York: Basic Books, 1982).

Donegan. Litoff observed that most late nineteenth-century doctors, as well as most middle- and upper-class Americans, complacently ignored the midwife. However, the arrival of millions of immigrants in the years after 1880 from eastern and southern Europe, where midwifery was a highly respected profession, coupled with the revelation that this nation's infant and maternal mortality rates were disturbingly high, heightened the visibility of and interest in midwives. Using Kobrin's earlier research on the early twentieth-century midwife debate as a guide, Litoff presented a detailed account of the positions of both the midwife's proponents and opponents. Although acknowledging the important role which obstetric specialists played in engineering the anti-midwife campaign, Litoff, like Kobrin, maintained that a vast array of social and cultural changes were responsible for the sharp decline in the number of midwife-attended births during the early years of the twentieth century. In addition, she argued that the low social status accorded the midwife contributed to a further eroding of her position. The portrait of the midwife that emerged in Litoff's study was that of the poor, immigrant, or black woman who was empirically trained and enjoyed little occupational prestige or professional identity. Isolated from each other by poverty, geography, and language barriers, midwives lacked the resources with which to stand up to their critics.[16] The latter sections of this book examined the origins of nurse-midwifery, the reasons for its slow acceptance by the medical profession, and the midwifery "renaissance" of the 1970s.

With the publication of *Midwives & Medical Men* and *American Midwives*, the field of midwifery studies entered a new stage. The research of Donegan and Litoff, along with the work of Scholten and Bogdan, had clearly illustrated that the historiography of American midwifery involved much more than simply portraying midwives as victims of a misogynous medical system. Now that the initial surveys had been completed, historians could turn their attention to the cultural milieu in which midwifery flourished and to learning more about the unique experiences of these nearly "forgotten women."[17]

---

[16] These themes are also detailed in Judy Barrett Litoff, "Forgotten Women: American Midwives at the Turn of the Twentieth Century," *The Historian* 40 (February 1978): 235–51.

[17] Of course, the issue of the "midwife as victim" was not completely laid to rest. For a recent work that emphasizes this theme, see Barbara Katz Rothman, *In Labor: Women and Power in the Birthplace* (New York: W. W. Norton & Co., 1982). On the other hand, Jane Pacht Brickman, in a 1983 article which recounted the story of the early twentieth-century midwife debate, specifically refuted the charges that the midwife was a victim of a sexist medical system. See Jane Pacht Brickman, "Public Health, Midwives, and Nurses, 1880–1930," in *Nursing History: New Perspectives, New Possibilities*, ed. Ellen Condliffe Lagemann (New York: Teachers College, Columbia University, 1983).

One of the most valuable recent sources on the world of the midwife of the early national era is Laurel Thatcher Ulrich's study of the Maine midwife, Martha Moore Ballard. Ulrich has demonstrated that Ballard's long-neglected diary is replete with information on the nature of her practice, the outcomes of her deliveries, and her relationship with other midwives and physicians. Ballard, like most other midwives of this era, was an apprentice-trained, older, married woman who had borne several children and who combined running a household with her midwifery practice. In addition, she treated the sick and knew how to make her own medicines. Ballard's diary entries also illustrate that she usually cooperated with local physicians and, according to Ulrich, that the "relations between doctors and midwives were less antagonistic and the two specialties less separate" than has often been supposed. Ulrich further determined that Ballard was an experienced, self-assured midwife whose maternal and infant mortality rates compared favorably with those of medical practitioners.[18]

Other researchers have turned their attention to questions relating to the ethnicity and race of early twentieth-century midwives. Of special importance were two very informative articles by Eugene Declercq on immigrant midwifery in Lawrence, Massachusetts. Basing his findings on an examination of the birth registration records filed with the city clerk of Lawrence between 1892 and 1915, as well as on interviews with the descendants of the midwives, Declercq was able to piece together a remarkably detailed picture of Lawrence's immigrant midwives, most of whom were from eastern and southern Europe. He compiled information on the ethnicity of the midwives and their clientele, the number of births they attended, their infant and maternal mortality rates, their education, and the fees they charged. He determined that Lawrence's midwives could be divided into three major categories: (1) "generalists midwives" who were very active and served a diverse ethnic population; (2) "active ethnic specialists" who concentrated their work in one ethnic group; and, (3) "granny midwives" who only occasionally attended

---

18 Laurel Thatcher Ulrich, "Martha Moore Ballard and the Medical Challenge to Midwifery," in *From Revolution to Statehood: Maine in the Early Republic*, ed. Charles E. Clark, James S. Leamon, and Karen Bowden (Hanover, NH: University Press of New England, 1988), pp. 165–83; Laurel Thatcher Ulrich, "'The Living Mother of a Living Child': Midwifery and Mortality in Eighteenth-Century New England," *William and Mary Quarterly*, 46 (Jan. 1989): 27–48; and Laurel Thatcher Ulrich, *A Midwife's Tale: The Life of Martha Ballard, Based on Her Diary 1785–1812* (New York: Alfred A. Knopf, 1990. An abridged version of Ballard's diary appears in Charles Eleventon Nash, *The History of Augusta: First Settlements and Early Days as a Town* (Augusta, ME: Charles E. Nash & Son, 1904).

births. Declercq concluded that, contrary to the popularly held image that midwives were dirty and ignorant, they were, as a rule, intelligent, independent women who were "generous with their time, flexible in accepting different kinds of payments and had outcomes that appear to be at least as good as if not better than contemporary local physicians."[19]

In a related article, Declercq examined the effect which the outlawing of midwifery in Massachusetts in 1907 had on midwives. To his surprise, he discovered that Lawrence midwives openly violated the law and that the percentage of midwife-attended births *increased* after midwifery was declared illegal, from 38% in 1907 to 40.9% in 1913. What made this discovery even more startling was the fact that Massachusetts was the center of anti-midwife sentiment in the United States and the only state to outlaw midwifery. Declercq attributed this paradox to the immigrant composition of Lawrence, the skills and standing of the midwives, the minimum fees which they charged, and their ability to circumvent the law by relying on the help of cooperative physicians.[20]

The extent to which the experiences of the midwives of Lawrence were shared by immigrant midwives in other communities has not yet been fully determined. Charlotte G. Borst's thoughtful and well-researched study of the training and practice of midwives in Wisconsin at the turn of the twentieth century demonstrated that Wisconsin's midwives, like those of Lawrence, could be divided into distinct groupings. By examining midwife licenses and other state and country records, Borst identified three types of midwives: (1) "neighbor women," usually native born, who occasionally attended the births of relatives and close friends; (2) "apprentice-trained midwives," also usually native born, who learned from older midwives and physicians; and (3) "school-educated midwives" who were overwhelmingly first or second generation immigrants. Borst, like Declercq, found evidence of a significant amount of cooperation among midwives and physicians. Further evi-

---

19 Eugene Declercq, "The Nature and Style of Practice of Immigrant Midwives in Early Twentieth Century Massachusetts." *Journal of Social History* 19 (Fall 1985): 113–29. The quotation appears on p. 124.

20 Eugene Declercq and Richard Lacroix, "The Immigrant Midwives of Lawrence: The Conflict Between Law and Culture in Early Twentieth-Century Massachusetts," *Bulletin of the History of Medicine* 59 (Summer 1985): 232–46. Mary Elizabeth Fiorenza investigated the midwifery laws in Illinois and Wisconsin during this same period and concluded that "the immediate effects of Illinois' and Wisconsin's midwifery laws might not have been dramatic, in relation to other factors. In the long run, however, such laws have played a critical role by perpetuating the authority of the medical view of childbirth." Mary Elizabeth Fiorenza, "Midwifery and the Law in Illinois and Wisconsin, 1877 to 1917" (M.A. thesis, University of Wisconsin-Madison, 1985), p. 112.

dence of this type of cooperation is detailed in Judy Barrett Litoff's survey of American midwifery since 1860.[21] By contrast, Nancy Schrom Dye's analysis of the medical case histories of the New York Midwifery Dispensary for the period between 1890 and 1920 revealed that dispensary doctors did not usually collaborate with the immigrant midwives from New York City's Lower East Side because "to cooperate with [them] . . . was professionally untenable."[22]

Other scholars have focused their attention on the experiences of the predominately black "granny" midwives of the South. In fact, studies of black midwifery were among the first to demonstrate the importance of examining closely the culture in which midwives practiced. Some of the most important research on this topic has come from anthropologists and sociologists. Anthropologist Molly C. Dougherty conducted interviews with black "granny" midwives from north Florida during the early 1970s. As a result, she concluded that these women were caught up in a system where their supernatural and technical abilities were highly respected within their own communities whereas the wider organization of health practitioners accorded them positions at the lowest level of the medical hierarchy. Dougherty maintained that, despite the tensions and conflicts generated by this system, southern "granny" midwives had "successfully incorporate[d] elements from the prestigious medical system while retaining the integrity of traditional [black American] rituals."[23]

---

21 Charlotte G. Borst, "The Training and Practice of Midwives: A Wisconsin Study," *Bulletin of the History of Medicine*, 62 (1988): 606–27. Litoff, *American Midwives*, pp. 103–5. Litoff determined that physicians and immigrant midwives from New Jersey and Connecticut often cooperated with each other. She also noted that during the 1920s, physicians in Georgia took the initiative in establishing a training and regulatory program for Georgia's mostly black midwives, and that many Georgia doctors also gave assistance and instruction to midwives.

22 Nancy Schrom Dye, "Modern Obstetrics and Working-Class Women: The New York Midwifery Dispensary, 1890–1920," *Journal of Social History* 20 (Spring 1987): 549–64. The quotation appears on page 554. For information about a French Canadian midwife who practiced in Maine from 1885 to 1935, see Roger Paradis, "Henriette, *la capuche*: The Portrait of a Frontier Midwife," *Canadian Folklore canadien* 3 (1981): 110–26.

23 Molly C. Dougherty, "Southern Lay Midwives as Ritual Specialists," in *Women in Ritual and Symbolic Roles*, ed. Judith Hoch-Smith and Anita Spring (New York: Plenum Press, 1978), p. 157. Molly C. Dougherty, "Southern Midwifery and Organized Health Care: Systems in Conflict," *Medical Anthropology* 6 (1982): 113–26. For information on "granny" midwives from North Carolina, see Beatrice Mongeau, "The 'Granny' Midwives: A Study of A Folk Institution in the Process of Social Disintegration" (Ph.D. dissertation, University of North Carolina, 1973) and Cathy Melvin Efird, "A Geography of Lay Midwifery in Appalachian North Carolina, 1925–1950" (Ph.D. dissertation, University of North Carolina, 1985).

Linda Holmes's investigation of the customs and practices of Alabama's "granny" midwives, also based on oral interviews, substantiated many of the findings of Dougherty. In addition, Holmes discussed the ways in which Alabama's black "granny" midwives "acted as significant tradition bearers in maintaining various customs and rituals" of African origin.[24]

As both Molly Dougherty and Linda Holmes have demonstrated, oral histories are an important source of information about the customs and rituals of black "granny" midwives. However, opportunities to interview these women are rapidly disappearing as many "granny" midwives are elderly and most states no longer issue lay midwifery licenses.[25]

Another valuable source of information on the customs and practices of "granny" midwives are the records of southern state boards of health. Molly Ladd-Taylor uncovered much useful information about the responses of southern "granny" midwives to midwifery training programs established under the Sheppard-Towner Maternity and Infancy Protection Act of the 1920s by analyzing the progress reports which the state boards of health sent to the federal Children's Bureau. Although these reports were written by white physicians and nurses who shared many of the racist assumptions of the era, Ladd-Taylor found that the picture of the midwives which emerged was that of assertive women who both welcomed the help and challenged the authority of Sheppard-Towner workers.[26]

---

[24] Linda Janet Holmes, "African American Midwives in the South," in *The American Way of Birth*, ed. Pamela Eakins (Philadelphia: Temple University Press, 1986), pp. 273–91. The quotation appears on p. 281. Linda Holmes, "Alabama Granny Midwife," *The Journal of the Medical Society of New Jersey* 81 (May 1984): 389–91.

[25] Another useful study of "granny" midwifery, based largely on oral interviews, is Debra Anne Susie, *In the Way of Our Grandmothers: A Cultural View of Twentieth-Century Midwifery in Florida* (Athens: University of Georgia Press, 1988). Additional information on the practices of "granny" midwives may be found in "Midwives and Granny Women," in *Foxfire 2*, ed. Eliot Wigginton (New York: Anchor Books, 1973); Chris Walters-Bugee, "And None of Them Left-Handed: The Midwife from Plains, Georgia," *Southern Exposure* 5 (Spring 1977): 4–12; Carole Merritt, *Homecoming: African American Family History in Georgia* (Atlanta: African American Family History Association, 1982); Beverly J. Robinson, *Aunt Phyllis* (Los Angeles: Women's Graphic Center, 1982); Lucie Bridgeforth, "Helping Them into the World," Memphis *Commercial Appeal*, March 24, 1985, pp. 16–19; and Endesha Ida Mae Holland, "Granny Midwives: Portrait of a Timeless Profession," *Ms.*, June 1987, pp. 48–51, 73–74. All of these accounts are based, in large part, on oral interviews and personal reminiscences.

[26] Molly Ladd-Taylor, "'Grannies' and 'Spinsters': Midwife Education Under the Sheppard-Towner Act," *Journal of Social History*, 22 (1988): 255–75.

While midwives exercised a virtual monopoly over childbirth during the colonial period and even as late as 1910 attended approximately one-half of all births, only a minuscule 0.05% of births were attended by midwives during the early 1970s. Around the middle of that decade, however, there was a small but significant shift away from physician-managed hospital births. Women who rejected the medical management of childbirth made it clear that the conventional approach, which routinely involved procedures such as fetal monitoring, the chemical stimulation of labor, episiotomies, and the separation of the mother from the newborn infant, was no longer acceptable.[27] In an effort to reassert control over childbirth, increasing numbers of women turned to midwives, and within a decade the number of midwife-attended births had more than quadrupled. This "renaissance" of midwifery prompted scholars to examine issues of special interest to the midwife's recent past.

Nancy Schrom Dye published an important article on Mary Breckinridge and the introduction of nurse-midwifery into the United States in the 1920s and 1930s.[28] Regi L. Teasley examined the issue of the similarities and differences in the ideologies of modern-day nurse-midwives and independent "lay" midwives.[29] A thoughtful study of the current debate over midwifery licensure may be found in Raymond G.

---

[27] Numerous works have appeared which critique the medical management of childbirth as practiced in the United States today. For examples of this type of writing, see Doris Haire, "The Cultural Warping of Childbirth" (Seattle: International Childbirth Education Association, 1972); Nancy Stoller Shaw, Forced Labor: Maternity Care in the United States (New York: Pergamon Press, 1974); and Suzanne Arms, Immaculate Deception: A New Look at Women and Childbirth in America (Boston: Houghton Mifflin, 1975).

[28] Nancy Schrom Dye, "Mary Breckinridge, the Frontier Nursing Service, and the Introduction of Nurse-Midwifery in the United States," Bulletin of the History of Medicine 57 (1983): 485–507. For additional information on this topic, see Josiah Macy, Jr. Foundation, The Training and Responsibilities of the Midwife (New York: Josiah Macy, Jr. Foundation, 1967); Report of a Macy Conference, The Midwife in the United States (New York: Josiah Macy, Jr. Foundation, 1968); Wanda C. Heistand, "Midwife to Nurse-Midwife: A History of the Development of Nurse-Midwifery Education in the Continental United States to 1965" (Ed.D. dissertation, Teachers College, Columbia University, 1976); Barbara Brennan and Joan Rattner Heilman, The Complete Book of Midwifery (New York: E. P. Dutton, 1977); and Carol Crowe-Carraco, "Mary Breckinridge and the Frontier Nursing Service," Register of the Kentucky Historical Society 76 (July 1978): 179–91. Two other earlier studies which are also useful are Shoemaker, History of Nurse-Midwifery (1947) and Breckinridge, Wide Neighborhoods (1952).

[29] Regi L. Teasley, "Nurse and Lay Midwifery in Vermont," in The American Way of Birth, ed. Pamela Eakins (Philadelphia: Temple University Press, 1986). Another useful study which compares nurse-midwifery and lay midwifery is Grace Granger Keyes, "Mexican-American and Anglo Midwifery in San Antonio, Texas" (Ph.D. dissertation, University of Wisconsin, 1985).

DeVries's *Regulating Birth: Midwives, Medicine, & the Law* (1985). Focusing on the states of Arizona, Texas, and California, DeVries analyzed both the beneficial and detrimental consequences of midwifery licensure. He argued that while legal recognition provided midwives with the immediate benefit of legitimacy, it also changed their profession to a standardized set of training programs and controls which had the potential to destroy the "uniqueness" of midwifery.[30] Judy Barrett Litoff produced a sourcebook on the early twentieth-century midwife debate which explored the relationship between the early debate and its contemporary counterpart.[31]

The replacement of midwives by physicians and what effect this has had on woman's losing control over childbirth continues to be debated. According to Catherine M. Scholten, the acceptance of physicians as birth attendants by urban, well-to-do women during the early decades of the nineteenth century resulted in women no longer dominating an area of medicine which, for centuries, had been their domain. Yet Judith Walzer Leavitt maintains that the transition of birth from the home to the hospital in the first third of the twentieth century, rather than the replacement of midwives by male physicians, was the most important factor which contributed to woman's loss of control over childbirth. On the other hand, Nancy Schrom Dye's analysis of the medical case histories of the New York Midwifery Dispensary at the turn of the twentieth century led her to conclude that "developments critical to the transformation from social to medical childbirth were well on their way to

---

[30] Raymond G. DeVries, *Regulating Birth: Midwives, Medicine, & the Law* (Philadelphia: Temple University Press, 1985). DeVries also analyzes this issue in "Midwifery and the Problem of Licensure," *Research in the Sociology of Health Care* 2 (1982): 77–120.

[31] Judy Barrett Litoff, *The American Midwife Debate: A Sourcebook on Its Modern Origins* (Westport, CT: Greenwood Press, 1986). The amount of primary source material on contemporary midwifery is voluminous. Two very useful first-person accounts are Ina May, *Spiritual Midwifery* (Summertown, TN: The Book Publishing Company, 1975) and Fran Leeper Bliss, *La Partera: Story of a Midwife* (Ann Arbor: University of Michigan Press, 1980). Two periodicals which are published specifically for midwives are the *Journal of Nurse-Midwifery* and *MANA News*. Worthy of special mention is the March/April 1989 issue of the *Journal of Nurse-Midwifery* which was devoted exclusively to a state-by-state examination of midwifery laws and regulations. Other journals which frequently publish articles related to contemporary midwifery include *Birth and the Family Journal*, *Mothering*, *Network News*, and *Women & Health*. The publications of the National Association of Parents and Professionals for Safe Alternatives in Childbirth also contain relevant information. See especially David Stewart and Lee Stewart, eds., *Safe Alternatives in Childbirth* (Chapel Hill, NC: NAPSAC, 1976) and Lee Stewart and David Stewart, eds., *21st Century Obstetrics Now* (Marble Hill, MO: NAPSAC, 1977).

completion before the hospital became the primary birthplace."[32] Clearly, the question of where and how women lost control over childbirth remains a multifaceted issue.

Recent efforts by scholars to learn more about the culture and cultural milieu of American midwives have proved of inestimable value and have considerably broadened our understanding of the midwife's often tenuous relationship to the medical profession. However, much additional information is still to be uncovered. Although only a few diaries, journals, and memoirs of midwives are known to exist, historians must continue to search archives, libraries, and the attics of private homes for writings of these types. Furthermore, historians have only just begun to make proper use of primary sources such as birth registration certificates, medical case histories, midwife licenses, and reports issued by state boards of health. Oral histories, especially of black "granny" midwives from the south, represent another largely untapped reservoir of information.

Over the past two decades, a small and insightful group of scholars has demonstrated that the once-neglected midwife has an important story to be told. Many valuable works have been published and several promising studies are currently under way. Just as important, a number of exciting research opportunities await those historians interested in exploring this new, and still growing, field of inquiry.

---

[32] Scholten, *Childbearing in American Society*, p. 48; Judith Walzer Leavitt, *Brought to Bed: Childbearing in America, 1750–1950* (New York: Oxford University Press, 1986), p. 4; Dye, "Modern Obstetrics and Working-Class Women," p. 560.

18

NURSES

Ellen D. Baer

"The Nurse question is the Woman question, pure and simple. We have to run the gauntlet of those historic rotten eggs."[1]

The irony that pervades the study of nursing and its history is that, as primarily women's work, it is ignored equally by traditional historians who focus more frequently on men's work and by feminist historians who choose more usually to celebrate women who have entered occupations previously considered men's province. As a consequence, nurses are the prototypically invisible women whose minds, hearts, and hands shaped a huge industry, yet whose story is essentially untold except by themselves—to preserve their memories, celebrate their triumphs, argue their point of view, or win support for their cause. As a result, nursing's historiography is inseparable from its social and cultural context. As nursing leaders extolled the virtues of their art, they summoned historical rhetoric in support of their work and they chronicled evidence simultaneously. To demonstrate this phenomenon as well as to document nursing's historiography, this chapter provides a brief overview of American "trained" nursing's post-Civil War reform origins; describes certain predominant themes in nursing's history; identifies the major American nursing historical scholarship that exists; and, concludes with a general suggestion regarding future study. Though "untrained" nursing existed forever as part of women's work, it has not been well studied. Usually, "untrained" nursing is mentioned or discussed in general histories of nursing, medicine, and hospitals, some of which are cited in this chapter.

CIVIL WAR ORIGINS

On December 21, 1862, in Falmouth, Virginia, across from Fredericksburgh, a man moved among the sick and wounded of the Army of

---

[1] Lavinia L. Dock, *A History of Nursing* (New York: G. P. Putnam's Sons, 1912). Vol. III, p. 33 attributes this quote to British Nurses' Association organizer and Florence Nightingale antagonist Ethel Fenwick (Mrs. Bedford) during the 1887 founding events.

the Potomac. He gave comfort as he could, candies for some, letter-writing for others, for as long as his supplies held out. What began as an odyssey to find his missing brother evolved into a chronicle of war and youth, suffering and sadness. His notes, scratched onto scraps of paper and tied together with string, documented the three-year journey of Walt Whitman through the Camp Hospitals of the Civil War. Spending his first day in a makeshift hospital, he described:

> a heap of amputated feet, legs, arms, hands, etc., a full load for a one-horse cart. Several dead bodies lie near, each cover'd with its brown woollen blanket. In the dooryard, towards the river, are fresh graves, mostly of officers, their names stuck on pieces of barrel staves or broken board, stuck in the dirt . . . The large mansion is quite crowded upstairs and down, everything impromptu, no system, all bad enough, but I have no doubt the best that can be done; all the wounds pretty bad, some frightful, the men in their old clothes, unclean and bloody . . .[2]

Any sick care that existed was given by ambulatory soldiers or by those wives, mothers, fathers, or brothers who succeeded in locating their injured kin.

The American society that emerged from the ashes of that war found systematic, public ways to accomplish many of its formerly private tasks. As the Industrial Revolution altered forever the home-based nature of human services, America's "middling" classes sought new ways to care for their dependent members by people other than kin, in places other than home. This "transfer of care of the sick and injured could not be accomplished to the satisfaction of the middle class unless the caretakers in the institution were guaranteed to be as reliable, respectable and clean (in all senses) as the mothers or sisters . . . formerly charged with the responsibility."[3] Antebellum sick-care institutions existed to serve the particular needs of specific groups—religious denominations, pioneer communities, the "deserving" poor, and disconnected persons. Each created a custodial role called "nurse" consistent with its mission. Religious sisters managed Roman Catholic, Lutheran, and Episcopal hospitals. Community women served for wages in hospitals for the

---

[2] Walt Whitman, *Memoranda During the War*, and *Death of Abraham Lincoln* (Camden, NJ, 1875–1876); reproduced in facsimile of the author's publication, Bloomington: Indiana University Press, 1962), p. 6.

[3] Joan Lynaugh, "Riding the Yo-Yo: The Worth and Work of Nursing in the 20th Century," *Transactions and Studies of the College of Physicians of Philadelphia*, series 5, 11:2 (1989): 201–17.

working poor. In big city almshouses, the progression from inmate to keeper to assistant nurse to nurse comprised a sort of job ladder available to the predominantly male population.[4] Though varied in motive and gender, what all these "nurses" shared (besides class) was ignorance as to any method or reasoned way to do their tasks. As one Bellevue lady visitor later described it:

> When the visitor entered the ward . . . a little boy of five years old had just been operated upon for stones in the bladder, an old woman was sitting by him trying good naturedly to soothe his cries but doing nothing to staunch the blood which was flowing from the wound.[5]

Following the lead of Florence Nightingale, who earlier solved England's same dilemma on the heels of its contemporary war, philanthropic, reform-minded American women introduced nurse-training schools to hospitals in 1873. The training schools provided simultaneous answers to several social agendas:

1. acceptable and meaningful work for single women seeking freedom and self-sufficiency in newly industrialized America;

2. "protection" of the women during their work in supervised enclaves called "schools";

3. respectable "middling" class caretakers for the sick;

4. certain ones from the above group who could be designated managers for the institutions in which the sick resided; and

5. an inexpensive labor force to staff the hospitals rapidly proliferating in number by the twentieth century's turn.

Apprenticed at their entry, the pupil-nurses acted as nurses immediately, gaining skills and information through occasional nighttime doctors' lectures and sporadic bedside instruction from the nursing superintendent on her rounds. After completing the two- (later three-) year "course," the graduate nurse entered private duty nursing in the

---

4   Charles E. Rosenberg, "From Almshouse to Hospital: The Shaping of Philadelphia General Hospital," Milbank Memorial Fund Quarterly/Health and Society, vol. 60, no. 1 (1982). See also, Wm. H. Williams, America's First Hospital: The Pennsylvania Hospital, 1751–1841 (Wayne, PA: Haverford House, 1976).
5   Elizabeth Hobson, Recollections of a Happy Life (New York: G. P. Putnam's Sons, 1916), pp. 65–66 report dated Nov. 22, 1872. Reported in Ellen D. Baer, "Nursing's Divided House—An Historical View," Nursing Research 34:1, p. 33.

homes of those able to pay or, later, did public health nursing.[6] Only a few graduate nurses remained in hospital employ, to supervise the pupil-nurses. From the outset, the women achieved great success in improving care, as evidenced by the increase in numbers of training schools in hospitals from 3 in 1873 to approximately 1,600 by World War I.[7] But they met with almost no success gaining recognition for their accomplishments. Long accustomed to women's bargain to exchange their labor for room and board and whatever perks accompanied the job of managing domestic households, American society did not readily accept single women, in quasi-domestic work like nursing, demanding anything more.

Historiography in nursing grew from this attitude. Nurses needed to state their case; to explain who they were, what they did, and why the work required specialized education, legislated registration, and professional recognition. Unwilling to allow society to give medicine full credit for health-care successes which often more accurately reflected good nursing, nursing's leaders, teachers, and organizers became its earliest informal historians.

HISTORY AS "LINCHPIN" FOR NURSING'S LEGITIMACY

Probably not coincidentally, American nursing's first "official" historians, Lavinia L. Dock and M. Adelaide Nutting, spent their early nursing years at Johns Hopkins University where "the study of history was the linchpin that could hold together both the science and the art of medicine and nursing."[8] Using these associations to good advantage, Hopkins's nursing superintendent Isabel Hampton (later Mrs. Hunter Robb) accepted the 1893 invitation of her colleagues, Hopkins physicians Henry Hurd and John Shaw Billings, to organize a nursing subsec-

---

[6] Susan Reverby, *Ordered to Care: The Dilemma of American Nursing, 1850–1945* (New York: Cambridge University Press, 1987), pp. 60–75, 95–117. See also Nancy Tomes, "'Little World of Our Own': The Pennsylvania Hospital Training School for Nurses 1895–1907," *Journal of the History of Medicine and Allied Sciences* 33 (1978): 507–30. See also Karen Buhler-Wilkerson, "Left Carrying the Bag: Experiments in Visiting Nursing, 1877–1909," *Nursing Research* 36: 42–47; and Karen Buhler-Wilkerson, "False Dawn, The Rise and Decline of Public Health Nursing, 1900–1930." In *Nursing History: New Perspective, New Possibilities*, ed. Ellen Lagemann (New York: Teachers College Press, 1983), pp. 89–106.

[7] Lavinia L. Dock and Isabel M. Stewart, *A Short History of Nursing* (New York: G. P. Putnam's Sons, 1920, 1925) 2nd ed, pp. 155–60 traces names and numbers of earliest training schools.

[8] Susan Reverby and David Rosner, ed., *Health Care in America: Essays in Social History* (Philadelphia: Temple University Press, 1979), p. 5.

tion for the Chicago World's Fair Congress of Charities, Correction and Philanthropy. The papers presented at the Fair contained nurses' first formal public statements about their art. These essays, heavily laced with social history, identified educational, economic, and political themes that persist in nursing in present times.

Isabel Hampton's "Educational Standards for Nurses" chided her hospital and medical colleagues for sending pupil-nurses to private homes to earn fees that the hospitals kept. Hampton politely called it making "philanthropists" of the pupil-nurses, though others have since criticized it as exploiting pupil-nurses while simultaneously providing unfair competition for graduate private duty nurses. Lavinia Dock (then assistant superintendent at Hopkins) speaking about "The Relation of Training Schools to Hospitals" decried "the power of the hospital to terminate its agreement, or to make conditions such that it is impossible for the school to continue its work." New York Hospital nurse-training school directress Irene Sutliffe (presenting a "History of American Training Schools") described the unique Waltham School that trained nurses in the homes of the sick, which gave her the idea for the settlement house where Lillian Wald trained.[9] Others spoke about various developing specialties such as "Nursing of the Insane," "District Nursing," "Midwifery as a Profession for Women"; or, gave the international picture through "The History of Workhouse Reform" in England, "Nursing in Scotland," France, Switzerland, Germany, ". . . Catholic Orders," and "Missionary Training Schools and Nursing." Even Florence Nightingale was represented by her final public paper, "Sick Nursing and Health Nursing,"[10] read by Hampton. The discussions that

---

[9] Isabel Hampton, "Educational Standards for Nurses" in *Nursing of the Sick, 1893*, Isabel A. Hampton et al. Papers and Discussions from the International Congress of Charities, Correction and Philanthropy, Chicago, 1893 (New York: McGraw Hill Book Co., 1949), p. 6. Lavinia Dock, "The Relation of Training Schools to Hospitals" in *Nursing of the Sick, 1893*, p. 14. Irene Sutliffe, "History of American Training Schools" in *Nursing of the Sick, 1893*, p. 90. Clearly impressed with this Waltham method, Miss Sutliffe initiated New York Hospital's Hudson Street Division where pupil-nurses like Lillian Wald gained the experience she later utilized in founding the Henry Street Settlement House.

[10] These papers were collected originally in: *Hospitals, Dispensaries and Nursing*, Papers and Discussions in the International Congress of Charities, Correction and Philanthropy, Section III, Chicago, June 12th to 17th, 1893, under the auspices of the World's Congress Auxiliary of the Worlds' Columbian Exposition, John S. Billings, M.D. and Henry M. Hurd, M.D., eds. (Baltimore: The Johns Hopkins Press, 1894). Reprinted in the 32-volume facsimile series *The History of American Nursing*, ed. Susan Reverby (New York: Garland, 1984). The nursing papers were later published separately under the sponsorship of the National League for Nursing Education as Hampton et al., *Nursing of the Sick, 1893*.

followed each paper revealed fledgling plans for a national association of
alumnae (later the American Nurses' Association) and superintendents'
society (later the National League for Nursing).

Subsequent nursing activities, textbooks, and journals reported similar "history" as introduction or benediction for the particular event or
manuscript. Like others seeking to legitimate their cause, nurses mixed
celebratory history and chronology into the presentation of their work
to the world. Unlike others, nursing's primary historical evidence became virtually indistinguishable from its secondary literature, with actors in events later providing the only written record and interpretation
of activities, as few non-nurse third parties took an interest in nursing
events until recently (1970s–1980s). As a result, nursing history came to
occupy a catch-22. Being of little previous interest to "real" historians,
nurses (mostly the leaders) recorded their own history. This then left
nursing open to be later criticized by historians such as Janet James for
using history "to enhance status and raise morale"[11] and Barbara Melosh
for having recorded mainly the perspective of the leaders.[12]

Without question, the leaders' political purposes shaped the message of their "histories." By presenting nursing in an inspirational and
heroic light, they hoped to attract women of a "better" type and discour-
age the "commercial woman" primarily seeking wages.[13] By strengthening the educational programs, they aspired to achieve for nursing the
reputation and power accruing to the middle class through the professions developing at the century's turn.[14] And, by attaching nursing
firmly to humanitarian, reform, and moral guardian ideals, nursing
leaders sought to co-opt womanly power and fend off the attacks of
physicians and others, "the steady general tendency . . . for men to take
control out of women's hands."[15] But, while these goals reinforced the
opportunity presented by nursing to women wishing to achieve, feel
accomplished, and remain womanly, they were at odds with some negative realities of the work: "A nurse's toil is great, her duties often
disgusting, her pecuniary remuneration small in comparison with her

---

[11] Janet Wilson James, "Writing and Rewriting Nursing History," *Bulletin of the History of
      Medicine* 58 (1984), p. 571.
[12] Barbara Melosh, *"The Physician's Hand": Work Culture and Conflict in American Nursing*
      (Philadelphia: Temple University Press, 1982).
[13] Isabel A. Hampton et al., *Nursing of the Sick, 1893*, pp. 2, 9–12. Joan Jacobs Brumberg
      and Nancy Tomes, "Women in the Professions: A Research Agenda for American
      Historians," *Reviews in American History* 10:2 (1982): 275–92.
[14] Brumberg and Tomes, "Women in the Professions," pp. 275–92.
[15] Dock, *A History of Nursing*, vol. III, p. 117.

requirements and her labors; so that there is nothing to invite the cooperation of the better class of women, save the highest motives which can influence the true Christian."[16]

The early strategies became albatrosses later. Nursing's early leaders persuaded a nineteenth-century audience of the rightness of their cause through the use of women's reformist and inspirational rhetoric, but these messages were not successful after World War I. By then, America's increasing love affair with science, technology, university education, and masculine enterprise ensured that nursing, which represented none of these, remained in limbo, struggling for professional recognition.[17] Leaders from nursing's earliest to its most recent generations, such as Lavinia Dock and Claire Fagin respectively, asserted their belief that the most fundamental cause of nursing's limbo was and is its gender-specific association.[18] The work itself is infused with femaleness, regardless of the gender of the nurse. As historian Nancy Tomes pointed out: "Women's professions have remained semi-professions because the prevailing views regarding woman's proper sphere could not accord her an autonomy and an expertise equal to a man's."[19] Nursing's historiography reflects these convoluted and complex themes of gender, class, race, and the manual nature of nursing work.

HISTORY BOOKS "To fire her zeal and to strengthen her purpose"[20]

The first and best history of nursing appeared in four volumes, two published in 1907 and two in 1912 by Putnam's. Called A History of

---

[16] Dr. H. R. Storer, *On Nurses and Nursing with Especial Reference to the Management of Sick Women* (Boston: Lee and Shepard, 1868), p. 11.

[17] Amitai Etzioni, *The Semi-Professions and Their Organization* (New York: The Free Press, 1969).

[18] Dock, *A History of Nursing*, vol. I, described cycles of "the position of women, socially and legally" (p. 96) throughout world history as relational with the role of nursing; "the ever-vigilant reluctance of men to admit women to positions of authority" (p. 112); the "dark period of nursing . . . the logical result . . . coincident with a subjection of women in general" (p. 500). Claire M. Fagin, "Professional Nursing . . . the Problems of Women in Microcosm," *Journal of the New York State Nurses' Association* 2:1 (1971): 7–13.

[19] Nancy Tomes, "Nursing Historiography Review Essay," unpublished manuscript (Philadelphia: University of Pennsylvania), p. 6.

[20] Dock and Stewart, *A Short History of Nursing*. Page v, preface to the first edition identifies the book as "prepared especially for the use of student nurses" in hope that "this story of her very ancient and honorable vocation will serve to fire her zeal and to strengthen her purpose . . ."

Nursing, the main author was Lavinia L. Dock, though M. Adelaide Nutting is listed as primary author in volumes I and II and credited as the creator of the project.[21] Still unrivaled in depth and breadth, these volumes traced sick care from earliest times to the events in which the two authors played primary roles. The first edition of volumes I and II carried the descriptive subhead: "The Evolution of the Methods of Care for the Sick from Earliest Times to the Foundation of the First English and American Training Schools for Nurses" and provided to the nursing student (for whom they were written) "both the inspiration which arises from cherished tradition, and the perspective which shows the relation of one progressive movement to others."[22]

Declaring from the outset their intention to demonstrate nursing as progress, Nutting and Dock early made clear that their definition of progress was twofold: Nursing as sick care and as women's work. In the preface to the first edition, the authors linked the nurses' destiny with "the general conditions of education and of liberty that obtain—as they rise, she rises, and as they sink, she falls."[23] From chapter 1, volume I, because nursing is documented from the perspective that it is "the oldest of the occupations of women and the youngest branch of medical science,"[24] the books provide a unique perspective to historians interested in all branches of women's history, from woman as worker to woman as physician, from biblical times to the early twentieth century. In addition, the descriptive, old-fashioned prose sets the historical mood quite successfully.

Volumes III and IV, authored only by Dock, are described in their first edition subhead as: "The Story of Modern Nursing. Presenting an Account of the Development in Various Countries of the Science of Trained Nursing with Special Reference to the Work of the Past Thirty Years." Hardly unbiased in any of the volumes, the material dealing with the author's contemporary activities is frankly political. Defending her choice to leave certain problems "untreated" in Volume III, "for want of space to do them justice," Dock preferred to describe the "advance in self-governing organisation" over the problems of "private nursing . . .

---

[21] M. A. Nutting and Lavinia L. Dock, *A History of Nursing* (New York: G. P. Putnam's Sons, 1907, 1912). In her 1932 "self-portrait" published in 1977 by *Nursing Outlook* 25:1, p. 26, Miss Dock stated that though Miss Nutting wrote only two of the chapters, the idea for the *History* was Nutting's.

[22] Nutting and Dock, *A History of Nursing,* vol. I, page v.

[23] Ibid.

[24] Ibid., p. 3.

the evils of commercial agencies . . . [and] the vast influx of young girls, of faulty rearing and imperfect education, into nursing, with the consequent dilution of standards . . ." Believing these latter topics to be more correctly debated in the professional press, Dock elected to document new events "resulting from the incessant efforts of women who have had no time to write down the history they have made and are busy making."[25] She thereby demonstrated the phenomenon (described in this chapter's introductory remarks) whereby nursing's history and historiography became inexorably intermingled.

As a feminist, a leading participant in the Henry Street Settlement House after leaving Hopkins, and the secretary of the International Council of Nurses (founded in 1899), Dock focused on nursing around the world and took the community view of nursing's practice in volumes III and IV. Her feminist convictions permeated all her writing, which illustrated her vivid belief that nursing represented women's first emancipated step after a century and a half of subjugation. Dock viewed nurses as "pioneer[s] in offering economic independence to women of education and good family whose only other alternative was 'governessing', or needlework."[26]

Only a few years after publication of volumes III and IV of the *History*, Dock joined with Isabel Stewart, assistant professor in Columbia University's Teachers College Department of Nursing and Health, to author the single volume *A Short History of Nursing* (1920). Mainly a condensation of the earlier volumes, the *Short History* was conceived of as a textbook for nursing students and is particularly useful as a guide to where and when events happened, and who was involved. There is less interpretation offered and many of the politically interesting comments of the longer *History* are omitted. Appendix I provides a helpful, brief timeline that integrates general history with social progress, medicine, nursing, and hospital events of note.

In competition for health care's publishing dollar, W. B. Saunders' answer to Putnam's Nutting and Dock was Minnie Goodnow's nine-edition *History of Nursing* (1916–1953) which became Josephine Dolan's in its tenth edition. Renamed *Nursing in Society* in its thirteenth edition (1973), the Christian basis for nursing practice that formed Goodnow's introductory 50 pages grew to 150 as Dolan sought to "superimpose . . . [nursing's history] on the history of mankind." Now in its fifteenth

25 Dock, *A History of Nursing*, vol. III, pp. vi–vii.
26 Dock and Stewart, *A Short History of Nursing*, pp. 9–10.

edition (1983), it is edited by M. Louise Fitzpatrick (formerly of Teachers College, currently dean of Villanova University's College of Nursing) and Eleanor Herrmann (formerly of Yale, now at the University of Connecticut at Storrs). The current edition is reinvigorated by its new editors who were trained as historians. Also published by Saunders, Richard Shyrock's A History of Nursing (1959)[27] represented the first social history of nursing that integrated nursing, medical, and nineteenth-century social history. This excellent work introduced historians and nurses. Though never as popular in schools of nursing as the nurse-historian textbooks, Shyrock's book set nursing in its appropriately larger context. It may provide a more familiar guide to women's historians needing orientation to nursing history.

Returning to the style reminiscent of Nutting and Dock, Mary M. Roberts (second editor of The American Journal of Nursing) compiled her American Nursing: History and Interpretation in 1954.[28] Begun as a celebratory venture to mark the professional journal's golden anniversary (1950), Roberts recorded nursing adventures in which she was a primary participant, observer, and interpreter. Utilizing her journal sources and editing skill, Roberts produced a lively narrative, rich in detail, that emphasized nursing's organizational history. Picking up where Nutting and Dock ended, she adopted their progressive theme and identified steps "forward" that included organization-building, book and journal production, educational standard-setting, fact-finding studies, public policy statements, two world wars, the Depression and the beginning "Atomic Age."

Identified by her Short History initiation as the legatee of Nutting and Dock, Isabel Stewart collaborated with Anne L. Austin (former professor of nursing at Western Reserve and author of the useful 1957 compilation of primary materials History of Nursing Source Book[29]) to update the Short History for its fifth edition in 1962. Confusingly renamed A History of Nursing,[30] the textbook's preface carried curricular

[27] M. L. Fitzpatrick and E. Herman, eds., Nursing in Society, 15th ed. (Philadelphia: W. B. Saunders, 1983). Richard Shyrock, A History of Nursing (Philadelphia: W. B. Saunders Co., 1959). See also Victor Robinson, M.D., White Caps: The Story of Nursing (Philadelphia: J. B. Lippincott, 1946) for an earlier non-nurse history of nursing. Dr. Robinson was professor of the history of medicine at Temple University in Philadelphia.

[28] Mary M. Roberts, American Nursing: History and Interpretation (New York: The Macmillan Co., 1954). Lavinia Dock is acknowledged as a manuscript reader.

[29] Anne L. Austin, History of Nursing Source Book (New York: G. P. Putnam's Sons, 1957).

[30] Isabel M. Stewart and Anne L. Austin, A History of Nursing, 5th ed. (New York: G. P. Putnam's Sons, 1962).

directives that reflected a major post-World War II nursing story. As nurse-educators and administrators increasingly sought advanced degrees, and schools of education offered them greater welcome than did liberal arts colleges, a teacher-ish tone crept into nursing's scholarly efforts.[31] Called a "normal school mentality" by Anselm Strauss,[32] self-conscious and pointed educational objectives diluted the intellectual effectiveness of this and subsquent histories of nursing. In this teacher mode, nursing authors used history to identify political trends and professional issues with which nursing students must learn to grapple prior to their entry into nursing practice. As with other facets of nursing education in this era, applicability became the all-important aspect of history. Lacking in critical analysis or interpretation, the once-florid drama presented by Nutting and Dock became pallid and dry.

The most recent of the textbook-type nursing histories were produced by two husband-wife teams in which the wives are nurses and the husbands are historians (Vern Bullough has now become a nurse as well). Bonnie and Vern Bullough (*The Emergence of Modern Nursing*, 1964)[33] created an able narrative that traced the familiar course of western altruisim. It provides informative reading for nursing students, but does not attempt to direct scholars to nursing's primary materials or competing interpretations of events. In the 1969 edition, the Bulloughs focused further on problems and professional issues in nursing. The best feature of both editions, the bibliography, became the primary focus of their publication *Nursing: A Historical Bibliography* (1981).[34] In her thoughtful 1984 article reviewing nursing-history research, Janet James identified important work missing from the 5,000-entry reference book.[35] The interested investigator, by combining James's notations with

---

[31] Ellen D. Baer, "'A Cooperative Venture' in Pursuit of Professional Status: A Research Journal for Nursing," *Nursing Research* 36:1 (1987): 18–25.

[32] Anselm Strauss, "The Structure and Ideology of American Nursing" in *The Nursing Profession: Five Sociological Essays*, ed. Fred Davis (New York: John Wiley, 1966), p. 74.

[33] Bonnie Bullough and Vern Bullough, *The Emergence of Modern Nursing* (New York: The Macmillan Co., 1964). In the 2nd edition, 1969, Vern Bullough is primary author.

[34] Bonnie Bullough, Vern Bullough, and Barrett Elcano, *Nursing: A Historical Bibliography* (New York: Garland, 1981). Vern Bullough has added nursing credentials to his academic history preparation. See also, Vern L. Bullough, Olga Church, and Alice P. Stein. *American Nursing: A Biographical Dictionary* (New York: Garland, 1988). See also, *Dictionary of American Nursing Biography*, ed. Martin Kaufman (New York: Greenwood Press, 1988).

[35] Janet James, "Writing and Rewriting Nursing History: A Review Essay," *Bulletin of the History of Medicine*, p. 583.

the Bulloughs', can be assured of covering most sources relevant to
nursing history through those time periods.

Philip and Beatrice Kalisch took an encyclopedic approach in *The
Advance of American Nursing* (1978, 1986).[36] Dates, numbers, and facts
appear against an impressive array of photographs, film clips, and paint-
ings unearthed by the Kalisches during their federally funded study of
nursing's image. A useful resource for factual data, the Kalisches' book
does not pretend to be a scholar's guide. The 1986 revised Chapter 20,
"Toward a New Era in Nursing," contains the best compilation of recent
nursing history currently available.

Smaller, local histories of specialty organizations, schools, personal
experiences, state developments, black nurses, and the like appeared
intermittently throughout the century. Elizabeth Carnegie's *The Path We
Tread* (1986), a history of black nursing; *My Cap and My Cape*, the
memoir of a Philadelphia woman's nursing life before marriage; Roberta
West's 1930 *History of Nursing in Pennsylvania*; and Mabel Staupers's
account of black nurses' organizational history in *No Time for Prejudice*
(1961) are good examples.[37] In addition, nursing's first sixty years of
literature is fully referenced in Virginia Henderson's annotated *Nursing
Studies Index*[38] and in the Cumulative Nursing Index and International
Nursing Index thereafter.

TRAINED TO BE *"An Intelligent Saint"*[39]

The introduction of nurses to analytical methods associated with
more critical historical research occurred at Teachers College of Columbia University. Higher education for nurses began in 1899 when
Teachers College agreed to Isabel Hampton Robb's plan to provide a

---

[36] Philip A. Kalisch and Beatrice J. Kalisch, *The Advance of American Nursing* (Boston: Little, Brown, 1978, 1986).
[37] M. Elizabeth Carnegie. *The Path We Tread: Blacks in Nursing 1854–1984* (Philadelphia: Lippincott, 1986); Mary Williams Brinton, *My Cap and My Cape* (Philadelphia: Dorrance & Co., 1950); Roberta West, *History of Nursing in Pennsylvania* (Pennsylvania State Nurses' Association, ND probably 1931); and Mabel K. Staupers, *No Time for Prejudice* (New York: The Macmillan Co., 1961).
[38] Virginia Henderson and Leo Simmons, *Nursing Studies Index* consists of four volumes divided chronologically and published in reverse order: Vol. I, 1900–1929, published in 1972; Vol. II, 1930–1949, published in 1970; Vol. III, 1950–1956, published in 1966; Vol. IV, 1957–1959, published in 1963 (Philadelphia: J. B. Lippincott Co.). Henderson was a Teachers College faculty member when she started the Index with Leo Simmons. She was on the faculty of Yale by its completion. Reprinted in the Garland Series, see note 10.
[39] Isabel Hampton, "Educational Standards for Nurses," *Nursing the Sick 1893*, p. 3.

'Hospital Economics' course for nursing teachers and administrators. The Teachers College program became important when M. Adelaide Nutting (Hampton's successor as Superintendent at Johns Hopkins) took charge of the course in 1907. As the major nursing spokesperson for half a century, Nutting, an inveterate collector, became the profession's archivist and, as previously noted, first historian. Isabel M. Stewart first assisted and then succeeded Nutting at Teachers College and carried forward all of her interests. As nurses sought broader-based advanced degrees in the 1960s, the stimulation of the women's movement, the presence of the Nutting Collection at Teachers College, and "a maze of late Victorian architecture"[40] inspired a trio of nursing doctoral students to do historical research in nursing.

Teresa Christy's account of the Teachers College program in *Cornerstone for Nursing Education* (1969) and her *American Journal of Nursing* "Portrait of a Leader" series made her the leading nurse-historian of her generation and Teachers College mentor to the generations that followed. JoAnn Ashley's angry *Hospitals, Paternalism and the Role of the Nurse* (1976) riveted a nursing world unused to the assertions of an "uppity" nurse, but earned criticism from historians for its selective use of data. The third nurse-historian, M. Louise Fitzpatrick, published her own history of *The National Organization for Public Health Nursing* (1975) and edited *Historical Studies in Nursing* (1978),[41] a compilation of nursing doctoral studies and methods of historical research developed by authors connected to the Teachers College program. Though still basically Whiggish in historiographic approach, these beginning efforts by nurses to use critical historical methods to analyze nursing's history moved nursing historiography into a new era.

Simultaneously, social historians, some of them nurses, discovered in nursing a good sample for studies of women's work, labor movements, health care, and domestic traditions. This growing body of work was presented at nursing history conferences organized around special

---

[40] Janet James, "Writing and Rewriting Nursing History," p. 573. The 84,000 items in the collection at Teachers College are available on microfiche as *The History of Nursing Microfiche Collection*, The Archives of the Department of Nursing Education, Teachers College, Columbia University (Ann Arbor, MI: UMI Research Collections, 1985).

[41] Christy and Ashley dissertations were published by Teachers College Press, New York, as were Fitzpatrick's edited *Historical Studies in Nursing*, and Ellen Condliffe Lagemann's *Nursing History: New Perspectives New Possibilities*. See also Fitzpatrick's *The National Organization for Public Health Nursing, 1912–1952: Development of a Practice Field* (New York: National League for Nursing, 1975).

nursing collections at Teachers College in New York and Mugar Library at Boston University. In 1981 major papers were presented at an Invitational Nursing History Conference at the Rockefeller Archive Center, and were later published as *Nursing History: New Perspectives, New Possibilities* (1983, ed. Ellen Condliffe Lagemann, also of Teachers College). Taught by bitter previous experiences with psychology, sociology, and other social sciences to be suspicious of exploitation by disciplines using nursing as a study sample to be criticized and discarded, nurses did not embrace the new interest of historians. In addition, those nurse-historians identified as leaders in nursing history felt compelled to protect their turf. Nurses' response to conference papers was harsh, and divisions developed between nurses studying history and historians studying nursing. Boston historians Janet James and Susan Reverby and Philadelphia historians Diana Long and Charles Rosenberg helped gradually to bridge the gap. As advisors to conferences, academic mentors to many participants' research, and leaders of regional seminars that included nurse-historians with historians of medicine, science, labor, technology, women's studies, and other relevant fields, they fostered excellent scholarship in a welcoming atmosphere and produced a cohort of nurses trained as historians as well as historians expert in nursing. Rosenberg's recognition that "Perhaps the most important single element in re-shaping the day to day texture of hospital life was the professionalization of nursing" in *The Care of Strangers* (1987)[42] signalled historians and assured nurses of his scholarly support for nursing's legitimate role in history. The founding of The American Association for the History of Nursing (AAHN) in the early 1980s created an institutional network and provided a yearly convention (since 1984) for nurse-historians (primarily) to share insights and present papers.

Several important books on nursing history have emerged to date from the Rockefeller papers, two of which are particularly important: Barbara Melosh's *The Physician's Hand: Work Culture and Conflict in American Nursing* (1982) and Susan Reverby's *Ordered to Care:*

---

[42] Charles E. Rosenberg, *The Care of Strangers* (New York: Basic Books, 1987), p. 8. For examples of nursing history produced by this cohort, see *Nursing Research*, 35th anniversary issue, 36: 1 (1987); and, Joan E. Lynaugh, "Narrow Passageways: Nurses and Physicians in Conflict and Concert Since 1875," in *The Physician as Captain of the Ship: A Critical Re-Appraisal*, ed. Nancy M. P. King et al. (Boston: D. Reidel Publishing Co., 1988).

The Dilemma of American Nursing, 1850–1945 (1987).[43] Reverby, who received the AAHN's first Lavinia L. Dock Award for historical nursing research and writing, argues that the true dilemma of nursing is "the order to care in a society that refuses to value caring."[44] It is hard to do a job that no one thinks is important yet everyone needs, because one is damned both ways. In attempting to solve that dilemma, nursing created secondary problems. It is these consequent dilemmas with which Melosh engages. She criticizes nursing leaders for being preoccupied with professional status, educational levels, legislative directives and similar agendas, rather than focusing on assisting the working nurses. But she discounts the underlying cause for their focus and, thereby, blames the victim. Reverby, on the other hand, acknowledges nursing's "dichotomy between the duty and desire to care for others and the right to control and define this activity."[45] More attuned to the work culture of nurses on the job, Melosh invests her interest in the "shared experience [of daily work], not the hope of professionalization, that shaped ordinary nurses' aspirations and ideology."[46] The difficulty with the work-culture approach is that it assumes that all nurses are the same and share in the same work culture, as is the case with physicians or lawyers who need only practice their profession. But nursing always comprised three practice foci: caring for patients, managing the institutions in which the patients resided, and training the pupil-nurses who gave the actual care. It has not been possible for nurses to do only one practice and ignore the others, for each depended on the other. In that sense, therefore, there were three work cultures, "that competed for status, students' time and their piece of the meager pie assigned to nursing by the institutions."[47] Using that perspective, Melosh's important book elaborates the culture of those nurses whose work was caring for patients.

Taken together, these two books create an excellent beginning to the newest phase of examining nursing history. The major variables that shaped nursing's development are gender- and class-related: lower status

---

[43] See notes 6 and 12.
[44] Susan M. Reverby, Ordered to Care: The Dilemma of American Nursing, 1850–1945 (New York: Cambridge University Press, 1957), p. 1.
[45] Ibid., p. 1 cites further literature on autonomy and altruism.
[46] Melosh, The Physician's Hand, p. 5.
[47] Ellen D. Baer, "Nursing's Divided Loyalties: An Historical Case Study," Nursing Research 38:3 (1989): 166–71.

work, restricted autonomy of practice, limited access to higher education, and lower pay that does not respond to the usual supply/demand
market forces. The effect of these interacting issues has been the attraction to nursing of lower socioeconomic recruits, who sometimes have
less ability, which is then used as a rationale for maintaining the restrictions that created the vicious cycle in the first place. Nursing offers
women's studies investigators the opportunity to explore every issue
that affects, or affected, women in America. In addition, nursing offers
feminist historians the opportunity to study women who have found the
satisfaction of achievement and success within the mainstream of wom-
en's work, connected to female traditions and possessed of a deep
women's culture.

CONCLUSION: ". . . those historic rotten eggs"

Within the context of gender-divided America, nursing provided a
place in medicine for women and women's work, needed but not honored. Segregated as nurses, women did their traditional tasks—caretaking, managing, coordinating disparate parts, attempting to meet everyone's needs no matter how much they conflicted with one another, and
never quite achieving their impossible goals. Now American society
moves further and further away from honoring women's roles. As our
most talented women strive to approximate more and more the life
patterns of men, the women's traditions inherent to nursing are in
danger of extinction or of being relegated to the interpretation and
practice of less gifted people.

Invented to ameliorate the harsher characteristics of an acquisitive
society, nursing represents three persistent women's dilemmas: nurses
are the prototypical women caretakers in a society that undervalues care;
nursing is an underfinanced personal service in a nation that honors
rational, entrepreneurial, and product-oriented capitalism; and, nurses
characterize the downside of America's gender-biased power structure.[48]
Feminists and women's studies researchers have avoided nurses and
nursing for these reasons. It has been too painful to look seriously at
nurses' experience because nurses represent women's inherently un-
valued place in American society. It has been easier to believe (hope?)

---

[48] The author's thinking about these issues has benefitted greatly from discussions with
Joan Lynaugh. See Joan E. Lynaugh and Claire M. Fagin, "Nursing Comes of Age,"
Image: The Journal of Nursing Scholarship 20:4 (1988): 184–90.

that it was the job or education or salary or whatever of nurses that made people uncomfortable about nursing.[49] To comprehend thoroughly how much nurses know, how important is their work, and how little they are credited, is to understand deeply the negative status of women in this society. Perhaps as we enter the last decade of the twentieth century, women will have the courage to look at these most pervasive ". . . rotten eggs."

---

[49] Claire M. Fagin and Donna Diers, "Nursing as Metaphor," *New England Journal of Medicine* 309 (1983): 116–17.

19

$\bullet \quad \bullet \quad \bullet \quad \underline{\hspace{3cm}} \quad \bullet \quad \bullet \quad \bullet$

PHYSICIANS

Regina Morantz-Sanchez

"The story of women in American medicine," observed the medical historian Richard Shryock in the *Journal of the American Medical Women's Association* in 1950, "involves chapters in the history of medicine, of women, and of American society; no one of which is intelligible save in relation to the others." Shryock's insightful comment was made in a brief but suggestive essay that raised a number of intriguing historical themes. Unfortunately, this early attempt to arouse the interest of professional historians in the subject of women physicians bore little fruit—at least not until the sweeping changes in focus that took place in historical writing in the early 1970s.[1]

This is not to say that there was no concern for chronicling women physicians' past achievements. But those who did so were usually women physicians themselves. Indeed, the first historical accounts of their struggles to enter the medical profession were penned by some of the earliest pioneers. While such studies provided much pertinent information for the researcher, they often lacked analytical sophistication. In many respects, they displayed both the advantages and disadvantages of "insider's history." Themes tended to center on individual women's achievements and collective struggles against discrimination.[2]

---

[1] Richard Shryock, "Women in American Medicine," *JAMWA* 5 (September 1950): 371–79. Similarly perceptive was an article on women physicians published fifteen years later by John B. Blake, another medical historian. His work anticipated many themes later fleshed out by other scholars. See Blake, "Women and Medicine in Ante-Bellum America," *Bulletin of the History of Medicine* 39 (March–April, 1965): 99–123.

[2] See for example, Rachel Bodley, *The College Story: Valedictory Address to the Twenty-Ninth Graduating Class of the Woman's Medical College of Pennsylvania, March 17, 1881* (Philadelphia: Grant, Faires & Rogers, Printers, 1881); Emily F. Pope, C. Augusta Pope, and

Probably the most penetrating of these early works was Mary Putnam Jacobi's essay "Woman in Medicine," which appeared in 1891, in
Annie Nathan Meyer's *Woman's Work in America*. Jacobi treated her
subject with intelligence, force, and a touch of ironical humor, the latter
aimed against those conservative colleagues who objected to .women
doctors. She argued that women's entrance into medicine was the result
of "two rival decorums" confronting each other at the end of the
eighteenth century. The first was the long-accepted control women
exerted over the practice of midwifery. The second, a newer protocol
catalyzed by advances in scientific medicine, dictated that safe deliveries
could best be accomplished by educated gynecologists, all of whom were
men. Forced to choose, many judged preserving female modesty in
childbirth more important than the breach of tradition involved in
letting "the ardent young girl into . . . medical school." Thus the "difficulties of educating a relatively few women in medicine were compelled
to -be accepted, in order to avert the far greater difficulties of medical
treatment for a very large number of women."[3]

But once in the profession, Jacobi observed, women physicians' struggle took on a life of its own, evolving, with a push from nineteenth-century
feminism, into an issue of equal opportunity. Jacobi believed that women
had as much right to be doctors as men; indeed, she thought them
particularly suited to the demands of clinical practice because of their skills
in translating scientific medical advances into new methods of treating the
sick. Although she admitted that their capacity to do science remained
unproved, she viewed the acceptance of women at Johns Hopkins Medical
School, an event that occurred just as her article was going to press, as
something that would open "an entire new horizon . . . before us."[4]

Emma L. Call, *The Practice of Medicine by Women in the United States* (Boston: Wright
and Potter, 1881); Clara Marshall, *The Woman's Medical College of Pennsylvania: An
Historical Outline* (Philadelphia: P. Blakiston & Son, 1897); Kate Campbell Hurd-Mead,
Medical Women of America (New York: Froben Press, 1933); Esther Pohl Lovejoy,
Women Doctors of the World (New York: Macmillan, 1957); Gulielma Fell Alsop, *The
History of the Woman's Medical College of Pennsylvania* (Philadelphia: J. B. Lippincott,
1950). The work of Frederick C. Waite, a professor of histology at Western Reserve
Medical School, also contributed much toward retrieving the little-known past of
nineteenth-century women physicians. Waite authored numerous articles on individual
women as well as the *History of the New England Female Medical College, 1848–1874*
(Boston: Boston University School of Medicine, 1950).
[3] Mary Putnam Jacobi, "Woman in Medicine," in Annie Nathan Meyer, ed., *Woman's
Work in America* (New York: Henry Holt, 1891), pp. 139–40. Blake made this point as
well. Blake, "Women and Medicine in Ante-Bellum America," p. 118.
[4] Jacobi, "Woman in Medicine," p. 205.

Unfortunately, the "new horizon" Jacobi anticipated did not materialize for at least another eighty years. Historical analysis of women physicians languished accordingly. In the early 1970s, however, a period of ferment in the historical profession generated new ways of asking old questions, stimulated the raising of new ones, and catalyzed the investigation of subject matter that had not previously been of interest to trained historians. Dubbed "social history," this fresh approach gave rise to several new fields of inquiry, two of which rekindled interest in the history of women physicians: women's history and the social history of medicine.

Some of the earliest work in women's history concentrated on the nineteenth century, where the emerging patterns of modern society were most visible. Scholars studied changes in the family and in sex roles, charted the evolution of the ideology of domesticity, and pondered the meaning of those changes for women. What role did women play in the process of modernization? Did they gain or lose power in the Victorian period? How did they view themselves and their roles in a society that still defined them as different and inferior to men? In what ways did they respond to efforts to constrict their access to the public sphere? One way to get at those questions was to look at women's occupations. Since medicine was second only to teaching as a profession for women in the nineteenth century, it was no accident that some historians eventually turned their attention to the study of women doctors.

If a renewed interest in gender as a category of analysis stimulated some of the early work on women doctors, then changes in the history of medicine accounted for the rest. In the late 1960s and early 1970s, critiques of contemporary medicine—some of them feminist—generated much interest in the history of health care.[5] In addition, younger scholars in the social history of medicine were turning away from the traditional celebrations of medical progress and heroism to concentrate on the social context of medical practice. Not always trained initially as medical historians, these researchers brought with them the perspectives

---

[5] See for example, Boston Women's Health Collective, *Our Bodies, Ourselves* (Boston: New England Free Press, 1971). Pauline Bart and Diane Scully, "A Funny Thing Happened on the Way to the Orifice: Women in Gynecology Textbooks," *American Journal of Sociology* 78 (January 1973): 1045–49; Barbara Ehrenreich and Deirdre English, *Witches, Midwives and Nurses* (New York: Feminist Press, 1971); Ellen Frankfort, *Vaginal Politics* (New York: Quadrangle Books, 1972); Naomi Weisstein, "Psychology Constructs the Female," and Phyllis Chesler, "Patient and Patriarch: Women in the Psychotherapeutic Relationship," in Vivian Gornick and Barbara K. Moran, eds., *Woman in Sexist Society* (New York: Basic Books, 1971).

of social history, cultural history, literary history, and the history of health policy. As a consequence, they were less interested in the internal history of medicine than in evaluating it as an artifact of culture. One of the most significant findings of the new work has been that technological advances have not inevitably improved patient care. Indeed some historians have even claimed that technology has often vitiated the doctor-patient relationship. In spite of these realities, the medical profession's power and prestige steadily improved at the end of the nineteenth and the beginning of the twentieth century. How and why did this occur? Many believed that science, though not yet technically valuable to physicians in spite of dramatic discoveries in the laboratory, wielded enormous cultural power—power that infused the organization of practice, the relationship of physician to patient, the development of new medical institutions, and the rising status of physicians. Interested in exploring the origins and social dimensions of that power, medical historians have lately sought to investigate the redefinitions of science generated by the bacteriological revolution. They have suggested that definitions of what has constituted science in medicine have changed over time. They have asked in what ways those changes can be linked to the domination of the medical profession by middle-class, white males.[6]

Historians of women and of medicine have thus shared an interest in questions about power and authority, though their differing perspectives have occasionally led to discordant conclusions. From the vantage point of feminist literary history, some feminist historians turned their attention to examining the power relationships between doctors and patients. Scholars like Ann Douglas, G. J. Barker Benfield, Barbara Ehrenreich, and Dierdre English put forth a mysogynist model of medical treatment, claiming that doctors' cultural prejudices biased both therapeutics and the doctor-patient relationship. Benfield, for example, depicted the rise of surgical gynecology as a function of male insecurity and hostility toward women. "Gynecologists' case histories," he wrote, "are suffused with male anxieties over, and attempts to deal with, women out of their place." Similarly, Ann Douglas characterized S. Weir Mitchell, the renowned neurologist who prescribed his "rest cure" to hundreds of "hysterical" Victorian middle-class women, as the spiritual brother of his generational predecessor, "the cauterizer, with his injections, leeches

---

[6] John Harley Warner, "Science in Medicine," *Osiris*, 2nd Ser. 1 (Fall, 1985): 37–58.

and hot irons," who spitefully nurtured a "veiled but aggressively hostile male sexuality and superiority."[7]

While medical historians countered by emphasizing the low prestige of doctors, the importance of considering the history of therapeutics, and the dependence of physicians on patient trust, other feminist scholars recognized that conspiracy models tending to reduce women to the role of victims were overly simplistic. Both groups concentrated on ferreting out the sources of scientific authority in medicine and demonstrating how biomedical theories were used to reinforce cultural assumptions about gender, class, and race. The work of Carroll Smith-Rosenberg and Charles Rosenberg, for example, examined Victorian perceptions of female life-cycle events like puberty and menopause and suggested that gynecological metaphors used by doctors to explicate such physiological crises represented and reinforced the extreme sex stereotyping of nineteenth-century society. In an article on female hysteria, Smith-Rosenberg pointed out that hysteria, characterized by male physicians as "the female malady," was actually a behavioral choice for some women overburdened by the task of living up to Victorian gender expectations, and that its symptoms merely carried to logical conclusion the Victorian image of woman as dependent, fragile, sensitive, and childlike.[8]

---

7 G. J. Barker-Benfield, *The Horrors of the Half-Known Life: Male Attitudes Toward Women and Sexuality in Nineteenth-Century America* (New York: Harper & Row, 1976), p. 89; Ann Douglas Wood, "'The Fashionable Diseases': Women's Complaints and Their Treatment in Nineteenth-Century America," *Journal of Interdisciplinary History* 4 (Summer 1973): 25–52; Ehrenreich and English, *Witches, Midwives and Nurses.*

8 See Regina Morantz's early critique which attempts to combine the approach of women's history and medical history, "The Lady and Her Physician," in Lois Banner and Mary Hartmann, eds., *Clio's Consciousness Raised: New Perspectives on the History of Women* (New York: Harper & Row, 1974). Some recent works in medical history (some of them by feminist scholars) which stress the limited power of physicians are John Harley Warner, *The Therapeutic Perspective: Medical Practice, Knowledge, and Identity in America, 1820–1885* (Cambridge: Harvard University Press, 1987); Judith Walzer Leavitt, *Brought to Bed: Childbearing in America, 1750–1850* (New York: Oxford University Press, 1986); Nancy Tomes, *"A Generous Confidence": Thomas Story Kirkbride and the Art of Asylum-Keeping* (Cambridge: Cambridge University Press, 1987); Joan Brumberg, *Fasting Girls: The Emergence of Anorexia Nervosa as a Modern Disease* (Cambridge: Harvard University Press, 1988). Carroll Smith-Rosenberg, "Puberty to Menopause: The Cycle of Femininity in Nineteenth-Century America," *Feminist Studies* 1 (Winter–Spring 1973): 58–73; Smith-Rosenberg and Charles Rosenberg, "The Female Animal: Medical and Biological Views of Women and Her Role in Nineteenth-Century America," *Journal of American History* 60 (Spring 1973): 332–56; Smith-Rosenberg, "The Hysterical Woman: Sex Roles and Role Conflict in Nineteenth-Century America," *Social Research* 39 (Winter 1972): 652–78. Charles Rosenberg published some excellent

Inevitably, questions raised regarding the ideology and behavior of male physicians led to the subject of women physicians. Ann Douglas Wood was one of the first to direct attention to them when she concluded her early examination of male treatment with some speculations on the attitudes of female practitioners. Building from the premise that women were victimized by male medical men, she suggested that nineteenth-century women doctors saw themselves as the saviors of their sex—the deliverers of women from the hands of the enemy. In Wood's story, the entrance of women into the medical profession was never a private struggle, but a political one. Indeed, she and several others characterized the women's medical movement as a "weapon in a social and political struggle for power between the sexes."[9]

These questions converged with others that women's historians were raising regarding women's status within and without the family in the nineteenth century. How did the ideology of separate spheres play itself out in women's lives? As the public sphere gradually became more complex and took on greater political importance, did women lose power? How was domesticity connected to women's efforts to enter professions like teaching and medicine, and what was the meaning of their visibility in the nineteenth-century reform movements?

As early as 1969, Gerda Lerner speculated that both middle-class and working-class women lost status, as universal manhood suffrage brought all white men, regardless of class, into the political arena. Equally culpable was nineteenth-century professionalization, with its preemption of esoteric knowledge and formal and informal legitimation in law and public acceptance. The development of educational requirements and professional societies institutionalized the exclusion of

---

work on race and class as well. See "The Bitter Fruit: Heredity, Disease, and Social Thought," *Perspectives in American History* 8 (1974): 189–235; and "Sexuality, Class, and Role," *American Quarterly* 25 (May 1973): 131–53. For more recent examples of this approach see Elaine Showalter, *The Female Malady: Women, Madness and English Culture, 1830–1980* (New York: Pantheon Books, 1985); Mary Poovey, "'Scenes of an Indelicate Character': The Medical Treatment of Victorian Women," and Thomas Laqueur, "Orgasm, Generation and the Politics of Reproductive Biology," in *Representations* no. 14 (Spring 1986): 137–68.

9 See Ann Douglas Wood, "'The Fashionable Diseases': Women's Complaints and Their Treatment in Nineteenth-Century America," *Journal of Interdisciplinary History* 4 (Summer 1973): 25–52, p. 28. See also Ehrenreich and English, *Witches Midwives and Nurses*; Virginia Drachman, "Women Doctors and the Women's Medical Movement: Feminism and Medicine, 1850–1895" (Ph.D. dissertation, SUNY Buffalo, 1976); Mary Roth Walsh, *"Doctors Wanted: No Women Need Apply": Sexual Barriers in the Medical Profession, 1835–1975* (New Haven: Yale University Press, 1977).

women from a wide range of activities—especially the delivery of health care—which they had previously claimed as their province. In the field of medicine, Lerner declared, "Women were the casualties of medical professionalization."[10]

Studies of the decline of female midwifery confirmed some of Lerner's hunches. Like Mary Putnam Jacobi before them, Jane Donegan, Catherine Scholtern, Richard and Dorothy Wertz, and others demonstrated how the management of childbirth gradually slipped from women's hands, as physicians acquired new anatomical knowledge and novel forceps technology, which allowed them to claim superior expertise.[11]

Yet in the first book-length study of women in the medical profession published by a professional historian, *'Doctors Wanted: No Women Need Apply': Sexual Barriers in the Medical Profession, 1835–1975*, Mary Roth Walsh found deliberate male hostility and intentional institutional discrimination to be more significant than professionalization in keeping women out of medicine. Walsh argued that women's entrance into medicine was part of the larger nineteenth-century struggle for female self-determination, and that feminism was crucial to women doctors' success in confronting the barriers of sexism.

Although institutional barriers existed from the very beginning, Walsh contended that in spite of them, the late nineteenth century was something of a "golden age" for women doctors, when they numbered

---

[10] "The Lady and the Mill Girl: Changes in the Status of Women in the Age of Jackson," *Midcontinent American Studies Journal* 10 (Spring 1969): 5–14, p. 6. See also Blake, "Women and Medicine," p. 107.

[11] See Jane Donegan, *Women and Men Midwives: Medicine, Morality and Misogyny in Early America* (Westport, CT: Greenwood Press, 1978); Judith Barrett Litoff, *American Midwives: 1860 to the Present* (Westport, CT: Greenwood Press, 1978); Richard W. Wertz and Dorothy C. Wertz, *Lying-In—A History of Childbirth in America* (New York: Free Press, 1977); Edna Manzer, "Woman's Doctors: The Development of Obstetrics and Gynecology," (Ph.D. dissertation, University of Indiana, 1979); Frances E. Kobrin, "The American Midwife Controversy: A Crisis of Professionalization," *Bulletin of the History of Medicine* 40 (July–August 1966): 350–63; Catherine Scholten, "'On the Importance of the Obstetrick Art': Changing Customs of Childbirth in America, 1760–1825," *William and Mary Quarterly* 34 (July 1977): 426–45. Judith W. Leavitt's masterful book on childbirth, *Brought to Bed: Childbearing in America, 1750–1950* (New York: Oxford University Press, 1986), has revised this thesis considerably by demonstrating that the medicalization of childbirth was much slower than historians had originally assumed. She suggests that women were not merely passive victims of medical intrusion, but often retained control over their confinement and mode of delivery throughout the nineteenth century, as long as the male physician came into the home. The major event in the social history of American childbirth was the transition from the home to the hosptial. See also Margarete Sandelowski, *Pain, Pleasure and American Childbirth* (Westport, CT: Greenwood Press, 1984).

10% or more of the enrollment in eighteen regular medical schools across the country. By 1900 their proportion in the profession rose as high as 18% in selected cities like Boston. These successes, achieved at a time "of rapid professionalization, when education requirements and licensing laws were fast becoming the norm" led Walsh to minimize professionalization as a barrier to women doctors. On the contrary, she argued, professionalization may have offered women their first real opportunity in medicine. By carefully spelling out the requirements for becoming a doctor, changes in the organization of medicine in the late nineteenth century actually favored women. "If one must acquire a medical degree, interested women could apply to medical colleges and if rebuffed could then go on to establish their own. If one must gain entrance into a medical society or obtain a license, women could rise to meet the requirements and, if rejected, could go on to raise the cry of injustice to gain support. In short," Walsh concluded, "it is possible to argue that it is easier to overcome a series of known obstacles than tilt at a series of shadowy spectres."[12]

Rejecting professionalization as the primary cause of women's marginalization in medicine allowed Walsh to concentrate on what she believed to be the real culprit: "the institutional barriers of sexism,"— entrance quotas, discriminatory hospital residency programs, and old boy networks—which, she argued, remained so resilient in the twentieth century that they continued to be "the central force in turning back the tide of women who, despite the obstacles, still aspired to careers in medicine." What made women particularly vulnerable to "male backlash" after 1900, she noted, was the decline in public feminism. In the final analysis, however, Walsh did not see how the very processes of professionalization institutionalized the discrimination that she so painstakingly exposed. Perhaps this was because her book, replete with important information regarding the history of women physicians, focused less on studying their career patterns than on attempting "to explain *why there are so few careers to study.*"[13]

In common with other historians of women, those studying women doctors focused at first on the ways in which women have been oppressed, both through individual mistreatment and through structural

---

12 Walsh, *"Doctors Wanted,"* pp. xvii, 14–15.
13 Ibid., pp. xvii, 14–15, xii. For the reluctance of medical societies to accept women see Martin Kaufman, "The Admission of Women to 19th-Century Medical Societies," *Bulletin of the History of Medicine* 50 (Summer 1976): 251–60.

discrimination. The documentation of the exclusion of women from the profession of medicine, and the demeaning attitudes of male physicians toward their women patients were a part of this stage. However, as more became known about the resistance and adaptations of women, both as physicians and as patients, the oppression model appeared increasingly inadequate.

In reviewing the work of Douglas, Benfield, and Smith-Rosenberg from the perspective of women's history and medical history, Regina Morantz-Sanchez reiterated Richard Shryock's observation that writing the history of women physicians must include chapters in the history of medicine. She emphasized the importance of evaluating treatment modalities in the light of nineteenth-century theories of disease, and cautioned that nineteenth-century medical therapeutics was indiscriminate in its harsh treatment of patients—men, women, and children alike.[14] How, she asked, had women physicians functioned "on their own terms" in a professional world dominated by men?[15]

She found that many women physicians derived power and autonomy from the nineteenth-century ideology of domesticity. A handful had participated in the nineteenth-century health-reform movement, a movement which legitimated new female responsibilities within and without the home, gave some women public roles as teachers of physiology and hygiene, and stimulated a few to professionalize their work by seeking formal medical training.[16]

In their public and private pronouncements, women doctors appeared to be motivated less by a desire to liberate their sisters from male medicine than they were determined to surpass their male colleagues in

---

[14] See also Gail Pat Parsons, "Equal Treatment for All: American Remedies for Male Sexual Problems, 1850–1900," *Journal of the History of Medicine* (Spring 1977): 56–71.

[15] "The Lady and Her Physician," in Lois Banner and Mary Hartman, eds., *Clio's Consciousness Raised: New Perspectives on the History of Women* (New York: Harper & Row, 1974); "Women in the Medical Profession: Why Were There So Few?" *Reviews in American History* 6 (June 1978): 163–70; "'The Connecting Link': The Case for the Woman Doctor in 19th-Century America," in Judith Walzer Leavitt and Ronald Numbers, eds., *Sickness and Health in America: Essays in the History of Health Care* (Madison: University of Wisconsin Press, 1978). See also Gerda Lerner, "Placing Women in History: Definitions and Challenges," in *The Majority Finds Its Past* (New York: Oxford University Press, 1979), p. 148.

[16] Regina Markell Morantz, "Making Women Modern: Middle-Class Women and Health Reform in 19th-Century America," *Journal of Social History* 10 (Summer 1977): 490–507; "Nineteenth-Century Health Reform and Women: A Program of Self-Help," in Guenter Risse, Ronald Numbers and Judith Leavitt, eds., *Medicine Without Doctors: Home Health Care in American History* (New York: Science History Publications, 1977).

bringing existing medical science into the home. As justification for their entrance into the profession, they used what Karen Offen has recently labeled "relational" arguments—ones that emphasized women's distinctive contributions to social welfare and made claims based on these contributions.[17] Their practice patterns among a constituency predominately of women and children bore out these intentions. Morantz-Sanchez's findings hinted at a complex relationship between female physicians, scientific values, and feminism, suggesting much diversity among women doctors in their approaches to women's issues.[18]

In her book, *Sympathy and Science: Women Physicians in American Medicine*, Morantz-Sanchez stressed the ideological dimension of medical professionalization and its effects on women's status, self-image, and accomplishments as doctors. She argued that women doctors at the end of the nineteenth century came into conflict with the dominant values of a new professional ethos, which included individualism, scientific objectivity, careerism, and rationality. As they struggled for an equal place in medicine, they experienced a tension between those professional values and their separate experience as women. As a minority and as women, they viewed professionalism from a different and more critical perspective than the majority of their male colleagues, often feeling more conflict between the dual commitment of medicine to "sympathy" and "science." While some accepted traditional Victorian assumptions about women's nature, arguing that women would always play a different role in medicine than men, others objected to female-centered, moralistic, and separatist standards for women. But the institutions they built and the specialties they chose often reflected an alternative resolution to this tension other than that chosen by their male colleagues. For example, some women's hospitals were slower to discard traditional holistic methods of care in favor of more technocratic approaches. In addition, in keeping with their nineteenth-century self-image, women physicians were over-represented in "feminine" specialties and in social medicine, especially in the first three decades of the twentieth century.[19]

The suggestion of all these historians that professionalization both

---

17 Karen Offen, "Defining Feminism: A Comparative Historical Approach," *Signs* 14 (Autumn 1988): 119–57.
18 Regina Markell Morantz, "'The Connecting Link'"; "From Art to Science: Women Physicians in American Medicine, 1600-1980," in *In Her Own Words; Oral Histories of Women Physicians*, edited with Cynthia Pomerleau and Carol Fenichel (Westport, CT: Greenwood Press, 1982), p. 16.
19 Regina Morantz-Sanchez, *Sympathy and Science: Women Physicians in American Medicine* (New York: Oxford University Press, 1985).

constricted and shaped the careers of women physicians in complex ways, especially at the end of the century when professional societies and educational institutions began to reflect what Burton Bledstein has called "the culture of professionalism," has been underscored in work on the history of other women professionals. Margaret Rossiter's *Women Scientists in America*, Rosalind Rosenberg's work on female social scientists, *Beyond Separate Spheres*, and Pnina Abir-Am and Dorinda Outram's edited collection, *Uneasy Careers and Intimate Lives, Women in Science, 1789–1979* recount how men in these professions viewed the entrance of women into the ranks with great ambivalence and took effective steps to marginalize them.[20]

Work on these other female professionals reinforced the notion that the founding of women's medical institutions in the nineteenth century was crucial to advancing women's status. Indeed, what women scientists lacked were the equivalent of the separate female medical schools, hospitals, and professional societies that offered students quality medical education, postgraduate training and the group support that allowed them to lobby for acceptance as full-fledged professionals.[21]

One important concern of the new research on women was whether there existed a distinct consciousness shared by women that contrasted with men's modes of behavior and perspectives on the world. A number of historians, including Nancy Cott and Carroll Smith-Rosenberg posited a separate women's culture in which dominant cultural stereotypes about women were absorbed and then recast by women themselves.[22] This research led some historians to speculate not only that women physicians exhibited a collective consciousness, but that their treatment modalities were at variance with those of their male colleagues.[23] Others

---

[20] Margaret Rossiter, *Women Scientists in America* (Baltimore: Johns Hopkins University Press, 1982); Rosalind Rosenberg, *Beyond Separate Spheres: Intellectual Roots of Modern Feminism* (New Haven: Yale University Press, 1982). See also Pnina B. Abir-Am and Dorinda Outram, eds., *Uneasy Careers and Intimate Lives: Women in Science, 1789–1979* (New Brunswick: Rutgers University Press, 1987).

[21] Walsh, *"Doctors Wanted,"* pp. 76–105; Morantz-Sanchez, *Sympathy and Science*, pp. 48–183.

[22] Smith-Rosenberg, "The Female World of Love and Ritual: Relations between Women in Nineteenth-Century America," *Signs* 1 (June 1975): 1–30; Nancy Cott, *The Bonds of Womanhood* (New Haven: Yale University Press, 1977).

[23] Virginia Drachman, "Women Doctors and the Women's Medical Movement," pp. 121–26; Patricia Branca, *Silent Sisterhood: Middle-Class Women in the Victorian Home* (Pittsburgh: Carnegie Mellon Press, 1975), pp. 62–73; Laurie Crumpacker, "Female Patients in Four Boston Hospitals of the 1890's," Paper delivered at the Third Berkshire Conference on the History of Women, October, 1974 (Copy on deposit at the Schlesinger Library, Radcliffe Women's Archives); Walsh, *"Doctors Wanted,"* pp. 76–105.

found that professionalism generally prevailed over female culture, albeit in complex ways.[24]

Virginia Drachman's book on the history of the New England Hospital for Women and Children, *Hospital with a Heart*, assessed the role of female-centered institutions in fostering a unique women's culture by focusing on the history of one of the most prominent of them.[25] While Drachman recognized the centrality of the New England Hospital's role, arguing that separatism was "the linchpin of almost all nineteenth-century women's lives," she also blamed separatism for the New England hospital's demise. After 1880, she found women were presented with increasing opportunities to study and work at male institutions. The lure of assimilation proved insurmountable to the policy makers at the New England, who became progressively more rigid in their organization of internships and residencies. Eventually, the institution's insensitivity to the mounting needs of young female medical graduates for more "hands-on" clinical experience—something they were able to get at coeducational establishments—made the hospital less attractive to aspiring women graduates.[26]

Drachman overemphasized the tension women physicians felt between separatism and assimilation. In the world of medicine, the separation she posited was never complete. There were always male faculty members at the women's medical schools, while male consultants gave advice and support to the women's hospitals. Hence, the boundaries between men and women in the nineteenth-century medical community were always permeable. Cora Marrett's study of female medical socie-

---

[24] Regina Morantz and Sue Zschoche, "Professionalism, Feminism and Gender Roles: A Study of the Therapeutics of Nineteenth-Century Male and Female Doctors," *Journal of American History* 67 (December 1980): 568–88. Contemporary research on differential therapeutics is also inconclusive, but women seem to spend more time with their patients. See Sue Fisher, *In the Patient's Best Interest* (New Brunswick: Rutgers University Press, 1982).

[25] Virginia Drachman, *Hospital with a Heart* (Ithaca: Cornell University Press, 1984). See Estelle Freedman, "Separatism as Strategy: Female Institution Building and American Feminism, 1870–1930," *Feminist Studies* 5 (Fall 1979): 512–29.

[26] Virginia Drachman, "Female Solidarity and Professional Success: The Dilemma of Women Doctors in Late-Nineteenth Century America," *Journal of Social History* 15 (Summer 1982): 607–19, and *Hospital with a Heart*. For a multicausal approach to the decline of the New England Hospital see Helena M. Wall, "Feminism and the New England Hospital," *American Quarterly* 32 (Fall 1980): 435–52. For a more recent article by Drachman that examines separatism among women physicians not necessarily connected with the New England Hospital see "The Limits of Progress: The Professional Lives of Women Doctors, 1881–1926," *Bulletin of the History of Medicine* 60 (Spring 1986): 56–72.

ties, for example, found that these were more likely to flourish in cities where men's societies were active. Women's admission to male societies apparently heightened their sensitivity to being a minority and, by bringing them together, gave them the chance to create separate and supplemental women's groups.[27] Moreover, Drachman overlooked other factors—like the resistance of older hospital staff to modern methods of medical education—that may well have been more important in the decline of the New England hospital than its tradition of being a woman's institution. Nevertheless, her work raised important questions regarding the nature of women's institutions and the problems women physicians faced at the end of the nineteenth century, when coeducation opened up new opportunities and medical professionalization generated fresh and less overt obstacles to women's advancement.

Historians now accept the centrality of professionalization to women physicians' experience in the late nineteenth and twentieth centuries. Because their work is informed by current historical literature on the professions, their definition of the professionalization process includes both institutional and cultural manifestations. Several studies, while attempting to describe and uncover the various effects of professionalization on women, go well beyond the oppression/victimization model to emphasize the various strategies women used to attain their goals in spite of consistent opposition.[28]

For example, Pnina Migdal Glazer and Miriam Slater also stressed the importance of understanding that women professionals' experience was different from men's in their book *Unequal Colleagues*. To view the history of women in the professions from the broadest possible perspective, their study offered four narrative vignettes of nine professional women active in four different fields—academia, medicine, research science, and psychiatric social work. They emphasized that the professional ideology that evolved at the beginning of the twentieth century

---

[27] Cora Marrett, "On the Evolution of the Women's Medical Societies," *Bulletin of the History of Medicine* 50 (Summer 1976): 251–60.

[28] For an excellent review of current thinking on women and the professions, see Joan Jacobs Brumberg and Nancy Tomes, "Women in the Professions: A Research Agenda for American Historians," *Reviews in American History* 30 (June 1982): 275–96. See also Burton Bledstein, *The Culture of Professionalism* (New York: Norton, 1976); Eliot Friedson, *Profession of Medicine* (New York: Dodd, Mead, 1975); Megali Larson, *The Rise of Professionalism* (Berkeley: University of California Press, 1977); E. Richard Brown, *Rockefeller Medicine Men, Medicine and Capitalism in America* (Berkeley: University of California Press, 1979), and JoAnne Brown, "Professional Language: Words That Succeed," *Radical History Review* 34 (January 1986): 33–51.

was one developed primarily by men and based on the male life cycle. Women who chose professional occupations were thus required to adapt themselves to a lifestyle much more easily suited to a man. Consequently they were forced to pursue various strategies of adjustment—the authors label these "separatism," "subordination," "superperformance," and "innovation"—which were wholly unnecessary for their male counterparts. For example, many chose not to marry because of perceived difficulties in balancing family life and career. Some formed lifelong relationships with women who were often more supportive of careers than husbands would have been. Others did marry but attained only modest professional achievement in the face of an insurmountable dual burden.[29]

Glazer and Slater's case-study approach has been used successfully by other historians to gain insight into how women physicians mediated between the demands of professional and private life. Barbara Sicherman in *Alice Hamilton, A Life in Letters*, proved particularly adept at revealing the complexity of Alice Hamilton's personal choices, as well as the constraints and benefits imposed on her by her gender.[30] In an article on early female psychiatrists, Constance McGovern contributed much to our understanding of how women managed their careers in one particular specialty.[31] Thomas Bonner has described how many women physicians in the late nineteenth century pursued postgraduate training in Europe, rather than be stymied in their career goals by discriminatory barriers.[32] The oral histories gathered by Morantz-Sanchez and published

---

[29] Pnina Migdal Glazer and Miriam Slater, *Unequal Colleagues: The Entrance of Women into the Professions, 1890–1940* (New Brunswick: Rutgers University Press, 1987). In this context, recent work on women in other professions has been especially helpful. See Jessie Bernard, *Academic Women* (University Park: Pennsylvania State University Press, 1964); Cynthia Fuchs Epstein, *Woman's Place: Options and Limits in Professional Careers* (Berkeley: University of California Press, 1970), and Epstein, *Women in Law* (New York: Basic Books, 1981); Helen Astin, *The Woman Doctorate in America: Origins, Career and Family* (New York: Russell Sage Foundation, 1969); Patricia Hummer, *The Decade of Elusive Promise, Professional Women in the United States, 1920–1930* (Ann Arbor: Research Press, 1976); Barbara Harris, *Beyond Her Sphere: Woman and the Professions in American History* (Westport, CT: Greenwood Press, 1978); Jonathan Cole, *Fair Science: Women in the Scientific Community* (New York: Free Press, 1979); Rosalind Rosenberg, *Beyond Separate Spheres: Intellectual Roots of Modern Feminism* (New Haven: Yale University Press, 1982); and Margaret Rossiter, *Women Scientists in America* (Baltimore: Johns Hopkins University Press, 1982).

[30] Alice Hamilton, *A Life in Letters* (Cambridge: Harvard University Press, 1984).

[31] Constance McGovern, "Doctors or Ladies? Women Physicians in Psychiatric Institutions, 1872–1900," *Bulletin of the History of Medicine* 53 (Fall 1979): 434–49.

[32] Thomas Neville Bonner, "Women Physicians Abroad: A New Dimension of Women's Push for Opportunity in Medicine, 1850–1914," *Bulletin of the History of Medicine* 62 (Spring 1988): 58–73.

in *In Her Own Words: Oral Histories of Women Physicians* suggested that many of the problems women faced in the twentieth century while coping with careers in medicine have been passed on from generation to generation.[33] These interviews indicate that it was not professional ideology per se that proved the greatest source of women's difficulties, but the professional ethos coupled with cultural beliefs about women's fundamental connection with family life.

Lest we dwell too much on ideology, self-image, and beliefs, Gloria Melnick Moldow's *Women Doctors in Gilded Age Washington: Race, Gender and Professionalization* has reminded us that the ethos of professionalism was always translated into concrete institutional restrictions. Her book detailed the ways in which professional barriers in one particular city arose at the end of the nineteenth century to bar from further advancement those who had already achieved a measure of success.[34] Moldow characterized the story of women physicians in the nation's capitol as one of "promise" and "disillusionment." Her work corroborates Mary Roth Walsh's theory of a "male backlash." Finding that women who came to the city in the 1860s seeking professional opportunity discovered a number of avenues available to them, the book vividly describes the gradual constriction of access to medical education, hospital training, and membership in professional societies. Male colleagues became increasingly uneasy with women's progress at the end of the century.

Moldow's work was also pathbreaking in its treatment of race. The presence in Washington, D.C. of Howard University, which offered a coeducational medical course to both blacks and whites, allowed her to provide something no other history of women physicians has: an account of the social origins, professional training, and subsequent practice patterns of the city's black women physicians, carefully placed in the context of evolving professional developments.[35] Using this material to

---

[33] Regina Morantz, Cynthia Pomerleau, and Carol Fenichel, eds., *In Her Own Words: Oral Histories of Women Physicians* (Westport, CT: Greenwood Press, 1982).

[34] Gloria Melnick Moldow, *Women Doctors in Gilded Age Washington: Race, Gender and Professionalization* (Urbana: University of Illinois Press, 1987).

[35] Dorothy Sterling, Darlene Clark Hine, and Margaret Jerrido have done excellent preliminary work ferreting out information on black women physicians. See Sterling, *We Are Your Sisters; Black Women in the Nineteenth Century* (New York: Norton, 1984), pp. 440–50; Hine, "Co-Laborers in the Work of the Lord: Nineteenth-Century Black Women Physicians," in Ruth Abram, ed., *"Send Us a Lady Physician": Women Doctors in America, 1835–1920* (New York: Norton, 1985), pp. 107–20; Jerrido, "Black Women Physicians, A Triple Burden," in Medical College of Pennsylvania *Alumnae News* 30 (Summer 1979): 4–5; and Jerrido, "Early Black Women Physicians," *Women*

excellent effect, Moldow fleshed out the consequences of black women physicians' double burden—that of being black and female. She illustrated how white male physicians, in barring blacks and women from their medical societies, at first lumped issues of race and sex together. But, when push came to shove, the "bonds of race and class" prevailed "over distinctions of sex," allowing white women to win membership. Sadly, racism also tarnished the efforts of white women physicians. They, too, excluded black women from their societies, while black medical organizations, no strangers to nineteenth-century theories of woman's place, shunned qualified female practitioners of their own race.[36]

Delving into questions of race has not been the only innovation of current historical studies. Despite the fact that most of the first generation nineteenth-century women physicians received sectarian medical training, scholarship on sectarian women physicians has lagged behind work on the regulars. Two books on women and water cure have begun to correct that imbalance. Jane Donegan's *"Hydropathic Highway to Health": Women and Water-Cure in Antebellum America* is particularly informative in describing how female water-cure physicians helped provide an alternative to allopathic care in the management of childbirth. It is also eloquent in describing the practice patterns and motivations of numerous female practitioners who attracted the patronage of thousands of ailing women.[37] Also important is Susan Cayleff's *Wash and Be Healed: The Water-Cure Movement and Women's Health*, a study of this special milieu of health seekers and caregivers.[38]

Using the hydropaths as a case in point, Cayleff argues that all the medical sects subscribed to more fluid notions of gender roles, and more readily appealed to the working classes.[39] Related to this thesis is her

---

& Health 5 (Fall 1980): 1–3. See also Janet Holmes, "The Life of Lena Edwards," *New Jersey Medicine* 85 (May 1988): 431–37.

[36] Moldow, *Women Doctors in Gilded Age Washington*, p. 104.

[37] Jane Donegan, *"Hydropathic Highway to Health": Women and Water-Cure in Antebellum America* (Westport, CT: Greenwood Press, 1986).

[38] Susan Cayleff, *Wash and Be Healed: The Water-Cure Movement and Women's Health* (Philadelphia: Temple University Press, 1987). For more on homeopathic women physicians see Chapter 11 in this volume.

[39] Although this was certainly true in general, homeopathic medical schools did occasionally discriminate against women. See William Barlow and David O. Powell, "Homeopathy and Sexual Equality: The Controversy over Coeducation at Cincinnati's Pulte Medical College 1873–1879," *Ohio History* 90 (Fall 1981): 101–13. For more on homeopathic women physicians, see Chapter 11 in this volume.

claim that hydropaths rejected the accoutrements of professionalization and were more "democratic" in the clinical encounter, enlisting the patient's cooperation in the cure.

Although both books are extremely suggestive, we know too little about how regular women physicians actually treated their patients to determine to what extent hydropathic physicians differed from them. Cayleff's work in particular opens up a new set of questions about gender, professionalization, and class. We know, for example, that most regular women physicians refused to consult with the sectarians, especially in the last third of the nineteenth century. What does this say about how the regulars balanced their professional and female identities? Further, how do we account for some women's deliberate and continued interest in sectarian medicine, even after regular medical schools gradually became willing to open their doors to female students? Several historians have asked how the therapeutics of women physicians differed from those of male colleagues, but no one yet has compared and contrasted the two groups of women.

It is clear that much progress has been made in the last decade. We have several rich and detailed studies of women physicians' entrance into the profession and the barriers erected against them. We have learned that, in spite of their professional socialization, they generally remained loyal to a tradition of holistic and humane care, one which manifested itself in their enthusiasm for public health and social medicine. In addition, historians have described their coping strategies, both on a personal and an institutional level. We have learned how feminism and female culture aided women struggling to become qualified professionals. We have discovered that women physicians were not a monolithic group, but a collection of individuals who differed among themselves on issues of separatism and assimilation, feminism and femininity, equality and difference, therapeutic issues, and their role in the profession. Notwithstanding this diversity, feminist theory has helped us to discover the ways in which the social construction of gender roles affected all of their lives, simply because of the fact that they were women.[40]

---

[40] For an introduction to this approach see Evelyn Fox Keller, *Reflections on Gender and Science* (New Haven: Yale University Press, 1985); Ruth Bleier, ed., *Feminist Approaches to Science* (New York: Pergamon Press, 1986); Regina Morantz-Sanchez, "The Compassionate Professional: Historical Notes on the Woman Physician's Dilemma," in Sharon S. Brehm, ed., *Seeing Female: Social Roles and Personal Lives* (Westport, CT: Greenwood Press, 1988); "The Many Faces of Intimacy: Professional Options and Personal Choices

Despite these very real achievements, much work remains to be done. Chronologically, the largest body of literature has focused primarily on the nineteenth and early twentieth centuries. We need more studies of the period after 1930.[41] Moreover, most, but not all women physicians were members of the white middle class, and we know far too little about black and ethnic practitioners. The dominant tendency thus far has been to focus on a mainstream professional model. Class is also a factor that has been little studied. How would the history of sectarian women in the nineteenth century and of women in osteopathy and chiropractic in the twentieth revise our current understanding of women physicians' past if questions regarding class were given more attention? In addition, social historians of the last decades have pointed to numerous ways in which medicine has been used as an instrument of social control.[42] Were women physicians social controllers as well? How did they relate to their patients, and did their patients—primarily women and children until recently—affect the way they practiced medicine? How did their membership in an elite profession, combined with their experience as women, affect their approach to issues of status, power, and economic domination?

Finally, feminist theorists have developed sophisticated critiques of the scientific model of objectivity that has dominated scientific research in the last several centuries. They have shown how the language of science served not only to validate a specific kind of analysis—for

among Nineteenth and Twentieth-Century Women Physicians," in Pnina Abir-Am and Dorinda Outram, eds., *Uneasy Careers and Intimate Lives, Women in Science, 1789–1979* (New Brunswick: Rutgers University Press, 1987); "Not Feminized but Humanized, Reflections on the Future of Women in the Profession," *New Jersey Medicine* 85 (May 1988): 363–70.

41 Ellen More's research promises more information about the twentieth century. See "The Blackwell Medical Society and the Professionalization of Women Physicians," *Bulletin of the History of Medicine* 61 (Winter 1987): 603–28; see also Judith Lorber, *Women Physicians, Careers, Status and Power* (New York: Tavistock, 1984), a helpful sociological study.

42 See for example Gerald N. Grob, "Rediscovering Asylums: The Unhistorical History of the Mental Hospital," in Morris Vogel and Charles E. Rosenberg, eds., *The Therapeutic Revolution: Essays in the Social History of American Medicine* (Philadelphia: University of Pennsylvania Press, 1979), pp. 135–57, for a review of some of this literature; Morris Vogel, "The Transformation of the American Hospital," in Susan Reverby and David Rosner, eds., *Health Care in America* (Philadelphia: Temple University Press, 1979); Rima Apple, "'To Be Used Only Under the Direction of a Physician': Commercial Infant Feeding and Medical Practice, 1870–1940," *Bulletin of the History of Medicine* 54 (Fall 1980): 402–17; Andrew Scull, "Humanitarianism or Control: Observations on the Historiography of Anglo-American Psychiatry," *Rice University Studies* 67 (1981): 21–41.

example, laboratory experiments under suitable controls, the precise measuring of results, the repetition of protocols—but to denigrate and devalue more subjective and informal modes of knowing increasingly identified with the feminine. At the end of the nineteenth century, the bacteriological revolution interjected this objective mode of inquiry into medical practice. How did women physicians respond to this development, and how did it affect their status in the profession?[43]

These are only a few of the new directions stimulated by current scholarship that has already enriched the history of medicine.[44] It has also become an integral part of the history of women. Moreover, each of these separate fields has had an enormous impact on the social history of American society. Indeed, Richard Shryock's modest claims for the gains to be made by the pursuit of women physicians' past have been more than fulfilled. Let us hope that the next decade will prove even more productive than the last.

---

[43] See Keller; Bleier; and Carolyn Merchant, *The Death of Nature* (San Francisco: Harper & Row, 1980); Sandra Harding, *The Science Question in Feminism* (Ithaca: Cornell University Press, 1986); C. MacCormack and M. Strathern, *Nature Culture and Gender* (Cambridge: Cambridge University Press, 1980); Carol McMillan, *Women, Reason and Nature* (Princeton: Princeton University Press, 1984); Sarah Ruddick, "Maternal Thinking," *Feminist Studies* 6 (Summer 1980): 342–67; Regina Morantz-Sanchez, "Not Feminized But Humanized."

[44] See John Harley Warner, "Science in Medicine," in Sally Gregory Kohlstedt and Margaret W. Rossiter, *Historical Writing on American Science*, pp. 37–58, originally published as volume one of *Osiris: A Research Journal Devoted to the History of Science and Its Cultural Influences* (Baltimore: Johns Hopkins University Press, 1986), for an excellent discussion of recent scholarship in this field.

• • • ─────── • • •

20

PHARMACISTS

Gregory J. Higby
with Teresa C. Gallagher

No other major American profession during the past fifty years has undergone feminization as rapidly as pharmacy. In 1950, only one in twenty-five pharmacists in the United States was a woman; today the ratio is one in four, and if current enrollment patterns continue, women should outnumber men in American pharmacy by the year 2015.[1] Despite this trend and the profession's expressed concern about it, the role of women in American pharmacy has not attracted substantial historical analysis. In contrast to the thousands of pages written by historians about women and other health-care professions and fields, analytical work about the history of women and American pharmacy has until recently totaled less than one *hundred* pages! Typical is the standard text, *Kremers and Urdang's History of Pharmacy*, which considers the position of women in American pharmacy in seventy-two words (followed by over a page on soda fountains).[2] The popular genre of books, state histories of pharmacy, usually have one or two pages at most sketching two or three prominent women practitioners.[3]

---

[1] *Fifth Report to the President & Congress on the Status of Health Personnel in the United States* (Washington, DC: USGPO, 1986).
[2] Glenn Sonnedecker, rev., *Kremers and Urdang's History of Pharmacy* (Philadelphia: Lippincott, 1976), pp. 308ff.
[3] Among the best are Edward R. Lewis, Jr., *Prairie State Pharmacy* (n.p.: Illinois Pharmacists Association, 1980), esp. pp. 142–45; Eunice Bonow Bardell, *Wisconsin Show Globe* (Madison: Wisconsin Pharmaceutical Association, 1983), esp. pp. 36–38; and David L. Cowen, *The New Jersey Pharmaceutical Association, 1870–1970* (Trenton: New Jersey Pharmaceutical Association, 1970), esp. pp. 108 and 117.

INTRODUCTION TO WOMEN
AND AMERICAN PHARMACY

To begin, one must gain some understanding of the history of pharmacy's professional development in the United States. This can be gained best by a reading of Part Three of Kremers and Urdang's History of Pharmacy, which contains about two hundred pages on American pharmacy. Although there are a few articles that address professionalization in American pharmacy, they do not differ significantly from this work.[4]

For the uninitiated, the history of pharmacy contains some rather confusing terminology. "Pharmacy" is a term applied to the science, art, and practice of compounding and dispensing medicines; it also is used to refer to the location where this activity takes place. The practitioners of this activity have, during various periods, been commonly called apothecaries (up to 1875), pharmaceutists (c. 1820–1860), druggists (c. 1750–1970), and pharmacists (c. 1870 to present). In addition, for most of the nineteenth century, employed pharmacists were called drug clerks.

Although drug shops appeared in Colonial villages and towns early on, an independent calling of pharmacy—totally apart from medicine—did not arise until about 1820. During Colonial times, apothecaries gained most of their income selling medicines to physicians or practicing medicine themselves in their shops. Written prescriptions intended for filling by a pharmacist did not become commonplace in American cities until the early 1800s. Physicians dispensed their own medicines, which were often compounded by their apprentices. Physicians continued to dispense drugs commonly until the late nineteenth century, especially in rural areas poorly served by drugstores. Many of these drugs were used by domestic healers, usually women, to make the medicines taken by the patients. Thus, domestic healers performed pharmaceutical as well as medical tasks.

During Colonial times through the early Republican era, a small number of women operated drug shops and small-scale medicine manufacturing businesses.[5] For example, Elizabeth Greenleaf owned and ran a

---

[4] See Gregory J. Higby, "Professionalism and the Nineteenth-Century American Pharmacist," Pharmacy in History 28 (1986): 115–24.

[5] J. H. Hoch and Q. Hoch, "Mrs. Masters and Her Tuscarora Rice," Journal of the American Pharmaceutical Association, NS 4 (1963): 577–78, 580.

drug shop in Boston from 1726 until her death in 1762, and Elizabeth Marshall took over a famous but floundering family pharmacy business in 1804 and restored its prominence.[6] In almost all cases where women owned shops, however, they had taken over from deceased fathers or husbands and continued to practice a mixture of pharmacy and medicine.

When pharmacy did become established as an occupation removed from medicine, around 1820, it did so in the setting of a commercial enterprise. This separation occurred at roughly the same time that the marketplace, once fairly open to women entrepreneurs, was becoming exclusively male.[7] Women disappeared from American pharmacy until the 1870s. More importantly, the apprenticeship system of the newly emerging occupation effectively blocked feminine involvement as practitioners of pharmacy.

AMERICAN PHARMACY EDUCATION BEFORE 1900

Until the present century pharmacists received the bulk of their training through apprenticeship. When retail pharmacies became common in urban areas during the first half of the nineteenth century, pharmacists not only compounded prescriptions but manufactured their own pharmaceutical ingredients: They purchased crude drugs in bulk (usually plant material), selected the medicinal parts of the plants, dried them, ground them (if necessary), and then stored them or used them to manufacture the basic preparations deemed official by the Pharmacopoeia or local practices. Grinding or triturating, sifting, macerating, pressing, filtering, and bottling required a bit of intelligence and a great deal of strength. Apothecaries gladly took on apprentices to do this back-breaking, difficult labor. Pharmacy was an art and a business, attempting to take on the image of a science, and recognized at most as a pseudo-profession. Formal education attracted few, except those attached to larger manufacturers or wholesalers (who were interested in

---

[6] [George Griffenhagen], "Who was the First Woman Pharmacist in America?" *Journal of the American Pharmaceutical Association*, NS 13 (1973): 637; and Alice Jean Matuszak, "History of Women in Pharmacy," *LKS Blue and Gold Triangle* (1986): 4–7.

[7] Gerda Lerner, "The Lady and the Mill Girl: Changes in the Status of Women in the Age of Jackson," *American Studies* 10 (Spring 1969): 8.

the newest techniques) or the very few tyros who aspired to working in the best, high-class establishments. Unlike medicine, school training did not supplant the apprenticeship system during the 1800s. The high value placed upon practical experience within the profession is shown by the fact that until 1868 all major pharmacy schools in the United States required four years of apprenticeship before conferring a diploma.

Pharmacy proprietors, of course, attempted to gain the respect afforded to professionals, but were considered tradesmen or artisans at best because of their general lack of education. Proud of their rigorous training, proprietors put their apprentices through long hours of work. A pharmacy's senior apprentice escaped the most strenuous tasks, but had the duty of sleeping at night in the back room, listening for his store's night bell. Even if a potential female apprentice could handle a fifty-pound carboy, a proprietor could not ask her to spend evenings away from home. Just as the average farmer of the mid-nineteenth century needed a large family to work his farm, so pharmacists needed strapping young apprentices.

Following the Civil War several changes occurred that made pharmacy both more attractive and more open to women. The manufacture of basic preparations, which had begun to shift over to large-scale manufacturers during the 1850s, was increasingly taken over by them following 1870. The most disgusting and time-consuming of the labors suffered by apprentices were now done in far-off factories and the "weaker sex" could now carry out most of the duties of a pharmacy apprentice. Still, apprenticeship in pharmacy was long and hard, a fact that probably discouraged many an aspiring "girl pharmacist."

From about 1875 to 1925 American pharmacy gradually adopted the values of the "new professionalism," i.e., restrictive educational requirements and paper credentials. To meet the demand for diplomas, established schools expanded enrollments and new schools appeared across the country. As competition among the schools increased, women (and their tuition) were welcomed. By attending certain schools like that of the University of Michigan (est. 1868), women could earn a diploma that could be used to get a job without first working through a long apprenticeship in a store.

The period of re-entry of women into American pharmacy during the 1870s, 1880s, and 1890s, has received almost all of the attention of historians working in this field. The two most widely cited articles on the history of women in American pharmacy deal with a specific aspect of this re-entry, women and pharmaceutical education: Glenn Sonne-- decker's "Women as Pharmacy Students in Nineteenth Century America,"[8] and Robert W. Culp's "The Education, Career Opportunities, and Status of American Women Pharmacists to 1900, Including a Directory."[9] Taken together, the two articles are only twenty-four pages long (with seven of those taken up by Culp's directory).

Both Sonnedecker and Culp came to their subjects in the early 1970s, as women began entering American pharmacy schools, and then the profession, in greater numbers. Sonnedecker paints a positive picture of American society opening up to women during the late nineteenth century, exemplified by women entering academic institutions. He contends that during the late nineteenth century, in contrast with medicine, "women began to be admitted to academic halls without public controversy among pharmacists or educators, although with occasional reluctance."

Restricted to the space allowed in a short presentation paper, Sonnedecker could do little more than describe the educational opportunities open to women in American pharmacy in the nineteenth century and offer some short comparisons to other health professions or pharmacy abroad. He ends his article with a two-sentence remark that deserves book-length analysis: "Of those [women] who ventured into practice, a majority, for several decades to come, would find their main opportunity in hospital pharmacy. Despite the newly opened doors of academia, there would be only slow growth in the number of women surmounting an encrusted tradition among laymen and pharmacists alike: That community pharmacy in America is a man's work."

Robert W. Culp looked at a similar sample—those American women who went to pharmacy school during the nineteenth century— from the broader point of view of a social historian. Culp makes reference to the role of women in domestic healing, especially during the Colonial period through the early republic, without exploring its importance. During that period there were, of course, a few famous women active in pharmacy, such as Jane Loring of Boston and Elizabeth Marshall of Philadelphia, but Culp cautions that it is "unwarranted to assume that American women made any serious inroads into the field of pharmacy during the early 1800s." He points to the 1870 census, which listed only 34 women among the 17,369 "traders and dealers in drugs and medicines."

---

[8] *Veröffentlichungen der Internationalen Gesellschaft für Geschichte der Pharmazie* 40 (1973): 135–41.
[9] *Transactions of the College of Physicians of Philadelphia* (1974): 211–27.

According to Culp, during the 1890s between two and four percent of American pharmacists were women. He gives two reasons for "such small numbers": societal resistance to women in the workplace generally and resistance to the entry of women from within pharmacy itself. With scant evidence, Culp argues that women were viewed by their potential male employers as too gossipy and lacking in the authoritativeness necessary in a position requiring the dispensing of advice as well as medicine.[10] Culp comes close to discussing the lack of a women's work culture within pharmacy, but he was apparently not familiar with the concept.

Culp closes his article with a valuable directory of American women pharmacists to 1900. He makes no claim for the completeness of this 243-member list, but it is the most comprehensive compiled. According to the author the directory was "derived from many sources, including several of the cited papers [sixteen in all], school catalogs, and news of the colleges published in the professional and trade journals of the period."

Unfortunately, Culp and Sonnedecker came to their mutual topic at the same time and thus neither could benefit from the other's work. They entered with different and obvious biases. As a social historian, Culp views pharmacy as one more misogynic profession. He contends that there was open hostility to women pharmacists during the period 1880 to 1920, in spite of the positive words of educators. As a historian interested in both American society and pharmacy, Sonnedecker possesses a more balanced viewpoint. He claims that pharmacy was more open to women than other American professions, but does allude to "an encrusted tradition among laymen and pharmacists" that retail pharmacy was reserved for men. Like other historical writers before and since, Sonnedecker and Culp do not even attempt to explore the reasons for this "tradition," which caused most women pharmacists to find their niche in hospital practice, laboratory work, or in homemaking.

The major problem with the articles by Culp and Sonnedecker is shared by almost all writers on the subject: they are narrowly focused on the issue of the entry of women into the profession via educational

---

[10] A brief examination of primary sources seems to corroborate Culp's assertions. For example, forty completed questionnaires sent out by Clara Abbott in 1898 to women pharmacists in Wisconsin testify to the fact that proprietors had little to no interest in hiring women pharmacists. They are housed in the Kremers Reference Files, F. B. Power Pharmaceutical Library, University of Wisconsin-Madison. There is no record of the publication of the survey's results.

institutions. No historian has yet to provide substantial analysis of the position of women in American pharmaceutical practice. While Sonnedecker specifically warns the reader that he is looking at students, Culp is not so straightforward. Both fail to emphasize that during the nineteenth century no state required formal education in pharmacy, and that the vast majority of practicing pharmacists, well into the twentieth century, did not have a pharmacy school diploma, but had passed a state examination with the help of cram schools or correspondence courses.[11]

SCHOOLS OF PHARMACY FOR WOMEN

In contrast to medicine, special professional schools for women were not part of the American pharmaceutical scene. Culp found references to an Olivia Institute for Women in Washington, D.C., which announced in 1895 that it would be teaching pharmacy, but no evidence that it ever opened its doors. The only school of this type that is known to have operated is the Louisville School of Pharmacy for Women (LSPW). Eunice Bonow Bardell, possessing a better understanding of pharmacy and the Louisville area than Culp, provides some valuable insights into this school's brief thirteen-year history.[12]

In her case study of the LSPW Bardell does mention that many Southern women following the Civil War were forced by circumstances—no husbands or male relatives to support them—to enter the job market, but she does not directly connect that post-1865 phenomenon with the increased interest of women in pharmacy beginning in the 1880s. In Louisville specifically, the rising number of women in pharmacy and the formation of the Louisville School of Pharmacy for Women can be attributed to one man, Joseph P. Barnum. During the early 1880s Barnum hired women to work in his pharmacy and he suggested that they attend the Louisville College of Pharmacy, but the College rebuffed them. Barnum responded by setting up the LSPW. With his pharmacy located in the building owned by the Polytechnic Society of Kentucky, an organization dedicated to the promotion of science, Barnum had a ready-made facility. With no apparent difficulty,

---

[11] Culp refers mistakenly to a "Pharmacy Law of 1885," implying it was national and required licensure. There has never been a national registry law for pharmacy in the United States. During the 1870s and 1880s, most states passed laws requiring registration.

[12] Eunice Bonow Bardell, "America's Only School of Pharmacy for Women," *Pharmacy in History* 26 (1984): 127-33.

Barnum enlisted the support of community leaders in 1883 and the school was incorporated by the Commonwealth of Kentucky on May 8, 1884. In accord with the Pharmacy Act of 1874, the graduates of this school would be granted licensure to practice pharmacy without examination.

Enrollment varied greatly at the school "from five students in 1883–1884 to twenty students in 1889–1890, with the exception of 1890–1891 when fifty-two students were reported." In 1887, one hundred fifty new pharmacists were elected as members of the Kentucky Pharmaceutical Association, including Barnum and nine female graduates of the LSPW. Despite the barriers put before them, women pharmacists in Kentucky had earned a measure of respect and recognition. Only a few years later, however, the LSPW lost its reason for being. By 1890 the Louisville College of Pharmacy opened its doors to women. The LSPW struggled on after 1892 when a fire at his store and the beginning of the 1890s depression put Barnum out of business.

Bardell's look at this unique institution in American pharmacy shows the value of local history or case studies that attempt to furnish context. Still, the motivations of those young women who entered pharmacy in the late nineteenth century are largely unexplored.

The short comparison between the status of women in pharmacy in the United States and in Canada contained in the article "Women in Ontario Pharmacy, 1886–1927"[13] by Ernst W. Stieb and others provides some answers to such questions. For example, they address the question of whether or not women came into pharmacy mainly through family businesses, concluding that they did. (Unfortunately, their data does not compare these women to men from the same time and place.) In addition, rural areas seemed more open to female pharmacists than did urban centers. This is attributed to the Victorian image of women, which was more prevalent in cities than in the countryside where men and women toiled side by side.

In their brief look at the American scene, Stieb, et al., emphasize one occurrence usually missed by other authors: that pharmacy schools in the United States openly invited women following the 1879 meeting of the American Conference of Pharmaceutical Faculties (the predecessor of today's American Association of Colleges of Pharmacy), which concluded that women should be welcomed to schools of pharmacy.

---

[13] *Pharmacy in History* 28 (1986): 125–34.

WOMEN AND THE PRACTICE
OF PHARMACY

To gain an understanding of the re-entry of women into American pharmacy in the late nineteenth century, the best source is still the contemporary and near-contemporary comments and chronicles of sister pharmacists.[14] The series of articles written about women and American pharmacy by Emma Gary Wallace, which appeared in twenty-two parts during 1912 in the journal *Pharmaceutical Era*, has been the starting point for almost every historical treatment to follow.[15] Usually authors have pulled a few facts out of Wallace's series without benefitting from her carefully worded, and sometimes profound insights. Later writers corrected a few of her small errors and have, no doubt, ignored her views as "quaint" and "Victorian." When prejudice is set aside, however, the voice of a woman pharmacist committed to the progress of her profession and her sex comes through strong and clear.

In classical fashion, Wallace begins her tale with the fall from grace in the Garden of Eden, through biblical stories and Greek mythology up to the "Oberlin College Movement," all in three pages. Her chronicle of women in American pharmacy starts with Dr. Susan Hayhurst, a graduate of the Woman's Medical College of Philadelphia in 1857 at the age of thirty-seven. In the chapters that follow, Wallace describes the varied achievements of American women pharmacists. Woman graduates of schools of pharmacy are listed chronologically in each geographic section of the nation.

Wallace's series is most valuable, aside from its accurate compilations of graduation lists and photographs of women, in its extended quotations from the letters of profiled women. For example, Miss H. Edna Byers of Los Angeles, California, is quoted for about 2500 words on her experiences and views on pharmacy.[16]

The success of the Wallace series inspired the editor of the *Era* to add a column on "Women in Pharmacy" to the regular features in the journal.[17] As a new departmental editor, Wallace brimmed with confi-

---

[14] For example, see Martha M. James, "That a Woman Makes as Good a Pharmacist as a Man Providing They Have Equal Advantages," *Proceedings*, Wisconsin Pharmaceutical Association 18 (1898): 32–37.

[15] Emma Gary Wallace, "Women in Pharmacy," *Pharmaceutical Era* 45 (1912): 17–20, 101–4, 181–84, 265–68, 328–32, 397–400, 462–64, 517–20, 578–81, 645–47, 701–3, 774–75.

[16] Ibid., pp. 397–99.

[17] Emma Gary Wallace, "Women in Pharmacy," *Pharmaceutical Era* 46 (1913): 21–22.

dence, and her column continued to document the efforts of women to make their place in pharmacy for the next dozen years.

Features on women in pharmacy appeared throughout the pharmaceutical trade press from about 1900 to 1930, those in the *Pharmaceutical Era* and the *Druggists Circular* being most noteworthy. Yet, aside from the series by Wallace, few articles touched on historical issues other than an occasional local history piece about "the first woman pharmacist" in a certain state or city. For example, of the four hundred-odd papers published by the American Pharmaceutical Association from its historical section for the period 1904 to 1967, only one dealt with a woman or women in pharmacy.[18]

This dearth of material is not surprising considering that during most of that period the number of women pharmacists remained relatively stable at 5–10% of the total. Lack of opportunity in retail pharmacy, where over 90% of pharmacists practiced until World War II, dissuaded women from entering pharmacy. In addition, laws restricting work hours for women discouraged owners from hiring women.[19] The vast majority of the fully independent female pharmacy practitioners, i.e., not belonging to an order or working in a family business, were in institutional practice, which had low status within the profession until the 1960s. Only the concurrent increase in prominence of institutional practice, the emergence of clinical pharmacy as a separate subdiscipline, and the rise in the number of women practitioners, made the position of women in the profession anything more than an academic curiosity. Since the rise of an independent occupation of pharmacy in the United States, the position of women within the profession has only been a serious issue for discussion during the period of re-entry (c. 1880–1915), during times of economic hardship, and since the recent influx (c. 1970 to the present); otherwise women pharmacists have been invisible, usually stuck away in hospital basements, institutional laboratories, or family drug stores.

The rise in the number of women and their increased commitment to the profession, starting around 1970, elicited a flurry of articles on "Women in Pharmacy." Aside from Culp and Sonnedecker, which appeared in journals outside the professional mainstream, or brief chro-

---

[18] J. H. Hoch and Q. Hoch, "Mrs. Masters and Her Tuscarora Rice," pp. 577–78, 580.
[19] Nellie A. Wakeman, "Women in Pharmacy," *American Journal of Pharmaceutical Education* 1 (1937): 146–50.

nologies,[20] almost all were ahistorical. An important exception is "Women in Hospital Pharmacy—A Study in Eight States," by Jo Ellen Austin and Mickey C. Smith.[21] Their literature review included brief synopses of previous models of women and work as put forward by J. B. Stern (1959), Caplow (1954), and Kykman and Stalnaker's report on women in medicine. Some of the straight statistical work, like that of Kenneth Kirk and Richard Ohvall,[22] provides extremely valuable data necessary to chart changes within the community of women within pharmacy, but with virtually no historical context.

An important step toward the creation of a framework for discussion of the role of women in American pharmacy occurred in 1977 when the American Pharmaceutical Association (APhA) invited sociologist Carol Kronus to write an article for its *Journal*. Kronus begins her germinal article by correcting a few widely held misconceptions about the contemporary history of women and work. The post-World War II rise in female employment, rather than being "meteoric," has been "slow and steady"; and most women who work are married, not single or widowed. As she puts it succinctly, the "real phenomenon we are experiencing is the widespread realization that the employed woman is the norm, not the abnormal."[23] Society is starting to adjust, finally, "to the cumulative impact of the working woman."

Of course, women have been coming into the work force, largely in positions determined by sexual occupational segregation: lawyers, doctors, and day laborers are generally men, while nurses, secretaries, and librarians are typically women. Despite accounts in the popular press of women judges or dragster drivers, sexual segregation in the workplace has changed little during the first two-thirds of the twentieth century. Kronus points to a series of studies showing the lack of change, especially in the professions.

---

[20] For example, William P. O'Brien, "Women In Pharmacy," *Louisiana Pharmacist* (January 1970): 12–13; and George B. Griffenhagen, "Woman Power," *Journal of the American Pharmaceutical Association*, NS 13 (1973): 609.

[21] *American Journal of Hospital Pharmacy* 28 (1971): 26–36.

[22] "Women in Pharmacy: Gratification or Discrimination," *Journal of the American Pharmaceutical Association*, NS 13 (1973): 610–13, 630; "Practice Patterns of Women Pharmacists," *Journal of the American Pharmaceutical Association*, NS 13 (1973): 614–17; and "Sex Differences in Pharmacy Student Career Planning and Aspirations," *American Journal of Pharmaceutical Education* 39 (February 1975): 37–40.

[23] Carol L. Kronus, "Women in Pharmacy: Trends, Implications, and Research Needs," *Journal of the American Pharmaceutical Association*, NS 17 (1977): 674.

After examining data on female pharmacy practitioners, Kronus came up with three trends: "First, in contrast to the slow increase in the general labor force, the proportion of women entering pharmacy is expanding at a rapid rate." In the health-care field, pharmacy is desegregating most rapidly. Second, rank segregation by sex is and has been common in pharmacy, with men in ownership or managerial positions and women rarely achieving such status. Third, women and men are divided into different types of pharmacy practice, with women overrepresented in institutional (hospital or clinic) practice. Kronus expressed the concern that women may overcrowd hospital pharmacy and thereby attract greater discrimination. The data did not allow her to answer a series of questions suggested by this last trend, i.e., are women attracted by the organizational factors of flexible hours, work environment, and opportunities for advancement in institutions? Do women prefer to avoid business dealings common in community practice? What about chain pharmacies is especially unattractive to women pharmacists?

After noting these trends, Kronus looked at the various sociological models used to study pharmacy, labelled by R. M. Kanter as "temperamental," "role-related," and "social-structural." She compared these approaches and their success in specific studies, and then concluded with a page of suggested research topics, several of which could benefit from historical analysis.

Soon after the Kronus article appeared, the APhA established the Task Force on Women in Pharmacy. Far from a whitewash, the *Final Report of the Task Force* aggressively dealt with the barriers and opportunities for women in the profession. Concerned with the future, the Task Force did not look beyond the beginning of the current feminization trend, which started in the 1970s. Even so, the report does document the place of women in American pharmacy as of 1980, which will benefit future historians.[24] Moreover, an annotated bibliography of eighty-four articles on women in pharmacy was also published as part of the Task Force project.[25] The lack of interest in historical questions is evident by the absence of a listing for history in the booklet's index.

---

[24] APhA Task Force, *Women in Pharmacy: Final Report* (Washington, DC: American Pharmaceutical Association, 1981).

[25] Alan P. Wolfgang and Kenneth W. Kirk, *Abstracts of Articles Written about Women in Pharmacy* (Washington, DC: American Pharmaceutical Association, 1982).

RECENT ADDITIONS TO THE LITERATURE

A recent issue of the journal of the American Pharmaceutical Association (now called *American Pharmacy*) had three short articles dealing with women and pharmacy.[26] Taken together, the first pair of articles demonstrate a renewed interest in exploring the historical roots of current trends; the last article shows that a decade after Kronus some of the difficult and controversial issues are now being confronted.

Shepherd and Proctor address an untouched and perhaps feared issue: women and pharmacy ownership. Unfortunately, the article is totally current without any retrospective data, and fails to discuss why women pharmacists *avoid* becoming owners. The findings of Shepherd and Proctor agree with the social-structural model of Kronus that negative expectations among potential women owners of pharmacies contribute significantly to today's low numbers. They conclude that for the "continued progress of pharmacy practice, it is crucial that women decide to become pharmacy owners. Pharmacy practice has its roots deeply embedded in pharmacy ownership, and the pharmacy entrepreneurial spirit should not be stifled because of the increased proportion of women pharmacists." Thus Shepherd and Proctor agree with Sonnedecker that only when women have achieved a secure position in community practice, the core of American pharmacy, can they be said to have reached an equal footing with men.

An important step to understanding the historical underpinnings of the role of women in American pharmacy has been taken in the tradition of Emma Gary Wallace. A labor of love, *Compounding WAS More Fun*, edited by Frances F. Curran, provides a resource for those interested in obtaining anecdotal evidence concerning women *practicing* pharmacy in the United States during the middle third of this century.[27] On behalf of the pharmacy fraternity for women, Lambda Kappa Sigma, Curran sent a circular letter to about 250 LKS members who had joined the organization before 1938. Seventy-two members responded with autobiographical sketches of one to five pages, mainly answering specific questions

---

26 "Women Pharmacy Faculty . . . ," pp. 18–22 and "Women in Pharmacy Education: The Pioneers," pp. 24–27 by Metta Lou Henderson and Tammy Lyn Keeney; and "Women and Pharmacy Ownership," by Marvin D. Shepherd and Kurt Proctor, *American Pharmacy*, NS 28 (May 1988).

27 Frances F. Curran, ed., *Compounding WAS More Fun!!! Life Experiences of Women of Lambda Kappa Sigma, the International Pharmacy Fraternity 1913–1938–1988* (Philadelphia: F. Curran and Lambda Kappa Sigma, 1988).

posed by Currran, such as why did you study pharmacy? where did you work? and so on. And although Curran asked, "What was the attitude of the public, physicians, or your fellow pharmacists toward a woman pharmacist and how did you handle it?" several ignored that difficult question. Perhaps the memories were too painful.

Although this is not a scientifically selected sample, the women do come from most parts of the nation and from different economic backgrounds. The career histories of the women follow the usual pattern of female professionals: they entered pharmacy during the 1930s because the work fascinated them, school was hard but enjoyable, getting employment was not difficult, and career was set aside to marry and raise a family. The expected pattern, however, breaks down because about half of the women returned to work (usually part time) after the nest was empty. They returned because although the demand for full-time employment has varied greatly in this century, there has always been a need for part-time work, especially for women, who could be paid less than men.

In addition to the seventy-two autobiographical sketches there are ten sketches on important women in LKS from information obtained from the fraternity files. These include some leading figures in American pharmacy, such as B. Olive Cole (1883–1971), the pioneer pharmacist-educator. The book concludes with two previously unpublished theses written by women who graduated from the Philadelphia College of Pharmacy in 1890. The second, by Carrie Emily Howard, addresses the issue of women and pharmacy, which is the subject of the essay.

Curran's book does not provide any analysis of these autobiographic sketches, but it does furnish an example of the valuable primary sources yet untapped by historians. Whether the results of surveys by Clara Abbott in 1898 or by Frances Curran 90 years later, the materials exist for serious historical work. The trade periodicals, beginning with the *Druggists Circular* in 1857, up through the 1950s, offer a frank and often chatty view of practice (and a woman's place in it).[28] And since 1960, reliable data has been collected by professional and educational groups that supplements the surveys mentioned above.

CONCLUSION

When I first wrote this review essay I was struck by the deficiencies in the historical literature. Aside from chronicles of the "first woman

---

[28] For example, "Walgreen Not in Favor of Women in Pharmacy," *Pharmaceutical Era* 61 (1925): 498.

pharmacist" in some state, locality, or institution, the literature rested on a handful of serious articles. Almost all of these concentrated on women and pharmaceutical education, perhaps a result of the academic connections of the authors and the availability of source material. Aside from saying that there was a moderate amount of resistance to women pharmacists during the late nineteenth century and early twentieth century among male practitioners and the public, analysis was almost totally lacking.

Since that first draft went to the editor, two excellent articles on women in pharmacy have appeared that surpass all previous pieces as far as scope. The first, published in the Autumn/Winter 1988 issue of *Caduceus* by Patricia Spain Ward, furnishes an overview to women in pharmacy previously unavailable; the second, by Teresa Gallagher and published in issue '2, 1989, of *Pharmacy in History*, provides serious analysis of the entry of women into American pharmacy in the period from 1870 to 1940. This scholarship is new and has not yet received thorough scrutiny by historians of the field.

As a starting point, Patricia Spain Ward's "Hygeia's Sisters: A History of Women in Pharmacy"[29] is superior to any other article in the literature. Utilizing most of the secondary sources mentioned in this chapter, plus significant primary research, Ward succeeds in placing the history of women pharmacists within the broader context of American health care. Despite the title, however, the article deals almost exclusively with American developments with an occasional reference to foreign events. In interpretation Ward does not differ greatly from previous authors and like Sonnedecker and Culp is most concerned with educational issues. What sets this work apart from that done previously is that Ward has the space and expertise to flesh out the subject matter and breathe life into it.

Although she begins in prehistoric times, Ward devotes much of her readable narrative to the period of struggle from 1870 to 1940. As a medical historian, she focuses on the differences between the entry of women into pharmacy and into medicine. By exploring these contrasts she makes her major original contribution to this subject. In addition to contrasting women physicians and pharmacists, Ward looks at those women in the late nineteenth century who received degrees in both disciplines and offers a few speculations as to why some women took this double path.

---

[29] *Caduceus* 4 (1988): 1-55.

A central figure in Ward's description of the period from 1870 to 1940 is Nellie Wakeman, a faculty member at the University of Wisconsin School of Pharmacy from 1913 to 1948. Wakeman was active in educational affairs dealing with women in pharmacy and her own career exemplified the struggle of women in academe.

As has been the case in the literature, Ward treats the last fifty or so years very lightly. But she does provide the basic facts showing the slow acceptance of women into the profession and the surprising increase that has occurred during the last generation.

All in all, "Hygeia's Sisters" is an excellent introduction to the subject. Unfortunately, the author concludes with hortatory prose that detracts from the essay's credibility.

Teresa Gallagher's "From Family Helpmeet to Independent Professional: Women in American Pharmacy, 1870–1940"[30] uses a different historical methodology with a degree of analysis absent since Kronus. Her perspective is that of the social scientist, with models, structures, and theory-driven arguments. Ward succeeded in placing pharmaceutical women in the larger context of health-care development; Gallagher puts the pursuit of women to achieve occupational status firmly within the context of the history of American professions.

In contrast to Ward's interest in women pharmacists as part of American health care, Gallagher's focus is pharmacy itself and its place in professional and commercial spheres between 1870 and 1940. This period was critical for the development of modern professionalism, prompting the central question Gallagher addresses: "What was the impact of professionalization on women's participation in the late nineteenth and early twentieth centuries?"[31] To answer the question, Gallagher analyzed data from enrollment lists and census records. In addition, using issues of the *Druggists Circular*, she extracted general opinions regarding women in pharmacy and compared those to professional and educational viewpoints expressed in the *Journal of the American Pharmaceutical Association* and the *American Journal of Pharmaceutical Education*.

Her conclusions are best summarized in this paragraph from the introduction to her article:

> In the late nineteenth and early twentieth centuries, professionalization processes enhanced women's access to pharmacy, and in contrast to

---

[30] *Pharmacy in History* 31 (1989): 60–77.
[31] Ibid., p. 60.

other male professions no formal barriers were erected against women's entry into the profession. One of the most important reasons for the relative openness of pharmacy to women was that it lagged behind other male professions in its development as a profession, and retained many characteristics of the trade model until well into the twentieth century. As pharmacy moved closer to the professional model in the 1920s and the 1930s, professionalization processes began to affect women in pharmacy as they had in other male professions around the turn of the century. Although by the early twentieth century women attained a position of relative equality in pharmacy education, informal discrimination against them in retail pharmacy prevented similar gains in employment, and the proportion of women in pharmacy remained at less than 10 percent.[32]

Beyond reaching these conclusions, Gallagher proposes important models for understanding the role of women in pharmacy between 1870 and 1940. For example, during the late nineteenth century, most women pharmacists came out of "family pharmacy," i.e., they were the wives or daughters of drug store owners. These women had learned their *trade* under the watchful eye of husbands and fathers. After 1900 a "new woman pharmacist" emerged, one who identified with the *profession* of pharmacy and the values of the new, modern professionalism. In contrast to the previous generation, new women pharmacists were college-educated and competed directly with men for jobs.

Gallagher's article is not without fault. For instance, it would have benefited from more attention paid to the growth of hospital pharmacy practice and the role of religious orders. Moreover, its cool, analytical style makes it more difficult to read than Ward's humanistic narrative.

In combination, the new articles by Ward and Gallagher take a large second step (the first being by Sonnedecker, Culp, and Kronus) toward a comprehensive understanding of women in American pharmacy. Because they cover each other's inadequacies so well, I recommend that they be read in tandem, preferably Ward first, followed by Gallagher.

When I first wrote this conclusion I was quite disappointed at the state of the literature on the history of women in American pharmacy. Ward and Gallagher have helped the situation greatly, but deficiencies remain. Like their predecessors, Ward and Gallagher concentrate largely on women in pharmacy education. We need more study of the nature of

---

[32] Ibid.

the *practice* of women pharmacists and whether it differed from the practice of men.

No doubt this will be done. American pharmacy is now in the midst of changing from a male-dominated to a female-dominated profession. This dramatic change and its causes should inspire some excellent studies in the near future.

SOME SPECULATIONS

When a comprehensive, book-length study of women in American pharmacy is completed, what might it reveal? After looking over the literature, a few speculations come to mind: First, a full-blown analytical history of women in pharmacy may be able to link the critical influx of women into American pharmacy with the changing paradigms of practice during the past 150 years. From its Colonial origins, through its emergence as an independent occupation, up through Reconstruction, pharmacy was an art, a "profession" of a special skill—how to make medicines out of crude drugs. A shift occurred following the Civil War when American pharmacy entered a period of about one hundred years, where applied chemistry and industrial technology prevailed. Professionalism changed from a base of art to one of science. The wise old "doc" was replaced by the "chemist on the corner." When academic training became available, women came into pharmacy in small numbers from the 1880s to the 1950s. Their entry coincided with the paradigmatic shift. The third change in pharmacy came in the mid-1960s, when the old product-orientation of professional practice was replaced by concern about the "patient." (The patrons of stores, who had been viewed as "customers" for 150 years, became "patients" almost overnight.) When this new approach to pharmacy practice, usually called "clinical pharmacy," gained general acceptance among educators in the early 1970s, female enrollment began its steep climb.

Second, in-depth historical treatment must examine a hidden aspect of women and American pharmacy that has received no attention from historians: the thousands (millions?) of prescriptions filled furtively by the untrained wives, daughters, and other female employees of male pharmacists. Many of the early women pharmacists came to be registered because of a family introduction to the occupation. Yet, an equal or perhaps greater number of women who compounded prescriptions in the late nineteenth century and early twentieth century did not. Mom and Pop drugstores were just that, with the wife often running the front of the store, including the ubiquitous lunch counter, and the husband filling prescriptions, talking to customers and doctors, in the back of the store. During especially busy times or when the husband was ill, the wife filled in as pharmacist. Until the 1940s, prescription departments were hidden away from public eye. Anyone, including wives and stock boys, could and did fill prescriptions without customer observation. As an occupation that only adopted academic professionalism in the 1930s, American pharmacy until the postwar era quietly tolerated wifely dispensers "trained" under the watchful eyes of a pharmacist-husband who had himself learned "the trade" as an apprentice.

Third, any sweeping history of women in American pharmacy will need to concentrate on the growth of hospital practice, an area of pharmacy almost ignored by historians.[33] For the first two centuries of hospital pharmacy, since Jonathan Edwards was appointed apothecary of the Philadelphia Hospital in 1755, up to 1942, when the American Society of Hospital Pharmacists was founded, hospital practice had low status within the profession. Most men studied or were trained in pharmacy in order to become proprietors (apothecaries or pharmacists), *not* to be employed practitioners (clerks). These men were attracted by the status given the pharmacy owner as businessman and professional man. There were no owners in hospitals, and once there a pharmacist was doomed to be a clerk forever. Moreover, hospitals paid poorly, usually less than any man would take; women, on the other hand, met resistance in the world of commerce and tolerated the poor wages. Thus, hospitals hired women, to whom they could pay less, and women pharmacists found a place to practice with far less prejudice.[34]

Beginning in the 1920s the situation began to change. As the pharmaceutical industry took over more and more of the production of end-dosage forms, the art and science of pharmacy practice declined in the retail setting, while hospital pharmacy remained a bastion of high pharmaceutical technology, art, and science. The seeds of a proud community were planted, which, after the difficult times of the Depression and World War, sprouted quickly in the postwar boom. An in-depth study

[33] The best source on hospital pharmacy remains a special issue of *Drug Intelligence and Clinical Pharmacy* 6 (1972): 425–56, which contains articles by Glenn Sonnedecker, Joseph Oddis, Alex Berman, and Donald Francke.
[34] "Women Graduates of the Philadelphia College of Pharmacy and Science," [unpublished compilation in College archives], August 12, 1942. Of thirty-eight surveyed, four were housewives, six worked for industry, fourteen worked in hospitals, and fourteen worked in retail pharmacies (five of which were family stores).

may well be able to correlate the ascendant status of hospital pharmacy and the rising enrollments of women as pharmacy students after 1965.

When a comprehensive, book-length history of women in American pharmacy is written that addresses issues such as these, it will no doubt make a significant and unique contribution to our general understanding of the profession of pharmacy.

BIBLIOGRAPHY

• • • ——— • • •

EDWARD T. MORMAN
WITH JILL GATES SMITH AND MARGARET JERRIDO

BIBLIOGRAPHY BY TOPIC

BIBLIOGRAPHY

◆ ◆ ◆ ──────── ◆ ◆ ◆

This bibliography complements the essays in this volume. The essays analyze contemporary scholarship on the history of American women in relation to health and medicine; the bibliography is a classified listing of some of the more important and pertinent recent works, along with certain classics in the field.

This bibliography is intended to direct readers to easily accessible books and journal articles. Dissertations are not listed, nor, in general, are biographies or works of narrow regional interest. Readers are encouraged to closely examine the references cited by the contributors to this volume, many of which are not included in this bibliography.

Historical scholarship on women and health is a new field, with vast opportunities for further work. The history of black women as physicians and nurses has only recently gained attention, while almost no work has yet been done on other women of color. In general there is room for much work on women in medicine which accounts for class, ethnicity, linguistic and cultural differences, and sexuality.

This bibliography reflects the current state of work in the field. Where it is weak, it should inspire the reader to start her or his own research project.

GENERAL SOURCES IN WOMEN'S STUDIES

I. Four key general reference sources.

Ballou, Patricia K. *Women: A Bibliography of Bibliographies*, 2d ed. Boston: G. K. Hall, 1986.

Lists several hundred books, pamphlets, journal articles, dissertations, etc., which contain substantial bibliographies. An excellent tool for identifying sources.

Women Studies Abstracts. New York: Rush, 1972–

This has become the basic periodic index in the field of women's studies in the U.S. It covers books and pamphlets as well as journal articles and book reviews. Published quarterly with an annual index.

Harrison, Cynthia E. *Women in American History: A Bibliography*. 2 vols.
Santa Barbara: ABC Clio, 1979–85.
   The vast majority of citations in these two volumes were drawn
from *America: History and Life* (see next section), but their subject
organization makes them useful for work restricted to women. Covers
the periodical literature almost exclusively, with some citations from
volumes of collected essays.

Notable American Women, 1607–1950: A Biographical Dictionary. 3 vols.
Cambridge: Belknap Press, 1971.

Notable American Women, the Modern Period: A Biographical Dictionary.
Cambridge: Belknap Press, 1980.
   Together, the four volumes of *Notable American Women* provide the
best access to quick biographical information about women who had
been omitted from American history before the resurgence of feminist
scholarship in the 1960s and 1970s. An important feature is an index by
field of endeavor. This is a good place to start identifying individual
women of importance in health care.

II. Access to information on women in science.
Herzenberg, Caroline L. *Women Scientists from Antiquity to the Present: An
Index*. West Cornwall, CT: Locust Hill Press, 1986.
   Indexes over one hundred books and articles which include infor-
mation on women scientists, physicians, and nurses.

Ogilvie, Marilyn Bailey. *Women in Science, Antiquity through the Nineteenth Century: A Biographical Dictionary with Annotated Bibliography*.
Cambridge: MIT Press, 1986.
   Useful both for its short articles on several hundred women scientists and for its excellent bibliography.

Searing, Susan E. *The History of Women and Science, Health, and Technology: a Bibliographic Guide to the Professions and the Disciplines*. Madison:
University of Wisconsin System Women's Studies Librarian, 1988.

Siegel, Patricia Joan, and Kay Thomas Finley. *Women in the Scientific
Search: an American Bio-Bibliography, 1724–1979*. Metuchen, NJ: Scare-
crow Press, 1985.
   A very useful source for people interested in women and health in
America. Each entry includes a critical assessment of further sources of
biographical information.

III. Other reference sources of narrower scope.

Conway, Jill K. *The Female Experience in Eighteenth- and Nineteenth-Century America: A Guide to the History of American Women.* New York: Garland, 1982.

Fishburn, Katherine. *Women in Popular Culture: A Reference Guide.* Westport, CT: Greenwood, 1982.

Hildenbrand, Suzanne, ed. *Women's Collection: Libraries, Archives and Consciousness.* New York: Haworth, 1986.

Loeb, Catherine R., Susan E. Searing, and Esther F. Stineman. *Women's Studies: A Recommended Core Bibliography, 1980–85.* Littleton, CO: Libraries Unlimited, 1987.

Sapiro, Virgina. *Women in American Society: An Introduction to Women's Studies.* Palo Alto, CA: Mayfield, 1986.

Stineman, Esther F., with the assistance of Catherine Loeb. *Women's Studies: A Recommended Core Bibliography.* Littleton, CO: Libraries Unlimited, 1979.

GENERAL WORKS ON WOMEN, HEALTH, AND MEDICINE

Fee, Elizabeth, ed. *Women and Health: The Politics of Sex in Medicine.* Farmingdale, NY: Baywood, 1982.

Leavitt, Judith Walzer, ed. *Women and Health in America: Historical Readings.* Madison: University of Wisconsin Press, 1984.
   This anthology gathers the best articles on women and health available through 1983. Many of the items cited in this bibliography originally appeared or are reprinted in the Leavitt reader. A major contribution to the development of the field.

Lewin, Ellen, and Virginia Oleson, eds. *Women, Health and Healing: Toward a New Perspective.* New York: Tavistock, 1985.

Marieskind, Helen I. *Women in the Health System: Patients, Providers, and Programs.* St. Louis: Mosby, 1980.

Rosser, Sue V., ed. *Feminism within the Science and Health Care Professions: Overcoming Resistance.* New York: Pergamon Press, 1988.

Rosser, Sue V. *Teaching Science and Health from a Feminist Perspective.* New York: Pergamon, 1986.

Ruzek, Sheryl B., Patricia Anderson, Adele Clark, Virginia Oleson, and Kristin Hill, eds. *Minority Women, Health and Healing in the U.S.: Selected Bibliography and Resources.* San Francisco: University of California Women, Health and Healing Program, 1986.

Sage: A Scholarly Journal on Black Women 2, no. 4 (Fall 1985).
    A special issue with 18 articles on Black women and health. Historical contributions include three essays on Black women doctors, a discussion of medical experimentation on slave women, and an analysis of the patient record of Olivia Davidson Washington (wife of Booker T. Washington) as she was dying.

Smith-Rosenberg, Carroll. *Disorderly Conduct: Visions of Gender in Victorian America.* New York: Knopf, 1985.
    Smith-Rosenberg has made a significant contribution to the agenda of women's history in the U.S. This book of collected essays includes her early articles on the biomedical construction of the nature of women, as well as her later, more groundbreaking work on sexuality and independent women's culture in nineteenth-century America.

Verbrugge, Martha. *Able-Bodied Womanhood: Personal Health and Social Change in Nineteenth-Century Boston.* New York: Oxford University Press, 1988.
    A contribution to our understanding of woman's self-conception in the nineteenth century. This book deals with the rise of popular physiology among women, the medical image of women, and the development of women's sports and physical culture.

Western Journal of Medicine 149, no. 6 (December 1988).
    This special issue on "Women and Medicine" includes 35 contributions dealing with five themes: (1) "controversial or neglected women's medical problems," (2) "the interactions of women, society and health care," (3) "women in medicine," (4) "epitomes about common, vexing, recurrent diagnostic and treatment dilemmas," and (5) "'testimonials' from women physicians who have managed their complicated lives successfully." Several of the articles include historical discussions.

Woloch, Nancy. *Women and the American Experience.* New York: Knopf, 1984.

Worcester, Nancy, and Mariamne H. Whatley, eds. *Women's Health: Readings on Social, Economic, and Political Issues.* Dubuque, IA: Kendall/Hunt Pub. Co., 1988.

GENERAL SOURCES IN HISTORY
OF AMERICAN MEDICINE

I. Three very important periodical indexes.

America: History and Life: A Guide to Periodical Literature. Santa Barbara, CA: Clio Press, 1964– .

Published since 1964, with some retrospective indexing, this is probably the most easily usable single tool for access to journal articles on American history and American studies in general. Using this with the *Bibliography of the History of Medicine* (see below) the researcher can be reasonably certain of identifying the vast majority of significant recent articles on the history of American medicine. Since it also indexes book reviews, it is a good source for books as well. *America: History and Life* is also available as an online database, accessible by most academic libraries.

Bibliography of the History of Medicine. Bethesda: National Library of Medicine, 1965– .

Published annually, its five-year cumulations make this a convenient source in spite of its cumbersome indexing. The National Library of Medicine (NLM) makes this available in machine-readable form as HISTLINE. Inquire at any medical library about access to the NLM computerized bibliographic system.

Current Work in the History of Medicine: an International Bibliography. London: Wellcome Historical Medical Library, 1954– .

The Wellcome is one of the largest libraries in the world devoted to history of medicine. Although in London, it provides excellent coverage for history of American medicine. *Current Work* is an extremely handy quarterly index, but it is best used for recent literature only, since it is not cumulated nor is there a corresponding online database.

II. Two major biographical sources.

Kaufman, Martin, Stuart Galishoff, and Todd L. Savitt, eds. *Dictionary of American Medical Biography.* 2 vols. Westport, CT: Greenwood Press, 1983.

This is a long-overdue, handy source, which complements the traditional Kelly and Burrage. The editors made a deliberate effort to identify people outside the medical mainstream, including women, members of minority groups, and irregular practitioners.

Kelly, Howard A., and Walter L. Burrage. *Dictionary of American Medical Biography; Lives of Eminent Physicians of the United States and Canada, from the Earliest Times.* New York: Appleton, 1928.

Until recently, this was the best general source of biographical information on American physicians. Although it is oriented to the traditional (i.e., white and male) profession, there are some entries for women missing from Kaufman, Galishoff, and Savitt (see above).

III. Some important recent general studies and collections of essays, which either emphasize women or which contain sections of particular relevance to women.

Beardsley, Edward H. *A History of Neglect: Health Care for Blacks and Mill Workers in the Twentieth-Century South.* Knoxville: University of Tennessee Press, 1987.

Fellman, Anita C., and Michael Fellman. *Making Sense of Self: Medical Advice Literature in Late Nineteenth-Century America.* Philadelphia: University of Pennsylvania Press, 1981.

Green, Harvey. *Fit for America: Health, Fitness, Sport and American Society.* New York: Pantheon Books, 1986.
    Green devotes ample attention to women in relationship to sport, exercise, and medical advice.

Grob, Gerald. *Mental Illness and American Society, 1875–1940.* Princeton: Princeton University Press, 1983.

Haber, Carole. *Beyond Sixty-Five: The Dilemma of Old Age in America's Past.* New York: Cambridge University Press, 1983.

Leavitt, Judith Walzer, and Ronald Numbers, eds. *Sickness and Health in America: Readings in the History of Medicine and Public Health,* 2d ed. Madison: University of Wisconsin Press, 1985.

Nissenbaum, Stephen. *Sex, Diet, and Debility in Jacksonian America: Sylvester Graham and Health Reform.* Westport, CT: Greenwood, 1980.

Pernick, Martin S. *A Calculus of Suffering: Pain, Professionalism, and Anesthesia in Nineteenth-Century America.* New York: Columbia University Press, 1985.

Reverby, Susan, and David Rosner. *Health Care in America: Essays in Social History.* Philadelphia: Temple University Press, 1979.

Rosenberg, Charles. *The Care of Strangers: The Rise of America's Hospital System.* New York: Basic Books, 1987.

Rosner, David and Gerald Markowitz, eds. *Dying for Work: Workers' Safety and Health in Twentieth Century America*. Bloomington: Indiana University Press, 1987.

Starr, Paul. *The Social Transformation of American Medicine*. New York: Basic Books, 1982.

Stevens, Rosemary. *In Sickness and in Wealth: American Hospitals in the Twentieth Century*. New York: Basic Books, 1989.

Warner, John Harley. *The Therapeutic Perspective: Medical Practice, Knowledge, and Identity in America, 1820–1885*. Cambridge: Harvard University Press, 1986.

Whorton, James C. *Crusaders for Fitness: The History of American Health Reformers*. Princeton: Princeton University Press, 1982.

WOMEN AS HEALTH-CARE PRACTITIONERS: REFERENCE SOURCES

Boquist, Constance, and Jeannette V. Haase. *An Historical Review of Women in Dentistry: an Annotated Bibliography*. Washington: U.S. Public Health Service Office of Health Resources Opportunity, 1977.

Brumberg, Joan Jacobs, and Nancy Tomes. "Women in the Professions: A Research Agenda for American Historians." *Reviews in American History* 10 (1982): 275–96.
 Places women physicians in the context of the more general problem of women's entry into the professions. In setting a research agenda, this article identifies key books and articles published in the 1970s.

Bullough, Vern L., Olga Maranjian Church, and Alice P. Stein. *American Nursing: a Biographical Dictionary*. New York: Garland, 1988.
Kaufman, Martin, Joellen Watson Hawkins, Loretta P. Higgins, and Alice Howell Friedman. *Dictionary of American Nursing Biography*. New York: Greenwood Press, 1988.
 These two biographical dictionaries, published within a few weeks of each other, are quite comparable in their coverage and quality. Bullough's work fits into his general work in nursing history, while Kaufman's serves as a supplement to his *Dictionary of American Medical Biography* (see above). Used together, they can guarantee access to information about any significant American nurse who has been the object of historical work.

Bullough, Bonnie, Vern L. Bullough, and Barrett Elcano. *Nursing, a Historical Bibliography*. New York: Garland, 1981.

A comprehensive bibliography, an excellent place to start work on nursing history.

Bullough, Bonnie, Vern L. Bullough, Jane Garvey, and Karen Miller Allen, assisted by Mary Boldt and Janice Fulton. *Issues in Nursing: An Annotated Bibliography*. New York: Garland, 1986.

Another comprehensive bibliography, covering topics including nursing ethics, nursing education, health-care delivery, and nursing specialties. Among the issues included is the feminist critique of nursing.

Chaff, Sandra L., Ruth Haimbach, Carol Fenichel and Nina B. Woodside. *Women in Medicine: A Bibliography of the Literature on Women Physicians*. Metuchen, NJ: Scarecrow, 1977.

Although a bit outdated, this still stands as the major bibliographic contribution to the field of women and medicine. Thousands of articles and books are included in chapters arranged by subject.

Nursing Studies Index, 1900–1960. New York: Garland, 1984. 4 vols.

Compiled at the Yale University School of Nursing and originally published in the early sixties; the current surge of interest in nursing history justified republication in 1984. This is probably the best single source of citations to the literature of nursing in the first half of this century.

WOMEN AS HEALTH-CARE PRACTITIONERS: PHYSICIANS

I. Books on women physicians in America.

Abram, Ruth J., ed. *Send Us a Lady Physician: Women Doctors in America, 1835–1920*. New York: Norton, 1985.

Dickstein, Leah J., and Carol C. Nadelson, eds. *Women Physicians in Leadership Roles*. Washington: American Psychiatric Press, 1986.

A mixed anthology, including several historical articles on women physicians in the United States.

Drachman, Virginia G. *Hospital with a Heart: Women Doctors and the Paradox of Separation at the New England Hospital, 1862–1969*. Ithaca: Cornell University Press, 1984.

Glazer, Pnina M., and Miriam Slater. *Unequal Colleagues: The Entrance of Women in the Professions, 1890–1940*. New Brunswick: Rutgers University Press, 1987.

Levin, Beatrice S. *Women and Medicine*. Metuchen, NJ: Scarecrow, 1980.
Brief biographies of women physicians stressing their motivations and their interest in women's health care.

Lightfoot, Sara Lawrence. *Balm in Gilead: Journey of a Healer*. Reading, MA: Addison-Wesley, 1988.
Lightfoot's biography of her mother, Margaret Morgan Lawrence, one of the first Black woman psychiatrists.

Lorber, Judith. *Women Physicians, Careers, Status and Power*. New York: Tavistock, 1984.

Moldow, Gloria. *Women Doctors in Gilded-Age Washington: Race, Gender, and Professionalization*. Urbana: University of Illinois Press, 1987.
Centers on the traditionally Black Howard University, whose medical school was among the earliest to be coeducational and at which many white women doctors were trained in the nineteenth century.

Morantz, Regina Markell, Cynthia S. Pomerleau, and Carol H. Fenichel, eds. *In Her Own Words: Oral Histories of Women Physicians*. Westport, CT: Greenwood, 1982.

Morantz-Sanchez, Regina Markell. *Sympathy and Science: Women Physicians in American Medicine*. New York: Oxford University Press, 1985.
A comprehensive history of women doctors in America that reflects the sensibilities of feminist history and the "new social history."

Sicherman, Barbara. *Alice Hamilton: a Life in Letters*. Cambridge: Harvard University Press, 1984.
Hamilton, who virtually founded the specialty of occupational medicine, met consistent institutionalized discrimination against women physicians throughout her early twentieth-century career.

Walsh, Mary Roth. *"Doctors Wanted: No Women Need Apply": Sexual Barriers in the Medical Profession, 1835–1975*. New Haven: Yale University Press, 1977.

II. Some recent articles on American medical women.

Blount, Melissa. "Surpassing Obstacles: Black Women in Medicine." *Journal of the American Medical Women's Association* 39 (1984): 192–95.

Bonner, Thomas Neville. "Medical Women Abroad: A New Dimension of Women's Push for Opportunity in Medicine, 1850–1914." *Bulletin of the History of Medicine* 62 (1988): 58–73.

Bonner, author of the standard work on American physicians who supplemented their education by spending time in European laboratories and clinics, here concentrates on the first generations of American women physicians.

Cole, Stephen. "Sex Discrimination and Admission to Medical School, 1929–1984." *American Journal of Sociology* 92 (1986): 549–67.
Cole argues that the small proportion of women among medical students from the 1930s through the 1960s was more a result of the career choices made by women than of systematic discrimination in admissions by medical schools.

Drachman, Virginia G. "Female Solidarity and Professional Success: the Dilemma of Women Doctors in Late Nineteenth-Century America." *Journal of Social History* 15 (1982): 607–19.

Drachman, Virginia G. "The Limits of Progress: the Professional Lives of Women Doctors, 1881–1926." *Bulletin of the History of Medicine* 60 (1986): 58–72.

Goodwin, Norma J. "The Black Woman Physician." *New York State Journal of Medicine* 85 (1985): 145–47.

Hildreth, Martha L. "Delicacy and Propriety: the Acceptance of the Woman Physician in Victorian America." *Halcyon* 9 (1987): 149–65.

Horn, Margo. "'Sisters Worthy of Respect': Family Dynamics and Women's Roles in the Blackwell Family." *Journal of Family History* 8 (1983): 367–82.

Jerrido, Margaret. "Early Black Women Physicians." *Women and Health* 5, no. 3 (Fall 1980): 1–3.

Kendall, Diana, and Joe R. Feagin. "Blatant and Subtle Patterns of Discrimination: Minority Women in Medical Schools." *Journal of Intergroup Relations* 11, no. 2 (1983): 8–33.

McGovern, Constance M. "Doctors or Ladies? Women Physicians in Psychiatric Institutions, 1872–1900." *Bulletin of the History of Medicine* 55 (1981): 88–107.

Marrett, Cora Bagley. "On the Evolution of Women's Medical Societies." *Bulletin of the History of Medicine* 53 (1979): 434–48.

Mathes, Valerie Sherer. "Native American Women in Medicine and the Military." *Journal of the West* 21, no. 2 (1982): 41–48.

Morantz, Regina Markell. "Feminism, Professionalism, and Germs: the Thought of Mary Putnam Jacobi and Elizabeth Blackwell." *American Quarterly* 34 (1982): 459–78.

   Blackwell and Jacobi were two major nineteenth-century American woman doctors. In this essay Morantz contrasts their careers and their scientific ideas to provide a rounded view of the first generations of American medical women.

Morantz, Regina Markell and Sue Zschoche. "Professionalism, Feminism, and Gender Roles: a Comparative Study of Nineteenth-Century Medical Therapeutics." *Journal of American History* 67 (1980): 568–88.

Morantz-Sanchez, Regina. "The Compassionate Professional: Historical Notes on the Woman Physician's Dilemma." In *Seeing Female: Social Roles and Personal Lives*, edited by Sharon S. Brehm, 113–122. Westport, CT: Greenwood, 1988.

More, Ellen. "The Blackwell Medical Society and the Professionalization of Women Physicians." *Bulletin of the History of Medicine* 61 (1987): 603–28.

New Jersey Medicine, volume 85, no. 5, May 1988.

   Special issue on women in medicine includes, among others, the following articles: Regina Markell Morantz-Sanchez, "Not Feminized but Humanized"; Estelle Brodman, "A Century of Women Physicians"; Barbara Smith Unwin, "Researching Women Physicians"; and Linda Janet Holmes, "The Life of Lena Edwards."

Smith, Jill Gates. "Women in Health Care Delivery: the Histories of Women, Medicine and Photography." *Caduceus* 1, no. 4 (Winter 1985): 1–40.

Wall, Helena M. "Feminism and the New England Hospital, 1949–1961." *American Quarterly* 32 (1980): 435–52.

Walsh, Mary Roth. "The Rediscovery of the Need for a Feminist Medical Education." *Harvard Education Review* 49 (1979): 447–66.

WOMEN AS HEALTH-CARE PRACTITIONERS: NURSES

[Interest in the history of nursing has accelerated greatly in the past few years, leading to a proliferation of studies of mixed quality. This section of the bibliography is therefore somewhat more selective than the others.]

I. Important recent books.

Buhler-Wilkerson, Karen, ed. *Nursing and the Public's Health: an Anthology of Sources.* New York: Garland Publishing, 1989.
A collection of key primary documents in the history of public health nursing, with an introduction that summarizes their significance and places them in context.

Bullough, Vern L. and Bonnie Bullough. *History, Trends, and Politics of Nursing.* Norwalk, CT: Appleton-Century-Crofts, 1984.

Carnegie, Mary Elizabeth. *The Path We Tread: Blacks in Nursing, 1854–1984.* Philadelphia: Lippincott, 1986.

Dammann, Nancy. *A Social History of the Frontier Nursing Service.* Sun City, AZ: Social Change Press, 1982.
The Frontier Nursing Service brought organized health care in the 1920s to a previously unserved remote area in rural Kentucky.

Fitzpatrick, M. Louise, ed. *Historical Studies in Nursing.* New York: Teachers College Press, 1978.

Freedman, Dan, and Jacqueline Rhoads, eds. *Nurses in Vietnam: the Forgotten Veterans.* Austin: Texas Monthly Press, 1987.
A collection of personal narratives by nurses who served in Vietnam.

Hine, Darlene Clark. *Black Women in the Nursing Profession: A Documentary History.* New York: Garland, 1985.
An anthology of documents significant in Black nursing history.

Hine, Darlene Clark. *Black Women in White: Racial Conflict and Cooperation in the Nursing Profession, 1890–1950.* Bloomington: Indiana University Press, 1989.

Jones, Anne Hudson, ed. *Images of Nurses: Perspectives from History, Art and Literature.* Philadelphia: University of Pennsylvania Press, 1988.

Kalisch, Philip A., and Bernice J. Kalisch. *The Advance of American Nursing,* 2d ed. Boston: Little, Brown, 1986.
A comprehensive textbook of nursing history which is in the tradition of Lavinia Dock and Adelaide Nutting's 1907 *History of Nursing* rather than the critical approach which has recently been gaining impetus.

Kalisch, Philip A., and Bernice J. Kalisch. *The Changing Image of the Nurse.* Menlo Park, CA: Addison-Wesley Health Sciences Division, 1987.

Kalisch, Philip A., Bernice J. Kalisch, and M. Scobey. *Images of Nurses on Television.* New York: Springer, 1983.

Lagemann, Ellen C., ed. *Nursing History: New Perspectives, New Possibilities.* New York: Teachers College Press, 1983.
     Contents include: Barbara Melosh, "Doctors, Patients, and 'Big Nurse': Work and Gender in the Postwar Hospital"; Susan Reverby, "'Something besides Waiting': the Politics of Private Duty Nursing Reform in the Depression"; Nancy Tomes, "The Silent Battle: Nurse Registration in New York State, 1903–1920"; Karen Buhler-Wilkerson, "False Dawn: the Rise and Decline of Public Health Nursing in America, 1900–1930"; and J. P. Brickman, "Public Health, Midwives, and Nurses, 1880–1930."

Marshall, Kathryn. *In the Combat Zone: an Oral History of American Women in Vietnam, 1966–1975.* Boston: Little, Brown, 1987.

Melosh, Barbara. *"The Physician's Hand": Work Culture and Conflict in American Nursing.* Philadelphia: Temple University Press, 1982.
     This book was a major breakthrough in bringing the methods of social history to studies of nursing.

Reverby, Susan, series editor. *"The History of American Nursing."* New York: Garland, 1984.
     This series of over thirty volumes includes reprints of classic works on nursing published in America.

Reverby, Susan. *Ordered to Care: the Dilemma of American Nursing, 1850–1945.* New York: Cambridge University Press, 1987.
     This is probably the most significant monograph in nursing history published in the last fifty years. No new work on the nursing profession in America can fail to address the issues raised here.

Stepsis, Ursula, and Dolores Liptak, eds. *Pioneer Healers: the History of Women Religious in American Health Care.* New York: Crossroad, 1989.
     A history of Catholic nursing orders and of other nuns involved in health care in this country. This is intended, in part, as a plea for more Catholic young women to consider the religious life.

Tayloe, Roberta Love. *Combat Nurse: a Journal of World War II.* Santa Barbara, CA: Fithian Press, 1988.

Webb, Christine. *Sexuality, Nursing and Health.* New York: Wiley, 1985.

II. A selection of recent articles.

Brown, Mary Louise. "One Hundred Years of Industrial or Occupational Health Nursing in the United States." *AAOHN Journal* 36 (1988): 433–36.

Buhler-Wilkerson, Karen. "Public Health Nursing: a Photographic Study." *Nursing Outlook* 36 (1988): 241–43.

Carnegie, M. Elizabeth. "Black Nurses at the Front." *American Journal of Nursing* 84 (1984): 1250–52.

Fiedler, Leslie A. "Images of the Nurse in Fiction and Popular Culture." *Literature and Medicine* 2 (1985): 79–90.

Garling, Jean. "Flexner and Goldmark: Why the Difference in Impact?" *Nursing Outlook* 33 (1985): 26–31.
    Contrasts the effects of the Flexner Report of 1910, which is viewed as central to the process of transforming medical education in the United States, with the Goldmark Report of 1923, whose limited effect on nursing education disappointed reformers in the field.

Hine, Darlene Clark. "The Ethel Johns Report: Black Women in the Nursing Profession, 1925." *Journal of Negro History* 67 (1982): 212–28.

Hine, Darlene Clark. "From Hospital to College: Black Nurse Leaders and the Rise of Collegiate Nursing Schools." *Journal of Negro Education* 51 (1982): 222–37.

James, Janet Wilson. "Isabel Hampton and the Professionalization of Nursing in the 1890s." In: *The Therapeutic Revolution*, edited by Morris J. Vogel and Charles E. Rosenberg, 201–44. Philadelphia: University of Pennsylvania Press, 1979.

Kalisch, Philip A., and Bernice J. Kalisch. "The Image of Nurses in Novels." *American Journal of Nursing* 82 (1982): 1220–24.

Matejski, Myrtle P. "Ladies' Aid Societies and the Nurses of Lincoln's Army." *Journal of Nursing History* 1, no. 2 (1986): 35–51.

Nursing Research 36, no. 1 (January–February 1987). Special issue on research in nursing history.
    Articles by several leading nurse-historians and other historians working in the field of nursing history: Joan Lynaugh and Susan Reverby, "Thoughts on the Nature of History"; Patricia O'Brien, "'All a Woman's Life Can Bring': the Domestic Roots of Nursing in Philadelphia, 1830–1885"; Ellen D. Baer, "'A Cooperative Venture' in Pursuit

of Professional Status: a Research Journal for Nursing"; Mary Madeline
Rogge, "Nursing and Politics: A Forgotten Legacy"; Mary Anderson
Hardy, "The American Nurses' Association Influence on Federal Fund-
ing for Nursing Education, 1941–1984"; Karen Buhler-Wilkerson and
Julie Fairman, "Missing Data: Nurses with their Patients"; Karen Buhler-
Wilkerson, "Left Carrying the Bag: Experiments in Visiting Nursing,
1877–1909"; Olga Maranjian Church, "From Custody to Community
in Psychiatric Nursing"; Julie A. Fairman, "Sources and References for
Research in Nursing History"; Joanne S. Stevenson, "Forging a Research
Discipline"; Rozella M. Schlotfeldt, "Defining Nursing: a Historic Con-
troversy"; and Charles Rosenberg, "Clio and Caring: an Agenda for
American Historians and Nursing."

Oderkirk, Wendell W. "Setting the Record Straight: a Recount of Late
Nineteenth-Century Training Schools." *Journal of Nursing History* 1, no.
1 (1985): 30–37.

Poslusny, Susan M. "Feminist Friendship: Isabel Hampton Robb, Lavinia Lloyd Dock and Mary Adelaide Nutting." *Image: Journal of Nursing
Scholarship* 21, no. 2 (Summer 1989): 64–68.

Reverby, Susan. "Nursing and Caring: Lessons from History." *Health/
PAC Bulletin* 18, no. 3 (Fall 1988): 20–23.
    An interview with Susan Reverby, in which she discusses the rela-
tionship between her scholarly work and her political activism in the
health rights movement.

Reverby, Susan. "The Search for the Hospital Yardstick: Nursing and
the Rationalization of Hospital Work." In: *Health Care in America*,
edited by Susan Reverby and David Rosner, 2d ed., pp. 206–18.
Philadelphia: Temple University Press, 1979.

Taylor, F. C., and G. Cook. "Alberta Hunter: a Celebration in Blues
(and Licensed Practical Nursing)." *Journal of Practical Nursing* 37, no. 1
(1987): 28–31.
    Alberta Hunter, who died in the early 1980s well into her eighties,
returned to her youthful career as a jazz singer after making her living as a
practical nurse for most of her adult life.

Tomes, Evelyn Kennedy, and Etherine Shaw-Nickerson. "Predecessors
of Modern Black Nurses: an Honored Role." *Journal of the National
Black Nurses Association* 1, no. 2 (1986): 72–78.
    A useful source on the role of Black women in providing health care
before the development of modern health professions.

Wagner, David. "The Proletarianization of Nursing in the United States." *International Journal of Health Services* 10 (1980): 271–90.

WOMEN AS HEALTH-CARE PRACTITIONERS: MIDWIVES

I. Books.
Buss, Fran Leeper. *La Partera, Story of a Midwife*. Ann Arbor: University of Michigan Press, 1980.

DeVries, Raymond G. *Regulating Birth: Midwives, Medicine and the Law*. Philadelphia: Temple University Press, 1985.

Donegan, Jane B. *Women and Men Midwives: Medicine, Morality and Misogyny in Early America*. Westport, CT: Greenwood, 1978.

Litoff, Judy Barrett, ed. *The American Midwife Debate: A Sourcebook on Its Modern Origins*. New York: Greenwood, 1986.

Litoff, Judy Barrett. *American Midwives, 1860 to the Present*. Westport, CT: Greenwood, 1978.

Logan, Onnie Lee, as told to Katherine Clark. *Motherwit: An Alabama Midwife's Story*. New York: E. P. Dutton, 1989.

Sullivan, Deborah A., and Rose Weitz. *Labor Pains: Modern Midwives and Home Birth*. New Haven: Yale University Press, 1988.

Susie, Debra Ann. *In the Way of Our Grandmothers: a Cultural View of Twentieth-Century Midwifery in Florida*. Athens: University of Georgia Press, 1988.
    A study of continuity and change in childbirth among southern Black women.

II. Articles.
Borst, Charlotte G. "The Training and Practice of Midwives: A Wisconsin Study." *Bulletin of the History of Medicine* 62 (1988): 606–27.

Declercq, Eugene R., and Richard Lacroix. "The Immigrant Midwives of Lawrence: the Conflict between Law and Culture in Early Twentieth-Century Massachusetts." *Bulletin of the History of Medicine* 59 (1985): 232–46.

Declercq, Eugene R. "The Nature and Style of Practice of Immigrant Midwives in Early Twentieth Century Massachusetts." *Journal of Social History* 19 (1985): 113–29.

Devitt, Neal. "The Statistical Case for Elimination of the Midwife: Fact Versus Prejudice, 1890–1935." *Women and Health* 4 (1979): 81–96, 169–86.

DeVries, Raymond G. "Midwifery and the Problem of Licensure." *Research in the Sociology of Health Care* 2 (1982): 77–120.

Dougherty, Molly C. "Southern Lay Midwives as Ritual Specialists." In *Women in Ritual and Symbolic Roles*, edited by Judith Hoch-Smith and Anita Spring, 151–64. New York: Plenum Press, 1978.

Dougherty, Molly C. "Southern Midwifery and Organized Health Care: Systems in Conflict." *Medical Anthropology* 6 (1982): 113–26.

Dye, Nancy Schrom. "Mary Breckinridge, the Frontier Nursing Service and the Introduction of Nurse-Midwifery in the United States." *Bulletin of the History of Medicine* 57 (1983): 485–507.

Holmes, Linda J. "Alabama Granny Midwife." *Journal of the Medical Society of New Jersey* 81 (1984): 389–91.

Litoff, Judy Barrett. "Forgotten Women: American Midwives at the Turn of the Century." *Historian* 40 (1978): 235–51.

Peterson, Karen J. "Technology as a Last Resort: the Work of Lay Midwives." *Social Problems* 30 (1983): 284–97.

Robinson, Sharon A. "A Historical Development of Midwifery in the Black Community: 1600–1940." *Journal of Nurse-Midwifery* 29 (1984): 247–50.

Rothman, Barbara Katz. "Midwives in Transition: the Structure of a Clinical Revolution." *Social Problems* 30 (1983): 262–71.

WOMEN AS HEALTH-CARE PRACTITIONERS: OTHER AREAS OF PRACTICE

Bardell, Eunice Bonow. "America's Only School of Pharmacy for Women." *Pharmacy in History* 26, no. 3 (1984): 127–33.

Fee, Elizabeth, and Barbara Greene. "Science and Social Reform: Women in Public Health." *Journal of Public Health Policy* 10 (1989): 161–77.

Fink, Leon, and Brian Greenberg. *Upheaval in the Quiet Zone: a History of Hospital Workers' Union, Local 1199.* Urbana: University of Illinois Press, 1989.

After organizing orderlies and other low-paid hospital personnel in New York City, Local 1199 attempted to duplicate its success elsewhere. Women constitute a large proportion of its membership and have recently been prominent in leadership positions.

Gallagher, Teresa Catherine. "From Family Helpmeet to Independent Professional: Women in American Pharmacy, 1870–1940." *Pharmacy in History* 31 (1989): 60–77.

Giangrego, Elizabeth. "AAWD: a Voice for Women in Dentistry." *Journal of the American Dental Association* 117 (1988): 441–45.

Hamilton, W. Alexander, and Penny R. Hamilton. "Sex and the Dental Practice: a Reinterpretation of the History of Dental Hygienists." *Bulletin of the History of Dentistry* 28 (October 1980): 64–68.

Henderson, Metta Lou, and Tammy Lynn Keeney. "Women in Pharmacy Education: the Pioneers." *American Pharmacy* 28, no. 5 (May 1988): 24–27.

Kirk, Kenneth W. "Women in Male-Dominated Professions." *American Journal of Hospital Pharmacy* 39 (1982): 2089–93.

Kirk, Kenneth W. and Marvin D. Shepard. "Women in Pharmacy— Where are We Now?" *American Pharmacy* 23, no. 2 (February 1983): 19–21.

Metaxas Quiroga, Virginia A. "Female Lay Managers and Scientific Pediatrics at Nursery and Child's Hospital, 1854–1910." *Bulletin of the History of Medicine* 60 (1986): 194–208.
    This article deals with women, not as health-care workers, but as overseers of hospital care in an era when Boards of Trustees played a much more immediate role in the management of institutions.

Motley, Wilma. "The Movement for Independent Practice of Dental Hygienists: from Evolution to Revolution." *Bulletin of the History of Dentistry* 36 (1988): 108–19.

Sacks, Karen. *Caring by the Hour: Women, Work and Organizing at Duke Medical Center.* Urbana: University of Illinois Press, 1988.
    Published in a series on labor history rather than medical history, this book looks seriously at the relationships among class, gender, and race among hospital workers. A contribution to the literature on Black women in the health-care system.

Shepherd, Marvin D., and Kurt A. Proctor. "Women and Pharmacy Ownership." *American Pharmacy* 28, no. 5 (May 1988): 28–36.

Ward, Patricia Spain. "Hygeia's Sisters: A History of Women in Pharmacy." *Caduceus* 4, no. 3–4 (Autumn/Winter 1988): 1–57.

GENDER AND HEALTH

Graney, Marshall J. "An Exploration of Social Factors Influencing the Sex Differential in Mortality." *Sociological Symposium* 28 (1979): 1–26.

Cutright, Phillips, and Edward Shorter. "The Effects of Health on the Completed Fertility of Nonwhite and White U.S. Women Born between 1867 and 1935." *Journal of Social History* 13 (1979): 191–97.

Gove, Walter R., and Michael Hughes. "Possible Causes of the Apparent Sex Differences in Physical Health: an Empirical Investigation." *American Sociological Review* 44 (1979): 126–46.

Gove, Walter R., and Michael Hughes. "Beliefs vs. Data: More on the Illness Behavior of Men and Women (A Reply to Marcus and Seeman)." *American Sociological Review* 46 (1981): 123–28.
These two articles present one side of a debate among sociologists about sex differences in health. For the other side, see Marcus and Seeman, below.

Haw, Mary Ann. "Women, Work and Stress: A Review and Agenda for the Future." *Journal of Health and Social Behavior* 23 (1982): 132–44.

Headen, Alvin E., and Sandra W. Headen. "General Health Conditions and Medical Insurance Issues Concerning Black Women." *Review of Black Political Economy* 14 (1985/86): 183–97.

Holden, Constance. "Why Do Women Live Longer than Men?" *Science* 238, no. 4824 (9 October 1987): 158–60.

Ibraham, Michel A. "Editorial: The Changing Health State of Women." *American Journal of Public Health* 70 (1980): 120–21.

Lewis, Charles E., and Mary Ann Lewis. "The Potential Impact of Sexual Equality on Health." *New England Journal of Medicine* 297 (1977): 863–69.

Marcus, Alfred C., and Teresa E. Seeman. "Sex Differences in Health Status: A Reexamination of the Nurturant Role Hypothesis (Comment

on Gove and Hughes, ASR February 1979)." American Sociological Review 46 (1981): 119–23.
Presents one side of a debate among sociologists about sex differences in health. For the other side, see Gove and Hughes, above.

Nathanson, Constance A. "Illness and the Feminine Role: A Theoretical Review." Social Science and Medicine 9 (1975): 57–62.

Nathanson, Constance A. "Sex, Illness and Medical Care: A Review of Data, Theory and Method." Social Science and Medicine 11 (1977): 13–25.

Nathanson, Constance A., and Gerda Lorenz. "Women and Health: The Social Dimensions of Biomedical Data." In Women in the Middle Years: Current Knowledge and Directions for Research and Policy, edited by Janet Z. Giele, 37–87. New York: Wiley, 1982.

Rossi, Alice S. "Life-Span Theories and Women's Lives." Signs 6 (1980): 4–32.

Shorter, Edward. "Women's Diseases Before 1900." In New Directions in Psychohistory, edited by Mel Albin, with the assistance of Robert J. Devlin and Gerald Heegan, 183–208. Lexington, MA: Heath, 1980.

Verbrugge, Lois M. "Sex Differentials in Health." Public Health Reports 97 (1982): 417–37.

Verbrugge, Lois M. "A Health Profile of Older Women with Comparisons to Older Men." Research on Aging 6 (1984): 291–322.

Verbrugge, Lois M., and Jennifer H. Madans. "Social Roles and Health Trends of American Women." Milbank Memorial Fund Quarterly/ Health and Society 63 (1985): 691–735.

Verbrugge, Lois M., and Deborah L. Wingard. "Sex Differentials in Health and Mortality." Women and Health 12, no. 2 (Summer 1987): 103–45.

Waldron, Ingrid. "Why Do Women Live Longer than Men?" Social Science and Medicine 10 (1976): 349–62.

WOMEN AS THE OBJECT OF MEDICAL AND SCIENTIFIC OBSERVATION

[see also "Gynecology and Women as Patients," below]

I. Important recent books.

Bleier, Ruth, ed. *Feminist Approaches to Science.* New York: Pergamon Press, 1986.

Bleier, Ruth. *Science and Gender: A Critique of Biology and Its Theories on Women.* New York: Pergamon, 1984.

Fausto-Sterling, Anne. *Myths of Gender: Biological Theories about Women and Men.* New York: Basic Books, 1985.

Gilligan, Carol. *In a Different Voice: Psychological Theory and Women's Development.* Cambridge: Harvard University Press, 1982.

Harding, Sandra, and Jean F. O'Barr, eds. *Sex and Scientific Inquiry.* Chicago: University of Chicago Press, 1987.
    A collection of articles reprinted from *Signs: Journal of Women in Culture and Society.* The section "Bias in the Sciences," in particular, contains five essays on the scientific construction of sex differences.

Hubbard, Ruth, Mary Sue Henifin, and Barbara Fried, eds. *Biological Woman: The Convenient Myth.* New York: Schenkman, 1982.
    A collection of feminist essays with a comprehensive bibliography.

Russett, Cynthia Eagle. *Sexual Science: the Victorian Construction of Womanhood.* Cambridge: Harvard University Press, 1989.

Sapiro, Virginia, ed. *Women, Biology and Public Policy.* Beverly Hills: Sage, 1985.
    A collection of articles on the biological and social construction of the nature of women.

Sayers, Janet. *Biological Politics: Feminist and Anti-Feminist Perspectives.* New York: Methuen, 1982.

Theriot, Nancy M. *The Biosocial Construction of Femininity: Mothers and Daughters in Nineteenth Century America.* Westport, CT: Greenwood, 1988.

II. Articles.

Bell, Susan E. "Changing Ideas: the Medicalization of Menopause." *Social Science and Medicine* 24 (1987): 535–42.

Bullough, Vern L. "Female physiology, technology and women's liberation." In *Dynamos and Virgins Revisited: Women and Technological Change in History*, edited by Martha Moore Trescott, 236–51. Metuchen, NJ: Scarecrow Press, 1979.

Fee, Elizabeth. "Nineteenth Century Craniology: The Study of the Female Skull." *Bulletin of the History of Medicine* 53 (1979): 415–33.

Harlow, Sioban D. "Function and Dysfunction: A Historical Critique of the Literature on Menstruation and Work." In *Culture, Society and Menstruation*, edited by Virginia Oleson and Nancy Fugate Wood, 39–50. Washington: Hemisphere, 1986.

Hawkins, Joellen W., and Cynthia S. Aber. "The Content of Advertisements in Medical Journals: Distorting the Image of Women." *Women and Health* 14, no. 2 (1988): 43–59.

McCrea. Frances B., and Gerald E. Markle. "The Estrogen Replacement Controversy in the USA and the UK: Different Answers to the Same Question?" *Social Studies of Science* 14 (1984): 1–26.

Skultans, Videa S. "Vicarious menstruation." *Social Science and Medicine* 21 (1985): 713–14.

Thomas, Samuel J. "Nostrum Advertising and the Image of Woman as Invalid in Late Victorian America." *Journal of American Culture* 5, no. 3 (1982): 104–12.

Valdiserri, Ronald O. "Menstruation and Medical Theory: An Historical Overview." *Journal of the American Medical Women's Association* 38, no. 3 (1983): 66–70.

Vertinsky, Patricia. "Exercise, Physical Capability, and the Eternally Wounded Woman in Late Nineteenth Century North America." *Journal of Sport History* 14 (1987): 7–27.

Vertinsky, Patricia. "'Of No Use without Health': Late Nineteenth Century Medical Prescriptions for Female Exercise through the Life Span." *Women and Health* 14, no. 1 (1988): 89–115.

OBSTETRICS, CHILDBIRTH, AND CHILDREARING

[see also "Women as Health Care Practitioners: Midwives," above]

I. Important recent books.

Apple, Rima D. *Mothers and Medicine: A Social History of Infant Feeding, 1890–1950.* Madison: University of Wisconsin Press, 1987.

Corea, Gena, ed. *Man-Made Women: How New Reproductive Technologies Affect Women.* London: Hutchinson, 1985.
   Collection of papers given at the 1984 Interdisciplinary Congress on Women.

Corea, Gena. *The Mother Machine: Reproductive Technologies from Artificial Insemination to Artificial Wombs.* New York: Harper and Row, 1985.

Eakins, Pamela S., ed. *The American Way of Birth.* Philadelphia: Temple University Press, 1986.
   A collection of essays by authors such as Nancy Schrom Dye and Barbara Katz Rothman, which share the point of view that medical obstetrics has served as a means of social control of women's lives.

Edwards, Margot, and Mary Waldorf. *Reclaiming Birth: History and Heroines of American Childbirth Reform.* Trumansburg, NY: Crossing Press, 1985.

Hoffert, Sylvia D. *Private Matters: American Attitudes toward Childbearing and Infant Nurture in the Urban North, 1800–1860.* Urbana: University of Illinois Press, 1989.

Ladd-Taylor, Molly. *Raising a Baby the Government Way: Mothers' Letters to the Children's Bureau, 1915–1932.* New Brunswick: Rutgers University Press, 1986.

Leavitt, Judith Walzer. *Brought to Bed: Childbearing in America, 1750 to 1950.* New York: Oxford University Press, 1986.
   This is the key work in the history of childbirth in America, addressing the basic question of how power relationships have changed. In contrast to the essays in *The American Way of Birth* (see above), Leavitt stresses the role of women themselves in the evolution of childbirth procedures.

Martin, Emily. *The Woman in the Body: A Cultural Analysis of Reproduction*. Baltimore: Johns Hopkins University Press, 1987.
Deals with childbirth in modern America using the methods of anthropological research.

Rothman, Barbara Katz. *Giving Birth: Alternatives in Childbirth*. New York: Penguin, 1984.
This book was previously published as *In Labor: Women and Power in the Birthplace*.

Rothman, Barbara Katz. *Recreating Motherhood: Ideology and Technology in a Patriarchal Society*. New York: Norton, 1989.

Sandelowski, Margarete. *Pain, Pleasure, and American Childbirth: from the Twilight Sleep to the Read Method, 1914–1960*. Westport, CT: Greenwood, 1984.

Scholten, Catherine M. *Childbearing in American Society, 1650–1850*. New York: New York University Press, 1985.

Shapiro, Thomas M. *Population Control Politics: Women, Sterilization, and Reproductive Choice*. Philadelphia: Temple University Press, 1985.

Wertz, Richard W., and Dorothy C. Wertz. *Lying-In: A History of Childbirth in America*. New York: Free Press, 1977. 2nd edition, 1989.

II. Articles.
Bogdan, Janet. "Care or Cure? Childbirth Practices in 19th-Century America." *Feminist Studies* 4 (1978): 92–99.

Cohen, Nancy Wainer, and Lois J. Estner. "Silent Knife: Cesarean Section in the United States." *Society* (New Brunswick) 21 (1983): 95–111.

Devitt, Neal. "The Transition from Home to Hospital Birth in the United States, 1930–1960." *Birth and the Family Journal* 4, no. 2 (1977): 47–58.

Drachman, Virginia G. "Gynecological Instruments and Surgical Decisions at a Hospital in Late Nineteenth-Century America." *Journal of American Culture* 3 (1980): 660–72.

Dye, Nancy Schrom. "Mary Breckinridge, the Frontier Nursing Service and the Introduction of Nurse-Midwifery in the United States." *Bulletin of the History of Medicine* 57 (1983): 485–507.

Dye, Nancy Schrom. "Modern Obstetrics and Working Class Women: the New York Midwifery Dispensary, 1890-1920." *Journal of Social History* 20 (1987): 549-64.

Dye, Nancy Schrom and Daniel Blake Smith. "Mother Love and Infant Death, 1750-1920." *Journal of American History* 73 (1986): 329-53.

Fitzpatrick, Ellen. "Childbirth and an Unwed Mother in Seventeenth-Century New England." *Signs* 8 (1983): 744-9.
Fitzpatrick provides commentary and the text of a seventeenth-century document.

Golden, Janet. "'Trouble in the Nursery': Physicians, Families and Wet Nurses at the End of the Nineteenth Century." In *To Toil the Livelong Day: American Women at Work, 1790-1980*, edited by Carol Groneman and Mary Beth Norton, 125-37. Ithaca: Cornell University Press, 1987.

Golden, Janet. "From Wet Nurse Directory to Milk Bank: The Delivery of Human Milk in Boston, 1909-1927." *Bulletin of the History of Medicine* 62 (1988): 589-605.

Hansen, Bert. "Medical Education in New York City in 1866-1867: A Student's Notebook of Professor Charles A. Budd's Lectures on Obstetrics at New York University." *New York State Journal of Medicine* 85 (1985): 488-97, 548-59.

Jones, Elise F. "Ways in which Childbearing Affects Women's Employment: Evidence from the U.S. 1975 National Fertility Study." *Population Studies* 36 (1982): 5-14.

Leavitt, Judith Walzer. "Birthing and Anesthesia: the Debate over Twilight Sleep." *Signs* 6 (1980): 147-64.

Leavitt, Judith Walzer. "'Science' Enters the Birthing Room: Obstetrics in America since the Eighteenth Century." *Journal of American History* 70 (1983): 281-304.

Leavitt, Judith Walzer. "Under the Shadow of Maternity: American Women's Responses to Death and Debility Fears in Nineteenth-Century Childbirth." *Feminist Studies* 12, no. 1 (1986): 129-54.

Miller, Lawrence G. "Pain, Parturition, and the Profession: Twilight Sleep in America." In: *Health Care in America: Essays in Social History*, edited by Susan Reverby and David Rosner, 19-44. Philadelphia: Temple University Press, 1979.

Milligan, B. Carol. "Nursing Care and Beliefs of Expectant Navajo Women (part 1)." *American Indian Quarterly* 8, no. 2 (1984): 83–101.

Nelson, Margaret K. "Working-Class Women, Middle-Class Women, and Models of Childbirth." *Social Problems* 30 (1983): 284–97.

Porges, Robert F. "The Response of the New York Obstetrical Society to the Report by the New York Academy of Medicine on Maternal Mortality, 1933–1934." *American Journal of Obstetrics and Gynecology* 152 (July 15, 1985): 642–49.

Powers, Marla N. "Menstruation and Reproduction: an Oglala Case." *Signs* 6 (1980): 54–65.

Siddall, A. Claire. "Bloodletting in American Obstetric Practice, 1800–1945." *Bulletin of the History of Medicine* 54 (1980): 101–10.

Suitor, J. Jill. "Husbands' Participation in Childbirth: a Nineteenth-Century Phenomenon." *Journal of Family History* 6 (1981): 278–93.

Treckel, Paula A. "Breastfeeding and Maternal Sexuality in Colonial America." *Journal of Interdisciplinary History* 29 (1989): 25–52.

Ulrich, Laurel Thatcher. "'The Living Mother of a Living Child': Midwifery and Mortality in Eighteenth-Century New England." *William and Mary Quarterly* ser. 3, 66 (1989): 27–48.

Weiss, Nancy Pottishman. "The Mother-Child Dyad Revisited: Perceptions of Mothers and Children in the Twentieth Century Child-Rearing Manuals." *Journal of Social Issues* 34, no. 2 (Spring 1978): 29–45.

Wertz, Dorothy C. "What Birth has Done for Doctors: a Historical View." *Women and Health* 8, no. 1 (Spring 1983): 7–24.

GYNECOLOGY AND WOMEN AS PATIENTS

[see also "Women as the Object of Medical and Scientific Observation," above]

I. Important recent books.

Apfel, Roberta J., and Susan M. Fisher. *To Do No Harm: DES and the Dilemmas of Modern Medicine.* New Haven: Yale University Press, 1984.

Bichler, Joyce. *DES Daughter: The Joyce Bichler Story.* New York: Avon, 1981.

Chavkin, Wendy, ed. *Double Exposure: Women's Health Hazards on the Job and at Home*. New York: Monthly Review Press, 1984.

Fenichell, Stephen, and Lawrence S. Charfoos. *Daughters at Risk: A Personal D.E.S. History*. Garden City, NY: Doubleday, 1981.

Golub, Sharon, ed. *Lifting the Curse of Menstruation: A Feminist Appraisal of the Influence of Menstruation on Women's Lives*. New York: Haworth, 1983.

McDonnell, Kathleen. *Adverse Effects: Women and the Pharmaceutical Industry*. Toronto: Women's Educational Press, 1986.

Mintz, Morton. *At Any Cost: Corporate Greed, Women, and the Dalkon Shield*. New York: Pantheon, 1985.

Perry, Susan, and Jim Dawson. *Nightmare: Women and the Dalkon Shield*. New York: Macmillan, 1985.

Ratcliff, Kathryn Strother, et al. *Healing Technology: Feminist Perspectives*. Ann Arbor: University of Michigan Press, 1989.
    Chapters deal with reproductive technologies, health care technologies, and technology-related disease.

Scully, Diana. *Men Who Control Women's Health: the Miseducation of Obstetrician-Gynecologists*. Boston: Houghton Mifflin, 1980.

Todd, Alexandra Dundas. *Intimate Adversaries: Cultural Conflict between Doctors and Women Patients*. Philadelphia: University of Pennsylvania Press, 1989.
    Based on research done observing doctor-patient interactions at the gynecological clinic of a community health center and at the private office of a successful gynecologist.

II. Articles.

Bale, Anthony. "'Hope in Another Direction': Compensation for Work-Related Illness Among Women, 1900–1960." *Women & Health* 15 (1989): 99–115.

Bauer, Carol, and Lawrence Ritt. "'The Little Health of Ladies,' An Anatomy of Female Invalidism in the Nineteenth Century." *Journal of the American Medical Women's Association* 36 (1981): 300–306.

Bell, Susan E. "A New Model of Medical Technology Development: A Case Study of DES." *Research in the Sociology of Health Care* 4 (1986): 1–32.

Gillam, Richard, and Barton J. Bernstein. "Doing Harm: the DES Tragedy and Modern American Medicine." *Public Historian* 9 (1987): 57–82.

Gosling, F. G., and Joyce M. Ray. "The Right to be Sick: American Physicians and Nervous Patients, 1885–1910." *Journal of Social History* 20 (1986): 251–67.

Haller, John S. "Trends in American Gynecology, 1800–1910: a Short History." *New York State Journal of Medicine* 89 (1989): 278–82.

Heifetz, Ruth. "Women, Lead and Reproductive Hazards: Defining a New Risk." In *Dying for Work: Workers' Safety and Health in Twentieth-Century America*, edited by David Rosner and Gerald Markowitz, 160–76. Bloomington: Indiana University Press, 1987.

Kaufert, Patricia A. "Myth and the Menopause." *Sociology of Health and Illness* 4 (1982): 141–65.

Longo, Laurence D. "Electrotherapy in Gynecology: the American Experience." *Bulletin of the History of Medicine* 60 (1986): 343–66.

Longo, Laurence D. "The Rise and Fall of Battey's Operation: a Fashion in Surgery." *Bulletin of the History of Medicine* 53 (1979): 244–67.

McClary, Andrew. "The Medicated Woman." *Pharos* 47, no. 3 (Summer 1984): 8–10.

McGregor, Deborah Kuhn. "Female Disorders and Nineteenth-Century Medicine: the Case of Vesico-Vaginal Fistula." *Caduceus* 3, no. 1 (Spring 1987): 1–30.

Nugent, Angela. "The Power to Define a New Disease: Epidemiological Politics and Radium Poisoning." In *Dying for Work: Workers' Safety and Health in Twentieth-Century America*, edited by David Rosner and Gerald Markowitz, 177–91. Bloomington: Indiana University Press, 1987.

Pearson, Willie, Jr., and Maxine L. Clark. "The Mal(e) Treatment of American Women in Gynecology and Obstetrics." *International Journal of Women's Studies* 5 (1982): 348–62.

Powers, Marla N. "Menstruation and Reproduction: an Oglala Case." *Signs* 6 (1980): 54–65.

Riessman, Catherine Kohler. "Women and Medicalization: a New Perspective." *Social Policy* 14, no. 1 (Summer 1983): 3–18.

Schroeder, Fred E. H. "Feminine Hygiene, Fashion and the Emancipation of American Women." *American Studies* 17 (1976): 101–10.

Scull, Andrew T., and Diane Favreau. "'A Chance to Cut is a Chance to Cure': Sexual Surgery for Psychosis in Three Nineteenth Century Societies." *Research in Law, Deviance and Social Control* 8 (1986): 3–39.

Scull, Andrew T., and Diane Favreau. "The Clitoridectomy Craze." *Social Research* 53 (1986): 243–60.

Sharpe, William D. "The New Jersey Radium Dial Painters: A Classic Case in Occupational Carcinogenesis." *Bulletin of the History of Medicine* 52 (1978): 560–70.

Summey, Pamela S., and Marsha Hurst. "Ob/Gyn on the Rise: The Evolution of Professional Ideology in the Twentieth Century." *Women and Health* 11 (1986): 103–22, 133–46.

Vertinsky, Patricia. "God, Science and Market Place: The Bases for Exercise Prescriptions for Females in Nineteenth Century North America." *Canadian Journal of History of Sport and Physical Education* 17 (1986): 38–45.

MENTAL HEALTH

I. Books.

Brumberg, Joan Jacobs. *Fasting Girls: The Emergence of Anorexia Nervosa as a Modern Disease.* Cambridge: Harvard University Press, 1988.

Chesler, Phyllis. *Women and Madness.* Garden City, NY: Doubleday, 1972.

Gilbert, Sandra M., and Susan Gubar. *The Madwoman in the Attic.* New Haven: Yale University Press, 1979.

Gomberg, E. S., and V. Franks, eds. *Gender and Disordered Behavior: Sex Differences in Psychopathology.* New York: Brunner Mazel, 1979.

Guttentag, Marcia, Susan Salasin, and Deborah Belle, eds. *The Mental Health of Women.* New York: Academic Press, 1980.

Howell, Elizabeth, and Marjorie Bayes, eds. *Women and Mental Health.* New York: Basic Books, 1981.

Lewin, Miriam, ed. *In the Shadow of the Past: Psychology Portrays the Sexes.* New York: Columbia University Press, 1984.

Rieker, Patricia P., and Elaine H. Carmen. *The Gender Gap in Psychotherapy*. New York: Plenum, 1984.

Walker, Lenore, ed. *Women and Mental Health Policy*. Beverly Hills: Sage, 1984.

Widom, Cathy S. *Sex Roles and Psychopathology*. New York: Plenum, 1984.

II. Articles.

Briscoe, Monica. "Sex Differences in Psychological Well-Being." *Psychological Medicine Monograph Supplement* 1 (1982): 1–46.

Dwyer, Ellen. "The Weaker Vessel: Legal versus Social Reality in Mental Commitments in Nineteenth Century New York." In: *Women and the Law: the Social Historical Perspective*, vol. 1, *Women and the Criminal Law*, edited by D. Kelly Weisberg. Cambridge, MA: Schenkman, 1982.

Himelhoch, Myra Samuels, and Arthur H. Shaffer. "Elizabeth Packard: Nineteenth Century Crusader for the Rights of Mental Patients." *Journal of American Studies* 13 (1979): 343–75.

McGovern, Constance M. "Doctors or Ladies? Women Physicians in Psychiatric Institutions, 1872–1900." *Bulletin of the History of Medicine* 55 (1981): 88–107.

McGovern, Constance M. "The Myths of Social Control and Custodial Oppression: Patterns of Psychiatric Medicine in Late Nineteenth Century Institutions." *Journal of Social History* 20 (1986): 3–23.
  McGovern argues against the notion that nineteenth-century mental hospitals were part of a system of institutional oppression.

McGovern, Constance M. "Psychiatry, Psychoanalysis, and Women in America: An Historical Note." *Psychoanalytic Review* 71 (1984): 541–52.

Mitchinson, Wendy. "Gynecological Operation on Insane Women: London Ontario, 1895–1901." *Journal of Social History* 15 (1982): 467–84.

Person, Ethel Spector. "Sexuality as the Mainstay of Identity: Psychoanalytic Perspectives." *Signs* 5 (1980): 605–30.

Spiegel, Allen D. "Temporary Insanity and Premenstrual Syndrome: Medical Testimony in an 1865 Murder Trial." *New York State Journal of Medicine* 88 (1988): 482–92.

Theriot, Nancy M. "Psychosomatic Illness in History: the 'Green Sickness' among Nineteenth-Century Adolescent Girls." *Journal of Psychohistory* 15 (1988): 461–80.

Waisberg, Jodie, and Stewart Page. "Gender Role Nonconformity and
Perception of Mental Illness." *Women and Health* 14, no. 1 (1988): 3–
16.

SEX, SEXUALITY, AND SEXUALLY
TRANSMITTED DISEASES
I. Books.

Barker-Benfield, G. J. *The Horrors of the Half-Known Life: Male Attitudes
toward Women and Sexuality in Nineteenth-Century America.* New York:
Harper and Row, 1976.

Butler, Anne M. *Daughters of Joy, Sisters of Misery: Prostitutes in the
American West, 1865–90.* Urbana: University of Illinois Press, 1985.

Connelly, Mark Thomas. *The Response to Prostitution in the Progressive
Era.* Chapel Hill: University of North Carolina Press, 1980.

D'Emilio, John, and Estelle B. Freedman. *Intimate Matters: A History of
Sexuality in America.* New York: Harper and Row, 1988.

Enrenreich, Barbara, Elizabeth Hess, and Gloria Jacobs, *Re-making Love:
The Feminization of Sex.* Garden City, NY: Doubleday, 1986.

Goldman, Marion S. *Gold Diggers and Silver Miners: Prostitution and
Social Life on the Comstock Lode.* Ann Arbor: University of Michigan
Press, 1981.

Hobson, Barbara Meil. *Uneasy Virtue: The Politics of Prostitution and the
American Reform Tradition.* New York: Basic Books, 1987.

Kern, Louis J. *An Ordered Love: Sex Roles and Sexuality in Victorian
Utopias—the Shakers, the Mormons, and the Oneida Community.* Chapel
Hill: University of North Carolina Press, 1981.

Maggiore, Dolores J. *Lesbianism: an Annotated Bibliography and Guide to
the Literature, 1976–1986.* Metuchen, NJ: Scarecrow, 1988.
    An excellent general bibliography on lesbianism, which includes a
chapter specifically on lesbian health issues.

Rosen, Ruth. *The Lost Sisterhood: Prostitution in America, 1900–1918.*
Baltimore: Johns Hopkins University Press, 1982.

550

BIBLIOGRAPHY

Sahli, Nancy Ann. *Women and Sexuality in America: A Bibliography.* Boston: Hall, 1984.

Sears, Hal D. *The Sex Radicals: Free Love in High Victorian America.* Lawrence: Regents Press of Kansas, 1977.

Stimpson, Catharine, and Ethel S. Pearson, eds. *Women: Sex and Sexuality.* Chicago: University of Chicago Press, 1980.
A collection of essays that originally appeared in *Signs.* Covers topics such as reproductive freedom, menstruation, pornography, prostitution, and lesbianism.

II. Articles.
Best, Joel. "Careers in Brothel Prostitution: St. Paul, 1865–1883." *Journal of Interdisciplinary History* 12 (1982): 597–619.

Cott, Nancy F. "Passionlessness: An Interpretation of Victorian Sexual Ideology, 1790–1850." *Signs* 4 (1978): 219–36.

Dubois, Ellen Carol, and Linda Gordon. "Seeking Ecstasy on the Battlefield: Danger and Pleasure in Nineteenth-Century Feminist Sexual Thought." *Feminist Studies* 9 (1983): 7–25.

Griswold, Robert L. "Law, Sex, Cruelty, and Divorce in Victorian America, 1840–1900." *American Quarterly* 38 (1986): 721–45.

Hirata, Lucie Cheng. "Free, Indentured, Enslaved: Chinese Prostitutes in Nineteenth-Century America." *Signs* 5 (1979): 3–29.

Hori, Joan. "Japanese Prostitution in Hawaii during the Immigration Period." *Hawaiian Journal of History* 15 (1981): 113–24.

Johnson, H. A. "The Other Flexner Report: How Abraham Flexner was Diverted from Medical Schools to Brothels." *Pharos* 49, no. 2 (Spring 1986): 9–12.

Kampmeier, Rudolph H. "Venereal Disease in the United States Army: 1775–1900." *Sexually Transmitted Diseases* 9 (1982): 100–103.

Rupp, Leila. "'Imagine My Surprise': Women's Relationships in Historical Perspective." *Frontiers: A Journal of Women's Studies* 5, no. 3 (Fall 1980): 61–70.

Sahli, Nancy. "Sexuality in 19th and 20th century America: the Sources and Their Problems." *Radical History Review* 20 (1979): 89–96.
A guide to research in this field.

Sahli, Nancy. "Smashing: Women's Relationships before the Fall." *Chrysalis* 8 (1979): 17–27.

Simmons, Christina. "Companionate Marriage and the Lesbian Threat." *Frontiers: A Journal of Women's Studies* 4, no. 3 (Fall 1979): 54–59.

Weinberg, Martin S., Rochelle Ganz Swensson, and Sue Kiefer Hammersmith. "Sexual Autonomy and the Status of Women: Models of Female Sexuality in U.S. Sex Manuals from 1950 to 1980." *Social Problems* 30 (1983): 312–24.

FAMILY PLANNING, BIRTH CONTROL, ABORTION, AND STERILIZATION

I. Books.

Davis, Nanette J. *From Crime to Choice: The Transformation of Abortion in America.* Westport, CT: Greenwood, 1985.

Gordon, Linda. *Woman's Body, Woman's Right: A Social History of Birth Control in America.* New York: Grossman, 1976.
    A groundbreaking book when it was first published, it remains a standard work.

Keller, Allan. *Scandalous Lady: The Life and Times of Madame Restell, New York's Most Notorious Abortionist.* New York: Atheneum, 1981.

Luker, Kristin. *Abortion and the Politics of Motherhood.* Berkeley: University of California Press, 1984.

McLaughlin, L. *The Pill, John Rock, and the Church: the Biography of a Revolution.* Boston: Little, Brown, 1982.

Mohr, James C. *Abortion in America: Origins and Evolution of National Policy, 1800–1900.* New York: Oxford University Press, 1978.

Petchesky, Rosalind Pollack. *Abortion and Woman's Choice: The State, Sexuality and Reproductive Freedom.* Boston: Northeastern University Press, 1985.

Reed, James. *The Birth Control Movement and American Society: From Private Vice to Public Virtue.* Princeton: Princeton University Press, 1983.

Rothman, Barbara Katz. *The Tentative Pregnancy: Prenatal Diagnosis and the Future of Motherhood.* New York: Viking, 1986.

Rubin, Eva R. *Abortion, Politcs, and the Courts: Roe v. Wade and Its Aftermath*, rev. ed. New York: Greenwood Press, 1987.

Van Horn, Susan Householder. *Women, Work, and Fertility, 1900–1986.* New York: New York University Press, 1988.

Ward, Martha C. *Poor Women, Powerful Men: America's Great Experiment in Family Planning.* Boulder: Westview Press, 1986.

Warren, Mary Anne. *Gendercide: The Implications of Sex Selection.* Totowa, NJ: Rowman and Allanhead, 1985.

II. Articles.

Anderton, Douglas L. "Urbanization, Secularization, and Birth Spacing: A Case Study of an Historical Fertility Transition." *Sociological Quarterly* 27 (1986): 43–62.

Anderton, Douglas L., and Lee L. Bean. "Birth Spacing and Fertility Limitation: A Behavioral Analysis of a Nineteenth Century Frontier Population." *Demography* 22 (1985): 169–83.

Aries, Nancy. "Fragmentation and Reproductive Freedom: Federally Subsidized Family Planning Services, 1960–80." *American Journal of Public Health* 77 (1987): 1465–71.

Borell, Merriley. "Biologists and the Promotion of Birth Control Research, 1918–1938." *Journal of the History of Biology* 20 (1987): 51–87.

Cates, Willard, Jr. "Abortion Attitudes of Black Women." *Women and Health* 2, no. 3 (November–December 1979): 3–9.

Combs, Michael W., and Susan Welch. "Blacks, Whites, and Attitudes toward Abortion." *Public Opinion Quarterly* 46 (1982): 510–20.

David, Paul A., and Warren C. Sanderson. "The Emergence of a Two-Child Norm among American Birth-Controllers." *Population and Development Review* 13 (1987): 1–41.

Davis, Angela Y. "Racism, Birth Control and Reproductive Rights." In *Women, Race and Class*, 202–21. New York: Random House, 1981.

Dawson, Deborah, Denise J. Meny, and Jeanne Claire Ridley. "Fertility Control in the United States before the Contraceptive Revolution." *Family Planning Perspectives* 12 (1980): 76–86.

DelCastillo, Adelaida R. "Sterilization: an Overview." In *Mexican Women in the United States: Struggles Past and Present*, edited by Magdalena Mora and Adelaida R. DelCastillo, 65–70. Los Angeles: UCLA Chicano Studies Resources Center, 1980.

Dryfoos, Joy G. "Family Planning Clinics—a Story of Growth and Conflict." *Family Planning Perspectives* 20 (1988): 282–87.

Fliess, Kenneth H. "Fertility, Nuptiality, and Family Limitation among the Wends of Serbin, Texas, 1854 to 1920." *Journal of Family History* 13 (1988): 251–63.

Goldstein, Michael S. "Creating and Controlling a Medical Market: Abortion in Los Angeles after Liberalization." *Social Problems* 31 (1984): 514–29.

Gordon, Linda. "Who is Frightened of Reproductive Freedom for Women and Why? Some Historical Answers." *Frontiers: A Journal of Women's Studies* 9, no. 1 (1986): 23–26.

Gordon, Linda. "The Long Struggle for Reproductive Rights." *Radical America* 15, no. 1–2 (1981): 75–88.

Hall, Elaine J., and Myra Mary Ferree. "Race Differences in Abortion Attitudes." *Public Opinion Quarterly* 50 (1986): 193–207.

Harper, John Paull. "Be Fruitful and Multiply: Origins of Legal Restrictions on Planned Parenthood in Nineteenth-Century America." In *Women of America: a History*, edited by Carol R. Berkin and Mary Beth Norton, 245–69. Boston: Houghton Mifflin, 1979.

Hofman, Brenda D. "Political Theology: the Role of Organized Religion in the Anti-Abortion Movement." *Journal of Church and State* 28 (1986): 225–47.

Kantrow, Louise. "Philadelphia Gentry: Fertility and Family Limitation among an American Aristocracy." *Population Studies* 34 (1980): 21–30.

Katz, Esther. "The History of Birth Control in the United States." In *History of Medicine*, edited by Rebecca Greene, 81–101. New York: Haworth Press, 1988. Also published in *Trends in History* 4, no. 2–3 (1988): 81–101.

Lewis, Jan, and Kenneth A. Lockridge. "'Sally Has Been Sick': Pregnancy and Family Limitation among Virginia Gentry Women, 1780–1830." *Journal of Social History* 22 (1988): 5–19.

McFalls, Joseph A., and George S. Masnick. "Birth Control and the Fertility of the U.S. Black Population, 1880 to 1980." *Journal of Family History* 6 (1981): 89–106.

Olasky, Marvin N. "Advertising Abortion during the 1830s and 1840s: Madame Restell Builds a Business." *Journalism History* 13, no. 2 (1986): 49–55.

Olasky, Marvin N. "Opposing Abortion Clinics: A New York Times 1871 Crusade." *Journalism Quarterly* 63 (1986): 305–10.

Ray, Joyce M., and F. G. Gosling. "American Physicians and Birth Control, 1936–1947." *Journal of Social History* 18 (1985): 399–411.

Reed, James. "Doctors, Birth Control, and Social Values, 1830–1970." In *The Therapeutic Revolution*, edited by Morris J. Vogel and Charles E. Rosenberg, 109–33. Philadelphia: University of Pennsylvania Press, 1979.

Reed, James. "Public Policy on Human Reproduction and the Historian." *Journal of Social History* 18 (1985): 383–98.

Reilly, Philip R. "Involuntary Sterilization in the United States: A Surgical Solution." *Quarterly Review of Biology* 62 (1987): 153–70.

Reilly, Philip R. "The Surgical Solution: The Writings of Activist Physicians in the Early Days of Eugenical Sterilization." *Perspectives in Biology and Medicine* 26 (1983): 637–56.

Rosoff, Jeannie I. "The Politics of Birth Control." *Family Planning Perspectives* 20 (1988): 312–20, 297.

Staggenborg, Suzanne. "Coalition Work in the Pro-Choice Movement: Organizational and Environmental Opportunities and Obstacles." *Social Problems* 33 (1986): 374–90.

Velez-I, Carlos G. "Se Me Acabo la Cancion: An Ethnography of Non-Consenting Sterilizations among Mexican Women in Los Angeles." In *Mexican Women in the United States: Struggles Past and Present*, edited by Magdalena Mora and Adelaida R. DelCastillo, 71–91. Los Angeles: UCLA Chicano Studies Resources Center, 1980.

WOMEN AND ALTERNATIVE OR SECTARIAN MEDICINE

I. Books.

Bordin, Ruth. *Woman and Temperance: The Quest for Power and Liberty, 1873–1900*. Philadelphia: Temple University Press, 1981.

Boston Women's Health Book Collective. *The New Our Bodies, Ourselves: a Book by and for Women*. New York: Simon and Schuster, 1984.

The modern feminist critique of medicine was codified in the first edition of *Our Bodies, Ourselves,* which was published in 1973. Not a scholarly book, this is a self-help manual with a clear political message.

Cayleff, Susan E. *Wash and Be Healed: The Water-Cure Movement and Women's Health.* Philadelphia: Temple University Press, 1987.

Donegan, J. B. *"Hydropathic Highway to Health": Women and Water-Cure in Antebellum America.* New York: Greenwood, 1986.

Numbers, Ronald. *Prophetess of Health: A Study of Ellen G. White.* New York: Harper and Row, 1976.
Ellen G. White was the founder of the Seventh-day Adventist movement in the United States. Her ideas about health and medical care are reflected in current day Adventist practice, propagated through the Loma Linda Medical School and the Loma Linda brand of vegetarian foods.

Padus, Emrika. *The Women's Encyclopedia of Healing and Natural Healing.* Emmaus, PA: Rodale Press, 1981.

Ruzek, Sheryl. *The Women's Health Movement: Feminist Alternatives to Medical Control.* New York: Praeger, 1978.

Stage, Sarah. *Female complaints: Lydia Pinkham and the Business of Women's Medicine.* New York: Norton, 1979.

II. Articles.

Barlow, William and David O. Powell. "A Case for Medical Coeducation in the 1870s." *Journal of the American Medical Women's Association* 35 (1980): 285-8.
Considers gender issues in homeopathy education.

Barlow, William, and David O. Powell. "Homeopathy and Sexual Equality: The Controversy over Coeducation at Cincinnati's Pulte Medical College, 1873-1879." *Ohio History* 90 (1981): 101-13.

Gartrell, Ellen G. "Women Healers and Domestic Remedies in 18th Century America: the Recipe Book of Elizabeth Coates Paschall." *New York State Journal of Medicine* 87 (1987): 23-29.

Gibbons, Russell W. "Forgotten Parameters of General Practice: the Chiropractic Obstetrician." *Chiropractic History* 2, no. 1 (1982): 27-33.

McIntosh, Karyl. "Folk Obstetrics, Gynecology, and Pediatrics in Utica, New York." *New York Folklore* 4 (1978): 49-59.

Gromala, Theresa. "Women in Chiropractic: Exploring a Tradition of Equity in Healing." *Chiropractic History* 3, no. 1 (1983): 59–63.

Jackson, Donald Dale. "If Women Needed a Quick Pick-Me-Up, Lydia Provided One." *Smithsonian* 15 (July 1984): 107–19.
An article about Lydia Pinkham, whose potion was a popular remedy outside the medical system.

Jaskoski, Helen. "'My Heart Will Go Out': Healing Songs of Native American Women." *International Journal of Women's Studies* 4 (1981): 118–34.

Morantz, Regina Markell. "Nineteenth-Century Health Reform and Women: A Program of Self-Help." In *Medicine Without Doctors*, edited by Guenter B. Risse, Ronald L. Numbers, and Judith Walzer Leavitt, 73–93. New York: Science History Publications, 1977.

Numbers, Ronald, and Rennie B. Schoepflin. "Ministries of Healing: Mary Baker Eddy, Ellen G. White, and the Religion of Health." In *Women and Health in America: Historical Readings*, edited by Judith Walzer Leavitt, 376–89. Madison: University of Wisconsin Press, 1984.

Sharp, Sharon A. "Folk Medicine Practices: Women as Keepers and Carriers of Knowledge." *Women's Studies International Forum* 9 (1986): 243–49.

NOTES ON CONTRIBUTORS

◆ ◆ ◆ ———————— ◆ ◆ ◆

Rima D. Apple is an Associate Editor of *Isis*. Her studies in women's health history have resulted in several publications, including *Mothers and Medicine: A Social History of Infant Feeding, 1890–1950* (University of Wisconsin Press, 1987). She is currently investigating the ideology of scientific motherhood.

Ellen D. Baer is a faculty member of the School of Nursing, University of Pennsylvania. Her publications reflect her interests in clinical nursing issues and the history of nursing.

Anthony Bale is currently a Post-Doctoral Fellow at Yale University in the School of Medicine. He has published extensively on the social aspects of health issues and litigation.

Edward H. Beardsley teaches in the History Department of the University of South Carolina. He recently published *A History of Neglect: Health Care for Blacks and Mill Workers in the Twentieth-Century South* (University of Tennessee Press, 1987).

Janet Carlisle Bogdan is on the faculty of LeMoyne College (Syracuse, New York) in the Department of Sociology. She is continuing her study of the transformation of childbirth in America.

Charlotte G. Borst is a member of the Department of History, University of Alabama at Birmingham. She has published on the history of midwifery in the United States.

Jonathan M. Butler has written extensively on the history of religions in the United States. Among his publications is *The Disappointed: Millerism and Millenarianism in the Nineteenth Century* (Indiana University Press, 1987), which he edited with Ronald L. Numbers.

Susan E. Cayleff is a member of the Department of Women's Studies, San Diego State University. Her publications in women's history include *Wash and Be Healed: The Water-cure Movement and Women's Health* (Temple University, 1987).

Adele E. Clarke teaches at the University of California, San Francisco, in the graduate programs of sociology and of the history of the health sciences. She is interested in the social relations of science and has written on feminist science and the history of the reproductive sciences.

Teresa C. Gallagher is a doctoral candidate at Stanford University in the School of Education. Her research concerns gender issues in education and employment.

Gregory J. Higby is the Director of the American Institute of the History of Pharmacy. His research focuses on the development of the pharmaceutical profession in the United States.

Margaret Jerrido is Associate Archivist of the Archives and Special Collections on Women in Medicine, Medical College of Pennsylvania. She is studying the history of black women physicians.

Molly Ladd-Taylor teaches at Northwestern University. She is editor of *Raising a Baby the Government Way: Mothers' Letters to the Children's Bureau, 1915–1932* (Rutgers University Press, 1986).

Judy Barrett Litoff teaches history at Bryant College (Providence, Rhode Island). Her publications in women's health history include *American Midwives, 1860 to the Present* (Greenwood Press, 1978) and *The American Midwife Debate: A Sourcebook on its Modern Origins* (Greenwood Press, 1986).

Joan E. Lynaugh is Director of the Center for the Study of the History of Nursing, University of Pennsylvania. Her research involves the history of the health professions. She recently published *Community Hospitals of Kansas City, Missouri—1870–1915* (Garland, 1989).

Regina Morantz-Sanchez teaches in the Department of History at the University of California, Los Angeles. She has published widely on the history of women physicians in the United States, including *Sympathy and Science: Women Physicians in American Medicine* (Oxford University Press, 1985).

Edward T. Morman is Curator of the Historical Collection and lecturer at the Institute of the History of Medicine, Johns Hopkins University. He recently published *Efficiency, Scientific Management and Hospital Standardization: An Anthology of Original Sources* (Garland, 1988).

Suzanne Poirier is on the faculty of the Department of Medical Education at the University of Illinois at Chicago. Her research focuses on the images of health and caring in literature.

Naomi Rogers is a member of the Department of History at the University of Alabama. Along with her work on sectarian medicine, she is completing a monograph on the early years of epidemic polio in the United States (Rutgers University Press, forthcoming).

Judith M. Roy teaches at Ball State University, where she is working on a history of Anglo-American gynecology in the nineteenth century.

Nancy Sahli is Director, Records Program, National Historical Publications and Records Commission, National Archives. Her research encompasses women's history, the history of sexuality and the development of bibliographic tools. Among her publications is *Women and Sexuality in America: A Bibliography* (G. K. Hall, 1984).

Rennie B. Schoepflin teaches at Loma Linda University-Riverside in the Department of History and Political Science. He has published several articles on Mary Baker Eddy and is working on a book-length study of Christian Science healing.

Jill Gates Smith is former Curator of Photographs, Archives and Special Collections on Women in Medicine, Medical College of Pennsylvania. She is particularly interested in the collection and preservation of historical photographs in women's history.

Nancy Tomes, on leave from the State University of New York at Stony Brook, is Acting Director of the Francis Clark Wood Institute for the

History of Medicine, The College of Physicians of Philadelphia. Her ongoing research in the history of mental health and psychiatry has resulted in many publications, including A *Generous Confidence: Thomas Story Kirkbride and the Art of Asylum-Keeping, 1840–1883* (Cambridge University Press, 1984).

Lois M. Verbrugge is a Research Scientist at the Institute of Gerontology, University of Michigan. She has published widely on sex differentials in health and health trends and futures of the American population.

Martha H. Verbrugge is a member of the Department of History of Bucknell University. Her research on the history of women's health includes *Able-Bodied Womanhood: Personal Health and Social Change in Nineteenth-century Boston* (Oxford University Press, 1988).

INDEX

INDEX

♦ ♦ ♦ ——————— ♦ ♦ ♦

Oudshoorn, Nelt, 32
Our Bodies, Ourselves, 332–33, 373
Ovariotomy, 173, 189
Owens-Adair, Bethenia, 298, 301

P

Packard, Elizabeth, 163–64
"Packard laws," 164
Pancoast, William, 242
Park, Roberta J., 374
Parkes, Alan S., 33
Parsons, Gail Pat, 179
Patterson, Daniel, 343
Patterson, James, 429
Peel, Robert, 350–51, 363
Penn Medical University, 292–93
Pennsylvania Hospital for the Insane, 167–68
Pennsylvania Hospital, 249, 251
Pentecostal Church, 338, 341, 358–59
Perkins, Frances, 419
Pernick, Martin, 185
Perry, Susan, 435
Person, Ethel Spector, 88–89
Petchesky, Rosalind Pollack, 237
Pharmaceutical industry: DES daughters' health risks, 431, 433; DES litigation, 432–33; DES use in high-risk pregancies, 431, 432; MER/29, 431; misconduct, 436–37; the "pill," 433–35; post-Civil War manufacturing, 500, 514; RU486, 234; thalidomide, 430, 431
Pharmacists: 497–99, 506, 514–15; apprentices, 498; barriers to women, 500; colonial apothecaries, 498–99; contemporary trends, 506–08; education of women, 499–503; employment of women, 506; institutional practice, 506; new professionalism, 500; post-Civil War and women, 500, 514; pre-1900, 499; profiles of women, 510; re-entry by women, 500–02, 505–07; schools for women, 503–04; status of women, 504; women and professionalism, 512–13
Pharmacopeia, United States, 499
Pharmacy: definition, 498; disappearance of women, 499; division of labor, 514–15; history of, 498–500, 514; practice by women, 505–08; re-entry of women,

502–06; schools for women, 503–04; styles of development, 514; women's ownership, 509. *See also* Pharmacists
Phelps, Elizabeth Stuart, 306
Phosphorus, match industry, 413–14
Phrenology, 84, 303
Physical education: feminism, 380–81; history and role of health, 370–71; instructors, 382–83; intercollegiate sports, 380–81; nineteenth century, 377; proponents, 381–82; sex-segregated, 380
Physicians: and abortion, 233–34; asylum work, 159–62, 166–67; black medical societies, 202 n.17; control over birthing, 214–15; credentials establishment, 201; dispensation of drugs, 498; and eighteenth-century self-help manuals, 313–14; elimination of midwives, 446–48; hospital deliveries, 197–98; misogynist model, 480–81; nineteenth-century gender bias, 158; nineteenth-century ideological conflict, 298–99; nineteenth-century mental illness treatment, 157, 160–62; obstetricians, 201–03; opening of societies and schools to blacks, 137; power over patients, 480–81; professionalism, 198, 486–87; racism, 491–92; sectarians as nonmedical role model, 304–05; sex discrimination, 288–89; specialization, 180–81, 200–01; specialty boards, 201–03; status, 480; transition from domestic medicine, 322–23, 326; in Victorian society, 184. *See also* Women physicians
Physiological lecture clubs, 385
Pickard, Madge, and R. Carlyle Buley, 320–21, 322
"Pill," the, 229. *See also* Birth control, Oral contraceptives
Pincus, Gregory, 227
Pinkham, Lydia, 325
Plagiarism, in medical literature, 84
Planned Parenthood clinics, 266
Plath, Sylvia, 143
Polak, John Osborn, 201
Polybrominated biphenyl (PBB), 424
Pomeroy, Wardell B., 96
Population: eugenics, 220, 221; future scenarios, 72–73, 74–77; shifting, 74–77; United States, 74–75

DATE DUE